Property and Conveyancing Library

THE LAW OF
MORTGAGES

AUSTRALIA AND NEW ZEALAND
The Law Book Company Ltd.
Sydney : Melbourne : Perth

CANADA AND U.S.A.
The Carswell Company Ltd.
Agincourt, Ontario

INDIA
N.M. Tripathi Private Ltd.
Bombay
and
Eastern Law House Private Ltd.
Calcutta and Delhi
M.P.P. House
Bangalore

ISRAEL
Steimatzky's Agency Ltd.
Jerusalem : Tel Aviv : Haifa

PAKISTAN
Pakistan Law House
Karachi

PROPERTY AND CONVEYANCING LIBRARY

THE LAW OF
MORTGAGES

by

EDWARD F. COUSINS B.A., LL.M.
Barrister of Gray's Inn and Lincoln's Inn

Assisted by

SIDNEY ROSS LL.B., M.Sc., Ph.D.
Barrister of Middle Temple and Lincoln's Inn

LONDON
SWEET & MAXWELL
1989

Published in 1989 by
Sweet & Maxwell Limited of
183 Marsh Wall, London E14.
Computerset by Promenade Graphics Limited.
Cheltenham, Gloucestershire.
Printed in Great Britain by
Richard Clay Limited, Bungay, Suffolk.

British Library Cataloguing in Publication Data
Cousins, Edward F.
The law of mortgages.
1. England. Mortgages. Law
I. Title
344.2064'364

ISBN 0–421–34410–5

PREFACE

The decision to publish this book was prompted by a perceived continuing and unfulfilled demand for a new practitioner's text on the law of mortgages.

Initially, it was envisaged that this project would involve the publication of a third edition of that valuable and now unobtainable work, *Waldock on the Law of Mortgages* (1949), the first edition of which having been written by Professor Hanbury and Mr. Waldock and published in 1939. But, at an early stage of this venture, owing to the considerable developments which have occurred in the field of mortgages since the publication of the second edition of Waldock, it was found necessary to revise, reconstruct and re-write substantial sections of this work.

It is in these circumstances that the *Law of Mortgages* was conceived, written, and now finally published, with all due acknowledgement to those remaining parts based upon (and hopefully, without any detraction from) the second edition of Waldock. It is my desire that this work will provide a useful and concise guide to practitioners and academics in the field of mortgages. I have attempted to set out the law as at June 30, 1989.

Finally, my thanks are due to colleagues and friends for their kindly criticisms and suggestions. I must also extend my thanks to my wife and children for their forebearance, large sections of this book having been written whilst on holiday in France and Spain during the Summers of 1987 and 1988.

LAW OF PROPERTY (MISCELLANEOUS PROVISIONS) ACT 1989

The Law Commission Report (No. 164), which deals with formalities for contracts for the sale of land, considered the defects of the existing law.[1] It concluded that, in view of the potential for injustice and the complex and uncertain state of the relevant law (particularly that relating to the doctrine of part performance), section 40 of the Law of Property Act 1925 was ripe for reform. Five proposals were considered. Part IV is devoted to the preferred scheme, which requires (with three exceptions) all contracts for the sale of land to be in writing signed by both parties. Part III of the Report deals with the reasons for rejection of the other four proposals.

The legislative response to the Law Commission's recommendations with respect to section 40 are contained in section 2 of the Law of Property (Miscellaneous Provisions) Act 1989; that section came into force on September 27, 1989, and section 40 is repealed.

The Law Commission recognised that the law relating to mortgages would be affected. Paragraph 4.3 of the report states that contracts to grant leases or mortgages, or options to purchase will be included, as well as contracts for sale. Paragraph 4.12 is concerned with the third of the three exceptions, namely, contracts made on a recognised investment exchange. A contract to sell a debenture is a contract within section 40 of the Law of Property Act 1925.[2] The Commission took the view that by the same reasoning, other forms of investment involving interests in land, perhaps unit trusts making such investments, would fall within the old section 40 and the proposed new provision. They concluded that debentures or other investments were not closely enough connected with the land to require such contracts to be subjected to the proposed formalities. Section 2(5)(c) excepts contracts regulated under the Financial Services Act 1986 from the requirements of the new Act.

Section 40(2) of the Law of Property Act 1925 preserves the doctrine of part performance.[3] Inherent in the recommendation that contracts should be made in writing is the consequence that the doctrine should no longer affect contracts concerning land. The Commission accepted, as one of the principles underlying its recommendations, that any reform should not increase the risk of injustice. The view expressed in Part V of the Report is that the tortious and restitutionary remedies available at law, and the equitable doctrines of promissory and proprietary estoppel, will be adequate to ensure that justice is done between the parties in cases where formalities have not been observed.

The Commission did not advert to the effect of their recommendations on the law relating to the creation of equitable mortgages, but it would appear inevitable that a deposit of title deeds, unaccompanied by a memorandum, can no longer create an equitable mortgage. Existing equitable mortgages by deposit are presumably unaffected.[4] For over 200 years a deposit of title deeds by way of security has been taken as showing a contract to create a legal mortgage and as an act of part performance of that contract.[5] A contract to create a legal mortgage can now be made only in accordance with the requirements of section 2 of the 1989 Act, and deposit of title deeds can no longer be part performance of such a contract. Questions will no doubt arise as to whether such a contract has effect as an equitable mortgage, by the operation of the principle that equity treats as done that which ought to be done.[6]

---

[1] More fully set out in (1985) Working Paper No. 92.

[2] *Driver* v. *Broad* [1893] 1 Q.B. 744.

[3] See paras. 3.23–3.26 in Appendix D of Working Paper 92, and section 1.9 of the Report.

[4] Section 2(7) of the new Act provides that nothing in the section shall apply to contracts made before the section comes into force. Sections 2 and 3 came into force on September 17, 1989, and section 40 of the Law of Property Act 1925 was repealed on that date.

[5] See, *e.g.* Megarry and Wade, *The Law of Real Property*, (5th ed., 1984) pp. 927–928, and cases cited at nn. 12, 13.

[6] Megarry and Wade, *op. cit.*, p. 927, and cases cited at nn. 4, 5, 7, 9 and 10.

CONTENTS

TABLE OF CASES

TABLE OF STATUTES

TABLE OF STATUTORY INSTRUMENTS

Chapter 1

THE NATURE OF A MORTGAGE

Introduction

There have been many attempts, both judicial and academic, to describe a mortgage. Two of the most famous attest to the difficulty of carrying out that task in a satisfactory manner. Lord Macnaghten was moved to say, in the case of *Samuel* v. *Jarrah Timber and Wood Paving Corporation*[1] that no-one, by the light of nature, ever understood an English mortgage of real estate; while Maitland described it as "one long *suppressio veri* and *suggestio falsi.*"[2]

The difficulties arise because, although the essence of a mortgage transaction is the charging of property as security for performance of an obligation, the transaction had for centuries been carried out by conveying an estate in land to the lender. These two facts were recognised by Lindley M.R. when he formulated his well-known description of a mortgage in the case of *Santley* v. *Wilde*[3]; a case in which the mortgage was taken not merely as security for the loan but, additionally, as security for a one-third share of future profits. This serves to demonstrate that mortgages can be raised to secure the performance of obligations other than the payment of debts.

The purpose of security is to afford to the obligee some additional means of enforcing the performance of the obligation by, or extracting the money equivalent from, the obligor. Thus a lender is often unwilling to rely solely on the borrower's personal credit, and requires a greater certainty of repayment than the mere possibility of enforcing the claim in an action of debt. The borrower can meet this requirement by offering personal security. In that case a third party undertakes to answer for the borrower's default by way of a personal commitment, and the lender has an action in debt against him if the borrower defaults. The surety may also reinforce his undertaking by giving a real security.

Real security is obtained when property is appropriated specifically to the satisfaction of a particular debt, so that that debt is a primary charge on the property. The lender whose right is protected by a real security is entitled to take that security for the discharge of his own secured debt, even to the extent of exhausting it entirely and withdrawing it altogether

---

[1] [1904] A.C. 323 at 326.
[2] Maitland, *Equity* (2nd ed., 1969), p. 182.
[3] [1899] 2 Ch. 474; see *post*, pp. 302, 303, 304.

from the pool of the borrower's assets available to the general creditor.[4] If, as is usual, the lender takes a personal covenant from the borrower to repay and the security is insufficient to discharge the debt, he can prove in the borrower's bankruptcy for the balance.[5]

By giving real security, the borrower has a property with which he cannot deal freely because it is incumbered, but he can release the property from its incumbrance by discharging his obligation to the lender, whatever the nature of the right which the lender acquired. This right to redeem is part of the borrower's equity of redemption. A mortgage deed generally contains a stipulation that the borrower shall repay on a fixed date which is, say, six months from the execution of the deed. The result, at law, of the borrower's failure to comply with this stipulation is that the property becomes vested in the lender. But in equity the borrower will be allowed to redeem the property after his default.[6] This arises even though the parties may have made time of the essence of the contract. This right to redeem will subsist until the lender has exercised such powers as he may have to destroy the borrower's equity of redemption by statute, foreclosure, sale or release[7] or until the borrower's right to redeem becomes statute-barred,[8] which can occur if the mortgage is a mortgage of real property or of a mixed fund[9] but not if it is a mortgage of personal property only.

In spite of judicial reluctance to accept it, there is a well established principle that the borrower will not be permitted to surrender to the lender his right to redeem, by any term of the mortgage contract[10]; though he may enter into a separate contract to give the lender a collateral advantage.[11]

In equity, it is a matter of substance, not of form, whether a transaction creates a security or transfers absolute ownership. If the true purpose of the transaction is to create a security, it will not assist the lender to disguise it as a conditional sale or a conveyance.[12] Where an agreement was intended only to create a security, that fact may be proved afterwards by parol evidence even though it contradicts the plain language of a deed.[13] Thus, where a conveyance of property was accompanied by a parol agreement for the defeasance of the deed on payment of a sum of money, it was

---

[4] *White* v. *Simmons* (1871) L.R. 6 Ch.App. 555.
[5] *Re London, Windsor and Greenwich Hotels Co. (Quatermaine's Case)* [1892] 1 Ch. 639. *Re Bonacino, ex p. Discount Banking Co.* (1894) 1 Mans. 59.
[6] *Seton* v. *Slade, Hunter* v. *Seton* (1802) 7 Ves. 265.
[7] *Weld* v. *Petre* [1929] 1 Ch. 33 at 43.
[8] Limitation Act 1980, s.17. In order to rely on that section, the mortgagee must be in possession in his character as mortgagee: *Hyde* v. *Dallaway* (1843) 2 H. 528.
[9] *Charter* v. *Watson* [1899] 1 Ch. 175.
[10] *Samuel* v. *Jarrah Timber and Wood Paving Corporation* [1904] A.C. 323, *per* Lord Halsbury L.C. See generally *post*, pp. 291 *et seq.*
[11] *Kreglinger* v. *New Patagonia Meat and Cold Storage Co.* [1914] A.C. 25; *cf. Noakes* v. *Rice* [1902] A.C. 24 and *Bradley* v. *Carritt* [1903] A.C. 253.
[12] *England* v. *Codrington* (1758) 1 Ed. 169; *Re Duke of Marlborough* [1894] 2 Ch. 133; *cf. Barnhart* v. *Greenshields* (1853) 9 Moo. P.C.C. 18; *Re Kent and Sussex Sawmills* [1947] Ch. 177.
[13] *Lincoln* v. *Wright* (1859) 4 De G. & J. 16.

held to be a fraud, in equity, for the grantee to refuse to give up the deed in return for the payment being made.[14] Nor is it conclusive in the lender's favour that the borrower makes two separate agreements, one to give security and one to purchase the mortgaged property; the court will declare the latter void if it appears that there was only one transaction.[15]

MORTGAGE SECURITY

A mortgage has been described as "a conveyance of land or an assignment of chattels as a security for the payment of a debt or the discharge of some other obligation for which it is given."[16] This description brings out the essential features of a mortgage: the provision of *security* by a *transfer of property rights*. Although mortgages are most commonly raised to secure a money debt, they may also be given to secure other obligations.

The mortgage transaction consists of a transfer of the legal or equitable title to property from the borrower, to the lender, to be held by the lender until all his claims under the mortgage are satisfied. The borrower's right is to have the title restored to him on fulfilment of his obligation to the lender even if he does not do so until after the contractual date for that fulfilment.

Although in certain circumstances the lender may assume possession of the property, his security does not depend on being in possession. If he wishes to apply the rents and profits to the satisfaction of the mortgage debt, his remedy is to appoint a receiver.[17] He cannot derive any personal profit from being in possession; indeed, he is accountable to the borrower not only for the profits which he does make but for those which he reasonably ought to have made.[18]

In order to protect both his own interests and those of persons who may deal with the borrower subsequent to the giving of security, the lender should ensure to the best of his ability that the borrower is not able to represent himself as being the owner of the property free from incumbrances. This means either taking the documents of title in addition to the conveyance, or registering his mortgage in whatever way is appropriate.

The lender's ultimate remedy is the destruction of the borrower's equity of redemption, which he can achieve by sale, without the intervention of the court if there is an express or statutory power of sale but not otherwise; or by foreclosure which can be decreed only by the court and which has the power to order sale instead.[19]

---

[14] *Re Duke of Marlborough* [1894] 2 Ch. 133.
[15] *Lewis* v. *Love (Frank)* [1961] 1 W.L.R. 261 and see the discussion at (1961) 77 L.Q.R. 163 (P. V. Baker): *cf. Reeve* v. *Lisle* [1902] A.C. 461.
[16] *Santley* v. *Wilde* [1899] 2 Ch. 474.
[17] L.P.A. 1925, s.109.
[18] *White* v. *City of London Brewery* (1889) 42 Ch.D. 237; *Shepherd* v. *Spansheath* (1988) E.G.C.S. 35.
[19] L.P.A. 1925, s.91.

Possessory securities: pledge and lien

A *pledge* of chattels is effected either by actual[20] or constructive
delivery, the latter being by delivery of documents,[21] and the creditor's
rights arise through his possession under the contract of pledge. The right
of the lender, or pledgee, is to retain the chattel until a proper tender of the
amount due is made.[22] As against the borrower, or pledgor, he may deny
him possession and, if the debt remains unsatisfied, he may after a reasonable time sell the chattel, though the borrower's right to redeem subsists
until the chattel is sold.[23]

The lender thus has a special property in the chattel,[24] but unlike a mortgagee, he is not at law the owner of it and therefore can never foreclose.[25]
Foreclosure is the destruction of an equity to redeem property which at law
is the property of the lender and is therefore unavailable to a pledgee.[26] On
the other hand, if a third party wrongfully removes the pledged chattel
from keeping, it is the lender who has the right to sue in conversion, since
that arises from ownership and possession, or from possession alone, or
from the immediate right to possession. Whilst the chattel is in pledge, the
borrower has none of these remedies.

If the lender returns the chattel to the borrower before he has discharged
the debt, the lender loses his special property in the chattel unless there is a
particular temporary purpose for the return and thereby is relegated to the
status of an unsecured creditor.[27]

A *possessory* lien gives the lender even less of a right against the borrower than a pledge. The right is a right to detain the chattel until a debt is
satisfied.[28] There is, in general, no right to realise the security by sale,[29]
though such a right can exist in special cases.

If the lender is in possession of the borrower's chattels under any of the
following circumstances, he has, provided that his possession remains continuous, a lien on the chattels until his debt is satisfied. If:

    (1) he has, expended labour, skill or money on them[30];
    (2) he is compellable by law to receive, or to perform services in
           respect of them[31];
    (3) he has saved them from loss or capture at sea.[32]

---

[20] *Re Morritt, ex p. Official Receiver* (1886) 18 Q.B.D. 222.
[21] *Official Assignee of Madras* v. *Mercantile Bank of India Ltd.* [1935] A.C. 53.
[22] *Halliday* v. *Holgate* (1868) L.R. 3 Ex. 299; *Yungmann* v. *Briesemann* (1892) 67 L.T. 642.
[23] *Carter* v. *Wake* (1877) 4 Ch.D. 605.
[24] *Donald* v. *Suckling* (1866) L.R. 1 Q.B.D. 585.
[25] *Carter* v. *Wake* (1877) 4 Ch.D. 605.
[26] *Donald* v. *Suckling* (1866) L.R. 1 Q.B.D. 585.
[27] *Reeves* v. *Capper* (1838) 5 Bing.N.C. 136; *North Western Bank* v. *Poynter, Son and Mac-
donalds* [1895] A.C. 56.
[28] *Lickbarrow* v. *Mason* (1787) 2 T.R. 63.
[29] *Smart* v. *Sandars* (1848) 5 C.B. 895.
[30] *Chase* v. *Westmore* (1816) 5 M. & S. 180.
[31] *Robins & Co.* v. *Gray* [1895] 2 Q.B. 501; *Marsh* v. *Commissioner of Police* [1945] K.B. 43.
[32] *Hartfort* v. *Jones* (1699) 1 Ld.Ray. 393.

Such liens arise by operation of law[33] and are known as common law liens; they secure only the particular debt which accrues to the lender by reason of his dealings with the chattels in his possession.

A similar right can be created by express contract or can arise by implication from trade or business usage.[34] Frequently such contractual liens, as they are generally termed, extend to cover the general balance between debtor and creditor, so that the indebtedness is not necessarily related to the chattel detained. Thus a solicitor's lien on papers which come into his possession in the course of business,[35] or a factor's lien on chattels,[36] gives him the right to detain against the general balance of his account. Whether the lien arises at common law, by contract or by implication, the rights under it depend on possession. So that if the lender returns the chattels to the borrower, or contracts on terms that the borrower may temporarily resume possession, or hand the chattels to a third party with the intent to abandon possession, his lien is lost. As with a pledge, there is an exception to this rule where, for some specific and temporary purpose, he delivers the chattels to the borrower or to a third party.[37]

Non-possessory securities: equitable lien

Like a lien at common law, an equitable lien can arise in respect of both real and personal property[38]; but unlike a common law lien, an equitable lien does not depend on possession of the property which is subject to the lien.[39] Further, the holder of an equitable lien has the power to realise his security by judicial sale[40] or the appointment of a receiver, whereas it is exceptional for the holder of a common law lien to have the power of sale.

The contrast is well illustrated by reference to the position of a vendor under a specifically enforceable contract for the sale of land. Thus, at common law the vendor would have a lien on the land or the deeds for the unpaid purchase money until he had conveyed the land to the purchaser or let him into possession of it, or handed over the deeds.

The equitable lien, however, persists irrespective of possession, so long as any part of the purchase money remains unpaid. Though it is liable to be defeated by a *bona fide* purchaser for value if it is not protected, as a general equitable charge in the case of unregistered land, or by notice, caution or substantive registration if the land is registered. The vendor's common law lien depending on his possession is an overriding interest if the land is registered, and thus does not require to be so protected.

---

[33] *Gladstone* v. *Birley* (1817) 2 Mer. 401.
[34] *Rushforth* v. *Hadfield* (1805) 7 East. 224.
[35] *Ex p. Sterling* (1809) 16 Ves. 258.
[36] *Kruger* v. *Wilcox* (1755) Amb. 252.
[37] *Reeves* v. *Capper* (1838) 5 Bing.N.C. 136.
[38] *Re Stucley* [1906] 1 Ch. 67; *Barker* v. *Stickney* [1919] 1 K.B. 121.
[39] *Goode* v. *Burton* (1847) 1 Ex. 189.
[40] *Neate* v. *Duke of Marlborough* (1838) 3 Myl. & Cr. 407.

A purchaser also has an equitable lien for his deposit[41] and costs of investigating title should he lawfully rescind the contract.[42] But if the purchase goes off through the purchaser's fault, the lien is lost.[43]

Non-possessory securities: the equitable charge

An equitable charge arises where specified property is appropriated to the discharge of an obligation without any right of ownership being transferred to the chargee. In many ways an equitable chargee is in the same position as the holder of an equitable lien. He is in the position of a secured creditor.[44] His interest is liable to be defeated if it is not protected in the appropriate manner. Since he has no title, he cannot foreclose or go into possession.[45] Judicial and academic indifference to strictness of terminology has led to the two terms being treated as largely interchangeable, and the most obvious distinction between them is that a lien arises by operation of law and a charge by act of parties. This, however, makes little, if any, difference to the remedies available.[46]

Distress

This is the least effective form of real security. The creditor does not get ownership or possession or the rights of a chargee, and the class of transaction in which it affords the creditor protection in a bankruptcy is very limited. Most commonly it is exercised by a landlord, whose power of distress entitles him to take and eventually sell chattels brought by the tenant on to the demised premises to satisfy a claim for rent. A licence to seize and sell annexed to a contract of pledge is also valid, since it is not caught by section 9 of the Bills of Sale Act 1882,[47] though in general, a licence to seize chattels given by contract expressly to secure a debt is a bill of sale for the purposes of that Act and is void because it cannot be made in the form required.[48]

MORTGAGE AND CHARGE

It has been stated, earlier, that a mortgage is a security accompanied by a transfer of property rights, while a charge is an appropriation of property to the satisfaction of an obligation without any such transfer. It therefore,

---

[41] *Whitbread & Co.* v. *Watt* [1902] 1 Ch. 835; but *cf. Combe* v. *Swaythling* [1947] Ch. 625 (no lien where deposit paid to stakeholder).
[42] *Kitton* v. *Hewett* (1904) W.N. 21; *Rt. Furneaux & Aird's Contract* (1906) W.N. 215; where the contract goes off because the vendor's title is defective, the lien extends to costs of proceedings to enforce specific performance, or of a vendor and purchaser summons.
[43] *Dinn* v. *Grant* (1852) 5 De G. & Sm. 451.
[44] *National Provincial and Union Bank of England* v. *Charnley* [1924] 1 K.B. 431 at 445, 446.
[45] *Tennant* v. *Trenchard* (1869) L.R. 4 Ch. 537.
[46] *Goode* v. *Burton* (1847) 1 Ex. 189; *Re Richardson, Shillito* v. *Hobson* (1885) 30 Ch.D. 396, *per* Fry L.J. at 403.
[47] *Re Townsend* (1886) 16 Q.B.D. 532.
[48] *Ibid.*

apparently, follows that a mortgagee, but not a chargee, should have the right to foreclose or to go into possession, while both should have the right to appoint a receiver or to realise the security by sale.

The distinction, nevertheless, is clouded not only by the judicial indifference referred to above, but by the draftsmen of the 1925 property legislation. In the definition section of the Law of Property Act[49] a mortgage is described as including "a charge or lien on any property for securing money or money's worth" whereas a mortgagee includes "a chargee by way of legal mortgage" but not the holder of a lien or an equitable chargee[50]; and while section 90 of the Act deals with orders for sale in reference to equitable mortgages, the section is actually entitled "Realisation of equitable charges by the court."

All this confusion, however, reflects reality when looked at from the point of view of the borrower. It is true that the lender has, *at law*, rights which differ according to whether he is a mortgagee or a chargee. As Harman J. said in *Four-Maids Ltd* v. *Dudley Marshall (Properties) Ltd.*[51]:

> "The right of the mortgagee to possession in the absence of some contract has nothing to do with default on the part of the mortgagor. The mortgagee may go into possession before the ink is dry on the mortgage unless there is something . . . whereby he has contracted himself out of that right."

A chargee has no such right against the chargor, as he is never owner of the property at law. And that same circumstance prevents him destroying the chargor's equity of redemption by foreclosure, a right confined to a mortgagee. The borrower, however, may find himself to be put in the same position, in practice, *vis-à-vis* the lender, whatever the lender's status.

If he cannot discharge the obligation, his right to redeem is as effectively destroyed by sale as by foreclosure; he loses possession as a result either of the appointment of a receiver or the making of a possession order.

The similarity in the borrower's position, whether his lender is a mortgagee or a chargee, is reflected by the provision allowing a legal mortgage to be created by means of a charge by deed expressed to be by way of legal mortgage.[52] Although the document is described as a charge, the lender, regardless of his lack of title, has all the powers of a legal mortgagee[53]: foreclosure, sale, possession, and the appointment of a receiver are all available to him.

---

[49] s.205(1)(xvi).
[50] L.P.A. 1925, s.205(1)(xvi).
[51] [1957] Ch. 317 at 320.
[52] L.P.A. 1925, s.85.
[53] *Ibid.* s.87.

CHAPTER 2

HISTORY OF THE LAW OF MORTGAGE[1]

COMMON LAW

The practice of giving rights over land as security for debt is of great antiquity. Until the end of the twelfth century the transaction was by way of lease by the mortgagor to the mortgagee, and was either a *vivum vadium* (live pledge, "vifgage") or a *mortuum vadium* (dead pledge, "mortgage") depending on whether the income from the land was, or was not, used in the discharge of the debt. In default of repayment either on the appointed day or, following an order of the court, after a reasonable time, the mortgagee took the fee simple.

Such transactions were not wholly satisfactory to the mortgagee since the *seisina ut de vadio* which he acquired was not protected by law, and it was also doubtful whether a term of years could be enlarged into a fee simple. Mortgages of freehold land were therefore made by conveyance of the fee simple, subject to the mortgagor's right to re-enter and determine the mortgagee's estate if the money were repaid on the named date. This was very onerous for the mortgagor, who would lose the land and yet remain liable for the debt if he did not repay it on the due date.

The usual form of the mortgage by reconveyance did not remain fixed, and by the beginning of the seventeenth century had developed into something resembling the modern pre-1926 form. It consisted of a conveyance of the fee simple with a covenant to reconvey if the money was paid on the due date. Mortgages by granting leases still existed, but their main use was for the purpose of raising portions terms. The effect of the mortgage, at common law, was not changed as a result of the change in form. The mortgagor still lost his land and remained liable for the debt, if he failed to pay on the due date, unless the mortgage provided otherwise. An alternative form was a conveyance subject to a condition that the conveyance would be avoided if the debt was repaid on the due date.

The important substantial, as distinct from formal, development was that the proprietary right of the creditor arose, not by virtue of a lease and the operation of a condition precedent, but by virtue of a grant and the operation of a condition subsequent. Although the mortgagee still went into possession under the later form, his protection was no longer based on that possession but on the title derived from the grant. The form underwent an apparently minor alteration in that the reconveyance was no

---

[1] For fuller treatments of the subject, see Pollock and Maitland, *The History of English Law* (2nd ed., 1911), Vol. 2, p. 119; Holdsworth, *History of English Law*; and the preface to Turner, *Equity of Redemption* (1931).

longer, in general, made on condition that the mortgagor was entitled to re-enter on discharging the debt, but, rather, subject to a proviso[2] that the mortgagee would reconvey the fee simple if the debt was paid on the due date. The advantage of this form was that proof of title depended on the reconveyance rather than on the date of payment of the money.

Thus the modern pre-1926 form of mortgage was by way of conveyance of the fee simple to the mortgagee, defeasible by a condition subsequent on a date fixed by the parties. The mortgagee thus enjoyed the following advantages:

(1) Absolute priority, in the absence of fraud, misrepresentation or gross negligence, over all later incumbrancers, by virtue of his legal title which gave him a right *in rem*.

(2) The right to custody of the title deeds.

(3) The power to convey the legal estate to a purchaser, in exercising his express or statutory power of sale, without applying to the court.

(4) The right to protect his security by going into possession.

(5) The right to apply to the court for a decree of foreclosure which, if granted, would destroy the mortgagor's equity of redemption and immediately vest the fee simple in him.

Similarly, leaseholds could be mortgaged by way of assignment of the term with a covenant to reassign. This, however, was not a popular form of mortgage because it created privity of estate between the landlord and the mortgagee,[3] who thus became liable on all such covenants in the lease as ran with the land, including the obligation to pay rent. Consequently, the alternative method, whereby the mortgagor granted a sub-lease, one day shorter than the lease, with a proviso for cesser on redemption, was generally adopted. This became one of the two methods for the mortgage of leaseholds permitted by the 1925 legislation. As a sub-tenant, the mortgagee would not be in privity of estate with the landlord and would not be liable on the covenants in the lease.[4]

But this method of creating mortgages of leaseholds led to two difficulties, both of which arose from the retention of a nominal reversion by the mortgagor. The mortgagee was not entitled to custody of the title deeds, nor could he, on exercising his power of sale, vest the whole of the mortgagor's lease in the purchaser. These were overcome by providing, in the mortgage deed, that the mortgagor declared himself a trustee of the nominal reversion for the mortgagee, and usually there was a clause permitting the mortgagee to appoint new trustees in place of the mortgagor. In this way the mortgagor could be compelled to assign his reversion to a

---

[2] As a result of *Cromwel's Case* (1601) 2 Co.Rep. 69(b) which decided that "proviso" makes a condition, the proviso for reconveyance subjected the mortgagee's estate to a condition subsequent.

[3] Under the doctrine in *Spencer's Case* (1583) 5 Co.Rep. 16.

[4] *Bonner* v. *Tottenham and Edmonton Permanent Investment Building Society* [1899] 1 Q.B. 161.

purchaser, without the need for the court to order an assignment. The mortgagee, therefore, had effective control of the nominal reversion.[5]

THE INFLUENCE OF EQUITY

The development of the law of mortgages was also affected by the laws relating to loans made at interest. Originally loans at interest were illegal, but later, from the sixteenth century onwards, maximum rates were fixed by the Usury Acts, with the result that the Court of Chancery took the view that a mortgage should be a security only.[6] It would no longer permit the mortgagee to profit from the fee simple, and would confine his benefit to the interest permitted by statute. Occupation, likewise, would yield no advantage to the mortgagee (except in the case of the now obsolete Welsh mortgage[7]) since he would be liable to the mortgagor for a full rent should he go into possession. Thus arose the modern type of mortgage under which the mortgagor remains in possession of the land and the conveyance of the fee simple is by way of security only.

The courts of equity, which had for many years relieved the mortgagor against forfeiture in special cases, at length established the rule that the mortgagor must be permitted to redeem his fee simple even though he did not pay on the due date.[8] The mortgagee had vested in him, as soon as the mortgage was made, an equitable interest whose measure was the difference between the value of the land and the amount of the debt, and one which he could enforce against anyone except a bona fide purchaser for value from the mortgagor without notice.

In addition to the contractual right to redeem at common law, which would rarely be exercised, the mortgagor obtained an equitable right to redeem which could not be exercised until the contractual date for redemption was past.[9] This right could be exercised only if the courts of equity thought it proper. Inequitable conduct on the part of the mortgagor would bar his right to redeem.

The equity of redemption

The equity of redemption is an interest which the mortgagor can convey, devise, entail, lease, mortgage or settle.[10] If the mortgagor dies intestate it will devolve subject to the intestacy rules.[11] It has been held that the equity of redemption in leasehold premises subject to a mortgage can pass to the Crown as *bona vacantia* where the mortgagor company has been dissolved.[12]

[5] *London and County Bank* v. *Goddard* [1897] 1 Ch. 642.
[6] *Thornborough* v. *Baker* (1675) 3 Swans. 628; (1676) 1 Ch.Ca. 283.
[7] Fisher and Lightwood, *Law of Mortgage* (10th ed., 1988), p. 7, n. (r).
[8] *Emanuel College, Cambridge* v. *Evans* (1625) 1 Rep.Ch. 18.
[9] *Brown* v. *Cole* (1845) 14 Sim. 427.
[10] *Pawlett* v. *Att.-Gen.* (1667) Hard. 465 at 469; *Fawcett* v. *Lowther* (1751) 2 Ves.Sen. 300.
[11] Administration of Estate Act 1925, ss.1, 3(1).
[12] *Re Wells* [1933] Ch. 29.

Prior to 1926, second and subsequent mortgages of freeholds would usually have been mortgages of the equity of redemption, since the legal fee simple would normally have been held by the first mortgagee. Until the enactment of the Conveyancing Act 1881, this led to the inconvenient situation that, on the mortgagee's death, the realty, that is, the legal estate, devolved on his devisee or heir who held it on trust for the persons entitled to the mortgage money, while the right to the money lent, being personalty, passed to the mortgagee's personal representatives. This complication was one of the factors which kept the mortgage by lease in being during the late nineteenth century.

As with subsequent mortgages of freeholds by conveyance, so subsequent mortgages of leaseholds by assignment were normally dealings with the equity of redemption. Subsequent mortgages of leaseholds made by sub-lease, however, did not involve any such dealing. Instead, further sub-leases were granted, each longer, usually by one day, than the sub-lease immediately before. Such mortgages, unlike subsequent mortgages by assignment, were legal, not equitable.

Destruction of the equity of redemption

Since an unfettered right to redeem would have nullified the intended effect of the mortgage transaction, that is, to enable the mortgagee to recover his capital, it was necessary to limit that right. The courts achieved this by a decree of forfeiture,[13] for which the mortgagee had to apply. The effect of such a decree was to destroy the equity of redemption,[14] including, of course, the right to redeem. The court, however, guarded against oppressive foreclosures by ordering a sale when the property was much more valuable than the debt, and the mortgagee then received only the balance due to him.[15]

The equity of redemption is likewise destroyed if the mortgagee, acting under his statutory power, makes a binding contract of sale of the mortgaged property,[16] and the exercise of an express power of sale has the same effect.

While the equity of redemption cannot be defeated by a stipulation in the mortgage that it will be extinguished if the debt is not paid by a specified date, it is open to the mortgagor to agree to release his equity of redemption by means of a separate and independent transaction subsequent to the mortgage.[17] Transactions have, however, been set aside as

[13] *How* v. *Vigures* (1628) 1 Rep.Ch. 32.
[14] Subject to rights to reopen the foreclosure; see *Thornhill* v. *Manning* (1851) 1 Sim.(N.S.) 451; *Coombe* v. *Stewart* (1851) 13 Beav. 111 and *Lancashire & Yorkshire Reversionary Interest Co.* v. *Crowe* (1970) 114 S.J. 435.
[15] *Rhymney Valley District Council* v. *Pontygwindy Housing Association Ltd.* (1976) 73 L.S. Gaz. 405.
[16] *Waring* v. *London and Manchester Assurance Co.* [1935] Ch. 310; *Property and Bloodstock Ltd.* v. *Emerton* [1968] Ch. 94; *Duke* v. *Robson* [1973] 1 W.L.R. 267; and see *post*, p. 237.
[17] *Reeve* v. *Lisle* [1902] A.C. 461.

clogging the equity of redemption where such a provision was part of the mortgage deed or contemporaneous with it.[18]

Finally, the mortgagor is barred from bringing an action to redeem any mortgaged land of which the mortgagee has been in possession for 12 years,[19] unless during that period the mortgagee in possession either receives a payment of principal or interest, or signs an acknowledgment of the mortgagor's title. An acknowledgment signed after the lapse of the 12 year period is of no effect if no payment has been received during the period.

LAW OF PROPERTY ACT 1925

Transitional provisions

The 1925 legislation abolished two forms of mortgage: it was no longer possible to create legal mortgages of freeholds by conveyance of the fee simple, or legal mortgages of leaseholds by assignment.

The transitional provisions which are contained in the Law of Property Act 1925, Schedule 1, Parts VII and VIII, include saving clauses which state that the subsisting rights of the parties are not to be affected by changes in mortgage forms.[20] In particular they expressly prescribe that a mortgagee of a legal estate made before January 1, 1926, and not protected by a deposit of title deeds or by registration of a land charge shall not obtain any benefit, by reason of its conversion into a legal mortgage, against a bona fide purchaser without notice, but was to retain, as against him, the status of an equitable interest.[21] It was therefore advisable to register pre-1926 mortgages which were not protected by a deposit of title deeds.

The effect of the provisions of Part VII on pre-1926 legal mortgages of freeholds is that:

(1) A first mortgage became a lease for 3,000 years without impeachment of waste, but subject to a provision for cesser on redemption corresponding to the right of redemption subsisting on January 1, 1926.[22]

(2) Second and subsequent mortgages were similarly converted into leases for one, two or more days longer than the term vested in the first mortgagee.[23]

(3) The legal fee simple was vested in the mortgagor or in the tenant

---

[18] *Fairclough* v. *Swan Brewery Co. Ltd.* [1912] A.C. 562.

[19] Limitation Act 1980, ss.16, 17. See *post*, pp. 400 *et seq.*

[20] L.P.A. 1925, s.39 provides for the effecting of the transition from the law prior to the commencement of the L.P.A. 1922, to the law enacted by that Act (as amended), by means of the provisions in Sched. 1.

[21] L.P.A. 1925, Sched. 1, Pt. VII, para. 6 does not apply to mortgages or charges registered or protected under the Land Registration Act 1925.

[22] *Ibid.* para. 1.

[23] *Ibid.* para. 2.

for life, statutory owner, trustee for sale, personal representative or other person of full age who, if all money owing on the security of the mortgage or mortgages had been discharged on January 1, 1926, would have been entitled to have the fee simple conveyed to him.[24]

(4) A sub-mortgage was converted into a lease for a term less by one day than the mortgage from which it was derived.[25]

The corresponding provisions in respect of leaseholds are contained in Part VIII of Schedule 1 and affect pre-1926 mortgages as follows:

(1) A first mortgage by assignment of a lease was converted into a sub-lease for a term of ten days less than the principal lease subject to a provision for cesser corresponding to the existing right of redemption.[26]

(2) Second and subsequent mortgages were similarly converted into sub-leases for terms at least one day less than the principal lease.[27]

(3) The provision as to the vesting of the principal lease corresponds to that for vesting of the legal fee simple, the person in whom it is to be vested being the person who would have been entitled to have the term assigned or surrendered to him.[28]

(4) A sub-mortgage was converted into a lease for a term less by one day than that of the mortgage from which it was derived.[29]

(5) The provisions of the Law of Property Act 1922, Schedule 15, paragraphs 2 and 5, which converted perpetually renewable leases to terms of 200 years and the Law of Property Act 1925, section 149(6) which converted leases for lives or marriages into terms of 90 years determinable after the death or marriage of the original lessee; apply to mortgage terms, with certain variations provided by the Law of Property Act 1925, Schedule 1, Part VIII, section 6.

Legal mortgages

Under the 1925 legislation legal mortgages of freeholds may now be created only by[30];

(1) A demise for a term of years absolute, subject to a provision for cesser on redemption; or

(2) A charge by deed expressed to be by way of legal mortgage.

By the first method, a long term, generally 3,000 years, is granted. The

[24] L.P.A. 1925, Sched. 1, Pt. VII, para. 3.
[25] *Ibid.* para. 4.
[26] *Ibid.* Pt. VIII, para. 1.
[27] *Ibid.* para. 2.
[28] *Ibid.* para. 3.
[29] *Ibid.* para. 4.
[30] *Ibid.* s.85(1).

provision for cesser is that the term shall cease when the loan is repaid, but since on repayment the term becomes a satisfied term and ceases automatically, it is not necessary.

Although the mortgagor now retains the legal estate, and is thus owner of the property both at law and in equity, the mortgagee does not suffer any disadvantage. The mortgagor can now create successive legal mortgages, by granting a series of leases each one day longer than the preceding lease,[31] and the substantial rights of the mortgagees will be their interests in the equity of redemption, not their nominal rights as reversioners.

Unlike a mortgagee by reconveyance, a mortgagee by demise before 1926 had no right to the title deeds, a fact which made mortgages by lease unpopular. But the 1925 legislation provided expressly that a mortgagee by demise should have the same right to the title deeds as if he had the fee simple.[32]

A purported conveyance of the fee simple by way of first mortgage now operates as a demise for 3,000 years without impeachment of waste, subject to cesser on redemption,[33] and each subsequent mortgage takes effect as a similar term one day longer than that granted to the immediately prior mortgagee.[34]

The second method does not create a term in the mortgagee, but he is given the same powers, protection and remedies as if he had a term of 3,000 years without impeachment of waste. In order to have effect at law, the charge must be by deed and be expressed to be by way of legal mortgage,[35] though it is not necessary to use the phrase as one complete expression.

Mortgages of leaseholds can be created only in two ways[36]:

(1) by sub-demise for a term of years absolute subject to cesser on redemption, the term being at least one day shorter than that vested in the mortgagor;
(2) by charge by deed expressed to be by way of legal mortgage.

Because the sub-term is shorter than the original term, the mortgage will not operate as an assignment, and mortgages of leaseholds by assignment are not permitted by the 1925 legislation. It is, in fact, usual to make the sub-term ten days shorter than the original term, so that subsequent mortgages can be accommodated[37] but the rule has been preserved that a subsequent lease can take effect in reversion on a lease of the same or

---

[31] A second legal mortgage for a term of the same length as, or shorter than, the first is still valid since it is binding on the lessor by estoppel. *Neale* v. *Mackenzie* (1836) 1 M. & W. 747.
[32] L.P.A. 1925, s.85(1).
[33] *Ibid.* s.85(2)(*a*).
[34] *Ibid.* s.85(2)(*b*).
[35] *Ibid.* s.87(1).
[36] *Ibid.* s.86(1).
[37] Although they can all be of the same length; *Neale* v. *Mackenzie* (1836) 1 M. & W. 747.

greater length. Consequently all the subsequent mortgages could be secured by terms of the same length and would take effect according to whatever rules determine their respective priorities.

A post-1925 purported mortgage by assignment of a lease takes effect as a sub-demise for a term of years absolute subject to cesser on redemption. A first or only mortgagee takes a sub-term ten days shorter than the original term and each subsequent mortgage takes a term one day longer than the immediately prior mortgage term, if this is possible.[38] The sub-term must, however, always be at least one day shorter than the original term.

The legal charge is generally considered to be more readily intelligible than the ordinary form of mortgage[39] which has in the past, attracted much academic and judicial criticism.[40] It provides a convenient method of mortgaging freeholds and leaseholds together.

Because the charge creates no sub-lease in favour of the mortgagee, it is generally thought that it does not amount to a breach of a covenant against sub-letting.[41] But if, as is usual, the covenant also prohibits parting with possession, there will be a breach if the mortgagee enforces his right to possession.

Equitable mortgages of legal interests

The power of an owner of land to create an equitable right in favour of a lender by way of security over the land is both old-established and unaffected by statute. But the pre-1926 type of mortgage by conveyance of the fee simple with a proviso for reconveyance on redemption which would have been an equitable mortgage if it was a second or subsequent mortgage, now takes effect as a mortgage by demise or sub-demise.

An equitable mortgage of a legal interest may be made either by an agreement to create a legal mortgage or by a deposit of title deeds. The first of these methods of creation rests on the principle that equity looks on that as done which ought to be done; but it is important to remember that the agreement must be specifically enforceable in order that that doctrine may operate. Consequently, an equitable mortgage cannot arise in this way unless the money has been advanced, since a contract to make a loan, even under seal, is not a specifically enforceable contract. Since an agreement to create a mortgage is a contract for the disposition of an interest in land, it must be evidenced in writing as required by section 40(1) of the Law of

---

[38] L.P.A. 1925, s.86(2).

[39] *Ibid.* Sched. 4 provides statutory forms of mortgage and transfer, but they are not commonly used nowadays.

[40] *Samuel* v. *Jarrah Timber and Wood Paving Corporation* [1904] A.C. 323, *per* Lord Macnaghten at 326; *Salt* v. *Marquess of Northampton* [1892] A.C. 1, *per* Lord Bramwell at 18; Maitland, *Equity* (2nd ed., 1949), p. 182.

[41] *Gentle* v. *Faulkner* [1900] 2 Q.B. 267; *Grand Junction Co. Ltd.* v. *Bates* [1954] 2 Q.B. 160. If a licence is required, it shall not unreasonably be withheld; L.P.A. 1925, s.86(1). Similarly a covenant against assignment is not hindered by the mention of a legal charge. But normally there is inserted into the lease a covenant against charging.

Property Act 1925 or supported by a sufficient act of part performance. An imperfect legal mortgage, such as an instrument which expresses itself to be a legal mortgage but is not a deed, may also be treated by equity as a contract to create a legal mortgage.

The mortgagee under a specifically enforceable contract to create a legal mortgage has the same remedies as if he held a legal mortgage by demise as in the Law of Property Act 1925, section 85(1).

The other way of creating an equitable mortgage of a legal interest is by deposit of title deeds; but that without more, is insufficient. There must be an intention to deposit the deeds by way of security. If that intention is evidenced by a memorandum of deposit under seal, the transaction then becomes a mortgage by deed for the purposes of the Law of Property Act 1925 and entitles the equitable mortgagee to exercise all the rights of a mortgagee by deed. Since, however, he cannot convey the legal estate to the purchaser, it is usual for the memorandum to contain either a power of attorney, or a declaration of trust, or both, in order to enable him to do so.

CHAPTER 3

MORTGAGES OF UNREGISTERED LAND

LEGAL MORTGAGES BY DEMISE

Freehold land

Both first and subsequent legal mortgages may be created by demise, but the later mortgages are no longer automatically equitable as was the case before the 1925 legislation. There is no necessity for the subsequent mortgage terms to be longer than the principal term, since at law the creation of a lease does not prevent the creation of a subsequent lease for a concurrent or even a shorter term. The subsequent lease is binding on the parties by estoppel.

The transitional provisions of the 1925 legislation do cause subsequent mortgages to take effect for terms longer by one, two or more days than the principal mortgage term, and the Law of Property Act 1925, section 85(2) causes a purported second or subsequent mortgage by conveyance of the fee simple, including an absolute conveyance with the deed of defeasance on redemption, to operate similarly.

The device of causing mortgages to operate as leases with a nominal reversion on the mortgagor is a conveyancing device to keep equities off the title, in accordance with the general principles underlying the 1925 legislation. However, it was seen to be necessary to remove various uncertainties as to the positions of the parties to the mortgage and this was done, in the case of mortgages of freehold land, by sections 85 and 88 of the Law of Property Act 1925, which make the following provisions:

(i) A first mortgagee has the same right to documents of title as if his security included the fee simple: section 85(1);

(ii) On a sale by a mortgagee under a power of sale, the conveyance to the purchaser operates to vest in him the whole of the mortgagor's estate, including the nominal reversion: section 88(1);

(iii) The mortgagor's nominal reversion will be vested in the mortgagee on a foreclosure order by the court; which also terminates his equity of redemption; and also when his equity of redemption becomes barred by lapse of time: section 88(2), (3);

(iv) Section 88(5) operates to extend the provisions of section 88(1), (2), (3) to a sub-mortgagee so as to enable him to acquire the nominal reversions of both his immediate mortgagor and the original mortgagor;

(v) On discharge of a mortgage debt, the mortgage term becomes a satisfied term and ceases automatically (section 116); this applies equally to sub-mortgages since section 5 restates the provisions of the Satisfied Terms Act 1845 so that they apply to underleases.

The replacement of mortgage by conveyance with mortgage by demise saves the mortgagor the cost of two conveyances; and, because of the provisions respecting satisfied terms, it is unnecessary to terminate the mortgage term by an express surrender. Normally, a properly executed receipt for the mortgage money is sufficient to put an end to the term.

The possibility of a series of legal mortgages of the same land altered the old rule whereby a legal mortgage automatically gave the mortgagee priority which was lost only by his own fraud, misrepresentation or gross negligence. Priority against subsequent purchasers now has to be secured by deposit of title deeds or by registration of the mortgage as a land charge.

Leasehold land

In practice, the 1925 legislation did not bring about substantial changes in the way in which leaseholds were mortgaged, because mortgages by assignment, which were converted into mortgages by sub-demise as a result of that legislation, were in any case rare. This state of affairs arose from the operation of the rule in *Spencer's Case*,[1] whereby the burden of a covenant which touched and concerned the land affected an assignee of a term.

By section 86(1) of the Law of Property Act 1925, the proper form of the mortgage is for the mortgagor of the land to make an underlease the term of which is shorter than that of the lease the subject-matter of the mortgage. Although an underlease for a concurrent term would be valid, the first mortgagee's term is made shorter, usually by ten days, so as to leave room for further legal mortgages of the same lease, each of which would be for a term one day longer than the term of the immediately prior mortgage. Section 86(2) puts this on a statutory basis in respect of successive mortgages of leases which purport to be created by assignment. Sections 86(1) and 89(1), (2), (3), (5) of the Law of Property Act 1925 make the same provisions in favour of a mortgagee or sub-mortgagee of leasehold land as are made by the corresponding subsections of sections 85 and 88 regarding freehold land.

Section 86(3) of the 1925 Act provides that sub-mortgages shall be made in the same way as other mortgages of leaseholds. If one person has advanced money on the security of a lease and wishes to raise money on the mortgaged property without calling in the mortgage, he can sub-mortgage the property to another by creating a mortgage term in the form of an underlease ten days shorter than the lease.

Contents of a deed of mortgage by demise

Generally

Certain matters must be included in a deed of mortgage by demise as a matter of formality and do not require detailed consideration here. These

---

[1] (1583) 5 Co.Rep. 16.

include the date of the mortgage, a statement of the parties and a recital of the loan agreement. Further, the Law of Property Act 1925 granted the mortgagee by deed certain statutory powers which obviated the need for these to be created by express covenants. These are: the power to grant leases while in possession: section 99(2); to realise a security by sale: sections 101(1), 103; and to appoint a receiver: sections 101(1)(iii), 109.

Testatum

This states that the mortgagee has paid to the mortgagor the sum agreed to be lent, and that the mortgagor acknowledges its receipt. The receipt is not, as between the parties, conclusive as to the amount paid,[2] and it is open to the mortgagor to show that a smaller amount was actually advanced and to claim redemption on payment of that amount. Section 67(1) provides that a receipt for consideration money or securities in the body of a deed shall be a sufficient discharge for the same to the person paying or delivering the same, without any further receipt for the same being endorsed on the deed.

Whereas the receipt may be inconclusive as between the parties to the deed, they themselves are estopped from denying its truth as against third parties.[3] The fact that one party to the deed is solicitor to the other does not fix a third party with any constructive notice or put him on inquiry. But where a solicitor takes a security from a client and the deed does not express the real nature of the transaction, extrinsic evidence is required to prove the amount of the debt and the bona fides of the transaction.[4]

Covenant for repayment

This is an express covenant by the mortgagor to pay the principal, together with interest at a stated rate. The mortgagor's personal obligation to repay is a speciality debt[5] and therefore, like the remedies against the land, subject to a 12 year limitation period.[6] The six year period appropriate to actions founded on simple contracts applies to the personal remedy on a simple contract debt charged on land in a document not under seal, and to a simple contract debt which is merely recited in a deed and which there is no express or implied promise to repay. The limitation period runs not from the date of the instrument but from the date of breach of the covenant.

It is usual to stipulate that the principal be repaid on a date shortly after the execution of the deed. Unless the mortgage otherwise provides, the statutory powers of sale and appointment of a receiver do not arise until this date is past. Further, there is normally a distinct covenant for payment

---

[2] *Mainland* v. *Upjohn* (1889) 41 Ch.D. 126.
[3] *Powell* v. *Browne* (1907) 97 L.T. 854; *Bickerton* v. *Walker* [1885] 31 Ch.D. 151: and see L.P.A. 1925, s. 68(1) for the effect, in favour of a purchaser, of a receipt.
[4] *Lewes* v. *Morgan* (1817) 5 Price 42; *Bateman* v. *Hunt* [1904] 2 K.B. 530.
[5] *Sutton* v. *Sutton* (1882) 22 Ch.D. 511.
[6] Limitation Act 1980, s.20(1). See *post*, pp. 404, 407.

of interest if the principal sum remains unpaid after the due date. If this is included the dates of payment and the rate of interest should be stated. But it is unclear that this is necessary, since it has been held that where there is a covenant to pay principal and interest, the covenant is to pay two distinct sums of money and can be enforced by two separate actions notwithstanding that the obligations are contained in the same instrument.[7]

A covenant to secure punctual payment is often inserted; this is expressed to be for the payment of a higher rate of interest, reducible on punctual payment, to the agreed rate. A written agreement specifying the rate of interest can be varied by a parol agreement, made for good consideration, to reduce the rate.[8] If the covenant to secure punctual payment is made in a form whereby the agreed rate of interest is to be increased if payment is not made punctually, it will be unenforceable as a penalty.[9] Covenants to secure punctual payment are strictly construed. If the payment is not made on the specified day, the mortgagee is entitled to demand the full rate. The fact that on one occasion he has accepted the reduced rate when payment was made late does not estop him from demanding the full rate in respect of a subsequent delayed payment.[10] Unless the covenant so stipulates, one late payment by the mortgagor will not deprive him of the benefit of the covenant in respect of future payments made punctually.

It is not necessary to stipulate that the principal be repaid on one fixed date. The principal may be made repayable by instalments, with a stipulation that its repayment shall not be otherwise enforced provided that the instalments and interest are duly paid. Where repayment of the principal by instalments is agreed, the parties are assumed to intend that, on default of regular payment of instalments, the whole debt shall become immediately payable. This may be provided for by one of the following covenants:

  (a) to pay the principal sum on a given date, with a proviso that if the sum is to be paid by the instalments stipulated, the lender will not require payment otherwise;
  (b) to pay in instalments with a proviso that if default is made in the payment of any instalment, the whole debt is to become immediately payable. Such a proviso is binding and will not be relieved against as a penalty.[11]

It is also possible to stipulate simply that the principal be repayable on demand, in which case it is implied that the mortgagor has a reasonable time in which to comply with the demand. The mortgage may, in such a case, provide that a demand is deemed to have been duly made once certain formalities have been observed.

[7] *Dickenson* v. *Harrison* (1817) 4 Price 282.
[8] *Lord Milton* v. *Edgworth* (1773) 5 Bro.P.C. 313.
[9] *Holles* v. *Wyse* (1693) 2 Vern. 389; *Strode* v. *Parker* (1694) 2 Vern. 316.
[10] *Maclaine* v. *Gatty* [1921] 1 A.C. 376.
[11] *Sterne* v. *Beck* (1863) 1 De G.J. and Sm. 595; *Wallingford* v. *Mutual Society* (1880) 5 App. Cas. 685.

Covenants implied by demise as beneficial owner

By demising the property as beneficial owner, the mortgagor gives the covenants implied by section 76 of the Law of Property Act 1925, in the mortgagee's favour. These are set out in full in Schedule 2, Parts III and IV, and comprise:

(a) Full power to convey and, in the case of a leasehold property, that the lease is in full force, unforfeited, unsurrendered, has not become void or voidable, and that all covenants and conditions have been observed;

(b) Quiet enjoyment if entry is made on default;

(c) Freedom from incumbrances other than those to which the mortgage is expressly made subject;

(d) Further assurance.

The habendum

This states the length of the term, that the lease is granted without impeachment of waste, and that there is a proviso for cesser on redemption.

Proviso for cesser on redemption

This normally states that if the mortgagor on a given day pays to the mortgagee the mortgage debt and interest, the mortgage term shall cease. An alternative proviso is that the mortgagee will, at any time thereafter and at the mortgagor's request and cost, surrender the term to the mortgagor or at his direction. A mortgagor cannot usually claim to be allowed to redeem before the day specified in the contract for payment of the principal, though he may do so if, before that date, the mortgagee has taken steps to recover payment.

Where there is a stipulation in a mortgage that the principal loan is not to be called in for a given period, there is usually a corresponding stipulation preventing the mortgagor from repaying or redeeming the mortgage, without the mortgagee's consent, until the period has expired. But the second stipulation if standing by itself may be held invalid as a clog on the equity of redemption, at any rate where the mortgagor is precluded from redeeming for an unreasonable length of time.

Covenants to repair and insure[12]

A mortgagee by deed has, by section 108(1) of the Law of Property Act 1925 a limited statutory power to insure the premises for loss or damage by fire to the extent specified in the mortgage deed or, if no amount is specified, up to two-thirds of the amount required to reinstate the property in the event of its total destruction. This power is excluded in the circumstances set out in section 108(2).

---

[12] See further pp. 332 *et seq.*, *post*.

By section 101(1)(ii), the premiums paid are a charge on the mortgaged property with the same priority and bearing the same rate of interest as the mortgage money. The premiums are a charge and cannot be recovered from the mortgagor as a debt, hence the mortgagor in practice has to covenant to insure, and breach of that covenant causes the mortgagee's power of sale to become exercisable.

Although a mortgagor is not obliged by statute to keep the mortgaged property in repair it is usual for him to covenant to do so.[13] Formerly, if the mortgage was a controlled mortgage[14] and the mortgagor failed to keep the property in a proper state of repair (measured by the general condition of the property at the date of the mortgage and not requiring that anything be done other than preserving that condition[15]) he lost his protection against the mortgagee's right to foreclose, sell or otherwise enforce his security.

Restriction on mortgagor's statutory powers of leasing[16]

These powers, which are conferred by section 99 of the Law of Property Act 1925, can be restricted or excluded by agreement[17] except in respect of mortgages of agricultural land[18] or where such exclusion or restriction would operate to prevent the carrying out of an order to grant a new tenancy of business premises.[19] The usual form of covenant is one not to grant a lease without the written consent of the mortgagee. But this does not prevent the mortgagor creating a lease which, as between himself and the tenant, is binding by estoppel. Such leases are not validated against the mortgagee by the Law of Property Act 1925, section 152.

Mortgagees' right to consolidate

Section 93(1) of the Law of Property Act 1925, provides that a mortgagor seeking to redeem any one mortgage is entitled to do so without paying any moneys due under any separate mortgage made by him, or by any other person through whom he claims, on property other than that comprised in the mortgage which he seeks to redeem; provided that no contrary intention is expressed in any one of the mortgage deeds and that at least one mortgage was made after 1881. It is therefore usual for the mortgage deed to contain a clause excluding the operation of section 93,

---

[13] But the mortgagee does have the right to have the security preserved from deterioration, see post, pp. 204 et seq.

[14] The provisions of the Rent Acts relating to controlled mortgages were repealed by the Housing Act 1980, s.152 and Sched. 26.

[15] Woodifield v. Bond [1922] 2 Ch. 40.

[16] See further post, pp. 337 et seq.

[17] Iron Traders Employers' Insurance Association Ltd. v. Union Land and House Investors Ltd. [1937] Ch. 313; Dudley and District Benefit Building Society v. Emerson [1949] Ch. 707; Rust v. Goodale [1957] Ch. 33.

[18] See Agricultural Holdings Act 1986, s.100, Sched. 14, para. 12(1)(2).

[19] Landlord and Tenant Act 1954, s.36(4).

although the restriction can equally well be excluded by a clause expressly preserving the mortgagee's right to consolidate.

Covenant against registration of title

The mortgagor usually covenants that no one shall be registered as owner of the mortgaged property, under the Land Registration Act 1925, without the mortgagee's consent.

Attornment clause

There is some doubt as to whether such a clause now has any value.[20] It was at one time usual for the mortgagor to attorn tenant: *(i)* at a nominal yearly rent; or *(ii)* at a rent reserved equivalent to the amount of interest payable annually; or *(iii)* at a full rack rent. The reason for creating the landlord-tenant relationship was to give the mortgagee the rights of a landlord as well as his right *qua* mortgagee; and in case *(ii)* above, to provide the right of distress as an additional security. Although such a clause would not confer the right of distress unless registered as a bill of sale,[21] its invalidity in that sense does not destroy the landlord-tenant relationship.[22] It is possible for a mortgagor to attorn tenant to a second mortgagee although he has already attorned tenant to the first mortgagee[23] and while the first mortgagee's rights under the mortgages are unaffected by the second attornment, that second attornment is valid by estoppel.

It has also been held that such a clause enables a mortgagee to enforce covenants given by a mortgagor's successor in title by virtue of the doctrine of privity of estate.[24] It was further held in the same case, that such a clause in a charge by way of legal mortgage created, not a tenancy at will, but a tenancy during the continuance of the security. This continued so long as the property was occupied by the mortgagor or persons deriving title under him, and subject to the mortgagee's right to determine the tenancy on giving the requisite period of notice. Where the clause requires that notice be given for determination of the tenancy, the mortgagee may not re-enter until that notice has been given.[25] Where the clause does not require notice to be given, commencement of possession proceedings operates as a determination[26] and thereafter no tenancy exists: Rent Act protection is not available and no statutory tenancy comes into existence. On the other hand it has been held that section 16 of the Rent Act 1957 (now section 5 of the Protection from Eviction Act 1977) might apply where the rent reserved by the attornment clause was a full rack rent or where the mortgagor was

---

[20] *Steyning and Littlehampton Building Society* v. *Wilson* [1951] Ch. 1018; *cf. Regent Oil Co. Ltd.* v. *J.A. Gregory (Hatch End) Ltd.* [1966] Ch. 402. See also *post*, p. 207.

[21] *Re Willis, ex p. Kennedy* (1888) 21 Q.B.D. 384.

[22] *Mumford* v. *Collier* (1890) 25 Q.B.D. 279; *Kemp* v. *Lester* [1896] 2 Q.B. 162.

[23] *Re Kitchin, ex p. Punnett* (1880) 16 Ch.D. 226, C.A.

[24] *Regent Oil Co. Ltd.* v. *J.A. Gregory (Hatch End)* [1966] Ch. 402.

[25] *Hinckley and Country Building Society* v. *Henny* [1953] 1 W.L.R. 352.

[26] *Woolwich Equitable Building Society* v. *Preston* [1938] Ch. 129; *Portman Building Society* v. *Young* [1951] W.N. 10.

required to reside on the premises.[27] It is therefore advisable, in order to safeguard against such protection being available to the mortgagor, for the clause to be in a form enabling the mortgagee to take possession without notice.

CHARGE BY WAY OF LEGAL MORTGAGE

The Law of Property Act 1925 provides that legal mortgages of both freeholds (section 85(1)) and leaseholds (section 86(1)) may be effected by a charge by deed expressed to be by way of legal mortgage. Section 87(1) provides that a chargee by deed expressed to be by way of legal mortgage shall have the same protection, powers and remedies as if he were a mortgagee by demise or sub-demise. By section 205(1)(xvi), "mortgage" includes any charge or lien on any property for securing money or money's worth, and "mortgagee" includes a chargee by way of legal mortgage. Nevertheless, a deed of charge does not convey any proprietary right to the chargee, so the mortgagor retains the full title instead of being left with only the nominal reversion. The charge, instead of demising the property merely states that the borrower, as beneficial owner, charges it by way of legal mortgage with the payment of the principal, interest and any other money secured by the charge. In addition, the charge differs substantially from a mortgage by demise in that it contains no proviso for redemption.

The words "as beneficial owner" in the charge fix the mortgagor with the same implied covenants as if the mortgage were by demise (Law of Property Act 1925, Schedule 2, Part III).

It has been suggested that it is uncertain whether the chargee can foreclose in the absence of a proviso for redemption or discharge. Foreclosure has been judicially described as the removal, by the court, of a stop put by the court itself on the mortgagee's title,[28] which would otherwise be absolute by reason of a breach of condition on the part of the mortgagor. A legal chargee, however, has no title from which a stop can be removed. Apparently, not even an express proviso for redemption could confer on him the right to foreclose. What is sometimes done is to insert a provision that, for the purposes of the charge, the legal right to redemption is to cease after the contract date.

It seems, however, that the words of sections 88(2) and 89(2) of the Law of Property Act 1925 clearly mean that a legal chargee has the right to foreclose; the only matter left uncertain is the event upon which that right arises and the provision referred to above has the effect of fixing that date in accordance with the natural view that the right arises as soon as the borrower is in default.

There is a special form of charge by way of legal mortgage, expressed to

---

[27] *Alliance Building Society* v. *Pinwill* [1958] Ch. 788; *Peckham Mutual Building Society* v. *Registe* (1981) 42 P. & C.R. 186. See further *post,* pp. 207, 467–468, and see *Bolton Building Society* v. *Cobb* [1966] 1 W.L.R. 1.
[28] *Carter* v. *Wake* (1877) 4 Ch.D. 605.

be a statutory mortgage, provided by the Law of Property Act 1925, Schedule 4, Form 1. This charge states the names of the parties, the sum lent, the rate of interest, the receipt of the money by the mortgagor, and the fact that the mortgagor, as beneficial owner, charges the named property with the principal and interest.

A mortgage when made in statutory form implies the following covenants:

(a) That the mortgagor will on the day stated pay to the mortgagee the stated mortgage debt with interest meanwhile at the stated rate; and thereafter will continue to pay interest at that rate, so long as the debt or any part of it remains unpaid, in half-yearly instalments, and this whether or not a judgment has been obtained under the mortgage.

(b) That if the mortgagor on the stated day pays to the mortgagee the mortgage debt and interest due, the mortgagee shall at the borrower's request and cost at any time thereafter discharge the mortgaged property or transfer the benefit of the mortgage as the mortgagor may direct.

Statutory forms of transfer are provided by the Law of Property Act 1925, Schedule 4, Forms 2 and 3 and a combined form of transfer is provided at Form 4. Schedule 4, Form 5 sets out a receipt on discharge of the statutory charge.

EQUITABLE MORTGAGES OF LEGAL INTERESTS

Arising from contract

Equitable securities in legal estates are either executory contracts to grant legal mortgages,[29] or charges[30] in the strict sense. While a mortgage is a conveyance of property subject to a right of redemption, a charge is not a conveyance but gives the chargee certain rights over the property charged. A typical contract creating an equitable charge arises where one party enters into a written contract to charge his realty with the payments of a sum of money to another.[31]

The security created by a contract to grant a legal mortgage has been described, both judicially and academically, as an equitable mortgage or an equitable charge. The basis of the distinction rests on the right of the party,

[29] *London County and Westminster Bank* v. *Tompkins* [1918] 1 K.B. 515.
[30] There have been many attempts to define "charge"; see *Re Sharland, Kemp* v. *Rozey (No. 2)* (1896) 74 L.T. 664; *National Provincial and Union Bank of England* v. *Charnley* [1924] 1 K.B. 431; cf. *Thomas* v. *Rose* [1968] 1 W.L.R. 1797.
[31] *Montagu* v. *Earl of Sandwich* (1886) 32 Ch.D. 525; but the express contract to give a charge was construed as a contract to give a mortgage, so the security was enforceable by foreclosure. Also *Cradock* v. *Scottish Provident Institution* (1893) 69 L.T. 380 affd. (1894) 70 L.T. 718, C.A. where an annuity was secured by a deed appointing a receiver of rents and profits; Romer J. held the deed to be a good equitable charge, but decreed foreclosure, not sale.

to whom the security is given, to a decree of specific performance.[32] Thus an instrument executed for the purpose of giving security in land will not give rise to an equitable mortgage if it is a voluntary settlement,[33] or a will,[34] or where statute prohibits the giving of security in the land.[35]

Agreements to give security in land are dispositions of interests in land and are, therefore, subject to the evidential requirements of the Law of Property Act 1925, section 40 but there are no specified words that need be used in order to create such agreements.[36] It is sufficient that the instrument manifests an intention to give security and in consequence, equitable mortgages have been held to be created by many types of instrument, including the following:

(i) a defective legal mortgage signed by the mortgagor or his agent[37];

(ii) a written agreement to create a security in consideration of a debt due or advance made[38]; but not in consideration of money to be advanced, since an unperformed agreement to lend money is not, normally, specifically enforceable[39];

(iii) an instrument charging property with a debt and containing a declaration that the debtor holds the property on trust for the creditor[40];

(iv) an authority for a creditor to sell land and retain his debt out of the proceeds[41];

(v) the appointment of a receiver to receive rents and pay money therefrom[42];

(vi) a power of attorney to a creditor to[43]:
　　(a) mortgage the debtor's land for payment of the debt
　　(b) to receive rents and profits and apply them in payment of principal or interest
　　(c) to enter up judgment in his favour[44];

(vii) an assignment of rent.[45]

---

[32] *Central Trust and Safe Deposit Co.* v. *Snider* [1916] A.C. 266; referring to *Freemoult* v. *Dedire* (1718) 1 P.Wms. 428.

[33] *Re Lloyd, Lloyd* v. *Lloyd* [1903] 1 Ch. 385; *Re Howell's Application* [1972] 1 Ch. 509.

[34] *Re Owen* [1894] 3 Ch. 220.

[35] *Metcalfe* v. *Archbishop of York* (1836) 1 My. and Cr. 547.

[36] *Mounsey* v. *Rankin* (1885) 1 Cab. and El. 496; *Cradock* v. *Scottish Provident Institution,* (1894) 70 L.T. 718.

[37] *Taylor* v. *Wheeler* (1706) 2 Salk. 449.

[38] *Eyre* v. *McDowell* (1861) 9 H.L.Cas. 619; *Parish* v. *Poole* (1884) 53 L.T. 35; *Capital Finance Co.* v. *Stokes* [1969] 1 Ch. 261.

[39] *Rogers* v. *Challis* (1859) 27 Beav. 175; *Larios* v. *Bonony y Gurety* (1873) L.R. 5 P.C. 346; *The South African Territories Ltd* v. *Wallington* [1898] A.C. 309. *cf.* the provision in the Companies Act 1985, s.195, making debentures specifically enforceable in respect of unpaid calls, and see *post*, p. 28.

[40] *London and County Banking Co.* v. *Goddard,* [1897] 1 Ch. 642.

[41] *Re Cook, ex p. Hodgson* (1821) 1 Gl. and J. 12.

[42] *Spooner* v. *Sandilands* (1842) 1 Y. & C.Ch. 390.

[43] *Ibid. Re Cook, ex p. Hodgson* (1821) 1 Gl. and J. 12; *Abbott* v. *Stratten* (1846) 3 J. & Lat. 603; *Re Parkinson's Estate* (1865) 13 L.T. 26.

[44] *Cook* v. *Fowler* (1874) L.R. 7 H.L. 27; Administration of Justice Act 1956, s.16.

[45] *Ex p. Wills* (1790) 1 Ves.Jun. 162.

A charge given by way of indemnity against rents equitably apportioned or charged exclusively on land in exoneration of other land and against the breach or non-observance of covenants or conditions is not a general equitable charge, nor is a loan with a provision for it to be satisfied out of the proceeds of letting or selling property. Neither of these is a charge on land or incorporeal hereditaments.[46]

Although in such cases the equitable mortgage arises out of the agreement to create a legal mortgage, the legal mortgage is not usually intended to be created, nor is it necessary that it should be.[47] Indeed, the mortgagee may find himself in a better position by relying on his equitable rights, as a legal mortgage must identify with particularity the lands mortgaged. Whereas it is sufficient that, in an equitable mortgage, the lands are described so that they may be identified either at once or when the security becomes enforceable.[48]

Thus such a mortgage arises immediately if the mortgagor agrees to charge all the realty, or all the realty and personalty, which he has at that time, or he subsequently acquires,[49] or he will have acquired at some specified future date. Such a mortgage is not void either for uncertainty, nor as being against public policy, as long as the property comprised in it can be ascertained at the time when it is sought to enforce the charge.[50] Even if the property is ascertainable only at a future date, the mortgage arises immediately and binds the property when ascertained.

But where the mortgagor agrees to charge sufficient of his property to secure a specified sum, there is initially only a personal covenant: no security arises until some property has been appropriated to the satisfaction of the obligation.[51] The same is true where the security is to be raised on only one of two specified properties; or if the agreement is to give security "on request." Specific performance will not be decreed until the property is specified or the request made.[52]

With one exception, executed consideration is necessary to make the agreement specifically enforceable; that exception is provided by section 195 of the Companies Act 1985 which makes debentures specifically enforceable in relation to unpaid calls.

It therefore follows that the mere existence of an antecedent debt is not valuable consideration for a security given by the debtor. In order for there to be valuable consideration, there must be an agreement, express or

[46] Land Charges Act 1972, s.2(4).
[47] Prior to 1971 the creation of an informal mortgage was a common method of avoiding the payment of stamp duty. The payment of stamp duty on mortgages was abolished by the Finance Act 1971, s.64.
[48] *Fremoult* v. *Dedire* (1718) 1 P.Wms. 429; *Montagu* v. *Earl of Sandwich* (1886) 32 Ch.D. 525; *Tailby* v. *Official Receiver* (1888) 13 A.C. 523.
[49] *Lyde* v. *Mynn* (1833) 1 My. & K. 683.
[50] *Ravenshaw* v. *Hollier* (1835) 4 L.J. Ch. 119.
[51] *Re Clarke, Coombe* v. *Carter* (1887) 36 Ch.D. 348; *Re Turcan* (1889) 40 Ch.D. 5; *Re Kelcey, Tyson* v. *Kelcey* [1899] 2 Ch. 530; *Syrett* v. *Egerton* [1957] 1 W.L.R. 1130 (such a charge cannot create a specific lien).
[52] *Shaw* v. *Foster* (1872) L.R. 5 H.L. 321.

implied, to give time or some further consideration, or there must be an actual forbearance which *ex post facto* may become the consideration to support the deed.[53] Thus it has been said:

> "It is quite enough if you can infer from the surrounding circumstances that there was an implied request for forbearance for a time, and that forbearance for a reasonable time was in fact extended to the person who asked for it."[54]

By contrast, the cases where the existence of an antecedent[55] debt has been held not to be good consideration for a voluntary increase of security are cases where that voluntary increase of the security was not known to the creditor, and could not have influenced him in the way of forbearance.

Arising from the deposit of title deeds

At one time, a deposit of title deeds without a memorandum created only a pledge of the deeds as chattels, giving the creditor the right to detain or sell the deeds as chattels, but no security over the land. Such transactions may still be carried out.[56] The law as to this was changed in a series of cases of which *Russel* v. *Russel*[57] was the first. In that case, a borrower, who subsequently became bankrupt, pledged a lease to a lender as security for money advanced to him and the lender brought an action for the sale of the leasehold. The jury decided that the lease had been deposited as security for the sums advanced and a sale was directed. In subsequent cases[58] this finding of fact was elevated into the principle that a deposit of deeds entitled the depositee to a mortgage and to have his lien effectuated. This so-called lien, however, is merely an implied contractual right to retain the deeds until the debt is paid, not a separate common law lien, and in consequence it cannot survive the avoidance of the security should that occur.[59]

The mere deposit of documents of title has not always been regarded as showing the intention to create an equitable mortgage. It is possible to deposit the deeds by way of pledge without the intention of binding the subject-matter of the deeds.[60]

---

[53] *Wigan* v. *English and Scottish Law Life Assurance Association* [1909] 1 Ch. 291.

[54] *Fullerton* v. *Provincial Bank of Ireland* [1903] A.C. 309 at 313; and see *Alliance Bank* v. *Broom* (1864) 2 Dr. & Sm. 289.

[55] *Glegg* v. *Bromley* [1912] 3 K.B. 474; Fletcher Moulton L.J.; and *cf. Holt* v. *Heatherfield Trust* [1942] 2 K.B. 1; *Combe* v. *Combe* [1951] 2 K.B. 215.

[56] *Swanley Coal Co.* v. *Denton* [1906] 2 K.B. 873, following *Barton* v. *Gainer* (1858) 3 H. & N. 387, in which it was held that an owner may separate his deeds from his estate and may grant the deeds as security, without the intention of binding their subject-matter; and see *Re Wallis and Simmonds (Builders) Ltd.* [1974] 1 W.L.R. 391.

[57] (1783) 1 Bro.C.C. 269; see also *Featherstone* v. *Fenwick* and *Hurford* v. *Carpenter*, noted in *ibid.* at 270. It took a long time for Lord Eldon to reconcile himself to the decision; see *Ex p. Coming* (1803) 9 Ves. 115 ("Lord Thurlow was of opinion, and that is not now to be disturbed"); *Ex p. Whitbread* (1812) 19 Ves. 209; *Ex p. Wright* (1812) 19 Ves. 255.

[58] *Edge* v. *Worthington* (1786) 1 Cox. Eq. Cas. 211, where Lord Kenyon M.R. held that parol evidence of the purpose for which the deeds were deposited was admissible to prove the agreement.

[59] *Re Molton Finance* [1968] Ch. 325.

[60] *Re Richardson, Shillito* v. *Hobson* (1885) 30 Ch.D. 396.

Sometimes it will be apparent from the nature of the transaction that the depositor had no intention of creating a mortgage (as where the deeds were deposited by mistake,[61] or so that they could be used for the preparation of a legal mortgage[62]) or where the deposit was made by way of indemnity without any agreement for a mortgage.[63] Again where only one joint tenant agreed to create a charge over property as security and deposited title deeds with the lender, it was held that there had been no effective deposit which could give rise to a charge in the absence of comment from the other joint tenants as first trustee of the legal estate.[64] Nevertheless there is now a presumption that a deposit of title deeds to secure a debt creates a charge on land,[65] the deposit being treated as a sufficient act of part performance. Further, it has been held that A may deposit deeds to his own land to secure a debt owed by B to C.[66] That presumption is rebuttable by evidence that the intention of the parties is to give the lender a right to the deeds themselves and not to give any security in the land. This reverses what had earlier been held. Some nineteenth century cases had laid down that either it was for the creditor to show affirmatively that the debtor intended to give a security over land or that there was no presumption at all and that evidence was required to decide what effect the depositor intended the deposit to give.[67]

It is not necessary to deposit all the title deeds in order to create an equitable mortgage by deposit. Such a mortgage has been held to have been created by depositing deeds relating to the property but not sufficient to show the depositor's title[68]; or deeds which are not complete but are material evidence of title[69]; or a single deed.[70] It is possible also to create an equitable mortgage by deposit of documents other than documents of title. Thus an equitable mortgage of a copyhold estate has been created by a deposit of a copy of the court roll.[71]

In one case the deposit of a receipt for purchase money containing a description of the property and a plan was held to be sufficient.[72] But a deposit of a map alone was held to be merely for the purpose of identifying the

---

[61] *Wardle* v. *Oakley* (1864) 36 Beav. 27.
[62] *Norris* v. *Wilkinson* (1806) 12 Ves. 192; where it was held that the deposit of deeds for the purpose of preparing a legal mortgage created neither a lien nor an equitable mortgage. Neither *Edge* v. *Worthington* (1786) 1 Cox. 211 nor *Ex p. Bruce* (1813) 1 Rose. 374 was cited to the court: and see *Hockley* v. *Bantock* (1826) 1 Russ. 141 for a directly contrary decision.
[63] *Sporle* v. *Whayman* (1855) 20 Beav. 607; *cf. Ex p. Coombe* (1810) 17 Ves. 369.
[64] *Thames Guaranty Ltd.* v. *Campbell* [1985] Q.B. 210.
[65] *Bank of New South Wales* v. *O'Connor* (1889) 14 App.Cas. 273.
[66] *Re Wallis and Simmonds (Builders) Ltd.* [1974] 1 W.L.R. 391.
[67] *Chapman* v. *Chapman* (1851) 13 Beav. 308; *Re McMahon, McMahon* v. *McMahon* (1886) 55 L.T. 763; *Dixon* v. *Muckleston* (1872) 8 Ch.App. 155.
[68] *Dixon* v. *Muckleston* (1872) 8 Ch.App. 155. *Roberts* v. *Croft* (1857) 24 Beav. 223.
[69] *Re Daintry, ex p. Arkwright* (1864) 3 Mont.D. & De G. 129; *Lacon* v. *Allen* (1856) 3 Drew. 579.
[70] *Ex p. Chippendale* (1835) 1 Deac. 67.
[71] *Ex p. Warner* (1812) 19 Ves. 202.
[72] *Goodwin* v. *Waghorn* (1835) 4 L.J.Ch. 172.

land to be mortgaged, and thus insufficient to create a mortgage by deposit.[73]

Where a series of mortgages is made by splitting up the title deeds and depositing some with each of the mortgagees, priority of the competing mortgages, in the absence of gross negligence by a prior mortgagee, depends on the date of their creation, that is, on the date of acquisition of the documents deposited.[74] Registration under the Land Charges Act 1972 is not available in respect of a mortgage protected by a deposit of title deeds. The creation of an equitable mortgage by deposit does not require delivery to the mortgagee himself. Delivery to his agent or trustee is sufficient, and it has been held that, where the mortgagor delivered deeds to his own solicitor to provide security for the mortgagee, the solicitor became a trustee for the mortgagee.[75] There is no sufficient delivery if the mortgagor executes a memorandum and hands over neither the deeds nor the memorandum.[76]

If an equitable mortgage by deposit is created, it is, in the absence of evidence to the contrary, security for further advances as well as the original loan. All that is required is clear parol evidence of such intention.[77] It would be pointless to insist on delivery of the deeds to the mortgagor and redelivery to the mortgagee in respect of every further advance.[78] This applies to all mortgages by deposit, whether accompanied by a memorandum or not, and is thus a case where parol evidence is admissible to vary the terms of a written memorandum. It must be stressed however that parol evidence, where there is a memorandum either in writing or by deed, is not admissible to show that the deposit was not for the purpose of giving security if the memorandum states that it was.[79]

Law of Property Act 1925, section 40 and the doctrine of part performance

Except with regard to the means of establishing priorty, there is no essential difference between a mortgage by deposit and a mortgage created in any other way. The presence or absence of the deeds can affect the mortgage contract in only one way, namely, to validate it in the event that there is no sufficient memorandum for the purpose of section 40 of the Law of Property Act 1925.[80] This validation is achieved by an extension of the doctrine of part performance.[81]

---

[73] *Simmons* v. *Montague* [1909] 1 I.R. 87 at 95; see also *Bank of Ireland Finance* v. *Daly* [1978] I.R. 79.
[74] *Roberts* v. *Croft* (1857) 24 Beav. 223.
[75] *Lloyd* v. *Attwood* (1858) 3 De G. & J. 614.
[76] *Ex p. Coming* (1803) 9 Ves. 115.
[77] *Ex p. Langston* (1810) 17 Ves. 227.
[78] *Ex p. Kensington* (1813) 2 Ves. & B. 79; *Re Ablett, ex p. Lloyd* (1824) 1 Gl. & J. 389, where the original creditors were partners, an oral agreement was held effective to charge further advances on the same security although there had been changes in the composition of the partnership.
[79] *Shaw* v. *Foster* (1872) L.R. 5 H.L. 321.
[80] *Re Beetham, ex p. Broderick* (1887) 18 Q.B.D. 766.
[81] *Russel* v. *Russel* (1783) 1 Bro.C.C. 269.

Under the usual application of that doctrine, the agreement would be enforceable in favour of the depositor only, since it is the performer of the act who is normally entitled to rely on it. But it is well settled that equitable mortgages by deposit are also enforceable in favour of the depositee. Neither the argument that an act of part performance renders the contract enforceable only for the benefit of the actor, nor the argument that it is unsound policy to dispense with the need for writing in contracts for security has prevented the development of the equitable mortgage by deposit into a permanent feature of the law of mortgages.[82]

Although there is no necessity for a memorandum it is advisable for one to be made[83] so as to avoid disputes between the parties as to the existence or extent of the security. The memorandum may be an informal document but in practice it is usually under seal, since an equitable mortgagee by deed has the statutory power of sale and appointment of a receiver.[84] He does not have the right to possession, however, unless there is an agreement to that effect.[85] No particular form of words is prescribed but it is desirable that the memorandum refers to the deposit of the deeds and states that such deposit was made with the intent that the land should be equitably charged with the repayment of the moneys advanced. Since an equitable mortgagee selling the security otherwise than by judicial sale has no power to make the conveyance to a purchaser,[86] the following provisions are normally inserted when the agreement is by deed:

(i) an appointment of the mortgagee as the mortgagor's attorney to make the conveyance on sale under the express or statutory power;

(ii) a declaration by the mortgagor that subject to his own right of redemption he holds the property on trust, to convey it as the mortgagee shall from time to time direct, together with an authorisation for the mortgagee to appoint, at any time, a new trustee in place of the mortgagor.[87]

PROPERTY WHICH CAN BE SUBJECT TO A MORTGAGE OF LAND

Fixtures

Both legal and equitable[88] mortgages of freehold and leasehold[89] land apply to all fixtures whether specified or not which are annexed to the land

---

[82] *Pryce* v. *Bury and Price* (1853) 2 Drew. 11; *Parker* v. *Housefield* (1834) 2 My. & K. 419; *Carter* v. *Wake* (1877) 4 Ch.D. 605.

[83] *Sporle* v. *Whayman* (1855) 20 Beav. 607.

[84] L.P.A. 1925, s.101.

[85] *Garfitt* v. *Allen* (1888) 37 Ch.D. 48; *Ocean Accident and Guarantee Corporation* v. *Ilford Gas Co.* [1905] 2 K.B. 493; *Vacuum Oil Co.* v. *Ellis* [1914] 1 K.B. 693.

[86] *Re Hodson and Howes' Contract* (1887) 35 Ch.D. 668.

[87] *London and County Banking Co.* v. *Goddard* [1897] 1 Ch. 642.

[88] *Re Lusty, ex p. Lusty* v. *Official Receiver* (1889) 60 L.T. 160.

[89] *Meux* v. *Jacobs* (1875) L.R. 7 H.L. 481; *Southport and West Lancashire Banking Co.* v. *Thompson* (1889) 37 Ch.D. 64. See also *post*, pp. 271–272.

at the date of the mortgage or become so during its continuance.[90] Fixtures which a tenant is entitled to retain as against his landlord pass with a mortgage by the tenant of his leasehold interest.[91] Rights of foreclosure, possession and statutory rights of sale extend to the interest in any fixtures or personal chattels affected by the mortgage.[92]

If chattels which are bailed under a hire or hire-purchase agreement, or agreed to be sold under a conditional sale agreement, become fixtures (other than trade fixtures) they become subject to the mortgage even if affixed after it was created.[93] If they are trade fixtures, the owner or creditor has no right against a prior legal mortgagee, without notice of the agreement, to sever and remove them; but he has such a right against a subseqent equitable mortgagee with or without notice.[94]

This right is displaced by the right of a legal mortgagee of the land who has taken possession under his security, but not by the right of an equitable mortgagee whose mortgage was created after the hire, hire-purchase or conditional sale agreement was entered into, even one who has appointed a receiver who has entered into possession.[95]

Renewable leases and enfranchisements

A first mortgagee takes the benefit of anything that either the mortgagor[96] or a subsequent mortgagee,[97] adds to the land to improve its value.

Where a lease is renewable and either the mortgagor or the mortgagee renews it, the renewed lease becomes part of the mortgage security.[98] If an option to purchase the freehold reversion, being part of the security, is exercised by the mortgagee, he is not entitled to retain the benefit of it. On redemption the mortgagor is entitled to get back the whole of his security, so on payment of principal, interest, costs and the purchase price of the reversion the mortgagor is entitled to a conveyance of the freehold.[99]

The freehold estate acquired by a tenant under the Leasehold Reform Acts 1967 and 1979 does not merge with his leasehold estate if the lease is mortgaged, since merger cannot occur when the charge and the land are owned by different people. Unless the parties agree otherwise, the lease

---

[90] *Mather* v. *Fraser* (1856) 2 K. & J. 536; *Walmsley* v. *Milne* (1859) 7 C.B.(N.S.) 115; *Longbottom* v. *Berry* (1869) L.R. 5 Q.B. 123; *Holland* v. *Hodgson* (1872) L.R. 7 C.P. 328; *Smith* v. *Maclure*, (1884) 32 W.R. 459; *Reynolds* v. *Ashby & Son* [1904] A.C. 466; *Ellis* v. *Glover and Hobson Ltd.* [1908] 1 K.B. 388; *Vaudeville Electric Cinema* v. *Muriset* [1923] 2 Ch. 74; *Hulme* v. *Brigham* [1943] 1 K.B. 152.

[91] *Meux* v. *Jacobs* (1875) L.R. 7 H.L. 481.

[92] L.P.A. 1925, ss.88(4), 89(4).

[93] As to whether a chattel has become a fixture, see *Holland* v. *Hodgson* (1872) L.R. 7 C.P. 328; *Crossley Bros* v. *Lee* [1908] 1 K.B. 86.

[94] *Hobson* v. *Gorringe* [1897] 1 Ch. 182; *Reynolds* v. *Ashby and Son* [1904] A.C. 466; *Ellis* v. *Glover and Hobson Ltd.* [1908] 1 K.B. 388.

[95] *Ibid.*

[96] *Re Kitchin, ex p. Punnett* (1880) 16 Ch.D. 226.

[97] *Landowners West of England & South Wales Land Drainage and Inclosure Co.* v. *Ashford* (1880) 16 Ch.D. 411.

[98] *Re Biss, Biss* v. *Biss* [1903] 2 Ch. 40; *Leigh* v. *Burnett* (1885) 29 Ch.D. 231.

[99] *Nelson* v. *Hannam* [1943] Ch. 59.

will continue to be the mortgage security. A mortgage term cannot be enfranchised.[1] If the mortgagor acquires an extended tenancy under sections 14 to 16 of the 1967 Act, the extended lease is part of the security and, by section 14(6), the mortgagee who was entitled to possession of the title deeds relative to the original lease has the same right in respect of those relative to the extended lease.

Mortgages of leaseholds—relief from forfeiture

If a mortgagor defaults on a lease subject to a legal mortgage and the lease is forfeited then any derivitive interests determine with the lease. By virtue of section 146(4) of the Law of Property Act 1925,[1a] however, where a lessor is proceeding by action or otherwise to enforce a right of re-entry or forfeiture under any covenant, proviso, or stipulation in a lease, or for non-payment of rent, an underlessee (which includes a mortgagee) may apply for relief from forfeiture either in the lessor's action (if any) or in any action brought by such person for that purpose.[1b]

The court may make an order vesting for the whole term of the lease or any less term the property comprised in the lease or any part thereof in the mortgagee upon such conditions as to the execution of any deed or other document, payment of rent, costs, expenses, damages, compensation, giving security or otherwise as the court in the circumstances of each case may think fit. But "in no case shall any such under-lessee be entitled to require a lease to be granted to him for any longer term than he had under his original sub-lease."[2]

A number of problems have arisen with regard to this statutory provision. The court is only able to grant relief under section 146(4) where the lessor is proceeding by action or otherwise. The ability of a mortgagee to seek and obtain relief from forfeiture ceases as soon as re-entry has been effected. But the mortgagee might be unaware of the impending forfeiture even though the lessor is bound to serve on the lessee a statutory notice under section 146 before proceeding to enforce the forfeiture either by action or re-entry.[2a] Further, such relief gives rise to the creation of a *new*

---

[1] *Re Fairview, Church Street, Bromyard* [1974] 1 W.L.R. 579.

[1a] Replacing Conveyancing Act 1892, S.4, and as amended by the Law of Property (Amendment) Act 1929, s.1.

[1b] For such a right to arise the mortgage must be by sub-demise or legal charge, see *Re Good's Lease* [1954] 1 W.L.R. 309; *Grand Junction Co. Ltd.* v. *Bates* [1954] 2 Q.B. 160; *Chelsea Estate Investments Trust Co. Ltd.* v. *Marche* [1955] Ch. 328.

[2] L.P.A. 1925, s.146(4). An apparent conflict occurs between these provisions, but it has been decided that the court will not grant a sub-lessee a term longer than his sub-lease, see *Ewart* v. *Fryer* [1901] 1 Ch. 499 at 515, and see *Factors Sundries Ltd.* v. *Miller* [1952] 2 All E.R. 630 at 634.

[2a] See *Rogers* v. *Rice* [1892] 2 Ch. 170; *Belgravia Insurance Company Ltd.* v. *Meah* [1964] 1 Q.B. 436. In the High Court the position of a mortgagee in such circumstances has been somewhat improved in that a lessor who commences forfeiture proceedings is required to notify any person entitled to relief from forfeiture of whom he is aware (see the Rules of the Supreme Court (Amendment Number 2) 1986 S.I. 1986 No. 1187 (L.9) rr.2 and 3. In the

lease in favour of the mortgagee and the new lease becomes the substituted security and is subject to the mortgagors' right of redemption.[2b]

Finally, it should be mentioned that the provisions of section 146 of the Law of Property Act 1925 do not affect the jurisdiction of the court with regard to the law relating to relief for non-payment of rent alone whether or not the lessor has actually re-entered by action or otherwise.

Goodwill

On the principle that anything added to the property by the mortgagor is an accretion for the mortgagor's benefit, the mortgagee is entitled to the goodwill which attaches to premises[3]; though it will be otherwise if the terms of the security show that only the premises were intended to be subject to the mortgage.[4] The mortgagee is not entitled to benefit from goodwill arising from the mortgagor's personal reputation.[5]

Compulsory purchase

Where land subject to a mortgage is to be compulsorily acquired, both the mortgagor and the mortgagee are entitled to a notice to treat and where the acquiring authority pays a lump sum into court in respect of both interests, the court will apportion the sum between them. It is, however, usual, unless the mortgagee is in possession, for the acquiring authority to treat with the mortgagor for the full value, leaving him to discharge the mortgage.

C.C.R. Ord. 6, r. 3 has been amended in an action for the recovery of land so that the particulars of claim must now state the name and address of any mortgagee or other underlessee known to the plaintiff to be entitled to such relief.

[2b] See *Chelsea Estates Investments Trust Co. Ltd.* v. *Marche* [1955] Ch. 328; *Cadogan* v. *Dimovich* [1984] 1 W.L.R. 609; *Official Custodian for Charities* v. *Mackey* [1985] Ch. 168; and see also *Official Custodian for Charities* v. *Mackey (No. 2)* [1985] 1 W.L.R. 1308. As the Law Commission Working Paper No. 99 *Land Mortgages* points out at para. 3.74 that as a result of a principle of privty of contract this has the effect of making the mortgagee liable on the covenants of the new lease throughout the term of the lease. See also the Law Commission Working Paper No. 95 *Landlord and Tenant—Privity of Contract and Estate*: duration of liability of parties to leases (1986) where it is concluded that the principle of privity of contract should be abrogated.

[3] *Cooper* v. *Metropolitan Board of Works* (1883) 25 Ch.D. 472.

[4] *Whitley* v. *Challis* [1892] 1 Ch. 64.

[5] *Cooper* v. *Metropolitan Board of Works* (1883) 25 Ch.D. 472.

CHAPTER 4

MORTGAGES OF REGISTERED LAND

CREATION OF MORTGAGES: RIGHTS OF PARTIES TO THE MORTGAGE

The Law of Property Act 1925, sections 85(3) and 86(3), apply the provisions of that Act in regard to the creation of mortgages, to land which is registered under the Land Registration Act 1925. Section 205(1)(xxii) of the Law of Property Act 1925, states that "registered land" has the same meaning as in the Land Registration Act 1925: that is, land or any estate in land the title to which is registered under the Land Registration Act 1925, or any enactment replaced by it; it includes any easement, privilege, right or benefit appendant or appurtenant to it.

By section 25(1) of the Land Registration Act 1925, the proprietor of any registered land may by deed:

"(a) charge the registered land with the payment at an appointed time of any principal sum of money with or without interest;

(b) charge the registered land in favour of a building society under the Building Societies Act[1] . . . , in accordance with the rules of that society."

A charge of registered land may be made by an instrument in the form prescribed by the Land Registration Rules 1925, rule 139 the general form of which set out in Schedule I as Form 45. Charges to secure annuities or further advances may be made as in Forms 46 and 47 respectively and combined with Form 45. By section 27(1) of the Land Registration Act 1925 a registered charge in Form 45 takes effect as a legal mortgage even if the words "by way of legal mortgage" are not used. In fact, Form 45 is not often used.

By section 25(2) of the Land Registration Act 1925, a charge may be in any form provided that:

"(a) the registered land comprised in the charge is described by reference to the register or in any other manner sufficient to enable the registrar to identify the same without reference to any other document;

(b) the charge does not refer to any other interest or charge affecting the land which—

(i) would have priority over the same and is not registered or protected on the register

---

[1] In the Land Registration Act 1925, the Acts referred to are the Building Societies Acts 1874 to 1894. By s.17(2)(*a*) of the Interpretation Act 1978 that reference can be taken as applying to the present Building Societies Act 1986.

(ii) is not an overriding interest."

The Land Registration Act 1925, section 26(1) provides that:

> "the charge shall be completed by the registrar entering on the register the person in whose favour the charge is made as the proprietor of such charge, and the particulars of the charge."

Section 63(1) of the Land Registration Act 1925 provides that, on the registration of a charge, a charge certificate shall be prepared, and must be delivered either to the proprietor or, if he so prefers, deposited in the registry. By section 63(4), the preparation, issue, indorsement and deposit in the registrary of the certificate shall be effected without cost to the proprietor.

Rule 262 of the Land Registration Rules 1925 deals with the form of the charge certificate. It must certify that the charge has been registered and must contain:

(a) an office copy of the charge;
(b) a description (if no description is contained in the charge) of the land affected;
(c) the name and address of the proprietor of the charge;
(d) a list of the prior incumbrances, if any, appearing on the register.

It must have the Land Registry Seal affixed and may contain such further particulars as the Registrar shall think fit, and notes of subsequent dealings shall be entered on the charge certificate, or if more convenient, a new certificate shall be issued. The Registrar also issues a charge certificate to the chargee, while the chargor is required to deposit the land certificate at the Registry, where it remains until the charge is cancelled.

Section 29 of the Land Registration Act 1925 provides that, subject to any entry to the contrary on the register, registered charges on the same land shall rank, as between themselves, according to the order in which they are entered on the register, and not according to the order in which they are created.

Section 66 of the Land Registration Act 1925, which is set out below, provides an alternative method of creating a security in registered land, and it is a common method of securing a temporary loan:

> "The proprietor of any registered land or charge may, subject to the overriding interests, if any, to any entry to the contrary on the register, and to any estates, interests, charges, or rights registered or protected on the register at the date of the deposit, create a lien on the registered land or charge by deposit of the land certificate or charge certificate; and such lien shall, subject as aforesaid, be equivalent to a lien created in the case of unregistered land by the deposit of documents of title or of the mortgage deed by an owner entitled for his own benefit to the registered estate, or a mortgagee beneficially entitled to the mortgage, as the case may be."

Rules 239 and 240 of the Land Registration Rules 1925 provide two methods of creating a mortgage by deposit of the land certificate. Rule 239 provides a formal method, and the notice of deposit operates as an ordinary caution under the Land Registration Act 1925, section 54:

"**239.**—(1) Any person with whom a land certificate or charge certificate is deposited as security for money may, by registered letter or otherwise, in writing give notice to the Registrar of such deposit, and of his name and address.

(2) The notice shall describe (by reference to the district and parish or place and number of the title) the land to which the certificate relates.

(3) On receipt of such notice the Registrar shall enter notice of the deposit in the Charges Register, and shall give a written acknowledgment of its receipt.

(4) Such notice shall operate as a caution under section 54 of the Act.

(5) The provisions of section 66 of the Act, and of these rules, as respects the deposit of a charge certificate, shall apply to the deposit of a certificate of sub-charge or of an incumbrance in like manner."

The procedure for creating a mortgage by way of notice of intended deposit is set out in rule 240; the notice does not have to be in any specified form, but rule 241 states the particulars which it must give:

"**240.** A person applying for registration as proprietor of land or of a charge may, whether the land or charge is already registered or not, create a lien on the land or charge equivalent to that created by a deposit of a certificate by giving notice in writing, signed by himself, to the Registrar, that he intends to deposit the land certificate or charge certificate, when issued, with another person as security for money.

241.—(1) The notice of such intended deposit shall state the name and address of the person with whom the certificate is to be deposited, and shall describe the land or charge to which the certificate relates by reference to the district or parish or place and number of the title or (in the case of unregistered land) by reference to the deed or document by which the land was last dealt with, or otherwise to the satisfaction of the Registrar.

(2) The Registrar shall enter notice of the intended deposit in the register and give a written acknowledgment of its receipt."

Section 66 of the Land Registration Act 1925 gives the proprietor of a registered charge the power to create a charge on the land by deposit of the charge certificate, and rules 163 to 166 of the Land Registration Rules 1925 deal with the powers of the proprietor of a charge or sub-charge and dispositions of sub-charges.

Unless and until a notice to the contrary has been entered on the register, a mortgagee or chargee of registered land has the same powers

and remedies as a legal mortgagee of unregistered land. Rule 141(2) of the
Land Registration Rules 1925 confers on the proprietor of a charge, while
in possession, or after a receiver has been appointed, or on such receiver's
behalf, the same powers as are conferred by sections 99 and 100 of the Law
of Property Act 1925, as extended by the instrument of charge or any
instrument varying the terms thereof; but subject to any contrary intention
expressed, a note of which shall, under an application to be made for that
purpose, be entered in the register. Section 28(1) of the Land Registration
Act 1925 confers these powers by means of the following implied covenants:

> (a) a covenant with the proprietor for the time being of the charge to
> pay the principal sum charged, and interest, if any, thereon, at
> the appointed time and rate; and
> (b) a covenant, if the principal sum or any part thereof is unpaid at
> the appointed time, to pay interest half-yearly at the appointed
> rate as well after as before any judgment is obtained in respect of
> the charge on so much of the principal sum as for the time being
> remains unpaid.

An additional implied covenant is provided, in the case of leasehold land,
by section 28(2) of the Land Registration Act 1925; *i.e.* to pay the rent and
observe the covenants and conditions contained in the lease, and to indemnify the chargee against all proceedings or claims arising out of breaches of
the covenants or conditions. If the mortgagee desires to enter and perform
the covenant himself, he will have to stipulate for the power to do so, as
section 28(2) does not confer that power on him.

As with rule 141 of the Land Registration Rules 1925, the contrary entry
on the register may be by way of a clause in the charge to the required
effect; and it is important for fiduciary owners and tenants for life of settled
land to make such entries, so as to avoid personal liability to pay the
mortgage debt.

The Land Registration Act 1925, section 25(3), invalidates any provision
in a charge which purports to:

> "(i) take away from the proprietor thereof the power of transferring
> it by registered disposition or of requiring the cessation thereof to be
> noted on the register; or
> (ii) affect any registered land or charge other than that in respect of
> which the charge is to be expressly registered."

Section 33 of the Land Registration Act 1925 contains the provisions
governing the transfer of registered charges and is as follows:

> "**33.**—(1) The proprietor of any registered charge may, in the pre-
> scribed manner, transfer the charge to another person as proprietor.
> (2) The transfer shall be completed by the registrar entering on the
> register the transferee as proprietor of the charge transferred, but the

transferor shall be deemed to remain proprietor of the charge until the name of the transferee is entered on the register in respect thereof.

(3) A registered transferee for valuable consideration of a charge and his successors in title shall not be affected by any irregularity or invalidity in the original charge itself of which the transferee did not have notice when it was transferred to him.

(4) On registration of any transfer of a charge, the term or subterm (if any) granted expressly or by implication by the charge or any deed of alteration shall, without any conveyance or assignment and notwithstanding anything to the contrary in the transfer or any other instrument, vest in the proprietor for the time being of the charge.

(5) Subject to any entry to the contrary on the register, the vesting of any term or subterm in accordance with this section in the proprietor of a charge shall, subject to the right of redemption, have the same effect as if such proprietor had been registered as the transferee for valuable consideration of the term or subterm."

The Land Registration Act 1925, section 31(1), gives the proprietor of a charge the power, by deed, in the prescribed manner, to alter the terms of the charge, but only with the consent of the proprietor of the registered land and the proprietors of all registered charges, if any, of equal or inferior priority, affected by the alteration. By section 31(3), the alteration is completed by the registrar entering it in the register.

PROTECTION OF MORTGAGEE

Mortgages may be created by transactions either on or off the land register. A registered charge is one the title to which has been examined by the registrar and its protection derives from the entry on the charges register. Securities off the register may be protected by one of the methods discussed below, but they are not entered on the charges register and no certificate is issued in respect of them.

The law relating to the protection of mortgages of registered land was substantially amended by section 26 of the Administration of Justice Act 1977, which incorporated a new section 106 into the Land Registration Act 1925. That new section is as follows:

"**106.**—(1) The proprietor of any registered land may, subject to any entry to the contrary on the register, mortgage, by deed or otherwise, the land or any part of it in any manner which would have been permissible if the land had not been registered and, subject to this section, with the like effect.

(2) Unless and until the mortgage becomes a registered charge—
   (a) it shall take effect only in equity, and
   (b) it shall be capable of being overridden as a minor interest unless protected as provided by subsection (3) below.

(3) A mortgage which is not a registered charge may be protected on the register by—

    (a) a notice under section 49 of this Act

    (b) any other such notice as may be prescribed, or

    (c) a caution under section 54 of this Act."

Section 101(1) of the Land Registration Act 1925 deals with the power of any person, whether the proprietor or not, having a sufficient interest in or power over registered land, to dispose of it, or create interests or rights in it. By section 101(2), all such interests or rights take effect as minor interests and are capable of being overridden by registered dispositions for valuable consideration. Section 101(3) deals with the protection of minor interests, which are expressed to take effect only in equity. This can be achieved by entry in the register of such notices, cautions, inhibitions and restrictions as the Act or rules made thereunder provide.

The former section 106 of the Land Registration Act 1925 provided a special form of caution for the protection of a mortgage by deed. As from August 29, 1977, the date of coming into force of section 26 of the Administration of Justice Act 1977, the Chief Land Registrar may arrange for the conversion of any mortgage, protected by a mortgage caution entered on the register before that date, into a registered charge. Rule 227 of the Land Registration Rules 1925 provides that on registration of a mortgage as a charge, all cautions relating to it shall be cancelled.

The relevant Land Registration rules have undergone some revision in the light of the 1977 Act. The Land Registration Rules 1977[2] revokes rule 223 of the 1925 Rules, substantially amends rule 228, which deals with the protection of sub-mortgages, but leaves rules 224 to 227 unaltered;

"**224.**—(1) A mortgage caution may be withdrawn at any time in the same manner and on the same conditions as an ordinary caution.

(2) A mortgage caution may be vacated, subject to the requisite evidence being furnished to the Registrar of the discharge of the mortgage.

225. On the lodgment for registration of any dealing with the land to which it relates, a mortgage caution shall be dealt with in the same manner as a caution under Section 54 of the Act, save that it cannot be warned off the register by service of notice on the cautioner; and the dealing, if registered, shall take effect subject to the rights, if any, protected by the mortgage caution.

226.—(1) If and when application is made to register the mortgage as a charge, the registration of the charge and of all dealings and devolutions affecting the mortgage shall have the same priority as the mortgage cautions by which they were respectively protected on the register, or such of them as are then subsisting and capable of taking effect.

---

[2] S.I. 1977 No. 2089.

(2) If the applicant is the person appearing by the register to be entitled to the benefit of the mortgage caution, the registration shall be made forthwith, and the applicant or his nominee shall be entered as proprietor of the charge.

(3) In other cases the application must be accompanied by proof of the applicant's title and shall be proceeded with as the Registrar shall direct."

The new rule 228 is as follows:

"**228.**—(1) The provisions of these rules and of section 26(2) of the Administration of Justice Act 1977 relating to mortgage cautions shall, subject to the necessary modifications, apply also to sub-mortgage cautions.

(2) Notice of the cancellation of a mortgage caution shall be served on the sub-mortgage cautioner.

(3) A sub-mortgage protected by a sub-mortgage caution shall not be registered as a sub-charge unless and until the principal mortgage is registered as a charge.

228A. The provisions of section 106 of the Land Registration Act 1925, as substituted by section 26(1) of the Administration of Justice Act 1977 shall, subject to any necessary modification, apply to a sub-mortgage created by the proprietor of a registered charge."

When the mortgage is created by notice of intended deposit, the registrar enters the notice in the register, and sends the land certificate to the chargee named.

As with an equitable mortgage of unregistered land, it is desirable, though not strictly necessary, for a memorandum to be executed, and, except for short-term securities, for it to be under seal and accompanied by a power of attorney for the mortgagee to make a registered disposition in case he should wish to exercise his statutory power of sale.

Although section 66 of the Land Registration Act 1925 describes the security so created as a lien, it contains the words "equivalent to a lien created in the case of unregistered land by the deposit of documents of title . . . " which, as explained earlier,[3] is by virtue of the anomalous extension of the doctrine of part performance, an equitable mortgage.

The mortgagee by deposit of the land certificate has the protection of section 64 of the Land Registration Act 1925 which requires its production to the registrar whenever any transaction specified in section 64(1) is carried out:

"—(1) So long as a land certificate or charge certificate is outstanding, it shall be produced to the registrar—

(*a*) on every entry in the register of a disposition by the proprietor of the registered land or charge to which it relates; and

(*b*) on every registered transmission; and

---

[3] See *ante*, pp. 26 *et seq.*

(*c*) in every case (except as hereinafter mentioned) where under this Act or otherwise notice of any estate right or claim or a restriction is entered or placed on the register, adversely affecting the title of the proprietor of the registered land or charge, but not in the case of the lodgement of a caution or of an inhibition or of a creditor's notice, or of the entry of a notice of a lease at a rent without taking a fine."

Section 64(2) provides that a note of every such entry or transmission shall be officially entered on the certificate, and gives the registrar the same powers of compelling the production of certificates as the Act gives him in respect of other documents.

In order for the mortgagee to avoid the possibility of losing his security as a result of temporarily giving up the certificate, he should produce it to the registrar himself; for rule 244 of the Land Registration Rules 1925 provides that if, while a notice of deposit or intended deposit is on the register, the certificate is left at the Registry for any purpose, it shall be dealt with, notwithstanding the notice, and shall be returned to the person leaving it or as he may in writing direct.

If a notice of deposit under rule 239 of the Land Registration Rules 1925 is entered on the register, the mortgagee has the additional protection conferred on a cautioner by section 55(1) of the Land Registration Act 1925; he will be entitled to notice of any intended disposition or entry on the register and will have 14 days in which to appear and to apply that the caution be continued. The caution also entitles the mortgagee to notice of any application for a new certificate and thus prevents his being prejudiced by such an application based on a false representation to the effect that the original has been lost or destroyed.

If an equitable charge is created, it ranks as a minor interest and may be protected by a notice or a caution as provided by sections 49(1)(*c*) and 54(1) of the Land Registration Act 1925, respectively.

CHAPTER 5

SECOND AND SUBSEQUENT MORTGAGES

GENERAL

Before 1926, second and subsequent mortgages of freehold land were necessarily equitable, as was also the case with leasehold land if the first mortgage was made by assignment. Subsequent mortgages of leasehold land could be legal if the first mortgage was made by sub-demise, each successive mortgage being by sub-demise for a term one day longer than the term of the previous mortgage.

It is now possible for second and subsequent mortgages of both freehold and leasehold land to be legal. These may be created by demise or sub-demise, as appropriate, or by charge expressed to be by way of legal mortgage. A second or subsequent mortgage, in addition to reciting the mortgagor's ownership and the agreement for the loan, should recite the state of the prior mortgage. This provides the mortgagee with a remedy under the implied covenants for title given by the mortgagor as beneficial owner in the event that the sum owing is greater than the sum recited. The demise or charge should be expressly made subject to any prior mortgage, and it is usual for the power of sale to be made exercisable on interest under a prior mortgage being in arrears for a specified number of days. There should also be a power for the subsequent mortgagee to settle and pass the accounts of prior mortgagees and a charge of the costs of so doing upon the mortgaged property.

The right to tack

A second or subsequent mortgagee may be exposed to the risk that a prior mortgagee will make further advances, ranking in priority to his mortgage, to the mortgagor. Before 1926, two classes of mortgagee had the right to tack further advances, namely an equitable mortgagee who acquired the legal estate, and a legal mortgagee who made a further advance. The right to tack is now regulated by section 94(1) of the Law of Property Act 1925:

> "After the commencement of this Act, a prior mortgagee shall have a right to make further advances to rank in priority to subsequent mortgages (whether legal or equitable)—
> (a) if an arrangement has been made to that effect with the subsequent mortgagees; or
> (b) if he had no notice of such subsequent mortgages at the time when the further advance was made by him; or

(c) whether or not he had such notice as aforesaid, when the mortgage· imposes an obligation on him to make further advances."

The subsection applies whether or not the prior mortgage was made expressly for securing further advances.

Therefore if B creates two mortgages, first in favour of L1 and then in favour of L2, on the same security, and then takes a further advance from L1, section 94(1)(a) of the Law of Property Act 1925 provides that L1 may, with the consent of L2, obtain priority for his further advance over that made by L2.

Section 94(1)(b) deals with the situation where L1 has no notice of L2's mortgage. He can, then, claim priority for his further advance over L2's advance. For this purpose, however, registration of L2's mortgage as a land charge constitutes actual notice, and it is therefore essential that L1 makes a Land Registry search in order to ascertain whether any subsequent mortgages have been created. Where a mortgage is made expressly for securing either a current account or other further advances, registration does not constitute notice for the purpose of depriving the prior mortgagee of his right to tack, and section 94(2) applies:

"a mortgagee shall not be deemed to have notice of a mortgage merely by reason that it was registered as a land charge . . . if it was not so registered at the time when the original mortgage was created or when the last search (if any) by or on behalf of the mortgagee was made, whichever last happened."

An intending second or subsequent mortgagee, on making a search and discovering that the prior mortgage has been made expressly to secure a current account or further advances, should therefore give notice, on completion of his mortgage, to the prior mortgagee. Another reason for giving such notice is that registration as a land charge is not notice for the purpose of the Law of Property Act 1925, section 96(2) which casts on a mortgagee having notice of subsequent mortgages, the duty to deliver the title deeds to the person next entitled in priority. Section 96(1) entitles the mortgagor, as long as his right to redeem subsists, to inspect and make copies of documents of title in the power or custody of the mortgagee; and section 205(1)(xvi) defines "mortgagor" as "any person . . . deriving title under the original mortgagor or entitled to redeem a mortgage according to his estate interest or right in the mortgaged property." Section 94(1)(c) applies where L1 by the terms of the mortgage is obliged to make further advances. In that case, neither registration nor actual notice of the existence of any subsequent mortgage deprives L1 of his right to tack; this provision reverses the pre-1926 common law rule.

The right to consolidate

It has also been suggested that a second mortgagee is exposed to the risk of having an earlier and a later advance by a first mortgagee of the same property consolidated against him. The doctrine of consolidation applied originally where the mortgagor created two mortgages on different properties, in favour of the same mortgagee, but was later extended to the case where the mortgages were originally created in favour of different mortgagees but subsequently became vested in the same person. By section 93(1) of the Law of Property Act 1925, the operation of the doctrine is excluded unless a contrary intention is shown in one or more of the mortgage deeds. There is one decision[1] in which consolidation was allowed in respect of three mortgages, the first two of the same property, the third being of that and other property. The judge expressed his unfamiliarity with the question and, while the decision has been accepted as authority for the propositions that: (i) the doctrine can be excluded by a provision in any one of the mortgage deeds; and (ii) that the right to consolidate exists where the mortgages become vested after the mortgagor's bankruptcy, it has never been subsequently cited as determining that the doctrine applies to successive mortgages of the same property.

Power of sale

A second or subsequent mortgagee may also be at risk of not recovering the amount of his security in the event of a prior mortgagee exercising his power of sale. Section 105 of the Law of Property Act 1925 provides that such a mortgagee holds the purchase money on trust, after prior mortgages have been paid off, to pay:

  (i) all expenses incidental to the sale;
 (ii) to himself, the principal, interest and costs due under the mortgage;
(iii) the surplus, if any, to the person entitled to the mortgaged property.

These words are defined so as to include subsequent mortgagees, and the prior mortgagee is a trustee of the surplus for those subsequent mortgagees of whose incumbrances he has notice. Registration as a land charge is notice for this purpose (Law of Property Act 1925, section 198(1)).

Although it has been decided that a mortgagee who exercises his power of sale is not a trustee of that power for the mortgagor, he owes a duty not only to act in good faith, but to take reasonable care to obtain the true market value of the mortgaged property at the date at which he sells it.[2] This is a statutory duty in the case of a building society mortgagee. It therefore ought to follow that, provided a second or subsequent mortgagee makes reasonable enquiries and takes reasonable precautions to satisfy himself that there is sufficient equity in the property to secure his advance, he should not be at much risk of loss on a sale by a prior mortgagee. In

---

[1] *Re Salmon, ex p. The Trustee* [1903] 1 K.B. 147; and see Megarry and Wade, *The Law of Real Property* (5th ed., 1984), p. 959, n. 28.
[2] *Cuckmere Brick Co. Ltd.* v. *Mutual Finance Ltd.* [1971] Ch. 949. See also *post*, Chap. 14 pp. 231 *et seq.*

practice, he often suffers loss resulting from the accumulated interest on the prior mortgage.

Trustees

By the Trustee Investment Act 1961, Schedule 1, Part II, paragraph 13, any mortgage of freehold property in England, Wales or Northern Ireland, or of any leasehold property of which the unexpired term is over 60 years, is an authorised narrower range investment requiring advice. Though trustees lending money on the security of such property do not obtain the protection of section 8 of the Trustee Act 1925 unless they comply with the provisions of subsection 1 of that section. Since section 8(1)(*b*) requires them to show that the amount of the loan does not exceed two-thirds of the value of the property, it may well be that second mortgages rarely comply with that provision.

Building societies

Formerly, section 32(1) of the Building Societies Act 1962 prohibited a building society from advancing money on the security of real property subject to a prior mortgage, except as provided by Schedule 5 to the Act or where the prior charge is in favour of the society. Section 32(2) fixed the directors jointly and severally with the liability for making good any loss occasioned to the society by the advance. The power of a building society to lend on second or subsequent mortgage has now been greatly extended by Part III of the Building Societies Act 1986, which is dealt with in Chapter 9.

PROTECTION

Unregistered land

A second or subsequent legal mortgagee will not, in general, have the title deeds, since they will normally be in the possession of the first mortgagee.

Section 2(4) of the Land Charges Act 1972 provides that a puisne mortgage (that is, one not protected by a deposit of title deeds) shall be registered as a class C(i) land charge, and, if not registered, it is void against a purchaser for value of any interest in the land. Equitable mortgages are registrable as general equitable charges, which belong to class C(iii), and failure to register has the same consequences.

Registered land

Here the method of protection depends on the way in which the first mortgage was created. If a first charge has been registered, the land certificate will have been deposited at the Registry in accordance with section 65 of the Land Registration Act 1925. A second legal mortgage can be registered and a charge certificate issued in respect of it. Section 29 of the 1925 Act provides that, subject to any entry to the contrary in the register, priorities among legal mortgages are determined by the order in which they were entered on the register. Form 45[3] contains stipulations altering the priority of charges under section 29.

Where the prior mortgage was created by deposit of the land certificate, that will be held by the prior mortgagee and protection will be by way of notice under the Land Registration Act 1925, section 49, if the depositee is willing to make the land certificate available, or otherwise by caution under the Land Registration Act 1925, section 54. The invariable practice of banks is to require a formal charge to be registered.

---

[3] Land Registration Rules 1925, Sched. I. See *ante*, p. 35.

CHAPTER 6

MORTGAGES OF PERSONAL CHATTELS

LEGAL MORTGAGES

A debt may be secured on personal chattels by way of pledge, charge or mortgage. Delivery of possession of the chattels to the lender is an essential element of a pledge, though possession may be constructive, as where a document of title to the chattel rather than the chattel itself is delivered. The pledgee acquires a so-called "special property" in the chattel. This term, however, has been criticised on the grounds that no proprietary right vests in him; but the term is too well established to be replaced by any supposedly more accurate expression.

Where security over the chattels is given by way of charge (or, as it is also termed, hypothecation) no transfer of possession occurs. The chargee obtains a right, in preference to other creditors, to apply the chattels to the satisfaction of the debt and, for the purpose of so doing, to trace the chattels into the hands of third parties other than those having a prior claim or purchasers of the legal title without notice of the charge. Since no transfer of ownership is brought about by the creation of a charge, the instrument creating it is not a bill of sale at common law. But section 4 of the Bills of Sale Act 1878 defines "bill of sale" so as to include any agreement which creates a charge or security over personal chattels.

Where the chattel is mortgaged, however, it is by way of assignment of the legal title with a proviso, express or implied, for reassignment on redemption, and possession is irrelevant to the mortgagee's title. The legal title will pass when the parties intend it to pass and the transfer of that title requires neither delivery nor writing. A legal mortgage of chattels may be created orally or in writing, but if possession is given by way of security without any express transfer of the title, it will be for the court to determine whether the intention of the parties was to create a mortgage or a pledge.

EQUITABLE MORTGAGES

Because the legal title to personal chattels cannot be split up, it is not possible to create a mortgage by demise, nor can a second legal mortgage be created. All subsequent mortgages are mortgages of the equity of redemption, and must, as dispositions of equitable interests, comply with the requirement of section 53(1)(c) of the Law of Property Act 1925 of being in writing signed by or on behalf of the mortgagor.

A valid mortgage of chattels may be created where the subject-matter is a specified chattel, or chattels in the mortgagor's possession at the time the mortgage was made. It is also possible to create a mortgage of goods which have not yet come into existence or which have not yet been acquired by the mortgagor.

At common law, a purported transfer of goods *inter vivos*, not at the time of the transfer owned by the transferor, could be effective only where the subject-matter of the transfer is either;

(1) potential produce of property already owned by the transferor and to be conveyed by the transfer, which itself operated to pass the legal title to the produce when it came into existence; or
(2) goods which the transferor had not yet acquired and the title to which passed to the transferee as a result of some further act of the transferor.

In equity, however, a transfer, or agreement for the transfer, of future goods, if made for value, vests the beneficial ownership of such goods in the transferee so soon as the transferor acquires them and without any new act of transfer on his part. This applies only when the goods are described sufficiently to be identifiable; and any property answering that description will be affected.

Fraudulent Transactions

The main reason for securing debts by way of mortgage, rather than pledging chattels, is that the debtor can retain the use and enjoyment of the mortgaged property while giving the creditor the desired security. The mortgagee's title does not depend on possession. While this arrangement may be satisfactory as between the creditor and the debtor, the retention of possession of the mortgaged chattel by the debtor opens the way to fraud.

In the first place, it is open to the debtor to enter into a collusive transaction whereby he is able to represent to his unsecured creditors that chattels are encumbered and thus unavailable to satisfy his debts to them. This danger was realised long ago and the Fraudulent Conveyances Act 1571 avoided any assurance of chattels made with intent to delay, hinder or defraud creditors. Continued possession of mortgaged chattels by the mortgagor was taken as raising a presumption of fraud for the purposes of that statute. But it seems nowadays to be accepted that such possession, like any other surrounding circumstance, is a matter to be taken into account in deciding whether the assurance of chattels was made bona fide.

The possession of chattels, subject to a mortgage bill of sale, by the mortgagor is, of course, entirely consistent with the mortgage contract and is, without more, insufficient to raise a presumption of fraud.

The relevant statutory provisions are now sections 423 to 425 of the Insolvency Act 1986, which in effect replace section 172 of the Law of

Property Act 1925.[1] That section provided that, with certain exceptions, conveyances of property made with intent to defraud creditors were void-able at the instance of the person prejudiced. The provisions of the 1986 Act introduce a new set of rules governing transactions intended to defeat and delay creditors. These enable the court, where a person has entered into a transaction of an undervalue with the purpose of defeating the claims of creditors or other persons, to make orders restoring the position to what it would have been had the transaction not been entered into and thus pro-tecting the interests of persons prejudiced.[1a]

This, however, is not the only danger associated with mortgages of chattels. A bona fide mortgage of chattels by an individual can lead to fraud, since, where the mortgagor remains in possession, there is nothing to show that the chattels are incumbered. He can thus obtain credit to which he is not entitled by falsely representing himself to be their unincum-bered owner. Mortgages or charges of chattels by companies require regis-tration.[1b]

Since there are no essential documents of title to chattels (except for bills of lading and similar documents) it is difficult for the mortgagee to prevent the mortgagor from dealing with the chattels as if he were the legal owner. The legislation originally enacted to deal with this problem applied only in the case of bankruptcy. It transferred to the trustee in bankruptcy all goods in the possession, order or disposition of the bankrupt with a reputation of ownership. The provisions relating to reputed ownership formerly con-tained in section 38(c) of the Bankruptcy Act 1914 have been repealed.[1c]

The protection which that legislation afforded to general creditors was, in any case limited, as all it did was to bring into the bankruptcy some chat-tels which would otherwise have been unavailable. Also, it did nothing to prevent them advancing credit on the strength of the ostensible ownership, nor did it in any way assist an execution creditor where there is no bank-ruptcy.

THE BILLS OF SALE ACTS

The earlier legislation

The first legislation enacted to deal with the two problems mentioned above[2] was the Bills of Sale Act 1854, the preamble to which read, in part:

---

[1] Repealed by the Insolvency Act 1985, s.235(3) and Sched. 10, Pt. III.

[1a] These sections should be compared with ss.238–241 and ss.339–341 of the Insolvency Act 1986, which confer similar powers on the court in relation to transactions at an undervalue and preferences. See *post*, pp. 106–111. See also the Consumer Credit Act 1974 and the law relating to extortionate credit bargains, *post*, pp. 146–152. It is also necessary to note the jurisdiction of the court to set aside or vary the terms of any extortionate credit com-pany; see Insolvency Act 1986, s.244. There are similar provisions in the case of bankrupts, see *ibid.* s.343.

[1b] Companies Act 1985, s.396(1)(c); see p. 52, *post.*

[1c] Insolvency Act 1985, s.235, Sched. 10, Pt. III. See also *post*, p. 96.

[2] Discussed in *Cookson* v. *Swire* (1884) 9 App.Cas. 653, *per* Lord Blackburn at 664; also see *Re Tooth, Trustee* v. *Tooth* [1934] 1 Ch. 616.

" . . . frauds are frequently committed upon creditors by secret bills of sale of personal chattels, whereby persons are enabled to keep up the appearance of being in good circumstances and possessed of property, and the grantees or holders of such bills of sale have the power of taking possession of the property of such persons, to the exclusion of the rest of their creditors."

The 1854 Act did not ascribe any particular meaning to the term "bill of sale," which is, at common law, a written instrument which effects a transfer of personal property.

It provided that every bill of sale of chattels, including mortgage bills of sale, whether absolute or conditional, whereby the grantee or holder was enabled to seize or take possession of any property comprised therein, should be registered. Want of registration would cause the bill to be avoided against the grantor's assignees in bankruptcy, against assignees for the benefit of creditors, and against execution creditors. Registration did not, however, amount to such a publication of change of ownership as would protect the grantee from the operation of the "reputed ownership" rule in bankruptcy.[3] The 1866 Act provided that registration should be renewed every five years.

The current Bills of Sale legislation

Purpose

The major Acts which now apply are the Bills of Sale Act 1878 and the Bills of Sale Act (1878) Amendment Act 1882. The Bills of Sale Acts 1890 and 1891 make some minor amendments to the main legislation.

The main purpose of the 1878 Act,[4] like its predecessors, was the protection of creditors against having their rights prejudiced by secret assurances under which chattels were permitted to remain in the apparent possession of those who had in fact parted with them. It invalidated all unregistered bills of sale against execution creditors and the grantor's trustee in bankruptcy, but not between grantor and grantee.

The 1882 Act was designed to prevent entrapment of the grantor by giving him an incomprehensible document to sign and to protect him from thereby having an oppressive bargain forced on him.[5] The 1882 Act changed the scope of the 1878 Act, which, from then on, applied only to bills of sale either by way of absolute assignment or which enabled the grantee to take possession of personal chattels otherwise than as security for the payment of money. Such bills are termed "absolute" bills. The 1882 Act applies only to bills of sale given as security for loans ("security" bills)

---

[3] *Badger and Williams* v. *Shaw and Walker* (1860) 2 E. & E. 472. Partnership assets are outside the "reputed ownership" provisions, as no partner has an exclusive right to them: *Re Bainbridge, ex p. Fletcher* (1878) 8 Ch.D. 218.

[4] *Manchester, Sheffield and Lincolnshire Railway Co.* v. *North Central Wagon Co.* (1888) 13 App.Cas. 554, *per* Lord Herschell at 560.

[5] *Ibid.*

and invalidates security bills, which do not conform to its provisions, as between grantor and grantee as well as between all other persons.

Application and scope of the Bills of Sale Act 1878

The 1878 Act defines "bill of sale," by section 4 as including:

" . . . bills of sale, assignments, transfers, declarations of trust without transfer, inventories of goods with receipt thereto attached, or receipts for purchase moneys of goods, and other assurances of personal chattels, and also powers of attorney, authorities, or licenses to take possession of personal chattels as security for any debt, and also any agreement, whether intended or not to be followed by the execution of any other instrument, by which a right in equity to any personal chattels, or to any charge or security thereon, shall be conferred";

and as excluding:

" . . . assignments for the benefit of the creditors of the person making or giving the same,[6] marriage settlements[7] transfers or assignments of any ship or vessel or any share thereof, transfers of goods in the ordinary course of business of any trade or calling, bills of sale of goods in foreign parts or at sea, bills of lading, India warrants, warehouse-keepers' certificates, warrants or orders for the delivery of goods, or any other documents used in the ordinary course of business as proof of the possession or control of goods, or authorising or purporting to authorise, either by indorsement or by delivery, the possessor of such document to transfer or receive goods thereby represented.":

and, additionally, the Bills of Sale Acts 1890 and 1891 exempt certain letters of hypothecation relating to imported goods.

Other charges exempted from the operation of the Bills of Sale Acts are:

(1) Debentures issued by any mortgage, loan, or other incorporated company (Bills of Sale (1878) Amendment Act 1882, section 17);

(2) Any instrument of charge or other security issued by a company which is required to be registered in the company's register of charges;

(3) Charges executed after September 14, 1967 by a society registered or deemed to be registered under the Industrial and

---

[6] In this exception "creditors" mean all the creditors: *General Furnishing and Upholstery Co.* v. *Venn* (1863) 2 H. & C. 153. It is sufficient if all the creditors have an opportunity of taking advantage of the deed by executing or assenting to it: *Boldero* v. *London and Westminster Loan and Discount Co.* (1879) 5 Ex.D. 47., although a time limit may be fixed within which a creditor must do so: *Hadley & Son* v. *Beedom* [1895] 1 Q.B. 646.

[7] Informal ante-nuptial agreements are within the exemption: *Wenman* v. *Lyon & Co.* [1891] 2 Q.B. 192, but post-nuptial settlements are not: *Ashton* v. *Blackshaw* (1870) L.R. 9 Eq. 510. Also see *Re Reis, ex p. Clough* [1904] 2 K.B. 769, C.A.

Provident Societies Act 1965, and which has registered offices in England or Wales, provided that an application for recording the charge is made in accordance with sections 1(1) and 8(2) of the Industrial and Provident Societies Act 1965;

(4) An agricultural charge (as defined by section 5(7) of the Agricultural Credits Act 1928) created by a farmer on all or any of his farming stock and other agricultural assets, in favour of a bank; and debentures issued by a society registered under the Industrial and Provident Societies Act 1965, or by an agricultural marketing board may be registered in like manner as an agricultural charge, if secured on farming stock and created in favour of a bank;

(5) Mortgages of aircraft registered in the United Kingdom Nationality Register and made on or after October 1, 1972;

(6) A mortgage of a ship or vessel or any share thereof.

By section 3 of the 1878 Act, its operation is restricted to bills of sale by which the grantee or holder has power, with or without notice, immediately or at any future time, to seize or take possession of any personal chattels comprised in or made subject to such bill of sale.

The Bills of Sale Acts deal with documents, not with transactions. Consequently, they do not apply where possession passes, as is the case when a pledge or lien is effected by physical change of possession and can be proved without reference to any document, even when accompanied by a collateral instrument regulating the rights of the parties as to the sale of the goods.[8] Possession can be constructive, as where a pledgor gives a delivery order to a warehouseman; this was held to be equivalent to actual possession by the pledgee.[9]

The Acts do not require that any transaction shall be put into writing. They only require that if a transaction is put in writing and is of a particular character, then it shall be registered, otherwise it shall be void.[10]

If the transaction is complete without any writing, so that the property intended to be dealt with passes independently of the writing, the Acts do not apply to any document merely confirming or referring to the transaction.[11] The transaction is not invalidated because such a document is afterwards drawn up and not registered. Thus where a motor car that was orally pledge as security for a debt owing was handed over to the pledgee, the transaction was not brought within the Acts because the registration book was handed over at the same time.[12]

If the transferee's title depends on a document, whether that document is a transfer, an agreement to transfer, or a document of title made at that

[8] *Re Hardwick, ex p. Hubbard* (1886) 17 Q.B.D. 690, C.A.
[9] *Grigg* v. *National Guardian Assurance Co.* [1891] 3 Ch. 206.
[10] *United Forty Pound Loan Club* v. *Bexton* [1891] 1 Q.B. 25 n.
[11] *Ramsay* v. *Margrett* [1894] 2 Q.B. 18, C.A.
[12] *Waight* v. *Waight and Walker* [1952] P. 282.

time as a record of the transaction, it will be a bill of sale[13] and the Acts will apply.

What constitutes a bill of sale?

There have been many cases in which tests have been suggested for determining whether a document is or is not a bill of sale. Thus, a receipt will be a bill of sale if it is a reduction into writing of the agreement between the parties with regard to the giving of the security.[14] In *Charlesworth* v. *Mills*[15] it was held that, if a document, even though a simple receipt for purchase money, was intended by the parties to it to be part of the bargain to pass the property in the goods, it was a bill of sale. In *Ramsey* v. *Margrett*[16] Lopes L.J. posed the questions:

(i) Was it necessary to look at the document to prove the plaintiff's title?
(ii) Did the document transfer any property?

This test was applied in *Youngs* v. *Youngs*[17] where a receipt to which an inventory of goods was attached was held to have been given as an assurance of title and to be part of the bargain which transferred the property.

In *Re Townsend, ex p. Parsons*[18] it was held that a document giving a licence to take immediate possession of goods as security for a debt was a bill of sale within section 4 of the 1878 Act. However, where goods were pledged as security for a loan and delivered to the pledgee, a document signed by the pledgor, recording the transaction and regulating the pledgee's right to sell the goods, was held not to be a bill of sale since possession had already passed independently of the document.[19] The reasoning in *Charlesworth* v. *Mills* was also applied to documents created after goods had been reduced into possession under a common-law lien.[20]

Certain instruments conferring powers of distress are declared to be bills of sale by section 6 of the 1878 Act, which was designed to confine powers of distress to their proper purpose of securing genuine leasehold rents. Before the Act, mortgages often contained an attornment clause whereby the mortgagor attorned tenant to the mortgagee at a rent equal to the mortgage interest, and the mortgagee was given power to distrain for

---

[13] *Marsden* v. *Meadows* (1881) 7 Q.B.D. 80 at 85.
[14] *Newlove* v. *Shrewsbury* (1888) 21 Q.B.D. 41, *per* Lord Esher M.R.
[15] [1892] A.C. 231, H.L.
[16] [1894] 2 Q.B. 18, C.A.
[17] [1940] 1 K.B. 760, C.A.
[18] *Re Townsend, ex p. Parsons* (1886) 16 Q.B.D. 532.
[19] *Re Hardwick, ex p. Hubbard* (1886) 17 Q.B.D. 690. In *Wrightson* v. *McArthur and Hutchinsons (1919) Ltd.* [1921] 2 K.B. 807, the contents of a room were constructively delivered by handing over the keys. A subsequently executed written licence to enter was held not to be a bill of sale.
[20] *Great Eastern Railway Co.* v. *Lord's Trustee* [1909] A.C. 109.

arrears. Such a clause has been held not to be a bona fide lease[21] but a lease to secure money and thereby coming with the ambit of section 6 below:

"Every attornment instrument or agreement, not being a mining lease, whereby a power of distress is given or agreed to be given by any person to any other person by way of security for any present future or contingent debt or advance, and whereby any rent is reserved or made payable as a mode of providing for the payment of interest on such debt or advance, or otherwise for the purpose of such security only, shall be deemed to be a bill of sale, within the meaning of this Act, of any personal chattels which may be seized or taken under such power of distress.

Provided, that nothing in this section shall extend to any mortgage of any estate or interest in any land tenement or hereditament which the mortgagee, being in possession, shall have demised to the mortgagor as his tenant at a fair and reasonable rent."

In summary, the section deems powers of distress conferred by way of security for debt to be bills of sale, except in respect of:

(i) mining leases;
(ii) leases, by mortgagees in possession, to their mortgagors at a fair and reasonable rent.[22]

Thus, a lease of a public house containing a power of distress for the price of goods sold was held to be a licence to take possession of personal chattels as security for a debt; this was deemed to be a bill of sale and was held void for want of registration.[23] Documents containing attornment clauses such as that referred to above are not altogether void. The landlord-tenant relationship created by such a clause exists for the purpose of giving the mortgagee the right to sue for possession or to enforce a proviso for re-entry for non-payment of rent. As the clause is merely "deemed" to be, rather than actually made into, a bill of sale, it will not be void for non-compliance with the statutory form.

Definition of personal chattels

In order for a document to be caught by the Bills of Sale Acts, it must not only be a bill of sale but must relate to personal chattels as defined by section 4 of the 1878 Act. The definition applies to both Acts, but where a security bill comprises some personal chattels as defined and some other property, it may be effectual with regard to that other property although

---

[21] *Re Willis, ex p. Kennedy* (1888) 21 Q.B.D. 384, C.A.; *cf. Green* v. *Marsh* [1892] 2 Q.B. 330. For attornment clauses, see *ante*, pp. 23–24 and *post*, pp. 207 *et seq*.
[22] *Re Roundwood Colliery Co. Ltd.* [1897] 1 Ch. 373, C.A.
[23] *Pulbrook* v. *Ashby & Co.* (1887) 56 L.J.Q.B. 376.

void, for non-compliance with the statutory form, as regarding the personal chattels.[24]

The 1878 Act defines "personal chattels," in section 4, as:

" . . . goods, furniture, and other articles capable of complete transfer by delivery, and (when separately assigned or charged) fixtures and growing crops, but shall not include chattel interests in real estate, nor fixtures (except trade machinery as herein-after defined),[25] when assigned together with a freehold or leasehold interest in any land or building to which they are affixed, nor growing crops[26] when assigned together with any interest in the land[27] on which they grow, nor shares or interests in the stock, funds, or securities of any government, or in the capital or property of incorporated or joint stock companies, nor choses in action, nor any stock or produce upon any farm or lands which by virtue of any covenant or agreement or of the custom of the country ought not to be removed from any farm where the same are at the time of making or giving of such bill of sale."

Thus a document transferring or charging those growing crops which are personal chattels within section 4 of the principal Act is registrable as a bill of sale[28] unless:

(1) the crops are industrial growing crops assigned by a transfer made in the ordinary course of business[29] or contained in an agricultural charge;

(2) the crops are farming stock or produce which by virtue of any agreement, covenant or custom of the country (*i.e.* prevalent usage of reasonable duration in the neighbourhood where the land is situated) ought not to be removed from the farm; or

---

[24] *Re Burdett, ex p. Byrne* (1886) 20 Q.B.D. 310, C.A. following *Pickering* v. *Ilfracombe Railway Co.* (1868) L.R. 3 C.P. 235, *per* Willes J. at 250; followed in *Re North Wales Produce and Supply Society* [1922] 2 Ch. 340. The case of *Davies* v. *Rees* (1886) 17 Q.B.D. 408 (and affd. *ibid.* at 499), was distinguished on the ground that it was a case where only personal chattels were mortgaged.

[25] By s.5, as machinery used in or attached to any factory or workshop, exclusive of (i) fixed motive power and its appurtenances; (ii) fixed power machinery, and (iii) steam, gas and water pipes.

[26] At common law, growing crops produced by agricultural labour (emblements, *fructus industriales*) or other growing crops (*fructus naturales*) after severance are "goods" but s.4 makes all growing crops "personal chattels" provided they are separately assigned or charged.

[27] s.7 of the 1878 Act applies both to growing crops and fixtures and provides that they shall not be deemed to have been separately assigned or charged: " . . . by reason only that they are assigned by separate words, or that power is given to sever them from the land or building to which they are affixed, or from the land on which they grow, without otherwise taking possession of or dealing with such land or building, or land, if by the same instrument any freehold or leasehold interest in the land or building to which such fixtures are affixed, or in the land on which such crops grow, is also conveyed or assigned to the same persons or person."

[28] *Re Phillips, ex p. National Mercantile Bank* (1880) 16 Ch.D. 104.

[29] *Stephenson* v. *Thompson* [1924] 2 K.B. 240.

(3) the document is otherwise excluded from the definition of a bill of sale or is exempted from the Acts by some other provision.

A mortgage of growing crops is a bill of sale only if the mortgagee is able to realise his security in the growing crops separately from his security in the land.[30] Only when growing crops are mortgaged incidentally in a mortgage of land are the Bills of Sale Acts excluded.[31] A mortgage of crops after severance is a bill of sale.[32] Fixtures affixed to mortgaged land, whether affixed before or after the date of the mortgage, form part of the security in the land and pass automatically to the mortgagee as realty unless the mortgage shows a contrary intention.[33] As with growing crops, a mortgage of fixtures is a bill of sale only where the mortgagee can realise his security in the fixtures apart from that in the land.[34]

Trade machinery, as defined in section 5 of the 1878 Act, is deemed to be a personal chattel for the purposes of that Act, and any mode of disposition of it by its owner which would be a bill of sale as to any other personal chattels is deemed to be a bill of sale within the meaning of the 1878 Act. Fixed trade machinery not expressly mentioned in a mortgage of property may pass as part of the mortgaged premises, and if there is no disposition of trade machinery as such, nor any power to sell separately, the mortgage is not a bill of sale.[35] If on the true construction of the instrument there is a power to sell it separately, the instrument is a bill of sale so far as the trade machinery is concerned.[36]

Choses in action, shares and interests in stock are all specifically excluded from the definition of personal chattels in section 4 of the 1878 Act. This includes shares in partnership assets even though they involve the right to specific chattels.[37] A mortgage of a reversionary interest in specific chattels settled as heirlooms has been held to be outside the Act,[38] as has a mortgage of rights under a hire purchase agreement where the chattels subject to the agreement was not mentioned.[39] But a charge on a car in a garage until sale and afterwards on the purchase money was held to be within the Act because the charge is primarily on the chattel which the chose of action, the prospective proceeds of sale, represents.[40]

There is a conflict of opinion as to whether future goods can be

---

[30] Ibid.
[31] Re Gordon, ex p. Official Receiver (1889) 61 L.T. 299.
[32] Re Phillips, ex p. National Mercantile Bank (1880) 16 Ch. D. 104.
[33] Reynolds v. Ashby [1904] A.C. 466.
[34] Re Yates (1888) 38 Ch.D. 112, C.A.; Small v. National Provincial Bank [1894] 1 Ch. 686, held, an intention to mortgage fixtures as chattels separately because fixtures grouped with movable chattels were clearly not part of the land. See also Reeves v. Barlow (1883) 12 Q.B.D. 436; Climpson v. Coles (1889) 23 Q.B.D. 465 as to building materials brought on to land where buildings are in course of erection.
[35] Re Yates (1888) 38 Ch.D. 112, C.A.
[36] Small v. National Provincial Bank [1894] 1 Ch. 686.
[37] Re Bainbridge (1878) 8 Ch.D. 218.
[38] Re Thynne [1911] 1 Ch. 282.
[39] Re Davis & Co., ex p. Rawlings (1888) 22 Q.B.D. 193.
[40] National Provincial and Union Bank of England v. Lindsell [1922] 1 K.B. 21.

"personal chattels" for the purposes of the Acts. Waldock[41] takes the view that chattels not yet in existence or which are not yet owned by a mortgagor are outside the definition since they are not "capable of complete transfer by personal delivery."[42]

In *Holroyd* v. *Marshall*[43] it was held that assignments of specific after-acquired property operate in equity to transfer an equitable title as soon as the assignee acquires the property. Such property is "specific" for the purpose of that doctrine if it is described by general words sufficiently precise to render the property intended to be comprised in the assignment ascertainable.[44] Regardless of the Bills of Sale Acts, assignments of after-acquired property create equitable mortgages which bind the property as soon as it comes into the hands of the mortgagor.[45] A valid mortgage of personalty can be created even though the mortgagor does not know the exact nature of the chattels,[46] or where the personal property is not yet in existence, provided he has an actual or potential interest in the source of the property.[47]

A security in an incomplete chattel may be created by way of a contract to complete the chattels and to assign both the materials appropriated for its completion and the chattel itself when finished.[48] If the view expressed by Waldock is correct, equitable mortgages of after-acquired property are outside the scope of the Acts; but it has been doubted.[49]

It has been suggested[50] on three grounds that whether a chattel is "capable of complete transfer by personal delivery" depends on its physical characteristics and not on its existence or ownership at the time the security is created. Those grounds are:

(1) The Bills of Sales Act 1878 which repealed and replaced the 1854 Act, added, in section 4, the following words to the definition of a bill of sale, "any agreement . . . by which a right in equity to any personal chattels, or to any charge or security thereon, shall be conferred" and the purpose of this addition was to catch agreements giving equitable rights over after-acquired property.

---

[41] Waldock, *Mortgages* (2nd ed., 1950), p. 87.
[42] *Brantom* v. *Griffits* (1877) 2 C.P.D. 212; *Thomas* v. *Kelly* (1888) 13 App.Cas. 506, *per* Lord Macnaghten at 518, affirming *Kelly & Co.* v. *Kellond* (1888) 20 Q.B.D. 569, C.A. See also Fisher and Lightwood, *Law of Mortgage* (10th ed., 1988), p. 88.
[43] (1862) 10 H.L.C. 191.
[44] *Tailby* v. *Official Receiver* (1888) 13 App.Cas. 523, H.L.; see also *Re Wait* [1927] 1 Ch. 606; *Syrett* v. *Egerton* [1957] 1 W.L.R. 1130.
[45] *Industrials Finance Syndicate Ltd.* v. *Lind* [1915] 2 Ch. 345, C.A.; mortgage of an expectancy in personalty under a will or intestacy is a valid equitable mortgage which matures when the property falls into possession.
[46] *Re Beattie, ex p. Kelsall* (1846) De G. 352.
[47] *Langton* v. *Horton* (1842) 1 Hare. 549.
[48] *Woods* v. *Russell* (1822) 5 B. & Ald. 942; *Reid* v. *Fairbanks* (1853) 13 C.B. 692.
[49] See *Re Reis, ex p. Clough* [1904] 2 K.B. 769 at 778; Sykes, *Law of Securities* (2nd ed., 1973), pp. 472 *et seq.* See also *Halsbury's Laws of England* (4th ed., 1973), Vol. 4, paras. 610 and 638.
[50] See *Halsbury's Laws, supra.*

(2) Section 5 of the 1882 Act, which is headed "Bill of sale not to affect after-acquired property," refers to "personal chattels . . . of which the grantor was not the true owner at the time of execution of the bill of sale" and, unless after-acquired property is within the definition, the section is inherently contradictory.

(3) Even were the section not self-contradictory, it could, unless after-acquired property is within the definition of "personal chattels" readily be evaded by the taking of a bill shortly before the grantor acquired the assets.

The effect of a document which purports to deal with both presently owned and after-acquired chattels is discussed as the validity of such documents is affected by section 9 of the 1882 Act.

If a document which is a bill of sale within the 1878 Act fails to comply with the provisions relating to form and registration,[51] it is void against the grantor's execution creditors, or his trustee in bankruptcy or his assignee for the benefit of creditors, in so far as it comprises any chattels which at the time of the execution of process, the filing of the bankruptcy petition, or of the assignment, are in his possession or apparent possession.

Goods remain in the grantor's apparent possession until something is done which clearly takes them out of his possession.[52]

Where two people live in the same house, they may each be in apparent possession, but the person who has the legal title is in possession. The nature of the relationship between them is irrelevant provided the two people have the common use of the chattels.[53]

A domestic servant living with his master has been held not to have common use of the chattels in the house.[54] Where two persons live in the same house and one purports to make a gift to the other, the gift will be avoided against the grantor's execution creditor or trustee in bankruptcy if there is no sufficient delivery. There must be such act of delivery or change of possession as would be unequivocally referable to an intention by the donor to transfer possession and title in the chattels to the donee.[55]

---

[51] Bills of Sale Act 1878, s.8.

[52] *Re Blenkhorn, ex p. Jay* (1874) 9 Ch.App. 697; goods are still in the grantor's apparent possession although the broker's men are in her house, but no longer when the men start to pack up and load the goods into vans.

[53] *Ramsay* v. *Margrett* [1894] 2 Q.B. 18; *French* v. *Gething* [1922] 1 K.B. 236 (husband and wife); *Youngs* v. *Youngs* [1940] 1 K.B. 760 (The principle does not apply as between a master and his domestic servant; But *cf.* as to the application of the doctrine of *Ramsey* v. *Margrett, supra* to a case where a woman was living with a man as his mistress; see the observations by Goddard L.J.); *Antoniadi* v. *Smith* [1901] 2 K.B. 589 (mother-in-law and son-in-law).

[54] *Youngs* v. *Youngs, supra.* But *cf. Koppel* v. *Koppel* [1966] 1 W.L.R. 802, C.A. (married man and housekeeper, where latter held to be living in house not as an ordinary paid domestic servant but as a person sharing a common establishment with the married man).

[55] *Hislop* v. *Hislop* [1950] W.N. 124 (gift by writing not under seal and no physical delivery of the chattels); *Re Cole (A Bankrupt), ex p. Trustees of the Property of the Bankrupt* [1964] Ch. 175, purported oral gift, no delivery).

Failure to comply with the requirements of form or registration does not invalidate an absolute bill of sale as between the parties to it.[56]

Application and scope of the Bills of Sale (1878) Amendment Act 1882

The 1882 Act applies to bills of sale given by way of security for the payment of money. It applies where the subject-matter of the bill of sale is "personal chattels" as defined by section 4 of the 1878 Act, provided that:

(a) those personal chattels should be capable of specific description, and should be specifically described therein[57];

(b) at the time of the execution, the grantor should be the true owner of those personal chattels.[58]

There are exceptions to these rules for growing crops, plant and trade machinery, and fixtures.[59]

The main provisions of the 1882 Act are:

(1) the restriction of the grantee's right of seizure to five specified causes[60];

(2) a brief and simple form of bill of sale, setting out clearly the consideration and terms of payment, incorporating by reference the statutory grounds of seizure and specifying the property comprised in the bill, was made obligatory[61];

(3) a bill of sale not in the prescribed form was made absolutely void in regard to the personal chattels comprised in it[62];

(4) a bill of sale in the prescribed form was made absolutely void, if not registered,[63] in contrast to the 1878 Act, under which unregistered absolute bills of sale remained valid between grantor and grantee;

(5) all bills of sale given in consideration of a sum less than £30 were made absolutely void[64];

(6) section 20 of the 1878 Act was repealed in regard to security bills of sale so that registration does not take goods comprised in security bills of sale out of the possession, order or disposition of a bankrupt grantor.[65]

The application of the Acts has been set out in the following frequently cited words:

"Those statutes do not require that any transaction shall be put in

---

[56] *Davis* v. *Goodman* (1880) 5 C.P.D. 128; *Tuck* v. *Southern Counties Deposit Bank* (1889) 42 Ch.D. 471.
[57] Bills of Sale Act (1878) Amendment Act (1882), s.4.
[58] *Ibid.* s.5.
[59] *Ibid.* s.6.
[60] *Ibid.* s.7.
[61] *Ibid.* s.8; and see the Schedule which sets out the form.
[62] *Ibid.* s.9.
[63] *Ibid.* s.8
[64] *Ibid.* s.12.
[65] *Ibid.* ss.3 and 15.

writing; they only require that if a transaction be put in writing and be of a particular character, then it shall be registered, otherwise it shall be void."[66]

This principle, usually paraphrased as "the Acts strike at documents, not transactions" is reinforced by section 62(3) of the Sale of Goods Act 1979 which provides that nothing in that Act or the 1893 Act affects the enactments relating to bills of sale.

Nevertheless the courts have regard to the substance of the transaction, and the intention of the parties is material in two respects. If a document is essential to the transaction whereby the property passes, it is a bill of sale,[67] but not if it is a mere record and is not intended to be essential, as where it is a receipt acknowledging the change in ownership.[68] Also, if a document is intended to conceal the fact that a transaction is a loan on security, it is caught by the Acts. Similarly, where a document purported to set out a hire-purchase agreement but the parties had no intention that the intending purchaser should ever become the owner of the chattels, it is also caught.[69]

If a contract, according to the tenor of the document and the intention of the parties, is a contract of hire with an option to purchase, it is outside the Acts.[70] The provision in a hire-purchase agreement giving the owner the power to re-take possession of the property does not make the agreement into a bill of sale. It has been said that if a contract of sale is genuinely intended to operate according to its tenor, so that the hire-purchase agreement is executed by the legal owner of the property, the transaction cannot be impeached as a colourable cloak for a mortgage.[71] This is so even if the parties initially contemplated a transaction by way of bill of sale and genuinely changed their intention.[72]

Seizure and sale of goods

The grantee of a security bill of sale may only seize the chattels comprised herein if one of the following conditions set out in section 7 apply:

"(i) If the grantor shall make default in payment of the sum or sums of

[66] *United Forty Pound Loan Club* v. *Bexton* [1891] 1 Q.B. 28 n., C.A., *per* Fry L.J.
[67] *Youngs* v. *Youngs* [1940] 1 K.B. 760.
[68] *Ramsay* v. *Margrett* [1894] 2 Q.B. 18.
[69] *Maas* v. *Pepper* [1905] A.C. 102, H.L.; and see *Re Walden, ex p. Odell* (1878) 10 Ch.D. 76, C.A.; *Re Watson* (1890) 25 Q.B.D. 27; *North Central Wagon Finance Co.* v. *Brailsford* [1962] 1 W.L.R. 1288; *Mercantile Credit Co.* v. *Hamblin* [1965] 2 Q.B. 242, C.A.
[70] *McEntire* v. *Crossley Bros. Ltd.* [1895] A.C. 457, H.L. See also *Helby* v. *Mathews* [1895] A.C. 471, *per* Lord M'naughten at 482: *Modern Light Cars Ltd.* v. *Seals* [1934] 1 K.B. 32; *Pacific Motor Auctions Pty. Ltd.* v. *Motor Credits (Hire Finance) Ltd.* [1965] A.C. 867, P.C.; for further discussions, see A. L. Diamond, (1960) 23 M.L.R. 399 at 516 and Crossley Vaines, *Personal Property* (5th ed., 1973), pp. 371 *et seq.* and 467 *et seq.*
[71] *Yorkshire Railway Wagon Co.* v. *McClure* (1882) 21 Ch.D. 309; *Manchester, Sheffield and Lincolnshire Railway Co.* v. *North Central Wagon Co.* (1888) 13 App.Cas. 554, H.L.
[72] *Beckett* v. *Tower Assets Co.* [1891] 1 Q.B. 1. Each case must be determined according to the proper inference from the facts; see *Johnson* v. *Rees* (1915) 84 L.J.K.B. 1276.

money secured by the bill at the time therein provided for payment,[73] or in the performance of any covenant or agreement contained in the bill and necessary for maintaining the security;

   (ii) If the grantor becomes bankrupt,[74] or suffers the goods to be
      distrained for rent, rates or taxes;

 (iii) If the grantor fraudulently removes or suffers the goods to be
      removed from the premises;

 (iv) If the grantor upon demand in writing unreasonably refuses to
      produce his last receipts for rent, rates and taxes[75];

  (v) If execution has been levied against the goods of the grantor
      under any judgment at law."

If even one instalment is unpaid, the grantee may seize the whole of the
goods as security for the whole of the money, even though the bill of sale
makes no such express provision.

When the right to seize has accrued, the grantee may not remove or sell
the goods until five clear days have elapsed.[76] Section 7 also provides that,
during that period, the grantee may apply to the High Court for relief and
the court, if satisfied that for any reason the cause of seizure no longer
exists, can restrain the grantee from removing or selling them or make such
other order as it thinks just. However, even after the five days have
elapsed, the grantor can exercise his equitable right to redeem so long as
the grantee has not sold the goods or foreclosed.[77]

Form and contents of a security bill of sale

The validity of a security bill of sale is dependent on it satisfying the
conditions of sections 8 and 9 of the 1882 Act and the Schedule thereto.
Section 8 states that:

"Every bill of sale shall be duly attested,[78] and shall be registered
under the principal Act within seven clear days after the execution
thereof, or if it is executed in any place out of England then within
seven clear days after the time at which it would in the ordinary course
of post arrive in England if posted immediately after the execution
thereof; and shall truly set forth the consideration for which it was

---

[73] *Re Wood, ex p. Woolfe* [1894] 1 Q.B. 605.

[74] This means what it says and does not mean "commits an act of bankruptcy"; *Gilroy* v.
Bowey (1888) 59 L.T. 223.

[75] What constitutes cause for seizure under this provision is dealt with in *Hammond* v.
Hocking (1884) 12 Q.B.D. 291; *Barr* v. *Kingsford* (1887) 56 L.T. 861; *ex p. Wickens* [1898]
1 Q.B. 543. *Re Wood, ex p. Woolfe* [1894] 1 Q.B. 605.

[76] Bills of Sale Act (1878) Amendment Act 1882, s.13. After the five days have elapsed, the
court can grant relief only under the general law applicable to mortgages: *Longden* v.
Sheffield Deposit Bank (1888) 24 S.J. 913.

[77] *Johnson* v. *Diprose* [1893] 1 Q.B. 512.

[78] By one or more credible witnesses none of whom is a party; compare s.10 of the 1878 Act
which provides that an absolute bill must be attested by a solicitor and that the attestation
must state that before the bill was executed the solicitor explained its effect to the grantor.

given[79] otherwise such bill of sale shall be void in respect of the personal chattels comprised therein."

Consideration, for the purpose of section 8, means, not the sum secured by the bill, but that which the grantor receives for giving it.[80] The consideration can include the cost of preparation of the bill, paid to a solicitor, if the grantor has agreed to pay it.[81]

"Truly" means with substantial accuracy according to either the mercantile or legal effect of the facts.[82] A clerical error will not invalidate a bill of sale if it appears otherwise from the document what the true consideration was[83]; and an approximate statement will suffice, if nearly accurate.[84] If the consideration is not truly set forth, the bill is avoided whether the untrue statement was made intentionally or accidentally, though in many of the cases, the untrue statement involved the concealment of a bonus or expenses, to be paid to the moneylender, within the statement of the consideration.[85] The avoidance is in respect of the personal chattels only, so the covenant for payment remains valid as a personal obligation, even though the security is void as between the parties as well as against third parties.[86]

Section 9 of the 1882 Act states that:

"A bill of sale made or given by way of security for the payment of money by the grantor thereof shall be void unless made in accordance with the form in the schedule to this Act annexed."

The Schedule is as follows:

"This Indenture made the   day of   , between A.B. of   of the one part, and C.D. of   of the other part, witnesseth that in consideration of the sum of £   now paid to A.B. by C.D., the receipt of which the said A.B. hereby acknowledges [or whatever else the consideration may be], he the said A.B. doth hereby assign unto C.D., his executors, administrators, and assigns, all and singular the several chattels and things specifically described in the schedule hereto annexed by way of security for the payment of the sum of £   , and interest thereon at the rate of   per cent. per annum [or whatever else may be the rate]. And the said A.B. doth further agree and declare that he will duly pay to the said C.D. the principal sum aforesaid,

---

[79] Which must not be less than £30, otherwise the bill is absolutely void; s.12 of the 1882 Act.
[80] Ex p. Challinor (1880) 16 Ch.D. 260; Darlow v. Bland [1897] 1 Q.B. 125; Criddle v. Scott (1895) 11 T.L.R. 222; Henshall v. Widdison (1923) 130 L.T. 607.
[81] London and Provinces Discount Co. v. Jones [1914] 1 K.B. 147.
[82] Credit Co. v. Pott (1880) 6 Q.B.D. 295.
[83] Roberts v. Roberts (1884) 13 Q.B.D. 794.
[84] Hughes v. Little (1886) 18 Q.B.D. 32; "£32 or thereabouts" held to be in accordance with the requirements of s.8.
[85] Richardson v. Harris (1889) 22 Q.B.D. 268; Re Cowburn, ex p. Firth (1882) 19 Ch.D. 419; Cohen v. Higgins (1891) 8 T.L.R. 8; Parsons v. Equitable Investment Co. Ltd. [1916] 2 Ch. 527.
[86] Heseltine v. Simmons [1892] 2 Q.B. 547.

together with the interest then due, by equal   payments of
£   on the   day of   [*or whatever else may be
the stipulated times or time of payment*]. And the said *A.B.* doth also agree
with the said *C.D.* that he will [*here insert terms as to insurance, payment of
rent, or otherwise, which the parties may agree to for the maintenance or
defeasance of the security*].

Provided always, that the chattels hereby assigned shall not be liable to
seizure or to be taken possession of by the said *C.D.* for any cause other
than those specified in section seven of the Bills of Sale Act (1878) Amendment Act 1882.

In witness, &c

> Signed and sealed by the said *A.B.* in the presence of me *E.F.* [*add
> witness' name, address, and description*].''

A bill given by way of security which is not substantially in accordance
with the above form is void, not only as between grantor and grantee in
respect of the assignment of personal chattels, but it is also void as a contract of loan in respect of the personal covenant to pay principal and interest.[87] This is so even if it purports to be an absolute bill.[88] The lender can
recover his money only in an action for money had and received but will
then be allowed only a reasonable rate of interest rather than the stipulated
rate.[89]

Where a bill is void *in toto*, this does not mean that the security of which
it forms a part is void *in toto*. If the security comprises personal chattels and
also property which does not fall within that description, and it is possible
to sever the security on the personal chattels from the security on the other
property, then the security will be void as to the personal chattels but good
as to the other property.[89a] But a bill of sale will be bad if it includes in the
schedule property other than personal chattels.[89b]

The phrase ''in accordance with the form in the Schedule'' was
considered in *Re Barber, ex p. Stanford*[90] It had already been decided that
a material departure, by way of addition, would cause the bill to be
avoided.[91] In *Re Barber, ex p. Stanford* the point to be decided was the
effect of inserting the words ''as beneficial owner'' after ''doth hereby
assign.'' This insertion altered the legal effect of the document, since by

---

[87] *Davies* v. *Rees* (1886) 17 Q.B.D. 408; *Smith* v. *Whiteman* [1909] 2 K.B. 437.
[88] *Madell* v. *Thomas & Co.* [1891] 1 Q.B. 230.
[89] *North Central Wagon & Finance Co. Ltd.* v. *Brailsford* [1962] 1 W.L.R. 1288; *Davies* v.
Rees, supra. In *Bradford Advance Co.* v. *Ayers* [1924] W.N. 152, 5% per annum was taken
as the appropriate rate of interest.
[89a] *Re O'Dwyer* (1886) 19 L.R. Ir. 19, where the instrument comprised a bill of sale of personal chattels and a mortgage of freehold or leasehold property. In *Re Burdett, ex p. Byrne*
(1888) 20 Q.B.D. 310, C.A.; a bill of sale of personal chattels and also of trade machinery
was excepted under s.5 of the Act of 1878.
[89b] *Cochrane* v. *Entwistle* (1890) 25 Q.B.D. 116, C.A.; but the mortgage will be effective as
regards the other property.
[90] (1886) 17 Q.B.D. 259.
[91] *Davis* v. *Burton* (1883) 11 Q.B.D. 537.

section 7 of the Conveyancing Act 1881[92] the words incorporated a covenant for immediate possession on default, which was inconsistent with the provisions of section 7 of the 1882 Act. An invalid addition cannot be saved by a proviso that conditions not in accordance with the statutory form are to be disregarded, since this would be a departure of a kind "calculated to mislead those whom it is the object of the statute to protect."[93]

There are 14 characteristics of a bill of sale, and a bill which departs from any of them is void, even if the legal effect of the bill is unaltered by the departure.[94] They are:

(1) the date of the bill;
(2) the names and addresses[95] of the parties;
(3) a statement of the consideration;
(4) an acknowledgment of receipt if the advance is a present advance;
(5) an assignment, by way of security, of personal chattels capable of specific description;
(6) securing of a fixed monetary obligation;
(7) statement of the sum secured,[96] the rate of interest[97] and the instalments by which repayment is to be made[98];
(8) agreed terms for maintenance[99] or defeasance of the security;
(9) a proviso limiting the grounds of seizure to those specified in section 7 of the 1882 Act;
(10) the description of the chattels to be in the schedule, not the body of the bill;
(11) execution by the grantor;
(12) attestation;
(13) name, address and description of the attesting witness;

---

[92] Now L.P.A. 1925, s.76.
[93] Re Barber, ex p. Stanford (1886) 17 Q.B.D. 259.
[94] Thomas v. Kelly (1886) 13 App.Cas. 506.
[95] Altree v. Altree [1898] 2 Q.B. 267; bill invalidated by omission of address even though these could have been ascertained from another source with reasonable certainty.
[96] The amount ultimately payable must be certain: Hughes v. Little (1886) 18 Q.B.D. 32.
[97] Which must be stated as a rate though not necessarily a percentage, Lumley v. Simmons (1887) 34 Ch.D. 698, C.A., and not a lump sum: Blankenstein v. Robertson (1890) 24 Q.B.D. 543.
[98] Both the amount repayable and the times of repayment must be certain: Attia v. Finch (1904) 91 L.T. 70 (interest); De Braam v. Ford [1900] 1 Ch. 142, C.A. (principal).
[99] These include covenants:
    (i) to repair and replace; Furber v. Cobb (1887) 18 Q.B.D. 494;
    (ii) to insure; Neverson v. Seymour (1907) 97 L.T. 788; Topley v. Crosbie (1888) 20 Q.B.D. 350;
    (iii) not to remove the goods without consent; Re Coton, ex p. Payne (1887) 56 L.T. 571; Furbes v. Cobb (1887) 18 Q.B.D. 494;
    (iv) to pay rent, rates and taxes on the premises where the chattels are situated; Goldstrom v. Tallerman (1886) 18 Q.B.D. 1; and to produce receipts therefor; Furbes v. Cobb (1887) 18 Q.B.D. 494; Cartwright v. Regan [1895] 1 Q.B. 900;
    (v) to permit the grantee to pay insurance premiums, rent, rates or taxes, and to add such payments to the security, on default by the grantor on such payments; Goldstrom v. Tallerman (1886) 18 Q.B.D. 1; Neverson v. Seymour (1907) 97 L.T. 788; Topley v. Crosbie (1888) 20 Q.B.D. 350;
    (vi) for further assurance of title; Re Cleaver, ex p. Rawlings (1887) 18 Q.B.D. 489.

(14) schedule describing the personal chattels.

Although superfluous material not altering the legal effect, such as recitals, will not avoid the bill[1] it must not be such as to confuse the grantor or destroy the simplicity which the Act was designed to attain.[2]

Maintenance of the security means the preservation of the security "in as good a plight and condition as at the date of the bill of sale."[2] Whilst defeasance of the security involves a provision which limits the operation of the bill or stipulates for its discharge on a stated event.

The scope for imposing defeasance clauses is very limited, since section 10(3) of the 1878 Act provides that any defeasance not contained in the body of the deed is deemed to be part of the bill and must be written on the same document as the bill prior to registration. If this is not done, the registration is void, which invalidates the bill as far as the personal chattels are concerned, though the covenant for payment remains valid. If the bill is a security bill, the defeasance must comply with the statutory form[3] and the conclusion of any covenant for defeasance which gives the grantee a power of seizure not in accord with sections 7 or 13 of the 1882 Act avoids the bill totally.[4]

Registration: section 8

The section is set out at page 62 and the provisions are the same as for registration of an absolute bill of sale.[5] On registration a true copy of the bill and an affidavit in support thereof must be filed with the registrar of bills of sale at the central office of the Royal Courts of Justice. The true copy of the bill must be accompanied by a copy of every schedule or inventory herein referred to, the affidavit must contain statements as to the time of making the bill, its due attestation and execution, the residence and occupation of the grantor and every attesting witness.[6] The registration must be renewed every five years,[7] as failure to do so avoids it even against the grantor[8]; but an assignment or transfer need not be registered.[9] If registration is not made within seven days the court may, on being satisfied that the omission to register was due to mistake or inadvertence, extend

---

[1] *Roberts* v. *Roberts* (1884) 13 Q.B.D. 794; *Re Morritt* (1886) 18 Q.B.D. 222.

[2] *Furber* v. *Cobb* (1887) 18 Q.B.D. 494; but the fact that two courts differ as to the construction of a bill does not lead to avoidance under this principle, *Edwards* v. *Marston* [1891] 1 Q.B. 225.

[3] *Smith* v. *Whiteman* [1909] 2 K.B. 437.

[4] *Davis* v. *Burton* (1883) 11 Q.B.D. 537; covenant giving a right of seizure for failure to produce rent receipts on demand; *Barr* v. *Kingsford* (1887) 56 L.T. 861; right of seizure for default in respect of a covenant not necessary for the maintenance of the security; *Lyon* v. *Morris* (1887) 19 Q.B.D. 139; express power to sell and seize immediately on default.

[5] Bills of Sale Act 1878, ss.8, 22.

[6] So that third parties can make all necessary inquiries before lending the grantor money or supplying him with goods on credit; *Jones* v. *Harris* (1871) L.R. 7 Q.B. 157, a decision under the Bills of Sale Act 1854.

[7] Bills of Sales Act (1878) Amendment Act 1882, s.11.

[8] *Fenton* v. *Blythe* (1890) 25 Q.B.D. 417.

[9] *Re Parker, ex p. Turquand* (1885) 14 Q.B.D. 636; *Marshall and Snelgrove Ltd.* v. *Gower* [1923] 1 K.B. 356.

the time for registration[10] but there is no power to extend the time for renewal of registration.[11]

Although all original registrations are in London, section 11 of the 1882 Act[12] directs the registrar to transmit copies of the bill of sale to the registrar of the county court in whose district the chattels are situated, if either the chattels are situated, or the grantor resides, outside the London bankruptcy district. The bill is not avoided by the failure of the registrar to transmit the copy to a county court registry.[13]

A bill of sale is vacated by an entry of satisfaction in the register.[14] On the filing of an affidavit showing that the grantee covenants to satisfaction being entered, the registrar orders a memorandum of satisfaction to be endorsed on the bill.

There is provision for the rectification of inadvertent errors in the register, but an order cannot be made for an affidavit to be filed correcting errors in the bill of sale or supporting affidavit.[15] Any order made for rectifying the register is made subject to rights which have already accrued to third parties.[16]

Because the register is open to inspection and search[17] the grantor may find it difficult to obtain further credit. Under the Bills of Sale Act 1854, registration could be avoided by giving successive bills of sale of the same property for the same debt before the seven day period had expired. This practice was stopped (except where the court is satisfied that the subsequent bill was given bona fide for the purpose of correcting a material error in the prior bills) by providing that the subsequent bill should be absolutely void to the extent of the repetition.[18]

Inventory and specific description

The Bills of Sale Act 1882, section 4 states that:

"Every bill of sale shall have annexed thereto or written thereon a schedule containing an inventory of the personal chattels comprised in the bill of sale; and such bill of sale, save as hereinafter mentioned, shall have effect only in respect of the personal chattels specifically described in the said schedule; and shall be void, except as against the grantor, in respect of any personal chattels not so specifically described."

The effect of this provision is that, if the bill has no schedule at all, it is absolutely void for all purposes, not being in accordance with the statutory

---

[10] Bills of Sale Act 1878, s.14.
[11] *Re Emery, ex p. Official Receiver* (1888) 21 Q.B.D. 405.
[12] The same provision for absolute bills of sale is in s.10 of the Bills of Sale Act 1878.
[13] *Trinder* v. *Raynor* (1887) 56 L.J.Q.B. 422.
[14] Bills of Sale Act 1878, s.15.
[15] *Crew* v. *Cummings* (1888) 21 Q.B.D. 420, C.A.
[16] *Ibid.* See also *Re Parsons, ex p. Furber* [1893] 2 Q.B. 122, C.A.
[17] Bills of Sale Act 1878, ss.12, 16; Bills of Sale Act (1878) Amendment Act 1882, s.16.
[18] Bills of Sale Act 1878, s.9.

form.[19] If it has a schedule in which some of the chattels are not "specifically described" it is void against third parties in respect of the chattels, but
it remains valid for all purposes as between grantor and grantee. Thus a bill
of sale which refers, in the Schedule, to some specifically described existing
chattels, and some after-acquired chattels, is void against third parties in
respect of the after-acquired chattels but otherwise valid. On the other
hand, if the body of the bill contains a mortgage of after-acquired chattels,
it is absolutely void for non-compliance with the statutory form.[20]

There must be an inventory; a general description such as
"stock-in-trade" is inadequate.[21] The chattels must be described as a business man would describe them,[22] and the degree of detail will vary from
case to case.[23] A more detailed description will be necessary when the
chattels mortgaged are part of a fluctuating stock-in-trade. There is very
little direct authority as to what constitutes a specific description, though it
has been said that "specifically" involves a description which helps to separate a chattel from the rest of the things of the same class.[24]

True ownership: section 5

Section 5 of the 1882 Act states that:

> "Save as herein-after mentioned,[25] a bill of sale shall be void, except
> as against the grantor, in respect of any personal chattels specifically
> described in the schedule thereto of which the grantor was not the true
> owner at the time of the execution of the bill of sale."

The term "true owner" includes an equitable owner or a trustee,[26] and is
not limited to "beneficial owner." If an owner of chattels has previously
executed a mortgage bill of sale he still owns the equity of redemption and
remains the true owner for the purposes of a second bill granted subject to
the first.[27] A mortgage bill of sale by a legal owner is valid even if third
parties have prior equitable interests in the chattels. If the grantor has
already made an absolute sale or gift of the chattels, he has transferred
both the legal and equitable title and is not the true owner; and it is irrelevant that the grantee has no notice of the sale or gift.[28] A hirer under a
hire-purchase agreement, being merely a bailee for use, is not the true

---

[19] *Griffin* v. *Union Deposit Bank* (1887) 3 T.L.R. 608.
[20] *Thomas* v. *Kelly* [1888] 13 A.C. 506.
[21] *Witt* v. *Banner* (1887) 20 Q.B.D. 114.
[22] *Roberts* v. *Roberts* (1884) 13 Q.B.D. 794, C.A., *per* Lindley L.J. at 806.
[23] *Davies* v. *Jenkins* [1900] 1 Q.B. 133; *Carpenter* v. *Deen* (1889) 23 Q.B.D. 566; *Hickley* v.
Greenwood (1890) 25 Q.B.D. 277; *Witt* v. *Banner, supra; Herbert's Trustee* v. *Higgins*
[1926] Ch. 794: *Davidson* v. *Carlton Bank Ltd.* [1893] 1 Q.B. 82.
[24] *Witt* v. *Banner, supra.*
[25] Bills of Sale Act (1878) Amendment Act 1882, s.6, creating exceptions to the avoidance
provisions in ss.4 and 5 in respect of growing crops, or fixtures, separately assigned, or
trade machinery.
[26] *Re Sarl, ex p. Williams* [1892] 2 Q.B. 591.
[27] *Thomas* v. *Searles* [1891] 2 Q.B. 408; *Usher* v. *Martin* (1889) 24 Q.B.D. 272.
[28] *Tuck* v. *Southern Counties Deposit Bank* (1889) 42 Ch.D. 471.

owner; thus he cannot create a valid mortgage of the chattel until he has exercised his option to purchase.[29]

A person beneficially entitled to chattels is the "true owner" to the extent of his interest[30]; but if two persons purport to assign goods jointly as grantor, the bill of sale will be valid only to the extent of the chattels which they own jointly.[31] A purported assignment "jointly and severally" of chattels some of which belonged to the husband and some to the wife was held absolutely void for non-compliance with the statutory form, which contemplates a single grantor.[32] But where a husband correctly assigned as sole grantor and the wife was made a party to the bill of sale for collateral purposes, the bill was held to be valid.[33]

Whenever a bill of sale is avoided as against third parties, a grantee cannot maintain title to the goods against such third parties, for example, the grantor's assignee under an assignment for the benefit of creditors, even though he has possession of the goods.[34]

Bankruptcy: section 15

By section 20 of the 1878 Act, chattels comprised in an absolute bill of sale are deemed not to be within the possession order and disposition of the grantor for the purpose of bankruptcy proceedings. But section 15 of the 1882 Act repealed this provision in respect of security bills and provided that the chattels comprised therein might be seized by the trustee in bankruptcy.[35] The provisions formerly contained in section 38 of the Bankruptcy Act 1914, which concerned the bankrupt's available property, are replaced by section 283 of the Insolvency Act 1986[35a] which define the bankrupt's estate. Section 306 of the Insolvency Act 1986[35b] provides for the vesting of the bankrupt's estate in the trustee, by operation of law, as soon as his appointment takes effect. Goods comprised in a security bill of sale can be distrained as for rates and taxes.[36] They are not protected against a distraining landlord,[37] who is entitled to exercise his right of distress during the five-day period provided by section 13 of the 1882 Act.[38]

---

[29] *Lewis* v. *Thomas* [1919] 1 K.B. 319.
[30] *Re Field, ex p. Pratt* (1890) 63 L.T. 289.
[31] *Gordon* v. *Goldstein* [1924] 2 K.B. 779, where a husband and wife purported to assign jointly chattels which belonged to the wife alone. The bill was held void against third parties under s.5.
[32] *Saunders* v. *White* [1902] 1 K.B. 472.
[33] *Brandon Hill Ltd.* v. *Lane* [1915] 1 K.B. 250.
[34] *Newlove* v. *Shrewsbury* (1888) 21 Q.B.D. 41.
[35] *Re Ginger* [1897] 2 Q.B. 461; approved, *Hollinshead* v. *Egan* [1913] A.C. 564, H.L.
[35a] Replacing s.130 of the Insolvency Act 1985, to which it corresponds.
[35b] Replacing s.153 of the Insolvency Act 1985, to which it corresponds, and restating more precisely and clearly the law formerly contained in s.18(1) of the Bankruptcy Act 1914. See also *post*, pp. 387, 388.
[36] Bills of Sale Act (1878) Amendment Act 1882, s.14.
[37] Law of Distress Amendment Act 1908, s.4.
[38] *London and Westminster Loan and Discount Co.* v. *London and North Western Railway Co.* [1893] 2 Q.B. 49.

Priority of bills of sale

It is possible to create successive security bills of sale because the grantor is still, after the execution of the first bill, the owner of the equity of redemption and is therefore the "true owner."[39] Where successive security bills of sale cover the same chattels in whole or in part, they rank in order of their registration.[40] An unregistered security bill of sale is void as to the security.[41]

However, where a grantor gives an absolute bill of sale, it remains valid between him and the grantee irrespective of registration, so that he has no title to, and ceases to be the true owner of, the chattels comprised therein. Since, by section 5 of the 1882 Act, a bill of sale of chattels not made by the true owner is void against third parties, an earlier absolute bill of sale, registered or not, has priority over a later registered bill of sale. The doctrine of notice, therefore, is irrelevant to the question of priorities.[42]

Section 10 of the 1878 Act applies whether the security created by the bill of sale is legal or equitable. A registered agreement to create a bill of sale will therefore prevail over a later, registered bill of sale. But if the legal title to chattels is acquired in good faith by someone who has no actual notice of the bill of sale, it will prevail over a registered equitable mortgage of chattels by bill of sale.[43] Registration merely fixes priorities between competing bills of sale and is not notice to all the world.

A legal mortgage of chattels created by bill of sale will not prevail against a third party who obtains title to the chattels from the mortgagor in the ordinary course of the mortgagor's business.[44] The grantee of a bill of sale over the grantor's stock-in-trade impliedly authorises the grantor to carry on the business, and bona fide purchasers of the chattels acquire a title valid against the grantee.[45] Nor does it matter that the bill of sale contains a covenant not to dispose of the chattels without consent.[46]

During the currency of the reputed ownership provisions security bills comprising goods in trade or business were considered to be precarious securities. *Re Ginger*[47] decided that, if a mortgagee wished to remove the false reputation of ownership he must either publicise his title or, once one of the causes under section 7 has arisen, take possession before he gets notice of an act of bankruptcy. That disadvantage has been eliminated by the abolition of the reputed ownership provisions.[48]

---

[39] *Thomas* v. *Searles* [1891] 2 Q.B. 408.
[40] Bills of Sale Act 1878, s.10.
[41] Bills of Sale Act (1878) Amendment Act 1882, s.8.
[42] See *Edwards* v. *Edwards* (1876) 2 Ch.D. 291, where the court refused to postpone the holder of a registered bill of sale to the holder of a prior unregistered bill of which he had express notice.
[43] *Joseph* v. *Lyons* (1884) 15 Q.B.D. 280.
[44] If title is obtained otherwise than in the ordinary course of the mortgagor's business, the purchaser is postponed to the mortgagee: *Payne* v. *Fern* (1881) 6 Q.B.D. 620.
[45] *National Mercantile Bank* v. *Hampson* (1880) 5 Q.B.D. 177.
[46] *Walker* v. *Clay* (1880) 49 L.J.Q.B. 560.
[47] [1948] 1 K.B. 705.
[48] By the Insolvency Act 1985, s.235, Sched. 10, Pt. III.

CHAPTER 7

MORTGAGES OF CHOSES IN ACTION

GENERAL PRINCIPLES

There is no precise definition of the term "chose in action,"[1] but it is generally regarded as including all forms of personalty not held in possession and which, if wrongfully withheld, must be recovered by action.[2] In contrast, a chose in possession is a tangible thing the possession of which will pass by delivery, and can be seized and sold in execution of a judgment in a personal action.

Choses in action, therefore, cover diverse forms of incorporeal personalty varying from simple contract debts to such specialised property as shares in a company, patents, copyrights and trade-marks. They also include equitable interests in a trust fund of personalty. Moreover, although they may not usually be regarded as including equitable interests in a trust fund of realty, it will be convenient to deal with those interests in this chapter, because their mortgages are governed by the same principles as choses in action. As it is not possible here to deal individually with every form of chose in action, the general principles of their mortgages are set out and then specific regard is directed to mortgages of equitable interests in trust funds, insurance policies, partnership shares and shares in a company all of which are particularly important in practice.

Mortgages of choses in action are expressly excluded from the operation of the Bills of Sale Acts.[3] They depend, in most cases, on the general law of assignment,[4] though the assignment of some choses in action is regulated by statute.[5]

At common law, the general rule was that no debt or other chose in action could be assigned without the debtor's consent. It was said that assignments would be:

---

[1] "Chose in action" is a known legal expression used to describe all personal rights of property which can only be claimed or enforced by action, and not by taking physical possession. *Torkington* v. *Magee* [1902] 2 K.B. 427 at 430, *per* Channell J.

[2] *British Mutoscope and Biograph Co.* v. *Homer* [1901] 1 Ch. 671.

[3] See the definition of "goods" in s.4 of the Bills of Sale Act 1878.

[4] For a more detailed treatment, see *Chitty on Contracts* (25th ed., 1983), Chap. 19; Bailey, (1931) 47 L.Q.R. 516; (1932) 48 L.Q.R. 248 and 547; Marshall, *Assignment of Choses in Action* (1950); Biscoe, *Credit Factoring* (1973).

[5] Bills of lading; Bills of Lading Act 1955, s.1. Policies of life assurance; Policies of Assurance Act 1867, s.1. Policies of marine assurance; Marine Insurance Act 1906, s.50(2). Shares in a company; Stock Transfer Act 1963 and Companies Act 1985, s.182(1). Negotiable instruments; Bills of Exchange Act 1882. Copyrights; Copyright Act 1956, s.36. Patents; Patent Act 1977, ss.30, 32.

"the occasion of multiplying contentions and suits of great oppression of the people, and the subversion of the due and equal execution of justice."[6]

This rule may have had its origin in the conceptual difficulties inherent in conceiving of the transfer of an intangible[7] but the possibility was recognised by statute in 1603.[8] At common law the Crown could both grant and receive choses in action by way of assignment,[9] and when the rules of the Law Merchant were incorporated into English law, mercantile choses in action became not only assignable but negotiable.[10] The difference is that, whereas an assignee takes subject to all defects in the assignor's title, a holder for value in due course gets a good title even though the person from whom he received it had not.

Apart from these exceptions, at common law the debtor had to be made a party to the assignment which, therefore, amounted to a novation, that is, the creation of a new contract between the assignor and the assignee. This involves the consent of all three parties that the original contract be extinguished and replaced by a new one.[11] It is thus necessary for the new contract to be supported by consideration.[12]

An alternative procedure is by acknowledgment,[13] whereby the creditor asks his debtors to pay some third party, and the debtor agrees to do so and informs the third party.[14] Assignment could also be made by power of attorney but this was normally revocable.[15] Equity, however, freely permitted the assignment of both legal and equitable choses in action.[16] The Judicature Act 1873, introduced a general form of statutory assignment, but before 1875 mortgages of choses in action, subject to the exceptions mentioned above, could be created only by equitable assignment. The equitable rules still govern mortgages of choses in action which do not comply with the statutory form and, as will be seen, *charges* of choses in action can only be created by equitable assignment. It is necessary, therefore, to consider two main methods of mortgaging choses in action: (i) by assignment in equity; and (ii) by statutory assignment.

---

[6] *Lampet's Case* (1612) 10 Co.Rep. 46 at 48(a).

[7] Holdsworth, *History of English Law*; Bailey (1931) 47 L.Q.R. 516.

[8] The statute 1 Jac. I, c. 15 permitted the assignment of the debts of a bankrupt.

[9] *Chitty on Contracts* (25th ed., 1983), p. 692.

[10] Milnes Holden, *The History of Negotiable Instruments in England Law* (1955).

[11] *Wilson* v. *Lloyd* (1873) L.R. 16 Eq. 60; *Miller's Case* (1876) 3 Ch.D. 391; *Perry* v. *National Provincial Bank* [1910] 1 Ch. 464; *Meek* v. *Port of London Authority* [1918] 2 Ch. 96.

[12] *Tatlock* v. *Harris* (1789) 3 Term Rep. 174; *Cuxon* v. *Chadley* (1824) 3 B. & C. 591; *Wharton* v. *Walker* (1825) 4 B. & C. 163.

[13] Davies, (1959) 75 L.Q.R. 220; Yates (1977) Conv.(N.S.) 49; Goff and Jones, *Law of Restitution* (3rd ed., 1986); *Chitty on Contracts* (25th ed., 1983), p. 727.

[14] *Wilson* v. *Coupland* (1821) 5 B. & Ald. 228; *Hamilton* v. *Spottiswoode* (1849) 4 Ex. 200; *Griffin* v. *Weatherby* (1862) L.R. 3 Q.B. 753. As to whether and in what circumstances consideration is required, see *Liversidge* v. *Broadbent* (1859) 4 H. & N. 603; *Shamia* v. *Joory* [1958] 1 Q.B. 448; Goff and Jones, *Law of Restitution* (3rd ed., 1986), pp. 519–521.

[15] Marshall, *Assignment of Choses in Action* (1950), pp. 67–69.

[16] *Wood* v. *Griffith* (1818) 1 Swanst. 43.

MORTGAGE BY EQUITABLE ASSIGNMENT

Equity makes a distinction between the assignment of legal choses, such as contract debts, and equitable choses such as legacies and trust interests. While both forms of chose in action are equally assignable, the assignee of a chose in equity may sue in his own name provided he has given notice to the holder of the fund.[17] An equitable assignment is absolute and complete without notice having been given to the debtor or fundholder, for notice does not render the title perfect,[18] and the validity of the assignment is not affected by the death or bankruptcy of the assignor before the holder of the fund receives notice. Furthermore, until the debtor receives notice, he is entitled to continue paying the original creditor[19]; and once the debtor has notice of the assignment, he cannot do anything to take away or diminish the rights of the assignee as they stood at the time of the notice.[20] Priorities between successive assignments are determined by the order in which the debtor or trustee receives notice of the assignee's title, in accordance with the rule in *Dearle* v. *Hall*.[21]

An equitable assignment can be made by an agreement between a debtor and his creditor that a specific chose in action which is, or will be in the hands of a third person, or is due from them and belongs to the debtor, shall be applied in discharge of the debt.

Thus, in *Brice* v. *Bannister*,[22] G, who owed a debt to P, was performing work for D who was paying him by instalments. Before the work was finished, and at a time when D had paid all the instalments then due, G directed D to pay £100 to P out of moneys due, or to become due, from D to G. G gave D written notice but he refused to be bound by it and continued to pay the money to G. It was held, by a majority of the Court of Appeal, that this was a valid assignment on which P was entitled to recover from D, notwithstanding D's payments to G., subsequent to the notice.

Alternatively, an equitable assignment can be made by an order given by a debtor whereby the holder of the fund is directed or authorised to pay it to the creditor.[23] There must be an engagement to pay the debt out of a particular fund.[24] A mere direction to pay money to a third person is not

---

[17] *Row* v. *Dawson* (1749) 1 Ves.Sen. 331; *Walker* v. *Bradford Old Bank* (1884) 12 Q.B.D. 511.

[18] *Ward* v. *Duncombe* [1893] A.C. 369.

[19] *Stocks* v. *Dobson* (1853) 4 De G. M. & G. 11.

[20] *Roxburghe* v. *Cox* (1881) 17 Ch.D. 520.

[21] (1823) 3 Russ. 1; see *post*, p. 80; and see also L.P.A. 1925, s.137(3) which provides that notice of an equitable assignment of trust interests is ineffective for the purpose of determining priority among competing interests unless in writing.

[22] (1878) 3 Q.B.D. 569, C.A. (Bramwell, Cotton L.JJ.; Brett L.J. *dissentiente*).

[23] *Row* v. *Dawson* (1849) 1 Ves. Sen. 331; *Burn* v. *Carvalho* (1839) 4 My. & Cr. 690; *Rodick* v. *Gandell* (1852) 1 De G.M. & G. 763; *Diplock* v. *Hammond* (1854) 5 De G.M. & G. 320; *William Brandt's Sons & Co.* v. *Dunlop Rubber Co.* [1905] A.C. 454; *Palmer* v. *Carey* [1926] A.C. 703, P.C.; *Cotton* v. *Heyl* [1930] 1 Ch. 510; *Re Warren* [1938] Ch. 725.

[24] *Watson* v. *Duke of Wellington* (1830) 1 Russ. & M. 602; *Percival* v. *Dunn* (1885) 29 Ch.D. 128; *Re Gunsbourg* (1919) 88 L.J.K.B. 479.

necessarily an assignment, for it may be a revocable mandate.[25] The direction itself gives the third person no right in the subject matter of the mandate and is revoked by any subsequent disposition of the property inconsistent with it.[26] Nevertheless, even in the case of an equitable chose, the assignor may for practical reasons have to be joined as a party when the assignment is not an absolute assignment of the whole debt. For, if the assignment is for part of the debt only, the assignor has to be joined in the action in order that the accounts may be correctly taken between the third parties, and that the debtor may be protected against a second action in respect of the same debt.[27] The modern practice in regard to joining an assignor is, unless the debtor waives the assignor's presence in court[28] to join him as a nominal plaintiff with an indemnity for costs, but, if he raises objection, to join him as a defendant.[29]

Where the assignment was absolute, the assignee could sue in his own sole name[30] before the Judicature Act and this position is unaltered. The provision for statutory assignment made by the Judicature Act 1873, section 25(6), did not "forbid or destroy equitable assignments or impair their efficacy in the slightest degree."[31]

If the assignment gives a right to payment out of a particular fund or property but does not transfer the fund or property, it is "by way of charge"[32] and so is an assignment of so much of a future debt as shall be sufficient to satisfy an uncertain future indebtedness.[33]

Whereas, prior to the Judicature Act 1873, an assignee of an equitable chose in action could sue in his own name provided that the assignment was absolute, the assignee of a legal chose in action could not. This arises because equity, having exclusive control of equitable interests, can allow an assignee of an equitable chose[34] to sue directly. But, in the case of a legal chose,[35] he has to have the assignor nominally a party before the court in order to bind the assignor's rights in the legal chose at common law. Equity, in fact, treats the assignor of a legal chose as trustee of his rights for the assignee.

---

[25] Bell v. London and North Western Railway (1852) 15 Beav. 548; Re Whitting, ex p. Hall (1879) 10 Ch.D. 615.

[26] Morrell v. Wootten (1852) 16 Beav. 197; cf. London & Yorkshire Bank v. White (1895) 11 T.L.R. 570 and The Zigurds [1934] A.C. 209.

[27] Re Steel Wing Co. [1921] 1 Ch. 349.

[28] William Brandt's Sons v. Dunlop Rubber Co. [1905] A.C. 454. R.S.C. Ord. 15, r. 6. and C.C.R. Ord. 5, r. 4, provide that no action shall be defeated by reason of the misjoinder or non-joinder of any parties.

[29] Bowden's Patents Syndicate v. Smith [1904] 2 Ch. 86.

[30] Cator v. Croydon Canal Co. (1841) 4 Y. & C. Ex. 593; Donaldson v. Donaldson (1854) Kay. 711.

[31] William Brandt's Sons & Co. v. Dunlop Rubber Co. [1905] A.C. 454 at 461, per Lord Macnaghten.

[32] Tancred v. Delagoa Bay and East Africa Rty. Co. (1889) 23 Q.B.D. 239.

[33] Jones v. Humphreys [1902] 1 K.B. 10; cf. Mercantile Bank of London v. Evans [1899] 2 Q.B. 613.

[34] A chose which could be sued for only in the Court of Chancery, e.g. an interest in a trust fund.

[35] A chose which could be sued for only in the common law courts, e.g. a contract debt.

After the Judicature Act came into operation, the position was that assignments of legal choses in action not complying with the statute continued to be valid in equity,[36] but both the assignor and the assignee had to be made parties to the proceedings.[37] If the assignor wishes to sue, he must join the assignee.[38]

It has been suggested that the rule requiring both the assignor and the assignee to be party to proceedings for enforcement of an equitable assignment of a legal chose in action serves a useful purpose only where the assignor has not wholly disposed of his interest, since in such cases it ensures that all parties with an interest in the chose are brought before the court. But that there is no need for the rule where, although the assignment is absolute, it takes effect only as an equitable assignment because, for example, it is not in writing.[39]

Subject to section 53(1)(c) of the Law of Property Act 1925 (which provides that a disposition of an equitable interest or trust subsisting at the time of the disposition must be in writing signed by the person disposing of the same or by his agent thereunto lawfully authorised in writing or by will), an equitable assignment is not required to be made in any particular form either from the point of view of evidence or of terminology. It may be verbal[40] and, couched in any language provided that the interest in the debt[41] is unmistakably made over to the assignee.[42] It is immaterial that the amount of the debt has not been ascertained at the time of the assignment.[43] Nor is an equitable assignment incomplete merely because notice has not been given to the debtor. Highly desirable though it is for an assignee to notify the debtor of his interest in order to bind the debtor not to pay out to any third party, an equitable assignment is by itself a perfect conveyance as between assignor and assignee.[44] Moreover, notice of an equitable assignment, when given, may be informal and even indirect, except in the case of trust interests, where notice must be in writing under section 137(3) of the Law of Property Act 1925.

Equitable assignments are thus virtually unrestricted by formal requirements. Mortgages of choses in action may still be created by these informal assignments operating only in equity. It is necessary only to make

---

[36] *William Brandt's Sons & Co.* v. *Dunlop Rubber Co.* [1905] A.C. 454.
[37] *Performing Rights Society Ltd.* v. *London Theatre of Varieties Ltd.* [1924] A.C. 1; *Williams* v. *Atlantic Assurance Co.* [1933] 1 K.B. 81; *Holt* v. *Heatherfield Trust Ltd.* [1942] 2 K.B. 1.
[38] *Walter and Sullivan Ltd.* v. *Murphy & Sons Ltd.* [1955] 2 Q.B. 584.
[39] *Chitty on Contracts* (25th ed., 1983), pp. 705–708.
[40] *Brown, Shipley & Co.* v. *Kough* (1885) 29 Ch.D. 848 at 854.
[41] Whereas there cannot be a statutory assignment of part of a debt or fund, there can be a good equitable assignment of a specified debt or fund: *Rodick* v. *Gandell* (1852) 1 De G.M. & G. 763; *Palmer* v. *Carey* [1926] A.C. 703, P.C.
[42] *William Brandt's Sons Ltd.* v. *Dunlop Rubber Co.* [1905] A.C. 454.
[43] *Crowfoot* v. *Gurney* (1832) 9 Bing. 372 at 376.
[44] *Gorringe* v. *Irwell India Rubber Works* (1886) 34 Ch.D. 128. An equitable assignment is good without notice against a trustee in bankruptcy: *Re Anderson* [1911] 1 K.B. 896, or against a judgment creditor: *Scott* v. *Lord Hastings* (1858) 4 K. & J. 633; *Holt* v. *Heatherfield Trust Ltd.* [1942] 2 K.B. 1.

the nature of the transaction plain.[45] Thus in *Tailby* v. *Official Receiver*[46] it was said:

> "It has long been settled that future property, possibilities and expectancies are assignable in equity for value. The mode or form of assignment is absolutely immaterial provided the intention of the parties is clear."

Conversely, it may be clear that the transaction is not an assignment as in *Re Danish Bacon Co. Staff Pension Fund Trusts*[47] where a revocable nomination which would not in any event become effective until the death of the nominator and might never affect any property at all, was held not fairly capable of being called an assignment.

MORTGAGE BY ASSIGNMENT UNDER THE LAW OF PROPERTY ACT 1925, SECTION 136

Section 25(6) of the Judicature Act 1873, introduced a new form of statutory assignment not limited to particular forms of choses in action. This section was, with negligible variations of language, re-enacted in section 136 of the Law of Property Act 1925, which provides as follows:

> "(1) Any absolute[48] assignment by writing[49] under the hand of the assignor (not purporting to be by way of charge only) of any debt[50] or other legal thing in action, of which express notice in writing has been given to the debtor, trustee or other person from whom the assignor would have been entitled to claim such debt or thing in action, is effectual in law (subject to equities having priority over the right of the assignee) to pass and transfer from the date of such notice—
> (a) the legal right to such debt or thing in action;
> (b) all legal and other remedies for the same; and
> (c) the power to give a good discharge for the same without the concurrence of the assignor:
> Provided that, if the debtor, trustee or other person liable in respect of such debt or thing in action has notice—
> (a) that the assignment is disputed by the assignor or any person claiming under him; or
> (b) of any other opposing or conflicting claims to such debt or thing in action;

---

[45] *German* v. *Yates* (1915) 32 T.L.R. 52.
[46] (1888) 13 App.Cas. 523 at 543 (assignment of future book debts in unspecified businesses not so vague as to be invalid).
[47] [1971] 1 W.L.R. 248.
[48] "Absolute" does not have the same meaning as in the Bills of Sale Act, where it means "not by way of security."
[49] No particular form of words is necessary: *Re Westerton* [1919] 2 Ch. 104; but an intention to transfer the interest must be shown: *Curran* v. *Newpark Cinemas Ltd.* [1951] 1 All E.R. 295; *Coulls* v. *Bagot's Executor and Trustee Co. Ltd.* (1967) 119 C.L.R. 460.
[50] This means "the entire debt"; see *Re Steel Wing Co.* [1921] 1 Ch. 349.

he may, if he thinks fit, either call upon the persons making claim thereto to interplead concerning the same, or pay the debt or other thing in action into court under the provisions of the Trustee Act 1925.

(2) This section does not affect the provisions of the Policies of Assurance Act 1867."

The opening words of the section at once raise the query whether statutory assignment is available at all for the creation of mortgages, for only absolute assignments not by way of charge are within its scope. It is, however, well established that an assignment in statutory form of a whole debt to a mortgagee, with the usual proviso for redemption and reconveyance, is an absolute assignment within section 136.[51] The same is true where an assignment is made apparently out and out, but, in fact, for purposes of security and the equity of redemption is merely implied,[52] or where a whole debt is assigned for the discharge of a liability subject to a trust for the repayment of any surplus to the assignor.[53]

In *Durham Bros.* v. *Robertson*,[54] S & Co. charged £1,080 due to them from R on completion of certain buildings as security for advances, and assigned their interest in that sum to D until the money with added interest was repaid to them. Unlike the cases cited earlier, this was held not to be an absolute assignment since the debtor would be uncertain as to whom he should pay the money unless he inquired into the state of accounts between the assignor and the assignee. The assignment is absolute only where the debtor is entitled to pay the whole debt to the assignee without further inquiry unless he is notified otherwise.

In that case, Chitty L.J. said[55]:

"The assignment of the debt was absolute: it purported to pass the entire interest of the assignor in the debt to the mortgagee, and it was not an assignment purporting to be by way of charge only. The mortgagor-assignor had a right to redeem, and on repayment of the advances a right to have the assigned debt reassigned to him. Notice of the assignment pursuant to the subsection would be given to the original debtor and he would thus know with certainty in whom the legal right to sue was vested."

The crucial point thus is whether the title of the assignee is absolute in the sense that the debtor, until he is informed to the contrary by notification, is entitled to pay the whole debt to the assignee without inquiry. The object of the section, in excepting assignments by way of charge, was to protect the debtor against repeated actions in respect of the same debt and against the risks involved in making payments dependent on the state of accounts

---

[51] *Tancred* v. *Delagoa Bay and East Africa Rty. Co.* (1889) 23 Q.B.D. 239.
[52] *Hughes* v. *Pump House Hotel Co.* [1902] 2 K.B. 190, C.A.
[53] *Comfort* v. *Betts* [1891] 1 Q.B. 737, C.A.; *Bank of Liverpool* v. *Holland* (1926) 43 T.L.R. 29.
[54] [1898] 1 Q.B. 765, C.A.
[55] *Ibid.* at 772.

between other parties. The assignment of an entire debt by way of mortgage is not inconsistent with this object because, for the time being, the mortgagee became *vis-à-vis* the debtor the absolute owner of the debt. Uncertainty in the state of accounts *between assignor and assignee* does not prevent an assignment from being absolute, if it does not affect the obligations of the debtor. So in *Hughes* v. *Pump House Hotel Co.*,[56] when debts had been assigned to a bank as continuing security to cover a current account, this was held to be a perfectly good statutory assignment.

A fortiori, a determinable interest of only part of a debt cannot be the subject of a statutory assignment.[57] This was illustrated by the facts of *Jones* v. *Humphreys*,[58] in which a schoolmaster assigned to a moneylender so much and such part of his salary as should be necessary to pay £22 10s. or any further sums advanced. This is precisely what the statute means by a charge as distinct from an absolute assignment. Such a charge cannot be created by statutory assignment, but is good in equity as a partial assignment of the debt. The practical effect is that the enforcement of the charge entails the joining of the assignor as a party to the proceedings against the primary debtor, *i.e.* in the present case the headmaster of the school. It also now seems settled that part of a debt cannot be assigned under section 136 on the ground that such an assignment is not "absolute." Accordingly the mortgage even of a specified portion of a debt can only operate in equity.[59] This was held to be the case in *Walter and Sullivan Ltd.* v. *J. Murphy and Sons Ltd.*[60] where A owed B £1,808, B owed C £1,558 and B gave A an irrevocable authority to pay £1,558 to C. This was held to be a good equitable assignment of the £1,558 by way of charge. It was also held that B and C were necessary parties to an action against A.

This rule has arisen because conflicting decisions might arise if either the existence or the amount of the debt was in dispute[61] and also because of the burden on the debtor which would be created if the creditor was allowed to split up the debt into several causes of action.[62]

Section 136 does not supersede the provisions of the Law Merchant or of particular statutes governing the assignment of special forms of property. Otherwise there appears to be little restriction on the kinds of choses in action which are assignable under the section. The words "any debt or other *legal* thing in action" have to be interpreted as not confined to legal choses properly so called. They cover any right which the common law did not look on as assignable because of it being a chose in action, but which

[56] [1902] 2 K.B. 190, C.A.
[57] *Jones* v. *Humphreys* [1902] 1 K.B. 10.
[58] *Ibid.*
[59] *Forster* v. *Baker* [1910] 2 K.B. 636; *Re Steel Wing Co.* [1921] 1 Ch. 349; *G. & T. Earle Ltd.* v. *Hemsworth RDC* (1928) 44 T.L.R. 605 at 758; *Williams* v. *Atlantic Assurance Co.* [1933] 1 K.B. 81 at 100; though the point was not originally free from doubt: *Brice* v. *Bannister* (1878) 3 Q.B.D. 569; *Skipper & Tucker* v. *Holloway & Howard* [1910] 2 K.B. 630.
[60] [1955] 2 Q.B. 584, C.A.
[61] *Re Steel Wing Co.* [1921] 1 Ch. 349 at 357.
[62] *Durham Bros.* v. *Robertson* [1898] 1 Q.B. 765, C.A.

equity dealt with as assignable.[63] This means that equitable as well as legal choses in action are assignable under the statute, but not rights such as contracts of personal service, which not even equity has ever regarded as being assignable.[64]

Assignment under section 136 has two requirements of form:

(1) The assignment itself must be in writing under the hand of the assignor.

(2) Written notice of the assignment must be given to the debtor. As the section does not say from whom, etc. notice is to issue, it may be given by the assignor, the assignee or his successors in title.

The notice must be given, otherwise the assignee cannot sue in his own name, but it can be given by the assignor, the assignee or their successors in title[65] at any time[66] before an action is brought. If there are joint debtors, notice must be given to both.[67] It is essential not only for a statutory assignment to be in writing, but also for the notice to be in writing. The requirement of notice in writing must be met even if the debtor cannot read and the assignment is brought to his attention in some other way.[68] Whereas notice of an equitable assignment simply operates to establish the right of the assignee against third parties, the notice of a statutory assignment is an integral part of the conveyance from the assignor to the assignee. The assignment takes effect from the date when the notice is received by the debtor, and if no written notice is given it takes effect in equity only.[69]

There is no need to state a date, but if the notice purports to identify the assignment by its date and the date is wrong, it will be invalid.[70] It has been suggested that the notice will be invalid unless the amount of the debt is correctly stated,[71] but, apart from any question of validity that might arise, it is prudent, before executing the assignment, to obtain a written admission from the debtor as to the amount of the debt assigned,[72] so as to prevent any dispute, when the assignee comes to realise the security, as to how much was due when the assignment was taken. As a creditor can

---

[63] *Torkington* v. *Magee* [1902] 2 K.B. 427, rvsd. [1903] 1 K.B. 644; *King* v. *Victoria Insurance Co.* [1896] A.C. 250; *Manchester Brewery* v. *Coombs* [1901] 2 Ch. 608; *Re Pain* [1919] 1 Ch. 38; *G. & T. Earle Ltd.* v. *Hemsworth R.D.C.* (1928) 44 T.L.R. 605.

[64] *Tolhurst* v. *Associated Portland Cement Manufacturers* [1903] A.C. 414.

[65] *Bateman* v. *Hunt* [1904] 2 K.B. 530.

[66] *Ibid.* See also *Compania Columbiana de Seguros* v. *Pacific Steam Navigation Co.* [1965] 1 Q.B. 101; including a time after the death of the assignor; *Walker* v. *Bradford Old Bank* (1884) 12 Q.B.D. 511; *Re Westerton* [1919] 2 Ch. 104 or assignee; *Bateman* v. *Hunt* [1904] 2 K.B. 530.

[67] *Josselson* v. *Borst and Gliksten* [1938] 1 K.B. 723.

[68] *Hockley and Papworth* v. *Goldstein* (1920) 90 L.J.K.B. 111.

[69] *Holt* v. *Heatherfield Trust Ltd.* [1942] 2 K.B. 1.

[70] *Stanley* v. *English Fibres Industries Ltd.* (1899) 68 L.J.Q.B. 839; *W. F. Harrison & Co.* v. *Burke* [1956] 1 W.L.R. 419, C.A.; *Van Lynn Developments Ltd.* v. *Pelias Construction Co. Ltd.* [1969] 1 Q.B. 607, explaining the *Harrison* case at 612; see also (1956) 72 L.Q.R. 321.

[71] *W. F. Harrison & Co.* v. *Burke,* [1956] 1 W.L.R. 419 at 421.

[72] *Matthews* v. *Walwyn* (1798) 4 Ves. 118.

assign by directing his debtors to pay the assignee it would appear that a single written document could serve as both assignment and notice.[73]

Apart from the statutory requirement, the giving of notice forms an important part of the assignee's protection. First, it binds the debtor, trustee or other person from whom the assignor would have been entitled to claim the debt or thing in action, to pay it or convey it to the assignee.[74] Secondly, it gives priority over subsequent dealings between the debtor and the assignor. Whether an assignment is statutory or equitable, the assignee takes subject to equities between the debtor and the assignor which existed before the debtor received notice of the assignment.[75] Finally, it establishes priority over other assignees, since it is provided by the Law of Property Act 1925, section 137(1) that priority among successive assignees of choses in action is regulated by the dates on which the debtor received notice of the assignments.

The rule in Dearle v. Hall

That provision, which derives from the rule in *Dearle* v. *Hall*,[76] applies to all mortgages of equitable interests in property of whatever description. The date of the notice itself is irrelevant to any question of priority. Where the notice is posted, it apparently takes effect when received, though it might be argued that, as between competing assignees, the first to post the notice should have priority. There is no express decision on the point.[77]

Once notice of an absolute assignment has been received by the debtor he is no longer liable to the assignor, but to the assignee,[78] and if he disregards such a notice and pays the assignor after having received it he will be liable to make a second payment to the assignee.[79] It is doubted whether he could then recover the first payment, as it has been made under a mistake of law, not of fact.[80] If however, a debtor pays his debt to the assignor by cheque but afterwards receives a notice that the debt has been assigned, he is not compelled to stop the cheque.[81]

The rule in *Dearle* v. *Hall*[82] must not be confused with the provision in section 136 of the Law of Property Act 1925 that the assignee takes subject to equities existing when the assignment takes effect of which the assignee

[73] *Curran* v. *Newpark Cinemas* [1951] 1 All E.R. 295.
[74] In the absence of notice, payment by the debtor to the assignor, or a relase by the assignor, will be good against the assignee: *Stocks* v. *Dobson* (1853) 4 De G.M. & G. 11.
[75] *Roxburghe* v. *Cox* (1881) 17 Ch.D. 520.
[76] (1828) 3 Russ. 1; see also *post*, pp. 350–353, 354, 360; and see also *Loveridge* v. *Cooper* (1823) 3 Russ 30. It seems that the rule originated earlier, but in the more restrictive form that the postponement of a prior assignee would occur only where the failure to give notice earlier was due to fraud or his gross negligence amounting to evidence of fraud. On this point see *Tourville* v. *Naish* (1734) 3 P.Wms. 307 and *Stanhope* v. *Verney* (1761) 2 Eden. 80.
[77] *Holt* v. *Heatherfield Trust Ltd.* [1942] 1 K.B. 1.
[78] *Cottage Club Estates* v. *Woodside Estates (Amersham) Ltd.* [1928] 2 K.B. 463.
[79] *Jones* v. *Farrell* (1857) 1 D. & J. 208; *Brice* v. *Bannister* (1878) 3 Q.B.D. 569.
[80] *Chitty on Contracts* (25th ed., 1983), p. 699, n. 69.
[81] *Bence* v. *Shearman* [1898] 2 Ch. 582.
[82] (1828) 3 Russ. 1.

has notice.[83] "Equities" include defects in the assignor's title and certain claims which the debtor has against the assignor. Thus an assignee of a contract affected by mistake or illegality normally has no greater rights than the assignor would have had, though an exception exists in the field of life assurance. It was held in *Beresford* v. *Royal Insurance Co.*[84] a case decided before the Suicide Act 1961, which decriminalised suicide, that a life assurance policy could not be enforced by the representative of an assured who had committed suicide, since it was against public policy to allow his estate to benefit from his crime. But, where the assignment was made before the suicide, the assignee was permitted to recover, since the benefit did not go to the criminal or his estate.[85] If a debtor has the right to set aside a contract for misrepresentation, the assignee takes subject to that right, unless it is excluded or modified by statute[86] or contract.[87] The purpose of the provision that the assignee takes subject to equities is to prevent the debtor being prejudiced by the assignment. If a debtor has a claim against the assignor, it is immaterial whether the assignee knew of the claim when he took the assignment.[88] Correlatively the debtor cannot do anything to take away or diminish the rights of the assignee as they stood at the time of the notice, once he has received notice of the assignment.[89]

These two rules are illustrated by the case of *Bradford Banking Co. Ltd.* v. *Briggs & Co. Ltd.*,[90] where it was held that an assignee of shares or debentures takes them subject to all equitable claims of the company which arose before notice of the assignment; but that, after notice, the company could not create any fresh equities. The rule that an assignee takes subject to equities is often excluded in debentures.

The ability of the debtor to rely, against the assignee, on a claim against the assignor depends on the way in which it arose. He can rely on a claim arising out of the contract assigned,[91] whenever the claim arose.[92] If the debtor's set-off against the assignor exceeds the amount of the debt, the assignee will recover nothing; but he is not liable to the debtor for the

---

[83] *Ord* v. *White* (1840) 3 Beav. 357; *Mangles* v. *Dixon* (1852) 3 H.L.C. 702; *Phipps* v. *Lovegrove* (1873) L.R. 16 Eq. 80; *Lawrence* v. *Hayes* [1927] 2 K.B. 111.

[84] [1938] A.C. 586.

[85] *White* v. *British Empire Mutual Life Assurance Co.* (1868) L.R. 7 Eq. 394.

[86] *Cf.* Bills of Exchange Act 1882, s.38(2); Marine Insurance Act 1906, s.50(2).

[87] *William Pickersgill & Sons Ltd.* v. *London and Provincial Insurance Co.* [1912] 3 K.B. 614; *Re Agra and Masterman's Bank, ex p. Asiatic Banking Corp.* (1867) 2 Ch.App. 391; *Re Blakely Ordinance Co., ex p. New Zealand Banking Corp.* (1867) 3 Ch.App. 154.

[88] *Athenaeum Society* v. *Pooley* (1858) 3 D. & J. 294; *Biggerstaff* v. *Rowatt's Wharf Ltd.* [1896] 2 Ch. 93.

[89] *Roxburghe* v. *Cox* (1881) 17 Ch.D. 520 at 526.

[90] (1886) 12 App.Cas. 29.

[91] *Business Computers Ltd.* v. *Anglo African Leasing Ltd.* [1977] 1 W.L.R. 578, in which the authorities reviewed extend this principle to claims closely connected with the contract assigned. See also *Newfoundland Government* v. *Newfoundland Ry. Co.* (1888) 13 App. Cas. 199 at 213.

[92] *Graham* v. *Johnson* (1869) LR. 8 Eq. 36; *William Pickersgill and Sons Ltd.* v. *London and Provincial Insurance Co.* [1912] 3 K.B. 614; *Banco Central S.A. and Trevelan Navigation Inc.* v. *Lingoss & Falce and B.F.I. Line*; *The Raven* [1980] 2 Lloyd's Rep. 266.

excess.[93] Among the equities which bind the assignee is the debtor's right to rescind for misrepresentation, provided, apparently, that the right has not been lost.[94]

If the claim arises out of some transaction other than the contract assigned, it can be set up against the assignee only if it arose before notice of the assignment was given to the debtor.[95] If it neither accrued due before notice was given, nor arose out of the contract to be assigned, or a contract closely connected with it, it cannot be set off.[96]

If an assignor does not acquire a right to the subject-matter of the assignment the assignee can take nothing, for example, where an assignment was made of money, to become due under a building contract, which the assignor failed to perform.[97] Nor can the assignee recover more from the debtor than the assignor could have done.[98]

CONSIDERATION

Whether consideration is necessary to support an assignment is a question between the assignor and the assignee.[99] The debtor has to pay the debt and his only concern is that all parties should be before the court, so that he does not have to pay twice. He cannot refuse to pay the assignee because the assignment was gratuitous.[1]

A statutory assignment of either an equitable or a legal chose in action is valid whether or not consideration is given.[2] There are, however, three situations where the existence or non-existence of consideration is relevant. First, where the purported assignment is of some right which either does not exist or has not yet been acquired by the assignor; secondly, where there is a voluntary equitable assignment; and, thirdly, where there is a defective statutory assignment.

Assignment of future property

A future chose in action cannot be the subject of an assignment, but only of an agreement to assign and such an agreement can be valid only when

---

[93] *Young* v. *Kitchin* (1878) 3 Ex.D. 127.

[94] *Stoddart* v. *Union Trust Ltd.* [1912] 1 K.B. 181. This decision has been criticised: see *Chitty on Contracts* (25th ed., 1983), p. 721; n 1308; Treitel, *Law of Contract* (7th ed., 1987), p. 510).

[95] *Stephens* v. *Venables* (1862) 30 Beav. 625; *cf. Watson* v. *Mid Wales Ry.* (1867) L.R. 2 P. 593. See also *Roxburghe* v. *Cox; Business Computers Ltd.* v. *Anglo African Leasing Ltd.*; and *Newfoundland Government* v. *Newfoundland Ry. Co.* (1888) 13 App.Cas 199.

[96] *Business Computers Ltd.* v. *Anglo African Leasing Ltd.* [1977] 1 W.L.R. 578 at 585; see also *Jeffryes* v. *Agra & Masterman's Bank* (1866) L.R. 2 Eq. 674; *Watson* v. *Mid Wales Ry. Co.* (1867) L.R. 2 C.P. 593; *Christie* v. *Taunton, Delmard, Lane & Co.* [1893] 2 Ch. 175; *Re Pinto Leite & Nephews, ex p. Desolivaes* [1929] 1 Ch. 221.

[97] *Tooth* v. *Hallett* (1869) L.R. 4 Ch.App. 242.

[98] *Dawson* v. *Great Northern and City Ry. Co.* [1905] 1 K.B. 260.

[99] *Re Rose* [1952] Ch. 499; *Letts* v. *I.R.C.* [1957] 1 W.L.R. 201; *Dalton (Smith's Administrative)* v. *I.R.C.* [1958] T.R. 45.

[1] *Walker* v. *Bradford Old Bank* (1884) 12 Q.B.D. 511.

[2] *Harding* v. *Harding* (1886) 17 Q.B.D. 442; *Re Westerton* [1919] 2 Ch. 104.

supported by consideration.[3] Rights which the prospective assignor has not yet acquired may fall into one of three categories. In the first are sums which are certain to become payable under an existing contract or other legal obligations and are treated as existing choses in action, even though the amounts which will be received are unascertained.[4] In the second are expectancies, as where the assignor hopes to receive sums under a contract not yet made, or to inherit from a person living at the date of the assignment.[5] The third, intermediate class comprises rights which may become due under an existing obligation but it is uncertain whether they will do so, because the obligation may terminate or is subject to a condition. Rights in the first category can be assigned without consideration; those in the second cannot. The decisions as to those in the third class are impossible to rationalise, though it seems clear that even where there is an existing chose in action capable of assignment, the proceeds of the chose may be a mere expectancy.[6]

Assignments of rights of action

A right of action arising out of tort has been held to be a chose in action.[6a] But it is not a "legal thing in action" within the meaning of section 136(1) of the Law of Property Act 1925. Generally, a bare right of litigation, such as the right to damages for a wrongful act[6b] is not assignable,[6c] on the principle that the law will not recognise any transaction savouring of maintenance or champerty.[7]

There is nothing unlawful however in the purchase of property which the purchaser can enjoy only by defeating existing adverse claims[7a] or in the

---

[3] *Meek* v. *Kettlewell* (1843) 1 Ph. 342; *Tailby* v. *Official Receiver* (1888) 13 App.Cas. 523; *Glegg* v. *Bromley* [1912] 3 K.B. 474; *Cotton* v. *Heyl* [1930] 1 Ch. 510.

[4] *Shepherd* v. *Federal Commissioners of Taxation* (1965) 113 C.L.R. 385.

[5] *Meek* v. *Kettlewell* (1843) 1 Ph. 342; *Re Tilt* (1896) 74 L.T. 163; *Re Ellenborough* [1903] 1 Ch. 697; *cf. Kekewich* v. *Manning* (1851) 1 De G.M. & G. 176.

[6] See *e.g. Glegg* v. *Bromley* [1912] 3 K.B. 474 (proceeds of a defamation action being brought by the assignor); *Norman* v. *Federal Commissioner of Taxation* (1963) 109 C.L.R. 9 (interest payable in the future as a loan which was not for a fixed period; dividends on shares already held which may become due in the future). In the following cases the subject-matter has been held to be an existing chose in action: *Walker* v. *Bradford Old Bank* (1864) 12 Q.B.D. 511 (sum standing to the assignor's credit at date of his death); *Hughes* v. *Pump House Hotel Co.* [1902] 2 K.B. 190 (sums payable to a builder under an existing contract). See also *post*, p. 84.

[6a] *Curtis* v. *Wilcox* [1948] 2 K.B. 474.

[6b] *e.g.* for assault, *May* v. *Lane* (1894) 64 L.J.Q.B. 236 at 238, *per* Rigby L.J.

[6c] *Dawson* v. *Great Northern and City Rly. Co.* [1905] 1 K.B. 260 at 271, *per* Stirling L.J.; *Fitzroy* v. *Cave* [1905] 2 K.B. 364 at 371; *Defries* v. *Milnes* [1913] 1 Ch. 98; *Holt* v. *Heatherfield Trust Ltd.* [1942] 2 K.B. 1; *Laurent* v. *Sale & Co.* [1963] 1 W.L.R. 829.

[7] The rule is unaffected by the Criminal Law Act 1967, which by s.13 abolishes the offences of maintenance and champerty and provides by s.14(1) that no person should be liable in tort for any conduct on account of it being maintenance or champerty. It is expressly provided by s.14(2) that the abolition of criminal and civil liability should not affect any rule of law as to the cases in which a contract is treated as contrary to public policy or otherwise illegal.

[7a] *Dickinson* v. *Burrell* (1866) L.R. 1. Eq. 337; *County Hotel and Wine Co Ltd.* v. *London and North Western Rly Co.* [1918] 2 K.B. 251 affd. on other grounds [1921] 1 A.C. 85; *Ellis* v. *Torrington* [1920] 1 K.B. 399.

assignment (for example, by mortgage) of property which is the fruit of litigation.[7b] In every case it is a question whether the purchaser's real object is to acquire an interest in the property, or merely to acquire a right to bring an action, either alone or jointly with the vendor.[7c] Thus the purchaser of a freehold reversion may take an assignment of the right to recover damages for dilapidations from the sub-tenant.[8] A creditor may assign his debt so as to enable another to sue for it.[8a] A person may buy shares in a company merely for the purpose of challenging, by legal proceedings, acts of the directors as being *ultra vires*.[8b] An assignment by an assured to his insurer of his rights against a contract breaker or tortfeasor is good, the enforcement of the cause of action being legitimately supported by the insurer's interest in recouping the amount of the loss which he has paid under the policy as a result of the act, neglect or default of the contract breaker or tortfeasor.[8c]

A solicitor purchasing from his client the subject-matter of a suit is in a different position from other purchasers. After his employment as such in the suit[9] he cannot purchase the subject-matter from his client[9a] although he may lawfully take a mortgage on it to secure costs and expenses already incurred.[9b]

Voluntary equitable assignments

The general principle to be derived from the decided cases is that an assignment of an existing chose in action need not be supported by consideration provided that the assignor has done everything within his power to transfer the property in the manner appropriate to its nature.[9c] In many cases the law will not treat a gift as valid unless it has been made in the prescribed way. Thus a gift of a chattel must be made either by deed of gift or by delivery of the chattel with the intent that the property shall pass.[9d]

[7b] *Glegg* v. *Bromley* [1912] 3 K.B. 474 at 484, C.A., *per* Vaughan Williams L.J. (the mortgage conferred no right on the mortgagee to interfere in the conduct of the proceedings).
[7c] *Dickinson* v. *Burrell* (1866) L.R. 1. Eq. 337; *Prosser* v. *Edmonds* (1835) 1 Y. & C. Ex. 481; *Harrington* v. *Long* (1833) 2 My. & K. 590; *Knight* v. *Bowyer* (1858) 2 De G. & J. 421.
[8] *Williams* v. *Protheroe* (1829) 5. Bing. 309; *Ellis* v. *Torrington* [1920] 1 K.B. 399.
[8a] *Fitzroy* v. *Cave* [1905] 2 K.B. 364 (even though the wish of that other person to enforce the debt arises from ill-feeling towards the debtor).
[8b] *Bloxam* v. *Metropolitan Rly. Co.* (1868) 3 Ch.App. 337 at 353.
[8c] *Compania Columbiana de Seguros* v. *Pacific Steam Navigation Co.* [1965] 1 Q.B. 101.
[9] *Knight* v. *Bowyer* (1858) 2 De G. & J. 421, C.A.; *Davis* v. *Freethy* (1890) 24 Q.B.D. 519.
[9a] *Wood* v. *Downes* (1811) 18 Ves. 120; *Simpson* v. *Lamb* (1857) 7 E. & B. 84; *Davis* v. *Freethy* (1890) 24 Q.B.D. 519.
[9b] *Anderson* v *Radcliffe* (1858) E.B. & E. 806.
[9c] *Kekewich* v. *Manning* (1851) 1 De G.M. & G. 176; *Milroy* v. *Lord* (1862) De F. & S. 264 *Harding* v. *Harding* (1886) 17 Q.B.D. 442; *Re Griffin* [1899] 1 Ch. 408; *German* v. *Yates* (1915) 32 T.L.R. 52; *Re Williams* [1917] 1 Ch. 1; *Holt* v. *Heatherfield Trust* [1942] 2 K.B. 1; *Re Rose* [1949] Ch. 78; *Re McArdle* [1951] Ch. 669; *Re Rose* [1952] Ch. 499; *Letts* v. *I.R.C.* [1957] 1 W.L.R. 201.
[9d] *Re Breton's Estate* (1881) 17 Ch.D. 416; *Cochrane* v. *Moore* (1890) 25 Q.B.D. 57; *Re Cole (A Bankrupt), ex p. Trustees of the Property of the Bankrupt* [1964] Ch. 175.

In *Milroy* v. *Lord*[10] the owner of shares in a company made a voluntary assignment of them by deed poll. This could not take effect as a gift since the legal title to the shares could be transferred only by execution of a proper instrument of transfer and registration of the transfer in the books of the company.

It was held that a voluntary settlement could not be valid and effectual unless the donor had done everything in his power which was necessary, having regard to the nature of the property comprised in the settlement, to transfer the property and render the settlement binding on him. That rule applies only to gifts which by law had to be made in a specified form.

The only formality required for the assignment of an equitable chose in action is that it must be in writing[10a]: so a voluntary settlement in writing of an equitable interest in a trust fund has been held binding on the settlor,[11] since he did not need to do anything else in order to transfer the property. Equitable assignments of legal choses in action are not required to be in writing. Unless the nature of the property brings special rules into play, there are no formal requirements for the transfer of legal choses in action[12] and it is necessary only for the donor to do all within his power to effect the transfer. If that has been done, it is immaterial that further steps need to be taken by the donee[13] or by some other third party.[14]

Defective statutory assignments

A statutory assignment may be ineffective as such, though it may take effect as an equitable assignment, if no written notice has been given to the debtor, or if it is not in writing, or if it is not an absolute assignment. Assignments which are conditional, or by way of charge, or are assignments of part of a debt, are not absolute.

Where the defect is want of notice, the assignment is effective although not supported by consideration.[15] Since it is not required by section 136 of the Law of Property Act 1925, that the assignor shall give the notice, he has done all within his power to transfer the property.

Where the defect is lack of writing, and the chose is equitable, the question of consideration does not arise because the assignment is void unless in writing. If it is a legal chose, want of consideration does not, by itself, invalidate the transfer. In *German* v. *Yates*[16] a voluntary oral assignment

---

[10] (1862) 4 De G.F. & J. 264; and see Turner L.J. at 274 for a statement of the rule. *Cf. Antrobus* v. *Smith* (1805) 12 Ves. 39 where a gift of shares failed because it was made in writing not under seal, contrary to the company's articles.

[10a] L.P.A. 1925, s.53(1)(*c*).

[11] *Kekewich* v. *Manning* (1851) 1 De G.M. & G. 176.

[12] See *Fortescue* v. *Barnett* (1834) 3 My. & K. 36, voluntary assignment, by deed, of a life insurance policy held binding on the assignor.

[13] *Re Paradise Motor Co. Ltd.* [1968] 1 W.L.R. 1125.

[14] *Re Rose, Midland Bank Executor and Trustee Co.* v. *Rose* [1949] Ch. 78; see also *Re Rose, Rose* v. *I.R.C.* [1952] Ch. 499.

[15] *Holt* v. *Heatherfield Trust Ltd.* [1942] 2 K.B. 1.

[16] (1915) 32 T.L.R. 52.

of a debt was held to bind the personal representatives of the assignor, and that the Judicature Act[17] had not destroyed equitable assignments or impaired them in any way.[18] In that case, it was held that the assignment was a perfect gift. But the problem which may arise is whether an oral assignment was a perfect gift or merely a promise to make a gift in the future. A voluntary promise to assign an equitable interest is not an assignment, and the fact that is made by means of signed writing is irrelevant. In *Re McArdle, Decd.*,[19] the following words were held to be incapable of being construed as an equitable assignment:

> "in consideration of your carrying out certain alterations and improvements to the property . . . we . . . agree that the executors shall . . . repay to you from the estate when so distributed £488 in settlement of the amount."

The works referred to had been carried out and it was held that the document purported to be a contract to assign, not an assignment, and thus required consideration. Since the consideration was past, the contract was unenforceable.

That case also suggests that a voluntary equitable assignment of part of a debt may be valid, but the reasoning by which that conclusion is arrived at has been criticised.

Where the assignment is not absolute because it is conditional, its effectiveness depends on the condition. If this is such as to require some further act to be done by the donor, the assignment will be ineffective, being an imperfect gift.

Finally, where there is an assignment by way of charge the question of consideration will not normally arise because the assignment will nearly always be made to secure a debt, and there will be consideration in the form of the assignee's advancing money or forbearance, or promising not to sue. Forbearance will amount to consideration only for a promise that is induced by it. Thus where a debtor executed a mortgage of an insurance policy in favour of his creditor, but the creditor did not know of the mortgage, it was held that his forbearance to sue for his antecedent debt was not consideration,[20] though it was said that he would have provided consideration if he had been told of the mortgage and forborne to sue on the strength of it. Forbearance may, it seems, be requested expressly[21] or impliedly.[22]

---

[17] The original provision enabling statutory assignments to be made was s.25(6) of the Judicature Act 1873.

[18] For a similar dictum see *William Brandt's Sons & Co.* v. *Dunlop Rubber Co.* [1905] A.C. 454 at 462.

[19] [1951] Ch. 669; see R. E. Megarry, (1951) 67 L.Q.R. 295 for a critical commentary and also see D. M. Stone, (1951) 14 M.L.R. 356; Treitel, *Law of Contract* (7th ed., 1987), p. 508.

[20] *Wigan* v. *English and Scottish Law Life Assurance Society* [1909] 1 Ch. 291.

[21] *Crears* v. *Hunter* (1887) 19 Q.B.D. 341.

[22] *Alliance Bank* v. *Broom* (1864) 2 Dr. & Sm. 289.

Assignments of Particular Choses in Action

Trust property

The 1925 property legislation provides for the mortgaging of equitable interests, in both realty and personalty, by assignment of the equitable interest subject to a proviso for reassignment on redemption. An interest in trust property was always freely assignable in equity, and the assignee could sue in his own name. If the whole interest was assigned, the assignor did not have to be made a party,[23] though his joinder was essential if he retained any interest, as where the assignment was conditional or by way of charge. The 1925 legislation did not alter this situation; it merely provided an alternative mode of assignment.

As between assignor and assignee the assignment is complete without notice to the trustee; notice is important for the reasons discussed earlier, which are to do with the interests of third parties.

The requirements of form arise, therefore, not from the provisions regulating statutory assignments but from section 53(1)(c) of the Law of Property Act 1925 which provides as follows:

> "A disposition of an equitable interest or trust subsisting at the time of the disposition, must be in writing, signed by the person disposing of the same, or by his agent, thereunto lawfully authorised in writing or by will."

In addition, it is usual for an assignment of trust property to be created by deed, since the assignee will then have the statutory powers conferred on a mortgagee by deed.[24] Because of the uncertain nature of limited or contingent interests in a trust property, the deed will contain various additional covenants and powers giving the assignee greater protection:

(1) Power for the assignee to protect his security by taking any proceedings, making any inquiries, giving any notices or obtaining any stop orders[25] necessary for that purpose.

(2) The assignment of a policy of life insurance or of insurance against a particular contingency, together with the assignment of the trust interest, and covenants by the assignor to pay the premiums and maintain the security.

Power is given to the court, under R.S.C. Ord. 50, r. 10 to make an order prohibiting the transfer, sale, delivery out, payment or other dealing with funds paid into court or any part of such fund or the income thereof, without notice to the applicant. A person:

---

[23] *Performing Rights Society* v. *London Theatre of Varieties Ltd.* [1924] A.C. 1.

[24] L.P.A. 1925, s.101.

[25] R.S.C. Ord. 50, r. 10. When a trust fund is paid into court, a "stop order" is equivalent to giving notice to the trustees: *Pinnock* v. *Bailey* (1883) 23 Ch.D. 497; *Montefiore* v. *Guedalla* [1903] 2 Ch. 26, C.A. Express notice should be given to the trustees.

(1) who has a mortgage or charge on the interest of any person in funds in court; or

(2) to whom that interest has been assigned; or

(3) who is a judgment creditor of the person entitled to that interest,

may apply to the court by summons in the cause or matter, or, if there is no cause or matter, by originating summons. Stop orders have priority, among themselves, in the order in which they were made,[26] but do not gain priority over existing incumbrancers who have given notice to the trustees before the stop order was made.[27] Express notice should also be given to the trustees.

While giving notice of the assignment to the trustees regulates priorities among assignees, it does not amount to taking possession of the trust interest unless the notice requires the payment of the income to be made to the assignee.[28] Until such notice is given, the trustees are entitled to continue to pay the income to the assignor, and in the interests of certainty it is advisable to insert a declaration in the assignment to the effect that the assignor is entitled to receive the income until the assignee otherwise directs.[29]

Even if the assignee notifies the trustees that all available monies are to be paid over to him it does not necessarily follow that the trustees must do so.[30] If the amount available exceeds the debt to the assignee and the trustees have notice of other assignments, they should pay over only such a sum as will discharge the principal, interest and costs.[31] If trustees are uncertain of the amount of the debt, they may refuse to pay over anything, even to the assignee first in priority, until an account has been taken.[32] They are trustees for all interested parties and need not pay monies, even to persons apparently entitled to them, without making inquiries.

Policies of life assurance

Before the Policies of Assurance Act 1867, mortgages of such policies were governed by the general law of assignment. Since rights under life assurance policies are legal choses in action, the assignee could not, under the pre-1867 general law, sue in his own name, but section 1 of the 1867 Act made this possible subject to compliance with the statutory formalities. The statutory provisions do not displace the previous law, so that an equitable assignment of a life assurance policy can still be made subject to the rules governing such assignments.

An assignment under the 1867 Act must be made in writing, either by an

---

[26] *Greening* v. *Beckford* (1832) 5 Sim. 195; *Swayne* v. *Swayne* (1849) 11 Beav. 463.

[27] *Livesey* v. *Harding* (1857) 23 Beav. 141; *Re Anglesey* [1903] 2 Ch. 727.

[28] *Re Pawson's Settlement* [1917] 1 Ch. 541; though *cf. Dearle* v. *Hall* (1828) 3 Russ. 1 at 58, *per* Lyndhurst L.C.

[29] Key and Elphinstone, *Precedents in Conveyancing* (15th ed., 1953–54), Vol. 2, p. 23.

[30] They may do so: *Jones* v. *Farrell* (1857) 1 De G. & J. 208.

[31] *Re Bell* [1896] 1 Ch. 1, C.A.

[32] *Hockey* v. *Western* [1898] 1 Ch. 350.

endorsement on the policy or by a separate instrument in the form given by the Schedule to the Act[33] or to the purpose and effect thereof. It has been held that a letter to the purported assignee, requesting him to instruct his solicitor to prepare an assignment, was not a valid assignment, either in equity or by statute and in consequence, notice to the insurance company by the purported assignee, B, that he was holding the policies as security for a debt was not a valid notice of assignment.[34] Likewise, an agreement to assign on request is not an assignment,[35] and a notice of the agreement is not a notice of the assignment. Consequently, the purported assignee did not, by informing the company of the agreement, gain priority over a prior equitable assignee, A, by deposit who had not given the company notice of such deposit. Indeed, the inability of the assignor to produce the policy was held to be constructive notice to B, in the circumstances of the case, of A's rights.[36] This accords with an earlier decision that, where the equities of two assignees are otherwise equal, possession of deeds gives the better equity.[37]

The assignee has no right to sue on the policy until written notice of the date and purport of the assignment has been given to the company. The policy must specify the place or places at which such notice may be given. The company is bound, on request and on payment of the prescribed fee, to give a written acknowledgment of receipt of notice, and that acknowledgment is conclusive, against the company, of such receipt.

The assignee takes subject to equities, including the right of the company to avoid the policy if full disclosure has not been made.

The 1867 Act provides that priorities between competing assignees are regulated by the order in which notice is given to the company,[38] but notice of a dealing not amounting to an assignment is ineffective. The provision does not apply where a subsequent assignee has notice, whether actual, constructive, or imputed, of a prior assignment,[39] as where money is lent on the security of an insurance policy which, being in the hands of a prior assignee, is not handed over. The non-delivery of the policy is constructive notice of the prior assignment. The subsequent assignee will obtain priority by giving notice first if he has no notice of the prior assignee, even though he was prevented from getting notice by fraudulent concealment of the prior assignment.

Mortgages of life assurance policies are made by way of assignment with a proviso for re-assignment. They normally contain covenants not to allow

---

[33] Policies of Assurance Act 1867, s.5.
[34] *Crossley* v. *City of Glasgow Life Assurance Co.* (1876) 4 Ch.D. 421.
[35] *Spencer* v. *Clarke* (1879) 9 Ch.D. 137.
[36] *Re Weniger's Policy* [1910] 2 Ch. 291.
[37] *Rice* v. *Rice* (1853) 2 Drew. 73.
[38] Policies of Assurance Act 1867, s.3. If a written request for an acknowledgment is made, the company must give an acknowledgment of receipt of notice, in writing, and this is conclusive against the company: Policies of Assurance Act 1867, s.6. The policy must specify the place at which notice of assignment is to be given: Policies of Assurance Act 1867, s.4.
[39] *Re Lake, ex p. Cavendish* [1903] 1 K.B. 151.

the policy to become void and to pay premiums and produce receipts therefore to the mortgagee, with power, in default, for the mortgagee to pay the premiums himself and charge them against the policy. The cost of paying premiums so as to keep the policy on foot is allowable, whether or not the policy contains an express provision to that effect.[40] A mortgagee by deed has the statutory power of sale given by the Law of Property Act 1925, section 101.

Since a creditor has an insurable interest in his debtor's life to the extent of the debt,[41] it is permissible for the creditor to take out a policy in his own name on the life of the debtor, instead of the debtor taking it out and assigning it to the creditor. The debtor should not take out a policy in the name of the creditor as the creditor, not being a party to the policy, would have no rights under it.[42] Thus where S took out a policy in his own name for the benefit of G, to mature in 17 years' time, and died five years after taking it out, it was held that G could not benefit as he was not a party to the policy and no declaration of trust in his favour had been made; nor did the Law of Property Act 1925, section 56(1) operate so as to confer any benefit on him.

Depending on circumstances, the policy may be the property of the debtor, mortgaged to the creditor, or it may belong to the creditor absolutely. There are three possible arrangements to consider:

(1) The debtor takes out the policy and pays the premiums. The policy is part of the security and belongs to the debtor.
(2) The creditor takes out the policy in the debtor's name, and pays the premiums without having any agreement with the debtor to charge the premiums to him. The policy is treated as having been taken out for the creditor's own protection and belongs to him.[43] This is so even where the creditor purported, in his own accounts, to charge the debtor with the premiums but there was no agreement to do so.
(3) The creditor takes out the policy but the premiums are by agreement chargeable to the debtor. There are two possible views:
   (a) the policy belongs to the debtor in equity, subject to security;
   (b) the policy belongs to the creditor and the stipulation that the debtor pays the premiums is a bonus for the creditor.
   There is a presumption in favour of (a) which can be rebutted by evidence showing that it was intended that the creditor should receive an outright bonus.[44]

---

[40] Gill v. Downing (1874) L.R. 17 Eq. 316.
[41] Morland v. Isaac (1855) 20 Beav. 389; see also Freme v. Brade (1858) 2 De G. & J. 582; Drysdale v. Piggot (1856) 8 De G.M. & G. 546; Bruce v. Garden (1869) 5 Ch.App. 32.
[42] Re Sinclair's Life Policy [1938] Ch. 799.
[43] Bruce v. Garden, supra.
[44] Salt v. Marquess of Northampton [1892] A.C. 1 at 16.

Where the policy is part of the security, the debtor has a right to redeem and any stipulation purporting to take away that right is void.[44a] Nor can the creditor claim the whole benefit of the policy if the debtor defaults in paying the premiums. He can only pay them himself to preserve the security and add them to the mortgage debt. He can acquire the security only by foreclosure.[45]

Life assurance policies are particularly hazardous in that they may be avoided by the suicide of the assured. It is contrary to public policy to allow the representatives of a wilful suicide to enforce a life policy,[46] and this rule has not been displaced by the Forfeiture Act 1982. That Act instigates the rule of public policy which may prevent a person who has unlawfully killed "another" acquiring a benefit from the death of that other and in certain circumstances provides for relief where a person has been guilty of unlawful killing. A mortgagee, being an assignee, cannot be in a better position than the representatives of the deceased assured unless the policy expressly provides for the preservation of rights of bona fide assignees for value.[47] Such provisions are not contrary to public policy, since they preserve the negotiability and hence the value to the assured, of the policy, and are frequently found in life policies.

Such a clause appeared in the policy the rights to which were in dispute in *Solicitors and General Life Assurance Society* v. *Lamb*.[48] L mortgaged a life policy and other securities to R and committed suicide. R relied on the clause against the insurance company to force the payment of the policy monies to him and also realised the other securities. The total exceeded the mortgage debt and the company claimed the surplus as against L's widow, advancing two arguments. They claimed that either the debt to R should be satisfied first out of the other securities, or that it should be apportioned rateably between the debt and the other securities. Both arguments were rejected, the court holding that the clause was inserted in the interests of the assured and created no equity in favour of the insurers in regard to monies payable to assignees.

The same principles were applied in *White* v. *British Empire Mutual Life Assurance Co.*[49] where the insurance company was the mortgagee. Other securities were also mortgaged to the company and it was held that, in the absence of any contractual provision entitling the company to repay itself out of the other securities, the widow of the assured could require the company to repay itself first out of the policy monies. The consequences of

---

[44a] *Salt* v. *Marquess of Northampton* [1892] A.C. 1 at 16.

[45] *Drysdale* v. *Piggot* (1850) 8 De G.M. & G. 546.

[46] *Beresford* v. *Royal Insurance Co.* [1938] A.C. 586. The principle was applied to prevent recovery on a policy of life insurance where the assured was executed for felony, although the policy did not expressly provide for this contingency: *Amicable Society* v. *Bolland* (1830) 4 Bligh. (N.S.) 194.

[47] *Ibid.* It has not been decided whether the security is avoided if the assured assigned the policy before committing suicide: *Hardy* v. *Motor Insurers Bureau* [1964] 2 Q.B. 745, C.A.

[48] (1864) 2 De G.J. & S. 251.

[49] (1868) L.R. 7 Eq. 394.

this decision in *Lamb's* case can be avoided if the clause provides for the preservation of the rights only of assignees who are independent third parties.[50]

A legal mortgage of a life assurance policy is discharged by reassignment, either in the form of an express reassignment or by way of statutory receipt. The form of receipt under paragraph 2 of Schedule 4 to the Building Societies Act 1986 is appropriate where a building society is the mortgagee,[50a] but discharge by simple receipt is satisfactory. The printed form of a mortgage of a life policy of banks and building societies and other institutional lenders usually, however, provide for an express reassignment. Notice of the discharge should be given to the insurance company.

Shares in partnerships

A share in a partnership confers the right to a share in the profits and, on dissolution, in the assets.[50b] It is a hazardous security, particularly as, by section 33 of the Partnership Act 1890, a partnership may, at the option of the other partners, be disolved if any partner suffers his share of the partnership property to be charged under the Act for his separate debt.

A mortgagee is not usually introduced into the partnership and by section 24(7) a partner may not, without the consent of all the other partners, introduce another partner into the firm. Unless he is so introduced, he has no right to interfere in the management of the partnership business,[51] to require accounts of partnership transactions, or to inspect partnership books.[52] He is not, however, precluded from impugning transactions made between the partners which are designed to deprive him of his rights.[53]

He is entitled, on a dissolution, to receive the mortgagor's share of the assets, and, for the purpose of ascertaining that share, to an account as from the date of dissolution.[54]

A mortgagee can enforce his security by foreclosure[55] and if the mortgage is made by deed, he has the statutory powers of sale and appointment of a receiver.

Although the mortgagee is entitled to share in the personal chattels of the partnership on dissolution, the mortgage is a mortgage of a chose in action and not a bill of sale,[56] and accordingly does not require registration. Notice of the mortgage should, however, be given to the other

---

[50] *Royal London Mutual Insurance Society* v. *Barrett* [1928] Ch. 411.
[50a] See s.13(7) and *post*, pp. 131 *et seq*.
[50b] See *post*, pp. 167 *et seq*.
[51] *Re Garwood's Trusts* [1903] 1 Ch. 236.
[52] *Bonnin* v. *Neame* [1910] 1 Ch. 732.
[53] *Watts* v. *Driscoll* [1901] 1 Ch. 294.
[54] *Ibid*.
[55] *Whetham* v. *Davey* (1885) 30 Ch.D. 574.
[56] *Re Bainbridge* (1878) 8 Ch.D. 218.

partners so as to establish priority as against other mortgagees and to bind them to pay over the share to the mortgagee.

Stocks and shares

Mortgages of stocks and shares are not regulated by the Bills of Sale Acts, such choses in action being outside the definition of "personal chattels" in section 4 of the Bills of Sale Act 1878. Stocks and shares had been made assignable at law before the Judicature Act 1873 provided for the legal assignment of choses in action. A company incorporated under the Companies Act 1985 may, by its articles of association regulate the transfer of its shares in any manner. By section 183(1) it is not lawful for a company to register a transfer of shares in the company without a proper intrument of transfer being delivered to it; unless the transfer is an exempt transfer within the Stock Transfer Act 1982; and a proper instrument of transfer is any instrument which will attract stamp duty. Transfers are therefore made for the nominal consideration of 50p.

The Stock Transfer Act 1963[57] provides that, notwithstanding anything in the articles of association of a company or any enactment or instrument relating thereto, fully paid up registered securities may be transferred by means of an instrument under hand, signed only by the transferor, whose signature need not be attested.

Legal mortgages of shares are created by transfer with a proviso for re-transfer, but it is not usual to mortgage shares in this way. Such a transaction gives the mortgagee both the rights and liabilities of a shareholder; thus he is subject to calls if the shares are not fully paid up and he may be compelled to vote in accordance with the wishes of the mortgagor[58]: on the other hand, he becomes entitled to the dividends.

An equitable mortgage of shares is usually created by a deposit of the share certificates with the mortgagee, together with a memorandum of deposit. While the mortgagor remains the registered owner, he must vote as the mortgagee directs.[59] It normally contains, *inter alia*, covenants by the mortgagor not to incur a forfeiture, to pay principal and interest, an undertaking by him to execute a registered transfer, a proviso for redemption, a power of sale, and a statement that the deposit is by way of security.

The deposit of the share certificates may also be accompanied by a transfer form executed by the mortgagor but with the date and the mortgagee's name left blank.[60] This allows the mortgagee to perfect his title by filling in the transfer and having it registered, provided that it is possible to transfer the shares merely by an instrument under hand.[61] Delivery of the blank transfer raises a presumption that the mortgagor has

---

[57] ss.1 and 2.
[58] *Puddephatt* v. *Leith* [1916] 1 Ch. 200; *Musselwhite* v. *C. H. Musselwhite & Sons Ltd.* [1962] Ch. 964.
[59] *Wise* v. *Lansdell* [1921] 1 Ch. 420.
[60] *Barclay* v. *Prospect Mortgages Ltd.* [1974] 1 W.L.R. 837.
[61] *Ortigosa* v. *Brown, Janson & Co.* (1878) 47 L.J.Ch. 168.

appointed the mortgagee his agent for the purpose of completing the transfer.[62] If, however, the shares are required to be transferred by deed, only an agent appointed by an instrument under seal can execute the deed,[63] and in such a case the deposit will be accompanied by a deed of mortgage containing a power of attorney authorising the mortgagee to execute a transfer of the shares to himself or a purchaser.[64]

Difficulties may arise if the mortgagor gives the mortgagee a blank transfer under seal and the mortgagee later executes it without having been given a power of attorney under seal or redelivering it to the mortgagor for re-execution by him. For in such circumstances the mortgagor has never acknowledged the deed as his own. He may be estopped from denying its validity as against a bona fide purchaser for value from the mortgagee without notice.[65] A transfer of the certificates without registration does not pass the legal title to the shares.[66] Nevertheless it is not a mere pledge but constitutes an equitable mortgage.[67] The equitable mortgagee can compel the mortgagor to execute a registered transfer of the shares and after default he is entitled to foreclose[68] or, after reasonable notice to the mortgagor, to sell the shares.[69]

Notice of the deposit of share certificates should be given to the company. This is not for the purpose of regulating priorities since by section 360 of the Companies Act 1985, no trust may be entered on the register of a company. The rule in *Dearle* v. *Hall*[70] does not apply to equitable mortgages of shares, priorities among which are governed by the same rules as applied to mortgages of land before 1926.

Since, by these rules, a bona fide purchaser of the legal estate without notice of a prior equitable mortgage takes in priority to it, it is advisable for the equitable mortgagee to acquire the legal title by having the transfer registered. Priority in time is only displaced if a second equitable assignee takes without notice of the first equity and then becomes registered as the legal owner of the shares.[71] The relevant time, in respect of notice acquired by the later mortgagee, is the time when he gave value for his interest. He is not adversely affected by notice acquired between the time he gave value and the time when he acquired the legal title.[72] This not only protects him against earlier equitable mortgages but against subsequent dealings

---

[62] *Colonial Bank* v. *Cady* (1890) 15 App.Cas. 267.
[63] *Powell* v. *London & Provincial Bank* [1893] 2 Ch. 555.
[64] *Hibblewhite* v. *M'Morine* (1840) 6 M. & W. 200; *Société Générale de Paris* v. *Walker* (1885) 11 App.Cas. 20; *Re Seymour, Fielding* v. *Seymour* [1913] 1 Ch. 475.
[65] *Earl of Sheffield* v. *London Joint Stock Bank* (1888) 13 App.Cas. 333; *Waterhouse* v. *Bank of Ireland* (1891) 29 L.R.Ir. 384; *London Joint Stock Bank* v. *Simmons* [1892] A.C. 201; *Fuller* v. *Glyn Mills, Currie & Co.* [1914] 2 K.B. 168.
[66] *Société Générale de Paris* v. *Walker, supra.*
[67] *Harrold* v. *Plenty* [1901] 2 Ch. 314.
[68] *Ibid.*
[69] *Deverges* v. *Sandeman* [1902] 1 Ch. 579.
[70] (1828) 3 Russ. 1. For the rule in *Dearle* v. *Hall*, see *ante*, pp. 80–82 and *post*, pp. 350–353.
[71] *Dodds* v. *Hills* (1865) 2 H. & M. 424.
[72] *Ortigosa* v. *Brown, Janson & Co.* (1878) 47 L.J. Ch. 168.

between a fraudulent mortgagor and an innocent third party. Although the non-production of the share certificates should put the third party on notice of a prior interest, the court may well uphold the title of the third party if the mortgagor gives him a plausible excuse for not providing the certificates and the company registers the transfer to him. Even where the company's articles of association state that certificates must be produced before transfers are registered, the company is not bound to require their production.[73] Dealings can be prevented by the service of a stop notice on the company under R.S.C. Ord. 50, rr. 11, 12. The effect is that the person or body on whom the stop notice is served shall not register a transfer of the securities or take any other steps restrained by the stop notice until 14 days after sending notice thereof by ordinary first class post to the person on whose behalf the stop notice was filed, but shall not by reason only of that notice refuse to register the transfer or to take any other step, after the expiry of that period. A mortgagor who, by putting a stop on registration, wrongfully obstructs the mortgagee in the exercise of his remedies is liable in damages for any resulting loss.[74]

Notice to the company, although not regulating priorities, may cause the company to become aware of conflicting claims and to defer registration, even, where appropriate, until the court has determined the rights of the conflicting parties.[75] It is doubtful whether a company is legally bound to delay so far,[76] but equally it is not bound to register a transfer which effectuates a fraud.[77] In *Ireland* v. *Hart*,[78] a solicitor was the registered owner of shares which he held in trust for his wife. He mortgaged them by deposit to H, who, being doubtful as to the mortgagor's financial stability, filled in his own name on the blank transfer which accompanied the deposit and applied for registration. In the meantime the directors of the company had learnt of the wife's interest. They deferred their decision and the court held that the wife's prior interest prevailed over H's later interest. It is only where the later equitable mortgagee has a "present, absolute and unconditional right" to be registered that he will gain priority; and this appears to be restricted to the case where the company has formally accepted the transfer and only a ministerial act by an officer of the company is required to complete the registration.

Notice to the company will also protect an equitable mortgagee against equities raised by the company after the notice has been given to it.[79] Thus, if the company by virtue of its articles of association has a first and paramount lien or charge on every share issued for all debts due from the

---

[73] *Rainford* v. *James, Keith and Blackman Co.* [1905] 1 Ch. 296; reversed on the facts [1905] 2 Ch. 147.
[74] *Deverges* v. *Sandeman* [1902] 1 Ch. 579.
[75] *Moore* v. *North Western Bank* [1891] 2 Ch. 599. See also *Simpson* v. *Molson's Bank* [1895] A.C. 270.
[76] *Ibid.*
[77] *Roots* v. *Williamson* (1888) 38 Ch.D. 485.
[78] [1902] 1 Ch. 522.
[79] *Rainford* v. *James, Keith and Blackman Co.* [1905] 2 Ch. 147.

holder, notice to the company of an equitable mortgage will cause further advances on the security of the same shares to rank after the equitable mortgage.[80] Further, if the company has actual notice that a shareholder does not own shares beneficially and makes advances to him, it does not acquire a lien on those shares for the debt.[81]

It has been held that a private company's lien arising out of a quasi-loan to a director had priority over a subsequent mortgage of the shares notwithstanding an agreement to postpone payment of the debt.[82] The equitable mortgagee of shares is, however, protected against claims by the mortgagor's trustee in bankruptcy without the necessity of giving notice to the company. "Things in action" are outside the "reputed ownership" provision[83] and shares are "things in action" within that exception.[84] Further, an equitable mortgagee by deposit does not leave the shares in the reputed ownership of the mortgagor, since he has not got the certificates and cannot deal with them without putting a third party on notice of some other interest.

When a mortgagor of shares either transfers the legal title to shares to a mortgagee, or puts into his hands a blank transfer, he enables the mortgagee to represent himself as being the beneficial owner of the shares. His beneficial interest is in the shares as security for the mortgage debt and if he transfers the shares he has the right only to assign the mortgage debt and his interest in the shares as security for it. The mortgagor, however, runs the risk of the mortgagee fraudulently transferring the shares to a third party, for value, without telling the transferee of his limited interest. When the mortgagee has perfected his legal title by registration of the transfer, the mortgagor can protect himself only by giving notice of his equity of redemption to the company as a result of which he may be able to intervene if the mortgagee attempts to make a fraudulent transfer.

Where the mortgagee is an equitable mortgagee, the rights of the parties will be determined by estoppel and by whether the person to whom the mortgagee transferred the shares is a bona fide purchaser for value without notice. When a mortgagor delivers share certificates and a blank transfer form, he confers on the mortgagee the right to do one of three things, namely to:

(1) complete his own legal title by filling in his name and registering himself as owner;

(2) sell the shares as mortgagee and fill in the name of the purchaser, having first given due notice to the mortgagor;

[80] *Bradford Banking Co. Ltd.* v. *Briggs & Co. Ltd.* (1886) 12 App.Cas. 29, applying *Hopkinson* v. *Rolt* (1861) 9 H.L.Cas. 514; *Mackereth* v. *Wigan Coal and Iron Co. Ltd.* [1916] 2 Ch. 293.

[81] *Reardon* v. *Provincial Bank of Ireland* [1896] 1 I.R. 532.

[82] *Champagne Perrier-Jouet S.A.* v. *H.H. Finch Ltd.* [1982] 1 W.L.R. 1359.

[83] This concept is now abolished; there is no provision in the Insolvency Act 1986 corresponding to s.38(c) of the Bankruptcy Act 1914. See also *ante*, p. 50.

[84] *Colonial Bank* v. *Whinney* (1886) 11 App.Cas. 426; *Re Collins* [1925] Ch. 556.

(3) assign the mortgage.

Even though the mortgagor has placed the *indicia* of title in the mortgagee's hands, he is not estopped from denying the mortgagee's right to deal with the shares in any other way.

In *France* v. *Clark*[85] F deposited share certificates with C, to secure a loan of £150, and also executed a blank transfer form. C then deposited both the certificates and transfer form with Q to secure his own debt to Q of £250. C died insolvent and Q then filled in his own name as transferee, sending on the transfer for registration. F gave notice to both the company and Q that he denied the validity of the transfer and it was not clear whether that notice was given before or after the registration in the name of C.

The Court of Appeal held that a transferee who takes a blank transfer and fills up the blanks in his own favour is not entitled to be treated as a bona fide purchaser for value without notice: and if he makes no inquiry he can take only the right that the mortgagee received from the mortgagor. Consequently, it was irrelevant whether the registration took place before or after the notice, as registration would give effect only to a prior valid transfer, but would not validate a document which, as between the mortgagee and his transferee, was of no effect. It was further held that the mortgagee had no authority to fill up the form for purposes foreign to the original contract, and thus Q had no title against F except as security for the £150 which F owed C. It would have been otherwise had the facts been such as to indicate that C had a general authority to deal with the shares; or if instead of shares they had been negotiable instruments such as bearer securities.

---

[85] (1883) 22 Ch.D. 830.

CHAPTER 8

MORTGAGE DEBENTURES

NATURE AND FORM OF A DEBENTURE

In its simplest form a debenture is an acknowledgment of a debt.[1] The usual reason for issuing a debenture is to secure a loan, most frequently by a company, but sometimes by an unincorporated association[2] or an individual. In such circumstances it will then contain a charge on the borrower's property, thereby becoming a mortgage debenture.

Where the borrower is a company, the debenture will normally contain a fixed charge on the company's land and a floating charge on the other assets.

In section 744 of the Companies Act 1985, "debenture" is defined as including debenture stock, bonds and any other securities of a company, whether constituting a charge on the assets of the company or not.[3] By reason of section 17 of the Bills of Sale Act (1878) Amendment Act 1882 (which excepts debentures from the ambit of the Act) and Schedule 1 to the Stamp Act 1891 (which deals with stamp duties on any mortgage, bond, debenture or covenant except a marketable security otherwise specially charged with duty) there have been many cases on the question whether a particular document is a debenture. From these, the following principles have emerged:

A document issued by a company which acknowledges a debt may be a debenture whether or not:

(1) it purports to be a debenture[4];
(2) it is under seal[5];
(3) it is one of a series[6];
(4) it is secured by any charge on any property of the company.[7]

As with a mortgage, it is substance, not form, that determines the nature of the document. Since any document in writing, except a bank note, containing a promise to pay, is a promissory note, the distinction between debentures and promissory notes is not clear and the nature of the document may

---

[1] *Edmonds* v. *Blaina Furnaces Co.* (1887) 36 Ch.D. 215; *Lemon* v. *Austin Friars Investment Trust Ltd.* [1926] Ch. 1.
[2] *Wylie* v. *Carlyon* [1922] 1 Ch. 51.
[3] There is no precise definition of the term: see *Levy* v. *Abercorris Slate and Slab Co.* (1887) 37 Ch.D. 260.
[4] *Edmonds* v. *Blaina Furnaces Co.*, *supra*; *Lemon* v. *Austin Friars Investment Trust Ltd.*, *supra*.
[5] *British India Steam Navigation Co.* v. *I.R.C.* (1881) 7 Q.B.D. 165.
[6] *Levy* v. *Abercorris Slate and Slab Co.*, *supra*.
[7] *Ibid.* See also *Speyer Bros.* v. *I.R.C.* [1908] A.C. 92.

have to be decided on the basis of inferences from surrounding circumstances.[8]

It is not necessary for a debenture to be issued under the company's seal, though it is usual. It is not clear whether the holders of a debenture issued under seal have the powers of sale of a mortgagee by deed under the Law of Property Act 1925, section 101. In *Blaker* v. *Herts and Essex Waterworks Company*[9] it was held that they did not. But all the cases which follow that decision deal with the right to sell where the property of the company has been acquired under statutory powers for public purposes.

The debenture usually contains a covenant by the company to pay a specified sum, at some specified place, to the registered holder or to a person named. The covenant also provides that payment should be made on a specified date or on the earlier occurrence of certain events, including:

(1) default in payment of interest;
(2) making of an effective order, or passing a resolution, for the winding up of the company.

It is also usual to provide for the appointment of a receiver in the event of either occurrence. Further, a covenant to pay interest in the meantime at a specified rate is usually included.

A debenture need not, but usually does, embody a charge. Sometimes there is a fixed charge on the company's land, and commonly there is a floating charge on the company's undertaking and all its property, present or future. If a certain class of assets is excepted, the exception applies to those assets from time to time, not merely those in existence at the date of the debenture.[10] All debentures to secure bank and other institutional lending are expressed to be payable on demand. There is sometimes a side letter which restricts the lender from making a demand except in specified circumstances.

Although it can be a single instrument, it is often one of a series. If that is so, it will be stated in the conditions endorsed thereon or annexed thereto, which may also state that all debentures in a series are to rank *pari passu*[11] as a charge of a specified priority. Other usual conditions regulate the assignment or transmission of the debenture, generally providing that the transferee takes free from equities. Such a condition may not always be effective; where a transferee gave value for debentures but the transferor had obtained them by misrepresentation, it was held that since the company had an equity to rescind against the transferor, the transferee could be in no better position.

Conditions also regulate the holding of meetings of debenture-holders and the validity of resolutions passed so as to bind a dissentient minority.[12]

---

[8] *British India Steam Navigation Co.* v. *I.R.C.*, *supra*.
[9] (1889) 41 Ch.D. 399.
[10] *Imperial Paper Mills of Canada* v. *Quebec Bank* (1913) 83 L.J.P.C. 67.
[11] *Re Mersey Rly. Co.* [1895] 2 Ch. 287.
[12] *British American Nickel Corporation Ltd.* v. *O'Brien* [1927] A.C. 369.

The power to pass resolutions affecting minority rights must be exercised by the majority for the benefit of the class as a whole.

Debentures may be issued as payable to registered holder, or to bearer, or to registered holder with interest coupons payable to bearer, or to bearer but with power for bearer to have them placed on a register and to have them withdrawn.[13] When a debenture is made payable to bearer, interest coupons are attached. The principal is payable on presentation of the debenture and the interest on delivery of the coupons. Where it is payable to the registered holder, only he can receive the principal or interest unless the debenture is issued with coupons payable to bearer.

A bearer debenture is a negotiable instrument transferable by delivery[14] and a holder in due course obtains title to it free from equities and from defects in the title of the transferor. Thus it has been held that a holder in due course may demand payment of the principal secured by a bearer debenture which was stolen, or obtained by fraud, or for which the consideration has totally or partially failed.[15]

A debenture payable to a registered holder is not a negotiable instrument, and is transferable in the same way as a chose in action. Unless, therefore, the debenture provides otherwise, the transferee will take subject to equities between the company and the transferor.[16] But since this makes such debentures unattractive as investments, a proviso is often inserted which states that the principal moneys and interest will be paid without regard to any equities between the company and the original or any intermediate holder of the debenture, or any set-off or cross claim.[17] Although, in general, an assignee of a chose in action can be in no better position than his assignor, a debtor is free to contract with his creditor on terms that he will not seek, against a transferee, to assert any rights that he has against the creditor.

Bearer securities attract stamp duty at the rate of three times the transfer duty and for this purpose a debenture payable to bearer but capable of being registered is a bearer security until a holder registers it in his name, upon which it becomes payable only to the registered holder. He may reconvert it into a negotiable security by cancelling the registration.

SECURITY OF DEBENTURES

It is usual to secure debentures by a security vested in trustees for the debenture holders, rather than in the debenture holders themselves. The

---

[13] See Palmer, *Company Law* (23rd ed., 1982), Chap. 43.

[14] *Edelstein* v. *Schuler & Co.* [1902] 2 K.B. 144.

[15] *Bechuanaland Exploration Co.* v. *London Trading Bank* [1898] 2 Q.B. 658.

[16] *Athenaeum Life Assurance Society* v. *Pooley* (1858) 3 De G. & J. 294.

[17] *Re Agra and Masterman's Bank* (1867) L.R. 2 Ch. 391; *Farmer* v. *Goy & Co.* [1900] 2 Ch. 149. If an unregistered transferee is also to take free of equities in favour of the company, it must be stated that the actual moneys, principal and interest, are to be transferable free from equities; see *Re Palmer's Decoration and Furnishing Co.* [1904] 2 Ch. 743; *Andrews* v. *Brown & Gregory* [1904] 2 Ch. 448.

debenture trustee is often a trust corporation. If this is not the case and there is a legal mortgage of the company's realty, the legal estate therein may not be vested in more than four persons. The trustees are under an express duty to protect the interests of the debenture holders and the vesting of the security in them greatly simplifies any common action on the part of the debenture holders, particularly the realisation of the security. The trust deed empowers the trustees to appoint a receiver and manager, or to enter and realise the security, in the event of the debenture becoming enforceable. Typically, it will contain a covenant for the repayment of the principal on a fixed date, or on the earlier occurrence of certain events and to pay interest meanwhile at a specified rate, a specific charge on the company's realty and a floating charge over all the company's other assets.

It should also provide for the remuneration of the trustees, who should not have any interest which conflicts with their duties as trustees; hence a debenture trustee should not be a shareholder. The remuneration is not payable in priority to the claims of stockholders, unless the trust deed expressly so provides.

By section 192(1) of the Companies Act 1985, any provision contained:

(1) in a trust deed for securing an issue of debentures;
(2) in any contract with the holder of debentures secured by a trust deed;

is void in so far as it would have the effect of exempting a trustee of the deed from, or indemnifying him against, liability for breach of trust where he fails to show the degree of care and diligence required of him as a trustee, having regard to the provisions of the trust deed conferring on him any powers, authorities or discretions.

Section 192(2) permits certain subsequent releases and the remainder of the section deprives the earlier sub-section of retrospective effect. A debenture trustee may, however, be protected by sections 30 and 61 of the Trustee Act 1925.

A debenture, whether a single instrument or one of a series, could charge only specific property of a company, for example, the realty, and in such a case it would have the same effect as an ordinary mortgage, being immediately effective and binding the mortgaged property in the hands of a third party taking it from the company. If the debenture is by deed, the debenture holder has the statutory power of sale and foreclosure in respect of the property specifically charged. This is not a satisfactory way of raising money to carry on the business of the company as a going concern, since it prevents the company from freely dealing with the mortgaged assets.

In consequence, mortgage debentures almost always create a floating charge. It is well settled that an assignment of specific future acquired property is valid in equity,[18] and future property is specific if described by

---

[18] *Holroyd* v. *Marshall* (1861) 10 H.L.C. 191.

general words sufficient to identify the property when acquired.[19] Future property so assignable can include future book debts.[20]

Such a security is a valid[21] equitable charge on the assets for the time being of the company, but it does not attach to any particular property. The company can deal with its assets so charged in the ordinary course of its business[22] until the charge crystallises[23] and the debenture holders become entitled to the security. If the company is wound up the charge crystallises automatically without any intervention by the debenture-holders. In addition, the debenture deed may contain conditions which lead to automatic crystallisation. Thus in *Re Manurewa Transport*[24] it was held that the charge crystallised automatically if the company attempted to mortgage any of its assets in breach of a restriction in the debenture. Crystallisation also occurs when the debenture holders take steps to enforce their security, as by appointing or applying to the court for the appointment of a receiver. Usually the power given to the debenture holder to appoint a receiver is made subject to the consent of the majority and a clause restraining enforcement of the security except with such consent is valid.[25] A provision that the principal shall become immediately payable if interest is a certain period in arrears will not be relieved against as a penalty.

Until the charge crystallises, the property may be dealt with in the ordinary course of business, even if this involves selling part of it and such dealings will bind the debenture-holders provided they are completed before crystallisation. A debenture-holder is not in the same position as an assignee of a chose in action. Until a floating charge has crystallised, unsecured creditors may set off debts due from the company to them against sums which they owe to the company,[26] whereas the assignee of a chose in action takes free from any set-off where the person claiming set-off had notice of the assignment at the time the debt was contracted.[27]

---

[19] *Tailby* v. *Official Receiver* (1888) 13 App.Cas. 523.
[20] *Re Yorkshire Woolcombers Association Ltd.* [1903] 2 Ch. 284; affirmed in *Illingworth* v. *Houldsworth* [1904] A.C. 355.
[21] The validity of floating charges was established in *Re Panama, New Zealand and Australian Royal Mail Co.* (1870) 5 Ch.App. 318.
[22] *Re Florence Land Co.* (1878) 10 Ch.D. 530.
[23] Farrar, (1976) 40 Conv. 397.
[24] [1971] N.Z.L.R. 909. It is not clear from the English reported cases whether "automatic" crystallisation clauses are effective. In *Re Brightlife* [1987] Ch. 200, Hoffmann J. preferred the decision in *Re Manurewa* to the contrary dicta in the Canadian cases, but did not find it necessary to decide any questions about automatic crystallisation. See also *Re Woodroffe's (Musical Instruments) Ltd.* [1986] Ch. 366 and *post*, pp. 104–105. See Farrar, *Company Law* (1st ed., 1985), pp. 216–218 and cases cited therein. See also *Stein* v. *Saywell* [1969] A.L.R. 481 (divided opinion in the High Court of Australia); *R.* v. *Churchill Consolidated Copper Corporation* (1978) 5 W.W.R. 652 (opposition to automatic crystallisation clauses in Canada).
[25] *Pethybridge* v. *Unibifocal Ltd.* [1918] W.N. 278.
[26] *Biggerstaff* v. *Rowatt's Wharf Ltd.* [1896] 2 Ch. 93.
[27] *Roxburghe* v. *Cox* (1881) 17 Ch.D. 520; *Edward Nelson & Co.* v. *Faber & Co.* [1903] 2 K.B. 367. For a review of the authorities on this topic see *Business Computers Ltd.* v. *Anglo-African Leasing Ltd.* [1977] 1 W.L.R. 578.

Priority of debentures

The vulnerability of a floating charge arises from two causes. As equitable charges on part or all of the present and future property of the company, they are postponed to later legal charges if the legal mortgagee had no notice of them.

Section 395 of the Companies Act 1985 provides:

"(1) Subject to the provisions of this Chapter, [*i.e.* ss.395–409] a charge created by a company registered in England and Wales and being a charge to which this section applies is, so far as any security on the company's property or undertaking is conferred by the charge, void against the liquidator and any creditor of the company, unless the prescribed particulars of the charge together with the instrument (if any) by which the charge is created or evidenced, are delivered to or received by the registrar of companies for registration in the manner required by this Chapter within 21 days after the date of the charge's creation.

(2) Subsection (1) is without prejudice to any contract or obligation for the repayment of the money secured by the charge; and when a charge becomes void under this section, the money secured by it immediately becomes payable."

This section also applies to a floating charge on the company's undertaking or property, by virtue of section 396(1)(*f*).

Prior to January 1, 1970, a land charge for securing money, created by a company, could be protected by registration either under section 10(5) of the Land Charges Act 1925 or section 95 of the Companies Act 1948.[28] As there was no official search available at the Companies Registry, a company search conferred no priority and was not conclusive as to its contents. By section 3(7) of the Land Charges Act 1972, all land charges for securing money, *other than floating charges*[29] created on or after January 1, 1970, must be registered, if registrable as land charges, at the Land Charges Registry. Floating charges can be registered only at the Companies Registry.

By section 396(1)(*d*), section 395 also applies to a charge on land wherever situated, or any interest in it, but not including a charge for rent or any other periodical sum issuing out of the land. This includes equitable charges by deposit of deeds and equitable sub-mortgages.

Further, section 198(1) of the Law of Property Act 1925[29a] provides that the registration of any instrument or matter under the Land Charges Act 1972, or any enactment which it replaces, in any register kept at the Land

---

[28] *Property Discount Corporation* v. *Lyon Group* [1981] 1 W.L.R. 300; *Barrett* v. *Hilton Developments Ltd.* [1975] Ch. 237; T. Flanagan and D. M. Hare, "Company Charges Relating to Land" [1982] Conv. 43.

[29] Described in *Government Stock and other Securities Investment Co.* v. *Manila Rly. Co.* [1897] A.C. 81; *Evans* v. *Rival Granite Quarries Ltd.* [1910] 2 K.B. 979, C.A.

[29a] As amended by the L.P.A. 1969, ss.24(1), 25(2).

Registry or elsewhere, "shall be deemed to constitute actual notice . . . to all persons and for all purposes connected with the land affected."

It therefore follows that registration at the Land Registry is notice of fixed charges on land, but since floating charges cannot be so registered, there is no deemed actual notice of them.

Where a company registered under the Companies Act creates a charge on registered land,[30] a purchaser will not be bound by the charge, even though it is registered at the Companies Registry, unless it is registered or protected on the register of title; this applies to both fixed and floating charges. Except where the Registrar so orders, no charge by a company is to be registered unless a duly signed certificate that the charge does not contravene the company's memorandum or articles of association is furnished.[31] If a debenture trust deed contains a specific charge capable of taking effect as a legal charge, it can be entered on the register as a registered charge. If it contains a floating charge, it can be protected by notice or caution, depending on whether the land certificate can or cannot be produced.

Purchasers of land from a company should always ascertain whether winding up procedures have commenced. Further, section 127 of the Insolvency Act 1986 which re-enacts section 522 of the Companies Act 1985 provides that in a winding up by the court, any disposition of the company's property is void unless the court orders otherwise. Further, if the land is subject to a floating charge, the charge will crystallise and although the company can convey land which is subject to a floating charge without the concurrence of the chargee, the purchaser is entitled to evidence of non-crystallisation. A certificate from either an officer of the company or, preferably, from the chargee should be obtained. By section 45(4)(b) of the Law of Property Act 1925, the purchaser must bear the expense of obtaining it. If the charge has crystallised, the chargee must join in the conveyance.

It should be noted that, if a charge on unregistered land is registered under the Land Charges Act 1972 but not under section 395 of the Companies Act, a mortgagee takes free of it since he is a creditor for the purpose of section 395, but a purchaser other than a mortgagee is bound by it.

Floating charges are also vulnerable because the company can go on dealing with the assets so charged.[32] Whether this arises because the debenture-holders have impliedly authorised the company to do so, or

---

[30] When such a charge is created, a certificate of registration under s.395 of the Companies Act 1985 should be lodged with application. If this is not done, a note is made on the register that the charge is subject to the provisions of that section.

[31] Land Registration Rules 1925, rr. 121(4) and 259. The certificate must be signed by the company's secretary or solicitor or by a director.

[32] *Foster* v. *Borax Co.* [1901] 1 Ch. 326 shows how comprehensive the company's power of alienation is. See also *Re Florence Land and Public Works Co., ex p. Moor* (1878) 10 Ch.D. 530; *Re Standard Manufacturing Co.* [1891] 1 Ch. 627; *Hubbuck* v. *Helms* (1887) 56 L.J.Ch. 536; *Nelson & Co.* v. *Faber & Co.* [1903] 2 K.B. 367; *Cretanor Maritime Co. Ltd.* v. *Irish Marine Management Ltd.* [1978] 1 W.L.R. 966, C.A.

because the company retains its ability to do so by virtue of the general law and its own memorandum and articles, is a matter of controversy.[33] But whichever explanation is correct, a floating charge which has not yet crystallised is postponed to a later fixed charge, whether legal[34] or equitable,[35] and whether the later incumbrancer has notice of the earlier floating charge or not.[36] This is the case whatever the nature of the assets charged.

Two propositions can be extracted from the decided cases. First, a company having created a floating charge on certain assets, cannot create a floating charge over those same assets ranking *pari passu* with or in priority to the earlier charge.[37] On the other hand, a later floating charge on a particular class of assets may be accorded priority over an earlier floating charge on the entire undertaking, depending on the words of the charge and the provisions as to creating further charges.[37a]

Secondly, a later mortgagee may be accorded priority over an earlier mortgagee even though the debenture restricts the company's power to create charges ranking in priority to or *pari passu* with the earlier floating charge. A later legal mortgagee will obtain priority unless he has knowledge both of the earlier charge and the restriction in it[38]; and the mere registration of the earlier floating charge is not notice of the restriction therein. Although it often happens that the registered particulars include a note of such a restriction, it is not a matter required to be entered by virtue of either section 397(1) or section 401(1) of the Companies Act 1985, and it has been doubted that anyone can be fixed with constructive notice of a matter not required to be registered.[39]

One of the advantages of appointing trustees of the debenture deed is that the trustees can take charge of the deeds should the company create an equitable charge by deposit and this will prevent any further dealings with the property charged on the basis that it is unencumbered. If a company

[33] See Pennington, (1960) 23 M.L.R. 630, and Pennington, *Company Law* (12th ed., 1985), Chap. 12; Farrar, *Company Law* (1st ed., 1985), Chap. 18, and Farrar, [1974] 38 Conv. 3; Goode, *Legal Problems of Credit and Security* (1982).
[34] *Re Florence Land and Public Works Co, ex p. Moor* (1878) 10 Ch. D. 530; *Re Colonial Trusts Corp., ex p. Bradshaw* (1879) 15 Ch.D. 465.
[35] *Wheatley v. Silkstone and Haigh Moor Coal Co.* (1885) 29 Ch.D. 715; *Re Castell and Brown Ltd.* [1898] 1 Ch. 315.
[36] *Re Hamilton's Windsor Ironworks* (1879) 12 Ch.D. 707; floating charge on company's undertaking, the debenture being specifically expressed to be a first charge, postponed to subsequent equitable charge created by deposit of title deeds.
[37] *Re Benjamin Cope & Sons* [1914] 1 Ch. 800.
[37a] *Re Automatic Bottle Makers* [1926] Ch. 412, where the first debenture expressly gave to the company very wide powers to charge its assets and entitling the later charge to priority over the earlier charge.
[38] *English and Scottish Mercantile Investment Co. v. Brunton* [1892] 2 Q.B. 700. In that case the restriction was held ineffective against a lien, arising by operation of law, in favour of the company's solicitor. And see *Robson v. Smith* [1895] 2 Ch. 118 (restriction ineffective against judgment creditor who obtained a garnishee order absolute).
[39] See Gower, *Modern Company Law* (4th ed., 1979), p. 475 and *cf. ibid.* (3rd ed., 1969), pp. 422–433; Palmer, *Company Law* (23rd ed., 1982), Vol. 1, para. 44–08, p. 572 and notes thereto; para. 44–16, p. 581 and notes thereto.

buys property with money advanced by a lender who is to have a charge thereon and the lender takes the title deeds, the charge takes priority over any debenture secured on that property.[40] The purchase is in effect a purchase of the equity of redemption.

Finally, debentures are vulnerable apart from the possibility of being postponed to later charges. Section 40(2) of the Insolvency Act 1986, replacing section 196(2), (5), of the Companies Act 1985, provides that, if the company is not at the time in the course of being wound up, the preferential debts shall be paid out of the assets coming to the hands of the receiver in priority to any claims for principal or interest in respect of the debentures. By section 40(3), payments made under the section shall be recouped, as far as may be, out of the assets of the company available for payment of general creditors.

Debenture holders may also be postponed as a result of dealings which are not voluntary acts of the company, as where payments have been made to a sheriff to get him out of possession,[41] or where a landlord has levied a distress before the floating charge has crystallised.[42] But where a judgment creditor has obtained a garnishee order, whether nisi[43] or absolute,[44] or has had goods of the company seized by the sheriff,[45] he does not obtain priority over the debenture holder if the charge crystallises before he obtains payment.[46]

Avoidance of Floating Charges

Section 239 of the Insolvency Act 1986 provides that where a company has at a relevant time[47] given a preference to any person, the liquidator or administrator may apply to the court for an order,[48] and the court shall, on

---

[40] Re Connolly Brothers Ltd. (No. 2) [1912] 2 Ch. 25, C.A.; Security Trust Co. v. Royal Bank of Canada [1976] A.C. 503, P.C. See also Lloyds Bank v. Rossett [1988] 3 W.L.R. 1301.

[41] Robinson v. Burnell's Vienna Bakery Co. [1904] 2 K.B. 624; Heaton and Dugard Ltd. v. Cutting Bros. Ltd. [1925] 1 K.B. 655.

[42] Re Roundwood Colliery Co. Ltd. [1897] 1 Ch. 373, C.A.; Re Bellaglade Ltd. [1977] 1 All E.R. 319.

[43] Norton v. Yates [1906] 1 K.B. 112.

[44] Cairney v. Back [1906] 2 K.B. 746.

[45] Davey & Co. v. Williamson & Sons Ltd. [1898] 2 Q.B. 194.

[46] Re Opera Ltd. [1891] 2 Ch. 154.

[47] The time at which a company gives a preference is a relevant time for the purposes of s.239 if the preference is given—(a) in the case of a preference which is given to a person connected with the company, at a time in the period of two years ending with the onset of insolvency; (b) in the case of a preference which is not such a transaction and is not so given, at a time in the period of six months ending with onset of insolvency; or (c) in either case, at a time between the presentation of a petition for the making of an administration order in relation to the company and the making of such an order on that petition: Insolvency Act 1986, s.240(1).

[48] For the former law, see Companies Act 1985, s.615, repealed by the Insolvency Act 1985, s.235, Sched. 10, Pt. II. Also see Farrar, [1983] J.B.L. 390 and the Report of the Review Committee on Insolvency Law and Practice (1982) Cmnd. 8558 (the Cork Report).

such application, make such order as it thinks fit for restoring the position to that which would have existed had the company not given that preference. A company gives a preference to a person if:

(a) that person is one of the company's creditors or a surety or guarantor for the company's debts or other liabilities; and

(b) the company does, or suffers anything to be done which (in either case) has the effect of putting that person in a position which, as the event of the company going into insolvent liquidation, would be better than the position in which he would have been if that act had not been done.[49]

The court shall not make an order under section 239 in respect of a preference given to any person unless the company which gave the preference was influenced in deciding to give it by a desire to produce the effect stated above.[50]

It is only necessary to establish, on the balance of probabilities, that the desire to produce that effect *influenced* the giver of the preference; it does not have to be the sole or dominant motive for giving it.[51] It is a question of fact in each case whether influence can be established, and where the giver's intentions have not been expressed, the court may infer the existence of the requisite influence from surrounding circumstances.[52] It will be open to the courts to develop a new test of influence in this context and the old law relating to fraudulent preferences will require careful review.[53] First, the section makes no reference to "fraudulent" preference, so there is no longer a statutory requirement to prove dishonesty. Secondly, establishing that the giver of the preference was acting principally in response to pressure from the creditor may not, without more, provide him with a defence.[54] It will be for the court to decide, on the evidence, whether the

---

[49] Insolvency Act 1986, s.239(4).

[50] *Ibid.* s.239(5). *Cf.* the former "dominant intention" test: *Peat* v. *Gresham Trust Ltd.* [1934] A.C. 252 at 260; *Re F.L.E. Holdings Ltd* [1967] 1 W.L.R. 1409; *Re F.P. and C.H. Matthews Ltd* [1982] Ch. 257.

[51] This is a significant departure from the position prior to the Insolvency Act 1986, where it was necessary to establish that the intent to prefer was the "substantial, effectual or dominant" view in the debtor's mind.

[52] See *R. M. Kushler Ltd* [1943] Ch. 248, where Lord Greene M.R. said: "It must be remembered that the inference to be drawn is of something which has about it, at the least, a taint of dishonesty . . . The court is not in the habit of drawing inferences which involve dishonesty or something approaching dishonesty, unless there are solid grounds for drawing them." The absence of the need to show that the preference is fraudulent may decrease the reluctance of the court to draw the necessary inference.

[53] *Re Lyons* (1934) 152 L.T. 201 (debtor's overdraft guaranteed by his father) might now be decided differently: *cf. Re F.L.E. Holdings, supra*, where the decision would be the same, it being held that there was no fraudulent preference because the company's dominant intention was not to prefer the bank but to keep on good terms with it.

[54] Earlier decisions on this point may have to be treated with caution: *Sharp* v. *Jackson* [1899] A.C. 419; *Re Cutts* [1956] 1 W.L.R. 728, C.A. If the company is under pressure to pay or give security to a particular creditor, it may not be able to exercise a free choice and the requisite desire may not be present.

desire to produce the effect influenced the decision to give the preference notwithstanding that pressure was also exerted.

Where, in the case of a company, the preference is given to a person connected with the company,[55] the company is presumed, unless the contrary is shown, to have been influenced by the desire to produce the effect stated above. Section 245 of the Insolvency Act 1986,[56] which provides for the avoidance of certain floating charges, states:

"(1) This section applies as does section 238, but applies to Scotland as well as to England and Wales.[57]

(2) Subject as follows, a floating charge on the company's undertaking or property created at a relevant time is invalid except to the extent of the aggregate of—

(a) the value of so much of the consideration for the creation of the charge as consists of money paid, or goods or services supplied, to the company at the same time as, or after, the creation of the charge,

(b) the value of so much of that consideration as consists of the discharge or reduction, at the same time as, or after, the creation of the charge, of any debt of the company, and

(c) the amount of such interest (if any) as is payable on the amount falling within paragraph (a) or (b) in pursuance of any agreement under which the money was so paid, the goods or services were so supplied or the debt was so discharged or reduced.

(3) Subject to the next subsection, the time at which a floating charge is created by a company is a relevant time for the purposes of this section if the charge is created—

(a) in the case of a charge which is created in favour of a person who is connected with the company, at a time in the period of 2 years ending with the onset of insolvency,

(b) in the case of a charge which is created in favour of any other person, at a time in the period of 12 months ending with the onset of insolvency, or

(c) in either case, at a time between the presentation of a petition for the making of an administration order in relation to the company and the making of such an order on that petition.

(4) Where a company creates a floating charge at a time mentioned in subsection (3)(b) and the person in favour of whom the charge is created is not connected with the company, that time is not a relevant time for the purposes of this section unless the company—

(a) is at that time unable to pay its debts within the meaning of section 123 in Chapter VI of Part IV, or

---

[55] Insolvency Act 1986, s.239(6).

[56] See the sources cited in n. 48 and particularly the Cork Report at pp. 1551–1566.

[57] Where an administration order is made in relation to a company or the company goes into liquidation.

(*b*) becomes unable to pay its debts within the meaning of that section in consequence of the transaction under which the charge is created.

(5) For the purposes of subsection (3), the onset of insolvency is—

(*a*) in a case where this section applies by reason of the making of an administration order, the date of the presentation of the petition on which the order was made, and

(*b*) in a case where this section applies by reason of a company going into liquidation, the date of the commencement of the winding up.

(6) For the purposes of subsection (2)(*a*) the value of any goods or services supplied by way of consideration for a floating charge is the amount in money which at the time they were supplied could reasonably have expected to be obtained for supplying the goods or services in the ordinary course of business and on the same terms (apart from the consideration) as those on which they were supplied to the company."[58]

Sections 488 to 674 of the Companies Act 1985 (except for sections 651 to 658) have been repealed by Schedule 12 to the Insolvency Act 1986. Sections 614 to 616 of the Companies Act 1985 are replaced by sections 238 to 241 of the Insolvency Act 1986. These provisions deal with the adjustment of prior transactions made by a company. The corresponding provisions in individual insolvencies are sections 339 to 342 of the Insolvency Act 1986. The purpose of the provision is to prevent persons, particularly directors, from converting themselves into secured creditors when the company is on the verge of collapse.

The operation of the provision seems to depend on whether there is a cash payment genuinely for the benefit of the company or whether its purpose is to prefer those negotiating the debenture. Two contrasting cases show the narrowness of the distinction:

(1) D was a director of X Co and a partner in D & Co who supplied goods to X Co. X Co owed D & Co some £1,954, they refused to supply any more goods until the debt was paid. Four months before X Co went into liquidation, and while it was insolvent, D agreed to lend X Co £3,000 on the security of a floating charge if X Co would pay D & Co the £1,954 out of the advance. It was later held that, as D wished to save X Co, the floating charge was valid; the whole £3,000 was cash paid to the company.[59]

(2) X Co, which was insolvent, created a floating charge in favour of Z for £900. Z was a nominee for Y who actually provided the money. On the day it was paid to X Co, the company paid out

---

[58] *Re Parkes Garage (Swadlincote) Ltd* [1929] 1 Ch. 139; *Mace Builders (Glasgow) Ltd. v. Lunn* [1987] Ch. 191.

[59] *Re Orleans Motor Co. Ltd* [1911] 2 Ch. 41, decided under the Companies (Consolidation) Act 1908.

£350 each in directors fees to A and B, and £200 to Y, who had guaranteed the company's overdraft to that extent. Less than 12 months later X Co went into liquidation and it was held that the £900 was not cash paid to the company and that the charge was invalid.[60]

Section 423 of the Insolvency Act 1986, below, is in Part XVI which contains provisions against debt avoidance applicable to England and Wales only. (compare section 245 which also applies in Scotland):

"(1) This section relates to transactions entered into in an undervalue; and a person enters into such a transaction with another person if—

(a) he makes a gift to the other person or he otherwise enters into a transaction with the other on terms that provide for him to receive no consideration;

(b) he enters into a transaction with the other in consideration of marriage; or

(c) he enters into a transaction with the other for a consideration the value of which, in money or money's worth, is significantly less than the value, in money or money's worth, of the consideration provided by himself.

(2) Where a person has entered into such a transaction, the court may, if satisfied under the next subsection, make such order as it thinks fit for—

(a) restoring the position to what it would have been if the transaction had not been entered into, and

(b) protecting the interests of persons who are victims of the transaction.

(3) In the case of a person entering into such a transaction, an order shall only be made if the court is satisfied that it was entered into by him for the purpose—

(a) of putting assets beyond the reach of a person who is making, or may at some time make, a claim against him, or

(b) of otherwise prejudicing the interests of such a person in relation to the claim which he is making or may make.

(4) In this section "the court" means the High Court or—

(a) if the person entering into the transaction is an individual, any other court which would have jurisdiction in relation to a bankruptcy petition relating to him;

(b) if that person is a body capable of being wound up under Part IV or V of this Act, any other court having jurisdiction to wind it up.

(5) In relation to a transaction at an undervalue, references here and below to a victim of the transaction are to a person who is, or is

---

[60] *Re Destone Fabrics Ltd* [1941] Ch. 319, C.A., decided under the Companies Act 1929.

capable of being, prejudiced by it; and in the following two sections the person entering into the transaction is referred to as 'the debtor.' "

This section, and sections 424 and 425 of the Insolvency Act 1986, replace Part IV of Schedule 10 to the Insolvency Act 1985 and section 172 of the Law of Property Act 1925 below:

"(1) Save as provided in this section, every conveyance of property, made whether before or after the commencement of the Act, with intent to defraud creditors shall be voidable, at the instance of any person thereby prejudiced.

(2) This section does not affect the operation of a disentailing assurance, or the law of bankruptcy for the time being in force.

(3) This section does not extend to any estate or interest in property conveyed for valuable consideration and in good faith or upon good consideration and in good faith to any person not having, at the time of the conveyance, notice of the intent to defraud creditors."

Chapter 9

BUILDING SOCIETY MORTGAGES

Power to Raise Funds and Borrow Money

The original purpose of building societies, as stated in the preamble to the Building Societies Act 1836, was to enable persons of moderate means to buy small properties. In the early societies, funds were derived from subscriptions, but societies also raised funds by the issue of shares and by receiving deposits or loans. The law relating to building societies was consolidated, first in the Act of 1874, then in the Act of 1962 which repealed almost all of the 1874 Act. The Building Societies Act 1986 received the Royal Assent on July 25, 1986, and many of its provisions have been brought into force.[1] Part II includes section 7 which deals with the power to raise funds and borrowing; this came into force on September 25, 1986. Part III, which deals with advances, loans and other assets, came into force on January 1, 1987. The Building Societies Act 1962 is intended to be repealed in its entirety and with certain exceptions has been repealed now that section 120(2) of the 1986 Act is in force.

Under the Building Societies Act 1962

Section 6 empowered societies to raise funds by the issue of shares, either fully paid up or to be paid by subscriptions with or without accumulating interest. The borrowing powers were regulated by sections 12 and 13 (restrictions on borrowing at the commencement of business), section 39(1), (powers to receive deposits or loans at interest for the purposes of the society) and sections 48 and 49 (suspension of borrowing powers). Section 40 provided that, if a building society received loans or deposits in excess of the statutory limits, the directors receiving the loans or deposits on its behalf would be personally liable for the excess. Further and importantly, section 32(1) prevented building societies from lending money on the security of any freehold or leasehold which was subject to a prior mortgage with certain exceptions, unless the prior charge was in favour of the society concerned.[2]

Under the Building Societies Act 1986

Section 7 gives the power to raise funds by the issue of shares to members, or to borrow money and receive deposits from any person,[3] to be

---

[1] Building Societies Act 1986 (Commencement No. 1) Order (S.I. 1986 No. 1560).
[2] The exceptions are for repeals of any provision in the Building Societies Acts of 1874 and 1894, Sched. 5 to the Building Societies Act 1960, ss.28–31 of the Building Societies Act 1962 and Pt. VII of the Building Societies Act (Northern Ireland) 1967.
[3] Which term includes a body of persons corporate or unincorporate: Interpretation Act 1978, s.5, Sched. 1.

applied for the purposes of the society. Section 8 regulates the proportion of liabilities which is to be in the form of shares. By section 7(3) and (15), a society's liabilities in respect of its non-retail funds and deposits must not exceed 20 per cent. (subject to variation by statutory instrument, but not to exceed 40 per cent. in any event) of its total liabilities in respect of shares and deposits. Section 8 provides that the principal of and interest on deposits must not exceed 50 per cent. of the aggregate of that amount and the principal and interest payable on shares. Section 9 deals with the central authorisation to raise funds and borrow money.[3a] A society must be authorised by the Building Societies Commission to raise funds and borrow money. Any authorisation may be made subject to conditions when granted (section 9) or subsequently (section 42). The procedure for applications for authorisation and the imposition of conditions is set out in Schedule 3.

UNAUTHORISED AND ILLEGAL BORROWING

Under former principles a borrowing which was not for the legitimate purposes of the society or exceeded the statutory limit created no debt or obligation to repay the money to the lender.[4] Thus in *Lougher* v. *Molyneux*[5] a loan was made in excess of the limit of £50 provided by section 46(*c*) of the Friendly Societies Act 1896. That Act also contained provisions making such a loan an offence punishable by a fine. It was held[6] that the money lent in contravention of a statutory prohibition was irrecoverable. In *Sinclair* v. *Brougham*[7] it was held that no action lay for such recovery by way of an action for money had and received.

These cases may be contrasted with *Re Coltman*.[8] By section 16 of the Friendly Societies Act 1875, trustees were authorised, under certain conditions, to lend money on securities, not including personal securities. The court held that the trustees had no power at common law to lend the society's money and could do so only as the statute permitted. Since, however, there was no express or implied prohibition and the money was not lent for an illegal purpose, the lending was not illegal, but merely unauthorised. The money was, therefore, recoverable.

The Building Societies Act 1986 provides, by section 9(1):

"Except to the extent permitted by subsection (3) below, a building society shall not raise money from members or accept deposits of

---

[3a] Building Societies (Non-Retail Funds and Deposits) Order 1987 (S.I. 1987 No. 378) made under the Building Societies Act 1986, s.7(9); operative on April 1, 1987; amends s.7 of the 1986 Act. It changes the coverage of that limited category.
[4] *Chapleo* v. *Brunswick Permanent Building Society* (1881) 6. Q.B.D. 696; *Brooks & Co.* v. *Blackburn Benefit Society* (1884) 9 App.Cas. 857.
[5] [1916] 1 K.B. 718.
[6] Relying on cases decided under the Moneylenders Act 1900; see *Victorian Daylesford Syndicate* v. *Dott* [1905] 2 Ch. 624 at 629.
[7] [1914] A.C. 398.
[8] (1881) 19 Ch.D. 64, C.A.

money unless there is in force an authorisation of the Commission granted under this section or treated as granted under this section by any provisions of this Act."

Section 9(11) makes it an offence, which is triable either way, to raise money or accept deposits of money in contravention of section 9(1), but provides that such contravention does not affect any civil liability in respect of the acceptance or of the money accepted.

POWERS TO MAKE ADVANCES

Under the Building Societies Act 1962

By section 8(1) of the 1962 Act, a building society may, if its rules so provide, advance money to a borrower who does not hold a share in the society. If the rules do not so permit, the loan is made by way of an advance, secured by a mortgage, of the total value of the shares for which the borrower has subscribed. If the borrower is a member holding partly paid up shares, the advance may consist only of the amount unpaid.

By section 1(1) of the 1962 Act, the purpose of a building society is to make advances to members out of the funds of the society by way of mortgage of freehold or leasehold land. A building society may not make an advance secured on the member's shares. The mortgage of land, although the primary security, is often not the only security, and collateral or additional security such as a guarantee or assignment of a life insurance policy is often taken.

Section 26(1) provides that, in determining the amount of an advance made by a building society to any of its members on the security of freehold or leasehold land, the society may not take into account the value of any additional security except such as is specified in Schedule III to the Act. Section 129(1) defines "additional security" as any security for the advance other than a mortgage of freehold or leasehold estate, whether effected by the person to whom the advance is made or any other person, and whether it is legal or equitable.

By section 33(1), a building society has the power to facilitate repayment of an advance made on the security of freehold or leasehold estate by making an additional advance to a member to cover the whole or part of a single premium payable in respect of a policy of life assurance. Section 33(2) states the conditions with which such a policy must comply for the advance to be permissible, and section 33(3) excludes the amount of such an advance from any determination as to whether it is excessive.

By section 28, where a society makes on advance to a member, to be used in defraying the purchase price of freehold or leasehold land and takes a security, other than a guarantee not secured by a change on property then, (except by leave of the court) no sums shall be recoverable, either by the building society or by any other person, in respect of the advance or of any security given for the advance, whether by the borrower or otherwise, unless, before any contract requiring the borrower to repay the advance is entered into, the society has given the borrower a notice in the prescribed form. By section 28(4), where a society fails to give the prescribed notice, the court may, on an application for leave or on an application made by the borrower, re-open the transaction and make such orders as to the sums recoverable, the security given and the exercise of rights conferred by that security, as it considers just.

Section 32(1) deals with the power of a building society to make advances on mortgages other than first mortgages. This power exists where the prior mortgage is in its own favour, or is a local authority charge taking effect under an Act or statutory instrument, or is a land improvement charge registered as a land charge. If the society postpones its first charge to a charge in favour of another mortgagee, it may not make a second advance.[9] By section 32(2), the directors authorising an unlawful advance on second mortgage are jointly and severally liable for any loss to the society covered by the advance. An advance on second mortgage prohibited by the statute is irrecoverable, the transaction is void and the borrower may recover his security. Nevertheless an order to vacate the charge may be refused even where the mortgage is void.

Sections 21 and 22 are concerned with the limits of and conditions governing special advances; limits are raised from time to time by the Building Societies (Special Advances) Orders.[10] A special advance is an advance made by a society on the security of a freehold or leasehold estate which is either:

(1) an advance of any amount to a body corporate;
(2) an advance exceeding £60,000 to a person other than a body corporate; or
(3) an advance to a person other than a body corporate who, after the advance is made to him, is indebted to the society for more than £60,000.

A person is considered to be indebted in an amount exceeding the limit of a special advance if the advance and all other debts, whether immediately repayable or not, exceed:

(a) £120,000 at the time the advance was made or;
(b) £60,000 at the sooner of:
    (i) the end of the financial year in which the advance was made;
    (ii) the end of three months beginning with the date of the advance.

Section 21(8) provides that, where an advance is made to two or more persons jointly, it is a special advance if the like advance made under the like conditions would have been a special advance if made to one of them.

The Chief Registrar may give permission for a society to exceed the

---

[9] *Portsea Island Building Society v. Barclay* [1895] 2 Ch. 298, C.A.
[10] The most recent of which is S.I. 1982 No. 1056.

ordinary limits. However, if a building society fails to comply with the provisions governing special advances it is liable to the maximum fine on summary conviction, as provided by section 32 of the Magistrates Courts Act 1980, while any officer who is in default is liable to the same fine or to three months imprisonment on summary conviction, and to a fine or two years' imprisonment if convicted on indictment.

Under the Building Societies Act 1986

The power to make advances is dealt with in Part III, sections 10 to 23 of the Act. The Act recognises fixed assets, commercial assets which are divided into three classes and liquid assets. The classification of commercial assets is specified by sections 10 to 19. Section 20 specifies the limits of the volume of business which societies may undertake, within each of the three classes.

Advances secured on land

This is dealt with by section 10(1)–(4) which states:

"**10.**—(1) A building society may make advances to members (in this Act referred to as 'advances secured on land') secured by—
    (*a*) a mortgage of a legal estate, or, as provided under subsection (*b*) below, an equitable interest in land in England and Wales or Northern Ireland, or
    (*b*) a heritable security over land in Scotland, and for that purpose may (in England and Wales or Northern Ireland) hold land with the right of foreclosure.
(2) Advances secured on land may, in accordance with sections 11 and 12—
    (*a*) be fully or partly secured by a mortgage of the legal estate or equitable interest in land in England and Wales or Northern Ireland, or
    (*b*) be fully secured by a heritable security over land in Scotland, and in this Part 'the basic security' means the security constituted by the legal estate in or heritable security over the land or, in a case where an equitable interest in land in England and Wales or Northern Ireland is or is also taken as security by virtue of this section, that constituted by that security or, as the case may be, the combined securities; and a reference to the land which is to secure an advance or on which an advance is secured is a reference to the estate or interest or the heritable security which constitutes or will constitute the basic security.
(3) The power to make an advance secured on land includes power, subject to the restriction imposed by subsection (4) below, to make, as a separate advance, an advance which is to be applied in or towards

payment of the deposit for the purchase of the land (in this Part referred to as 'an advance for a deposit for the purchase of land.')

(4) The restriction referred to is that an advance for a deposit for the purchase of land must not exceed 10 per cent. of the total amount to be paid for the purchase of the land."

Section 10(1), unlike section 1(1) of the 1962 Act, refers expressly to mortgages of a legal estate. Section 13 of the Building Societies Act 1874, from which the provision in the 1962 Act derived, simply empowered building societies to make advances on security in land. At that time "estate" had a more general connotation and would not have been confined to legal estates. For the purposes of the 1986 Act, the advance, to be "an advance secured by land" must be at least partly secured by a mortgage of a legal estate. Strictly, an advance which is to be applied towards payment of the deposit cannot be secured by a mortgage of a legal estate, because at the time of making such an advance the borrower will not have a legal estate but only the equitable interest arising under his contract to purchase.

Further, section 10(5)–(10) states:

"(5) An advance shall be treated for the purposes of this Act as secured by a mortgage of a legal estate in registered land in England and Wales or Northern Ireland notwithstanding that the advance is made before the borrower is registered as proprietor of the estate.

(6) A building society may advance money on the security of an equitable interest in land in England and Wales or Northern Ireland if the equitable interest is an equitable interest in land of a description and is created in circumstances prescribed in an order made by the Commission with the consent of the Treasury under this subsection and any conditions prescribed in the order are complied with.

(7) Any powers conferred on building societies by an order under subsection (6) above may be conferred on building societies of a description specified in the order or all building societies other than those of a description so specified.

(8) The power to make an order under subsection (6) above includes power—
  (a) to prescribe the circumstances in which the power conferred by section 17(1) on building societies of the description specified therein is to be available to them; and
  (b) to make such incidental, supplementary and transitional provision as the Commission considers necessary or expedient.

(9) An instrument containing an order under subsection (6) above shall be subject to annulment in pursuance of a resolution of either House of Parliament.

(10) The power to make advances secured on land includes power to make them on terms that include provision as respects the capital element in the mortgage debt (with or without similar provisions as respects the interest element)—

(*a*) that the amount due to the society may be adjusted from time
to time by reference to such public index of prices other than
housing prices as is specified in the mortgage;

(*b*) that the amount due to the society may be adjusted from time
to time by reference to such public index of housing prices as is
specified in the mortgage;

(*c*) that the amount due to the society at any time shall be determined by reference to a share, specified or referred to in the
mortgage, in the open market value of the property at that
time;

and, in cases where the amount due to the society in respect of capital
exceeds the amount advanced, references in this Act to the repayment
of an advance include references to payment of the excess."

From January 1, 1987, building societies were empowered[10a] to advance
money on the security of three types of equitable interest. The first is a
leaseholder's right to acquire the freeehold or a greater leasehold interest,
and it is the only prescribed equitable interest to which section 17(10) of
the Building Societies Act 1986 applies. By virtue of that section, a building society which does not for the time being have a qualifying asset holding[10b] may acquire, hold and dispose of residential land so as to enable it to
make advances on the security of such an interest. The second is an easement, profit or similar right appurtenant to the land the legal estate in
which is security for the advance. The third is a development contract
which is protected by registration as an estate contract or by notice or
restriction.

When a building society advance is made in order to finance the purchase of registered land, the purchaser will not have the legal estate vested
in him at completion, though the mortgage deed will be executed, and the
advance made, at that time. The purpose of section 10(5) is to treat the
advance as if it were secured by a mortgage of a legal estate immediately on
completion, although the legal estate does not vest in the purchaser until
his registration as proprietor.[11] A mortgage of an equitable interest will
qualify as security for "an advance secured on land" only where the equitable interest falls within section 10(6). Section 10(10) makes provision,
which the 1962 Act did not, for index-linked mortgages, though the general
law does not prevent them being made. In *Nationwide Building Society* v.
Registrar of Friendly Societies[12] it was held that the 1962 Act did not prevent building societies entering into such mortgages, provided that the
mortgage specified that in the event of a downward movement in the index,
the sum repayable by the borrower should be no less than the amount orig-

---

[10a] Building Societies (Prescribed Equitable Interests) Order 1986 (S.I. 1986 No. 2099).
[10b] At present £100 million; this can be varied by statutory instrument—Building Societies
Act 1986, s.118(2), (3).
[11] Land Registration Act 1925, ss.19(1), 22(1) and 69(1).
[12] [1983] 1 W.L.R. 1226.

inally advanced. Section 10(10) does not contain such a provision. The final subparagraph provides for mortgages where the debt is defined by reference to the value of a specified share of the property ("equity mortgages"). There has been doubt as to whether the general law permitted such mortgages,[13] though a clause providing for repayments to be linked to the rate of exchange of the Swiss franc was held not to be contrary to public policy.[14]

Class 1 and class 2 advances

"**11.**—(1) The provisions of this section and section 12 define what is a class 1 advance and what is a class 2 advance for the purpose of the requirements of this Part for the structure of commercial assets and when an advance may, for those purposes, be treated partly as a class 1 advance and partly as a class 2 advance.

(2) Class 1 advances are advances as to which the society when it makes the advance is satisfied that the advance is an advance secured on land and that—

(*a*) the borrower is an individual;

(*b*) the land is for the residential use of the borrower or a dependant of his of a prescribed description;

(*c*) the amount advanced will not exceed the value of the basic security (after deducting from that value any mortgage debt of the borrower to the society outstanding under a mortgage of the land); and

(*d*) subject to subsection (5) below, no other mortgage of the land which is to secure the advance is outstanding in favour of a person other than the society;

and which are not made on terms as respects the capital element of the mortgage debt authorised by section 10(10)(*b*) or (*c*).

(3) Subject to any order made under section 12(1), the requirement subsection (2)(*b*) above shall be treated as satisfied if no less than 40 per cent. of the area of the land is used for residential purposes by the borrower or a dependant of his of a prescribed description.

(4) Class 2 advances are advances as to which the society when it makes the advance—

(*a*) either is not satisfied that the requirements for the time being of subsection (2) above are fulfilled or is satisfied that any of them is not fulfilled, but

(*b*) is satisfied that the advance is an advance secured on land, and

(*c*) is satisfied, where the amount advanced will exceed the value of the basic security (after deducting from that value any mortgage debt of the borrower outstanding under a mortgage of the

[13] *Samuel* v. *Jarrah Timber and Wood Paving Corporation* [1904] A.C. 323.
[14] *Multiservice Bookbinding* v. *Marden* [1979] Ch. 84; *Davies* v. *Directloans Ltd.* [1986] 1 W.L.R. 823.

land) that the excess will be secured by the taking of security of
a prescribed description in addition to the basic security, and
   (d) is satisfied that no, or no more than one, other mortgage of the
land which is to secure the advance is outstanding in favour of a
person other than the society.
   (5) The requirement in subsection (2)(d) and (4)(d) above shall be
treated as satisfied if the advance is made on terms that the other
mortgage is redeemed or postponed to the basic security."

The definition of class 1 and class 2 advances refer to the society being
"satisfied" of various matters. This wording is to cover the case where the
society and the borrower enter into a bona fide contract which later turns
out to be invalid by reason, inter alia, of defective title.

The commercial assets of a society consist of its class 1, 2 and 3 assets;
class 1 and 2 advances are, respectively, class 1 and 2 assets[15] and indeed
are the only significant categories of those assets.

Section 20 deals with the commercial asset structure[16] and provides, in
effect, that class 1 assets shall form at least 90 per cent. of the total commercial assets.[16a] This, in turn, means that building societies' business will
continue to be largely their traditional business of lending money on residential mortgages.

Class 2 advances involve a higher risk than class 1 advances. They do not
have to be fully secured on the mortgaged property,[17] and they can be
made where one prior mortgage, other than a mortgage to the society, or
one which is to be redeemed or postponed, is outstanding.[18] Registered
local land charges are disregarded when determining whether the land is
subject to a prior mortgage.[19] It will be seen that the power to grant second
mortgages, when the first mortgage was granted by a lender other than the
society, is far wider than before. Advances secured by mortgages linked to
a public index of housing prices,[20] or under equity mortgages[21] are class 2
advances.[22]

Under the 1962 Act, advances to corporate bodies,[23] and advances
which caused the borrower's indebtedness to exceed a specified figure,[24]
most recently £60,000,[25] were "special advances" subject to the restrictions

---

[15] Building Societies Act 1986, s.11(8).
[16] Ibid. s.20(2)(a).
[16a] The percentage of class 2 and 3 assets which a building society may hold will be increased
   from January 1, 1990; Building Societies (Limit on Commercial Assets) Order 1988 (S.I.
   1988 No. 1142).
[17] Ibid. s.11(4)(c).
[18] Ibid. s.11(4)(d); compare the Building Societies Act 1962, s.32(1).
[19] Building Societies Act 1986, s.12(9)(a).
[20] Ibid. s.10(10)(b).
[21] Ibid. s.10(10)(c).
[22] Ibid. s.11(4).
[23] Building Societies Act 1962, s.21(1)(a).
[24] Ibid. s.21(1)(b), (c).
[25] Building Societies (Special Advances) Order 1982 (S.I. 1982 No. 1056).

imposed by that Act on special advance lending. Now, however, an advance, however large, to an individual may qualify as a class 1 advance.

Section 11(3) of the 1986 Act deals with the case where the borrower, or a dependant of his, is not occupying the whole of the premises for residential purposes and is apparently worded so as to exclude shared or common parts of the premises from calculation should there be a division into two parts. Whether any particular part is "for residential use" can be specified by the Building Societies Commission.[26]

Difficulties may arise if an advance for a deposit for the purchase of land is made in accordance with section 11(6) and the purchase is not completed within six months. Section 16(2) provides as follows:

> "Advances fully secured on land do not constitute loans under this section except that an advance for a deposit for the purchase of land shall, if the purchase is not completed within the period of six months beginning with the date of the advance, be treated after the end of that period as a loan under this section and shall accordingly cease to be a class 1 or class 2 advance."

Further, section 11(6)–(15) provides that:

> "(6) An advance for a deposit for the purchase of land is also a class 1 or class 2 advance according as it is made with a view to the making of a class 1 or class 2 advance secured on the land.
>
> (7) Advances which would be class 2, and not class 1, advances by reason only that the extent of the residential use of the land is not such as to satisfy the requirement in subsection (2)(b) above shall be treated as class 1 advances if and to the extent prescribed by an order under section 12(5).
>
> (8) For the purposes of the requirements of this Part for the structure of commercial assets—
>
> (a) class 1 advances constitute class 1 assets, and
>
> (b) class 2 advances constitute class 2 assets,
>
> and accordingly the aggregate amount of mortgage debts outstanding in respect of class 2 advances counts in accordance with section 20 towards the limit applicable to class 2 assets under that section.
>
> (9) For the purposes of subsections (2) and (4) above, where a building society makes an advance by instalments, any reference to the time when the society makes the advance is a reference to the time when it pays the first of the instalments, disregarding for this purpose any instalment which is to be applied towards payment of the deposit in respect of the purchase of the land which is to secure the advance.
>
> (10) Subject to subsection (11) below, any land to which a building society becomes absolutely entitled by foreclosure or by release or other extinguishment of a right of redemption—

---

[26] Building Societies Act 1986, s.12(1)(a). The Building Societies (Residential Use) Order 1987 (S.I. 1987 No. 1671) specifies circumstances in which land is for a person's residential use for the purposes of s.11(2).

(a) shall as soon as may be conveniently practicable be sold or converted into money,[27] and

(b) shall, until the sale or conversion, constitute a class 1 asset if
the advance secured on the land was a class 1 advance and a
class 2 asset if it was a class 2 advance.

(11) Where a building society which has for the time being adopted
the powers conferred by section 17 becomes entitled to land as mentioned in subsection (10) above, and the land is land that may be held
under that section, then, if the society—

(a) elects to hold the land under that section, or

(b) without such an election, retains the land after the expiry of the
period of twelve months immediately following the date on
which it so becomes entitled to the land,

the society shall be taken to hold the land under that section.

(12) An election under subsection (11) above shall be made by resolution of the board of directors and shall be irrevocable.

(13) If a building society contravenes subsection (10) above the
society shall be liable on summary conviction to a fine not exceeding
level 5 on the standard scale and so shall any officer who is also guilty
of the offence.[28]

(14) For the purposes of this Act, the mortgage debt at any time, in
relation to an advance secured on land, is the total amount outstanding at that time in respect of—

(a) the principal of the advance;

(b) the interest on the advance; and

(c) any other sum which the borrower is obliged to pay the society
under the terms of the advance.

(15) The reference in subsection (10) above to land to which a building society becomes absolutely entitled by foreclosure includes a reference to land which a building society has acquired by virtue of a decree
of foreclosure under section 28 of the Conveyancing and Feudal
Reform (Scotland) Act 1970."

The power to lend to individuals other than by class 1 or class 2 advances
is dealt with in section 16. Moreover, section 16(11) enables loans to constitute class 3 loans for the requirements of Part III of the Act for the structure of commercial assets, and section 16(12) provides that a society which
does not for the time being have a qualifying asset holding[29] does not have
the power to make such loans.

Where the advance is payable by instalments, a difficulty may arise if
another incumbrance is created of which the society has notice. By section
94(1)(b) of the Law of Property Act 1925, a prior mortgagee has a right to

[27] Building Societies Act 1962, s.109(1).
[28] Cf. Building Societies Act 1962, s.109(2).
[29] Building Societies Act 1986, s.118. At present the aggregate commercial assets must exceed
£100 million, but this can be varied by statutory instrument.

make further advances to rank in priority to subsequent mortgages if he had no notice of subsequent mortgages at the time the advance was made by him. But, if the prior mortgagee is obliged to make further advances, section 94(1)(c) preserves that priority. The mortgage therefore should contain such an obligation.

Although section 11(10) of the 1986 Act creates a primary duty on the society to sell or convert the land into money on becoming absolutely entitled, it may, if it has a qualifying asset holding, make use of its power to hold and develop the land for commercial purposes.[30] Land held under these powers is a class 3 asset: but if not so held, pending sale or conversion it remains an asset of the same category as the advance secured on it.

Section 12 makes various supplementary provisions respecting class 1 and 2 advances as follows:

"**12.**—(1) The Commission, by order in a statutory instrument, may as respects class 1 advances—

(a) specify the circumstances in which land is for a person's residential use,

(b) specify who are to be a person's dependants, and

(c) make such other incidental and supplementary and such transitional provision as the Commission considers necessary or expedient

for the purposes of section 11(2); and in that subsection 'prescribed' means prescribed in an order under this subsection.

(2) Without prejudice to the generality of subsection (1)(c) above, an order may prescribe evidence on which a building society is to be entitled to be satisfied (in the absence of evidence to the contrary) that the requirements of section 11(2) are fulfilled as respects an advance secured on land.

(3) The Commission, by order in a statutory instrument, may as respects class 2 advances—

(a) specify descriptions of security falling within this subsection which for the purposes of paragraph (c) of section 11(4), may be taken for class 2 advances in addition to the basic security; and

(b) make such other incidental or supplementary and such transitional provision as it considers necessary or expedient for the purposes of paragraph (c) or (d) of that subsection;

and in that subsection 'prescribed' means prescribed in an order under this subsection.

(4) The descriptions of additional security which fall within subsection (3)(a) above are guarantees, indemnities or other contractual

---

[30] Building Societies Act 1986, s.17. The Building Societies (Business Premises) Order 1987 (S.I. 1987 No. 1942) provides that where less than 30% of the area of premises occupied by a building society is used for the society's business, the premises are treated as held under s.17 and are class 3 assets.

promises made by virtue of, or by a public body established by or under, any enactment for the time being in force."[31]

While the Building Societies Commission is empowered to prescribe evidence on which a building society may be satisfied that the requirements of section 11(2), which deals with class 1 advances are fulfilled, there is no corresponding provision in respect of class 2 advances.

It is further provided by section 12 that:

"(8) For the purpose of facilitating the repayment to a building society of a class 1 advance or a class 2 advance, the society may make to the borrower, by way of addition to the advance, a further advance of or towards the cost of a single premium payable in respect of an appropriate policy of life assurance; and a sum added to an advance under this subsection shall be treated as not forming part of the advance for the purpose of determining whether the requirements of section 11(2) or (4) are satisfied with respect to the advance. . . .

(13) In this section 'appropriate policy of life assurance,' with reference to an advance, means a policy of insurance which satisfies the following requirements, that is to say—
  (a) the life assured is that of the person to whom the advance is made or his spouse, his son or his daughter, and
  (b) it provides, in the event of the death, before the advance has been repaid, of the person on whose life the policy is effected, for payment of a sum not exceeding the amount sufficient to defray the sums which are, at and after the time of the death, payable to the society in respect of the advance and any addition made in respect of the premium."

These provisions[32] enable a society to advance a further sum for the borrower to meet or contribute to the cost of a single premium mortgage protection policy. Such a further advance does not affect the classification of the initial advance as class 1 or class 2.

Local land charges

It is important here to consider the provisions of section 12(9) of the 1986 Act:

"Where an advance secured on land in England and Wales or Northern Ireland is made, then, for the purpose of determining whether the land is subject to a prior mortgage for the purposes of section 11(2)(d) or (4)(d) above, any outstanding charge over the land which is registered—
  (a) in the case of land in England and Wales, in the appropriate local land charges register, and

---

[31] As under s.442 of the Housing Act 1985.
[32] Building Societies Act 1962, s.33.

    (*b*) in the case of land in Northern Ireland, in the statutory charges register under section 87 of, and Schedule 11 to the Land Registration Act (Northern Ireland) 1970,
shall be disregarded."

Section 11(2)(*d*) and (4)(*d*) state respectively that an advance cannot be made on the security of land subject to one or more than one prior mortgage. Section 12(9) provides that registered local land charges are to be disregarded, but says nothing about unregistered local land charges. Section 10(1) of the Local Land Charges Act 1975, states that failure to register or disclose a local land charge shall not affect its enforceability and also provides for compensation.

The Building Societies Act 1962, Schedule 1, defined the local land charges to be excluded for the purpose of section 32 of that Act, as follows:

"Any charge over land in Great Britain acquired by a local authority under an Act of Parliament or under an instrument made under an Act of Parliament, being a charge which takes effect by virtue of the Act or instrument."

"Local authority" is defined as an authority being within the meaning of the Local Loans Act 1875, an authority having power to levy a rate.

Thus a building society could, under the 1962 Act, advance a second mortgage on property subject to *any* local land charge, provided that it had advanced the first mortgage. The question whether the local land charge was registered or unregistered did not need to be considered since before the coming into operation of the Local Land Charges Act 1975, unregistered local land charges were avoided as regards the charge, though the debt remained outstanding. This is no longer the case; an unregistered charge is now enforceable. Since section 12(9) of the Building Societies Act 1986 disregards only registered local land charges for the purpose of section 11(2)(*d*) and (4)(*d*), there is the possible anomaly that the existence of an unregistered local land charge would prevent a further advance being made, whereas the existence of a registered local land charge would not.

Leasehold charges

Another possible difficulty arises where a charge on leasehold property is created in favour of the landlord.

The case of *Re Abbots Park Estate (No. 2)*[33] involved a scheme of management under section 19 of the Leasehold Reform Act 1967. Section 19(10) of that Act provided that a certificate given or scheme approved under that section should be registered under that Act as a local land charge. It was held that if the scheme created a charge or mortgage in favour of the landlord, as section 19(8) permits, it would, unless expressly postponed to any future building society mortgage, prohibit a building society from making an advance on the property. In spite of the suggestion

[33] [1972] 1 W.L.R. 1597.

by Pennycuick V.-C. that that position might be considered with a view to a possible legislative amendment, it remains unchanged.

Valuation

Valuation is dealt with in section 13 of the 1986 Act, which resembles section 25 of the 1962 Act, its purpose being to ensure that adequate arrangements are made for assessing the adequacy of the security for any advance which is to be fully secured[34] on land:

> "**13.**—(1) It shall be the duty of every director of a building society to satisfy himself that the arrangements made for assessing the adequacy of the security for any advance to be fully secured on land which is to be made by the society are such as may reasonable by expected to ensure that—
>
> > (*a*) an assessment will be made on the occasion of each advance whether or not any previous assessment was made with a view to further advances or re-advances;
> >
> > (*b*) each assessment will be made by a person holding office in or employed by the society who is competent[35] to make the assessment and is not disqualified under this section from making it;
> >
> > (*c*) each person making the assessment will have furnished to him a written report on the value of the land and any factors likely materially to affect its value made by a person who is competent to value, and is not disqualified under this section from making a report on, the land in question;
> >
> > but the arrangements need not require each report to be made with a view to a particular assessment so long as it is adequate for the purpose of making the assessment."

The duty of the directors is not to assess, personally, the adequacy of the society's securities, but to ensure that the arrangements for making those assessments comply with the requirements of the section. Failure to carry out that duty does not attract penalties.[36] However, section 45 of the 1986 Act, which deals with the criteria for prudent management, provides as follows:

> "(1) If it appears to the Commission[37] that there has been or is, on the part of a building society or its directors, a failure to satisfy any one of the following criteria of prudent management[38] it shall be entitled to

---

[34] *i.e.* an advance qualifying as a class 1 or class 2 advance; see s.10(11) of the Building Societies Act 1986.

[35] But no longer "prudent" or "experienced"; *cf.* s.25(2) of the Building Societies Act 1962.

[36] There is no provision corresponding to s.25(4) of the Building Societies Act 1962.

[37] The general functions and powers of the Building Societies Commission are set out in the Building Societies Act 1986, s.1.

[38] *Ibid.* s.45(3).

assume for the purposes of its relevant prudential powers[39] that the failure is such as to prejudice the security of the investments of shareholders or depositors."

One of the criteria of prudent management is the maintenance of the requisite arrangements for assessing the adequacy of securities for advances secured on land.

Another difference between the present section 13 and the previous section 25 is that, formerly, no assessment was required where a further advance was made without further security being taken. Now, there should be an assessment on every occasion when an advance is made, whether or not further security is taken. Employees, as well as officers,[40] of the society are now authorised to assess the adequacy of the security but certain persons are now disqualified from doing so, which was not formerly the case.[41]

Section 13 provides further that:

"(3) In relation to any land which is to secure an advance where the advance is to be made following a disposition of the land, the following persons are disqualified from making an assessment of the security of authorising the making of the advance, that is to say—

(a) any person, other than the building society making the advance,[42] having a financial interest in the disposition of the land and any director, other officer or employee of his or of an associated[43] employer; and

(b) any person receiving a commission[44] for introducing the parties to the transaction involving the disposition and any director, other officer or employee of his.

(4) Any person who, being disqualified from doing so—

(a) makes a report on any land which is to secure an advance,

(b) makes an assessment of the adequacy of the security for an advance, or

(c) authorises the making of an advance,

and in the case of a person making a report does so knowing or having reason to believe that the report will be used or is likely to be used for the purposes of the advance, shall be liable on summary conviction to a fine not exceeding level 4 on the standard scale."

There are minor alterations as to disqualification from making a valuation report[45] contained in section 13(2):

---

[39] Either the imposition on conditions on a society's authorisation to raise funds or borrow money, or the revocation thereof, under ss.42, 43, respectively, of the 1986 Act: see also s.45(2).

[40] Cf. s.25(1)(a) of the 1962 Act.

[41] Building Societies Act 1986, s.13(1)(b).

[42] To cover the case where the society wishes to make an advance to a purchaser who is buying property from the society itself.

[43] Defined by the Building Societies Act 1986, s.13(5).

[44] Defined by ibid. s.13(6).

[45] Cf. ss.25(3) to 25(6) of the 1962 Act.

"In relation to any land which is to secure an advance, the following persons are disqualified from making a report on its value, that is to say—

(a) the directors and any other officer or employee of the society who makes assessments of the adequacy of securities for advances secured on land or who authorises the making of such advances;

(b) where the society has made, or undertaken to make, to any person a payment for introducing to it an applicant for the advance, that person;

(c) where the advance is to be made following a disposition of the land any person having a financial interest in the disposition of the land and any director, other officer or employee of his or of an associated employer; and

(d) where the advance is to be made following a disposition of the land, any person receiving a commission for introducing the parties to the transaction involving the disposition and any director, other officer or employee of his."

Overseas property

The power to make advances secured on land overseas is dealt with in section 14, and these may also be classified as either class 1 or class 2 advances.[46] Building societies which have qualifying asset holdings may now make advances on the security of land in the Isle of Man,[46a] Jersey[46b] or Guernsey and Alderney.[46c]

Class 3 assets

Section 15 gives power to make loans for the purchase of mobile homes: types of security have been prescribed[47] and the present limit of an advance to an individual is £15,000.[48] The limit of an unsecured advance to an individual under section 16 is now £10,000. Section 17 gives power to hold and develop land as a commercial asset, and the bodies in which a building society may invest have been specified in a number of statutory instruments.[49] The Treasury may confer powers to hold other descriptions of class 3 assets.[50-51]

---

[46] Building Societies Act 1986, s.14(1)(c).
[46a] Building Societies (Isle of Man) Order 1987 (S.I. 1987 No. 1498).
[46b] Building Societies (Jersey) Order 1987 (S.I. 1987 No. 1872).
[46c] Building Societies (Guernsey and Alderney) Order 1988 (S.I. 1988 No. 1394).
[47] Building Societies (Mobile Homes) Order 1986 (S.I. 1986 No. 1877).
[48] Building Societies (Limits on Lending) Order 1988 (S.I. 1988 No. 1197), made under ss.15(7) and 16(8).
[49] Building Societies (Designation of Qualifying Bodies) Order 1986 (S.I. 1986 No. 1715); Orders 1987 S.I.s Nos. 1871, 2018, and 1988 S.I. No. 23 were consolidated in 1988 (S.I. No. 1196) which was amended by S.I. 1988 No. 1393.
[50-51] Building Societies (Credit Facilities) Order 1987 (S.I. 1987 No. 1975) and Building Societies (Commercial Assets and Services) Order 1988 (S.I. 1988 No. 1141).

REDEMPTION, TRANSFER AND DISCHARGE OF A
BUILDING SOCIETY MORTGAGE

Building society loans are governed by the general law of mortgages.[52] The main difference between building society mortgages and other mortgages is the incorporation of the society's rules into the mortgage. The mortgage usually provides that the mortgagor shall be bound by any alteration of the rules, and, while a society has extensive powers to alter its rules,[53] such alteration must be one which could reasonably be considered as within the contemplation of the members of the society when the contract of membership was made.[54]

Redemption

Borrowers under building society mortgages have the same right to redeem as any other mortgagors.[55] The rules of a building society must provide for the manner in which advances are to be made and repaid, and the conditions on which a borrower may redeem the amount due from him before the end of the period for which the advance was made.[56] In the case of a "permanent" building society[57] the covenant for repayment is for the payment of an aggregate amount representing principal plus interest, by equal instalments over a stated period of years, together with any other sums which may become due under the rules of the society.

Where an advance is made to a member of a "terminating" society,[58] the covenant provides for the payment of subscriptions, fines and all other sums due under the rules of the society until the advanced member shall have paid the full amount due from an investing member, plus periodical sums called redemption monies, which are, in fact, interest.[59] The advance is of a sum, usually less a discount, equal to the amount to which the member would have been entitled on the termination of the society had he remained an investing member.

The 1986 Act contemplates the dissolution of building societies by members' consent,[60] or its winding-up, voluntarily or by the court.[61] The rules of a society must specify the entitlement of members to participate in the surplus assets, in the event of dissolution by consent or winding-up.[62] Section 92 of the 1986 Act provides as follows:

[52] *Provident Permanent Society* v. *Greenhill* (1878) 9 Ch.D. 122, and see *post*, p. 000.
[53] *Rosenberg* v. *Northumberland Building Society* (1889) 22 Q.B.D. 373; *Wilson* v. *Miles Platting Building Society* (1887) 22 Q.B.D. 381, n; *Bradbury* v. *Wild* [1893] 1 Ch. 377. Also see Sched. 2, para. 6 to the 1986 Act.
[54] *Hole* v. *Garnsey* [1930] A.C. 472.
[55] *Provident Permanent Society* v. *Greenhill* (1878) 9 Ch.D. 122.
[56] Sched. 2, para. 3(4) to the 1986 Act; *cf.* s.4(1)(*g*) of the 1962 Act.
[57] One whose rules do not contemplate the termination of the society on any particular date.
[58] One whose rules contemplate the termination of the society on a fixed date or on the occurrence of a specified event, *e.g.* that the amount of each share has reached a specified sum.
[59] *Fleming* v. *Self* (1854) 3 De G.M. & G. 997.
[60] Building Societies Act 1986, s.86(1)(*a*) and s.87.
[61] *Ibid*. ss.86(1)(*b*), 88 and 89.
[62] *Ibid*. Sched. 2, para. 3(4).

"Where a building society is being wound up or dissolved by consent, a member to whom an advance has been made under a mortgage or other security, or under the rules of the society, shall not be liable to pay any amount except at the time or times and subject to the conditions set out in the mortgage or other security, or in the rules, as the case may be."

Whether the society is "permanent" or "terminating," the mortgage normally contains a clause whereby default in the payment of any one instalment will render due immediately the entire amount advanced. Such a clause is not invalid as a penalty clause.[63]

Transfer and discharge

Under the general law a mortgagee is entitled to transfer his security either absolutely or by way of sub-mortgage, with or without the mortgagor's consent. But where the mortgagee is a building society, the relation between the mortgagor, as member, and the society, prevents this unless the mortgagor consents or special provision is made.[64] A transfer, however, may be made under an amalgamation or transfer of engagements.[65]

In the absence of special provision or the consent of the mortgagor it may be that the society can only assign the mortgage debt,[66] and even if a transfer is possible the transferee may not be able to exercise the power of sale and will not be in the same position as the society for the purpose of exercising the mortgagee's rights.[67] Thus in *Re Rumney and Smith*[68] it was held that trusts and powers for sale could be exercised only by the person authorised to do so by the instrument creating the trust or power.

A society can discharge a mortgage by executing a reconveyance or surrender in favour of the owner of the equity of redemption or of the reversion expectant on the mortgage term or of such persons, being *sui juris*, as the owner may direct.

A receipt[69] operating as a reconveyance or release of property mortgaged to a building society may be given under section 115 of the Law of Property Act 1925. Such a receipt must:

(1) state the name of the person conveying the money;
(2) be executed either by the chargee by way of legal mortgage or the person in whom the mortgaged property is vested and who is legally entitled to give a receipt for the mortgage money; and
(3) be indorsed on, annexed to or written at the foot of the mortgage.

---

[63] *Protector Endowment and Annuity Loan Co.* v. *Grice* (1880) 5 Q.B.D. 592.
[64] *Sun Building Society* v. *Western Suburban and Harrow Road Building Society* [1920] 2 Ch. 144.
[65] ss.93, 94 and Sched. 2, Pt. III, of the 1986 Act; *cf.* ss.18–20 of the 1962 Act.
[66] *Re Rumney and Smith* [1897] 2 Ch. 351.
[67] *Sun Building Society* v. *Western Suburban and Harrow Road Building Society* [1920] 2 Ch. 144.
[68] [1897] 2 Ch. 351.
[69] For the form of such a receipt, see the L.P.A. 1925, s.115(1), (5) and Sched. 3.

Except where the land is registered land subject to a registered charge, such a receipt operates as a release reconveyance or surrender and discharges the property from all principal and interest secured by the mortgage and all claims thereunder. If the person stated in the receipt to have paid the money is not the person entitled to the immediate equity of redemption, the receipt operates, not as a discharge, but as a transfer to him.[70]

The Law of Property Act 1925, section 115(9), provides as follows:

"The provision of this section relating to the operation of a receipt shall (in substitution for the like statutory provisions relating to receipts given by or on behalf of a building, friendly industrial or provident society) apply to the discharge of a mortgage made to any such society, provided that the receipt is executed in the manner required by the statute relating to the society . . . "

The relevant statute is now the Building Societies Act 1986; paragraph 2 of Schedule 4 to the Act, which reproduces section 37 of the 1962 Act, reads as follows[71]:

"**2.**—(1) When all money intended to be secured by a mortgage given to a building society has been fully paid or discharged, the society may endorse on or annex to the mortgage one or other of the following—

(a) a receipt in the prescribed form under the society's seal, countersigned by any person acting under the authority of the board of directors;

(b) a reconveyance of the mortgaged property to the mortgagor;

(c) a reconveyance of the mortgaged property to such person of full age, and on such trusts (if any), as the mortgagor may direct.

(2) Where in pursuance of sub-paragraph (1) above a receipt is endorsed on or annexed to a mortgage, not being a charge or incumbrance registered under the Land Registration Act 1925, the receipt shall operate in accordance with section 115(1), (3), (6) and (8) of the Law of Property Act 1925 (discharge of mortgages by receipt) in the like manner as a receipt which fulfils all the requirements of subsection (1) of that section.

(3) Section 115(9) of the Law of Property Act 1925 shall not apply to a receipt in the prescribed form endorsed or annexed by a building society in pursuance of sub-paragraph (1) above; and in the application of that subsection to a receipt so endorsed or annexed which is not in that form, the receipt shall be taken to be executed in the manner required by the statute relating to the society if it is under the

---

[70] L.P.A. 1925, s.115(2)(a).

[71] s.13(7) of the Building Societies Act 1986 provides that Sched. 4, which contains supplementary provisions as to mortgages, shall have effect.

society's seal and countersigned as mentioned in sub-paragraph (1)(*a*) above.

(4) The foregoing sub-paragraphs shall, in the case of a mortgage of registered land, have effect without prejudice to the operation of the Land Registration Act 1925 or any rules in force under it.

(5) In this paragraph—

'mortgage' includes a further charge;

'the mortgagor,' in relation to a mortgage, means the person for the time being entitled to the equity of redemption; and

'registered land' has the same meaning as in the Land Registration Act 1925."

Under the 1962 Act, Schedule 6 sets out the prescribed form, which is as follows:

The [   ] Building Society hereby acknowledge to have received all moneys intended to be secured by the within [*or* above] written deed.

In witness whereof the seal of the society is hereto affixed this day of   by order of the board of directors [*or* committee of management]

In the presence of

> By authority of the board of directors [*or* committee of management] [other witnesses if any, required by the society.]

Under the 1986 Act, paragraph 3(1) of Schedule 4 empowers the Chief Registrar to prescribe the form of documents but at the time of writing no form had been prescribed.

It will be seen that a building society receipt in the old form cannot operate as a transfer since it does not state the name of the payer of the money.[71a]

The discharge of a charge or incumbrance registered under the Land Registration Act 1925, is excluded from the ambit of the Law of Property Act 1925, section 115 by virtue of subsection (10) thereof. The Land Registration Act 1925, section 35, however, provides that:

"(1) The registrar shall, on the requisition of the proprietor of any charge, or on due proof of the satisfaction (whole or partial) thereof, notify on the register in the prescribed manner, by cancelling or varying the original entry or otherwise, the cessation (whole or partial) of the charge, and thereupon the charge shall be deemed to have ceased (in whole or part) accordingly.

(2) On the notification on the register of the entire cessation of a registered charge whether as to the whole or part of the land affected thereby, the term or sub-term implied in or granted by the charge or

---

[71a] See *post*, p. 475.

by any deed or alteration so far as it affects the land to which the discharge extends, shall merge and be extinguished in the registered
estate in reversion without any surrender."

The discharge of a registered charge will generally be effected by a receipt
in the form prescribed by the Building Societies Act. But where the registered charge is a mortgage in unregistered form, discharge may be effected
by statutory receipt. Otherwise the discharge should be in Form 53.[72] The
registrar is however at liberty to accept and act upon any other proof of
satisfaction of a charge which he may deem sufficient.[73]

A statutory receipt is a final discharge, and after it has been given no
claim can be made by the society in respect of any sum secured by the
mortgage.[74] The receipt can be delivered as an escrow and if that is done,
the mortgagee may prove that the mortgage has not been paid off.[75]

---

[72] Land Registration Rules 1925, r. 152 and Sched.
[73] *Ibid.* r. 151.
[74] Even if given under a mistake: *Harvey* v. *Municipal Permanent Investment Building Society*
  (1884) 26 Ch.D. 273; *London and County United Building Society* v. *Angell* (1896) 65
  L.J.Q.B. 194; *contra, Farmer* v. *Smith* (1859) 4 H. & N. 196.
[75] *Lloyds Bank* v. *Bullock* [1896] 2 Ch. 192.

CHAPTER 10

AGRICULTURAL MORTGAGES AND CHARGES

ORDINARY MORTGAGES AND CHARGES

Since 1900, a considerable body of legislation has come into existence affecting persons engaged in agriculture, which has among its objects, the improvement of the position of tenants of agricultural land, and the provision of finance for farmers over a longer period and on more favourable terms than would be available from the usual commercial lending institutions. Most of the legislation enacted for the first purpose is outside the scope of this work. But one area dealt with is the mechanism, introduced by the Agricultural Holdings Act 1948 and now contained in the Agricultural Holdings Act 1986[1] for securing compensation payments due from the landlord to the tenant of an agricultural holding by means of a charge on the holding.

The perceived need for long-term finance was provided in the Agricultural Credits Act 1928, which also set up a registration system that regulated both priority between agricultural charges and the validity of such charges against third parties. Unlike the charges to secure compensation payments, these charges are outside the ambit of the Land Charges Act 1972.

Apart from this legislation, it is possible to create mortgages of farm stock and agricultural land which are governed, respectively, by the ordinary law of bills of sale and of mortgages.

"Agricultural land" is defined by section 109(1) of the Agriculture Act 1947 as:

> "land used for agriculture which is so used for the purposes of a trade or business, or which is designated by the Minister for the purposes of this subsection, and includes any land so designated as land which in the opinion of the Minister ought to be brought into use for agriculture"

subject to the exceptions in favour of pleasure and private gardens, allotments and sports and recreation grounds.

In addition to the normal commercial sources of money, the Agricultural Mortgage Corporation Limited, established by Part I of the Agricultural Credits Act 1928, is empowered to make loans on mortgages of agricultural land of up to two thirds the value of the mortgaged property, and to make loans under the Improvement of Land Acts 1864 and 1899. These long-term loans may be made repayable by yearly or half-yearly instalments of

---

[1] Repealing the whole of the Agricultural Holdings Acts 1948 and 1984.

capital and interest over a period of 60 years or on such other terms as the corporation's memorandum or articles may permit and the mortgage may be made irredeemable for the period during which the instalments are repayable.

Before the enactment of section 18 of the Conveyancing Act 1881 (now replaced by section 99 of the Law of Property Act 1925) neither the mortgagor nor the mortgagee alone could make a lease which would be valid against the other, unless that power was expressly given by the mortgage deed. By the Law of Property Act 1925, section 99(13), the remainder of the section applies only if and in so far as a contrary intention is not expressed by the mortgagor and the mortgagee in the mortgage deed, or otherwise in writing. The Agricultural Holdings Act 1986 Schedule 14, paragraph 12,[2] however, provides that the statutory powers of leasing cannot be excluded in the case of a mortgage of agricultural land made after March 1, 1948. Section 99(3)(i) restricts the term of the lease which may be granted to 21 years in the case of an agricultural lease. Where a lease fails to comply with the terms of section 99, but was made in good faith and the lessee has entered under it, section 152(1) of the Law of Property Act 1925 effectuates the lease in equity as a contract for the grant, at the lessee's request, of a valid lease of like effect as the invalid lease, subject to such variations as may be necessary in order to comply with the statutory power.

In *Pawson* v. *Revell*[3] the owners of a farm which was mortgaged in 1949 granted an oral tenancy of it at a yearly rent payable quarterly. The agreement did not contain the proviso for re-entry necessitated by section 99(7), which was applicable, by virtue of section 99(17), to an oral letting. It was held that the combined effect of section 152(1) and 152(6) of the Law of Property Act 1925 was to validate the exercise of the power of leasing.

Section 152(6) provides that:

> "Where a valid power of leasing is vested in or may be exercised by a person who grants a lease which, by reason of the determination of the interest of the grantor or otherwise, cannot have effect and continuance according to the terms thereof independently of the power, the lease shall for the purposes of this section be deemed to have been granted in the intended exercise of the power although the power is not referred to in the lease."

Section 85(2) of the Agricultural Holdings Act 1986 provides that:

> "Where a sum becomes due to a tenant of an agricultural holding in respect of compensation from the landlord, and the landlord fails to discharge his liability within the period of one month from the date on which the sum becomes due, the tenant shall be entitled to obtain from the Minister an order charging the holding with payment of the amount due."

---

[2] This provision was originally made by s.95 of, and Sched. 7, para. 2 to, the Agricultural Holdings Act 1948.

[3] [1958] 2 Q.B. 360, C.A.

By section 2(2) of the Land Charges Act 1972, such a charge is registrable as a Class A land charge; and by section 85(6), (8), of the Agricultural Holdings Act 1986 such a charge, or likewise a charge under section 74 of the Agricultural Holdings Act 1948,[4] shall rank in priority to any other charge, however and whenever created or arising. Charges created under those sections rank, as between themselves, in order of their creation.

A mortgagee, whether legal or equitable, who has not taken possession is not entitled to growing crops which have been removed by the mortgagor between the time of demand and the time of recovery of possession, but he is entitled to all crops growing on the land when he takes possession,[5] unless under an express contract of tenancy between the mortgagor and himself, the mortgagor can claim them as emblements.[6] Since the severance of the crops converts them into personal chattels, a mortgagee who has not taken possession before the mortgagor's bankruptcy has no right to them as against the mortgagor's trustee in bankruptcy.[7]

If an ordinary mortgage or charge of a farm includes a covenant that the mortgagor shall not, without the consent of the mortgagee, include any growing crops in an agricultural charge, a breach of that covenant will bring the statutory power of sale under section 101 of the Law of Property Act 1925 into operation.

Agricultural Charges

The nature and mode of creation of an agricultural charge are dealt with by section 5 of the Agricultural Credits Act 1928. Since an agricultural charge is a mortgage within the meaning of section 205(1)(xvi) of the Law of Property Act 1925, the part of that Act relating to the rights and powers of mortgagees and mortgagors applies to agricultural charges.

Section 5 of the Agricultural Credits Act 1928 provides as follows:

> "(1) It shall be lawful for a farmer as defined by this Act by instrument in writing to create in favour of a bank as so defined a charge (hereinafter referred to as an agricultural charge) on all or any of the farming stock and other agricultural assets belonging to him as security for sums advanced or to be advanced to him or paid or to be paid on his behalf under any guarantee by the bank and interest, commission and charges thereon.
>
> (2) An agricultural charge may be either a fixed charge, or a floating charge, or both a fixed and a floating charge.
>
> (3) The property affected by a fixed charge shall be such property

---

[4] This section, which dealt with recovery of compensation where a contract of tenancy is not binding on a mortgagee, was repealed by s.10(2) and Sched. 4 to the Agricultural Holdings Act 1984 which itself was repealed by the Agricultural Holdings Act 1986, but charges created under the 1948 Act are still in existence.

[5] *Bagnall* v. *Villar* (1879) 12 Ch.D. 812.

[6] *Re Skinner, ex p. Temple and Fishe* (1882) 1 Gl. & J. 216.

[7] *Re Phillips, ex p. National Mercantile Bank* (1880) 16 Ch.D. 104.

forming part of the farming stock and other agricultural assets belonging to the farmer at the date of the charge as may be specified in the charge, but may include—

(*a*) in the case of live stock, any progeny thereof which may be born after the date of the charge; and

(*b*) in the case of agricultural plant, any plant which may whilst the charge is in force be substituted for the plant specified in the charge.

(4) The property affected by a floating charge shall be the farming stock and other agricultural assets from time to time belonging to the farmer, or such part thereof as is mentioned in the charge.

(5) The principal sum secured by an agricultural charge may be either a specified amount, or a fluctuating amount advanced on current account not exceeding at any one time such amount (if any) as may be specified in the charge, and in the latter case the charge shall not be deemed to be redeemed by reason only of the current account having ceased to be in debit.

(6) An agricultural charge may be in such form and made upon such conditions as the parties thereto may agree, and sureties may be made parties thereto.

(7) For the purposes of this Part of this Act—

"Farmer" means any person (not being an incorporated company or society) who, as tenant or owner of an agricultural holding, cultivates the holding for profit; and "agriculture" and "cultivation" shall be deemed to include horticulture, and the use of land for any purpose of husbandry, inclusive of the keeping or breeding of live stock, poultry, or bees, and the growth of fruit, vegetables, and the like;

["Bank" means an institution authorised under the Banking Act 1987,[8] a bank within the meaning of [the Trustee Savings Banks Act 1981[9]] or the post office, in the exercise of its powers to provide banking services.]

"Farming stock" means crops or horticultural produce, whether growing or severed from the land, and after severance whether subjected to any treatment or process of manufacture or not; live stock, including poultry and bees, and the produce and progeny thereof; any other agricultural or horticultural produce whether subjected to any treatment or process of manufacture or not; seeds and manures; agricultural vehicles, machinery, and other plant; agricultural tenants' fixtures and other fixtures which a tenant is by law authorised to remove;

"Other agricultural assets" means a tenant's right to compensation

---

[8] s.5(7) amended by the Banking Act 1987, s.108(1), Sched. 6, para. 2; but not so as to affect the validity of, or the rights and obligations of the parties to, an agricultural charge made before October 1, 1987.

[9] As amended by the Trustees Savings Bank Act 1985, ss.4(3), 7(3) and Sched. 4.

under the Agricultural Holdings Act 1986, except unde sections 60(2)(*b*) or 62,[10] for improvement, damage by game, disturbance or otherwise, and any other tenant right."

An agricultural charge is deemed, by section 8(1) of the 1928 Act not to be a bill of sale within the meaning of the Bills of Sale Acts 1878 and 1882, and an instrument creating such a charge is, by section 8(9), exempt from stamp duty.

Registration of agricultural charges

By section 9(1):

"Every agricultural charge shall be registered under this Act within seven clear days after the execution thereof, and, if not so registered, shall be void as against any person other than the farmer: Provided that the High Court on proof that omission to register within such time as aforesaid was accidental or due to inadvertence may extend the time for registration on such terms as the Court thinks fit."

By section 9(8)

"Registration of an agricultural charge under this section shall be deemed to constitute actual notice of the charge, and of the fact of such registration, to all persons and for all purposes connected with the property comprised in the charge, as from the date of registration or other prescribed date, and so long as the registration continues in force:

Provided that, where an agricultural charge created in favour of a bank is expressly made for securing a current account or other further advances, the bank, in relation to the making of further advances under the charge, shall not be deemed to have notice of another agricultural charge by reason only that it is so registered if it was not so registered at the time when the first-mentioned charge was created or when the last search (if any) by or on behalf of the bank was made, whichever last happened."

By the Land Charges Act 1972, section 18, Schedule 3, paragraph 7, a schedule relating to official searches in the register of agricultural charges was added to the Act.[11] Registration is effected by sending a memorandum of the charge in form AC1, and the fee, to the Agricultural Credits Superintendent at the Land Charges Registry, Plymouth.

A fixed charge gives the bank the right to seize the property subject to the charge on the occurrence of any event authorising seizure, and to sell it after five clear days or such lesser period as the charge allows. The proceeds of the sale must be applied towards the discharge of the monies or liabilities secured, and the cost of seizure and sale; the surplus must be

[10] Amended by the Agricultural Holdings Act 1986, s.100 and Sched. 14, para. 16.
[11] Substituting s.9(7) of the Agricultural Credits Act 1928.

returned to the farmer. The usual events authorising seizure are breach of covenant to repay or of any other covenant, death of the farmer, his becoming bankrupt or making a composition or arrangement with creditors, the levying of distress or execution against the property charged, and the removal or disposal by the farmer of any of the property charged otherwise than by way of sale in the ordinary way of trading as a farmer.

The farmer may remain in possession of the property charged, and may sell it, but, unless otherwise agreed, the proceeds of any sale must be paid to the bank to be applied to the discharge of the monies secured, as must any insurance money or compensation received by the farmer for destruction of beasts under the Animal Health Act 1981 or of plants, under the Plant Health Act 1967.

Section 6(3) and (4) of the Agricultural Credits Act 1928 is as follows:

> "(3) Subject to compliance with the obligations so imposed, a fixed charge shall not prevent the farmer selling any of the property subject to the charge, and neither the purchaser, nor, in the case of a sale by auction, the auctioneer, shall be concerned to see that such obligations are complied with notwithstanding that he may be aware of the existence of the charge.
>
> (4) Where any proceeds of sale which in pursuance of such obligation as aforesaid ought to be paid to the bank are paid to some other person, nothing in this Act shall confer on the bank a right to recover such proceeds from that other person unless the bank proves that such other person knew that the proceeds were paid to him in breach of such obligation as aforesaid, but such other person shall not be deemed to have such knowledge by reason only that he has notice of the charge."

Section 7(1), which deals with the effect of a floating charge, is as follows:

> "(1) An agricultural charge creating a floating charge shall have the like effect as if the charge had been created by a duly registered debenture issued by a company:
> Provided that—
> (a) the charge shall become a fixed charge upon the property comprised in the charge as existing at the date of its becoming a fixed charge—
>   (i) upon [bankruptcy order][12] being made against the farmer;
>   (ii) upon the death of the farmer;
>   (iii) upon the dissolution of the partnership in the case where the property charged is partnership property;
>   (iv) upon notice in writing to that effect being given by the bank on the happening of any event which by virtue of the charge confers on the bank the right to give such a notice;

---

[12] As amended by the Insolvency Act 1985, s.235 and Sched. 8, para. 6.

(*b*) the farmer, whilst the charge remains a floating charge, shall be subject to the like obligation as in the case of a fixed charge to pay over to the bank the amount received by him by way of proceeds of sale, in respect of other agricultural assets, under policies of insurance, or by way of compensation, and the last foregoing section shall apply accordingly: Provided that it shall not be necessary for a farmer to comply with such obligation if and so far as the amount so received is expended by him in the purchase of farming stock which on purchase becomes subject to the charge."

Priorities of agricultural charges

Priorities between agricultural charges are regulated by section 8(2) to (6) of the Act, which are as follows:

"(2) Agricultural charges shall in relation to one another have priority in accordance with the times at which they are respectively registered under this Part of this Act.

(3) Where an agricultural charge creating a floating charge has been made, an agricultural charge purporting to create a fixed charge on, or a bill of sale comprising any of the property comprised in the floating charge shall, as respects the property subject to the floating charge, be void so long as the floating charge remains in force.

(4) [. . .][13]

(5) Where a farmer who is adjudged bankrupt has created in favour of a bank an agricultural charge on any of the farming stock or other agricultural assets belonging to him, and the charge was created within three months of the date of the presentation of the bankruptcy petition and operated to secure any sum owing to the bank immediately prior to the giving of the charge, then, unless it is proved that the farmer immediately after the execution of the charge was solvent, the amount which but for this provision would have been secured by the charge shall be reduced by the amount of the sum so owing to the bank immediately prior to the giving of the charge, but without prejudice to the bank's right to enforce any other security for that sum or to claim payment thereof as an unsecured debt.

(6) Where after the passing of this Act the farmer has mortgaged his interest in the land comprised in the holding, then, if growing crops are included in an agricultural charge the rights of the bank under the charge in respect of the crops shall have priority to those of the mortgage, whether in possession or not, and irrespective of the dates of the mortgage and charge."

[13] s.8(4) was repealed by the Insolvency Act 1985, s.235, Sched. 10, Pt. III.

CHAPTER 11

MORTGAGES OF LAND AND THE CONSUMER CREDIT ACT 1974

APPLICATION OF THE ACT

Types of agreement

An agreement may be unregulated, partially regulated, regulated, or exempt.

Unregulated agreements are those which do not attract the operation of the Act at all, either because English law does not apply to them or because none of the debtors is an individual. Section 43(2)(*c*) refers to such agreements, but the Act does not define them.

Partially regulated agreements are agreements which are exempt from certain specific provisions of the Act. They include pledges of documents of title and some purchase-money arrangements secured by a mortgage of land.

Regulated agreements[1] are defined by section 189(1) as consumer credit or consumer hire agreements, other than exempt agreements.

Exempt agreements which are not affected by the Act except for the provisions of section 137 to 140, which apply to extortionate credit bargains.

Definitions

By section 189(1), a land mortgage includes any security charged on land and thus a rentcharge is a land mortgage; but by section 2 of the Rentcharges Act 1977, no new rentcharges can validly be created. Section 189(1) also defines "land" as including an interest in land, whether freehold or leasehold.

Exempt consumer credit agreements are of two types. Section 16(1) exempts land mortgages or agreements relating thereto where the creditor is a specified body, while section 16(5) empowers the Secretary of State to exempt certain other consumer credit agreements by order.[1a] Section 181 provides for the amendment of monetary limits by statutory instrument.

Section 8(2) defines a consumer credit agreement as a personal credit agreement by which the creditor provides the debtor with credit not exceeding £5,000. By the Consumer Credit (Increases of Monetary Limits) Order 1983 (S.I. 1983 No. 1878)[2] the upper limit was raised to £15,000 with

---

[1] s.126 of the Act provides that a land mortgage securing a regulated agreement is enforceable only by an order of the court; see *post*, p. 247.

[1a] The Consumer Credit (Exempt Agreements) Order (No. 2) (S.I. 1985 No. 757) presently in force, is further amended by (S.I. 1985 No. 1736); (S.I. 1985 No. 1918); (S.I. 1986 No. 1105); (S.I. 1986 No. 2186); (S.I. 1987 No. 1578).

[2] At the time of writing there have been no further orders.

effect from May 20, 1985, the date after the coming into force of the entire Act.

Exempt agreements are dealt with by section 16 of the Act. Section 16(1), as amended,[3] reads:

"(1) This Act does not regulate a consumer credit agreement where the creditor is a local authority, [. . .] or a body specified, or of a description specified, in an order made by the Secretary of State, being—

(*a*) an insurance company,

(*b*) a friendly society,

(*c*) an organisation of employers or organisation of workers,

(*d*) a charity,

(*e*) a land improvement company,

(*f*) a body corporate named or specifically referred to in any public general Act, or

[*ff* a body corporate named or specifically referred to in an order made under sections 156(4), 444(1) or 447(2)(*a*) of the Housing Act 1985, section 2 of the House Purchase Assistance and Housing Corporation Guarantee Act 1978 or section 31 of the Tenants' Rights, etc. (Scotland) Act 1980, or Articles 154(1) or 156AA of the Housing (Northern Ireland) Order 1981 or Article 10(6A) of the Housing (Northern Ireland) Order 1983; or]

[(*g*) a building society]

[(*h*) an authorised institution or wholly-owned subsidiary (within the meaning of the Companies Act 1985) of such an institution.]"

The relevant order is the Consumer Credit (Exempt Agreements) (No. 2) Order[3a] and the specified bodies are listed in Part I of the Schedule thereto. Provided that the creditor is a local authority, and the agreement falls within section 16(2) of the Act, it is an exempt agreement. Section 16(2) reads:

"(2) Subsection (1) applies only where the agreement is—

(*a*) a debtor-creditor-supplier agreement financing—

(i) the purchase of land, or

(ii) the provision of dwellings on any land, and secured by a land mortgage on that land, or

(*b*) a debtor-creditor agreement secured by any land mortgage; or

(*c*) a debtor-creditor-supplier agreement financing a transaction which is a linked transaction in relation to—

(i) an agreement falling within paragraph (*a*), or

(ii) an agreement falling within paragraph (*b*) financing—

---

[3] By the Building Societies Act 1986, s.120(1), (2) and Scheds. 18, 19 Housing and Planning Act 1986, s.22; Banking Act 1987, s.88.

[3a] S.I. 1985 No. 757 as amended by S.I. 1986 No. 2186, S.I. 1987 No. 1578 and S.I. 1988 No. 707.

(*aa*) the purchase of any land, or

(*bb*) the provision of dwellings on any land,

and secured by a land mortgage on the land referred to in paragraph

(*a*), or, as the case may be, the land referred to in sub-paragraph

(ii)."

Where the creditor is a building society authorised under the Building Societies Act 1986, an institution authorised under the Banking Act 1987, or a wholly owned subsidiary of such an institution, or a specified body under the above order, the agreement is exempt provided that it falls within Article 2(2) of the order. The effect of Article 2(2) is to narrow the range of exempt debtor-creditor agreements; the position in regard to debtor-creditor-supplier agreements is unaltered, as all such agreements within sections 16(2)(*a*) or (*c*) of the Act are within Article 2(2). Building Societies lost their automatic exemption from January 1, 1987.

As to debtor-creditor agreements, not all such agreements secured by land mortgages are exempt, as section 16(2)(*b*) formerly provided: the exemption applies only to the agreements specified in sub-paragraphs (*b*) and (*c*) of Article 2(2), which read:

"(*b*) a debtor-creditor agreement secured by any land mortgage [to finance]—

(i) the purchase of land; or

(ii) the provision of dwelling or business premises on any land; or

(iii) subject to paragraph (3) below, the alteration, enlarging, repair or improvement of a dwelling or business premises on any land;

(*c*) a debtor-creditor agreement secured by any land mortgage to refinance any existing indebtedness of the debtor whether to the creditor or another person, under any agreement by which the debtor was provided with credit for any of the purposes specified in heads (i) to (iii) of sub-paragraph (*b*) above."

For the purposes of the Act, a "building society" has the meaning given to it by section 1 of the Building Societies Act 1962[4]; "local authority," in relation to England and Wales, means the Greater London Council,[5] a county, London borough, or district council, the Common Council of the City of London, or the Council of the Isles of Scilly. Debtor-creditor-supplier and debtor-creditor agreements are defined in sections 12 and 13, respectively. The essential difference between them is that, in a debtor-creditor agreement there is either no supplier of goods or services, or there

---

[4] The 1962 Act has been repealed by the Building Societies Act 1986, s.120(2), Sched. 19, Pt. I, however, by s.1(4) a building society was defined as a society incorporated under the 1962 Act "or any enactment repealed by this Act." The words in quotation marks are omitted in the definition in s.119 of the 1986 Act.

[5] The definition of "local authority" has not been amended despite the abolition of the Greater London Council by the Local Government Act 1985, s.1.

is no arrangement between the supplier and the creditor. Whereas in a debtor-creditor-supplier agreement, the supplier is either the creditor or a party to actual or contemplated arrangements between himself and the creditor.

It therefore follows that the exemption provided by section 16(2)(a) is effective when credit is extended by the vendor, or the builder, or a third party lender who has made arrangements with the vendor or builder, as the case may be, and where the advance is secured on the land purchased or to be built on. A dwelling, for the purpose of this provision, is any accommodation designed wholly or mainly for living or sleeping in, rather than for business. A debtor-creditor agreement secured by a land mortgage will be an exempt agreement under Article 2(2)(b) provided that it is to finance the purchase of land or the provision of dwelling or business premises on any land, and that the creditor is an authorised bank or building society or body specified in Part I of the Schedule.

Agreements to finance the alteration, enlarging, repair or improvement of a dwelling or business premises on any land are not necessarily exempt agreements even when the creditor is one of the specified bodies.[5a] The exemption under Article 2(2)(b)(iii) may apply *either* because the creditor is a creditor under an agreement of the type specified in Article 2(3)(i)(a) or (b), *or* because the agreement has been made as a result of any such services as are described in section 4(3)(dd) of the Housing Act 1985 and which are certified as having been provided by one of the bodies specified in Article 2(3)(ii)(a–f).

The bodies listed[5a] various insurance companies, friendly societies and ecclesiastical charities, are exempt agreements.

CANCELLATION AND WITHDRAWAL

Part V of the Act deals with the withdrawal by an intending debtor or hirer from a prospective regulated agreement, and with cancellation by a debtor or hirer of a regulated agreement already entered into. Most land mortgages are exempt agreements by virtue of section 8(2) and section 16, but even where a land mortgage is a regulated agreement, it can be excluded from the operation of Part V by a determination under section 74 of the Act, which provides as follows[6]:

"(1) This Part (except section 56) does not apply to:—
(a) a non-commercial agreement, or
(b) a debtor-creditor agreement enabling the debtor to overdraw on a current account, or

---

[5a] Specified in the Sched. to the Consumer Credit (Exempt Agreements) (No. 2) Order 1985 (S.I. 1985 No. 757) as amended by (S.I. 1985 No. 1736); (S.I. 1985 No. 1918); (S.I. 1986 No. 1105); (S.I. 1986 No. 2186); (S.I. 1987 No. 1578); (S.I. 1988 No. 707); (S.I. 1988 No. 990).

[6] A new s.3A was added, and s.4 altered as indicated by the deletion of the words in square brackets, by the Banking Act 1979, s.38(1).

(c) a debtor-creditor agreement to finance the making of such payments arising on, or connected with, the death of a person as may be prescribed.

(2) This Part (except sections 55 and 56) does not apply to a small debtor-creditor-supplier agreement for restricted-use credit

(3) Subsection (1)(b) or (c) applies only where the Director so determines, and such a determination:—

"(a) may be made subject to such conditions as the Director thinks fit, and

(b) shall be made only if the Director is of opinion that it is not against the interests of debtors."

(4) If any term of an agreement falling within subsection (1)[(b) or](c) or (2) is expressed in writing, regulations under section 60(1) shall apply to that term (subject to section 60(3)) as if the agreement were a regulated agreement not falling within subsection (1)(b) or (c) or (2)."

A non-commercial agreement is a consumer credit agreement or a consumer hire agreement not made by the creditor or owner in the course of a business carried on by him.

Few land mortgages would, in fact, be excluded by the operation of section 74, but they are excluded from the cancellation provisions of sections 67 to 73. Instead, section 58(1) provides a special mechanism whereby the debtor or hirer under certain land mortgage transactions gets, in effect, the right to withdraw. Although the Act does not expressly give that right, the debtor or hirer is always free to withdraw until he has signed the written regulated agreement and an agreement to enter a regulated agreement is not enforceable against him. Section 58 reads:

"(1) Before sending to the debtor or hirer, for his signature, an unexecuted agreement in a case where the prospective regulated agreement is to be secured on land (the "mortgaged land"), the creditor or owner shall give the debtor or hirer a copy of the unexecuted agreement which contains a notice in the prescribed form indicating the right of the debtor or hirer to withdraw from the prospective agreement, and how and when the right is exercisable, together with a copy of any other document referred to in the unexecuted agreement.[7]

(2) Subsection (1) does not apply to—

(a) a restricted-use credit agreement to finance the purchase of the mortgaged land, or

(b) an agreement for a bridging loan in connection with the purchase of the mortgaged land or other land."

The reason for the provisions of section 58(1) is the administrative inconvenience which is likely to arise from the registration and almost immedi-

---

[7] The Consumer Credit (Cancellation Notices and Copies of Documents) Regulations 1983 (S.I. 1983 No. 1557) as amended by (S.I. 1984 No. 1108), (S.I. 1985 No. 666) are partly made under s.58(1) of the Consumer Credit Act 1974.

ate de-registration of mortgages, were they cancellable. The exceptions in section 58(2) apply to certain transactions where there is a need for finance to be provided rapidly and the delay provided by section 58(1) might be prejudicial. Section 61, below deals with the signing of regulated agreements:

"(1) A regulated agreement is not properly executed unless—

(a) a document in the prescribed form itself containing all the prescribed terms and conforming to regulations under section 60(1) is signed in the prescribed manner both by the debtor and hirer and by or on behalf of the creditor or owner, and

(b) the document embodies all the terms of the agreement, other than implied terms, and

(c) the document is, when presented or sent to the debtor or hirer for signature, in such a state that all its terms are readily legible."

(2) In addition, where the agreement is one to which section 58(1) applies, it is not properly executed unless—

"(a) the requirements of section 58(1) were complied with, and

(b) the unexecuted agreement was sent, for his signature, to the debtor or hirer by post not less than seven days[8] after a copy of it was given to him under section 58(1), and

(c) during the consideration period, the creditor or owner refrained from approaching the debtor or hirer (whether in person, by telephone or letter, or in any other way) except in response to a specific request made by the debtor or hirer after the beginning of the consideration period, and

(d) no notice of withdrawal by the debtor or hirer was received by the creditor or owner before the sending of the unexecuted agreement."

(3) In subsection (2)(c), "the consideration period" means the period beginning with the giving of the copy under section 58(1) and ending—

(a) at the expiry of seven days after the day on which the unexecuted agreement is sent, for his signature, to the debtor or hirer, or

(b) on its return by the debtor or hirer after signature by him. whichever first occurs.

(4) Where the debtor or hirer is a partnership or an unincorporated body of persons, subsection (1)(a) shall apply with the substitution for 'by the debtor of hirer' of 'by or on behalf of the debtor of hirer.' "

The provisions of section 61(2) are additional to, not in substitution for, those of section 61(1), so, not only must the form and content of the agree-

---

[8] It is thought that this means seven clear days excluding both the date of delivery of the copy and the date of sending the agreement for signature: R. v. Turner [1910] 1 K.B. 346; Re Hector Whaling Ltd. [1936] Ch. 208.

ment be as provided by section 60, but the requirements of section 58 must be met if that section applies.

Section 59 prevents the debtor or hirer having a prospective agreement enforced against him.

"(1) An agreement is void if, and to the extent that, it purports to bind a person to enter as debtor or hirer into a prospective regulated agreement.

(2) Regulations may exclude from the operation of subsection (1) agreements such as are described in the regulations."[9]

Although the cancellation provisions of sections 67 to 73 do not apply to land mortgages, section 57(4) applies section 57(1) to non-cancellable agreements, and, by section 57(1), the rights of the parties after withdrawal are the same as those conferred by section 69 where the agreement was cancellable. Section 57 states that:

"(1) The withdrawal of a party from a prospective regulated agreement shall operate to apply this Part to the agreement, any linked transaction and any other thing done in anticipation of the making of the agreement as it would apply if the agreement were made and then cancelled under section 69.

(2) The giving to a party of a written or oral notice which, however expressed, indicates the intention of the other party to withdraw from a prospective regulated agreement operates as a withdrawal from it.

(3) Each of the following shall be deemed to be the agent of the creditor or owner for the purpose of receiving a notice under subsection (2)—

(a) a credit-broker or supplier who is the negotiator in antecedent negotiations, and

(b) any person who, in the course of a business carried on by him, acts on behalf of the debtor or hirer in any negotiations for the agreement.

(4) Where the agreement, if made, would not be a cancellable agreement, subsection (1) shall nevertheless apply as if the contrary were the case."

Linked transactions are defined by section 19 of the Act. Not only is the transaction and any linked transaction cancelled, but so is any offer by the debtor or hirer or his relative, to enter into a linked transaction, unless in both cases the linked transaction is exempted by regulation by virtue of section 69(5). Section 69(4) provides that cancelled agreements are to be treated as if they had never been entered into.

If the relevant agreement is a debtor-creditor-supplier agreement financing the supply of goods or doing of work in an emergency, or financing the supply of goods which have become incorporated by act of the debtor or

---

[9] Consumer Credit (Agreements to Enter Prospective Agreements) (Exemptions) Regulations 1983 (S.I. 1983 No. 1552).

his relative in any land or thing not itself comprised in the agreement or any linked transaction, the cancellation or withdrawal affects only those provisions that relate to the provision of credit, or require payment of an item in the total charge for credit. But the obligation of the debtor to pay for the work or supply of goods is unaffected.[9a]

EXTORTIONATE CREDIT BARGAINS[9b]

Statutory control over extortionate credit bargains formerly derived from the Moneylenders Act 1900, as amended by the Moneylenders Act 1927.[10] Under those enactments only loans made by persons who were money-lenders within the meaning of the earlier Act, and certain pawnbroking transactions were caught, and there was a presumption under section 10(1) of the 1927 Act that any interest charge of over 48 per cent. per annum was excessive. In addition, the courts had an equitable jurisdiction to relieve against harsh and unconscionable bargains.

The provisions of the Moneylenders Acts, which have been progressively repealed as various parts of the Consumer Credit Act 1974 have come into force, and were totally repealed on May 19, 1985, have been replaced by sections 137 to 140 of the Consumer Credit Act. Two important differences between the new and the former provisions are that the new provisions apply to all "credit bargains" as defined in section 137, *infra*, and the statutory presumption as to excessive interest rates has been abolished:

"(1) If the court finds a credit bargain extortionate it may reopen the credit agreement so as to do justice between the parties.

(2) In this section and sections 138 to 140—
 (a) 'credit agreement' means any agreement between an individual (the 'debtor') and any other person (the 'creditor') by which the creditor provides the debtor with credit of any amount, and
 (b) 'credit bargain'—
  (i) where no transaction other than the credit agreement is to be taken into account in computing the total charge for credit, means the credit agreement, or
  (ii) where one or more other transactions are to be so taken into account, means the credit agreement and those other transactions, taken together."

Section 138(1) defines "extortionate" whilst section 138(2) to (5) sets out

[9a] s.69(2).
[9b] Where the mortgagor is a company, the court has jurisdiction to set aside or vary the terms of any extortionate credit transactions. It is similar to the jurisdiction under the Consumer Credit Act in respect of extortionate credit bargains. But it is only exercisable in respect of transactions entered into within 3 years before the day on which the company goes into liquidation or an administration order is made—see Insolvency Act 1986, s.244(1) and also s.343 for analogous provisions in the case of bankrupts.
[10] Repealed by the Consumer Credit Act 1974, s.192(3) and Sched. 5.

the evidential matters which the court is to take into account in determining whether a credit bargain is extortionate:

"(1) A credit bargain is extortionate if it—

    (a) requires the debtor or a relative of his to make payments (whether unconditionally, or on certain contingencies) which are grossly exorbitant, or

    (b) otherwise grossly contravenes ordinary principles of fair dealing.

(2) In determining whether a credit bargain is extortionate, regard shall be had to such evidence as is adduced concerning—

    (a) interest rates prevailing at the time it was made,

    (b) the factors mentioned in subsections (3) to (5), and

    (c) any other relevant considerations.

(3) Factors applicable under subsection (2) in relation to the debtor[11] include—

    (a) his age, experience, business capacity and state of health; and

    (b) the degree to which, at the time of making the credit bargain, he was under financial pressure, and the nature of that pressure.

(4) Factors applicable under subsection (2) in relation to the creditor include—

    (a) the degree of risk accepted by him, having regard to the value of any security provided[12];

    (b) his relationship to the debtor; and

    (c) whether or not a colourable cash price was quoted for any goods or services included in the credit bargain.

(5) Factors applicable under subsection (2) in relation to a linked transaction include the question how far the transaction was reasonably required for the protection of debtor or creditor, or was in the interest of the debtor."

The general equitable jurisdiction of the courts to set aside "harsh and unconscionable" bargains was supplemented by section 1(1) of the Money-lenders Act 1900. Where a transaction was caught by this provision, the court had power to re-open it where there was evidence that the interest and other charges were excessive and that the transaction was harsh and unconscionable or otherwise such that the court of equity would give relief. Before 1900, courts of equity had set aside two classes of bargain. Where the bargain was with an expectant heir,[13] the onus was on the purchaser to prove that it was fair, just and reasonable, and if he failed to discharge that

---

[11] The cases of *Samuel* v. *Newbold* [1906] A.C. 461, *Poncione* v. *Higgins* (1904) 21 T.L.R. 11 and *Glaskie* v. *Griffin* (1914) 111 L.T. 712 contain decisions on similar factors under the old provisions.

[12] For relevant decisions see *Kruse* v. *Seeley* [1924] 1 Ch. 136; *Verner-Jeffreys* v. *Pinto* [1929] 1 Ch. 401; *Reading Trust Ltd.* v. *Spero* [1930] 1 K.B. 492.

[13] *Earl of Aylesford* v. *Morris* (1873) L.R. 8 Ch.App. 484; *Earl of Chesterfield* v. *Janssen* (1750) 2 Ves.Sen. 125; *Nevill* v. *Snelling* (1880) 15 Ch.D. 679.

burden, the transaction would be set aside. But, regardless of the relationship between the parties to the bargain, it would be set aside on the ground of unconscionableness if the court considered that the creditor had taken a grossly unfair advantage of the debtor. In *Samuel* v. *Newbold*[14] it was decided that these two grounds were quite distinct.

The Consumer Credit Act 1974 contains no power to re-open transactions which are otherwise such that the court would give relief. It may be, however, that a loan made on the credit of the borrower's expectancy,[14a] but without taking a security over it, would be set aside unless the lender could prove that the terms were fair and reasonable. Such a loan is outside section 174 of the Law of Property Act 1925 which provides that a sale or loan on the security of a reversion is not voidable merely by reason of undervalue, but preserves the jurisdiction of the court to set aside unconscionable bargains.

The power of courts of equity to set aside unconscionable bargains was reviewed in *Multiservice Bookbinding Ltd.* v. *Marden*.[15] It is clear from that judgment that courts will not set aside bargains which are improvident or contain terms which are, by normal standards, unreasonable. A bargain cannot be unfair and unconscionable unless one of the parties to it has imposed the objectionable terms in a morally reprehensible manner and thus in a way that affects his conscience. The categories of unconscionable bargains are not limited.

A bargain may be set aside where advantage is taken of a poor, ignorant or weak-minded person, or one who is for some other reason in need of special protection. In *Fry* v. *Lane*[16] it was held that there were three requirements to be satisfied if a bargain were to be held unconscionable: (i) poverty and ignorance of the plaintiff; (ii) sale at an undervalue; and (iii) lack of independent advice. In *Cresswell* v. *Potter*[17] Megarry J. explained "ignorant" as meaning "ignorant in the context of property transactions in general and conveyancing documents in particular." In *Backhouse* v. *Backhouse*,[18] Balcombe J. considered that a party who had executed a document under the emotional strain of an impending or actual marriage breakdown, might be relieved as being in a position of unequal bargaining power, under the principle enunciated by Lord Denning M.R. in *Lloyds Bank* v. *Bundy*.[19] In *Samuel* v. *Newbold*[20] it was said that a transaction

[14] [1906] A.C. 461.
[14a] See *post*, pp. 312, 313.
[15] [1979] Ch. 84. Here the court refused to apply the test of "reasonableness" to an indexation clause in the mortgage made between the parties. The time test was whether the bargain was "unfair and unconscionable." Held: stipulation valid and enforceable, reflecting *Tresider-Griffin* v. *Co-operative Insurance Society Ltd.* [1956] 2 Q.B. 127. See also *Davies* v. *Directloans Ltd.* [1986] 1 W.L.R. 823.
[16] (1888) 40 Ch.D. 312.
[17] Reported as a note (p. 255) to *Backhouse* v. *Backhouse* [1978] 1 W.L.R. 243.
[18] *Ibid.*
[19] [1975] Q.B. 326 at 329.
[20] [1906] A.C. 461.

might fall within the description because of the borrower's extreme necessity and helplessness, or because of the relationship in which he stood to the lender, or because of his situation in other ways. That was a case in which the circumstances of the transaction and the "monstrous" rate of interest charged (418 per cent.) were each sufficient to characterise the bargain as harsh and unconscionable.

Whether the bargain is extortionate has to be determined as at the date of the agreement.[21] If the bargain as struck is not extortionate, the borrower will not be relieved merely because its terms become more onerous in the light of subsequent events.[22]

The Consumer Credit Act 1974, section 138 deals with the matters to which the court shall have regard if evidence of them is adduced. It is for the party, not the court, to call the evidence, and the court cannot call for any evidence or direct a party to do so against his wishes. Further, by section 139 it is only the debtor or a surety who can apply to re-open the transaction. The court cannot do so of its own motion in proceedings brought by a creditor.

Although section 138 directs the court to have regard to evidence adduced of factors applicable to the debtor and to the creditor, it does not follow that any weight will necessarily be placed on such evidence. The older decisions strongly suggest that, before the bargain can be set aside, the court must find that the creditor knew of the circumstances which made the debtor particularly vulnerable and unfairly took advantage of them. Although abnormally high interest rates may be taken as conclusive evidence of unfair dealing, they may on the other hand be intended genuinely to reflect the risk involved in lending. As Darling J. said in *Jackson* v. *Price*[23]: "If you had to lend a mutton chop to a ravenous dog, on what terms would you lend it?"

It is for the debtor to show, on the balance of probabilities, the existence of any fact on which he relies for the purpose of establishing any matter referred to in section 138(3) and, if it is relevant, the creditor's knowledge of that fact. If he fails to do so, the court will not take the matter into account; but if he succeeds, it is for the creditor by virtue of section 171(7) to show that, despite those facts, the bargain was not extortionate. In regard to section 138(4)(*c*), the 1974 Act does not provide a definition of the words a "colourable cash price" but this denotes a price artificially inflated so as to conceal the actual rate of charge. The question whether a credit bargain is extortionate has been considered in two recent cases.

In *Davies* v. *Directloans Ltd.*[24] it was held impermissible and unnecessary to look outside the Act at earlier authorities, in order to ascertain the meaning of the word "extortionate" in section 138(1), and that it does not

---

[21] *Harris* v. Classon (1910) 27 T.L.R. 30.
[22] *Multiservice Bookbinding Ltd.* v. *Marden* [1979] Ch. 84 and see *Davies* v. *Directloans Ltd.* [1986] 1 W.L.R. 823.
[23] (1909) 26 T.L.R. 106 at 108.
[24] [1986] 1 W.L.R. 823.

necessarily mean the same as "harsh and unconscionable."[25] Whereas out-side the Act a bargain cannot be unfair and unconscionable:

> "unless one of the parties to it has imposed the objectionable terms in a morally reprehensible manner, that is to say, in a way which affects his conscience"[26]

within the Act it is not necessary or permissible to consider whether the creditor's behaviour has been morally reprehensible but only whether one or other of the conditions of section 138(1) is fulfilled.

In determining whether a credit bargain is extortionate, section 138(2)(*a*) lays down that the prevailing rate of interest at the time the bargain was made is a factor to be considered. It was held that regard should be had to the true rate of interest, that is, the annual percentage rate of charge calculated in accordance with the Consumer Credit (Total Charge for Credit) Regulations 1980[27] even though the regulations did not apply to the loan in question. *Coldunell* v. *Gallon*[28] was primarily concerned with the question whether A can avoid a transaction with B on the grounds of undue influence exerted by C, and decided that for such avoidance it must be shown that C was acting as B's agent. At first instance the transaction in that case was set aside both on that ground and on the ground that the bargain was extortionate within the definition in section 138(1)(*b*). On appeal it was held that C was not B's agent, and the burden on B of showing the bargain not to be extortionate was discharged, so far as section 138(1)(*b*) was concerned, by demonstrating that the bargain was on its face a proper commercial bargain and that B had acted in the way that an ordinary commercial lender would be expected to act.

Section 139 is concerned with the methods by which the extortionate credit bargain may be re-opened, and is set out below, excluding sub-sections (6) and (7) which apply to Scotland and the Northern Ireland, respectively:

> "(1) A credit agreement may, if the court thinks just, be reopened on the ground that the credit bargain is extortionate—[29]
>> (*a*) on an application for the purpose made by the debtor or any surety to the High Court, county court or sheriff court; or
>> (*b*) at the instance of the debtor or a surety in any proceedings to

---

[25] *Cf.* Goode, *Introduction to the Consumer Credit Act 1974* (1979), p. 370; *Castle Phillips Finance Co. Ltd.* v. *Khan* [1980] C.C.L.R. 1 at 3.

[26] *per* Browne–Wilkinson J. in *Multiservice Bookbinding Ltd.* v. *Marden* [1979] Ch. 84 at 110. This judgment was approved by the C.A. in *Alec Lobb (Garages) Ltd.* v. *Total Oil (Great Britain) Ltd.* [1985] 1 W.L.R. 173. In the latter case, a majority of the C.A. was of the view that there was no general doctrine of "reasonableness" independent of undue influence and duress. Equity controls only unconscionable and not unreasonable bargains. See *Lloyds Bank* v. *Bundy* [1975] Q.B. 326 at 339; *Nationwide Building Society* v. *Registry and Friendly Societies* [1983] 1 W.L.R. 1226; and *Davies* v. *Directloans Ltd.* [1986] 1 W.L.R. 823.

[27] S.I. 1980 No. 51.

[28] [1986] Q.B. 1184. See also *Davies* v. *Directloans Ltd.*, *supra.*

[29] The onus of proof is on the creditor: s.171(7).

which the debtor and creditor are parties, being proceedings to enforce the agreement, any security relating to it, or any linked transaction; or

(c) at the instance of the debtor or a surety in other proceedings in any court where the amount paid or payable under the credit agreement is relevant.

(2) In reopening the agreement, the court may, for the purpose of relieving the debtor or a surety from payment of any sum in excess of that fairly due and reasonable, by order—

(a) direct accounts to be taken, or (in Scotland) an accounting to be made, between any persons,

(b) set aside the whole or part of any obligation imposed on the debtor or surety by the credit bargain or any related agreement,

(c) require the creditor to repay the whole or part of any sum paid under the credit bargain or any related agreement by the debtor or a surety, whether paid to the creditor or any other person,

(d) direct the return to the surety of any property provided for the purposes of the security, or

(e) alter the terms of the credit agreement or any security instrument.

(3) An order may be made under subsection (2) notwithstanding that its effect is to place a burden on the creditor in respect of an advantage unfairly enjoyed by another person who is a party to a linked transaction.

(4) An order under subsection (2) shall not alter the effect of any judgment.

(5) In England and Wales, an application under subsection (1)(a) shall be brought only in the county court in the case of—

(a) a regulated agreement, or

(b) an agreement (not being a regulated agreement) under which the creditor provides the debtor with fixed-sum credit not exceeding [the county court limit] or running-account credit on which the credit limit does not exceed [the county court limit]."[30]

Section 140 provides as follows:

"Where the credit agreement is not a regulated agreement, expressions used in sections 137 to 139 which, apart from this section, apply only to regulated agreements, shall be construed as nearly as may be as if the credit agreement were a regulated agreement."

The effect of section 139(4) is that, once the creditor has obtained a judgment to recover a loan or enforce a security, the debtor cannot be

---

[30] Words in square brackets were inserted by the County Courts Act 1984, Sched. 2.

relieved under section 139(2). But the court retains its inherent or statutory jurisdiction to set aside a judgment obtained in default of notice of intention to defend or of defence, or given in the absence of the defendant, or where a new trial is ordered. In High Court proceedings once a notice of intention to re-open a credit agreement has been served by the debtor or surety in accordance with R.S.C. Ord. 83, r. 2, the creditor cannot, without leave of the court, obtain judgment in default of notice of intention to defend or of defence (R.S.C. Ord. 83, r. 3). The corresponding provision in county court proceedings is contained in C.C.R. Ord. 49, r. 4.

CHAPTER 12

LOCAL AUTHORITY MORTGAGES[1]

A local authority or county council may, subject to any economic restraints imposed on such authorities, advance money for the purpose of acquiring, constructing, altering, enlarging, repairing or improving houses, for acquiring buildings for conversion into houses or flats, for carrying out such conversions, or for paying off loans for such purposes. The powers of local authorities to make such advances are effectively controlled by central government by restrictions on borrowing[2] and the imposition of cash limits. Local authority capital expenditure on housing is determined through the Housing Investment Programme, which involves submissions by local authorities relating to levels of expenditure planned for their areas. One of the heads of such expenditure is lending to private persons for house purchase and improvement.

There were formerly several statutes under which local authorities had power to make advances and to borrow money for the purposes set out above, but these have been repealed.[3] The powers are contained in the consolidating Act, that is, the Housing Act 1985, which came into force on April 1, 1986. The first statutes under which local authorities were given such powers were the Small Dwellings Acquisition Acts 1899–1923. Under those Acts a local authority could advance money to a resident in any house in its area to enable him to acquire the ownership of the house, or to enable a person to construct a house in which he intended to reside. The usefulness of that provision was severely restricted, since an advance could be made only if, in the opinion of the local authority, the market value of the house to be acquired did not exceed £5,000.[4]

Originally the advance could not exceed 90 per cent. of the market value of the house as determined by a valuation made on behalf of the local authority[5] but later, 100 per cent. advances were permitted.[6] The severity of the restriction meant, however, that most loans were made under section 43 of the Housing (Financial Provision) Act 1958.[7] Consequently, the Law Commission recommended, at paragraph 38(i) of their report on the consolidation of the Housing Acts, that the provisions of the 1899–1923 Acts should be re-enacted only to the extent that they are still required for the purposes of advances made before the commencement date of the Housing

---

[1] For the lending powers of other public authorities, see *post*, p. 189.
[2] For the borrowing powers of local authorities, see *post*, p. 189.
[3] See the Housing (Consequential Provisions) Act 1985, Sched. 1.
[4] Small Dwellings Acquisition Act 1899, s.1(1); Housing Act 1949, s.44(1).
[5] Housing Act 1923, s.22(*d*).
[6] House Purchase and Housing Act 1959, s.3(1).
[7] Re-enacted by the Housing Act 1985, ss.435, 436.

Act 1985. That recommendation has been effected by section 456 of the 1985 Act.[8]

The powers formerly available to local authorities under the Housing (Financial Provisions) Act 1958[9] are preserved by section 436 of the Housing Act 1985.

Section 435(1) of the 1985 Act gives local authorities power to make loans, or to make advances to repay previous loans, for the acquisition, construction, alteration, enlargement, improvement or repair of houses, or for the conversion of buildings into houses or their acquisition for such conversion. Before making an advance the local authority must be satisfied that the resultant house will be fit for human habitation, or in the case of a house to be acquired, is or will be made fit.[10] The purpose of this provision is to assist owner-occupiers who already have loans secured by a mortgage and to whom the original lender is unwilling to make a further advance; and it applies whether or not the original lender was a local authority. Because the local authority is empowered to make a loan which is large enough to pay off the existing mortgage debt as well as to pay for improvements, the borrower is not faced with the difficulties of a second mortgage. In order to prevent the borrower from using the part of the loan not required to pay off the mortgage debt for purposes other than meeting his housing needs, it is provided[11] that no such advance shall be made unless the local authority is satisfied that the primary effect will be to meet the borrower's housing needs. Advances may be made to "any persons." "Person" is not defined in the Act but in view of the necessity for the local authority to be satisfied that housing needs are being met, it would seem that "persons" means "natural persons" and does not include bodies corporate. A local authority may, however, make loans to housing associations.[12]

The terms of advances are set out in section 436. The amount of the advance must not exceed the value of the mortgaged security in the case of a house or houses to be acquired, or in any other case, the value which it is estimated the mortgaged security will bear when the construction, conversion, alteration, enlargement, repair or improvement has been carried out.[13] The advance together with interest must be secured by a mortgage on the property.[14] The mortgage must provide for repayment of the principal either by instalments (of equal or unequal amounts) beginning on the date of the advance or a later date or at the end of a fixed period (with or without a provision allowing the authority to extend the period) or on the

---

[8] The provisions of Sched. 18 to the Housing Act 1985 have effect with respect to advances made under the Small Dwellings Acquisition Acts 1899–1923 before April 1, 1986.

[9] As amended by the Local Government Act 1974, s.37(2). The section was partly repealed by the Housing Act 1980, s.152, Sched. 25(9), Sched. 26.

[10] Housing Act 1985, s.439.

[11] *Ibid.* s.439(3), re-enacting s.43(2A) of the Housing (Financial Provisions) Act 1958.

[12] Housing Associations Act 1985, ss.58 *et seq.*

[13] Housing Act 1985, s.436(3). There must be a valuation on behalf of the local authority. Except in cases of advances for acquiring houses, the advance may be made by instalments as the works proceed.

[14] Housing Act 1985, s.436(3).

happening of a specific event before the end of that period and for the payment of instalments of interest[15] throughout the period beginning on the date of the advance and ending when the whole of the principal is repaid.[16] In either case, the balance outstanding is payable on demand if there is a breach of any of the conditions of the advance and the borrower may repay on any of the usual quarter days after giving a month's notice of his intention.[17]

The provisions as to local authority mortgage interest rates formerly contained in section 110(1),[18] (2) of the Housing Act 1980 are re-enacted by section 438(1) of the 1985 Act. A local authority may give assistance[19] by way of waiver or reduction of payments of property requiring repair or improvement,[20] or by making partially interest-free loans to first time buyers for the first five years of the loan.[21] Those provisions do not apply to loans made by local authorities under section 228 of the Housing Act 1985.[22] That section casts a duty on local housing authorities to offer a loan, to be secured by a mortgage of the applicant's interest in the dwelling concerned, to a person who is liable:

(1) to incur expenditure in complying with an improvement notice served, or undertaking accepted, under Part VII of the Housing Act 1985; or

(2) to make a payment as directed by a court under section 217(5) thereof;

Advances may be made in addition to other assistance given by the local authority in respect of the same house under any other Act or any other provisions of the Housing Act 1985.[23]

SECURE TENANT'S RIGHT TO A MORTGAGE

Secure tenant's right to buy

A secure tenancy is a tenancy of a dwelling-house[24] which is let as a separate dwelling and in respect of which

---

[15] For interest, see the Housing Act 1985, s.438 and Sched. 16.

[16] This is subject to s.441 (waiver or reduction of payments in case of property requiring repair or improvement) and s.446(1)(b) (assistance for first time buyers: part of loan interest free for up to five years) s.436(5).

[17] Housing Act 1985, s.436(6).

[18] As amended by the Housing and Building Control Act 1984, s.64, Sched. 11.

[19] Housing Act 1985, s.438(1).

[20] Ibid. s.441.

[21] Ibid. s.446(1)(b).

[22] The exemption is conferred by s.438(3) of the Housing Act 1985, containing provisions formerly in s.110(14) of the Housing Act 1980.

[23] Housing Act 1985, s.435(4). e.g. under ss.132–135 of the Housing Act 1985 (right to mortgage) or under ss.460 et seq of the 1985 Act (improvement and other grants).

[24] In this context "dwelling-house" means a house or part of a house: Housing Act 1985, s.112(1). For land let together with a dwelling-house, see s.112(2).

(a) the interest of the landlord belongs to one of a specified list of authorities or bodies[25]; and

(b) the tenant is an individual and occupies the dwelling-house as his only or principal home; or, where the tenancy is a joint tenancy, that each of the joint tenants is an individual and at least one of them occupies the dwelling-house as his only or principal home.[26]

A secure tenant has the right to buy, at discounted prices, either;

(a) the freehold of his dwelling-house if the landlord owns the freehold; or

(b) a long lease of it at a low rent if the landlord does not own the freehold or if the dwelling-house is a flat (whether or not the landlord owns the freehold)[27] and to leave the whole of the price outstanding on a mortgage repayable over 25 years[28] provided that the relevant conditions and exceptions stated in sections 118 *et seq.* of the Housing Act 1985 are satisfied.[29]

The right to a mortgage

Although a tenant of public sector accommodation who has the right to buy may seek private finance, institutional lenders may be reluctant to advance the money.

A secure tenant who has the right to buy has the right, subject to the relevant provisions of the Housing Act 1985;

(a) to leave the whole or part of the aggregate amount oustanding on the security of a first mortgage of the dwelling-house; or

(b) if the landlord is a housing association, to have the whole or part of that amount advanced to him on that security by the Housing Corporation.[30]

---

[25] *i.e.* a local authority, a new town corporation, an urban development corporation, the Development Board of Rural Wales, the Housing Corporation, a housing trust which is a charity, or a registered housing association other than a co-operative housing association and an unregistered housing association which is a co-operative housing association: Housing Act 1985, s.80(1), (2).

[26] Housing Act 1985, s.81.

[27] *Ibid.* s.118(1) containing provisions formerly in the Housing Act 1980, s.1(1), (2), as amended, in the case of s.1(1) by the Housing and Building Control Act 1984, s.1(2). Where a secure tenancy is a joint tenancy then, whether or not each of the joint tenants occupies the dwelling-house as his only principal home, the right to buy belongs jointly to all of them or to such one or more of them as may be agreed between them; but such an agreement is not valid unless the person or at least one of the persons to whom the right to buy is to belong occupies the dwelling-house as his only or principal home: s.118(2) reinforcing provisions formerly in s.4(1) of the 1980 Act.

[28] Housing Act 1985, Sched. 7.

[29] For details of the right to buy see further, s.119 and Sched 4. (qualifying period); s.120 and Sched. 5, as amended by the Housing and Planning Act 1986, s.1 (exceptions to the right to buy); s.121 (circumstances in which the right cannot be exercised); ss.122–125, as amended by the Housing and Planning Act 1986, s.4 (the procedure for exercising the right); ss.126–131 and Sched. 4, as amended by the Housing and Planning Act 1986, s.2 (the purchase price and discount).

[30] Housing Act 1985, s.132.

The procedure for exercising the right to a mortgage

A secure tenant cannot exercise his right to a mortgage unless he claims to exercise it by the prescribed period in writing and, where a tenant has claimed[31] to exercise the right to buy and that right has been established, whether by the landlord's admission or otherwise,[32] the landlord shall serve on the tenant a notice complying with section 125. The notice must inform the tenant of his right to a mortgage,[33] the effect of the sections of the Act which deal with the procedure for claiming to exercise that right[34] and must be accompanied by a form for use by the tenant in claiming to exercise the right to a mortgage.

Section 134 deals with the tenant's notice claiming to exercise the right to a mortgage and provides as follows:

"(1) A secure tenant cannot exercise his right to a mortgage unless he claims to exercise it by notice[35] in writing served on the landlord, or, if the landlord is a housing association, on the Housing Corporation.

(2) The notice must be served within the period of three months beginning with the service on the tenant of—

(*a*) where he exercises his right under section 128 (determination of value by district valuer), the notice under subsection (5) of that section (further notice by landlord after determination), or

(*b*) where he does not exercise that right, the notice under section 125 (landlord's notice of purchase price and other matters),

or within that period as extended under the following provisions.

(3) Where there are reasonable grounds for doing so, the landlord or, as the case may be, the Housing Corporation shall by notice in writing served on the tenant extend (or further extend) the period within which the tenant's notice claiming to exercise his right to a mortgage must be served.

(4) If in such a case the landlord or Housing Corporation fails to do so, the county court may by order extend or further extend that period until such date as may be specified in the order."

By section 135 the landlord or Housing Corporation must, as soon as practicable after the service on it of the section 134 notice, serve on the tenant a notice in writing of the amount and terms of the mortgage. The notice specifies that:

"(1) As soon as practicable after the service on it of a notice under sec-

---

[31] By written notice served on the Landlord, Housing Act 1985, s.122(1), in the form prescribed by the Housing (Right to Buy) (Prescribed Form) Regulations 1984 (S.I. 1984 No. 1175).

[32] Housing Act 1985, s.125(1).

[33] *Ibid.* s.125(5)(*b*).

[34] *Ibid.* ss.134, 135.

[35] The notice must be in Form 4 prescribed by the Housing (Right to Buy) (Prescribed Forms) Regulations 1980 (S.I. 1980 No. 1465).

tion 134, the landlord or Housing Corporation shall serve on the tenant a notice in writing stating—

  (a) the amount which, in the opinion of the landlord or Housing Corporation, the tenant is entitled to leave outstanding or have advanced on the security of the dwelling-house,

  (b) how that amount has been arrived at, and

  (c) the provisions which, in the opinion of the landlord or Housing Corporation, shall be contained in the deed by which the mortgage is to be effected.

(2) The notice shall be accompanied by a form for use by the tenant in claiming, in accordance with section 142(1), to be entitled to defer completion and shall also inform the tenant of the effect of subsection (4) of that section (right to serve further notice claiming mortgage).

(3) Where, in the opinion of the landlord or Housing Corporation, the tenant is not entitled to a full mortgage, the notice shall also inform the tenant of the effect of the provisions of this Part relating to the right to be granted a shared ownership lease and shall be accompanied by a form for use by the tenant in claiming to exercise that right in accordance with section 144(1).

(4) The Housing Corporation shall send to the landlord a copy of any notice served by it on the tenant under this section."

Form of mortgage

The provisions formerly in sections 18 and 151 of the Housing Act 1980, as amended and partly repealed, are not contained in Schedule 7 to the Housing Act 1985[36]:

"1. The deed shall provide for repayment of the amount secured in equal instalments of principal and interest combined.

  2.—(1) The period over which repayment is to be made shall be—

  (a) 25 years, or

  (b) where the mortgagor's interest in the dwelling-house is leasehold and the term of the lease is less than 25 years, a period equal to the term of the lease,

or, at the option of the mortgagor, a shorter period.

(2) The period mentioned in sub-paragraph (1) may be extended by the mortgagee.

(3).—(1) The Secretary of State may by order—

  (a) vary the preceding provisions of this Schedule, or

  (b) prescribe additional terms to be contained in the deed,

but only in relation to deeds executed after the order comes into force.

(2) An order under this paragraph—

  (a) may make different provision with respect to different cases or

---

[36] Unless the parties agree to the contrary, the deed must conform with the provisions of Sched. 7 to the Housing Act 1985.

descriptions of case, including different provision for different areas, and
  (b) shall be made by statutory instrument which shall be subject to annulment in pursuance of a resolution of either House of Parliament.
  4. The deed may contain such other provisions as may be—
    (a) agreed between the mortgagor and the mortgagee, or
    (b) determined by the county court to be reasonably required by the mortgagor or the mortgagee."

The amount to be secured

Section 133(1) sets out the amount which a secure tenant is entitled to have advanced to him or have left outstanding:

"(1) The amount which a secure tenant exercising the right to a mortgage is entitled to leave outstanding, or have advanced to him, on the security of the dwelling-house is, subject to the limit imposed by this section, the aggregate of—
    (a) the purchase price;
    (b) so much of the costs incurred by the landlord or the Housing Corporation as is chargeable to the tenant under section 178(2) (costs), and
    (c) any costs incurred by the tenant and defrayed on his behalf by the landlord or the Housing Corporation."

Section 133(2) specifies the limits in the cases where the right to a mortgage belongs to one or more than one person. These limits are based on the available annual income of the person or persons who have the right to a mortgage, and by section 133(3) the Secretary of State is empowered to make regulations[37] providing for the calculation of the amount to be taken into account as a person's available annual income and for specifying a factor by which it is to be multiplied.

Transfer of local authority mortgages is now regulated by section 7 of the Local Government Act 1986.[38] The transfer cannot be made without the prior written consent of the mortgagor, or all the mortgagors if more than one, and the Secretary of State may make regulations[39] specifying the information to be given to the mortgagor and prescribing forms.

Completion

The Housing Act 1985 contains detailed provisions as to the period for completion and notices to complete.[40]

[37] By virtue of the Housing (Consequential Provisions) Act 1985, s.2, the Housing (Right to Buy) (Mortgage Limit) Regulations 1980 (S.I. 1980 No. 1423) have effect as if made under s.133(3) of the Housing Act 1985.
[38] The section came into force on March 26, 1986.
[39] Local Authorities (Disposal of Mortgages) Regulations 1986 (S.I. 1986 No. 1028).
[40] s.140 (landlord's first notice to complete); s.141 (landlord's second notice to complete); s.142 (when tenant is entitled to defer completion).

Right to a shared ownership lease

Where a secure tenant has claimed to exercise the right to buy and:

(a) his right has been established and his notice claiming to exercise it remains in force;

(b) he has claimed the right to a mortgage but is not entitled, or treated as entitled, to a full mortgage[41]; and

(c) he is entitled to defer completion;

he has the right to be granted a shared ownership lease of the dwelling-house in accordance with the relevant provisions of the Housing Act 1985.[42] A shared ownership lease means a lease:

(a) granted on payment of a premium calculated by reference to a percentage of the value of the dwelling or the cost of providing it; or

(b) under which the tenant (or his personal representatives) will or may be entitled to a sum calculated by reference, directly or indirectly, to the value of the dwelling.[43]

Under a shared ownership lease the tenant purchases an initial share[44] of a leasehold dwelling-house with the right to purchase further shares[45] until the whole has been acquired.[46] The Act contains notice and other provisions for the completion of a shared ownership lease equivalent to those in relation to the right to buy and to a mortgage.[47]

A deed by which a mortgage is effected where the tenant exercises both the right to a mortgage and the right to be granted a shared ownership lease shall, unless otherwise agreed between the parties, conform with Schedule 7 to the Housing Act 1985 (terms of mortgage granted in pursuance of right to a mortgage) and without prejudice to that, with Schedule 9 to that Act (right to further advances)[48]

Registration of title

On the conveyance of the freehold or the grant of a lease under the right to buy or on a conveyance of the freehold where the tenant under a shared ownership lease has acquired a 100 per cent. interest in the dwelling-house and consequently the right to the freehold, section 123 of the Land Regis-

---

[41] s.133(5).
[42] ss.143 *et seq*. Where the right to buy belongs to two or more persons jointly, the right to be granted a shared ownership lease also belongs to them jointly: s.143(2).
[43] Housing Act 1985, s.622.
[44] Not less than 50 per cent.: Housing Act 1985, s.145(3).
[45] In tranches of 12.5 per cent. or such other percentages as the Secretary of State may by order prescribe: Housing Act 1985, s.145(2).
[46] For the terms of a shared ownership lease, see Housing Act 1985, Sched. 8. In particular para. 9 prohibits the disposal of part of the dwelling-house, other than exempt disposals, when the tenant's total share is less than 100 per cent.
[47] Housing Act 1985, ss.144–150, 152, 153.
[48] *Ibid*. s.151(4).

tration Act 1925 (compulsory registration of title) applies even though the dwelling-house is not in an area of compulsory registration or the lease would not normally require registration.[49]

Where the landlord's title to the dwelling-house is not registered, the landlord must give the tenant a certificate or the form approved by the Chief Land Registrar stating that the landlord is entitled to convey the freehold or make the grant subject only to such incumbrances, rights and interests as are stated in the conveyance or grant or summarised in the certificate.[50] Such certificate is to be accepted by the Chief Land Registrar as sufficient evidence of the facts stated in it.[51]

Repayment of discount on early disposal

If a purchaser under the right to buy or the right to be granted a shared ownership lease disposes[52] of the dwelling-house or his share within five years of the acquisition, the purchaser must repay the discount, reduced by 20 per cent. for each complete year which has elapsed since the acquisition.[53] The liability to repay is a charge on the dwelling-house, taking effect as if it had been created by deed expressed to be by way of legal mortgage[54] and having priority immediately after any legal charge securing an amount: (i) left outstanding by the tenant in exercising the right to buy or the right to be granted a shared ownership lease; (ii) advanced to him by an approved lending institution[55] for the purpose of enabling him to exercise that right; or (iii) further advanced to him by that institution.[56]

---

[49] Housing Act 1985, s.154.

[50] *Ibid.* s.154(2), (4).

[51] *Ibid.* s.154(5). The landlord must indemnify him if a claim is successfully made against him under s.83 of the Land Registration Act 1925, as amended.

[52] For relevant disposals, see Housing Act 1985, s.159.

[53] Housing Act 1985, s.155. For exempted disposals, see s.160.

[54] *Ibid.* s.156(1). Such charge is a land charge for the purposes of s.59(2) of the Land Registration Act 1925; s.156(3).

[55] *e.g* a building society, bank, etc: see s.156(4)–(6).

[56] Housing Act 1985, s.156(2); but the landlord may at any time by written notice served on an approved lending institution postpone the charge created by the liability to repay to a legal charge securing an amount advanced or further advanced to the tenant by that institution.

CHAPTER 13

PARTIES TO MORTGAGES

ABSOLUTE OWNERS

General

Generally an absolute owner of property who is not subject to any incapacity[1] may mortgage the property in exercise of the full powers of alienation with which he is invested.[2]

Co-owners

Where land is owned by more than one person, such persons may be beneficially interested in the land either jointly or as tenants in common. In such a case the legal estate in the land will be held by not more than four of the co-owners as joint tenants upon trust for sale for the co-owners as joint tenants or tenants in common.[3]

As trustees for sale the co-owners may mortgage the land under their statutory powers.[4] But where the same persons are both the trustees and the beneficiaries, they may mortgage by virtue of their powers as absolute owners and need not rely upon the statutory powers.[5]

Where a legal mortgage of land is made to several persons, the legal estate vests in the mortgagees or the first four named as joint tenants upon trust for sale. By virtue of section 111 of the Law of Property Act 1925 where the mortgage is made to several mortgagees jointly or the mortgage money is expressed to belong to them on a joint account, then unless a contrary intention is expressed in the mortgage the mortgage monies are (as between the mortgagees and the mortgagor) deemed to be and remain, monies belonging to the mortgagees on joint account.[6-7] Thus, persons dealing in good faith with several mortgagees may assume that the mortgagees are entitled to the mortgage monies on a joint account unless a contrary intention is expressed in the instruments relating to the mortgage.[8]

[1] See post, pp. 163 et seq.
[2] See Coke on Littleton, 223a.
[3] L.P.A. 1925, ss.34–36; Settled Land Act 1925, s.36; Trustee Act 1925, s.34.
[4] For the mortgage powers of trustees for sale, see post, pp. 173 et seq.
[5] A purported mortgage by one co-owner may operate as a mortgage of his beneficial interest, and in the case of a beneficial joint tenancy of freehold land it severs the joint tenancy; cf. Cedar Holdings Ltd. v. Green [1981] Ch. 129. Quaere the position with regard to leasehold interest as mortgages are made by demise since 1925.
[6-7] Replacing the Conveyancing Act 1881, s.61.
[8] L.P.A. 1925, s.113(1)(a).

Persons subject to disabilities

(a) Bankrupts

For the position in the insolvency of the mortgagee and mortgagor, see pages 387 to 389.

(b) Infants

Borrowing powers The law applicable to contracts by minors[9] is now governed by the Minors' Contracts Act 1987[9a] which applies to any contracts made by minors after June 9, 1987. Section 1 of that Act disapplies the Infants Relief Act 1874, which invalidated certain contracts made by minors and prohibited actions to enforce contracts ratified after majority. It also disapplies the Betting and Loans (Infants) Act 1892, section 5 of which invalidated contracts to repay loans advanced during minority.

Under section 1 of the 1874 Act all contracts with minors for the repayment of money lent, or for goods supplied or to be supplied (other than contracts for "necessaries" which were binding on the infant), and all accounts stated with minors, were rendered "absolutely void." It did not, however, invalidate any contract into which a minor might enter by statute or the rules of common law or equity except those which under the existing law were voidable. The disapplication of that section will, therefore, result in the contracts in question again becoming subject to the rules of common law.

The disapplication of section 2 of the 1874 Act means that on a minor reaching the age of majority, his ratification of an otherwise unenforceable contract entered into by him as a minor is effective. However, section 2, while not abolishing the common law rules, imposed a bar on proceedings to enforce ratification (whether or not there was "new consideration") of a minor's contract, by providing that no action should be brought for that purpose. The removal of this procedural bar serves to reinstate the relevant rules of common law.

Further, the 1987 Act disapplies section 5 of the Betting and Loans (Infants) Act 1892, which rendered void any new agreements by a minor, after attaining his majority, to repay a loan made to him while a minor. It also invalidates any negotiable instrument given in connection with such an agreement. In doing so the new law makes any such new agreement and any such negotiable agreement effective.

The effect of the 1987 Act is essentially to restore the common law position before 1874 whereby a loan to a minor could not be enforced against a minor, except in the case of necessaries, but the infant could, upon attaining his majority, ratify the contract.

---

[9] The Family Law Reform Act 1969 reduced the age of majority to 18 (s.1). For the alternative "minor", see s.12.

[9a] The Act gives effect to the recommendations in the Law Commission's Report on "Law of Contract: Minors' Contracts" (Law Com. No. 134). The Law Commission identified several areas where the existing law was unsatisfactory and produced a draft bill upon which this Act is based.

Further, section 3(1) of the new Act extends the power of the court,[9b] if it is just and equitable to do so, to require a minor who has acquired property under an unenforceable contract to restore it. This is the case even where there has been no fraud on the part of the minor.[10] The power will also be exercisable where the minor has, on the ground of his minority, repudiated the contract under which he acquired the property. The court's power is limited to ordering the transfer of property acquired under the contract, or property representing it.[10a]

An infant cannot hold a legal estate in land, and consequently cannot be a legal mortgagor.[11] Thus, although an infant may be a member of a building society and may give all necessary receipts[11a] he cannot execute a valid mortgage to secure advances made to him by the society.[11b] An equitable mortgage made by an infant is unenforceable, but an infant can ratify if upon attaining his majority.[12] Where the mortgage was made to secure monies lent for the purchase of necessaries the mortgage is voidable and not absolutely void.[13] As the disposition is voidable and not void it is binding if the infant fails to repudiate it within a reasonable time after attaining his majority.[14] Where an infant has executed such a mortgage and subsequently upon attaining full age charges the premises with a further advance and has confirmed the earlier mortgage, he cannot redeem without paying off the sum advanced during his infancy.[14a]

Where an infant is beneficially entitled to any property. The court may direct the trustees to raise money by mortgage of the property or order them to apply the capital or income for the minor's maintenance, education or benefit.[15] Powers of management of a minor's lands may be conferred on the trustees appointed for the purpose, or if there are none so appointed then the trustees of the settlement under which the minor is entitled. The specified powers do not include a power to mortgage, but the power generally to deal with the land in a proper and due course of man-

[9b] That is the High Court or, within the financial limit of its general jurisdiction in actions of contract, a county court.
[10] Under the old law that power was confined to cases where the minor induced the other party to enter into the contract by fraud.
[10a] According to the Law Com. Report No. 134 the words "property representing property" are to be interpreted as referring to the general principle of tracing. Thus, if the minor has sold or exchanged the goods acquired under the contract, he can be compelled to pay over the price, or hand over the goods received in exchange. But if he has consumed or otherwise "dissipated" the goods or their proceeds, he cannot be required to pay to the seller a sum equivalent to the purchase price, or to the value of the goods.
[11] L.P.A. 1925, s.1(6). For the effect of a conveyance to an infant, see L.P.A. 1925, s.19; Settled Land Act 1925, s.27.
[11a] Building Societies Act 1986, s.5, Sched. 2, para. 5(3)(a); but cannot vote or hold office: *Nottingham Permanent Benefit Building Society* v. *Thurstan* [1903] A.C. 6.
[11b] *Ibid.* but the Society in this case was entitled to a loan on the property for the purchase monies.
[12] *Gardner* v. *Wainfur* (1920) 89 L.J.Ch. 98.
[13] *Martin* v. *Gale* (1876) 4 Ch.D. 428 at 431; *Edwards* v. *Carter* [1893] A.C. 360.
[14] *Edwards* v. *Carter* [1893] A.C. 360.
[14a] *Gardner* v. *Wainfur* (1919) 89 L.J.Ch. 98.
[15] Trustee Act 1925, s.53.

agement may comprehend such a power.[16] Personal representatives also have power of mortgaging property during the minority of a beneficiary.[17] Under the Settled Land Act 1925, a binding disposition of an infant's land may be made by the statutory owner which permits sales, exchanges, leases and mortgages on certain terms.[17a]

Lending powers The repeal of the Infants Relief Act 1874 by the Minors' Contracts Act 1987 means that a contract of loan can be enforced by an infant.

Mortgages to infants Since the Law of Property Act 1925 an infant cannot be an estate owner. Thus he cannot hold a legal estate in land[18] nor can he be a legal mortgagee.[19] Any attempt to grant or transfer a legal mortgage or charge to one or more persons who are all infants operates as an agreement for valuable consideration to execute a proper mortgage or transfer when the infant or infants attain full age[20] or majority[21] and in the meantime the mortgagor or transferor holds the beneficial interest in the mortgage debt, if any, on trust for the persons intended to benefit.[22] The infant's beneficial interest in the mortgage debt should be registered as an estate contract. If the mortgage is made to an infant or infants together with a person or persons of full age it will operate to vest the legal estate in the person of full age as if the infants were not named but subject to the infant's beneficial interest.[23]

Where an infant is beneficially entitled to any property, the court may direct the trustees to raise money by mortgage of the property in order to apply the capital or income for the minor's maintenance, education or benefit.[24] Personal representatives also have powers of mortgaging property during the minority of a beneficiary.[25] Under the Settled Land Act 1925 a binding disposition of an infant's land may be made by the statutory owner which permits sales, exchanges, leases and mortgages on certain terms.[26]

(c) Persons suffering from mental disorder

Any deed executed by a person suffering from such mental disorder as to render him incapable of understanding its effect when its nature and con-

[16] Settled Land Act 1925, s.102.
[17] Administration of Estates Act 1925, ss.33 and 39.
[17a] Settled Land Act 1925, s.102.
[18] L.P.A. 1925, s.1(6).
[19] *Ibid.* s.119(6).
[20] *Ibid.*
[21] By virtue of the Family Law Reform Act 1969, s.1(1) the age of majority was reduced to 18 years as from January 1, 1970, and the moment at which a person attaining his majority (or any other age) has been altered to the first moment of the relevant anniversary of his birth (*ibid.* s.9).
[22] L.P.A. 1925, s.19(4), (6). See also s.19(1) and the Settled Land Act 1925, s.27(1).
[23] L.P.A. 1925, s.19(5), (6) proviso.
[24] Trustee Act 1925, s.53.
[25] Administration of Estates Act 1925, ss.33 and 39.
[26] s.102.

tents are explained to him, is absolutely void as a matter of law even if no receiver has been appointed under section 99 of the Mental Health Act 1983.[27] Thus, a voluntary conveyance of a person suffering from a mental disorder may be set aside even against a subsequent purchaser for valuable consideration without notice.[28] But a deed executed during a lucid interval for valuable consideration is binding provided that no receiver has been appointed under section 99 and the person suffering from the mental disorder understood its nature and effect.[29] Similarly, a deed executed before the supervention of mental disorder is binding.[30]

Where, however, a receiver has been appointed under section 99 of the 1983 Act, the mentally disordered person probably cannot exercise any power of disposition, *inter vivos*, over his property even during a lucid interval, by reason of the fact that upon the making of such an order his property passes out of his control to the receiver[31] and any disposition made by him is inconsistent with that passing of control, and consequently is void.[32]

The position prior to the Mental Health Act 1959 was similar where there was a finding of insanity by inquisition[33] except that a will made during a lucid interval was valid.[34]

Under the Mental Health Act 1983, Part VII, the Lord Chancellor and nominated judges, or the Court of Protection, are invested with very wide powers of ordering or authorising dispositions and other transactions concerning the patient's property.[35] In practice, subject to appeal to a nominated judge, the jurisdiction is exercised by the master, deputy master, or a nominated officer of the Court of Protection. These powers include the power to appoint a receiver[36] who may exercise any of the powers under the 1983 Act under the direction of the court.[37] Such powers can be invoked, therefore, provided that it is for the benefit of the person suffering from the mental disorder or his family or other persons for whom he might have been expected to provide.[38] In a proper case of emergency these powers may be exercised even before the issue of incapacity has been

---

[27] See, *e.g. Price* v. *Berrington* (1849) 7 Hare 394 at 402; on Appeal (1851) 3 Mac. & G. 486.
[28] *Elliott* v. *Ince* (1857) 7 De G.M. & G. 475; *Manning* v. *Gill* (1872) L.R. 13 Eq. 485.
[29] *Towart* v. *Sellers* (1817) 5 Dow.231; *Selby* v. *Jackson* (1844) 6 Beav. 192; *Jenkins* v. *Morris* (1880) 14 Ch.D. 674; *Drew* v. *Nunn* (1879) 4 Q.B.D. 661.
[30] *Affleck* v. *Affleck* (1857) 3 Sn. & G. 394.
[31] There is some doubt since the Mental Health Act 1983 the point at which a person loses all legal capacity. The appointment of a receiver is now more of an administrative function and the intervention by the court is of greater importance with regard to the question of control of the patient's affairs.
[32] *Re Marshall, Marshall* v. *Whateley* [1920] 1 Ch. 284.
[33] *Re Walker* [1905] 1 Ch. 160.
[34] *Ibid.* at 172.
[35] ss.94(2) and 96(1)(*b*).
[36] s.99.
[37] *Ibid.* s.99.
[38] *Ibid.* ss.95 and 96. As to the meaning of "property" see *Re E* [1984] 1 W.L.R. 320, on appeal *Re E* [1985] 1 W.L.R. 245.

determined.[39] One of these powers is the power to charge the patient's property.[40] The court has also authorised the loan of a patient's money upon mortgage.[41] But, there is no power to make a disposition which the patient could not himself have made if he were of sound mind.[42]

Partners

An ordinary partner has an implied authority under the Partnership Act 1890[43] as an agent of the partnership and the other partners to pledge or mortgage partnership property and to give a receipt thereof. This implied authority, however, only arises when the dealing is for the purpose of raising money for the carrying on in the usual way of the partnership business and is in accordance with the partnership objects. It does not arise if the partner so acting has in fact no authority to act for the firm, and the person with whom he is dealing either knows that he has no authority, or does not know or believe him to be a partner. This authority does not arise in the case of a mortgage by deed of partnership property.

Mortgage of personal property

Provided that there is no notice of fraud or want of authority, a partner[44] may mortgage or pledge the personal property of the partnership for the ordinary purposes of the firm.[45] But such a transaction will not be binding upon the firm if made in order to secure the partner's personal debt without the knowledge and consent of the other partners.[46] The mortgagee must prove such knowledge and consent[47] or circumstances in which such knowledge and consent might reasonably be inferred. But, if it can be shown that the mortgagee is unaware[48] that the security is partnership property, then the transaction will not be set aside.[49] The authority to mortgage partnership property continues after dissolution for the purpose of winding up the affairs of the partnership and to complete any unfinished transactions at that date.[50]

Mortgage of real property

Where partners hold the legal estate of the partnership property, either freehold or leasehold, as beneficial owners they are empowered to mort-

[39] *Ibid.* s.98.
[40] *Ibid.* s.96(1)(*b*).
[41] *Re Ridgeways* (1825) Hog. 309.
[42] *Pritchard* v. *Briggs* [1980] Ch. 338 at 409.
[43] See s.5, and see *Re Bourne, Bourne* v. *Bourne* [1906] 2 Ch. 427.
[44] A limited partner does not have power to bind the firm, see the Limited Partnerships Act 1907, s.6(1).
[45] See the Partnership Act 1890, s.5.
[46] *Re Litherland, Ex p. Howden* (1842) 2 Mont.D. & De G. 574.
[47] *Shirreff* v. *Wilks* (1800) 1 East. 48.
[48] *Snaith* v. *Burridge* (1812) 4 Taunt. 684.
[49] *Reid* v. *Hollinshead* (1825) 4 B. & C. 867.
[50] Partnership Act 1890, s.38; *Butchart* v. *Dresser* (1853) 4 De G.M. & G. 542; *Re Bourne, Bourne* v. *Bourne* [1906] 2 Ch. 427.

gage the legal interest as joint tenants holding the same as statutory trustees for sale.[51] However, one partner is unable to bind the other partners by executing a mortgage deed of partnership property without the concurrent and express authority under seal to do so.[52] Further, where one partner executes a mortgage deed on behalf of the partnership that partner alone may be bound, and not the firm, unless he can demonstrate that his signature was with the special authority of the firm and conditional upon the firm being bound.[53] Where, however, there is an equitable mortgage made by deposit of the title deeds, or the mortgage itself is not required to be effected by deed, the general rule set out above with regard to the implied authority vested in a partner will apply.

Lending powers of partners

A partner has authority to lend the firm's money on mortgage when such a transaction is part of the firm's ordinary business.[54-55]

Mortgage of share in partnership

A share in a partnership is a right to share in the profits and, in the event of dissolution, to share in the division of the assets. It is, in the nature of things, a somewhat speculative form of security, but a partner may freely mortgage his share to cover his private debts. On the other hand, a partner is by statute precluded from introducing a new partner into the firm without the consent of all the existing partners.[56] The fact that a mortgagee is not normally introduced into the partnership materially increases the hazards of taking a partnership share as security, for he has no voice whatever in the management of the business. His rights are set out in section 31 of the Partnership Act 1890, and are broadly as follows:

(1) During the partnership he is not entitled either to interfere in the management of the partnership business or to require accounts of partnership transactions or to inspect books. He is entitled to the profits but must accept the account of profits agreed between the partners.

(2) On dissolution, he is entitled to receive the mortgagor's share of the assets and, for the purpose of ascertaining that share, he is entitled to an account from the other partners as from the date of dissolution.

A mortgagee is thus in a very weak position in regard to maladministration of the partnership business. But section 31 does not, of course, preclude

---

[51] L.P.A. 1925, ss.34 and 36(1); Settled Land Act 1925, s.36(4). See also the Trustee Act 1925, ss.16, 17; L.P.A. 1925, s.28(1).

[52] Harrison v. Jackson (1797) 7 Term Rep. 207; Steiglitz v. Egginton (1815) 1 Holt N.P. 141.

[53] Elliot v. Davis (1800) 2 Bos. & P. 338; Cumberlege v. Lawson (1857) 1 C.B.N.S. 709.

[54-55] Re Land Credit Co. of Ireland, Weikersheim's Case (1873) 8 Ch.App. 831; but see Niemann v. Niemann (1889) 43 Ch.D. 198.

[56] Partnerships Act 1890, s.24(7).

him from impugning transactions between the partners which are designed to over-reach him. It is only a genuine partnership transaction with which he has no right to concern himself.[57]

It remains to observe that, as a mortgage of a partnership share is essentially a mortgage of a chose in action, it is not a bill of sale despite the fact that, on dissolution, the mortgagee is entitled to share in the personal chattels of the partnership.[58] The mortgage does not, therefore, require registration as a bill of sale. Notice of the mortgage should, however, be given to the other partners in order to bind them to pay over the share to the mortgagee and to establish his priority against other assignees as the mortgagee takes subject to the equities subsisting between the partners.

Married women

Generally, a married woman is not subject to any disability and she can acquire, retain and dispose of property as if she were unmarried (*a feme sole*). The courts have a special jurisdiction over property disputes between husband and wife.

First, under the Married Women's Property Act 1882.[59] In any question between husband and wife as to the title to or possession of property, either party may apply in a summary manner to the court, and the judge may make such order with respect to the property in dispute as he thinks fit. Further, in matrimonial proceedings, under the Matrimonial Causes Act 1973, as amended, the court has a wide jurisdiction, *inter alia*, to make property adjustment orders.

Secondly, and more important with regard to the law of mortgages, by virtue of the Matrimonial Homes Act 1983.[60] Where one spouse is entitled[61] to occupy a dwelling-house, which is or has at some time been the matrimonial home, by virtue of a beneficial estate or interest or contract or by virtue of any enactment giving him or her a right to remain in occupation, and the other spouse is not so entitled, then, subject to the provisions of the Act, the spouse not so entitled has certain statutory rights, known as "rights of occupation," in the dwelling-house.[62]

These rights are as follows:

    (1) if in occupation of the dwelling-house, a right not to be evicted or

---

[57] *Watts* v. *Driscoll* [1901] 1 Ch. 294.

[58] *Re Bainbridge* (1878) 8 Ch.D. 218.

[59] s.17, as amended by the Matrimonial Causes (Property and Maintenance) Act 1958, s.7 (extending and clarifying the power of the court to order a sale); Matrimonial Proceedings and Property Act 1970, s.39; and the Law Reform (Miscellaneous Provisions) Act 1970, s.2 (extending the power of the court to engaged couples who terminate their engagement).

[60] Consolidating and amending earlier legislation including the Matrimonial Homes Act 1967 which gave a statutory right of occupation of the matrimonial home to a spouse, whether a husband or a wife. This development occurred after the collapse of the concept of the deserted wife's equity as a result of the decisions by the House of Lords in *National Provincial Bank Ltd.* v. *Ainsworth* [1965] A.C. 1175.

[61] Matrimonial Homes Act 1983, s.1(10).

[62] *Ibid.* s.1(1).

> excluded from the house or any part of it by the other spouse, except with the leave of the court; or
>
> (2) if not in occupation, a right with the leave of the court to enter into and occupy the house.[63]

Where a spouse has an equitable interest in a dwelling-house or in the proceeds of sale of it, but does not have the legal fee simple or a legal term of years absolute in it, either solely or jointly, he or she is to be treated as not being entitled to occupy the house by virtue of that interest.[64]

Unless these rights have been previously terminated by an order of the court, they continue so long as the marriage subsists. The court has a wide discretion to act as it considers just and reasonable for the purposes of declaring, enforcing, restricting or terminating these rights having regard to the conduct and respective needs and financial resources of the spouses and the needs of the children and to all the circumstances of the case.[65] Whilst these rights exist, the court may also prohibit, suspend or restrict the exercise of the rights of occupation of *either* spouse, and may require *either* spouse to permit their exercise by the other.[66] This is so even if the legal estate is vested in both spouses jointly or if both have contractual or statutory rights of occupation.[67]

Rights of occupation as a charge on the dwelling-house

Where the owning spouse is entitled to occupy the dwelling-house by virtue of an *estate* or *interest*, as opposed to a contract or statute, the rights of occupation of the non-owning spouse are a charge on that estate or interest. This charge has the like priority as if it were an equitable interest created at whichever is the latest of (*i*) the date of the marriage; (*ii*) the date when the spouse so entitled acquired the estate or interest; and (*iii*) January 1, 1968 (the date of commencement of the Matrimonial Homes Act 1967).[68] In the case of unregistered land this charge is registerable under the Land Charges Act 1972, section 2(7), as a Class F land charge which is a new class created to cover the statutory rights of spouses in the matrimonial home.[69] Registration, renewal of registration, or cancellation, should be applied for on the forms now specified in Schedule 2 to the Land Charges Rules 1974. In the case of registered land registration of the Class F land charge is effected by registration of a notice under the Land Registration Act 1925.[70] It is specified that the spouse's rights of occupation shall not be an overriding interest notwithstanding that the spouse is in actual

---

[63] *Ibid.* s.1(1)(*a*), (*b*).
[64] Matrimonial Homes Act 1983, s. 1(11).
[65] *Ibid.* s. 1(2), (3).
[66] *Ibid.* s.1(2).
[67] *Ibid.* s.9. The right to possession on the part of a mortgagee is to be disregarded: s.9(4).
[68] *Ibid.* s.2.
[69] See the Land Charges Act 1972, s.2(1), (7), and the Land Charges Rules 1974, Sched. 2.
[70] See the Matrimonial Homes Act 1983, s.2(8) and the Land Registration (Matrimonial Homes) Rules 1983 (S.I. 1983 No. 40). A caution may no longer be lodged, s.2(9).

occupation of the dwelling-house.[70a] Thus, whilst the owning spouse is alive and the marriage subsists the non-owning spouse can enforce this charge against third parties provided that such charge has been duly registered in the case of a purchaser before completion of the purchase, otherwise it will be void.[71] The charge may be registered as soon as the non-owning spouse is in occupation,[72] or where the charge arises out of the right to enter and occupy the dwelling-house even before the court has given leave to enter and occupy. Thus, a spouse *not* in occupation may make an effective registration in certain circumstances.[73]

Where the non-owning spouse's rights of occupation are a charge on the estate or interest of the owning spouse, and that estate or interest is the subject of a mortgage then if this charge is registered as a land charge after the date of creation of the mortgage the charge shall, for the purposes of section 94 of the Law of Property Act 1925,[74] be deemed to be a mortgage subsequent in date to the early mortgage.[75] Such a charge, however, was void against persons who represent creditors in the bankruptcy or insolvency of the owning spouse.[76] However after 1986, the charge, if duly registered, continues notwithstanding the insolvency of the owning spouse and is binding on the trustee in bankruptcy of the owning spouse or on his personal representatives.[77] Finally, it should be mentioned that the Matrimonial Homes Act, 1983 may apply to several dwelling-houses at the same time. But where it extends to two or more such houses, it is registerable against any one of them at any one time and only the later registration in time may stand.[78]

Postponement of priority of charge and release of rights of occupation

A non-owning spouse entitled to a charge may agree in writing that any other charge on, or interest in, that estate or interest shall rank in priority to the charge to which that spouse is entitled.[79] Further, a spouse so entitled may by a release in writing release those rights in whole or in part.[80] The registration of the charge may be cancelled by the non-owning spouse.[81] Where a contract is made for the sale of the dwelling-house or for the grant of a lease in respect of that house the rights of occupation of the non-owning spouse shall be deemed to have been released on the delivery

---

[70a] Matrimonial Homes Act 1983, s.2(8)(*b*).

[71] See *Miles* v. *Bull* [1969] 1 Q.B. 258; *Wroth* v. *Tyler* [1974] Ch.30. The definition of a "purchaser" includes a mortgagee, see the Land Charges Act 1972, s.17(1).

[72] See *Miles* v. *Bull* [1969] 1 Q.B. 258.

[73] See *Watts* v. *Waller* [1973] 1 Q.B. 153.

[74] This section regulates the rights of mortgagees to make further advances ranking in priority to subsequent mortgages (as amended by the Law of Property (Amendment) Act 1926).

[75] Matrimonial Homes Act 1983, s.2(10).

[76] *Ibid.* s.2(7) now repealed by the Insolvency Act 1985, Sched. 10.

[77] See the Insolvency Act 1986, s.336(2); Administration of Insolvent Estates of Deceased Persons Order 1986 (S.I. 1986 No. 1999).

[78] s.3.

[79] Matrimonial Homes Act 1983, s.6(3).

[80] *Ibid.* s.6(1).

[81] Land Charges Act 1972, s.16(1); Land Charges Rules 1974 (S.I. 1974 No. 1286).

to the purchaser or lessee or his solicitor on completion of the contract of an application for the cancellation of the registration of the charge, or the lodging of such an application at H.M. Land Registry, whichever first occurs, by the spouse entitled to the charge. Thus, where a prospective mortgagee ascertains that a Class F land charge (or notice) is registered, he should therefore require the spouse entitled to the charge to release such rights and apply for the cancellation of the registration, or to postpone the priority of the charge.

Mortgage payments made by non-owning spouse

Where a spouse is entitled to rights of occupation, any payment or tender made or other thing done by that spouse in or towards satisfaction of the liability of the other spouse in respect of, *inter alia*, mortgage payments, shall whether or not it was made or done in pursuance of an order of the court be as good as if made or done by the other spouse.[81a] Further, in respect of such mortgage payments, the person to whom the payment is made may treat it as having been made by the owning spouse, but this shall not affect any claim of the spouse making the payment against the other spouse to any interest in the dwelling-house by virtue of such payment.[82] If the non-owning spouse is able to make such payments in respect of the mortgage then that person is entitled to be joined as a defendant in possession proceedings brought by the mortgagee against the mortgagor.[83]

FIDUCIARY OWNERS

Mortgages by personal representatives

Personal representatives have always been able to raise money by mortgaging the deceased's personal estate, which includes leasehold, for the payment of debts and funeral and testamentary expenses.

By virtue of sections 2 and 39 of the Administration of Estates Act 1925, personal representatives now have the power to mortgage both the real and personal estate of the deceased. With regard to the deceased's real estate, by section 2 of the Act a personal representative has the same powers of disposition as a personal representative had before 1926 in respect of leaseholds.[84] With regard to both the real and personal estate of the deceased, by section 39 of the Act, personal representatives have, for the purposes of administration or during the minority of any beneficiary or the subsistence of any life interest or until the period of distribution arrives, the same powers and discretions, which includes the power to raise

---

[81a] Matrimonial Homes Act 1983, s.1(5).

[82] See *Hastings & Thanet Building Society* v. *Goddard* [1970] 1 W.L.R. 1544; see also *post* p. 319.

[83] Matrimonial Homes Act 1983, s.8(2).

[84] Administration of Estates Act 1925, s.2(1). In relation to deaths after 1925, s.2 replaces with amendments the Land Transfer Act 1897, s.2(2), and the Conveyancing Act 1911, s.12.

money by way of mortgage or charge, whether or not by the deposit of documents, as a personal representative had before 1926 with regard to personal estate.[85] A personal representative also has all the powers conferred by law on trustees for sale.[86] In the case of land the power may be exercised by the personal representatives by way of legal mortgage.

In the case of a mortgage of real estate[87] all the personal representatives must concur or an order of the court must be obtained.[88] An exception arises, however, where probate is granted to one or some of two or more persons named as executors, whether or not power is reserved to the other or others to prove, when a mortgage may be made by the proving executor or executors for the time being.[89]

Powers of trustees under the Settled Land Act

By virtue of the Law of Property Act 1925[90] the powers of trustees for sale have been extended. Before 1926 trustees for sale had no powers, *inter alia*, of mortgaging the trust property or otherwise dealing with the land except by way of sale. After 1925 trustees for the sale of land have, until sale, all the powers of a tenant for life of settled land and the trustees of a settlement under the Settled Land Act 1925, which includes the powers of mortgaging and management, but which are subject to the same restrictions which govern a tenant for life.[91] The powers are exercisable with the consents, if any, required for sale.[92] But if any requisite consents cannot be obtained, any person interested may apply for an order of the court in order to give effect to the proposed transaction. The powers also include the power to purchase land for the purposes of investment,[93] and a power to apply to the court under the Settled Land Act 1925 to effect a transaction which the settlement does not authorise. If the trustees refuse to exercise any of their statutory powers, the court has power, if it thinks fit, to order the trustees to act.[94]

Despite the fact that all the powers belong to the trustees, in certain circumstances such powers must be exercised in accordance with the wishes of the beneficiaries. In the case of a trust for sale which is either created by statute or an intention is demonstrated that the statute is to apply[95] the trustees must, so far as practicable, consult the persons of full age for the time being beneficially interested in possession in the rents and profits of

---

[85] Administration of Estates Act 1925, s.39(1)(i).
[86] *Ibid.* s.39(1)(ii), (iii).
[87] "Real Estate" includes chattels real, and leasehold; see the Administration of Estates Act 1925, ss.3(1) and 55(1)(xix).
[88] *Ibid.* ss.2(2) and 55(1)(ii).
[89] *Ibid.* s.2(2). But see *Fountain Forestry Ltd.* v. *Edwards* [1975] Ch. 1.
[90] s.28(1).
[91] See *post* p. 176.
[92] L.P.A. 1925, s.28(1).
[93] *Ibid.* s.28(1); Settled Land Act 1925, s.73(1)(xi); *Re Wellsted's Will Trusts* [1949] Ch. 296.
[94] L.P.A. 1925, s.30.
[95] *Ibid.* s.26(3) (as substituted by the Law of Property (Amendment) Act 1926, s.7, (Sched.)) and s.205(1)(xxix).

the land until sale, and must, so far as is consistent with the general interest of the trust, give effect to the wishes of such persons, or in the case of disputes, to the wishes of the majority in terms of value. But, in any case, a purchaser, which includes a mortgagee, is not concerned to see that the trustees have complied with this requirement.[96] In a proper case, however, a beneficiary may restrain a trustee who seeks to sell in breach of the statutory requirement.[97]

Under a trust for sale all the powers in relation to land are discharged by the trustees, but under a settlement it is the tenant for life who exercises such powers. By virtue of the Law of Property Act 1925 a trust for sale means an "immediately binding trust for sale."[98] The same definition is used in the Settled Land Act 1925,[99] and as a consequence only an "immediate binding trust for sale" falls inside its purview. Thus, to constitute a trust for sale for the purposes of the Law of Property Act there must be not only a trust to sell and not a mere power of sale, and this trust must be immediate, but the trust for sale must be "binding." Complications have arisen, however, with regard to the definition of the word "binding." A problem arose with regard to the displacement of the Settled Land Act at the moment when an effective trust for sale was created. Equitable interests, such as an equitable mortgage or charge, created paramount to the trust did not prevent it from being an immediate binding trust for sale, and there was some judicial concern manifested towards the possibility of a later trust for sale displacing outstanding interests created by a prior settlement which might be overlooked by the trustees for sale despite being bound by such prior interests.

But it would seem that the existence of paramount equitable charges such as jointure rent charges or portions charges[1] sufficient to constitute the land as settled land may well prevent the legal estate from vesting in the trustees for sale,[2] and thus prevent such interest being displaced by a trust for sale even when the trustees for sale have been approved or appointed by the court or consist of a trust corporation and are therefore able to overreach such paramount equitable interests.[3]

Further, where a legal estate in land is vested in trustees for sale and by reason of the exercise of any equitable power or under any trust affecting the proceeds of sale any principal sum is required to be raised, then, unless the claim is satisfied out of the net proceeds of sale, the trustees for sale shall, if so requested in writing, be bound, *inter alia*, to create such legal

---

[96] L.P.A. 1925, ss.26(3) and 205(1) (xxix).
[97] *Waller* v. *Waller* [1967] 1 W.L.R. 451; and see *Re Jones* [1931] 1 Ch. 375.
[98] s.205(1)(xxix).
[99] s.117(1)(xxx).
[1] Settled Land Act 1925, s.1(1)(v)
[2] *Ibid.* s.7(5).
[3] By virtue of the L.P.A. 1925, s.2(2) (as amended by the Law of Property (Amendment) Act 1926, s.7, Sched.). For cases on the subject see *Re Parker's Settled Estates* [1928] Ch. 247; not following *Re Leigh's Settled Estates (No. 1)* [1926] Ch. 852 (and see *Re Leigh's Settled Estates (No. 2)* [1927] 2 Ch. 13); *Re Norton* [1929] 1 Ch. 84; *Re Sharpe's Deed of Release* [1939] Ch. 51.

estates, to take effect in priority to the trust for sale, as may be required for raising the money by way of legal mortgage.[4] Mortgages can also be made pursuant to the powers conferred upon the trustees for sale in the following circumstances:

(1) by co-owners of full age who are entitled in undivided shares at the commencement of the Law of Property Act 1925,[5] or as joint tenants[6];

(2) in respect of a legal estate conveyed to an infant jointly with one or more persons of full age[7];

(3) with the consent of the persons of full age, not being annuitants, interested in possession in the net rents and profits, on a partition between the beneficiaries under a trust for sale the trustees may provide by way of mortgage the payment of equality money.[8]

Private trustees

In the case of land other than land which is settled land under the Settled Land Act 1925,[9] a private trustee may not mortgage trust property unless he is expressly or impliedly authorised to do so by the instrument creating the trust,[10] or pursuant to a power conferred by statute or pursuant to a court order.[11–12]

Where trustees are authorised by the trust instrument, if any, creating the trust, or by law, to pay or apply capital monies subject to the trust for any purpose or in any manner, they have, and are deemed always to have had, power to raise, *inter alia*, money by way of mortgage of all or any part of the trust property for the time being in possession.[13] This power is available notwithstanding anything to the contrary in the instrument, if any, creating the trust, but it does not apply to trustees of property held for charitable purposes, or to trustees of settled land not being also statutory owners.[14] Further, trustees for sale have, in relation to land, all the powers of a statutory owner.[15]

With regard to settled land, however, any powers to mortgage which are conferred upon the trustees are exercisable not by them, unless they are the statutory owners for the time being, but by the tenants for life or statu-

---

[4] L.P.A. 1925, s.3(1)(*b*)(ii). This includes a charge by way of legal mortgage, see *ibid.* s.205(1)(xvi).

[5] Sched. 1, Pt. IV, para. 1(2). By virtue of s.35 of the Act persons holding land upon the statutory trusts hold as trustees for sale.

[6] L.P.A. 1925, s.36.

[7] *Ibid.* s.19(2).

[8] *Ibid.* s.28(3).

[9] See *post*, p. 176.

[10] *Re Bellinger* [1898] 2 Ch. 534; *Re Suenson-Taylor's Settlement Trusts* [1974] 1 W.L.R. 1280.

[11–12] See the Trustee Act 1925, s.57. In the case of settled land, see the Settled Land Act 1925, s.54.

[13] Trustee Act 1925, s.16(1). "Possession" includes receipt of rents and profits or the right to receive the same, if any; *ibid.* s.68(10).

[14] *Ibid.* s.16(2).

[15] L.P.A. 1925, s.28(1), and see *ante*, p. 173.

tory owner by way of additional powers, and as if conferred by the Settled Land Act 1925.[16] By virtue of section 17 of the Trustee Act 1925, a mortgagee advancing money on a mortgage purporting to be made under any trust or power vested in trustees is not concerned to see that the money is wanted, or that no more than is wanted is raised, or otherwise as to its application. But as the mortgage money is capital money the mortgagee must not pay it to fewer than two trustees unless the trustee is a trust corporation.[17]

Power to lend money on mortgage

Trustees are only able to lend money on mortgage if authorised by the trust instrument in the case of personal property, or pursuant to the statutory power to do so under the Trustee Investments Act 1961 in the case of real property (either freehold or leasehold), unless expressly prevented from doing so by the instrument creating the trust.[18] A tenant for life has no power to mortgage or charge the legal estate for his own benefit or use. If he wishes to do so he can mortgage his own beneficial interest.

LIMITED OWNERS

Tenants for life and statutory owners

Generally

An important class of persons having power to raise money by way of a legal mortgage over the settled property is the tenant for life or statutory owner under the Settled Land Act 1925 as trustees or parties interested under the settlement.[19] The requisite vesting instrument must have been made vesting the legal estate in the settled land in the tenant for life or statutory owner,[20-21] and the loan must be required for certain specified purposes. Where there is no tenant for life or person otherwise having, either under the Act or by the settlement, the powers of a tenant for life, then the trustees of the settlement may exercise those powers for the purposes of the Act as statutory powers.[22] A settlement includes any instrument or instruments whereby a fee simple or term of years absolute is limited in trust for an infant, or for any person contingently or where the

---

[16] See *ante*, p. 173.
[17] L.P.A. 1925, s.27(2); Law of Property (Amendment) Act 1926, s.7 and Sched. In order to avoid the difficulty of the beneficiaries having to join in giving a receipt for the mortgage monies, or to investigate whether or not the trustees were the duly appointed trustees of the trust in question (see *Re Blaiberg & Abrahams* [1899] 2 Ch. 340) it became the common practice to insert a "joint account clause" where two or more persons lent money. After 1881 such a clause is now unnecessary.
[18] Trustee Investments Act 1961, s.1(1), (3), Sched. 1, Pt. II, para. 13, Pt. IV, para. 5. See also generally *Lewin on Trusts* (16th ed., 1964).
[19] See the Settled Land Act 1925, s.107.
[20-21] *Ibid.* s.13.
[22] See the Settled Land Act 1925, ss.23, 26 and 117(1)(xxvi).

land stands charged with family charges.[23] The tenant for life also has the power to create a settlement for the express purpose of overreaching equitable interests and powers.[24] There are two classes of purpose for which a mortgage may be made, namely, purposes paramount to the settlement, and purposes for giving effect to equitable interests under the settlement. It should be noted, however, that in the absence of a contrary provision in the settlement itself[25] a tenant for life has no power to mortgage or charge the legal estate for his own benefit or use. If he wishes to do so he can mortgage his own beneficial interest.

Mortgages paramount to equitable interests under the settlement

The tenant for life or statutory owner has power by a legal mortgage[26] to raise money for certain specified purposes, namely where money is required[27] for any of the following purposes:

(1) discharging an incumbrance[28] on the settled land or parts thereof[29];
(2) paying for any improvement authorised by the Act or by the settlement[30];
(3) equality of exchange;
(4) redeeming a compensation rent charge[31] in respect of the extinguishment of manorial incidents and affecting the settled land[32];
(5) satisfying any claim under the Landlord and Tenant Act 1927 for compensation for an improvement[33];
(6) paying a coast protection charge or expenses incurred in carrying

---

[23] *Ibid.* s.1(1)(ii)(*d*), (iii).
[24] *Ibid.* s.72 and the L.P.A. 1925, s.2. An estate owner also has the powers of a tenant for life; in particular the power to make overreaching conveyances under the Settled Land Act 1925, s.21.
[25] See *Re Egerton's Settled Estates* [1926] Ch. 574.
[26] Or charge by way of legal mortgage, see the Settled Land Act 1925, s.117(1)(xi).
[27] "Required" means reasonably required having regard to the circumstances, see *Re Clifford* [1902] 1 Ch. 87; *Re Bruce* [1905] 2 Ch. 372 at 376.
[28] *i.e.* of a permanent nature and not any annual sum payable only during a life or lives or during a term of years absolute or determinable, see the Settled Land Act 1925, s.71(2).
[29] This includes, *e.g.* local charges for making up streets, see *Re Smith's Settled Estate* [1901] 1 Ch. 689; *Re Pizzi* [1907] 1 Ch. 67.
[30] See the Settled Land Act 1925, s.83 and Sched. 3.
[31] Such power is conferred by the L.P.A. 1922, s.139(3); the Manorial Incidents (Extinguishment) Rules 1925 (S.R. & O. 1925 No. 810), r. 15; and also see the Manorial Incidents (Extinguishment) (Amendment) Rules 1935 (S.R. & O. 1935 No. 1241), r. 2.
[32] Settled Land Act 1925, s.71(1)(i)—(iii), (vi), (ix). Other purposes were also specified by s.71(1) namely, the raising of money by mortgage for extinguishing manorial incidents, for compensating the stewards on the extinguishment of manorial incidents and discharging expenses incurred in connection with the extinguishment for commuting any additional rents made payable on the conversion of a perpetually renewable leasehold interest into a long term and for satisfying any claims for compensation by an agent of the lessor in respect of loss of fees on conversion (see s.71(1)(iv) (v), (vii), (viii)). They are either repealed or spent by Statute Law (Repeals) Act 1969, s.1, Sched., Pt. III.
[33] Landlord and Tenant Act 1927, s.13(2).

out work under a works scheme under the Coast Protection Act 1949[34];

(7) paying certain expenses and making certain payments under the Landlord and Tenant Act 1954[35];

(8) paying certain sums recoverable under the Town and Country Planning Act 1971[36];

(9) discharging any sum payable in respect of betterment levy under the Land Compensation Act 1967 in so far as that sum represents the whole or part of the principal amount of the levy[37];

(10) paying expenses incurred by a tenant for life or statutory owner in connection with proceedings for enfranchising leaseholds or obtaining extensions of leases under the Leasehold Reform Act 1967, and paying compensation in connection with exercise of certain overriding rights of a landlord under that Act[38];

(11) paying the costs of any transaction authorised under the foregoing heads or by sections 69 or 70 of the Settled Land Act 1925.[39]

Thus, the tenant for life may raise the money so required on the security of the settled land or any part thereof, and the money so raised shall be capital money for that purpose, and may be paid or applied accordingly. For this purpose it must be paid to the trustees of the settlement.[40] As has already been noted the mortgage must be a legal mortgage, which includes a charge by way of legal mortgage, and the tenant for life or statutory owner cannot make an equitable mortgage.[41]

Overreaching effects of paramount mortgage of settled land

A legal mortgage made by the tenant for life or statutory owner under the statutory powers is effectual to give the mortgagee a title to discharge free from all the limitations, powers, and provisions of the settlement and from all estates, interests and charges subsisting or to arise thereunder, but subject to and with the exception of:

(1) all legal estates and charges by way of legal mortgage having priority to the settlement;

(2) all legal estates and charges by way of legal mortgage which has been conveyed or created for securing money actually raised at the date of the deed; and

(3) all leases and grants at fee-farm rents or otherwise, and all grants of easements, rights of common, or other rights or privileges which: (a) were before the date of the mortgage granted or made

---

[34] Coast Protection Act 1949, s.11(2)(a).
[35] Landlord and Tenant Act 1954, Sched. 2, para. 6.
[36] Town and Country Planning Act 1971, s.275.
[37] Land Compensation Act 1967, s.92.
[38] Leasehold Reform Act 1967, s.6(5), Sched. 2, para. 9(1).
[39] Settled Land Act 1925, s.71(1)(ix).
[40] Ibid. s.75.
[41] Ibid. s.72(1).

for value in money or money's worth, or agreed so to be, by the tenant for life or statutory owner, or by any of his predecessors in title, or any trustees for them, under the settlement, or under any statutory power, or are at that date otherwise binding on the successors in title of the tenant for life or statutory owner; and (*b*) are at that date protected by registration under the Land Charges Act 1925 if capable of registration thereunder.[42]

Notwithstanding registration under the Land Charges Act 1925 of an annuity within the meaning of Part II of that Act or of a limited owner's charge or a general equitable charge within the meaning of that Act, a mortgage under the Settled Land Act 1925 operates to overreach such annuity or charge.[43]

Shifting incumbrances

By virtue of section 69 of the Settled Land Act 1925, where there is an incumbrance[44] affecting any part of the settled land (whether capable of being overreached on the exercise by the tenant for life of his powers under the Act or not) then *Re Knight's Settled Estates*[45] illustrates that the tenant for life, with the consent of the incumbrancer, may charge that incumbrance on any other powers of the settled land, or on all or any part of the capital money or securities representing capital money subject or to become subject to the settlement, whether already charged therewith or not, in exoneration of the first mentioned part and the tenant for life may by a legal mortgage or otherwise make provision accordingly.

Variation and consolidation of securities

By section 70 where an incumbrance affects any part of the settled land, the tenant for life may, with the consent of the incumbrancer, vary the rate of interest charged and any other provisions of the instrument, if any, creating the incumbrance and with the like consent, charge that incumbrance on any part of the settled land, whether already charged therewith or not, or on all or any part of the capital money or securities representing capital money subject or to become subject to the settlement, by way of additional security, or of consolidation of securities. The tenant for life may by a legal mortgage or otherwise make provision accordingly.

Costs

The court may direct that a tenant for life may also raise by a legal mortgage of the settled land or any part thereof, any costs, charges or expenses

---

[42] *Ibid.* s.72(2).
[43] *Ibid.* s.72(3).
[44] Incumbrance in this section includes any annual sum payable during a life or lives or during a term of years absolute or determinable, but in any such case an additional security must be effected so as only to create a charge or security similar to the original charge or security, see s.70(2).
[45] [1918] 1 Ch. 211.

to be paid out of the property subject to the settlement.[46] The costs of the summons for leave to raise by mortgage such costs, may be added and raised.[47]

Additional powers under the settlement

The settlement may confer powers to mortgage additional to or larger than those conferred by the Settled Land Act 1925,[48] but any power of mortgaging conferred on the trustees of the settlement or other persons for any purpose, whether or not provided for by the Act, is exercisable by the tenant for life or statutory owner, as if it were an additional power conferred on the tenant for life,[49] and operates as if it were conferred by the Act on the tenant for life.[50]

Additional powers authorised by order of the court

By virtue of section 64 of the Settled Land Act 1925 the court has a statutory jurisdiction to authorise the tenant for life to effect any transaction affecting or concerning the settled land, or any part thereof, or any other land not otherwise authorised by the Act or the settlement[51] if in the opinion of the court it would be for the benefit of the settled land, or any part thereof for the persons interested under the settlement.[52] But it must be a transaction which could have been validly made by an absolute owner.[53] The transactions which may be authorised include any sale, exchange, assurance, grant, lease, surrender, re-conveyance, release, reservation, or other disposition; any purchase or other acquisition; any covenant, contract or option; any application of capital money and any compromise or other dealing or arrangement.[54] Thus, the court has authorised a tenant for life to raise a mortgage on the settled land to pay off his debts which had arisen from the expenses of maintaining the land.[55] Further, this jurisdiction empowers the court to sanction a proposed scheme on behalf of those who are unable to consent (for example an infant) which alters the beneficial interest under the settlement,[56] having as its object or effect to reduce liability for tax, including estate duties, which

---

[46] See the Settled Land Act 1925, ss.92 and 114.
[47] *Re Pizzi* [1907] 1 Ch. 67 at 71.
[48] s.109(1).
[49] Settled Land Act 1925, s.108(2).
[50] *Ibid.* s.109(2).
[51] See *Re Symons* [1927] 1 Ch. 344 at 354.
[52] See *Re Cleveland Literary and Philosophical Society's Land* [1931] 2 Ch. 247.
[53] Settled Land Act 1925, s.64(1) as amended by the Settled Land and Trustee Acts (Court's General Powers) Act 1943, s.2. Certain words were repealed by the Statute Law (Repeals) Act 1969, s.1, Sched., Pt. III. By virtue of s.1 of the 1943 Act the jurisdiction of the court was extended to enable it, in particular circumstances, to make an order authorising expenses of management to be treated as a capital outgoing notwithstanding that in other circumstances the expense could not have been so treated. This provision was amended and made permanent by the Emergency Laws (Miscellaneous Provisions) Act 1953, s.9.
[54] See the Settled Land Act 1925, ss.64(2), as amended, and s.109(1).
[55] *Re White-Popham Settled Estates* [1936] Ch. 725.
[56] See *Re Simmons* [1956] Ch. 125.

could not normally be effected under the general law prior to the enactment of the Variation of Trust Acts 1958.[57]

Tenant for life as trustee—limits on powers

The tenant for life not only has the estate[58] vested in him on trust for himself and the other beneficiaries under the settlement, but also he is in the position of a trustee in relation to the exercise of his statutory powers.[59] Thus, the tenant for life will be restrained by injunction from creating a mortgage which is prejudicial or unjust to the interests of the beneficiaries,[60] and the court will treat the creation of any such mortgage as a breach of trust. Thus, a tenant for life is not entitled to attempt to preserve a heavily incumbered estate by mortgaging it, if by doing so he prejudices the interests of existing equitable incumbrances.[61] But, provided that the tenant for life acts in good faith and has proper regard to his statutory duty under the Act in relation to the interests of all parties entitled under the settlement, the court will not normally interfere with the discretion of a tenant for life as to the exercise of those powers.[62]

If, however, a trustee fails to see that he is acting unjustly despite being honest and acting within the letter of his trust, it is the duty of the court to interfere.[63]

Payment of capital money to trustees and protection of mortgages

Since money raised by virtue of the statutory powers is capital money it must be paid either to the trustees of the settlement, for the purposes of the Settled Land Act 1925, of whom there must be not fewer than two persons as trustees of the settlement, unless the trustee is a trust corporation[64] or into court, at the option of the tenant for life.[65] The tenant for life must also give notice to each of the trustees of the settlement of his intention to mortgage or charge the land, and, if known, to the solicitor for the trustees.[66] This, however, must be a notice of each specific transaction contemplated by the tenant for life,[67] and a general notice does not suffice.[68] But a mortgagee dealing in good faith with the tenant for life is not con-

---

[57] See, e.g. Chapman v. Chapman [1954] A.C. 429.
[58] Settled Land Act 1925, s.16(1); and see Re Boston's Wills Trust [1956] Ch. 395 at 405.
[59] See the Settled Land Act 1925, s.107.
[60] Hampden v. Earl of Buckinghamshire [1893] 2 Ch. 531 at 543, 544.
[61] Ibid.
[62] Ibid.; and see Re Richardson [1900] 2 Ch. 778 at 790.
[63] Hampden v. Earl of Buckinghamshire [1893] 2 Ch. 531 at 544; Re Gladwin's Trust [1919] 1 Ch. 232; and see Re Charteris, Charteris v. Biddulph [1917] 2 Ch. 379 at 394. The title of the estate mortgaged by the tenant for life is not affected by this provision, but it causes the tenant for life to be personally bound as a trustee, see Re Marquis of Ailesbury's Settled Estates [1892] 1 Ch. 506 at 535, 536.
[64] Settled Land Act 1925, s.94.
[65] Ibid. ss.75(1), 94.
[66] Ibid. s.101(1).
[67] See Re Ray's Settled Estates (1884) 25 Ch.D. 464.
[68] i.e. under the Settled Land Act 1925, s.101(2).

cerned to make any enquiry with regard to the giving of the notice.[69] Further, a mortgagee paying his advance to the trustees is not concerned to see that the money advanced is required for any purpose under the Act or that no more than is wanted is raised.[70]

Mortgages to give effect to equitable interests

Further, by virtue of section 16 of the Settled Land Act 1925, the estate owner is a statutory trustee of the settled land for giving effect to the equitable interests. Thus, where:

"(a) any principal sum is required to be raised on the security of the settled land, by virtue of any trust, or by reason of the exercise of an equitable power affecting the settled land, or by any person or persons who under the settlement is or are entitled or together entitled to or has to have a general power of appointment over the settled land, whether subject to any equitable charges or powers of charging subsisting under the settlement or not; or

(b) the settled land is subject to any equitable charge for securing money actually raised and affecting the whole estate the subject of the settlement;

the estate owner shall be bound, if so requested in writing, to create such legal estate or charge by way of legal mortgage as may be required for raising the money or giving effect to the equitable charge."[71]

It is therefore possible to raise money under this provision for portions.

But this is subject to the proviso that so long as the settlement remains subsisting, any legal estate or charge by way of legal mortgage so created shall take effect and must be expressed to take effect subject to any equitable charges or powers of charging subsisting under the settlement which have priority to the interests or powers of the person or persons by or on behalf of whom the money is required to be raised, or legal effect is required to be given to the equitable charge, unless the persons entitled to the prior charges or entitled to exercise the powers consent in writing to the same being postponed. But it is not necessary that such consent be expressed in the instrument creating such estate or charge by way of legal mortgage.[72] Further, effect may be given by means of a legal mortgage[73] to an agreement for a mortgage, or a charge or lien, whether or not arising by operation of law, if the agreement, charge or lien ought to have priority over the settlement.[74]

The Act also provides for the means of settling doubts as to whether any

---

[69] Settled Land Act 1925, s.101(5).
[70] Settled Land Act 1925, ss.95 and 110(1) and the Trustee Act 1925, s.17.
[71] Settled Land Act 1925, s.16(1)(iii); See also the Land Registration Act 1925, s.90; and the Land Registration Rules 1925, r. 144.
[72] Settled Land Act 1925, s.16(1)(iii) proviso; Land Registration Rules 1925, r. 156.
[73] Which includes a legal charge, see the Settled Land Act 1925, s.117(1)(xi).
[74] Settled Land Act 1925, s.16(4).

and what legal estate ought to be created under the foregoing provisions[75] by application to the court for directions and for vesting orders in case of refusal or neglect by the tenant for life, or any other difficulty.[76]

Overreaching effect of mortgage and protection of mortgagee

Provided that the mortgage or legal charge is expressed to be made pursuant to section 16 of the Settled Land Act 1925, it takes effect in priority to all the trusts of the settlement and equitable interests and powers subsisting or to arise under the settlement except those to which it is expressly made subject, and shall so take effect whether the mortgagee or chargee has notice of any such trusts, interests or powers, and further the mortgagee or chargee shall not be concerned to see that a case has arisen to authorise the mortgage or charge or that no money than was wanted was raised.[77] But, if the deed is to take effect under the Act and to overreach the beneficial interests there is one important condition which must be observed. The mortgagee or chargee must require that any capital money payable in respect of the transaction must be paid either:

(1) to or by the direction of all the trustees of the settlement who must be either two or more in number or a trust corporation[78]; or

(2) into court.[79]

This rule applies notwithstanding anything to the contrary in the settlement.

Mortgage of land subject to family charges

The meaning of settled land was extended by the Settled Land Act 1925[80] to include, not only the normal case of land limited in trust for any person in possession, but to various other cases where land is not vested in some person absolutely and beneficially.

Thus, land is settled land where it is subject to family charges, such as an annuity or jointure rent charge and charges for portions. In the circumstances the estate owner subject to such family charges only has the powers of a tenant for life[81] and can only create a legal mortgage free from such charges if the Settled Land Act procedure as to the appointment of trustees and the execution of a vesting deed are observed.[82] But, in a limited class of case provided by section 1 of the Law of Property (Amendment) Act 1926 which allows settled land to be dealt with as if it were not settled, the estate owner may make a legal mortgage subject to such charges as if the

---

[75] *i.e.* Under the Settled Land Act 1925, s.16.
[76] *Ibid.* s.16(6), (7).
[77] *Ibid.* s.16(2).
[78] *Ibid.* s.18(1)(*b*), (*c*); L.P.A. 1925, s.2(1)(i).
[79] Settled Land Act 1925, s.18(1)(*b*).
[80] *Ibid.* s.1(1).
[81] *Ibid.* s.1(1)(v).
[82] *Ibid.*

land had not been settled land and without compliance with the Settled
Land Act procedure.

Mortgage to tenant for life

A mortgage or charge of the settled land may be made to the tenant for
life.[83] In such a case the trustees of the settlement have, in addition to their
powers as trustees, all the powers of a tenant for life as to negotiating and
completing the transaction.[84]

Mortgage by trustees where tenant for life has ceased to have a substantial interest

If it is shown to the satisfaction of the court that the tenant for life:

(1) has ceased to have a substantial interest in the land by reason of
bankruptcy, assignment, incumbrance, or otherwise; and
(2) either consents to an order being made or has unreasonably
refused to exercise any of the powers conferred on him by the
Settled Land Act 1925;

then by virtue of section 24(1) of the Settled Land Act 1925:

"the court may, upon the application of any person interested in the
settled land or the part thereof affected, make an order authorising
the trustees of the settlement to exercise in the name and on behalf of
the tenant for life, any of the powers . . . in relation to the settled land
or the part thereof affected, either generally and in such manner and
for such period as the court may think fit, or in a particular instance."

Once such an order has been made it prevents the tenant for life from exercising any of the powers affected by the order.[85] But a person dealing with
the tenant for life is not affected by it unless and until it has been registered
under the Land Charges Act 1972 as an order affecting land. Such an order
does not vest the legal estate nor the statutory powers in the trustees who
do not become the statutory owner. The order merely authorises the
trustees to exercise the statutory powers on behalf of the tenant for life and
in his name. Further, the provision does not apply to statutory owners and
is limited to tenants for life.[86]

Mortgage of tenant for life's beneficial interest

It is possible for the tenant for life to mortgage his beneficial interest in
the trust fund. Such an interest is necessarily equitable, but as it is an equitable thing in action within the meaning of section 136 of the Law of Prop-

---

[83] *Ibid.* s.13.
[84] *Ibid.* s.68(2).
[85] Settled Land Act 1925, s.24(2), and see the Land Charges Act 1972, s.6.
[86] *Re Craven Settled Estates* [1926] Ch. 985.

erty Act 1925, it is capable of legal assignment.[87] However, a mortgage of an equitable interest is normally by way of an equitable mortgage.[88]

Tenants in tail

Power of tenant in tail to mortgage

A tenant in tail in possession will normally have the legal estate, either freehold or leasehold, in the entailed property vested in him as estate owner on the trusts of the settlement.[89] In such circumstances he has the statutory power of a tenant for life to mortgage. Where he has only an equitable interest in the land entailed, which is the usual case,[90] he has special statutory powers of disposing of his equitable interest in the entailed land[91] apart from the general powers of disposition conferred on limited owners under the Settled Land Act 1925, Part II, sections 38 to 72. The tenant in tail[92] can put an end to the settlement by barring the entail,[93] then by virtue of his legal estate the tenant in tail becomes the absolute owner in equity and can mortgage. But unless the legal estate in the entailed land is vested in the tenant in tail[94] he can only mortgage the equitable interest in the land. By virtue of his special statutory powers of disposition the tenant in tail in possession may execute by deed a mortgage in the form of a conveyance of his equitable interest in fee simple or any less interest in the land.[95] If, however, the tenant in tail is not in possession, unless the mortgage is made with the consent of the protector of the settlement,[96] it will only convey to the mortgagee an equitable interest in the nature of a base fee. This is unimpeachable during the survival of the issue of the tenant in tail, but is voidable upon the death of the survivor of that issue by the person next entitled in remainder on the estate tail.[97]

Extent of disentailment by mortgage

When a tenant in tail mortgages the land entailed under his special statutory powers pursuant to the Fines and Recoveries Act 1833,[98] generally the

[87] *Re Pain* [1919] 1 Ch. 38; *Earle Ltd.* v. *Hemsworth R.D.C.* (1928) 44. T.L.R. 605; and see *ante*, pp. 76 *et seq.*
[88] See *ante*, pp. 76 *et seq.*
[89] Settled Land Act 1925, ss.4(2), 6(*b*), 7(1)–(4), 9(2), 20(1)(i), 117(1)(xxviii).
[90] See the L.P.A. 1925, s.1. (1), (3).
[91] See the Fines and Recoveries Act 1833, s.15, and the Law of Property (Amendment) Act 1924, s.9, Sched. 9, by which the Fines and Recoveries Act 1833 remains in force only as regards dealings with entailed interests as equitable interests.
[92] As to the circumstances of family charges constituting a settlement, see the Settled Land Act 1925, s.1. (1)(v), and *ante*, p. 183, and the power of a person beneficially entitled to land subject to such family charges to convey or create a legal estate subject to the charges, see the Law of Property (Amendment) Act 1926, s.1, and *ante*, p. 183.
[93] See the Fines and Recoveries Act 1833, s.15.
[94] See n. 89 above.
[95] See the Fines and Recoveries Act 1833, ss.15, 40.
[96] *Ibid.* ss.22–28, 32.
[97] *Ibid.* s.34.
[98] s.15.

entail is wholly barred in equity to the extent of the interest created by the mortgage, irrespective of any intention to the contrary express or implied in the mortgage deed.[99] But if the mortgage only creates an interest *pur autre vie*, a term of years, a charge unsecured by a term of years, or a greater interest, then the entail is barred only so far as is necessary to give effect to the mortgage, notwithstanding any intention express or implied to the contrary.[1]

Agreement to disentail

The 1833 Act also provides that a disposition by a tenant in tail in contract is of no force and that the courts are not to give effect to defective dispositions.[2] But it would seem that an agreement by a tenant in tail to disentail for the purpose of executing a legal mortgage may be specifically enforced against the tenant in tail himself.[3] But it cannot be specifically enforced against the issue in tail if the tenant in tail dies before conveying,[4] unless the remainder man was a party to the mortgage transaction.[5]

Mortgage by charity trustees

By section 29 of the Settled Land Act 1925 land vested in trustees for charitable, ecclesiastical or public[6] trusts or purposes was made settled land, so that the trustees have the powers of a tenant for life and trustees of a settlement under the Act.[7] The powers are exercisable subject to such consents or orders of any kind being obtained as would, if the Act had not been passed, have been requisite if the transaction were being effected under an express power conferred by the instrument creating the trust.[8] But the land does not become settled land for all purposes. Thus a conveyance to a charity need not be made by a vesting deed and trust instrument, nor is a sole trustee prevented from giving a good receipt for capital money if the scheme governing the charity so authorises.

Further, by virtue of section 29 of the Charities Act 1960 no land which forms part of the permanent endowment of a charity, or is or has been occupied for the purposes of the charity, may be mortgaged or charged without an order of the court or the Charity Commissioners, or the Secretary of State for Education and Science.[9] This provision applies to any land which is held by or in trust for a charity and is or has at any time been

---

[99] See the Fines and Recoveries Act 1833, s.21.
[1] Fines and Recoveries Act 1833, s.21, proviso.
[2] *Ibid.* ss.40, 47.
[3] *Bankes* v. *Small* (1887) 36 Ch.D. 716.
[4] See *Att.-Gen.* v. *Day* (1749) 1 Ves.Sen. 218 at 224; *Hinton* v. *Hinton* (1755) 2 Ves.Sen. 631 at 634.
[5] See *Pryce* v. *Bury* (1853) 2 Drew 11.
[6] See *Re Cleveland Literary and Philosophical Society's Land* [1931] 2 Ch. 247.
[7] Settled Land Act 1925, s.29(1).
[8] *Re Booth & Southend-on-Sea Estates Co's Contract* [1927] 1 Ch. 579.
[9] See the Charities Act 1960, s.29(1), (2); Secretary of State for Education and Science Order (S.I. 1964 No. 490). The concurrent jurisdiction of the Minister of Education for Educational Charities was abolished by the Education Act 1973, s.1(1), (5).

occupied for the purposes of the charity as it applies to land forming part of the permanent endowment thereof. But in the case of land not forming part of the permanent endowment a mortgage entered into without such an order is valid in favour of a person who, at the time or later, acquires in good faith a charge on the land for money or money's worth.[10] A transaction entered into without the requisite order is void,[11] save that where a contract for sale or lease "subject to" the requisite order being obtained is not prohibited under the Act.[12]

There are a number of exceptions to the requirement for the obtaining of such an order.[13] First, a transaction authorised by statute or taking effect thereunder or under a scheme does not require consent. Secondly, certain charitable bodies are exempt,[14] such as the Universities of Oxford, Cambridge, London and Durham, together with industrial and provident societies and friendly societies. Thirdly, there are a large number of excepted charities by orders or regulations, such as religious charities which are subject only to modified restraint.[15]

CORPORATIONS

Borrowing powers of corporations

The powers of a corporation to mortgage its property are limited by reference to any express or implied authorisation to do so. Thus, in the case of a company incorporated under the Companies Act 1985 (or its statutory predecessors) its express powers to mortgage are contained in the objects and purposes specified in the Memorandum of Association.[16] Similarly, a public utility company incorporated by a special act of Parliament has the powers conferred by the special act and the Companies Clauses Consolidation Act 1845[17] which enables such a company to raise money by way of mortgage of property subject to certain conditions.[18] Further, a corporation created by Royal Charter, prima facie, is empowered to mortgage on the basis that it has all the rights and powers possessed by an ordinary person.[19]

In the case of companies incorporated under the Companies Act for trading or commercial purposes, there is an implied power to mortgage the

---

[10] See the Charities Act 1960, s.29(2).
[11] *Bishop of Bangor* v. *Parry* [1891] 2 Q.B. 277.
[12] *Haslemere Estates Ltd.* v. *Baker* [1982] 1 W.L.R. 1109: and see *Richards (Michael) Properties Ltd.* v. *Corporation of Wardens of St. Saviour's Parish, Southwark* [1975] 3 All E.R. 416.
[13] Charities Act 1960, s.29(3).
[14] *Ibid.* Sched. 2.
[15] *Ibid.* s.29(4).
[16] *Ashbury Railway Carriage and Iron Co.* v. *Riche* (1875) L.R. 7 H.L. 653.
[17] s.38. See also generally *Palmer's Company Law* (1987).
[18] Companies Clauses Consolidation Act 1845, ss.38–55. In the case of nationalised corporations the powers of the particular body to raise money by way of mortgage are contained in the statute creating the particular body.
[19] *Jenkin* v. *Pharmaceutical Society of Great Britain* [1921] 1 Ch. 392 at 398.

company's property even though the memorandum of association is silent provided that there is no positive prohibition preventing it.[20] But such an implication will not be made in the case of a non-trading company which can mortgage its property only if it is expressly authorised to do so by its Memorandum of Association. A limited company by its Articles of Association usually delegates to the directors of the company the exercise of the power to mortgage.[21] There is usually a limitation[22] on the amount which can be borrowed without the sanction of a general meeting. But, the express, or implied, power to borrow is limited to borrowing for authorised and legitimate purposes.[23]

In the case of any party to a transaction dealing with a company in good faith, such transaction being decided upon by the directors, the said party is not bound to inquire as to the capacity of the company to enter into it or as to any limitation on the powers of the directors under the Memorandum or Articles of Association. In other words, it must be deemed to be a transaction which is within the capacity of the company to enter, unless the contrary is proved.[24]

In the case of companies incorporated by the Companies Act 1985, it is not usually legitimate for one company to charge its property as security for the debts of another company, for example, its parent or holding company. But, if it is proposed that a subsidiary company should guarantee a loan made to the holding company the Memorandum of Association of the subsidiary company can be altered so as to ensure that it has the appropriate authorisation to enter into such a transaction.

Further, where a company incorporated under the Companies Act 1985 enters into a transaction whereby it charges the property of the company, such a transaction shall be void against the liquidator and any creditor of the company unless the prescribed particulars of the charge together with the instrument, if any, by which the charge is created or evidenced, are delivered to or received by the registrar of companies for registration as required within 21 days after the date of its creation, but without prejudice to any contract or obligation for repayment of the money thereby secured.[25] When the charge becomes void under this section the money secured thereby shall immediately become payable. Finally, the object of the company will usually include an express power to make advances and

---

[20] *Re Patent Ivory Manufacturing Co. Howard* v. *Patent Ivory Manufacturing Co.* (1888) 38 Ch.D. 156; *General Auction Estate and Monetary Co.* v. *Smith* [1891] 3 Ch. 432.

[21] *Re Irish Club Co. Ltd.* [1906] W.N. 127. A company limited by guarantee cannot charge the amounts which the members have undertaken to contribute in the event of a winding up.

[22] See, *e.g.* Companies Act 1985, Table A, Part I, reg.

[23] *Introductions Ltd.* v. *National Provincial Bank* [1970] Ch. 199.

[24] See the European Communities Act 1972, s.9(1); see further *Buckley on the Companies Act* (14th ed.) pp. 241 *et seq.*

[25] Companies Act 1985, s.395. For a more detailed analysis of these provisions in particular the effect of non-registration, registration otherwise than under the Act, and rectificiation see *Buckley on the Companies Act* (14th ed.). For mortgaged debentures see *ante*, pp. 98 *et seq.*

lend money, secured by way of mortgage.[26] But in the absence of such an express power a company has an implied power to do so provided that it is in the ordinary course of its business and in furtherance of its objects.

PUBLIC AUTHORITIES

The borrowing power of local authorities

Local authorities have statutory powers of mortgaging, their powers being defined by the relevant Act or being implied.[27] Further, under the Local Government Act 1972,[28] a local authority may with the consent of the sanctioning authority,[29] borrow such sums as may be required for the acquisition of land, for building and for other defined statutory purposes. A person lending money to a local authority is not bound to inquire whether the borrowing is or was legal or regular or whether the money was properly applied and he is not prejudiced by any illegality or irregularity in such matters or by the misapplication or non-application of any such money.[30] Such money may be raised by mortgage, or by the issue of stock, debentures or bonds,[31] but the most common method of raising money is by the issue of stock or bonds. Local authorities may also borrow money for certain specified purposes under general Acts of Parliament.[32]

Lending powers of local authorities[33]

A local authority or county council may, subject to any economic restraints imposed on such authorities, advance money for the purpose of acquiring, constructing, altering, enlarging, repairing or improving houses, for converting buildings into houses or flats, for acquiring houses for that purpose or for paying off a loan for such purposes. Before making an advance the local authority must be satisfied that the resultant house will be fit for human habitation, or in the case of a house to be acquired is or will be made fit.[34]

Other public authorities

Further, other public authorities have statutory powers, where required, both to advance money on mortgage or to mortgage property. Such powers are conferred by the statutes regulating the authority in question. Thus, water authorities,[35] and internal drainage boards[36] may raise money on

[26] See further *Buckley on the Companies Act* (14th ed.).
[27] *Baroness Wenlock* v. *River Dee Co.* (1883) 36 Ch.D. 675.
[28] s.172, Sched. 13, and see the Local Government Act 1985, ss.70, 71, 75, 76.
[29] Usually the Secretary of State for the Environment.
[30] Local Government Act 1972, Sched. 13, para. 20.
[31] Local Government Act 1972, Sched. 13, para. 2.
[32] See, *e.g.* Housing Act 1985, s.451.
[33] See further *ante*, Chap. 12, p. 153.
[34] Housing Act 1985, s.451.
[35] See the Water Act 1973, s.2(8), Sched. 3, para. 2.
[36] See the Land Drainage Act 1976, s.87.

mortgage. The Agricultural Mortgage Corporation Limited has power to make advances by way of mortgage,[37] and to issue debentures.[38] The National Trust may also borrow money by way of mortgage of its alienable property.[39-40]

HOUSING ASSOCIATIONS

Housing associations[41-42]

By virtue of the Housing Act 1985 a Housing Association[43-44] is "a society, body of trustees or company established for the purpose of, or amongst whose objects or powers are included those of, providing, constructing, improving, or managing, or facilitating or encouraging the construction or improvement of houses or hostels, being a society, body of trustees or company who do not trade for profit or whose constitution or rules prohibit the issue of any capital with interest or dividend exceeding the rate for the time being prescribed by the Treasury, whether with or without differentiation as between share and loan capital."[45] A housing association may be either an industrial and provident society,[46] a company registered under the Companies Act 1985,[47] or unincorporated. It may also be a charity.[48] It may or not be registered under the Housing Associations Act 1985 and the land which it acquires may or may not be grant-aided.[49-50]

The housing corporation

The housing corporation was established by Part I of the Housing Act 1964. Its functions were extended by the Housing Act 1974 and are now consolidated in the Housing Associations Act 1985. It is a body corporate with perpetual succession and has a common seal. The objects of the Housing Corporation are to promote and assist the development of registered housing associations and unregistered self-build societies, to facilitate the proper performance of the functions of such associations and to publicise their aims and principles. Further, it is to establish and maintain a register of housing associations and to exercise supervision and control over them and to undertake the provision of dwellings for letting or sale and of hostels and the management of dwellings or hostels provided by the Corpor-

---

[37] See the Agricultural Credits Act 1928, ss.1, 2.
[38] See the Trustee Investments Act 1961, s.1, Sched. 1, Part II, para. 8. Part IV, paras. 1, 2, 4.
[39-40] See the National Trust Act 1907, s.22.
[41-42] As to the history and the development of the various types of housing associations see (Craddock), (1959) 23 Conv. (N.S.) 3.
[43-44] This includes a housing society.
[45] Housing Associations Act 1985, s.1(1).
[46] See *post*, p. 191.
[47] See *ante*, p. 187.
[48] See *ante*, p. 186.
[49-50] See the Housing Associations Act 1985, s.9(1), Sched. 1.

ation.[51] The housing corporation also has certain borrowing powers[52] and it also is empowered to make loans to housing associations.[53] By virtue of section 9 of the 1985 Act a registered housing association may, not, *inter alia*, mortgage any land, and an unregistered association may not, *inter alia*, mortgage grant-aided land, except with the consent of the Housing Corporation.[54]

INDUSTRIAL AND PROVIDENT SOCIETIES[55]

Generally the rules of each society must provide whether it may enter into loans or receive money on deposit from members or other persons, and if so, under what conditions, on what security and to what amounts.[56] Such mortgages and charges over the property of industrial and provident societies do not require registration with the Chief Registrar of Friendly Societies. A mortgagee is not bound to inquire as to the relevant authorisation for the mortgage by the society, and the society's receipt is a good discharge for all monies arising from such a transaction.[57]

Charges may be created by industrial and provident societies on their personal chattels free from the provisions of the Bills of Sale Acts 1878 and 1882 if an application is lodged within 14 days at the central office established under the Friendly Societies Act 1896 to record the charge.[58]

A registered industrial and provident society may by its rules provide for advances of money to members on the security of real or personal property or, if the society is registered to carry on banking business, in any manner customary in the conduct of such business.[59] Further, advances can be made to members of agricultural, horticultural, or forestry societies for agricultural, horticultural or forestry purposes without security.[60]

FRIENDLY SOCIETIES

Generally, provided that a registered society or branch's rules permit it to hold land and buildings, such land can be mortgaged.[61]

The trustees of a registered society or branch may, with the consent of the committee or of a majority of the members present and entitled to vote in a general meeting, invest the funds of the society or branch or any part

---

[51] *Ibid.* s.75.
[52] *Ibid.* ss.92, 93.
[53] *Ibid.* s.79(1).
[54] If, however, the association is a registered charity and the mortgage requires consent or an order under s.29 of the Charities Act 1960, such consent under the Housing Associations Act is not required.
[55] Building Societies are dealt with in Chap. 9, *ante*, p. 112.
[56] Industrial and Provident Societies Act 1965, s.1 and Sched. 1.
[57] *Ibid.* s.30(1).
[58] *Ibid.* s.1.
[59] *Ibid.* s.21.
[60] *Ibid.* s.12.
[61] Friendly Societies Act 1974, s.51 which implies a power to borrow, and see s.23(2).

thereof, *inter alia*, upon any security expressly directed by the rules of the society or branch, not being a personal security, but only as authorised by the provisions of the Friendly Societies Act 1974 with respect to loans[62] and in any investments authorised by law for investment of trust funds.[63] The Act also makes provisions for loans to members out of a separate loan fund.[64]

---

[62] Friendly Societies Act 1974, ss.48 and 49.
[63] *Ibid.* s.46(1)(*d*), (*e*).
[64] *Ibid.* s.49.

CHAPTER 14

RIGHTS, DUTIES AND REMEDIES OF THE MORTGAGEE OR CHARGEE

INTRODUCTION

The essential feature of lending money by means of a mortgage is that the lender becomes a secured creditor of the borrower. The lender's rights and remedies enable him to enforce his rights against the mortgaged property in the event of a default by the borrower. He will have first call on the mortgaged property on the assumption that he is the first and only mortgagee. By reason of the fact that in earlier times the mortgage contract was in essence regarded as an investment by the the mortgagee, the principles of law became established during the course of the nineteenth and the early part of the present century to the effect that the mortgagee should have complete freedom to realise his security in the event of default on the part of the mortgagor. Most of the mortgagee's rights and remedies as developed are now enshrined in statutory enactments, in particular the Law of Property Act 1925.

These principles, however, must now be viewed in the light of the various developments which have occurred in recent years which have tended to temper the strict application of the mortgagee's remedies. The reason for this is simple: since the 1930s, and more particularly since the last war, successive governments have placed strong emphasis on home ownership. Concomitant with this has been the growth in lending by the building societies, and latterly by the banks, who provide funds for the purchase of dwelling-houses secured by way of mortgage. Thus, the traditional rights and remedies of the mortgagee have required some readjustment in order to meet the changing role of the mortgage. Substantial restrictions have been placed on the mortgagee's ability to realise his security both by statute and by the courts in order to provide a measure of protection for a mortgagor in the occupation of his own home, the result being to "temper the wind to the shorn lamb."[1] But the process of erosion of the mortgagee's remedies must not be exaggerated. In this context it must be remembered that although there has been an enormous growth in institutional lending for home ownership the number of defaults is small in comparison with the total. The reason for this is not that building societies and banks necessarily fail to enforce their security (and there is some evidence that building societies in particular "hold back" in times of crisis), but more that such institutional lenders will, prior to lending, usually make

---

[1] *Redditch Benefit Building Society* v. *Roberts* [1940] Ch. 415 at 420 and *post*, p. 241.

extensive enquiries into the potential borrower's means in order to ensure that he or she can service the level of borrowing.

Mortgagee's interest limited to the security

The mortgagor is in equity the beneficial owner of the mortgaged property until his interest is lost to him by the realisation of the security, or by lapse of time. The corollary is that the mortgagee's interest in the property is solely as a security until he acquires full beneficial ownership by a decree for foreclosure absolute, or by lapse of time. This principle was clearly stated in the case of *Thornborough* v. *Baker*[2-4] where Lord Nottingham held that, in a mortgage of land, if redemption took place after the death of the mortgagee, the redemption moneys must be paid to the personal representatives and not to his heir-at-law. At that date the legal title to land necessarily passed to the heir-at-law whereas the title to a contract debt passed to the personal representatives. Lord Nottingham's decision thus meant that the substance of a mortgagee's interest is not his title to the mortgage property which he holds as security, but his right to the mortgage moneys. Although at law the mortgagee's title is made absolute by the passing of the contract date for redemption, in equity it is his beneficial interest in the title which remains his security for enforcing payment of the mortgage debt. Hence, the legal title in the hands of the heir-at-law could not carry any beneficial interest in the mortgage debt which belonged to the personal representatives and in equity was held on the latter's behalf to enforce the debt. In other words, although at law his title gives to a mortgagee a right to the property, in equity his interest in the mortgage comprises his debt, his use of the title as security for the debt and nothing more.[5]

Mortgagee not a trustee

A mortgagee has, therefore, two titles, the title to the mortgaged property, which he holds subject to the mortgagor's equity of redemption, and his own beneficial interest in the property as a security. At first sight a mortgagee seems to be very like a trustee, for he holds a title to give effect to equitable rights vested in himself and another. But, although there is some analogy between the conceptions of mortgage and trust, a mortgagee is not a trustee.[6] It has been said repeatedly that no fiduciary relationship arises between a mortgagor and a mortgagee until the latter has been paid off.[7] Then, the mortgagee does indeed become a trustee of the legal estate, if the mortgage has been redeemed,[8] and of the surplus proceeds of sale if

---

[2-4] (1676) 1 Ch.Cas. 283.

[5] This position was altered by s.30 of the Conveyancing Act 1881, and the Land Transfer Act 1897, both of which have now been replaced as to deaths after 1925 by the Administration of Estates Act 1925, ss.1(1), 3(1)(ii). But the principle is still of importance.

[6] *Marquis of Cholmondely* v. *Lord Clinton* (1820) 2 J. & W. 1; and see Turner, *Equity of Redemption* (1931), Chap. 8.

[7] *Kennedy* v. *De Trafford* [1897] A.C. 180.

[8] *Taylor* v. *Russell* [1892] A.C. 244.

the property has been sold under a power of sale.[9] But a mortgagee is not a trustee of the power of sale, for the power of sale is given to the mortgagee for his own benefit to enable him to realise his security,[10] although such power must be exercised bona fide and with reasonable care.[11] Thus, until a mortgagee has been satisfied, his interest in the property is essentially adverse to that of the mortgagor, but this is never so between a trustee and a *cestui que trust*. The suggestion that a mortgagee acts in a fiduciary capacity was strongly attacked by Plumer M.R., in the case of *Marquis of Cholmondely* v. *Lord Clinton*,[12] in a passage which would seem to leave no room for further argument. Yet, in one form or another, the fallacy has reappeared from time to time, and in the more recent case of *Allen and Clarke* v. *O'Hearne & Co.*[13] the Privy Council had occasion again to deny the trusteeship of a mortgagee.

There are, in fact, several points on which the characters of mortgagee and trustee diverge. The most conspicuous are:

(1) A legal mortgagee has, in general, an absolute right to take possession of the mortgaged property, whereas dispossession of a *cestui que trust* would be a breach of trust[14];

(2) Purchases by trustees from their beneficiaries are regarded with the utmost jealousy. Whereas mortgagees are free to purchase the equity of redemption as the relationship is considered to be that of vendor and purchaser unless and until the mortgagor is able to show any fraud or oppression on the part of the mortgagee or when there is pressure and inequality of bargaining position, and the mortgagee has obtained the purchase at a nominal or insufficient price. Undervalue alone will not be sufficient to set the transaction aside[15];

(3) In foreclosure proceedings the court actually assists a mortgagee to acquire the equity of redemption, whereas such a thing is unthinkable in the case of a trustee;

(4) A mortgagee in possession may, while a trustee in possession never can, acquire a title under the statute of limitation[16];

(5) Apart from his duty to act in good faith and with reasonable care particularly with regard to the obtaining of a full price (see

---

[9] *Rajah Kishendatt Ram* v. *Rajah Mumtaz Ali Khan* (1879) L.R. 6 Ind.App. 145; *Banner* v. *Berridge* (1881) 18 Ch.D. 254.

[10] See *Warner* v. *Jacob* (1882) 20 Ch.D. 220 at 224; and see *post*, pp. 228 *et seq* for the various duties of the mortgagee as vendor.

[11] For power of sale see *post*, pp. 220 *et seq*, and see *Cuckmere Brick Co. Ltd.* v. *Mutual Finance Ltd.* [1971] Ch. 949; *Bishop* v. *Bonham* [1988] 1 W.L.R. 742. See *post*, pp. 231 *et seq*. With regard to the duties of building societies and the exercise of the power of sale, see Building Societies Act 1986, s.13(7) and Sched. 4, para. 1 and pp. 229 *et seq*.

[12] (1820) 2 J. & W. 1 at 182 *et seq*.

[13] [1937] A.C. 213 at 219.

[14] *Marquis of Cholmondely* v. *Lord Clinton* (1820) 2 J. & W. 1, at 183.

[15] *Knight* v. *Marjoribanks* (1849) 2 Mac & G. 10; *Ford* v. *Olden* (1867), L.R. 3 Eq. 461, and see *post*, pp. 229 *et seq*.

[16] *Cf. Re Alison, Johnson* v. *Mounsey* (1879) 11 Ch.D. 284.

above), a mortgagee, in exercising his powers, need have little
regard for the mortgagor's interest, whereas that is the whole
duty of the trustee[17];

(6) A mortgagee in possession is liable to account on the footing of
wilful default without it being specially pleaded, whereas a special
case must be made out for charging a trustee with wilful default.[18]

Thus, a mortgagee is plainly not a trustee for the mortgagor.

That being so, a mortgagee, not being a trustee, is entitled to exercise
the legal and equitable rights which he obtains by the mortgage solely to
advance his own interests. The only restraints upon him are those which
require him to act not only in good faith[19] but also with reasonable care[20]
particularly with regard to taking reasonable care to obtain the best
price.[21] The only other restraints upon the mortgagee are the equitable
rules which establish and regulate the mortgagor's right of redemption.
This means that as the mortgagee's interest is limited to his security, so
long as any right of redemption still exists, he cannot make any personal
profits out of the mortgaged property beyond those which result directly
from the mortgage bargain. Thus an accretion to the mortgaged property,
for example by the exercise of an option to purchase, benefits the mortgagee by enlarging his security, but it belongs to the mortgagor.[22] Similarly, any profits from the property, which are intercepted by the
mortgagee after exercising his legal right to take possession, must be
placed to the credit of the mortgagor. The only beneficial interest of the
mortgagee in the property until foreclosure is as a security for the mortgage
debt.

Part of a mortgagee's security derives directly from his title to the property or from rights granted by the mortgage agreement. Not all his rights
are, however, expressed in the agreement because equity, in subjecting his
title to the equity of redemption, at the same time provides him with rights
and remedies for the protection and realisation of his security. Thus, the
right to possession of the property follows from his legal title but the right
to foreclose or to obtain the judicial appointment of a receiver or a judicial
sale are equitable rights. The legal and equitable rights and remedies of the

---

[17] *Davey* v. *Durrant, Smith* v. *Durrant* (1857) 1 De G. & J. 535; but see *post*, p. 228 for the
mortgagee's duties as vendor.
[18] *Dobson* v. *Land* (1850) 8 Hare 216 at 220.
[19] *Tomlin* v. *Luce* (1889) 43 Ch.D. 191; and see *Cuckmere Brick Co. Ltd.* v. *Mutual Finance
Ltd.* [1971] Ch. 949.
[20] In *Standard Chartered Bank Ltd.* v. *Walker* [1982] 1 W.L.R. 1410 and *American Express
International Banking Corporation* v. *Hurley* [1985] F.L.R. 350, the liability of the mortgagee to the mortgagor's guarantor was considered to be a matter of tort. But the relationship between the mortgagee and the guarantor is a matter of contract, (see Lord Scarman
in *Tai Hing Cotton Mill Ltd.* v. *Liu Chong Hing Bank Ltd.* [1986] 1 A.C. 80 at 96; *National
Bank of Greece S.A.* v. *Pinios (No. 1)* [1989] 1 All E.R. 253; and see *post*, p. 231.
[21] *Cuckmere Brick Co. Ltd.* v. *Mutual Finance Ltd.* [1971] Ch. 949, in which *Kennedy* v. *De
Trafford* [1897] A.C. 180 was explained. See also *Holohan* v. *Friends Provident and Century Life Office* [1966] I.R. 1; *Bishop* v. *Bonham* [1988] 1 W.L.R. 742. See *post*, p. 231.
[22] *Nelson* v. *Hannam* [1943] Ch. 59.

mortgagee, both in and out of court, make up the sum total of the mortgagee's security and will now be examined in detail.

THE EXERCISE BY THE MORTGAGEE OF HIS RIGHTS AND REMEDIES

Foreclosure, sale and the personal action on the covenant for payment may be termed *final* remedies arising from the nature of the security, their object being to recover capital and to obtain a final settlement from the mortgagor. Entry into possession and the appointment of a receiver, on the other hand, are not normally final remedies. It is true that a mortgagee in possession, after meeting outgoings and the mortgage interest, is entitled to apply surplus rents and profits to the discharge of the principal and a receiver appointed by the mortgagee may do the same, if so directed. But the surplus is not usually large enough to enable the principal to be paid off except over a longer period than is acceptable to the mortgagee. Consequently entry into possession and the appointment of a receiver are essentially interim remedies employed out of court to protect the security and keep down the interest—very often as a preliminary step to the realisation of the security by foreclosure or sale.

A mortgagee's choice of remedy naturally depends on the particular circumstances both of the mortgaged property and of the debtor. If the property is worth the money secured by the mortgage, or if it is likely to increase in value with good management, foreclosure may be the best course. In other cases, if the property is let to tenants or otherwise produces appreciable income, the appointment of a receiver out of court followed by a sale may provide the simplest means of realising the mortgage. If, however, the mortgagor is in possession, there is nothing for the receiver to receive and the fact that vacant possession cannot be given is an obstacle to sale. Then recourse may be had to a summons for possession followed by a sale out of court. A personal action on the covenant for payment is always available as an additional remedy where the security is insufficient to meet the mortgage debt. It has, of course, particular value where the mortgagor has other property which can be reached by a judgment.

Concurrent exercise of a mortgagee's rights and remedies

Once the mortgagor is in default the mortgagee is entitled to pursue all his remedies concurrently. He may simultaneously take proceedings to obtain foreclosure or sale, possession or the appointment of a receiver, delivery of the title deeds and payment on the personal covenant. If he has any collateral securities, he may also enforce these at the same time.[23] If his mortgage empowers him to sell or to appoint a receiver out of court, he may exercise these powers despite the fact that he has already begun proceedings for foreclosure.[24] There are, however, two qualifications on the

[23] *Lockhart* v. *Hardy* (1846) 9 Beav. 349; *Palmer* v. *Hendrie* (1859) 27 Beav. 349 at 351.
[24] *Stevens* v. *Theatres Ltd.* [1903] 1 Ch. 857.

right to exercise remedies concurrently. Once an order nisi for foreclosure has been obtained, the leave of the court is necessary for a sale out of court.[25] Secondly, if a mortgagee takes proceedings for foreclosure and for payment on the personal covenant concurrently, he must do so in the *same* proceedings. As it is open to him to ask for foreclosure and for judgment on the covenant in the *same* action, the duplication of the concurrent actions will be regarded as vexatious. He may, as will be seen, take separate proceedings for foreclosure and payment *successively* but, if he does so *concurrently*, the action on the covenant will be struck out as vexatious.[26]

Successive exercise of remedies

A mortgagee may also pursue his remedies successively. The fact that he has enforced one remedy does not prevent him from afterwards pursuing another, unless by enforcing the first he has paid himself off. If a judgment on the covenant is only partially satisfied, or if after a sale there is a deficiency, a mortgagee may still pursue any other remedy that, in the circumstances, is open to him.[27] Even foreclosure absolute does not prevent him from bringing an action on the covenant for payment; if he does so, he reopens the foreclosure, because a person cannot receive payment and keep the estate.[28] Only if he sells the estate after foreclosure are his remedies at an end; he can then no longer return the estate, and has no further rights against the mortgagor.[29] A secured creditor is, therefore, largely outside the rule that separate proceedings must not be brought for different forms of relief claimed in respect of the same transaction.

OUT OF COURT RIGHTS AND LIABILITIES OF THE LEGAL MORTGAGEE

Right to custody of the title deeds

The general rule is that muniments of title follow the legal title, so that the holder of the legal title has a prima facie right to custody of the title deeds.[30] Formerly, this meant that legal mortgagees in fee were, as against the mortgagor, entitled to the deeds,[31] but that legal mortgagees by demise including, of course, most mortgagees of leasehold interests were not entitled to custody of the mortgagor's title deeds.[32] But, mortgages of freeholds and leaseholds were required by sections 85 and 86 of the Law of Property Act 1925 to be by demise and those sections, at the same time,

---

[25] *Stevens* v. *Theatres Ltd* [1903] 1 Ch. 857.
[26] *Williams* v. *Hunt* [1905] 1 K.B. 512.
[27] *Lockhart* v. *Hardy* (1846) 9 Beav. 349 at 355.
[28] *Perry* v. *Barker* (1806) 13 Ves. 198.
[29] *Lockhart* v. *Hardy* (1846) 9 Beav. 349. A bona fide purchaser without notice gets a good title, *Lloyds & Scottish Trust* v. *Britten* (1982) 44 P. & C.R. 249. See also *post*, pp. 248, 261, 263.
[30] As to what is meant by "title deeds" see *Clayton* v. *Clayton* [1930] 2 Ch. 12 at 21. The meaning is used in its widest sense, *i.e.* all documents necessary to prove title.
[31] *Smith* v. *Chichester* (1842) 2 Dr. & War. 393.
[32] *Wiseman & Benley* v. *Westland, Fisher, Benson, Davis & Stanbridge* (1826) 1 Y. & J. 117.

provided for the *first* legal mortgagee to have a right to custody of the deeds. Thus, a first legal mortgagee of a freehold interest has the same right to the deeds as if his title included the fee, whereas a first legal mortgagee of a leasehold interest has the same right to custody of the deeds as if his mortgage had been created by assignment of the lease, instead of by demise. A mortgagee of a leasehold interest is therefore in a better position than he was before the Act, unless he was then a mortgagee by assignment of the lease, which was unusual. An equitable mortgagee, however, not having the legal title, has no right to the deeds as against the mortgagor, unless he stipulates for that right in the contract. Such a stipulation is, of course, almost invariably found in a first equitable mortgage. Thus, generally, the non-possession of the title deeds by the holder of the legal title constitutes notice to a subsequent mortgagee that the property in question is subject to a mortgage. Also the possession of the title deeds by the first legal mortgagee will usually provide difficulties for the mortgagor in raising further finance on the security of the property or otherwise dealing with it to the disadvantage of the first legal mortgagee.

But a first legal mortgagee's rights to the deeds, though absolute against the mortgagor, will not prevail against an equitable mortgagee, who has already obtained the deeds and of whose incumbrance the legal mortgagee therefore has notice.[33] Nor would it prevail, even against a subsequent equitable incumbrancer in possession of the deeds, if the gross negligence of the legal mortgagee in not obtaining the deeds has induced the equitable incumbrancer to believe that there was no prior legal mortgage.[34] In other words, the right to the deeds may sometimes involve the question of competing priorities and the legal mortgagee's normal right to the custody of the deeds may sometimes be displaced.[35]

Registered land

In the case of registered land, however, there are no title deeds on which the first legal mortgagee can take possession. In the case of a registered charge, which is the most common form of legal mortgage, being a charge by way of legal mortgage, the mortgagor deposits his land certificate with the Land Registry, who then issue a "charge certificate" to the mortgagee as proprietor of the registered charge.[36] It is also possible for a mortgagor to arrange a mortgage by a deposit of a land certificate, and this procedure is usually found in the case of short-term loans. But difficulties can occur in the use of such a procedure particularly with regard to the question of priority.

---

[33] It is just conceivable that the legal mortgagee might have a right to the deeds in such a case, see *Agra Bank* v. *Barry* (1874) L.R. 7 H.L. 135, and *post*, p. 348.

[34] See *post*, p. 348.

[35] Since the Judicature Act 1873, it is in all cases the duty of the court to give complete relief by ordering the delivery of the deeds to the incumbrancer, who has priority. *Re Cooper, Cooper* v. *Vesey* (1882) 20 Ch.D. 611; *Re Ingham, Jones* v. *Ingham* [1893] 1 Ch. 352.

[36] See s.27 of the Land Registration Act 1925, and see *ante*, Chap. 4, p. 35.

Liability of the mortgagee in possession of deeds to produce them

Before 1882 a mortgagor could not compel his mortgagee to produce the title deeds for inspection without tendering the mortgage moneys[37] and this was so even though the deeds were required for the purpose of negotiating a loan to pay off the existing mortgage.[38] This rule still applies to any mortgages created before January 1, 1882, but it is reversed with regard to later mortgages by section 96(1) of the Law of Property Act 1925,[39] which provides as follows:

> "A mortgagor, as long as his right to redeem subsists, shall be entitled from time to time, at reasonable times, on his request, and at his own cost, and on payment of the mortgagee's costs and expenses in this behalf, to inspect and make copies or abstracts of or extracts from the documents of title relating to the mortgaged property in the custody or power of the mortgagee."

Moreover, the section expressly forbids any contracting out of the above provision. It will also be noted that the subsection does not entitle the mortgagor to *borrow* the title deeds.

A mortgagee's liability under section 96 is not limited to producing the title deeds for the mortgagor only, because "mortgagor" also includes "any person from time to time deriving title under the original mortgagor or entitled to redeem a mortgage according to his estate, interest, or right in the mortgaged property."[40] Presumably, in the case of trust property, the liability is only to produce the deeds to the trustees unless, owing to the default of the trustees, the beneficiaries are admitted to redeem in their place. But in the case of settled land the primary liability is, of course, to the life-tenant who holds for all persons entitled under the settlement,[41] and he is entitled to production of the title deeds. Whether a vested remainderman has a right to the production of the deeds is uncertain. He certainly had the right before 1926, when his remainder was a legal estate, and it may well be that this right still exists, although his interest is now equitable only. Logically, his right should be confined to the case when he has the consent of the life-tenant to redeem, which he must obtain before he can redeem the mortgaged property.[42]

A mortgagee, whose debt has been satisfied, must at once deliver up any deeds which are in his possession.[43] When the person redeeming is not the mortgagor, he has a right to keep the mortgage alive for his own benefit,

---

[37] *Browne* v. *Lockhart* (1840) 10 Sim. 420.
[38] See Coote, *Mortgages* (9th ed., 1927), Vol. 2, p. 841.
[39] Replacing s.16 of the Conveyancing Act 1881.
[40] L.P.A. 1925, s.205(1)(xvi).
[41] See the Settled Land Act 1925, s.107(1).
[42] In *Halsbury's Laws of England* (4th ed., 1980), Vol. 32, para. 757, the view is expressed that as the vested remainderman has a right to redeem he therefore has the statutory right to production of the title deeds.
[43] See *Graham* v. *Seal* (1918) 88 L.J.Ch. 31.

and is entitled to the deeds. But when it is the mortgagor who redeems, a mortgagee is not always obliged to hand over the deeds to him: on the contrary, if he has notice of puisne incumbrances, it is his duty to deliver the deeds to the incumbrancer next in priority of whom the mortgagee has notice.[44] If he does not do so he is liable to make good any loss resulting to the incumbrancer concerned. In this instance, however, contrary to the general rule that registration is notice, registration under the Land Charges Act 1972 or in a local register is *not* deemed to be equivalent to actual notice. Accordingly, there is no need to make a search at either registry before handing over the deeds, although a mortgagee is bound to search the appropriate registries before he distributes any surplus after a sale.[45] Thus, a mortgagee is under no liability to persons of whose interest he has neither actual nor constructive notice, even though they have registered their incumbrances.[46]

Liability for loss of deeds

A mortgagee, whose mortgage includes the deeds, must be ready to give up the deeds when the debt is satisfied.[47] This duty arises from the fact that the deeds are part of the mortgaged property and the mortgagor is entitled to the return of the whole of his property.[48] Thus, a mortgagee's liability for loss of the deeds arises, not from breach of contract, nor from negligence as a bailee, but from the breach of his duty to return the property. This being so, a mortgagor cannot fix the mortgagee with liability, except when he is offering to redeem. This somewhat questionable state of affairs arises as a result of the provisions of section 13 of the Law of Property Act 1925 which, in effect, preserves the principle of the pre-1926 law, which was that the mortgagee, being owner of the land, was also owner of the deeds and could not be liable for losing his own property.[49] During the currency of the security the mortgagor has, it is true, a right to inspect the deeds under section 96 of the Law of Property Act and presumably might be able to bring an action against the mortgagee for damages for breach of his statutory duty under that section, but such damages could not include a sum for the permanent loss of the deeds.[50]

The loss of the deeds does not prevent a mortgagee from pursuing his

---

[44] *Corbett* v. *National Provident Institution* (1900) 17 T.L.R. 5.

[45] See *post*, p. 235.

[46] See Law of Property (Amendment) Act 1926, s.7 and the L.P.A. 1925 Schedule of Minor Amendments, which alters s.96(2) of the L.P.A. 1925 to this extent. See also L.P.A. 1969, s.16(2), Sched. 2 Pt. I; Land Charges Act 1972, s18(6).

[47] See *Schoole* v. *Sall* (1803) 1 Sch. & Lef. 176.

[48] See *Gilligan and Nugent* v. *National Bank* [1901] 2 I.R. 513.

[49] In the case of *Browning* v. *Handiland Group Ltd.* (1976) 35 P. & C.R. 345 it was held that a mortgagee owed no duty of care in relation to the documents of title and thus the mortgagor was unable to recover the loss incurred when a projected sale failed as a result of the loss of the deeds.

[50] See *Gilligan and Nugent* v. *National Bank* [1901] 2 I.R. 513.

remedies.[51] It only exposes him to an obligation to make compensation, should the mortgagor offer to redeem.[52] At one time the liability to make compensation was absolute, but now the court has jurisdiction to give relief in cases of accident. The practice appears to be as follows:

(1) When a mortgagor is prevented from redeeming by reason of the absence of the deeds, he has an absolute right to take out a summons for redemption for the sole purpose of having an inquiry as to the loss of the deeds.[53] The object of the proceedings is to establish the fact of the loss in a way which will satisfy future purchasers from the mortgagor and the mortgagee will be made to bear the costs of the action. The offer of an indemnity is not enough; the master's inquiry is a protection to which the mortgagor is absolutely entitled.[54] The position is the same when redemption is forced upon the mortgagor in a foreclosure action.[55]

(2) If the master certifies that the loss was not due to any negligence or wilful default on the part of the mortgagee, the mortgagor is entitled only to an indemnity against future charges and expenses which may result from the absence of the deeds.[56]

(3) But if the loss is found to have been due to the negligence or other default of the mortgagee, the mortgagor is entitled both to an indemnity and to immediate compensation.[57] Compensation will cover the expense of procuring new copies of deeds where that is possible and of office-copies of any proceedings taken to establish the loss, and in addition a sum by way of damages for future difficulties in proving title. This last is, however, confined to extra expense in proving title, and may not include a speculative amount for possible depreciation of the market value of the estate caused by the lack of the deeds.[58]

(4) If the result of the inquiry is that the deeds are found not to be lost, but to be in the hands of a third party, the mortgagor will be directed to bring an action for their recovery, the expenses of the action to be debited to the mortgagee.[59]

(5) If a mortgagor has given notice to redeem and then been prevented from doing so owing to the loss of the deeds, interest ceases to run from that date when redemption was due to take place, even though he does not hand over his money. He cannot

[51] *Baskett* v. *Skeel* (1863) 11 W.R. 1019.
[52] *Stokoe* v. *Robson* (1815) 19 Ves. 385.
[53] *James* v. *Rumsey* (1879) 11 Ch.D. 398.
[54] *Lord Midleton* v. *Eliot* (1847) 15 Sim. 531.
[55] *Stokoe* v *Robson* (1815) 19 Ves. 385; *Shelmardine* v. *Harrop* (1821) 6 Madd. 39.
[56] *Shelmardine* v. *Harrop* (1821) 6 Madd. 39, where the mortgagee was robbed.
[57] *Hornby* v. *Matcham* (1848) 16 Sim. 325.
[58] *Ibid.*; *Brown* v. *Sewell* (1853) 11 Hare 49.
[59] *James* v. *Rumsey* (1879) 11 Ch.D. 398.

be expected to part with his money except in return for his whole security.[60]

Right to maintain the security

A mortgagee is entitled to take all steps necessary to perfect and protect his security, and may debit the mortgagor with any costs or charges which he incurs thereby. Thus a legal mortgagee who discovers a defect in his title may call upon the mortgagor to remedy it if that becomes possible.[61] The rule is not, of course, confined to mortgages. "The doctrine of the Court of Chancery," said Cranworth L.C., in the case of *Smith* v. *Osborne*,[62] is "that if a man contracts to convey, or to mortgage, or to settle an estate, and he has not at the time of his contract a title to the estate, but he afterwards acquires such a title as enables him to perform his contract, he shall be bound to do so." On this principle an equitable mortgagee has a right to call for the execution of a legal mortgage and to charge the mortgagor with the costs of repairing it.[63] He may enforce this right, even though the mortgagor has begun proceedings for redemption.[64] Moreover, an equitable mortgagee who has begun proceedings for foreclosure may obtain an interim injunction to prevent dealings with the legal estate intended where there are grounds for believing that the mortgagor intends to do something improper with the legal estate.[65]

Rights against third parties

A mortgagee may protect the security against third parties who impeach the mortgagor's title by claiming a title paramount; he may take any proceedings necessary to defend the mortgagor's title and may add the costs to the mortgage debt.[66] It is, however, necessary to distinguish carefully between cases where third parties are attacking or dealing vexatiously with the mortgagor's title and cases where the mortgagee's own title to the security is impeached by third parties. In the latter case the mortgagee must bear the cost of defending himself.[67] An unusual application of this rule occurred in the case of *Re Smith's Mortgage, Harrison* v. *Edwards*[68] in which a first mortgagee sold under his power of sale and realised a sufficient sum to provide something for the second mortgagee. The mortgagor, however, impeached the sale and the first mortgagee incurred costs

---

[60] *Lord Midleton* v. *Eliot* (1847) 15 Sim. 531; *James* v. *Rumsey* (1879) 11 Ch.D. 398.
[61] *Seabourne* v. *Powel* (1686) 2 Vern. 11.
[62] (1857) 6 H.L.C. 375 at 390.
[63] *National Provincial Bank of England* v. *Games* (1886) 31 Ch.D. 582.
[64] *Grugeon* v. *Gerrard* (1840) 4 Y. & C. (Ex.) 119.
[65] *London & County Banking Co.* v. *Lewis* (1882) 21 Ch.D. 490.
[66] *Sandon* v. *Hooper* (1843) 6 Beav. 246, on appeal (1844) 14 L.J.Ch. 120, L.C.
[67] *Parker* v. *Watkins* (1859) John 133.
[68] [1931] 2 Ch. 168.

in establishing its validity. He was not, as against the second mortgagee, allowed to add these costs to his mortgage debt, for he was defending himself rather than the title to the mortgaged property.

Right to preserve the substance of the security

A mortgagee is also entitled to preserve the substance of his security. A legal mortgagee is to a large extent able to protect his security against the acts of the mortgagor by reason of his legal ownership, but every mortgagee, legal or equitable has a general right in equity, as against the mortgagor, to hold the security undiminished in value.[69] Thus, if a mortgagor is wasting the security by cutting timber,[70] or by removing fixtures included in the security,[71] he may be restrained from doing so, provided that the security is shown to be insufficient. But even when the mortgagor's acts do not amount to waste, they may be restrained if it be shown that the security is insufficient and will be prejudiced. For example, mortgagors of tolls were restrained from reducing the toll fees, the security being insufficient.[72]

A mortgagee may similarly interfere to prevent depreciation of the security from other causes. He may, for example, restrain by injunction a subsequent incumbrancer from dealing with the property to his prejudice.[73] If the mortgage comprises licensed premises, he may take part in proceedings to obtain the renewal of the licence.[74] Again, in a case where part of the mortgagee's security was taken under the Land Clauses Acts, he was entitled to be served with notices, and even to claim compensation for "injurious affection" of other lands.[75] Also, where the property is to be compulsorily acquired, the mortgagee as well as the mortgagor is entitled to be served with the notice to treat.[76] Other examples arise in the cases where a mortgagee is entitled to take possession of the property in order to prevent deterioration of his security by vandalism[77] or to prevent injury to the property,[78] or to enforce a restrictive covenant.[79]

A mortgagee's right to take proceedings in respect of damage done to

---

[69] *McMahon* v. *North Kent Iron Works Co.* [1891] 2 Ch. 148, where the mortgage debt was not even yet due.

[70] *Harper* v. *Aplin* (1886) 54 L.T. 383.

[71] *Ackroyd* v. *Mitchell* (1860) 3 L.T. 236; *Ellis* v. *Glover and Hobson, Ltd.* [1908] 1 K.B. 388.

[72] *Lord Crewe* v. *Edleston* (1857) 1 De G. & J. 93; *cf. Re Humber Ironworks Co.* (1868) 16 W.R. 667.

[73] *Legg* v. *Mathieson* (1860) 2 Giff. 71 where a judgment creditor had been restrained at the suit of the prior mortgagee, even before the mortgage debt had become due, from taking possession of the property under the legal right acquired by the former elegit.

[74] *e.g.* he can appeal to the Crown Court against non-renewal of the licence, see *Garrett* v. *St. Marylebone, Middlesex JJ.* (1884) 12 Q.B.D. 620.

[75] *R.* v. *Clerk of the Peace for Middlesex* [1914] 3 K.B. 259.

[76] *Cooke* v. *L.C.C.* [1911] 1 Ch. 604.

[77] See *Western Bank Ltd.* v. *Shindler* [1977] Ch. 1.

[78] *Matthews* v. *Usher* [1900] 2 Q.B 535 at 538; *Turner* v. *Walsh* [1909] 2 K.B. 484 at 487.

[79] *Fairclough* v. *Marshall* (1878) 4 Ex.D. 37.

the mortgaged property by third parties largely depends on his title. If he is a legal mortgagee, or if his contract gives him a right, he may go into possession and avail himself of possessory remedies. He may sue for trespass and, whether his mortgage is legal or equitable, the doctrine of trespass by relation back applies to enable him to sue for trespasses committed before his entry.[80] Similarly, a mortgagee of goods, if he is in possession or has an immediate right to possession, may bring an action in trespass or conversion or seek the recovery of the goods under the provisions of the Torts (Interference with Goods) Act 1977.[81] But, if the mortgagee under the terms of the mortgage is not able either expressly or impliedly to obtain possession until the occurrence of a certain event, for example, a demand for payment and default, proceedings cannot be commenced unless and until the event has occurred.[82] A different picture emerges, however, in the case of an equitable mortgagee. He may stipulate for a right to possession in his contract, but otherwise he can have no right to possession without first enforcing his contract for a legal mortgage.

Although a mortgagee may thus be able to protect his security against third parties, it is not often necessary for him to do so. As a rule, the protection of the property is as much in the interests of the mortgagor as of the mortgagee and action is usually taken by the mortgagor, the mortgagee only being joined as a party where that is necessary.[83] A mortgagor in possession has by virtue of his possession and of the rights given to him in equity and statute, a wide power to take proceedings in defence of the mortgaged property.[84] It is generally only when the mortgagor refuses or is unable to take action that the mortgagee will find it necessary to assert his own rights.[84a]

Right to enter into possession

The legal title which he obtains by his conveyance gives to a legal mortgagee[85] the immediate right to commence an action for possession of the mortgaged security subject to any agreement to the contrary. Normally,

---

[80] *Ocean Accident and Guarantee Corporation* v. *Ilford Gas Co.* [1905] 2 K.B. 493.
[81] But for the recovery of title deeds themselves no action will lie under the 1977 Act; see *post*, p. 314.
[82] *Bradley* v. *Copley* (1845) 1 C.B. 685; a future right to possession is not of course enough, so that a mortgagee cannot sue if he has covenanted to give the mortgagor possession until default: *ibid. Cf. White* v. *Morris* (1852) 11 C.B. 1015, where the mortgagee was allowed to sue when he was a *trustee* to give the mortgagor possession.
[83] See *Van Gelder, Apsimon & Co.* v. *Sowerby Bridge United District Flour Society* (1890) 44 Ch.D. 374. But see in the case of leasehold interests the mortgagee's right to seek relief from forfeiture under the court's inherent jurisdiction or pursuant to statute, *e.g.* s.146(4) of the L.P.A. 1925 *ante*, p. 33.
[84] See the L.P.A. 1925, ss.98 and 141(2).
[84a] *e.g.* this may arise in the case where the mortgagee wishes to seek relief from forfeiture under L.P.A. 1925, s.146(4); see *ante*, pp. 33 *et seq*.
[85] A chargee by way of legal mortgage has a corresponding statutory right by virtue of s.87(1) of the L.P.A. 1925, and see *ante*, p. 24.

the right arises at once on the execution of the conveyance and is based upon the legal estate or interest which the mortgagee acquires as a result of the mortgage.[86] Once the right has arisen, the court will not by injunction restrain the mortgagee from exercising his right.[87] This is so even if there has been no default on the part of the mortgagor,[88] or that a bill of exchange has been given for the debt,[89] or that a considerable time has elapsed, provided that the action for possession is not statute-barred.[90] Alternatively, the mortgagee can enter into receipt of the rent and profits by serving notice on the tenant to pay their rents to himself instead of to the mortgagor.[91]

Qualifications and restrictions

But this right is subject to a number of qualifications and restrictions.

(1) As indicated above, the mortgage deed itself may contain an express term under which the mortgagee contracts out of his right to possession of the property for a given term, provided that the mortgagor maintains the repayments due under the mortgage. This may amount to a redemise or merely to a personal covenant by the mortgagee not to interfere with the mortagor's enjoyment.[92]

(2) An agreement restricting the mortgagee's right may be implied into the mortgage deed to the effect that the mortgagee has surrendered his right to take possession of the property. But in the absence of an express term it is clear that the court will not lightly restrict the mortgagee's right and it has shown considerable reluctance to do so.[93] But it would seem that the court will more readily imply such a term in circumstances where the principal

---

[86] " . . . before the ink is dry on the mortgage . . . ", per Harman J. in Four-Maids Ltd. v. Dudley Marshall (Properties) Ltd. [1957] Ch. 317 at 320; Westminster City Council v. Haymarket Publishing Ltd. [1981] 1 W.L.R. 677 at 696. See also Alliance Permanent Building Society v. Belrum Investments [1957] 1 W.L.R. 720; Western Bank Ltd. v. Shindler [1977] Ch. 1; Mobil Oil Co. Ltd. v. Rawlinson (1982) 43 P. & C.R. 221.

[87] Marquis of Cholmondeley v. Lord Clinton (1820) 2 J. & W. 1 at 181; this, of course, is one of the points of difference between mortgagees and trustees. See also London Permanent Benefit Building Society v. De Baer [1969] 1 Ch. 321.

[88] Birch v. Wright (1786) 1 T.R. 378 at 383; Four-Maids Ltd. v. Dudley Marshall (Properties) Ltd. [1957] Ch. 317; see Rogers v. Grazebrook (1846) 8 Q.B. 895. But see post, p. 207.

[89] Bramwell v. Eglington (1864) 5 B. & S. 39.

[90] Wright v. Pepin [1954] 1 W.L.R. 635.

[91] See post, p. 000. See also Horlock v. Smith (1842) 6 Jur. 478; or merely not to pay the rent to the mortgagor, Heales v. M'Murray (1856) 23 Beav. 401; see also Kitchen's Trustee v. Madders and Madders [1949] Ch. 588. Affd. [1950] Ch. 134; Mexborough U.D.C. v. Harrison [1964] 1 W.L.R. 733 at 736, 737.

[92] Wilkinson v. Hall (1837) 3 Bing. N.C. 508; Doe d. Parsley v. Day (1842) 2 Q.B. 147. Such contractual restrictions are not common.

[93] See Esso Petroleum Co. Ltd. v. Alstonbridge Properties Ltd. [1975] 1 W.L.R. 1474; Western Bank Ltd. v. Shindler [1977] Ch. 1. See [1979] Conv. 266 (R. J. Smith).

moneys are repayable by instalments which is usual in building society (and bank) mortgages.[94] Once there has been a default, however, on the part of the mortgagor, a term restricting the mortgagee's right to possession, whether express or implied, ceases to operate whilst the default continues to occur. Then the mortgagee must take into account a number of the following factors before going into possession of the security:

(a) If a security is land which is already let on a lease binding on the mortgagee, either by reason of the fact that the lease was made prior to the creation of the mortgage, or it is a subsequent lease binding upon him, the mortgagee cannot physically go into possession, however he can enter into receipt of the rents and profits by serving notice on the tenants to pay their rents to himself instead of to the mortgagor.[95]

(b) If the mortgagee desires to seek possession of the premises it is usually advisable to do so by means of court proceedings, and not by physically taking possession. This is especially so if the mortgage deed contains an attornment clause (for the relationship of landlord and tenant is created during the continuance of the security)[96] or if a dwelling-house is the subject of the mortgage in question. If a mortgagee attempts to re-enter premises he *may* be guilty of an offence under the Criminal Law Act 1977.[97] In the case of a dwelling-house an unlawful eviction of a residential occupier *may* also be a criminal offence pursuant to the provisions of the Protection from Eviction Act 1977.[98] But if the premises are vacant or have been abandoned by the mortgagor and the mortgagee has reasonable cause to believe that the residential occupier has ceased to reside therein, or the mortgagor has consented to the taking of possession, then the mortgagee can take possession. Further, if there is an attornment clause it must be remembered that as the *substance* of the transaction is that of a mortgage in relation to which the attornment clause plays an ancillary part, the tenancy is outside the protection of the

---

[94] See *Birmingham Citizens Permanent Building Society* v. *Caunt* [1962] Ch. 883.

[95] See *ante*, n. 9.

[96] See *Regent Oil Co. Ltd.* v. *J.A. Gregory (Hatch End) Ltd.* [1966] Ch. 402. See also *ante*, p. 23. Such clauses are now rare.

[97] *i.e.* of using violence to secure entry, see s.6 (replacing the Forcible Entry Acts 1381–1623, s.13). By virtue of s.6(2) it is no defence that the mortgagee is entitled to possession of the premises.

[98] See ss.2, 3. But there is nothing contained in the Act which affects the jurisdiction of the High Court in possession proceedings in a case where the former tenancy was not binding on the mortgagee (s.9(3)); and see *Bolton Building Society* v. *Cobb* [1965] 1 W.L.R. 1. See also *Midland Bank Ltd.* v. *Monobond* [1971] E.G.D. 673 and *London Goldhawk Building Society* v. *Eminer* (1977) 242 E.G. 462. It is also possible that the mortgagee's right is restricted by virtue of the Administration of Justice Act 1970, s.36 (see *post*, pp. 243 *et seq.*, 501 *et seq.*). See also [1983] Conv. 293 (A. Clarke).

Rent Act 1977, the Protection from Eviction Act 1977, and the Agricultural Holdings Act 1986.[99] Also, unless the attornment clause so provides, there is normally no need for the mortgagee to serve a notice to quit or a demand for possession on the mortgagor.[1]

(c) In the case of a mortgage which secures a regulated agreement under the Consumer Credit Act 1974, it is only enforceable pursuant to an order of the court.[2]

(3) Another way in which a mortgagee may find his desire to go into possession obstructed is by the fact that a receiver has already beeen appointed by the court at the instance of a third party. In such a case he cannot enter into possession, unless his right to do so was specially reserved by the court in the order appointing the receiver. His proper course is, either to apply to the court for the discharge of the receiver, or for leave to bring an action for the recovery of the land.[3] If the mortgagee is prevented from exercising his right by the mortgagor he may bring an action to eject the mortgagor.[4]

(4) A practical factor which tends to inhibit the exercise of the mortgagee's right to possession is the strict liability to account which is placed upon a mortgagee in possession. He is liable to account strictly "on the footing of wilful default." This means that he must account not only for such sums as he actually does receive, but also for all that he ought to have received had he managed the property with due diligence.[5]

(5) A mortgagee cannot obtain a possession order where the property in question is subject to an overriding interest under section 70(1) of the Land Registration Act 1925.[6] By analogy, the claim to an overriding interest by the occupiers of the mortgaged property may inhibit the mortgagee's entry into possession, if the mortgagor or some other person claiming a beneficial interest in

---

[99] Except possibly in the case where there was a full rack rent or the mortgagor was required to reside in the premises see *Portman Building Society* v. *Young* [1951] 1 All E.R. 191; *Alliance Building Society* v. *Pinwill* [1958] Ch. 788; *Peckham Mutual Building Society* v. *Registe* (1980) 42 P. & C.R. 186; *Steyning and Littlehampton B.S.* v. *Wilson* [1951] Ch. 1018 and see *ante*, p. 23.

[1] *Hinkley Building Society* v. *Henny* [1953] 1 W.L.R. 352. As the status of the mortgagor in possession has been likened to that of a tenant at sufference who can be ejected without any possession, (see further *ante*, p. 23), and *post*, pp. 284 *et seq*.

[2] s.126. See also *Encyclopedia of Consumer Credit Law*, para. 2.127, and see generally *ante* Chap. 11, pp. 140 *et seq* and *post*, p. 247.

[3] *Thomas* v. *Brigstocke* (1827) 4 Russ. 64.

[4] *Doe d. Roby* v. *Maisey* (1828) 8 B. & C. 767.

[5] *Chaplin* v. *Young (No. 1)* (1864) 33 Beav. 330. at 337, 338. See also *White* v. *City of London Brewery Co.* (1889) 42 Ch.D. 237 and *Shepherd* v. *Spansheath* (1988) E.G.C.S. 35; and further *post*, p. 212.

[6] See *Williams & Glyn's Bank Ltd.* v. *Boland* [1981] A.C. 487 except where such overriding interests have been overreached. *City of London Building Society* v. *Flegg* [1988] A.C. 54; see *post*, pp. 361–366.

the property seeks to restrain the mortgagee from taking possession.

(6) Reference should also be made to the court's general discretion and its specific statutory discretion to grant a stay in a possession action brought by a mortgagee.[7]

What amounts to possession

Where a mortgagee is in personal occupation of land or has obtained actual possession of chattels, his possession is beyond argument. But when his alleged entry into possession consists merely of some interference with the mortgaged property, it may be doubtful whether or not his acts amount to a taking of possession. Nor is this an academic question, for a mortgagee, by entering into possession renders himself liable to account to the mortgagor with considerable strictness for the profits which he has received while in possession.[8] Indeed, for this reason the court will not readily hold a mortgagee to be in possession, unless it is clearly established that such was his position.[9] In the case of *Noyes* v. *Pollock*[10] the Court of Appeal ruled that to be in possession a mortgagee must have so far interfered with the mortgaged property as to take over its control and management. The mortgagee's receipt of certain rents, even by cheques made out by the tenants themselves, was there held not to be enough for it was not shown that he had taken over the power of management.[11] Similarly a mortgagee does not, by foreclosing, render himself liable to account as the mortgagee in possession if the foreclosure is reopened: he must have gone on to control and manage the property.[12] Moreover, even when a mortgagee is admittedly in possession, it must also be shown that he took possession in his capacity as mortgagee without reasonable grounds for believing himself to hold in another capacity.[13] A mortgagee who is in possession as tenant[14] to the mortgagor, as a life-tenant,[15] or as a purchaser[16] under a sale which turns out to be invalid, cannot be called on to account as a mortgagee in possession, for his possession does not rest on his character as mortgagee. A similar position arose where possession was taken under a forfeiture, and not as a mortgagee.[17] On the other hand, once a mortgagee has

---

[7] See *post*, pp. 240 *et seq*.

[8] See *ante*, p. 208 and *post*, pp. 446 *et seq*.

[9] *Gaskell* v. *Gosling* [1896] 1 Q.B. 669.

[10] (1886) 32 Ch.D. 53; but see *Mexborough Urban District Council* v. *Harrison* [1964] 1 W.L.R. 733 at 736, 737, where the mortgagee gave notice to the tenants not to pay rent to the mortgagor.

[11] *Contra* the positions where the mortgagee gives notice to the tenants to pay their rents to him, see *Horlock* v. *Smith* (1842) 11 L.J.Ch. 157.

[12] *Re Loom, Fulford* v. *Reversionary Interest Society Ltd.* (1910) 2 Ch.D. 230.

[13] *Parkinson* v. *Hanbury* (1867) L.R. 2 H.L. 1; *Gaskell* v. *Gosling* [1896] 1 Q.B. 609 at 691; *Page* v. *Linwood* (1837) 4 Cl. & Finn. 399.

[14] *Page* v. *Linwood* (1837) 4 Cl. & Finn. 399.

[15] *Lord Kensington* v. *Bouverie* (1855) 7 De. G.M. & G. 156; see also *Whitbread* v. *Smith* (1854) 3 De G.M. & G. 727.

[16] *Parkinson* v. *Hanbury* (1867) L.R. 2 H.L. 1.

[17] *Blennerhassett* v. *Day* (1812) 2 Ball & B. 104 at 125.

entered into possssion as mortgagee and taken upon himself the burden which is imposed on all mortgagees who are in possession, he must continue to perform the duty, and he cannot, when he pleases, elect to give it up. Nor, in the absence of special circumstances, will the court assist him to give it up by appointing a receiver under an express or statutory power.[18]

Where the mortgaged property has a bounded and defined area, entry on to part will be regarded as entry on the whole.[19] But the mortgagee may limit his possession to part only so as not to render himself liable for default in respect of that part still occupied by the mortgagor.[20]

Rights and liabilities of a mortgagee in possession

Right to receive rents and profits   As long as the mortgagor remains in possession,[21] he is entitled to take all the profits from the security without being in any way obliged either to account for them or to apply them in discharging the mortgage interest.[22] But, equally, once the mortgagee goes into possession he is entitled to take the rents and profits by virtue of his legal or equitable ownership conferred upon him by the mortgage.[23]

On such entry into possession the mortgagee is entitled to the rents and profits in respect of any tenancies created before the mortgage or otherwise binding upon the mortgagee under an express or statutory power.[24] This may involve the requirement on the part of the mortgagee to have paid to himself all arrears of rent existing on entry into possession.[25] He may even claim an increased rent despite the fact that the agreement relating to such increase was made after the date of the mortgage.[26]

But, where there is in existence a tenancy which is not binding on the mortgagee by virtue of the fact that it has been created after the mortgage and was not pursuant to any express or statutory power[27] there is no contractual nexus between the tenant and the mortgagee, and thus the mortgagee is not entitled to demand payment of the rents as such from the tenant. But, after notice from the mortgagee the tenant should thereafter pay the rent to the mortgagee and not the mortgagor, since on recovery of possession the mortgagor would be entitled to recover the rents from the tenant as puisne profits.[28-29] Further, on entry by the mortgagee his pos-

---

[18] *Re Prytherch, Prytherch* v. *Williams* (1889) 42 Ch.D. 590; *County of Gloucester Bank* v. *Rudry Merthyr Colliery Co.* [1895] 1 Ch. 629; but the mortgagee may relieve himself by appointing a receiver under an express or statutory power—see *Refuge Assurance Co.* v. *Pearlberg* [1938] Ch. 687. See also *post*, p. 217 as to the mortgagee's statutory power.

[19] *Low Moor Co.* v. *Stanley Coal Co. Ltd.* (1876) 34 L.T. 186, C.A.

[20] *Soar* v. *Dalby* (1852) 15 Beav. 156; *Simmins* v. *Shirley* (1877) 6 Ch.D. 173.

[21] See *post*, pp. 284 *et seq.*

[22] *Trent* v. *Hunt* (1853) 9 Exch. 14.

[23] *Cockburn* v. *Edwards* (1881) 18 Ch.D. 449 at 457; see L.P.A. 1925, s.141.

[24] *Ibid.*

[25] *Moss* v. *Gallimore* (1779) 1 Doug. K.B. 279; *Rogers* v. *Humphreys* (1835) 4 Ad. & El. 299 at 314.

[26] *Burrowes* v. *Gradin* (1843) 1 Dow. & L. 213.

[27] See *post*, pp. 333 *et seq.*

[28-29] *Pope* v. *Biggs* (1829) 9 B. & C. 245 at 257; *Underhay* v. *Read* (1887) 20 Q.B.D. 209; and see *Rusden* v. *Pope* (1868) L.R. 3 Exch. 269 at 275.

session relates back to the date of the mortgage and he is able to recover any accrued sums in respect of rent due within six years prior to his entry.[30] This position applies despite the fact that strictly the action for recovery of puisne profits is an action in trespass which normally requires the person claiming the sums due to have been in possession during that time.[31]

Although, generally, the mortgagee will be able to recover from the tenant the accrued rents due within six years prior to his entry or commencement of any action brought by him, he can only recover those rents which the tenant had failed to pay to the mortgagor. But, if the tenant had paid rent to the mortgagor in advance and before it was due, this does not constitute a good payment against the mortgagee in respect of those sums accruing due after notice of the mortgage has been given to the tenant, and the tenant is liable to pay those sums over again to the mortgagee.[32]

A mortgagee's object in going into possession is to intercept the profits from the mortgaged property, and to utilise them for the discharge of his claims under the mortgage. Thus, after paying any outgoings, such as rents, rates and taxes, insurance premiums, etc., he may apply the profits to the payment of his interest on the mortgage debt, on the expense of improvements and then, if he so desires, to the reduction of the capital account.[33]

Right to carry on business   A mortgagee in possession has full powers to manage the mortgaged property. In the case of business premises the mortgagee may carry on the business for a reasonable time with a view to its sale as a going concern and for such purpose he is able to use the name of the firm to do so.[34] Where there is a mortgage of a business as a going concern, the mortgagee in possession is entitled to be recouped in respect of any losses incurred without negligence in carrying it on out of the proceeds of sale.[35] If the mortgage includes the goodwill of the business of a publican, the mortgagee on taking possession is entitled to call upon the mortgagor to concur in obtaining a transfer to the mortgagee of the existing licence.[36] Once the mortgagee enters into possession of the business, he, in effect, becomes the owner of the business and stands in the mortgagor's place,[37]

---

[30] *Barnett* v. *Earl of Guildford* (1855) 11 Exch. 19; *Ocean Accident & Guarantee Corp. Ltd.* v. *Ilford Gas Co.* [1905] 2 K.B. 493 at 498; and see Limitation Act 1980, s.19.

[31] See *Turner* v. *Cameron's Coalbrook Steam Coal Co.* (1850) 5 Exch. 932; see also *Wheeler* v. *Montefiore* (1841) 2 Q.B. 133.

[32] *De Nicholls* v. *Saunders* (1870) L.R. 5 C.P. 589; *Cook* v. *Guerra* (1872) L.R. 7 C.P. 132; *Lord Ashburton* v. *Knocton* [1915] 1 Ch. 274 at 282; *Smallmas Ltd.* v. *Castle* [1932] I.R. 294. *Contra* the position where the tenant has paid a lump sum in satisfaction of all rents accruing during the term and no inquiry of the tenant is made by the mortgagee, he is bound by such payment. See *Green* v. *Rheinberg* (1911) 104 L.T. 149; *Grace Rymer Investments Ltd.* v. *Waite* [1958] Ch. 831 at 847.

[33] *Re Knight, ex p. Isherwood* (1882) 22 Ch.D. 384; *Re Coaks, Coaks* v. *Bayley* [1911] Ch. 171.

[34] *Cook* v. *Thomas* (1876) 24 W.R. 427.

[35] *Bompas* v. *King* (1886) 33 Ch.D. 279.

[36] *Rutter* v. *Daniel* (1882) 30 W.R. 801.

[37] *Chaplin* v. *Young (No. 1)* (1864) 33 Beav. 330 at 337.

but he does not render himself liable on the existing contracts of the business unless they are specifically adopted so as to effect a novation. It would also seem that the fact that a mortgagee takes possession of a business does not of itself operate as a dismissal of the employees employed in that business.[38] Other contractural and statutory provisions might apply, however, and reference should be made to standard works on employment law and transfer of undertakings e.g. Transfer of Undertakings (Protection of Employment) Regulations 1981 (S.I. 1981 No. 1794).

Right to emblements   A mortgagee entering into possession of agricultural land is entitled as against the mortgagor or his trustee in bankruptcy to emblements[39] and the mortgagor is not so entitled.[40] The mortgagee on entering into possession is entitled to all the growing crops and the mortgagor, or any person claiming under him, such as his trustee in bankruptcy, may be restrained by injunction from cutting and removing crops on the mortgaged land.[41] However, if the mortgagee has not taken possession of the mortgaged property before the mortgagor's bankruptcy, and the crops had been cut or removed before the bankruptcy, such action converts the crops into personal chattels so that they belong to the mortgagor's trustee in bankruptcy.[42] Further, in the case of an agricultural holding which is occupied under a tenancy not binding on the mortgagee, then the tenant is, as against the mortgagee who takes possession, entitled to any compensation which would otherwise be due to him from the mortgagor with regard to crops, improvements, tillages or other matters connected with the holding pursuant to the provisions of the Agricultural Holdings Act 1986.[43] If the tenancy is from year to year or for a term not exceeding 21 years at a rack rent, the mortgagee must normally give the occupier six months' written notice before he deprives him of possession, and if he so deprives him, compensation is due to the occupier for his crops and for expenditure on any unexhausted improvement made in the expectation of the remaining full term of the tenancy.[44]

Right to grant leases[45]   This is dealt with under the section entitled "rights common to both parties."

Liability to account   A mortgagee, by taking possession becomes the manager of the property in which the beneficial interest still belongs to the mortgagor.[46] In consequence, he has certain duties to the mortgagor. Thus, he is bound to be diligent in collecting the rents and profits and will

---

[38] Per Fry L.J. in Reid v. Explosives Co. (1887) 19 Q.B.D. 264 at 267, 269.
[39] Keech v. Hall (1778) 1 Doug. K.B. 21.
[40] Birch v. Wright (1786) 1 Trn. Rep. 378 at 383; Moss v. Gallimore (1779) 1 Doug. K.B. 279 at 283.
[41] Bagnall v. Villar (1879) 12 Ch.D. 812.
[42] Re Phillips, ex p. National Mercantile Bank (1880) 16 Ch.D. 104.
[43] See Agricultural Holdings Act 1986, s.60; see also Lloyds Bank Ltd. v. Marcan [1973] 1 W.L.R. 1387.
[44] See Agricultural Holdings Act 1986, s.85.
[45] See post, pp. 333 et seq.
[46] See Noyes v. Pollock (1886) 32 Ch.D. 53.

have to give the mortgagor credit not only for the rents and profits which he actually receives, but also for the rents and profits which, but for his own gross negligence or wilful default, he might have received.[47] But, although a mortgagee is bound to be diligent, he is not bound to speculate with the mortgaged property and if he does, he must himself bear the losses.[48]

The mortgagee may enter into possession of the property in order to protect his security,[49] in which case he is not liable to account for any notional rent, where sale is contemplated within a reasonable period.[50] But, more frequently, the mortgagee's object in going into possession is either to sell the property, or to intercept the net rents and profits therefrom, and to utilise them for the discharge of his claims under the mortgage. After paying any outgoings, he may apply the profits to the payment of his interest, and, if he so desires, to the reduction of the capital account. But a mortgagee cannot be made to accept the return of his capital in instalments,[51] so that if the profits are more than sufficient to meet the interest, he need not apply the surplus in reduction of capital. He may hand over the surplus to the mortgagor, unless he has received notice from a later incumbrancer to divert it to him. If, however, he retains the surplus in his own hands, as he is fully entitled to do, he will have to account for it when the final accounts are taken. The question may then arise whether, by so doing, he is to be held to have gradually reduced the capital indebtedness of the mortgagor, and correspondingly his own claim for interest.

As a mortgagee cannot be made to accept payment by instalments, he cannot be compelled to account until either he attempts to realise his security or the mortgagor seeks to redeem.[52] It makes no difference that the mortgagee is in possession; he cannot be made to render periodical accounts. But when the time comes for the mortgage account to be taken, the fact that the mortgagee has been in possession does considerably affect the terms of the order directing the account. The special nature of the account arises from the fact that the mortgagee has in his own interest assumed control over property which, beneficially, does not belong to him.[53]

The first principle of the account is that the mortgagee is entitled to have nothing from the property except his security; he cannot, by going into possession, make a personal profit or reap any personal advantage beyond what is due to him under the mortgage. Although he may have credit for

---

[47] *Hughes* v. *Williams* (1806) 12 Ves. 493. *Parkinson* v. *Hanbury* (1867) L.R. 2 H.L. 1; see also *Chaplin* v. *Young (No.1)* (1864) 33 Beav. 330.

[48] *Hughes* v. *Williams* (1806) 12 Ves. 493. See also *Shepherd* v. *Spansheath* (1988) E.G.C.S. 35.

[49] See, *e.g. Western Bank Ltd.* v. *Shindler* [1977] Ch. 1.

[50] *Norwich General Trust* v. *Grierson* [1984] C.L.Y. 2306; see also Law Commission Working Paper No. 99: *Land Mortgages* (1986) para. 3.25.

[51] *Nelson* v. *Booth* (1858) 3 De G. & J. 119 at 122; *Wrigley* v. *Gill* [1906] 1 Ch. 165.

[52] See *Tasker* v. *Small* (1837) 3 My. & Cr. 63.

[53] *Eyre* v. *Hughes* (1876) 2 Ch.D. 148 at 162.

his proper expenditure, he cannot charge a commission for his own time and trouble.[54]

Secondly, he may have credit only for such expenditure on repairs and outgoings as is reasonably necessary. He may charge for reasonable improvements which permanently increase the value of the property, but not for extraordinary improvements made without the consent of the mortgagor.[55] If he could charge for every improvement, he might add so considerably to the mortgagor's indebtedness as to make it impossible for him to redeem and thus "improve" him out of his property altogether.[56]

Thirdly, the mortgagee being under a duty to be diligent,[56a] is accountable for rents and profits on the footing of wilful default.[57] As Jessel M.R., pointed out in *Mayer* v. *Murray*,[58] the case of a mortgagee in possession is the only one in which the charge of wilful default need not be raised in the pleadings. This means that the mortgagor will be credited not only with the profits which the mortgagee in fact received, but also with those which, but for his gross negligence or wilful default, he would have received.[59] A mortgagee who personally occupies the mortgaged property, will be charged a fair occupation rent.[60] For example, a brewer mortgagee, who takes possession of a public house and lets it as a tied house, will be liable to account for the additional rent the house would have commanded as a free house.[61] A mortgagee's duty does not, however, go so far as to compel him to make the most of the mortgaged property: he is not bound to speculate with it[62]; he is not even bound to make special exertions to get the highest possible rent or the largest possible profit.[63] He is liable only for gross negligence or wilful default. The fact that the account is on the

---

[54] *Langstaffe* v. *Fenwick*; *Fenwick* v. *Langstaffe* (1805) 10 Ves. 405; *Re Wallis, ex p. Lickorish* (1890) 25 Q.B.D. 176; but he may stipulate for such payment in the mortgage contract, since now there is no objection to a collateral advantage as such: *Biggs* v. *Hoddinott* [1898] 2 Ch. 307.

[55] *Shepard* v. *Jones* (1882) 21 Ch.D. 469; see also *Scholefield* v. *Lockwood* (1863) 33 L.J.Ch. 106; *Tipton Green Colliery Co.* v. *Tipton Moat Colliery Co.* (1877) 7 Ch.D. 192, and see *post*, p. 217.

[56] *Sandon* v. *Hooper* (1844) 14 L.J.Ch. 120.

[56a] See *Sherwin* v. *Shakespear* (1854) 5 De G.M. & G. 517.

[57] *Hughes* v. *Williams* (1806) 12 Ves. 493; *Shepherd* v. *Spansheath* (1988) E.G.C.S. 35. Wilful default also means he is liable for damage to the *corpus* of the property. *National Bank of Australasia* v. *United Hand-in-Hand & Co.* (1879) 4 A.C. 391, P.C.

[58] (1878) 8 Ch.D. 424 at 427; see also *Lord Kensington* v. *Bouverie* (1855) 7 De G.M. & G. 134 at 156.

[59] *Brandon* v. *Brandon* (1862) 10 W.R. 287; *Shepherd* v. *Spansheath, supra*; *Noyes* v. *Pollock* (1886) 32 Ch.D. 53.

[60] *Lord Trimleston* v. *Hamill* (1810) 1 Ball & B. 377 at 385; *Marriott* v. *Anchor Reversionary Co.* (1861) 3 De G.F. & J. 177 at 193, see also *Fyfe* v. *Smith* [1975] 2 N.S.W.L.R. 408; but not, of course, where the premises have no letting value, see *Marshall* v. *Cave* (1824) 3 L.J.(o.s.) Ch. 57; and letting value, *White* v. *City of London Brewery* (1889) 42 Ch.D. 237 either by reason of their physical condition or a local trading slump. See also Law Commission Working Paper No. 99, *Land Mortgages*, (1986), para. 3.24.

[61] *White* v. *City of London Brewery* (1889) 42 Ch.D. 237 and see *Shepherd* v. *Spansheath, supra*.

[62] *Hughes* v. *Williams* (1806) 12 Ves. 493. See also *Shepherd* v. *Spansheath, supra*.

[63] See *Wragg* v. *Denham* (1836) 2 Y & C. Ex. 117.

footing of wilful default need not, therefore, unduly alarm a prudent man of business. Maitland however, sets up a further objection by suggesting[64] that the account against a mortgagee in possession is often taken with annual rests, *i.e.* that at each half-year[65] if there was an excess of profit of receipts over interest charges, the surplus must be taken to have gone in reduction of the capital debt, so that interest is afterwards allowed only on the reduced amount. But such an account is only ordered in exceptional circumstances.[66]

The general rule is that the account of rents and profits runs on from beginning to end without reference to the question whether the mortgagee has at any particular time had in his hands more than sufficient to pay the interest, the reason being that a mortgagee is not bound to accept payment by instalments and is entitled to have the account taken as a whole. To this rule there appear to be two exceptions: *(i)* where the mortgagee has claimed the property as his own, denying the mortgagor's right to redeem[67]; and *(ii)* where the interest was not in arrear when the mortgagee went into possession.[68] In the second case the mortgagee is considered to have elected to take his money in instalments, so that he must set off the excess of receipts and interest against the principal[69]: but, once he is in possession, the mere fact that afterwards the interest ceased to be in arrear will not render him liable to make rests; he cannot safely give up possession so that there is no evidence of an intention to take his money in instalments.[70] It is true that in some older cases[71] it is suggested that even when interest was in arrear at the time of entry, the mortgagee must account with rests, where the annual profits greatly and notoriously exceed the interest. But these cases cannot now be relied on,[72] and the true principle seems to be that the court only directs an account with rests by way of penalising the mortgagee when he fails to treat the mortgage property as a security. If he enters when his interest is genuinely in arrears, such a penalty is out of place.[73] If, however, the profits do greatly exceed the interest, the mortgagee must be capable of restoring the property to the mortgagor as soon as his whole debt is satisfied, for, if afterwards he continues in possession,

---

[64] *Maitland, Equity* (2nd ed.), p. 187.

[65] Or at the end of each full year, as the case may be.

[66] *Wrigley* v. *Gill* [1905] 1 Ch. 241; *Ainsworth* v. *Wilding* [1905] 1 Ch. 435.

[67] *National Bank of Australasia* v. *United Hand-in-Hand & Co.* (1879) 4 A.C. 391; see *Wrigley* v. *Gill* [1905] 1 Ch. 241, P.C.; *Incorporated Society in Dublin* v. *Richards* (1841) 1 Dr. & W. 258.

[68] *Shephard* v. *Elliot* (1819) 4 Madd. 254.

[69] This presumption will not be made if, interest not being in arrear, he entered to protect the security; *Patch* v. *Wild* (1861) 30 Beav. 99.

[70] *Davis* v. *May* (1815) 19 Ves. 383; *Latter* v. *Dashwood* (1834) 6 Sim. 462; but if he settles an account with the mortgagor, capitalising the arrears, he must go out of possession or he will be treated as if he had entered when no rent was in arrear; *Wilson* v. *Cluer* (1840) 3 Beav. 136.

[71] *e.g. Uttermare* v. *Stevens* (1851) 17 L.T.(o.s.) 115; see also *Wilson* v. *Cluer* (1840) 3 Beav. 136.

[72] *Nelson* v. *Booth* (1858) 3 De G. & J. 119; *Wrigley* v. *Gill* [1905] 1 Ch. 241.

[73] *Per* Warrington J. in *Wrigley* v. *Gill* [1905] 1 Ch. 241 at 249.

he will have to pay interest to the mortgagor on such further sums as he receives by way of profits.[74] He is not entitled to use the mortgagor's money, and therefore, if the latter can establish that at any particular date the whole debt was paid off, an account will be taken against the mortgagee from that date charging him compound interest on the excess of rents and profits over outgoings with annual rests.[75]

Thus although the account is taken against a mortgagee in possession with some strictness,[76] this need not deter a mortgagee from enforcing his right if the occasion arises for its exercise, and if he keeps in mind that the property does not cease to be the mortgagor's. Mortgagees, particularly building societies, do in practice go into possession a great deal more frequently than is commonly supposed,[77] but only as a last resort.

Liability for waste   Prior to 1926 the mortgagee formerly held the legal estate in fee simple and was thus an absolute owner at law and so was not liable for waste. After 1925 the mortgagee holds by virtue of a term of years, but this is normally expressed to be without impeachment of waste.[78] In equity the mortgagee on redemption must hand back to the mortgagor the property unimpaired, and he may not destroy any part of it unless the security is deficient. But he must make good any such loss to the mortgagor in taking the accounts.

Although a mortgagee will be liable for waste if he causes unnecessary injury to the property, such as cutting timber when the security is not shown to be defective,[79] it must, however, be remembered that if the mortgage is by deed executed after 1881, section 101(1)(iv) of the Law of Property Act 1925 gives a mortgagee in possession the power to cut and sell timber and other trees right for cutting which were not planted or left standing for shelter or ornament, and he may contract for this to be done on the terms of the contract being completed within one year. The power, however, may be varied or excluded by the mortgage deed,[80] and a felling licence may be necessary.[81] Further, even when a mortgagee in possession has no power to cut timber (*i.e.* the statutory power has been excluded) he will not be restrained by injunction from so doing, unless the security is sufficient.[82] This reflects the position prior to 1926 in that the mortgagee of the fee simple might cut timber by virtue of his ownership without committing waste at law, but in equity he would be restrained unless the security was insufficient or defective. All profits from the sale of timber must, of course, be brought into the account for the benefit of the mortgagor. It

---

[74] *Wilson* v. *Metcalfe* (1826) 1 Russ. 530.
[75] *Ashworth* v. *Lord* (1887) 36 Ch.D. 545 at 551.
[76] For the practice in taking the accounts see *post*, pp. 434 *et seq.*
[77] See Law Commission Working Paper No. 99, *Land Mortgages* (1986), para. 1.3.
[78] See L.P.A. 1925, ss.85(2), 86(2), 87(1), Sched. 1, Pt. VII, paras. 1, 2.
[79] *Withrington* v. *Banks* (1725) Cas temp King 30.
[80] L.P.A. 1925, s.101(3), (4).
[81] Felling licences are obtained from the Forestry Commission.
[82] *Millett* v. *Davey* (1862) 31 Beav. 470.

should also be added that the mortgagee may not open new mines[83] but he has the right to work mines already opened.[84] But, again, the court will not interfere if a new mine is opened provided that there is no wanton destruction.[85]

Liability for repairs   The mortgagee is bound to maintain the property in necessary repair but only so far as the rent and profits allow him to do so.[86] He will be liable for any deterioration consequent on his neglect to perform this duty. Provided that such repairs and improvements are necessary and reasonable,[87] the cost of effecting the same will be charged to the mortgagor in the accounts.[87a] If the security is leasehold property the rule is especially strict and he will be liable for a forfeiture of the lease occasioned by his breach of a repairing covenant.[88] He need not spend his own money on the upkeep of the security. Accordingly he will only be liable for neglect to effect necessary repairs to the extent of surplus rents and profits after providing for the interest to which he is entitled under the mortgage.[89] A mortgagee may construct new houses in substitution of ruinous old houses,[90] but he is not bound to expend money in rebuilding.[91] Although the mortgagee may without the mortgagor's consent make reasonable and beneficial improvements to the property[92] he cannot make excessive or permanent improvements unless he obtains the mortgagor's consent, or there is acquiescence on the part of the mortgagor after notice to him.[93] The reason for this is that the mortgagee must not improve the mortgagor out of his estate which would have the effect of preventing him from redeeming the property.

Right to the appointment of a receiver

There are two ways in which a mortgagee may obtain the appointment of a receiver: *(i)* by himself making the appointment under a power in the mortgage contract; and *(ii)* by an application to the court for a receiver to

---

[83] *Ibid.* at 475.
[84] *Elias* v. *Snowden Slate Quarries Co.* (1879) 4 App.Cas. 454.
[85] *Millett* v. *Davey* (1862) 31 Beav. 470 at 476.
[86] But improvements and repairs not strictly necessary he does at his own risk, unless he first obtains the mortgagor's consent as these may affect the mortgagor's power to redeem, see *Sandon* v. *Hooper* (1844) 14 L.J.Ch. 120.
[87] *Richards* v. *Morgan* (1753) 4 Y. & C.Ex. 570. See also *Moore* v. *Painter* (1842) 6 Jur. 903; *Powell* v. *Trotter* (1861) 1 Drew. & Sm. 388; *Tipton Green Colliery Co.* v. *Tipton Moat Colliery Co.* (1877) 7 Ch. 192.
[87a] *Scholefield* v. *Lockwood* (1863) 4 De G.J. & Sm. 22 L.C.; *Tipton Green Colliery Co.* v. *Tipton Moat Colliery Co.* (1877) 7 Ch.D. 192.
[88] *Perry* v. *Walker* (1855) 3 Eq.Rep. 721.
[89] *Richards* v. *Morgan* (1753) 4 Y. & C.Ex. 570.
[90] *Hardy* v. *Reeves* (1799) 4 Ves. 466 at 480; *Newman* v. *Baker* (1860) 8 C.B. (N.S.) 200; *Marshall* v. *Cave* (1824) 3 L.J. (O.S.) Ch. 57.
[91] *Moore* v. *Painter* (1842) 6 Jur. 903.
[92] *Shepard* v. *Jones* (1882) 21 Ch.D. 469 at 479; see also *Powell* v. *Trotter* (1861) 1 Drew. & Sm. 388.
[93] *Sandon* v. *Hooper* (1844) 14 L.J.Ch. 120; *Bright* v. *Campbell* (1885) 54 L.J.Ch. 1077.

be appointed by the court.[94] A mortgagee places a receiver in control of the mortgaged property for the same reasons as he goes into possession himself; either the security is in danger of being squandered by the mortgagor, or else he is anxious to intercept the profits and apply them to the discharge of the mortgage debt. Appointing a receiver has a great advantage over going into possession, since by this means the property can be taken out of the mortgagor's control without the mortgagee having to assume any responsibilities towards the mortgagor and there is only one minor disadvantage, which is that lapse of time does not confer a title to the land in the case of a receiver.[95]

If the appointment is made by the mortgagee under a power in the mortgage deed the receiver will be treated as the agent of the mortgagor, while if the appointment is made by the court, the receiver will become an officer of the court. In neither case is the mortgagee responsible for the acts of the receiver. But if the receiver is not expressed to be the agent of the mortgagor, he will be the agent of the mortgagee.[95a]

History

Before 1860 a mortgagee had no power to appoint a receiver unless he had expressly stipulated for it in the mortgage. Consequently, if, having no such power, he did appoint a receiver, it was equivalent to going into possession, and the receiver was his agent.[96] Well-drawn mortgages, however, invariably contained such a power and also a statement that the receiver, when appointed, was to be considered the agent of the mortgagor; and the mortgagee was liable to account strictly in the same way as if he had taken possession or the receiver had been his agent.[97] In 1860 Lord Cranworth's Act[97a] made this power statutory for mortgages created by deed, but the power was confined to the case of rents and profits from land. In 1881, section 19 of the Conveyancing Act widened the scope of the statutory power, and this section is now replaced by section 101 of the Law of Property Act 1925. All mortgages executed after 1881 are governed by provisions now contained in sections 101 and 109 of the Law of Property Act 1925.

Scope of the power

The effect of these sections is that in every mortgage made by deed after 1881, the mortgagee shall have a power to appoint a receiver unless the parties specifically exclude the power. The power is made subject to detailed conditions, which regulate the position of the receiver when

---

[94] See post, p. 266.
[95] Contra the position in the case of a mortgagee in possession.
[95a] Deyes v. Wood [1911] 1 K.B. 806.
[96] Quarrell v. Beckford (1816) 1 Madd. 269.
[97] Cf. Jefferys v. Dickson (1866) 1 Ch.App. 183 at 190; cf. Rigby L.J., in Gaskell v. Gosling [1896] 1 Q.B. 669 at 692.
[97a] Power of Trustees, Mortgagees, etc. Act 1860.

appointed, unless the parties otherwise provide.[98] Under the Act the power is not exercisable until the mortgage money is due, and even then only in circumstances when the mortgagee would be entitled under section 103 to exercise his statutory power of sale, that is, one of the three enabling events mentioned in section 103 must have occurred. Third parties are not, however, bound to ascertain whether the circumstances have justified his appointment when they make payments to the receiver. Further, a mortgagee in possession is not prevented from appointing a receiver.[99]

Procedure

The original nomination in writing of the receiver and his subsequent removal or replacement in writing are all matters for the mortgagee and are for his benefit.[1] The receiver is bound to insure the mortgaged property at the direction of the mortgagee and requires the authority of the mortgagee before he can execute even necessary repairs,[2] moreover, by section 99(19) of the Law of Property Act 1925, after the appointment of a receiver, the power to grant leases vests in the mortgagee, and can only be exercised by the receiver on delegation from the mortgagee. But although the mortgagee has this considerable control over the receiver, the latter, under section 109, is deemed (unless the mortgage deed provides otherwise) to be the agent of the mortgagor,[3] and is to have sole responsibility for the receiver's acts.[4] Since it has frequently been decided[5] that a receiver is the mortgagor's agent, not merely for the receipt of profits, but for all purposes, the receiver's acts will necessarily bind the mortgagor in relation to third parties.

Application of receipts

The Act empowers a receiver to take all necessary steps to collect the income, whether by action, distraint or otherwise, in the name of the mortgagor or of the mortgagee to the full extent of the mortgagor's estate or interest, and to give effectual receipts for such income. The income must be applied by the receiver in the following order:

    (1) in discharging rents, taxes and other outgoings;
    (2) in meeting charges having priority over the mortgage under which he is a receiver;

---

[98] s.101(3). As to these conditions, see s.109. Many institutional mortgages expressly provide that the statutory power shall arise *and* be exercisable on the execution of the mortgage. See also *post*, p. 224. In practice, many of the statutory powers are varied by the mortgage deed, particularly in relation to the receiver's remuneration. See *post*, p. 219.

[99] *Refuge Assurance Co. Ltd.* v. *Pearlberg* [1938] Ch. 687.

[1] See *Re B. Johnson & Co. (Builders) Ltd.* [1955] Ch. 634 at 644.

[2] *White* v. *Metcalf* [1903] 2 Ch. 567.

[3] For the position of a receiver appointed by debenture holders, see *Deyes* v. *Wood* [1911] 1 K.B. 806.

[4] See *Portman Building Society* v. *Gallwey* [1955] 1 W.L.R. 96; *Contra* the position where the mortgage provides otherwise, or the mortgagee represents the receiver as being his agent; see *Chatsworth Properties* v. *Effiom* [1971] 1 W.L.R. 144.

[5] *Re Hale, Lilley* v. *Foad* [1899] 2 Ch. 107; *Law* v. *Glenn* (1867) L.R. 2 Ch. 634.

(3) in paying the expenses of management, *i.e.* his own commission, insurance premiums, and the cost of proper repairs directed by the mortgagee;

(4) in paying his mortgagee's interest under the mortgage;

(5) any surplus he may appropriate to the discharge of the principal debt if so directed in writing by the mortgagee: otherwise he must pay it over either to the holder of the equity of redemption or to any subsequent incumbrancer who has given notice of his charge.

The statutory power of appointing a receiver is confined to mortgagees whose mortgages are created by deed. Where the mortgage is not by deed and there is no express power in the contract, a receiver can be appointed by the mortgagee only at the price of becoming a mortgagee in possession. The receiver will then be the agent of the mortgagee.

Finally, it should be noticed that a receiver is sometimes appointed at the same time as the mortgage is executed and as part of the mortgage agreement. This occurs when it is obvious that the mortgage interest will not be paid without employing a substantial portion of the income from the mortgaged property for that purpose. The appointment is made in the name of the mortgagor in order that the receiver may be his agent, and is generally effected by a separate instrument which the receiver holds as evidence of his authority.[6]

Finally, it should be stated that the statutory power to appoint a receiver usually renders it unnecessary to apply to the court to appoint a receiver.

Right to realise the security by sale out of court

History

A mortgagee of stocks or shares[7] and a mortgagee of personal chattels, who is in possession,[8] have an implied power to sell their security when the mortgagor is in default, unless the contrary is stated in the mortgage. A mortgagee of land, however, has no such implied power, and can only sell by virtue of an express or statutory power,[9] or with the mortgagor's consent. Indeed, until the end of the eighteenth century,[10] a mortgage of land could not be realised except through the tedious and expensive medium of proceedings such as foreclosure proceedings in Chancery. Attempts were occasionally made to give the mortgagee power to sell, but such attempts, perhaps owing to a doubt whether the power would infringe the rule con-

---

[6] Not when the mortgagee's solicitor is appointed; the appointment is then made by the mortgage deed to save the expense of two deeds.

[7] *Wilson* v. *Tooker* (1714) 5 Bro.Parl.Cas. 193; *Lockwood* v. *Ewer, Child (Lady)* v. *Chanstilet* (1742) 2 Atk. 303; *Kemp* v. *Westbrook* (1749) 1 Ves. Sen. 278; *Deverges* v. *Sandeman, Clark & Co.* [1902] 1 Ch. 579; *Stubbs* v. *Slater* [1910] 1 Ch. 632.

[8] *Re Morritt, ex p. Official Receiver* (1886) 18 Q.B.D. 222.

[9] *Re Rumney and Smith* [1897] 2 Ch. 351. At common law he could, of course, transfer his mortgage but this would be subject to the mortgagor's equity of redemption and willing purchasers would be difficult to find.

[10] Holdsworth, *History of English Law*, Vol. 7, p. 160.

cerning clogs on the equity of redemption, were not common. In the first years of the nineteenth century more attention was paid to the possibility of realising mortgages out of court through powers.[11] The legality of powers of sale was established, and, after some doubts about the need for the concurrence of the mortgagor in the sale[12] and some further experiments with trusts, express powers of sale became a regular feature of every mortgage deed.[13] Since the ordinary form of these express powers adequately protected the mortgagor,[14] they were a legitimate improvement of the creditor's remedies for realising his security. At the same time the need to protect the interests of both parties necessitated the insertion of a very elaborately drawn clause until the legislature introduced a statutory power of sale satisfactory to creditors.

Lord Cranworth's Act 1860.   This Act largely failed because the power of sale contained in it was less satisfactory to creditors than the usual express power and did not induce them to omit the express power. The Act was repealed by the Conveyancing Act, 1881, but remains in force for mortgages created between 1860 and 1882.[15] Even then it is of importance in the exceptional case when the mortgage did not contain an express power.[16]

Power of sale under the Law of Property Act 1925.   The statutory power of sale in the Conveyancing Act 1881, was satisfactory to creditors and led to the omission of express powers; that Act has, however, been repealed, the relevant provisions being replaced by sections 101–107 of the Law of Property Act 1925. The power of sale contained in the 1925 Act as in the 1881 Act is modelled on the express power of sale in common use before 1882, and is so adequate that the statutory power is almost invariably relied on. It is introduced into all mortgages made by deed[17] created after 1881 and an express power is only found in mortgages made by deed when there is some special reason for departing from the statutory power.

Scope of the power

Section 101(1) of the Law of Property Act 1925 provides as follows:

"A mortgagee, where the mortgage is made by deed, shall, by virtue of this Act, have the following powers, to the like extent as if they had been in terms conferred by the mortgage deed, but not further (namely):
(i) A power, when the mortgage money has become due, to sell, or to concur with any other person in selling, the mortgaged property, or any part thereof, either subject to prior charges or not,

---

[11] It is significant that the delays of the Chancery courts were at their worst during this period.
[12] Set at rest in *Corder* v. *Morgan* (1811) 18 Ves. 344.
[13] *Cf. Clarke* v. *Royal Panopticon* (1857) 4 Drew. 26.
[14] By requiring the mortgagor to be given six months' notice of the intention to sell.
[15] *Re Solomon and Meagher's Contract* (1889) 40 Ch.D. 508.
[16] The number of such mortgages still in existence must now be few.
[17] L.P.A. 1925, s.101(1).

and either together or in lots by public auction or by private contract, subject to such conditions respecting title, or evidence of title, or other matter, as the mortgagee thinks fit, with power to vary any contract for sale, and to buy in at an auction, or to rescind any contract for sale, and to resell, without being answerable for any loss occasioned thereby; . . . "

This power is ample; the sale may be of the whole property or only of a part; it may be by public auction or by private contract, and the wording of the Act does not mean that the property must first have been put up for auction before the mortgagee can proceed to sell by private contract.[18] The mortgagee may vary or cancel a sale, and an ineffectual attempt to sell does not affect his power to enter into a new contract for sale.[19]

Subsection (2)[20] carries the scope of the power still further, for it allows a mortgagee when exercising his power:

(1) to impose covenants or conditions on either the land sold or the land retained for the purpose of restricting the user of the land or of protecting rights of working mines or minerals;

(2) To sell mines or minerals apart from the surface, to grant or reserve rights of way and other easements and privileges, and to grant or reserve wayleaves, powers, easements, or privileges in connection with the working of mines or minerals.

This subsection confers powers, which were not included in the Conveyancing Act 1881 and were only introduced by the Conveyancing Act 1911,[21] with the result that in the Law of Property Act 1925, they are confined to mortgages executed after December 31, 1911. If the mortgage was executed before that date, the mortgagee can probably not impose conditions at all,[22] but he may sell mines or minerals if he obtains the leave of the court to do so.[23]

The statutory power of sale set out in section 101 may be varied or extended by the agreement of the parties, and if so varied or extended, will take effect in its altered form just as if the alterations had been part of the provisions contained in the Act.[24] Consequently, it is not necessary to set out an express power unless the mortgagee's requirements are widely different from the statutory power. Finally, although this was already assumed from the law relating to express powers,[25] section 106(2) of the Law of Property Act 1925 distinctly states that the power of sale conferred by the Act does not affect the right of foreclosure.

[18] *Davey* v. *Durrant, Smith* v. *Durrant* (1857) 1 De G. & J. 535.
[19] This had already been decided by the Privy Council: *Henderson* v. *Astwood, Astwood* v. *Cubbold, Cobbold* v. *Astwood* [1894] A.C. 150 at 162, P.C.
[20] The *ipsa verba* of the statute are not employed in this instance.
[21] s.4.
[22] Fisher & Lightwood, *Law of Mortgages* (10th ed., 1988), p. 381.
[23] *Buckley* v. *Howell* (1861) 29 Beav. 546.
[24] s.101(3).
[25] *Perry* v. *Keane* (1836) 6 L.J.Ch. 67; *Wade* v. *Hanham* (1851) 9 Hare 62.

Who may exercise the power

The statutory power may be excluded by agreement, but, subject to this, it is introduced into every "mortgage" *made by deed*, whether the mortgage is legal or equitable and whether its subject-matter is realty or personalty. It is thus given to a chargee by way of legal mortgage and to the holder of "any charge or lien on property for securing money or money's worth"[26]; it is given also to the proprietor of a registered charge, unless a contrary entry has been made on the register.[27] The result is that the holder of *any* mortgage, charge,[28] or equitable lien on any kind of property is entitled to the statutory power so long as the security was created by deed. There is, however, one exception: the statutory power of sale has been held not to be incorporated in a document governed by the Bills of Sale (1878) (Amendment) Act 1882.[29] Subject to this exception, section 101 of the Law of Property Act 1925 applies alike to realty and personalty or any interest in it or any thing in action.[30] Section 102 further ensures that the mortgagee of an undivided share in land, who took his security before 1926, shall not lose his statutory or express power of sale by reason of the conversion of his interest into a share in personalty.

Co-mortgagees. The effect of a mortgage to several mortgagees is that, unless a contrary intention is expressed in the mortgage deed, the mortgage debt is deemed to be held upon a joint account[31]; this means that the power of sale is exercisable by the original mortgagees jointly and that, if one dies, the survivors may sell without joining his personal reprsentatives in the sale. In the case of land, if the mortgagees exceed four in number, the first four are the statutory trustees on behalf of all the mortgagees and the sale must be made through them, or, if one dies, the survivors of them.[32]

Transferees. The statutory power is exercisable by a transferee of the mortgage debt in the same way as by the original mortgagee, for section 106(1) provides[33]:

"The power of sale conferred by this Act may be exercised by any per-

---

[26] L.P.A. 1925, s.205(1)(xvi), which defines "mortgage" to include these.

[27] Land Registration Act 1925, s.34(1) and see *Lever Finance* v. *Trustee of the Property of Needleman* [1956] Ch. 375.

[28] Debenture holders in a *public* company have no power of sale, but otherwise debenture holders appear to be entitled to the statutory power: *Deyes* v. *Wood* [1911] 1 K.B. 806. Coote, *Mortgages* (9th ed. 1927), p. 910, *contra*, following Kay J., in *Blaker* v. *Herts and Essex Waterworks Co.* (1889) 41 Ch.D. 399, but *Deyes* v. *Wood* seems to limit Kay J.'s statement.

[29] *Re Morritt, ex p. Official Referee* (1886) 18 Q.B.D. 222; *Calvert* v. *Thomas* (1887) 19 Q.B.D. 204.

[30] L.P.A. 1925, s.205(1)(xvi), (xx). It may be noted that Lord Cranworth's Act did not extend to personalty, being limited to *hereditaments*.

[31] *Ibid.* s.111; trustees hold on a joint account. And see Trustee Act 1925, s.18.

[32] L.P.A. 1925, s.34(2).

[33] In any case s.205(1)(xvi) states that "mortgagee" includes any person from time to time deriving title under the original mortgagee.

son for the time being entitled to receive and give a discharge for the mortgage money."

Transferees include sub-mortgagees, who may either sell the mortgage debt only, leaving the original mortgagor's equity of redemption outstanding, or else sell, as assignees of the mortgage, and destroy also the original equity of redemption. It is necessary to include a word of warning in circumstances where the power of sale is express and not statutory since the original mortgage does not in terms extend the power of sale to assignments, the power cannot be transferred.[34] An express power should therefore either incorporate the language of section 106(1) or otherwise provide for assignment of the power.

Personal representatives.   The personal representatives of the mortgagee and, after the necessary assents have been given, the persons beneficially interested in the mortgage moneys may exercise the statutory power of sale, in virtue of section 106(1). But, again, this will not be so in the case of an express power unless provided in the mortgage deed.[35]

Conditions for the power of sale

When the power arises.   There are three conditions which must be fulfilled before the power of sale arises:

(a) the mortgage must be made by deed (as in the case of all legal mortgages); and

(b) the mortgage money must have become due—*i.e.* the legal date for redemption must have passed. In most mortgages there is inserted a legal date for redemption, but if there is no such clause and the mortgage debt is repayable by instalments, the power of sale arises as soon as any instalment is in arrear[36];

(c) there is no contrary intention in the mortgage deed.

When the power becomes exercisable.   Although the statutory power of sale *arises* at that time, it cannot—without express variation of the statutory requirements by the parties—*be exercised* unless at least one of the conditions set out in section 103 of the Law of Property Act 1925 has been satisfied, namely:

(a) Notice requiring payment of the mortgage money[36a] has been

---

[34] *Re Rumney* v. *Smith* [1897] 2 Ch. 351.
[35] *Re Crunden and Meux's Contract* [1909] 1 Ch. 690.
[36] *Payne* v. *Cardiff Rural District Council* [1932] 1 K.B. 241. But, if the mortgage money is not due (*i.e.* the interest is in arrear, but the principal is not) the statutory power does not arise, although the court may be able to order a sale in lieu of foreclosure pursuant to the L.P.A. 1925, s.91(2). See *Twentieth Century Banking Corporation* v. *Wilkinson* [1977] Ch. 99.
[36a] *i.e.* money or money's worth secured by mortgage—L.P.A. 1925, s.205(1)(xvi).

served on the mortgagor or one of two or more mortgagors, and default has been made in payment of the mortgage money, or of part thereof, for three months after such service[37]; or

(b) Some interest under the mortgage is in arrear[38] and unpaid for two months after becoming due[39]; or

(c) There has been a breach of some other provision contained in the mortgage deed[40] or in the 1925 Act,[41] or in an enactment replaced by that Act which should have been observed or performed by the mortgagor or by someone who concurred in making the mortgage.[42]

Although the occurrence of one of these circumstances is normally a condition precedent to the exercise of the statutory power, the mortgage contract may, and usually does, exclude the restrictions. On the other hand, it has been suggested that a clause allowing for sale without any notice might be considered oppressive, and will be so considered, if there is any fiduciary relationship between the parties.[43]

Notice under section 103 must be served on the mortgagor, and "mortgagor" includes any person deriving title under the original mortgagor.[44] Who ought to be served when there are later incumbrancers is an unsettled point; the course generally adopted is to give notice to the mortgagor himself and to the incumbrancer highest in priority.[45] The form of notice contemplated by section 103 is probably a demand for immediate payment, with a threat that if at the end of three months the money has not been paid, the power will be exercised: but a notice is just as good if it is merely a notice to pay at the end of three months from the date of the notice.[46] The notice must be in writing, and the serving of the notice is in all respects governed by the general provisions as to notices contained in section 196 of the Law of Property Act 1925. A person entitled to notice may waive it,

---

[37] L.P.A. 1925, s.103(i), and see *Barker* v. *Illingworth* [1908] 2 Ch. 20.

[38] It is for the mortgagee to prove affirmatively that the interest is in arrear, and it seems that a mortgagee in possession is not entitled to say that the interest is in arrear merely because he receives nothing on account of interest from the mortgagor. He must show that the interest is in arrear in spite of the receipt of rents and profits: *Cockburn* v. *Edwards* (1881) 18 Ch.D. 449 at 459, 463; *Wrigley* v. *Gill* [1905] 1 Ch. 241.

[39] L.P.A. 1925, s.103(ii).

[40] *e.g.* breach of covenants to repair or insure; see *Braithwaite* v. *Winwood* [1960] 1 W.L.R. 1257.

[41] See *Public Trustee* v. *Lawrence* [1912] 1 Ch. 789 (failure to deliver counterpart of lease as required by s.99(8)).

[42] L.P.A. 1925, s.103(iii).

[43] *Miller* v. *Cook* (1870) L.R. 10 Eq. 641; *Cockburn* v. *Edwards* (1881) 18 Ch.D. 449; this will not be so if the security was not given for a fresh loan but for obtaining more time for payment: *Pooley's Trustee* v. *Whetham* (1886) 33 Ch.D. 111.

[44] L.P.A. 1925, s.205(1)(xvi).

[45] Omission to give notice to an incumbrancer may expose the mortgagee to an action for damages (*Hoole* v. *Smith* (1881) 17 Ch.D. 434); this decision would appear to apply to the statutory power by virtue of the definition of 'mortgagor' given in the text.

[46] *Barker* v. *Illingworth* [1908] 2 Ch. 20.

but he must then join in the conveyance to the purchaser.[47] Finally, although a sale cannot take effect until the expiry of the notice required by section 103, the contract of sale may be entered into before that time, the contract being conditional on the mortgagor not discharging the mortgage.[48]

Protection of purchasers

The importance of the distinction between the power of sale *arising* and the power of sale being *exercisable* cannot be underestimated. If the power has not arisen the mortgagee has no statutory power of sale at all. Any sale by him in purported exercise of the statutory power does not give a good root of title and will not transfer the legal estate to a purchaser, but will only transfer his mortgage, *i.e.* it will only be effective to transfer to the purchaser the rights of mortgagee as mortgagee. Thus, a purchaser must ascertain whether or not the power of sale has arisen. But as the question of its exercisability is a matter between the mortgagor and the mortgagee, this does not normally concern the purchaser of the legal estate.

Thus, if the power of sale has arisen, but is not exercisable, the mortgagee can give a good root of title which is not impeachable, and the only recourse open to the mortgagor is a remedy in damages against the person exercising the power of sale.[49] But in this regard it is necessary to consider the provisions of section 104(2) of the Law of Property Act 1925 in the light of the case law preceding this legislation. The subsection corresponds with the usual clause in an express power and provides as follows:

"(2) Where a conveyance is made in exercise of the power of sale conferred by this Act, or any enactment replaced by this Act, the title of the purchaser shall not be impeachable on the ground:
(a) that no case had arisen to authorise the sale; or
(b) that due notice was not given; or
(c) where the mortgage is made after the commencement of this Act, that leave of the court, when so required, was not obtained; or
(d) whether the mortgage was made before or after such commencement, that the power was otherwise improperly or irregularly exercised;
and a purchaser is not, either before or on conveyance[50] concerned to see or inquire whether the case has arisen to authorise the sale, or due notice has been given, or the power is otherwise properly and regularly exercised; but any person damnified by an unauthorised, or

---

[47] *Selwyn* v. *Garfit* (1888) 38 Ch.D. 273.
[48] *Major* v. *Ward* (1847) 5 Hare 598.
[49] See the L.P.A. 1925, s.104(2).
[50] "Or on conveyance" was inserted to overrule the case of life interests etc. *Life Interest and Reversionary Securities Corporation* v. *Hand-in-Hand Fire and Life Insurance Society* [1898] 2 Ch. 230.

improper, or irregular exercise of the power, shall have his remedy for damages against the person exercising the power.[50a]

(3) A conveyance on sale by a mortgagee, made after the commencement of this Act, shall be deemed to have been made in exercise of the power of sale conferred by this Act unless a contrary intention appears."[51]

Thus, proof of title is simplified and all that the purchaser need do is to satisfy himself that the power of sale has arisen and he need not inquire whether it has become exercisable.[52] Further a purchaser is under no obligation to make inquiries as to the regularity of the sale, and the protection given to him by the terms of the subsection enures to him as soon as the contract is signed and is not dependent on completion having been obtained.[53] The existence of the power of sale is proved by the document creating the power, *i.e.* the form of the mortgage deed itself, and the redemption date specified in it.

But a number of authorities appear to lay down the rule—that when the purchaser had actual notice of an irregularity such as a defect in the mortgagee's power to sell,[54] or of facts which make the proposed sale impossible or inconsistent with a proper exercise of the power,[55] the sale will be set aside,[56] and the purchaser's title will be impeached.[57] It has been stated that in the circumstances " . . . to uphold the title of a purchaser who had notice of impropriety or irregularity in the exercise of the power of sale would be to convert the provisions of the statute into an instrument of fraud. . . . "[58]

Having regard to the above, several comments need to be made. First, the cases which establish the apparent qualification to the express provisions of section 104(2) are in the main decided upon express, as opposed to statutory, powers of sale, and generally precede the 1925 legislation.[59] Secondly, the only case of importance since 1925 is that of *Lord Waring* v.

[50a] The reference to a remedy in damages does not create a special statutory remedy, nor does it refer to a common law action for damages, but is a reference to the mortgagor's equitable proceedings to hold the mortgagee to account on the footing of wilful default—*McGinnis* v. *Union Bank of Australia Ltd.* [1935] V.L.R. 161.

[51] This renders it unnecessary to state in the conveyance that the conveyance is made in exercise of a sale under the statutory power as this is presumed.

[52] *Bailey* v. *Barnes* [1894] 1 Ch. 25 at 35.

[53] s.104 expressly overrules life interests, etc. *Life Interest and Reversionary Securities Corporation* v. *Hand-in-Hand Fire and Life Insurance Society* [1898] 2 Ch. 230.

[54] *Jenkins* v. *Jones* (1860) 2 Giff 99. *Parkinson* v. *Hanbury* (1867) L.R. 2 H.L. 1.

[55] *Selwyn* v. *Garfitt* (1888) 38 Ch.D. 273; *Bailey* v. *Barnes* [1894] 1 Ch. 25.

[56] *Bailey* v. *Barnes* [1894] 1 Ch. 25; *contra* Fisher & Lightwood, *Law of Mortgage* (10th ed., 1988), p. 387 which suggests having regard to the authority that the purchaser is liable to have the sale set aside not only if he took with actual notice of an irregularity but also if he took with constructive notice. *cf.* also *Parkinson* v. *Hanbury* (1860) 1 Dr. & Sm. 143.

[57] *Lord Waring* v. *London & Manchester Assurance Co. Ltd.* [1935] Ch. 310 at 318.

[58] See *Bailey* v. *Barnes* [1894] 1 Ch. 25 at 30, *per* Stirling J., but note that that statement was made in relation to s.21(2) of the Conveyancing Act 1881, which is reproduced in the first part only of s.104(2).

[59] See, *e.g. Jenkins* v. *Jones* (1860) 2 Giff 99; *Parkinson* v. *Hanbury* (1867) L.R. 2 H.L. 1; *Selwyn* v. *Garfitt* (1888) 38 Ch.D. 273; and *Bailey* v. *Barnes* [1894] 1 Ch. 25.

London & Manchester Assurance Co. Ltd.[60] in which dicta in *Bailey* v. *Barnes*[61] were approved *obiter*. Thirdly, there has been no case, as yet, in which the court has expressly had to consider the wording of section 104(2). In these circumstances it would seem that the present position is as follows—provided that the purchaser does not *actually know* of any irregularity he will obtain a good unimpeachable title, and the mortgagor's remedy is in damages against the person exercising the power of sale. Further, it would seem that there is no obligation upon the purchaser to make the inquiries which a suspicious purchaser should make, and that the purchaser will not have constructive notice of any irregularity or impropriety in the exercise of the power of sale which would have been revealed by such inquiries. But the conveyance may be set aside if the purchaser takes with knowledge of any impropriety in the sale, in the sense of what would have come to his knowledge had he not shut his eyes to suspicious circumstances, rather than the usual sense related to failure to inquire, whether that knowledge be by way of actual or constructive notice.[62]

Sale

Mode of sale.   The sale will in most cases be made under the provisions of section 101 of the Law of Property Act 1925, without reference to the court.[63] This gives to the mortgagee a wide discretion as to the manner in which he exercises his power. It may be by auction or by private contract. It may be of the whole or part of the property, and may be made subject to easements or restrictive covenants. It may include the grants of easements and privileges, and may separate the mines and minerals from the ownership of the surface. But the section gives no power to sell timber apart from the land,[64] or trade machinery apart from the buildings containing it,[65] nor to grant an option.

The sale may be made either free of or subject to prior charges. This is important when there are successive incumbrancers; a puisne incumbrancer, who is desirous of selling, has two choices: *(i)* he may sell subject to the prior charges; or *(ii)* he may sell free of prior charges by arranging to discharge them out of the proceeds of sale. If the latter alternative is adopted he must either obtain the concurrence of the prior incumbrancers

---

[60] [1935] Ch. 310. *Holohan* v. *Friends Provident and Century Life Office* [1966] I.R. 1; *Forsyth* v. *Blundell* (1973) 129 C.L.R. 477. See also *Property and Bloodstock Ltd.* v. *Emerton*; *Bush* v. *Property and Bloodstock Ltd.* [1968] Ch. 94.

[61] [1894] 1 Ch. 25 at 30, 34, which seems to suggest that there is a different standard from that usually applied in relation to the doctrine of notice.

[62] See *Bailey* v. *Barnes* [1894] 1 Ch. 25 at 30, 34; *Holohan* v. *Friends Provident and Century Life Office* [1966] I.R. 1.

[63] There is an exception in the case where a mortgage provides that a power of sale shall be exercisable in the case of bankruptcy. In such a case leave of the court is required, but it does not concern the purchaser; see L.P.A. 1925, s.104(2). Also, in those cases where the mortgaged property is occupied by the mortgagor (in particular dwelling-houses) presumably the mortgagee will wish to have vacant possession prior to sale which will normally necessitate court proceedings.

[64] Cf. *Cholmeley* v. *Paxton* (1825) 3 Bing. 207.

[65] *Re Yates, Batcheldor* v. *Yates* (1888) 38 Ch.D. 112.

in the sale,[66] or else he must make use of the procedure provided by section 50 of the Law of Property Act 1925, in which case he obtains leave to pay into court a sum sufficient to cover the requirements of the prior charges, plus any costs or expenses likely to be incurred.

Mortgagee as vendor.   The courts have repeatedly affirmed that a mortgagee is not a trustee for the mortgagor until his debt has been satisfied.[67] It follows that a mortgagee, in exercising his power of sale, is not a trustee of the power[68]; on the contrary, the power arises by contract with the mortgagor and forms part of the mortgagee's security, so that he is entitled to look after his own interests when making the sale.[69] In *Warner* v. *Jacob*[70] Kay J., stated the general principle at common law of the mortgagee's position thus:

> "A mortgagee is, strictly speaking not a trustee of the power of sale. It is a power given to him for his benefit, to enable him the better to realise his debt. If he exercises it bona fide for that purpose, without corruption or collusion with the purchaser, the court will not interfere, even though the sale be very disadvantageous, unless, indeed, the price is so low as in itself to be evidence of fraud."

So strong was this principle that a mortgagee has been held not to be a trustee of the power of sale, even when the mortgage is created in the form of an express trust for sale.[71]

Price.   At common law, therefore, the general rule flowing from this principle was that the duty of a mortgagee, exercising his power of sale, merely should act in good faith in the *conduct of the sale*.[72] If the sale was bona fide he need not consult the interests of the mortgagor, so that it would be no ground for setting aside a sale that a larger price could have been obtained if the sale had been delayed.[73] The court would not inquire into a mortgagee's motive for exercising his power,[73a] provided the sale itself was

---

[66] A complication arises in the case of registered land. The prospective purchaser can insist on the vendor/mortgagee procuring his registration of the charge (see Land Registration Act 1925, s.110(5)), but without the concurrence of the *first* mortgagee with whom the Land Certificate may have been deposited this cannot be done.

[67] *Marquis of Cholmondely* v. *Lord Clinton* (1820) 2 J. & W. 1; *Taylor* v. *Russell* [1892] A.C 244; *Sands to Thompson* (1883) 22 Ch.D. 614; Turner, *Equity of Redemption* (1931) pp. 166 *et seq.*; and see *ante*, pp. 194 *et seq.* But even if the mortgagee is not a trustee, he is bound to take reasonable care to obtain a true market value of the mortgaged property, see *Cuckmere Brick Co. Ltd.* v. *Mutual Finance Ltd.* [1981] Ch. 949; and see *post*, pp. 231 *et seq.*

[68] *Kennedy* v. *De Trafford* [1897] A.C. 180; *Cuckmere Brick Co. Ltd.* v. *Mutual Finance Ltd.* [1971] Ch. 949.

[69] *Farrar* v. *Farrars, Ltd.* (1888) 40 Ch.D. 395 at 398, *per* Chitty, J.

[70] (1882) 20 Ch.D. 220 at 234.

[71] *Kirkwood* v. *Thompson* (1865) 2 De G. J. & Sm. 613; *Locking* v. *Parker* (1872) L.R. 8 Ch.App. 30. But this principle probably should now be qualified in the light of the *Cuckmere* case, see *post*, pp. 231 *et seq.*

[72] *Kennedy* v. *De Trafford* [1897] A.C. 180. Lord Herschell, however, deprecated any attempt to define exhaustively the words "acting in good faith."

[73] *Davey* v. *Durrant, Smith* v. *Durrant* (1857) 1 De G. & J. 535.

[73a] See *Nash* v. *Eads* (1880) 25 S.J. 95.

fair, and neither spite nor any other indirect motive would invalidate the sale. The mortgagee was not a trustee of the power in any sense.[74]

But, at the same time, obviously, the question of the price to be obtained by the mortgagee in respect of the security is of importance to the mortgagor. He is the person interested in the balance of the proceeds of sale after payment of the mortgage debt by the mortgagee exercising his power of sale (and the debt of any other mortgagee interested in the security). In short, the mortgagor's interests must not be sacrificed.

Thus, the general rule must now be viewed in the context of subsequent legislation and case law particularly with regard to the question of price and the earlier authorities may need some reappraisal.

In the case of building societies an important inroad into the above rule has been made by the Building Societies Act 1986,[74a] (replacing earlier legislation) which imposes a duty on building societies to take reasonable care to ensure that the price for which the property is sold is the best price that can reasonably be obtained. At one time it was considered that this was a special rule placing a more onerous duty on building society mortgagees than on other mortgagees.

Vaisey J. in the case of *Reliance Permanent Building Society* v. *Harwood-Stamper*[75] held that not only must building society mortgagees take reasonable care to obtain a fair price[75a] but also to have converted mortgagees under a building society mortgage into fiduciary vendors. Indeed he was inclined to think that, if there is a striking disparity between the amount realised and the amount of the mortgage debt, the section places an onus on the mortgagees to show that they have fulfilled their obligations under the Act. At the same time he emphasised that a building society mortgagee, although a fiduciary vendor, retains as mortgagee:

(1) the right to prefer his own convenience in recovering his money at once to the mortgagor's advantage in delaying the sale;
(2) the right to employ the various methods of sale allowed by section 101 of the Law of Property Act 1925;
(3) the protection of section 106(3) of the Law of Property Act 1925 against liability for any involuntary loss in connection with the exercise of the power of sale.

But in the case of *other* mortgagees the question of a duty of care to ensure that the best price be obtained was unresolved and the common law rule enunciated above, remained, that is in the absence of evidence of

---

[74] *Belton* v. *Bass, Ratcliffe & Gretton Ltd.* [1922] 2 Ch. 449; *Nash* v. *Eads* (1880) 25 S.J. 95; *Colson* v. *Williams* (1889) 58 L.J.Ch. 539.

[74a] s.13(7), Sched. 4, para. 1.

[75] [1944] Ch. 362, considering the terms of the Building Societies Act 1939, s.10, (substantially reproduced in the Building Societies Act 1986, s.13(7)).

[75a] See the comments of Salmon L.J. in the *Cuckmere* case (*post*, p. 231) with regard to the distinction made by Vaisey J. between "proper price" and "best price" ([1971] 2 All E.R. 633 at 644–646).

fraud a sale would not be set aside.[76] Indeed, it was well settled that selling at an undervalue did not by itself constitute *male fides*. In *Adams* v. *Scott*,[77] for example, it was alleged that property sold for £12,000 was worth £20,000, but Wood V.-C., declared that mere undervalue was not enough to justify interference with the sale without proof of fraud. Where there was fraud, however, the court would grant an injunction to restrain the completion of a sale, or would set aside a completed sale.[78] If the property has reached the hands of a purchaser for value without notice of the fraud, an action for damages will lie against the mortgagee.

But as the law developed, although proof of fraud was essential in order to set aside a sale otherwise executed in accordance with the terms of the mortgagee's power, yet the mortgagee would be made to account for his careless handling of the sale. A mortgagee was not to be regarded as a trustee, but he would be treated as a reasonable man of business. Dicta of Lord Herschell L.C.,[79] and Lindley L.J.,[80] were sometimes cited in support of the proposition that, in the absence of fraud, a mortgagee was only liable for selling at an undervalue if he wilfully or recklessly sacrifices the property of the mortgagor. But this seemed to put the rule too favourably for the mortgagee, for in *Tomlin* v *Luce*[81] a mortgagee was held responsible for the blunder made by an otherwise competent auctioneer, whom he had employed. The error of the auctioneer was accidental, though serious, and reckless seems too strong a word for his conduct, let alone that of his employer's. The Privy Council in *McHugh* v. *Union Bank of Canada*[82] defined the duty of a mortgagee more broadly:

"It is his duty to behave in conducting the realisation of the mortgaged property as a reasonable man would behave in the realisation of his own property, so that the borrower may receive credit for the fair value of the property sold."

The true rule as it developed was that a mortgagee must use reasonable care to get a fair or proper price,[83] and if he did not, he would be debited in his mortgage account with the full value of the mortgaged property *at the date of the sale*.[84]

But it was not until 1971 that this rule finally received full judicial recog-

---

[76] See *Warner* v. *Jacob* (1882) 20 Ch.D. 220; and see *ante*, pp. 228 *et seq*.

[77] (1859) 7 W.R. 213.

[78] *Bettyes* v. *Maynard* (1883) 49 L.T. 389; *Haddington Island Quarry Co. Ltd.* v. *Hudson* [1911] A.C. 727; *Lord Waring* v. *London and Manchester Assurance Co.* [1935] Ch. 310.

[79] *Kennedy* v. *De Trafford* [1897] A.C. 180 at 185; this dictum does not in fact support the proposition.

[80] *Kennedy* v. *De Trafford* [1896] 1 Ch. 762 at 772, C.A.

[81] (1889) 43 Ch.D. 191.

[82] [1913] A.C. 299 at 311, P.C.

[83] *Colson* v. *Williams* (1889) 58 L.J.Ch. 539; *Reliance Permanent Building Society* v. *Harwood-Stamper* [1944] Ch. 362.

[84] *Wolff* v. *Vanderzee* (1869) 20 L.T. 350; *Deverges* v. *Sandeman, Clarke & Co.* [1902] 1 Ch. 579; for a statement of the measure of the mortgagee's liability, see *Tomlin* v. *Luce* (1889) 43 Ch.D. 191.

nition in the English courts. In the case of *Cuckmere Brick Co. Ltd.* v. *Mutual Finance Ltd.*[85] the Court of Appeal has now held that a mortgagee at common law is under a duty to " . . . take reasonable care to obtain the true market value of the mortgaged property."[86] Thus, if a mortgagee in exercising his power of sale in respect of a plot of building land advertises the property and fails to mention that there is in existence planning permission for the erection of 100 flats, he will be accountable to the mortgagor for the difference between the proper price which could have reasonably been obtained and the price actually obtained.[87] This would seem now to place upon *any* mortgagee the same duty of care to obtain the best price reasonably obtainable as has been imposed upon building societies since 1939.

Further decisions in 1982 and 1985 held that this duty of care is also owed to the guarantor of the mortgaged debt as well as to the mortgagor.[88] It may be added that in a sale, otherwise bona fide, the price is none the less a fair price, although part, or even the whole of the purchase price is left on mortgage, but the mortgagee must, of course, have debited himself in the mortgage account with the full amount of the purchase price.[89]

But a number of points remain for consideration. First, now that the law has been clarified in that *any* mortgagee is required to act not only in good faith but also with reasonable care, how far does this duty extend? Having regard to the earlier cases, it appears that the mortgagee is under no duty to advertise the security, nor is he bound to sell it by auction.[90] Further, a mortgagee is under no duty to delay the sale in order to obtain a better price.[91] Again, the mere fact that a mortgagee in exercising his power of sale omits a material point of which he is ignorant (for example, planning permission) does not of itself justify a finding of negligence.[92] Also the mortgagee is not required to put the property into good repair.[93] The answer is that the mortgagee is entitled to proceed to a forced sale to real-

---

[85] [1971] Ch. 949, explaining *Kennedy* v. *De Tafford* [1897] A.C. 180. See also *Holohan* v. *Friends Provident and Century Life Office* [1966] I.R. 1. The *Cuckmere* principle has since been applied in *Palmer* v. *Barclays Bank Ltd.* [1971] 23 P. & C.R. 30; *Bank of Cyprus (London) Ltd.* v. *Gill* [1980] 2 Lloyd's Rep. 51; *Standard Chartered Bank Ltd.* v. *Walker* [1982] 1 W.L.R. 1410; *Tse Kwong Lam* v. *Wong Chit Sen* [1983] 1 W.L.R. 1394; *Bishop* v. *Bonham* [1988] 1 W.L.R. 742. See also "*The Calm C*", *Gulf and Fraser Fisherman's Union* v. *Calm C Fish Ltd.* [1975] 1 Lloyd's Rep. 189.

[86] *Cuckmere Brick Co. Ltd.* v. *Mutual Finance Ltd.* [1971] Ch. 949 at 966, *per* Salmon L.J.

[87] *Ibid.*, *per* Salmon L.J., who held that the proper price is the same as the true market value.

[88] *Standard Chartered Bank Ltd.* v. *Walker* [1982] 1 W.L.R. 1410, C.A., a case where there was a sale by a receiver under a debenture of a private company which was guaranteed by the directors personally; *American Express International Banking Corpn.* v. *Hurley* [1985] F.L.R. 350.

[89] *Davey* v. *Durrant, Smith* v. *Durrant* (1857) 1 De G. & J. 535; *Kennedy* v. *De Trafford* [1897] A.C. 180; *Belton* v. *Bass, Ratcliffe and Gretton Ltd.* [1922] 2 Ch. 449.

[90] *Davey* v. *Durrant, Smith* v. *Durrant* (1857) 1 De G. & J. 535 at 560; *Bank of Cyprus (London) Ltd.* v. *Gill* [1980] 2 Lloyd's Rep. 51.

[91] *Davey* v. *Durrant, Smith* v. *Durrant, ante*, at 553; *Bank of Cyprus (London) Ltd.* v. *Gill, ante.*

[92] *Palmer* v. *Barclays Bank* (1972) 23 P. & C.R. 30.

[93] *Waltham Forest London Borough Council* v. *Webb* (1974) 232 E.G. 461.

ise his security irrespective of his motive for selling.[94] Provided that he acts bona fide and takes reasonable care to ensure that the price is the best reasonably obtainable *in the circumstances*, then such actions are justifiable.

The duty of care imposed on a selling mortgagee by the *Cuckmere* principle, being essentially in the nature of an obligation implied by law, is capable, therefore, of being excluded by agreement.[94a] But the courts may not reject exclusion clauses where the exempting words are clear and are susceptible to one meaning only, however unreasonable. The result therefore may be[94b] that where such clauses authorise the mortgagee to exercise the power of sale with absolute discretion, the power is nonetheless subject to the implicit restriction that it should be exercised properly within the limits of the general law, that is, with the exercise of reasonable care to obtain a proper price.[94c]

Secondly, what of the position of the auctioneer or estate agent handling the sale on behalf of the mortgagee? In other words, does a mortgagee discharge his duty to the mortgagor if he places the sale in the hands of a reputable agent? As yet, there has been no case directly on this point as in all the cases it is the mortgagee who has been held liable for his agent's negligence. But it is clear that the mortgagee would usually have a claim to an indemnity from the agent. In addition, there are a number of suggestions that the mortgagor himself may have an action directly against the agent for negligence,[95] but the correctness of this proposition raises some doubt in view of the fact that normally there is no duty of care owed to a third party in the case of economic loss.[96] Finally, despite the fact that the law now seems to have been clarified by the *Cuckmere* case, is it strictly correct to state that the duties owed by building society mortgagees and other mortgagees are identical having regard to the various developments set out above? It had previously been considered that building societies alone owed a special duty since the enactment of section 10 of the Building Societies Act 1939.

---

[94] *Farrar* v. *Farrars Ltd.* (1888) 40 Ch.D. 395 at 398; and see *Adams* v. *Scott* (1859) 7 W.R. 215.

[94a] *Bishop* v. *Bonham* [1988] 1 W.L.R. 742 at 752, *per* Slade L.J. In the case of building society mortgages *exclusion* of limitability is presently *excluded*, see Building Societies Act 1986, Sched 4; para. 1(2).

[94b] *Photo Production Ltd.* v. *Securicor Transport Ltd.* [1980] A.C. 827 at 850, *per* Lord Diplock, cited by Slade L.J. in *Bishop* v. *Bonham* (*ante*); see also *George Mitchell (Chesterhall) Ltd.* v. *Finney Lock Seeds* [1983] Q.B. 284 at 312; *Chitty on Contracts*, (25th ed., 1983) Vol. 1, para. 878.

[94c] *Bishop* v. *Bonham* [1988] 1 W.L.R. 742.

[95] Cross L.J. in *Cuckmere Brick Co. Ltd.* v. *Mutual Finance Ltd.* [1971] Ch. 949 at 973; *Garland* v. *Rulp, Pay &* (1984) 271 E.G. 106; *Piodeth* v. *Castle Phillips Finance Co Ltd.* (1986) 279 E.G. 1355; and see (1986) *Conv.* 442 (Thompson).

[96] See *e.g. D. & F. Estates* v. *Church Commissioners for England* [1989] A.C. 177. This case did not overrule *Junior Books* v. *Veitchi Co.* [1983] A.C. 520 but applied the dissenting judgment of Lord Brandon in the earlier case. Presumably, therefore, where there is a similar uniquely proximate relationship as occurred in the *Junior Books* case, such a duty of care will continue to be owed.

Identity of purchaser. The sale must be a true sale. A mortgagee cannot sell to himself, either alone or with others, even though the price be the full value of the property sold.[97] Such a sale may restrained or be set aside or ignored.[98] It is not so much that there is the conflict between interest and duty, which prevents a trustee from acquiring the trust property, as the impossibility of the contract. A man cannot make an agreement with himself. Nor can he disguise the fact that he is both buyer and seller by employing an agent or trustee to purchase for him.[99] The same principle prevents a solicitor or other agent employed to conduct the sale from becoming a purchaser.[1] But a sale by a mortgagee to a company of which he is a shareholder, or even director, or a sale by a mortgagee company to one of its members, is not necessarily invalid.[2] As Lindly L.J. said[3]:

> "A sale by a person to a corporation of which he is a member is not, either in form or in substance, a sale by a person to himself. To hold that it is, would be to ignore the principle which lies at the root of the legal idea of a corporate body, and that idea is that the corporate body is distinct from the persons composing it. A sale by a member of a corporation to the corporation itself is in every sense a sale valid in equity as well as at law."

At the same time, although such a sale is not a nullity, it may be impeached on the ground of fraud or other irregularity,[4] and the fact that the mortgagee has a substantial interest in the company will throw upon the mortgagee and the company the burden of affirmatively proving the bona fides of the sale. In *Farrar* v. *Farrars, Ltd.*[5] this burden was discharged; in *Hodson* v. *Deans*[6] it was not, and the sale was accordingly upset.

The mortgagor himself may bid at an auction and become the purchaser, and in the case of co-mortgagors one may purchase from the mortgagee without the concurrence of the others. Nor can the others impeach the sale on the ground that they were not notified of the name of the purchaser, for there is no fiduciary relationship between co-mortgagors to render such a

---

[97] *National Bank of Australasia* v. *United Hand-in-Hand and Band of Hope* (1879) 4 App. Cas. 391; see also *Martison* v. *Clowes* (1882) 21 Ch.D. 857.

[98] See *Williams* v. *Wellingborough Borough Council* [1975] 1 W.L.R. 1327 where a purported transfer to itself by the local authority was held to be void. See also Housing Act 1980, s.112.

[99] *Downes* v. *Grazebrook* (1817) 3 Mer. 200; *National Bank of Australasia* v. *United Hand-in-Hand etc., Co.* (1879) 4 A.C. 391.

[1] *Martinson* v. *Clowes* (1882) 21 Ch.D. 857; *Lawrence* v. *Galsworthy* (1857) 30 L.T.(o.s.) 112; *Hodson* v. *Deans* [1903] 2 Ch. 647; but not if the agent was not employed in the conduct of the sale: *Guest* v. *Smythe* (1870) L.R. 5 Ch.App. 551; *Nutt* v. *Easton* [1899] 1 Ch. 873.

[2] *Tse Kwong Lam* v. *Wong Chit Sen* [1983] 1 W.L.R. 1394.

[3] *Farrar* v. *Farrars, Ltd.* (1888) 40 Ch.D. 395 at 409.

[4] *Tse Kwan Lam* v. *Wong Chit Sen* [1983] 1 W.L.R. 1349

[5] (1888) 4 Ch.D. 395.

[6] [1903] 2 Ch. 647.

notification necessary.[7] Further, there is no objection to a purchase by a puisne incumbrancer,[8] and the effect of such a purchase from a first mortgagee, exercising his power of sale, is quite different from a mere purchase of the first mortgage. The sale carried out in pursuance of a power created by the mortgagor cancels the latter's equity of redemption, so that the puisne incumbrancer obtains an absolute irredeemable title.[9]

Distribution of surplus proceeds of sale.   Sale under a power of sale cancels the equitable right to redeem, but it by no means destroys the equitable interest of the mortgagor *vis-à-vis* the mortgagee. Consequently, as on a sale under an express or statutory power of sale, the mortgagee becomes a trustee of the surplus proceeds of sale for the mortgagor and other interested parties.[10] In the case of an express power, he is an express trustee if the mortgage contains an express trust of the proceeds of sale[11]; otherwise he is a constructive trustee.[12] In the case of a statutory power, the Law of Property Act 1925, section 105 expressly states that the mortgagee is a trustee of the purchase-money and provides for its application in this order:

(1) if the sale is "free from incumbrances" and there were some *prior* incumbrancers, in the discharge of their claims;

(2) in the payment of all costs, charges or expenses properly incurred by the mortgagee, incidental to the sale and any attempted sale[13];

(3) in discharging his own debt under the mortgage[14];

(4) the *residue* is to be paid to the person entitled to the mortgaged property, or authorised to give receipts for the proceeds of the sale (*i.e.* the next incumbrancer, or, if none, the mortgagor).[15]

When the persons interested in the equity of redemption have lost their titles under the Limitation Act 1980, the mortgagee holds the proceeds of sale free of any obligation to account to them, even if he has purported to

---

[7] *Kennedy* v. *De Trafford* [1897] A.C. 180.

[8] *Parkinson* v. *Hanbury* (1860) 1 Dr. & Sm. 143; affirmed (1867) L.R. 2 H.L. 1; *Rajah Kishendatt Ram* v. *Rajah Mumtaz Ali Khan* (1879) L.R. 6 Ind.App. 145, P.C.

[9] *Shaw* v. *Bunny* (1865) 2 De G. J. & Sm. 468.

[10] *Rajah Kishendatt Ram* v. *Rajah Mumtaz Ali Khan* (1879) L.R. 6 Ind.App. 145, P.C.

[11] *Locking* v. *Parker* (1872) L.R. 8 Ch. 30; *Weld-Blundell* v. *Synott* [1940] 2 K.B. 107.

[12] *Banner* v. *Berridge* (1881) 18 Ch.D. 254, where Kay J. said that the fiduciary relationship did not arise unless a surplus was proved. *Cf. Sands* to *Thompson* (1883) 22 Ch.D. 614; *Thorne* v. *Heard and Marsh* [1895] A.C. 495.

[13] Including any statute-barred interest, see *post*, p. 414. A mortgagee who exercises his power of sale may retain *all* arrears of interest out of the proceeds of sale as this is not recoverable by action.

[14] This is so irrespective of any cross-claim by the mortgagor against the mortgagee—see *Samuel Keller (Holdings) Ltd.* v. *Martin's Bank Ltd.* [1971] 1 W.L.R. 43; and see *Inglis* v. *Commonwealth Trading Bank of Australia Ltd.* (1972) 126 C.L.R. 161.

[15] The concluding words of s.105 are not accurate in that it states that the residue " . . . shall be paid to the person entitled to the mortgaged property." This literally means the *purchaser* and not any subsequent mortgagee or the mortgagor, if none. It would seem that the phrase must be construed with the following additional words inserted " . . . to the person *who immediately before the sale was* entitled to the mortgaged property." See *British General Insurance Co. Ltd.* v. *Att.-Gen.* [1945] L.J.N.C.C.R. 113 at 115.

sell under the power of sale in the mortgage.[16] But any person still interested in the residue, whether as a puisne mortgagee or as a holder of the ultimate equity of redemption, is entitled to an account from the mortgagee as to his disbursements under the first three headings. Indeed, the mortgagee must have his accounts settled before he can get a discharge from the person with a first claim on the surplus[17]; if the latter disputes the account, the mortgagee can apply to have the account taken by the court.[18]

The destination of the residue depends on what has happened to the equity of redemption; if there is one person solely entitled, there is no difficulty, but the equity of redemption may have been settled, incumbered, or have devolved upon several persons with partial interests.

(1) Settlement. The money must be paid to the trustees or into court.

(2) Successive incumbrances. The money belongs to the incumbrancers according to their priorities. Each successive incumbrancer holds the balance on trust to satisfy his own claim and to pass on the balance, if any. Accordingly, the mortgagee is liable to any incumbrancer, of whose charge he knows, if he pays over the money to the mortgagor.[19] This means, in the case of a legal mortgage of land, that he must search at the Land Registry, because registration has the same consequences as actual notice.[20] He is not, however, under such a duty to state his accounts correctly to other incumbrancers as to estop him from claiming repayment, if in error he pays over to the second mortgagee more than is in fact left—after discharging his own mortgage.[21] The mortgagee, as a trustee of the money, appears to have three ways of obtaining his discharge. Either he may distribute the whole fund, paying to a puisne incumbrancer only what is due to him on his mortgage,[22] or else he may pay the whole fund over to the incumbrancer next entitled and obtain a discharge from him. The latter will then hold the residue on the trusts set out in section 105 of the Law of Property Act 1925.[23] Thirdly, if in doubt as to the priorities, he may pay the money into court.[24]

---

[16] *Young* v. *Clarey* [1948] Ch. 191.
[17] See *Eley* v. *Read* (1897) 76 L.T. 39.
[18] *Chadwick* v. *Heatley* (1845) 2 Coll. 137.
[19] *West London Commercial Bank* v. *Reliance Permanent Building Society* (1885) 29 Ch.D. 954.
[20] L.P.A. 1925, s.198(1).
[21] *Weld-Blundell* v. *Synott* [1940] 2 K.B. 107.
[22] *Re Bell, Jeffrey* v. *Sayles* [1896] 1 Ch. 1; but, strictly, it is the right of the next incumbrancer to have the whole surplus paid over to him, and therefore his claims must be allowed on that footing, *i.e.* the first incumbrancer cannot limit him to six years' arrears of interest: *Re Thomson's Mortgage Trust, Thomson* v. *Bruty* [1920] 1 Ch. 508.
[23] *Cf.* s.107(2) which covers such a receipt by a puisne incumbrancer.
[24] *Re Walhampton Estate* (1884) 26 Ch.D. 391; and see Trustee Act 1925, s.63 (as amended by the Administration of Justice Act 1965, s.36(4), Sched. 3).

(3) Several owners of the equity of redemption.   Being a trustee, he must regulate his payments in accordance with the strict rights of the parties and give the beneficiaries all proper allowances.[25] In case of difficulty he may apply to the court for guidance.

Finally, if there is a surplus and the mortgagee does not distribute it, he will be charged simple interest on the balance in his hands in favour of persons interested in the equity of redemption; and it will not make any difference that there is delay in applying to have the money paid out.[25a] He will not, however, be charged interest if distribution is prevented by disputes concerning priorities.[25b]

Effect of a sale.   The effect of a sale under a power of sale is to destroy the equity of redemption and to constitute the mortgagee a trustee of the surplus proceeds for the persons interested according to their priorities.[25c] It vests the whole of the estate of the mortgagor in the purchaser,[26] subject to any prior mortgage, but free from the selling mortgagee's mortgage and all subsequent incumbrances (including the mortgagor's equity of redemption). The subsequent interests are overreached (if transferred into the proceeds of sale[27]). In the case of registered land the purchaser must register his interest.[28] That the mortgagor's right to redeem is utterly gone is well illustrated by the case of *Shaw* v. *Bunny*,[29] where a puisne incumbrancer purchased the estate from the first mortgagee, selling under an express power. The fact that the purchaser had been under an obligation to allow the mortgagor to redeem the property as to the puisne incumbrance did not prevent his purchase from conferring on him a title absolute and irredeemable. Moreover, under the equitable doctrine of conversion the destruction of the equity of redemption takes place as soon as there is a binding contract for sale (even if it is conditional), not upon completion. In *Lord Waring* v. *London and Manchester Assurance Co.*,[30] the court was invited to say that the mortgagor might redeem at any time before the execution of the conveyance: the result would be that a mortgagee could only give a conditional contract for sale, and his ability to find a purchaser might be seriously prejudiced. But the power to sell is a power to bind the mortgagor by sale, and the court had no hesitation in deciding that the contract by itself is enough to defeat the equity of redemption. If the mortgagee has, in exercise of his power of sale, entered into a contract for the sale of property, the mortgagor cannot stop the sale by tendering the

---

[25] *Re Cook's Mortgage, Lawledge* v. *Tyndall* [1896] 1 Ch. 923.
[25a] *Eley* v. *Read* (1897) 76 L.T. 39.
[25b] *Mathison* v. *Clarke* (1855) 25 L.J.Ch. 29; presumably he would have to account for interest actually produced by the surplus, as, *e.g.*, if he put it to deposit.
[25c] *Rajah Kishendatt Ram* v. *Rajah Mumtaz Ali Khan* (1879) L.R. 6 Ind. App. 145.
[26] L.P.A. 1925, ss.88(1), 89(1), 104(1).
[27] *Ibid.* s.2(1)(iii).
[28] Land Registration Act 1925, s.19 as amended by the Land Registration Act 1986, s.4(3).
[29] (1865) 2 De G.J. & Sm. 468; *S.E. Rly. Co. (Directors, etc.)* v. *Jortin* (1857) 6 H.L.C. 425. (1865) 2 De G.J. & Sm. 468.
[30] [1935] Ch. 310.

moneys due.[31] Further a contract made by the mortgagor has no effect on the mortgagee's power of sale.[32]

The sale also has consequences for the mortgagee. He has taken steps to realise his security, and therefore the interest ceases to run as from the date of sale so that he cannot charge the mortgagor with an additional six months' interest after the sale.[33] On the other hand, sale is not like fore-closure, and does not necessarily put an end to the mortgage debt. If there is a surplus after discharging the debt, the transaction is, of course, con-cluded, save for the distribution of the surplus. But if the amount realised is less than what is due on the mortgage, the mortgagee may still sue on the personal covenant for the deficiency: the rule that a mortgagee disables himself from suing for the debt by putting it out of his power to reconvey does not apply to a sale under a power given by the mortgage.[34]

The conveyance. A power to make conveyance on sale is not automati-cally attendant on a power to sell, and it is therefore necessary to consider how the conveyance is made upon a sale by a mortgagee. Formerly, in the case of express powers, the power to sell in a mortgage by conveyance did carry with it the power to convey, because the mortgagee was holder of the title. But in mortgages of land by demise or sub-demise (the usual method of mortgaging leasehold), the mortgagor's reversion caused a difficulty which was usually got over by declaring the mortgagor a trustee of the reversion for the mortgagee.[35] Again, in equitable mortgages the mort-gagee, having no legal title, had no power to convey, and it was necessary to provide for this by giving the mortgagee a power of attorney to convey the property upon a sale.[36] The law is still the same for mortgagees by con-veyance of personalty and for equitable mortgagees with express powers. But legal mortgages of land today must be by demise or sub-demise, or by legal charge, and whether the power to sell is express or statutory the mort-gagor's reversion causes no difficulty, because section 88(1) of the Law of Property Act 1925 provides for mortgages or legal charges of the fee, that whether the mortgagee sells under express or statutory power:

> "(a) the conveyance by him shall operate to vest in the purchaser the fee simple in the land conveyed subject to any legal mortgage having priority to the mortgage in right of which the sale is made and to any money thereby secured, and thereupon;
> (b) the mortgage term or the charge by way of legal mortgage and any subsequent mortgage term or charges shall merge or be extinguished as respects the land conveyed; and such conveyance may, as respects

---

[31] *Ibid.*, and see *Property and Bloodstock Ltd.* v. *Emerton, Bush* v. *Property & Bloodstock Ltd.* [1968] Ch. 94. See also *post*, pp. 239 *et seq.*
[32] *Duke* v. *Robson* [1973] 1 W.L.R. 267.
[33] *Cf. West* v. *Diprose* [1900] 1 Ch. 337.
[34] *Re McHenry, McDermott* v. *Boyd, Barker's Claim* [1894] 3 Ch. 290.
[35] *London and County Banking Co.* v. *Goddard* [1897] 1 Ch. 642.
[36] *Re Hodson and Howes' Contract* (1887) 35 Ch.D. 668 at 671, *per* North J. " . . . he can convey all he has; but he cannot convey the legal estate," and see *post*, pp. 268–269.

the fee simple, be made in the name of the estate owner in whom it is vested."

Section 89(1) of the Law of Property Act 1925 contains parallel provisions for mortgages of leasehold interests with one important difference. The mortgagor's nominal reversion expectant on the mortgagee's sub-term will vest in the purchaser upon a sale, but application may be made to the court to have the reversion kept alive as a protection to the purchaser against onerous covenants in the original lease. If the purchaser acquires the whole leasehold interest formerly vested in the mortgagor, he will be in the position of an assignee and bound by the covenants under the doctrine in *Spencer's Case*.[37] Applications to the court under this section will be uncommon, and there is no guidance as to what the court will consider a sufficient reason for allowing a purchaser to escape from performance of the covenants.[38] Further, where a licence to assign is required on sale by a mortgagee, such licence shall not be unreasonably refused.

So much for sales under express powers, which will not often occur. Conveyances consequent upon the exercise of *statutory* powers, under which most sales take place, are provided for by section 104(1) of the Law of Property Act 1925, which states that the mortgagee shall have power:

> "by deed to convey the property sold *for such estate and interest therein as he is by the Act authorised to sell or convey or may be the subject of the mortgage*, freed from all estates, interests and rights to which the mortgage has priority, but subject to all estates, interests and rights which have priority to the mortgage." [author's emphasis].

The words in italics require explanation. Under a statutory power the mortgagee has the advantage of sections 88(1) and 89(1) of the Law of Property Act 1925, so that a *legal* mortgagee of leasehold or freehold property may sell and convey a larger estate than was the subject of the mortgage, *i.e.* the mortgagor's reversion may be included; but that in all other cases the mortgagee can only convey the interest which was mortgaged to him, unless the mortgage gives him powers additional to that in the statute. This latter point causes no inconvenience to a legal mortgagee of personalty or to a mortgagee of an equitable interest by assignment. The mortgagor's whole title is transferred to them, and section 104 merely confirms the right to make a conveyance of a title already vested in them. But when the legal owner of land or personalty has created a mere equitable security by contract, the "subject-matter of the mortgage" is the *equitable* interest (*i.e.* the power over the equity of redemption) transferred to the mortgagee, and section 104 does not therefore confer[39] a power to convey the

---

[37] (1583) 5 Co.Rep. 16a.

[38] See Wollstenholme & Cherry, *Conveyancing Statutes* (13th ed.).

[39] This narrow interpretation was doubted in *Re White Rose Cottage* [1965] Ch. 940 at 951, where it was suggested that s.104(1) gives an equitable mortgagee power to sell the legal estate. Also in Fisher & Lightwood, *Law of Mortgage* (10th ed., 1988), pp. 402, 403, approval is given to this interpretation and it is suggested that s.104 of the Law of Property

mortgagor's legal title to a purchaser.[40] This is a serious disability. It is, however, the universal practice to provide for this by giving an equitable mortgagee a power of attorney to convey on behalf of the mortgagor,[41] indeed, *ex abundanti cautela*, the mortgagor is usually in addition made a trustee of the legal title for the mortgagee. If no such precaution is taken, the conveyance cannot be made without either the mortgagor's concurrence or an application to the court.

Deeds.   Section 106(4) of the Law of Property Act 1925 provides that when the statutory power has become exercisable, the person entitled to sell may demand and recover from any person, other than someone with a prior interest in the mortgaged property, all deeds or documents relating to the title or to the property which a purchaser might be entitled to demand and recover from him. It should be noticed that this will apply to deeds in the hands of a *prior* mortgagee whose debt is discharged out of the purchase-moneys or under section 50 of the Law of Property Act 1925.

Injunctions to restrain sale.   When there is evidence of fraud or some other irregularity in the sale which would justify it being set aside, an injunction will be granted by the court to restrain the sale provided that the purchaser had *actual* notice of the fraud or irregularity or of facts which make the proper exercise of the power impossible.[42] Otherwise the mortgagor will be left to his remedy in damages against the mortgagee.[43]

The court will also restrain a sale when the mortgagee is obstructing redemption by the mortgagor. Thus, if a tender of the mortgage debt has been made and declined,[44] or if an offer to redeem has been made and the mortgagee has disputed the right to redeem,[45] the mortgagee will be restrained from *attempting* to exercise his power of sale,[46] similarly if, upon motion to restrain the sale, the amount claimed is paid into court.[47] But no injunction will be granted if the mortgagor merely expresses an intention to

---

Act 1925 approximates in its effect rather to Lord Cranworth's Act 1860, than to the Conveyancing Act 1881. This seems an odd way of regarding the section, since Lord Cranworth's Act *did* enable a mortgagee to convey the mortgagor's whole interest (*Re Solomon and Meagher's Contract* (1889) 40 Ch.D. 508), whereas the 1881 Act, like the 1925 Act, did not.

[40] "The mortgaged property" under the L.P.A. 1925, s.101(1)(i).
[41] See *post*, pp. 268–269.
[42] See *ante*, pp. 226 *et seq.*
[43] *Prichard* v. *Wilson* (1864) 10 Jur. (N.S.) 330. This is on the assumption that the sale is pursuant to the statutory power which contains the clause for the protection of purchasers (see *ante* pp. 225 *et seq.*), or to a well-drawn express power containing such a clause. If the express power contains no such clause then the general doctrine of actual or constructive notice applies.
[44] Even without a tender for costs: *Jenkins* v. *Jones* (1860) 2 Giff. 99.
[45] *Rhodes* v. *Buckland* (1852) 16 Beav. 212; but not if the dispute is only as to the amount due: *Gill* v. *Newton* (1866) 14 L.T. 240.
[46] But note the position if there is in existence a binding contract of sale between the mortgagee and the purchaser in the absence of fraud or some other irregularity, *ante*, pp. 225 *et seq*.
[47] *Whitworth* v. *Rhodes* (1850) 20 L.J.Ch. 105.

redeem,[48] not even if he has begun an action for redemption[49]; it is only on the terms of *payment* that the power of sale will be restrained. Consequently, the court will always, when granting an injunction, insist on payment into court of the amount due as a condition of restraining the sale.[50] Even an order *nisi* for foreclosure in an action brought by the mortgagee does not necessarily put a restraint on the exercise of his power to sell out of court, but until foreclosure absolute he may sell with the leave of the court.[51] Finally, it may be noticed that in special cases, where there is a fiduciary relationship between the mortgagor and mortgagee, the court, without altogether restraining the sale, may interfere and control the rights of the parties.[52]

Implied power of sale at common law.   The mortgagee of personal chattels, if they are in his possession, and in any case the mortgagee of stocks and shares has[53] a power of sale implied at common law. When the mortgage is by deed, the common law power is displaced by the power given by section 101 of the Law of Property Act 1925, but the implied power is still serviceable when there is no deed. If the mortgage fixes a day for payment, the implied power is exercisable immediately after default on that date. If no date is fixed, then it is exercisable after the mortgagor has been given reasonable notice to pay the debt and has defaulted.[54] It appears from the same case that in a mortgage of shares a month or even a fortnight may be sufficient notice.[55]

Rights and Remedies of the Legal Mortgagee for Enforcing the Security in Court

Proceedings for possession

The legal title which he obtains by his conveyance gives to a legal mortgagee and a chargee by way of legal mortgage the right to enter into actual possession of the mortgage security from the moment the mortgage is created.[56] If the security is land, which is already let on leases binding the mortgagee, he cannot, of course, go into possession physically, but he can enter into receipt of the rents and profits by serving notice on the tenants to pay their rents to himself instead of to the mortgagor.[57] Normally, the right arises at once on the execution of the conveyance. If, however, (as now

---

[48] *Matthie* v. *Edwards* (1847) 16 L.J.Ch. 405.
[49] *Davies* v. *Williams* (1843) 7 Jur. 663.
[50] *Warner* v. *Jacob* (1882) 20 Ch.D. 220; *Macleod* v. *Jones* (1883) 24 Ch.D. 289.
[51] *Stevens* v. *Theatres Ltd.* [1903] 1 Ch. 857.
[52] *Macleod* v. *Jones* (1883) 24 Ch.D. 289.
[53] See *ante*, p. 220.
[54] *Deverges* v. *Sandeman* [1901] 1 Ch. 70 at 73, *per* Farwell, J., affirmed [1902] 1 Ch. 579.
[55] [1902] 1 Ch. 579.
[56] See *ante*, p. 205.
[57] *Horlock* v. *Smith* (1842) 6 Jur 478; or merely not to pay the rents to the mortgagor: *Heales* v. *M'Murray* (1856) 23 Beav. 401.

rarely happens) the mortgage deed contains a covenant for quiet enjoyment until default is made on the day fixed for payment (or any similar provision) the right is suspended.[58] Further once the right has arisen, the court will not by injunction restrain the mortgagee from exercising his right.[59] Indeed, until 1936 it was true to say that a legal mortgagee had an absolute right to possession which he could enforce summarily by obtaining judgment for possession in the King's Bench Division. Thus if it was necessary to commence proceedings for possession of the mortgaged premises instead of relying upon physical entry, the court would afford to the mortgagee the same summary remedy which he had by virtue of his title to enable him to enforce the security.

Discretion at common law

An amendment to the Rules of Court in 1936,[60] however, materially affected the enforcement of a mortgagee's right to possession. All proceedings by a mortgagee for payment or for possession were thenceforth assigned to the Chancery Division[61] with the express object of excluding summary proceedings by a mortgagee in the King's Bench Division where no regard was had to the Chancery practice of granting equitable relief to the mortgagor in proper cases. The reason for the amendment was that summary proceedings for possession were usually taken against mortgagor-purchasers of small dwelling-houses and it was desired to give the court discretion to "temper the wind to the shorn lamb."[62] Proceedings for possession therefore had to be taken by writ or originating summons in the Chancery Division, and judgment for possession became discretionary but only by leave of the Master.[63] Moreover, practice directions authorised Masters, when the defendant was in arrears with any instalment, to give him an opportunity of paying off the arrears by adjourning the summons if the circumstances warranted such a course. The mortgagee in the case of *Hinckley and South Leicestershire Permanent Benefit Building Society* v. *Freeman*[64] sought to impeach these directions as *ultra vires* on the ground that they conflicted with a mortgagee's established right to immediate possession but they were upheld by the court. The change in the procedural rules of court thus gave the court some measure of control over the mortgagee's exercise of his right to possession.

But this practice, which had continued for some 26 years, was terminated abruptly by the decision of Russell J. in the case of *Birmingham Citi-*

---

[58] *Wilkinson* v. *Hall* (1837) 3 Bing. N.C. 508; see *ante*, p. 206, and *post*, p. 286.
[59] *Marquis of Cholmondely* v. *Lord Clinton* (1820) 2 J. & W. 1, 181; this, of course, is one of the points of difference between mortgagees and trustees. See also *ante*, pp. 194 *et seq*.
[60] On the recommendation of the Supreme Court Rules Committee.
[61] Under R.S.C. 1883, Ord. LV, rr. 5A, 5C. Now R.S.C. Ord. 88, rr. 1, 2. Also see *Norwich Union Life Assurance Society* v. *Preston* [1957] 1 W.L.R. 813.
[62] *Redditch Benefit Building Society* v. *Roberts* [1940] Ch. 415 at 420.
[63] R.S.C. Ord. 88, r. 7 (Formerly R.S.C. 1883, Ord. LV, r. 5A).
[64] [1941] Ch. 32.

zens' Permanent Building Society v. *Caunt*[65] who declared that this jurisdiction was without legal foundation. The court had no power to order an
adjournment if the mortgagee objected to such a course, save for a short
period of up to 28 days, and only when the mortgagor had reasonable pros-
pects of paying off the whole mortgage debt, or otherwise satisfying the
mortgagee in full.[66]

The present position is somewhat obscure, but this discretionary jurisdiction in the High Court would still seem to be extant. If, however, the
mortgagor has no reasonable prospect of satisfying the mortgagee within a
short period of time, an adjournment will be refused.[67] It should be added
that the strict approach of the courts based upon commercial considerations is also exemplified in those decisions where despite the fact that the
mortgagor has a cross-claim which may exceed the mortgage debt, the
courts have still refused an adjournment.[68]

In the case of *Quennel* v. *Maltby*[69] the possibility of a wider equitable
discretion was raised. There it was held by the Court of Appeal that a
mortgagee would not be granted possession by the court if he was seeking
to exercise his right for purposes other than the protection or enforcement
of his security. In that case the mortgagee was seeking possession of a
dwelling-house which, contrary to the terms of the mortgage with Barclays
Bank, had been let to students. Thus, whilst the tenancies enjoyed the protection of the Rent Act 1977 *vis-à-vis* the mortgagor landlord, their tenancies were not binding on the mortgagee.[70] The mortgagee refused to
commence possession proceedings against the tenants. The mortgagor then
arranged for his wife to pay off the mortgagee and to take a transfer of the
mortgage, thereby becoming the mortgagee. Possession proceedings were
then commenced by her to obtain vacant possession of the premises. It was
held by the court that she was acting as agent for the landlord mortgagor
and thus could not assert the rights of the original mortgagee to evict tenants of the mortgagor. Lord Denning M.R. relied on a wider inherent
equitable discretion of the courts to prevent a mortgagee or a transferee
from him from obtaining possession of a dwelling-house contrary to the
justice of the case when there was an ulterior motive, namely, to gain possession of the premises in order to resell it at a profit.[71] But the narrower
ground of agency preferred by Templeman L.J.[72] probably provides a preferable justification as such an action for possession if commenced directly

---

[65] [1962] Ch. 883.
[66] See now the statutory discretion, *post*, pp. 243 *et seq.*
[67] *Ibid.* See also *Robertson* v. *Cilia* [1956] 1 W.L.R. 1502; *Four-Maids Ltd.* v. *Dudley Mar-shall (Properties) Ltd.* [1957] Ch. 317; *Braithwaite* v. *Winwood* [1960] 1 W.L.R. 1257.
[68] See *Samuel Keller (Holdings) Ltd.* v. *Martins Bank Ltd.* [1971] 1 W.L.R. 43; *Mobil Oil* v. *Rawlinson* (1981) 261 E.G. 260; *Citibank Trust Ltd.* v. *Aviyor* [1987] 1 W.L.R. 1157; *Barclays Bank plc* v. *Tennet* (unreported), C.A. (Civ. Div.) Transcript No. 242, 1984.
[69] [1979] 1 W.L.R. 318.
[70] See *Dudley and District Benefit Building Society* v. *Emerson* [1949] Ch. 707, and *ante*, p. 22 and *post*, pp. 335, 337, 338.
[71] *Quennel* v. *Maltby* [1979] 1 W.L.R. 318 at 323.
[72] *Ibid.* at 324.

by a landlord would have failed by virtue of the protection afforded to the tenants by the 1977 Act.[73]

Statutory discretion

Under the Administration of Justice Acts 1970 and 1973.   Following the recommendations of the Payne Committee,[74] sections 36 to 38 of the Administration of Justice Act 1970 were specifically enacted in the case of mortgages of dwelling-houses in order to reverse the decision of *Birmingham Citizens Permanent Building Society* v. *Caunt*.[75] Whether the action is brought in the High Court or the county court,[75a] the Administration of Justice Act 1970, as amended, provides the court with certain powers to adjourn the proceedings, stay the order for possession, or postpone the date for delivery of possession.[76] Section 36 of the 1970 Act provides as follows:

> "(1) Where the mortgagee under a mortgage of land which consists of or includes a dwelling-house brings an action in which he claims possession of the mortgaged property, not being an action for foreclosure in which a claim for possession of the mortgaged property is also made, the court may exercise any of the powers conferred on it by subsection (2) below if it appears to the court that in the event of its exercising the power the mortgagor[76a] is likely to be able within a reasonable period to pay any sums due under the mortgage[76b] or to remedy a default consisting of a breach of any other obligation arising under or by virtue of the mortgage.
> (2) The court—
> (a) may adjourn the proceedings, or
> (b) on giving judgment, or making an order, for delivery of possession of the mortgaged property, or at any time before the execution[77]; of such judgment or order, may—

---

[73] The existence of such an extension to the jurisdiction is to be doubted, see R. J. Smith [1979] Conv. 266; R. A. Pearce [1979] C.L.J. 257.

[74] Report of the Committee on the Enforcement of Judgment Debts 1969, (Cmnd. 3908).

[75] [1962] Ch. 883. These powers are not dependant upon default by the mortgagor: see *per* Buckley L.J. and Scarman L.J. (*contra* Goff L.J.) in *Western Bank Ltd.* v. *Schindler* [1977] Ch. 1 and see *ante*, p. 206.

[75a] For the position where the county court has exclusive jurisdiction in mortgage actions, see *post*, Appendix III.

[76] Unless the mortgage secures a regulated agreement within the meaning of the Consumer Credit Act 1974, in which case the 1974 Act applies, (see *ante*, pp. 140 *et seq.*).

[76a] By s.39(1) "mortgagee" and "mortgagor" include any person deriving title under the original mortgagee or mortgagor. Thus a tenant of a mortgagor may be able to avail himself of these powers, but *quare* the position where the tenancy has been created after the mortgage and is therefore not binding on the mortgagee.

[76b] Meaning the arrears due at the date of the hearing, *Middlesbrough Trading and Mortgage Co. Ltd.* v. *Cunningham* (1974) 28 P. & C.R. 69.

[77] It would seem that these words have overruled the decision in *London Permanent Benefit Building Society* v. *De Baer* [1969] 1 Ch. 321. But there has been no decision, as yet, as to whether these words mean "before execution is complete" or "before execution has been commenced."

(i) stay or suspend execution of the judgment or order, or

(ii) postpone the date for delivery of possession,

for such period or periods as the court thinks reasonable.

(3) Any such adjournment, stay, suspension[77a] or postponement as is referred to in sub-section (2) above may be made subject to such conditions with regard to payment by the mortgagor of any sums secured by the mortgage or the remedying of any default as the court thinks fit.

(4) The court may from time to time vary or revoke any condition imposed by virtue of this section."

Thus, the purpose of section 36 was to mitigate the severity of the legal rule that a mortgagee is entitled to possession of the mortgaged property by giving some protection to a mortgagor of a dwelling-house who had fallen into temporary financial difficulties over the payment of his instalments in allowing him a reasonable time to make good his default.[77b]

But, unfortunately, it soon became apparent that those cases in which it was likely that the jurisdiction would be invoked were the very cases where the whole principal sum had become due by reason of the fact that most building society mortgages contain a provision making the whole principal sum due in the case of default. The reference in section 36 to "a reasonable period to pay any sums due under the mortgage" had the effect of confining the operation of the section to relatively few cases where the mortgagor was reasonably likely to be able to pay off the whole of the sums due under the mortgage.[78] If the mortgagor was already in difficulties in his instalments, the chances of his being able to pay off the whole principal sum was obviously somewhat slim. In the case of the *Halifax Building Society* v. *Clark*[79] the wife of the mortgagor invoked the provisions of section 1(5) of the Matrimonial Homes Act 1967 (now the Matrimonial Homes Act 1983, section 1(5))[80] which obliged the mortgagee to accept payment from her although her husband was the owner of the mortgaged property. She sought an adjournment of the mortgagee's action for possession as she was in a position to pay the current instalment and also the accumulated arrears, with the support of social security. But, in that case, the court held that such an action would not be sufficient to justify the invocation of its power to adjourn the mortgagee's claim for possession as the "sums due" under the mortgage amounted to the whole of the capital sum under the accelerated payments clause and she clearly was not in a position to pay that.

[77a] For enforcement of suspended orders, see *The Supreme Court Practice 1988*, Vol. 1, para. 88/2–7/19, and *Practice Direction (Possession Order: [1972] Issue of Execution) [No. 7 of 1972]* 1 W.L.R. 240.

[77b] *per* Griffiths L.J. in *Bank of Scotland* v. *Grimes* [1985] Q.B. 1179 at 1190.

[78] *Halifax Building Society* v. *Clark* [1973] Ch. 307; but *cf. First Middlesbrough Trading & Mortgage Co. Ltd.* v. *Cunningham* (1974) 28 P. & C.R. 69 where this case was not followed.

[79] [1973] Ch. 307.

[80] See *ante*, pp. 169–172.

As a result, section 8 of the Administration of Justice Act 1973 was designed to overturn that decision. Section 8, in effect, redefines "sums due under the mortgage" as " . . . such amounts as the mortgagor would have expected to be required to pay if there has been no provision for earlier payment."

Thus, section 8 of the 1973 Act restored what was presumed to be the original intention of the 1970 Act, and, in effect, provides that where the mortgage entitles or permits the mortgage debt to be repaid by instalments, or otherwise defers payment of the whole or any part of the sum, and there is also a term rendering the whole sum due in the event of a default, then the court may nevertheless exercise its powers pursuant to section 36 of the 1970 Act provided that the mortgagor is likely to be able to pay off the outstanding instalments. Clearly, by virtue of these provisions an instalment mortgage is now included within the terms of the sections where there was a six-month legal date for redemption, and also an endowment mortgage is similarly included as it is a mortgage which otherwise permits deferred repayment.[81]

In the case of *Western Bank Limited* v. *Schindler*[82] a majority of the Court of Appeal was even prepared to hold that section 36 of the 1970 Act was applicable even in the absence of a default by the mortgagor.[83] This was an unusual case in that the mortgage made no provision for the payments of capital or interest until 10 years after its execution. The mortgagor, however, failed to pay the premium due on the life assurance policy and the policy lapsed. The debt was therefore inadequately secured and in the event it was held that it was not a proper case for the exercise of statutory discretion in the mortgagor's favour. But, the contrary opinion of Goff L.J. is probably to be preferred in that he was of the view that section 36 of the 1970 Act had no application in any event.

Further, in the case of *Habib Bank Ltd.* v. *Tailor*[84] it was held that if the loan is not one which otherwise permits deferred repayment then the statutory discretion does *not* apply. This may have serious consequences for the mortgagor.[85] In that case the mortgagor secured an overdraft on his current account with his bank by a charge on his home the sums being repayable on demand. As the bank could therefore not sue on a supporting mortgage until such a demand had been made the court held that section 8 of the 1973 Act did not apply as it was not a mortgage which permitted deferred repayment. As a consequence any relief had to be sought under

---

[81] *Centrax Trustees Ltd.* v. *Ross* [1979] 2 All E.R. 952; *Bank of Scotland* v. *Grimes* [1985] Q.B. 1179. The section also empowers the court to adjourn foreclosure actions but not to make suspended orders in such cases.
[82] [1977] Ch. 1.
[83] *Ibid.* at 12, 13, 15, 19, 26. See also *Royal Trust Co. of Canada* v. *Markham* [1975] 1 W.L.R. 1416.
[84] [1982] 1 W.L.R. 1218.
[85] But not all mortgages in which the loan is expressed to be on demand fall within this category, see S. Tromans [1984] Conv. 91.

section 36 of the 1970 Act, and as we have seen, this would not be possible unless the mortgagor could demonstrate to the court that he could repay the whole of the debt within a reasonable period.

It should also be added that where the mortgage falls within the provisions of section 8 of the 1973 Act, the court's discretion also extends to foreclosure actions whether or not possession is also sought in the same proceedings.[86]

Finally, it must be remembered that the conditions for the grant of an adjournment are strict. The court's discretionary powers are only exercisable if there is a likelihood of the mortgagor being able to pay the sums due (*i.e.* the arrears and also the current instalments) within a reasonable period, or, that he will seek a speedy sale of the mortgaged property to discharge the arrears and the mortgage debt.[87] Thus the court should not grant an indefinite adjournment and the period must be fixed or ascertainable.[88] In any event, these powers are *not* exercisable where the mortgagor is unable to comply with the original payment schedule. Thus the court has no power to order payment of instalments at a reduced level, for example, payment of interest only.

Consumer Credit Act 1974.   The Act has provided a complex series of safeguards in many different types of credit transactions. Most mortgages are not included within its terms since generally it only applies where the credit provided does not exceed £15,000[89] and where the mortgagor is an "individual," and the mortgagee is not an exempt lender as defined by section 16 of the Act.[89a] This definition of exempt lender includes some building societies,[89b] local authorities, large assurance companies and other cases specified by ministerial order. The purpose of the Act in so far as it regulates mortgage lending, in effect, is to provide safeguards for borrowers raising finance by way of second mortgages. With regard to those transactions to which the Act does apply, however, (*i.e.* "regulated agreements"), such agreements must be in the form prescribed by regulations in order to ensure that the mortgagor is aware of his rights and duties, the

---

[86] Administration of Justice Act 1973, s.8(3), and see *Lord Marples of Wallasey* v. *Holmes* (1975) 31 P. & C.R. 94.

[87] *Royal Trust Company of Canada* v. *Markham* [1975] 1 W.L.R. 1416. *Mobil Oil* v. *Rawlinson* (1982) 43 P. & C.R. 221; *Bank of Scotland* v. *Grimes* [1985] Q.B. 1179; *Citibank Trust Ltd.* v. *Aviyor* [1987] 1 W.L.R. 1157.

[88] The usual time given for possession if no order is made under the Administration of Justice Acts 1970–1973, is 28 days after service, see *Barclays Bank* v. *Bird* [1954] Ch. 274 at 282, *per* Harman J.

[89] (S.I. 1983 No. 1878), applying this limit to new transactions from May 20, 1985. Up until this date the original limit applies of £5,000.

[89a] As amended by the Building Societies Act 1986, s.120(1), (2); the Housing and Planning Act 1986, s.22; the Banking Act 1987, s.88.

[89b] From January 1, 1987, building societies lost their automatic exemption from the Consumer Credit Act 1974 when the major part of the Building Societies Act 1986 came into force; see Consumer Credit (Exempt Agreements) (No. 2) Order 1985 (S.I. 1985 No. 757) as amended by (S.I. 1985 No. 1736), (S.I. 1985 No. 1918), (S.I. 1986 No. 1105), (S.I. 1986 No. 2186), (S.I. 1987 No. 1578), (S.I. 1988 No. 707) and (S.I. 1988 No. 991).

amount and rate of the total charge for credit, and the protection and remedies provided by the Act.[90]

The agreement must contain all the agreed terms, except implied terms and must be signed by both parties. Also, the mortgagee must supply the mortgagor with a copy of the proposed agreement seven days in advance of execution, and must not approach him in the meantime in order to give him an opportunity to withdraw. If the agreement fails to comply with the requirements of the Act, it is improperly executed and enforceable only on an order of the court.[91] If the mortgagor is in default the mortgagee must serve a default notice under the provisions of section 87 of the Act before he can recover possession of the goods or land. If the mortgagor complies in due time with the requirements of the default notice, the breach is treated as if it had never occurred.[92] The mortgage is only enforceable by order of the court.[93] The court has a wide discretion to make a "time order" under section 129(1) of the Act, under which the mortgagor is given time to pay by such instalments and at such time as the court having regard to the means of the mortgagor considers reasonable. The court can also make a suspended order for possession under section 135 of the Act.[94]

Regulated mortgages under the Rent Act 1977.[95]   Finally, mention should be made of the provisions of the Rent Act 1977 (as amended)[96] which impose special statutory restrictions on the right of a mortgagee to take possession of mortgaged premises in the case of regulated mortgages. These mortgages are now rare as the provisions of the 1977 Act generally have no application unless the mortgage was created before the relevant date.[97] Thus these complex provisions are of limited importance, and it is suggested that further reference be made to the standard works on the Rent Act 1977.[98]

Foreclosure or judicial sale

Generally

Equity, having created the equity of redemption, also provides means whereby a mortgagee may free his title from the equity. Otherwise a mortgagee would suffer a serious injustice, since, even when in urgent need of his capital, he would have no means of compelling its restoration.[99] He

[90] ss.60, 61.
[91] ss.58, 61 and 65.
[92] s.89.
[93] s.126 (or, if the mortgagor consents, s.173(3)). The "court" is the county court, see s.189(1).
[94] For a fuller explanation of the terms of the Consumer Credit Act 1974, see *ante*, pp. 140 *et seq*.
[95] Controlled mortgages were abolished by the Housing Act 1980, s.152 and Sched. 26.
[96] ss.131, 132, as amended by the Housing Act 1980, s.152 and Scheds. 25, 26.
[97] Usually December 8, 1965, but in any event no later than August 14, 1974.
[98] See, *e.g.* Pettit, *Private Sector Tenancies* (1981); Arden and Partington, *Housing Law* (1983); Megarry, *The Rent Acts* (11th ed., 1988).
[99] *Campbell* v. *Holyland* (1877) 7 Ch.D. 166 at 171, *per* Jessel, M.R.

might go into possession or appoint a receiver, but even so the rents and profits might do no more than pay him his interest. Consequently, although jealous to protect the equity of redemption, the court allows a mortgagee to destroy the equitable right to redeem *with its own assistance*. This assistance takes the form of an order either for foreclosure or for a judicial sale. By the former, a mortgagee's title is made absolute by the court, the effect of which is to transfer the legal estate from the mortgagor to the mortgagee.[1] By the latter, the security is, under the supervision of the court, sold freed from the equity of redemption. In the Republic of Ireland, foreclosure orders have never been favoured,[2] and there judicial sale is the remedy for a mortgagee as well as for a chargee. In England, on the other hand, the natural remedy given by the court to a mortgagee is foreclosure, and judicial sale is available to him only as an alternative, which the court may in its discretion grant him in the course of proceedings for foreclosure.[3] The realisation of his security in court in one of these two ways is, historically, the primary remedy of a mortgagee. But today a mortgagee will nearly always possess either an express or statutory power to sell out of court,[4] and will not be obliged to seek the court's assistance. Further, the courts have shown a reluctance to order foreclosure. Consequently it is a remedy which now has only limited importance and it has been suggested that it should be replaced by the simple remedy to order a judicial sale as in the Republic of Ireland. On the other hand, the power of the court to order foreclosure is still of some interest, since a mortgagee may desire to retain the mortgaged property in his own hands and to obtain the balance of its value.[5]

The right of foreclosure

In England and Wales the right to foreclose is inherent in the nature of mortgage,[6] and in no other form of security. It was for this reason that the test of a security, being a mortgage rather than a mere charge, is the availability to the creditor of the remedy of foreclosure. The only exceptions being *(i)* the old Welsh mortgage, in which any realisation of the security is

---

[1] *i.e.* by vesting the mortgagor's fee simple or term of years in the mortgagee, see L.P.A. 1925, ss.88(2), 89(2). In the case of registered land an order for foreclosure is completed by registration of the proprietor of the charge as proprietor of the land and by cancellation of the charge, (Land Registration Act 1925, s.34(3)). Prior to 1925 the remedy of foreclosure terminated the mortgagor's equity of redemption leaving the mortgagee with an unencumbered interest.

[2] *Re Cronin* [1914] 1 I.R. 23, 29; *Harpur* v. *Buchanan* [1919] 1 I.R. 1, 4; but the jurisdiction to give foreclosure, though not exercised, appears to exist: *Shea* v. *Moore* [1894] 1 I.R. 158 at 163, n, *per* Porter, M.R.

[3] L.P.A. 1925, s.91(2) and see *post*, p. 257.

[4] See *ante*, pp. 220 *et seq*. In practice a mortgagee will only seek the remedy of foreclosure where the security is deficient but there is a prospect that the value of the property will improve.

[5] For a modern case illustrating the difficulties which can be encountered in foreclosure proceedings, see *Lloyds & Scottish Trust Ltd.* v. *Britten* (1982) 44 P. & C.R. 249 and see *post*, pp. 261, 263.

[6] *Re Bogg* [1917] 2 Ch. 239 at 255.

impossible[7] and *(ii)* mortgages given by public utility companies where the impossibility of foreclosure arises not from the form of mortgage but from the property being in public use.[8] All other mortgages, whether their sub-ject-matter is realty or personalty,[9] and whether the mortgage is legal or equitable, give rise to this remedy. Thus an equitable mortgagee of a legal estate by express contract or by deposit of title deeds may foreclose,[10] while a mortgagee of an equitable interest in property may foreclose the equitable interest leaving the legal title outstanding in a third party.[11] Simi-larly, a mortgagee of personal chattels[12] and of a share in a partnership,[13] and a debenture holder may foreclose.[14] But, apart from statute, the rem-edy of a chargee is sale, not foreclosure.[15] A chargee with a charge by way of legal mortgage is a statutory exception to this rule, because the Law of Property Act 1925[16] gives him precisely the same remedies as a legal mort-gagee.

Restrictions on the equity of redemption by order of the court.   Foreclosure is the prerogative only of a mortgagee, because foreclosure presupposes a title in the creditor which has become absolute at law through the breach of a condition.[17] Under his contract a mortgagee's title to the property becomes absolute when the mortgagor fails to redeem in accordance with the terms of the proviso for redemption. Equity then intervenes on behalf of the mortgagor to give him a right to redeem notwithstanding that failure, and thus puts a stop on the absolute title of the mortgagee. But there has to be a stage at which a mortgagee can finally enforce his security. Foreclosure, as Jessel M.R., indicated,[18] is no more than the court's removal from the mortgagee's title of the stop which the court itself imposed. Foreclosure is therefore always an act of the court: today a mortgagee usually has power to sell his security out of court, but he cannot become the beneficial owner of the security except under the authority of the court. In *Re Farnol, Eades, Irvine & Co.*[19] Warrington J. said:

> "Foreclosure as a thing which can be done by a person has no mean-ing. Foreclosure is done by the order of the court, not by any person. In the strict legal sense it is nothing more than the destruction of the equity of redemption which previously existed."

[7] See *Coote on Mortgages* (9th ed., 1927), Vol. 1, Chap. III, p. 35.
[8] *Gardner* v. *London, Chatham and Dover Rly. Co.* (1867) 2 Ch. App. 201.
[9] *General Credit and Discount Co.* v. *Glegg* (1883) 22 Ch.D. 549.
[10] *Pryce* v. *Bury* (1853) 2 Drew 41; *Frail* v. *Ellis* (1852) 16 Beav. 350.
[11] *Cf. Slade* v. *Rigg* (1843) 3 Hare 35.
[12] *Kemp* v. *Westbrook* (1749) 1 Ves.Sen. 278.
[13] *Redmayne* v. *Forster* (1866) L.R. 2 Eq. 467.
[14] *Sadler* v. *Worley* [1894] 2 Ch. 170.
[15] *Tennant* v. *Trenchard* (1869) L.R. 4 Ch. 537.
[16] See *ante*, p. 222, and see Land Registration Act 1925, s.34(1).
[17] *Bonham* v. *Newcomb* (1684) 1 Vern. 232 affd. (1689) 1 Vern. 233n H.L.
[18] " . . . the court simply removes the stop it has itself put on." *Per* Jessel M.R. in *Carter* v. *Wake* (1877) 4 Ch.D. 605 at 606. See also *Heath* v. *Pugh* (1882) 7 A.C. 235.
[19] [1915] 1 Ch. 22 at 24.

Nature of default giving rise to foreclosure. It follows that the right to foreclosure cannot arise until the mortgagor is in default *under the proviso for redemption*[20] and repayment has become due at law. The importance of this is that not every breach of his contract by a mortgagor will give a mortgagee the right of foreclosure: the breach must bring into effect the condition rendering the mortgagee's title absolute, and therefore must concern the proviso for redemption. In *Williams* v. *Morgan*,[21] a mortgage made in 1900 contained a covenant for the payment of the principal in 1914, with interest half-yearly in the meanwhile, but the proviso for redemption permitted redemption in 1914 on payment of the capital and of such interest as might then be due and unpaid. The mortgagor defaulted in payment of interest before 1914, but Swinfen-Eady J. held that under this deed no right to foreclose could arise until 1914. The covenant for payment and the proviso for redemption were distinct stipulations, and it would have been altering the plain language of the deed to incorporate the terms of the covenant for payment into the proviso for redemption. The mortgagor's default did not, therefore, constitute a default under the proviso for redemption, so that the mortgagee was not entitled to a foreclosure.

But this does not mean that the mortgagor's default must be in the repayment of capital. Even when the mortgagee has debarred himself from calling in the capital for a definite period of years, default in the payment of any instalment of interest will entitle him to foreclose if the proviso for redemption was made conditional on the punctual payment of interest.[22] The point is that the terms of the covenant for payment of interest must have been incorporated into the proviso for redemption. The same principle applies to a mortgagor's other covenants. Thus, in a mortgage of leaseholds, the mortgagor's breach of his covenant to observe the terms of the lease will give rise to a right of foreclosure only if the performance of the covenant was expressly incorporated in the proviso for redemption.[23] If such a covenant and the proviso for redemption are expressed as distinct stipulations, the court will not, by construction, incorporate the covenant into the proviso for redemption.[24]

The time when foreclosure becomes available is therefore the moment the mortgagor makes default under the proviso for redemption. The default which usually calls into being the right of foreclosure is the failure to repay the principal on the date named in the contract for redemption,

---

[20] In a mortgage of a legal estate a proviso for redemption is not strictly necessary, since by mere payment the mortgage term becomes a satisfied term: therefore a forfeiture clause would be sufficient, but a proviso for redemption is found in practice often *Contra* bank mortgages which are usually payable on demand and contain no such proviso.

[21] [1906] 1 Ch. 804.

[22] *Burrowes* v. *Molloy* (1845) 2 Jo. & Lat. 521; *Edwards* v. *Martin* (1856) 25 L.J.Ch. 284; *Kidderminster Mutual Benefit Building Society* v. *Haddock* [1936] W.N. 158; *Twentieth Century Banking Corporation Ltd.* v. *Wilkinson* [1977] Ch. 99.

[23] *Cf. Seaton* v. *Twyford* (1870) L.R. 11 Eq. 591; if in an equitable mortgage by contract to create a legal mortgage the mortgagee agrees not to foreclose for a given period, the court will imply that this is conditional on the perfomance of covenants. *Ibid.*

[24] *Turner* v. *Spencer* (1894) 43 W.R. 153.

usually six months after the execution of the mortgage deed. If no date is fixed, or if the money is repayable on demand, then the right arises after a demand has been made and a reasonable time has been allowed for compliance with the demand.[25] As a rule the right to foreclose and the equitable right to redeem arise simultaneously on the passing of that date without redemption. There is, however, no objection to a mortgagee precluding himself from foreclosing during any period of whatever length, and the mortgagor need not be under a corresponding obligation not to redeem.[26] As a mortgagee requires no protection when making the agreement, he cannot obtain relief on the ground of want of mutuality even when he has not made his agreement to forbear conditional on the punctual payment of interest.[27] Therefore he almost invariably makes forbearance conditional on such payment of interest, in order that a failure to pay interest may lift the bar to foreclosure.[28] Nor will he afterwards lose his right to foreclose by accepting payment of the interest: to revive the bar he must actually *waive the breach of the condition*.[29]

The right to foreclose, once it has arisen, continues to be available so long as any part of the mortgage debt remains unpaid.[30]

Persons entitled to foreclosure

Foreclosure is available to a mortgagee, legal or equitable, and to the holder either of a registered charge or a charge by way of legal mortgage. The right to foreclose also belongs to persons who become entitled to the mortgage by assignment or devolution and also to a trustee in bankruptcy.[30a] Thus, in addition to an incumbrancer solely entitled, the following persons may foreclose:

> (1) Express assignees of the mortgage. The assignee's right is, however, subject to the state of the accounts between mortgagor and mortgagee at the date of the assignment and also to any equities then existing in the mortgagor's favour.[31] An assignment of the debt without the security leaves the right to foreclose in the original mortgagee.[32]

---

[25] *Fitzgerald's Trustee* v. *Mellersh* [1892] 1 Ch. 385; *Balfe* v. *Lord* (1842) 2 Dr. & War. 480.

[26] *Ramsbottom* v. *Wallis* (1835) 5 L.J.Ch. 92; *Kreglinger* v. *New Patagonia Meat & Cold Storage Co. Ltd.* [1914] A.C. 25.

[27] *Burrowes* v. *Molloy* (1845) 2 Jo. & Lat. 521.

[28] The way such an agreement is framed is to have the ordinary proviso for redemption putting the mortgagor in default after six months followed by a separate covenant not to call in the money for the period specified, the covenant being made conditional on the regular payment of interest.

[29] *Keene* v. *Biscoe* (1878) 8 Ch.D. 201.

[30] A foreclosure decree will not, however, be made in respect of costs only: *Drought* v. *Redford* (1827) 1 Moll. 572.

[30a] A judgment creditor who has obtained a charging order under the Charging Orders Act 1979 is in the position of an equitable mortgagee.

[31] *Withington* v. *Tate* (1869) L.R. 4 Ch. App. 288; *Turner* v. *Smith* [1901] 1 Ch. 213.

[32] *Morley* v. *Morley* (1858) 25 Beav. 253; he will, however, be a trustee of the security for the assignee.

(2) Sub-mortgagees are assignees and may foreclose on the original mortgagor on similar terms.[33]

(3) Co-mortgagees. Each must foreclose the whole mortgage, not merely his own share.[34] Co-ownership of land involves statutory trusts and co-mortgagees of land ought presumably to foreclose through the trustees.

(4) Trustees. The beneficiaries must proceed through their trustees.[35]

(5) Personal representatives before assent or transfer.[36]

(6) Trustee in bankruptcy in the case of the bankruptcy of the mortgagee.[37]

Parties to the action

If there are several persons beneficially interested in the mortgage moneys, they must all be represented in the action; and in accordance with the general rule, trustees and personal representatives sufficiently represent the persons for whom they act.[38] In the case of co-mortgagees *all* must be joined[39]; if they are willing to concur in the proceedings, they will be made plaintiffs; if not, they must be made defendants.[40] If land has been mortgaged to several co-mortgagees, there will be a statutory trust[41] and foreclosure must take place through the trustees. Clearly, when the money was advanced out of a joint account (as in the case of trustee-mortgagees), the personal representatives of a deceased co-mortgagee need not be joined. Moreover under section 111 of the Law of Property Act 1925 co-mortgagees are to be deemed joint tenants—subject to any statement to the contrary—both when the money is expressed to be advanced out of a joint account and when the mortgage is merely made to them jointly. Even in the rare case when a mortgage of land is not made upon a joint account, the personal representatives of a deceased co-mortgagee probably need not be joined, since foreclosure will always take place through statutory trustees, who are necessarily joint tenants. In a mortgage of personalty, however, the fact that the money neither was, nor could be deemed to be, advanced out of a joint account would necessitate the joinder of the personal representative, because personalty is not subject to the statutory trusts.[42] It may be added that in an action by debenture holders all must be

---

[33] See *Hobart* v. *Abbott* (1731) 2 P.Wms. 643; *Norrish* v. *Marshall* (1821) 5 Madd. 475.

[34] *Davenport* v. *James* (1847) 7 Hare 249; *Luke* v. *South Kensington Hotel Co.* (1879) 11 Ch.D. 121; as to the effect of decree in the case of an equitable mortgage, see *Re Continental Oxygen Co.*, *Elias* v. *Continental Oxygen Co.* [1897] 1 Ch 511.

[35] *Wood* v. *Williams* (1819) 4 Madd. 186.

[36] Administration of Estates Act 1925, ss.1, 3.

[37] See *ante*, p. 388.

[38] R.S.C. Ord. 15, rr. 12, 13.

[39] *Davenport* v. *James* (1847) 7 Hare 249.

[40] See *Luke* v. *South Kensington Hotel Co. Ltd.* (1879) 11 Ch.D. 121.

[41] Law of Property Act 1925, s.34(2).

[42] *Cf. Vickers* v. *Cowell* (1839) 1 Beav. 529.

before the court either as plaintiffs or defendants[43]; this is usually achieved by a representative action under R.S.C. Ord. 15, r. 12.

In foreclosure, as in redemption, actions, all persons interested in the equity of redemption *must* be before the court in order that they may be bound by the accounts, and in general, beneficiaries are sufficiently represented by their trustees. In foreclosure suits, however, so anxious is the court that no party shall be deprived of his opportunity to redeem that it will readily allow beneficiaries to be joined, if it appear that the trustees may be unable to redeem.[44-45] Who, in general, has a right to redeem and is entitled to be joined as defendant has already been investigated at length in connection with redemption and with the maxim, *redeem up, foreclose down*. The details need not be repeated here, but the general principle is that all persons must be joined who will be affected by the accounts taken in the action, so that in a foreclosure action all persons acquiring interests in the property *subsequent to the mortgage* must be joined.[46] Thus, a mortgagee must foreclose not only on the mortgagor, but on all persons claiming through him, including puisne incumbrancers.[47] He may, however, foreclose without at the same time claiming to redeem *prior* incumbrancers[48]; one may not redeem up without foreclosing down, but one may foreclose down without redeeming up, because prior incumbrancers will not be affected by the accounts taken in the foreclosure. On the same principle a mortgagee may foreclose on the mortgagor without at the same time redeeming his own sub-mortgage.

Procedure

If the amount actually advanced does not exceed the county court limit,[49] proceedings for foreclosure may be taken in the county court[50]; otherwise foreclosure proceedings must be brought in the High Court, and are assigned by the Supreme Court Act 1981 to the Chancery Division.[51] The High Court does *not* necessarily have jurisdiction[52] to hear and determine an action in which a mortgagee claims possession and the mortgaged property consists of or includes a dwelling-house. In such cases the county

---

[43] *Re Continental Oxygen Co.*, *Elias* v. *Continental Oxygen Co.* [1897] 1 Ch. 511; *Westminster Bank Ltd.* v. *Residential Properties Improvement Co. Ltd.* [1938] Ch. 639.

[44-45] *Goldsmid* v. *Stonehewer* (1852) 9 Hare, Appendix XXXVIII.

[46] A person entitled to redeem who has not been made a defendant will not be bound by the foreclosure: *Gee* v. *Liddell* [1913] 2 Ch. 62.

[47] See *Keith* v. *Butcher* (1884) 25 Ch.D. 750.

[48] *Rose* v. *Page* (1829) 2 Sim. 471; *Slade* v. *Rigg* (1843) 3 Hare 35.

[49] At present £30,000: see County Courts Act 1984, s.23; County Courts Jurisdiction Order 1981 (S.I. 1981 No. 1123). *Jurisdiction and Procedure*. Where the sum originally advanced exceeded the county court limit but is reduced by payment or otherwise, to below that sum, the county court would appear to have jurisdiction to hear the action—see *Shields, Whitley and District Amalgamated Model Building Society* v. *Richards* (1901) 84 L.T. 587.

[50] *i.e.* the court for the district in which the land or any part of it is situate C.C.R., Ord. 4, r. 3; where the mortgage comprises property other than land action may be commenced in the court or the district in which the defendant resides or carries on business.

[51] s.61(1), Sched. 1; R.S.C. Ord. 88, rr. 1, 2.

[52] See *ante*, Appendix III.

court has exclusive jurisdiction even if the amount outstanding is above the county court limit,[52a] except where any part of the land is situated in Greater London or where the net annual value for rating is above the county court limit.[53] This exclusive jurisdiction of a county court, however, does not apply to an action for foreclosure or sale in which a claim for possession of the mortgaged property is also made.[54] Thus (and subject to the above considerations) a mortgagee in a foreclosure action is under no compulsion to commence proceedings in the county court when his advance is less than £30,000. Moreover, he will be allowed his costs in the High Court on the High Court Scale, unless there is a special ground for treating resort to the High Court as unreasonable.[55]

For example, when the mortgagee and mortgagor both resided in the same district, costs on the county court scale only were allowed.[56]

In the High Court foreclosure action may be begun, either by writ or by originating summons the choice being governed by R.S.C. Ord. 5. In the Chancery Division mortgage actions are normally commenced by originating summons[57] except where fraud is alleged or, for example, where there is the likelihood of a substantial dispute as to fact.[58] In the High Court the originating summons must describe the property and the mortgage under which the claim is made.[58a]

A mortgagee may bring his action for foreclosure only, so that his claim is merely that an account be taken of what is due to him on the mortgage in respect of principal, interest and costs, and that the court may foreclose the mortgage. In such an action the court may, at the instance of any interested party, direct a sale, although the claim is for foreclosure.[59] But in any case the mortgagee himself may favour a sale, and then his claim is for an account, and for foreclosure or sale. Furthermore, if he is a mortgagee in possession his claim for an account must refer to that fact, and he should

[52a] See R. v. Judge Dutton Briant, ex p. Abbey National Building Society [1957] 2 Q.B. 497.

[53] At present £1,000, see County Courts Act 1984, ss.21, 147(1) (enlarged by the Administration of Justice Act 1970, Sched. 2).

[54] See the County Courts Act 1984, ss.21, 147(1) (replacing the Administration of Justice Act 1970, s.37(2)). But, and importantly, the action for foreclosure or sale must be a genuine one for that relief and the claim for foreclosure or sale not merely added as a device to take the proceedings outside the county court's exclusive jurisdiction in possession proceedings; see The Trustees of Manchester Unity Life Insurance Collecting Society v. Sadler [1974] 1 W.L.R. 770. Often the claim will include payment, possession of the mortgaged property, foreclosure or sale together with other relief in the same proceedings. The mere claim for foreclosure or sale, however, does not itself render the action one for foreclosure or sale. The test is to have regard to the nature of the relief which the plaintiff genuinely seeks. Thus a claim for possession under a mortgage is usually treated as an action for recovery of land within s.21 of the County Courts Act 1984 and not as an action for foreclosure within s.23, see West Penwith Rural District Council v. Gunnell [1968] 1 W.L.R. 1153.

[55] Brown v. Rye (1874) L.R. 17 E.Q. 343. The provisions of the County Courts Act 1984, s.20 (which provides rules for the limitation of recoverable costs in actions founded on contract and tort) do not apply to foreclosure actions.

[56] Simons v. McAdam (1868) L.R. 6 Eq. 324; Crozier v. Dowsett (1885) 31 Ch.D. 67.

[57] R.S.C. Ord. 5, r. 2.

[58] Ibid. r 4.

[58a] The Supreme Court Practice 1988, Vol. 1, para. 88/2–7/24.

[59] See ante, p. 248 and post, p. 257.

make a specific claim to be allowed such sums as have been properly expended by him on the mortgaged property. If a mortgagee is not in possession and is asking for foreclosure rather than sale, an order for possession will be necessary when the mortgagor proves obstructive. The court, it is true, has jurisdiction to make an order for possession without any demand for such an order having been made in the writ or summons,[60] and may make the order even after the foreclosure decree has been made absolute.[61] Nevertheless, if the mortgagor is expected to prove obstructive, it is advisable to claim the order specifically, since the court will not make the order *ex parte* where it was not asked for in the writ or summons.[62-63] Again, a mortgagee is entitled to pursue all his remedies concurrently, and will frequently combine with his foreclosure action a claim for judgment on the mortgagor's personal covenant to pay the mortgage debt. Such actions must be commenced in the Chancery Division if the High Court is the appropriate forum.[64] But it must be remembered that if a mortgagee sues on the personal covenant *after* foreclosing he reopens the foreclosure.[65]

A mortgagee who starts proceedings for foreclosure cannot bring an action on the personal covenant concurrently in the Queens Bench Division, since it was open to him to combine this remedy with his foreclosure suit. Thus, such an action will be treated as vexatious, and be stayed.[66] Further, although a mortgagee may obtain judgment for payment and foreclosure in the same action, the two claims are quite distinct. For example, a foreclosure decree gives the mortgagor six months in which to redeem, but the judgment on the covenant is for immediate payment, as there is no rule in equity that a sum of money immediately payable at law shall not be payable until after six months have elapsed.[67]

Where foreclosure has taken place by reason of the failure of the plaintiff in a mortgage action for redemption to redeem, the defendant in whose favour the foreclosure has taken place may apply, by way of motion or summons, for an order for delivery to him of possession of the mortgaged property and the court may make such order thereon as it thinks fit.[67a]

Order for account to be taken

Since a mortgagor is entitled to have an account the decree will first direct that the appropriate account be taken, unless, of course, the parties have already agreed to it. But, although a mortgagor has this right to an account, the court in exceptional cases will stay the taking of it, unless he is prepared to give security for the costs of the account. For if it is highly

---

[60] *Salt* v. *Edgar* (1886) 54 L.T. 374.
[61] *Jenkins* v. *Ridgley* (1893) 41 W.R. 585.
[62-63] *Le Bas* v. *Grant* (1895) 64 L.J.Ch. 368.
[64] R.S.C. Ord. 88, r. 2; and see Supreme Court Act 1981, s.61(1), and see *ante*, p. 253.
[65] See *post*, p. 261.
[66] *Earl Poulett* v. *Viscount Hill* [1893] 1 Ch. 277; *Williams* v. *Hunt* [1905] 1 K.B. 512.
[67] *Farrer* v. *Lacy, Hartland & Co.* (1885) 31 Ch.D. 42; see also *Dymond* v. *Croft* (1876) 3 Ch.D. 512.
[67a] R.S.C. Ord. 88, r. 7.

improbable that the mortgaged property will prove sufficient to satisfy the mortgage debt, it is unfair to the mortgagee to increase the costs of his foreclosure unnecessarily.[68] The court's direction for the account is subject to variation to meet the special circumstances of the mortgage. For example, a mortgagee in possession must account for rents and profits, and there may be a claim for special allowances or expenses.[69] In any event, if a claim on the personal covenant has been joined with a foreclosure action it is necessary to have two distinct accounts. The reason is obvious: a foreclosure decree allows six months for redemption, and the foreclosure account will include an allowance of six months' additional interest, but in an action on the covenant a mortgagee will obtain judgment for immediate payment of the sum due, and correspondingly will not be entitled to additional interest. Again, if the mortgagee is in possession, judgment for the payment on the covenant cannot include in the amount to be paid any allowances or expenses in connection with the mortgaged property.[70] Similarly, judgment on the covenant carries with it a right only to the costs of proceedings on the covenant, and the costs of a foreclosure must therefore go into the mortgage account only. Plainly, the two accounts must be taken separately.[71]

Foreclosure nisi

The court, it has been said, continues to regard a mortgagee's title as a mere security, and will not cancel the equity of redemption without first giving the mortgagor a further opportunity to redeem. A foreclosure decree is granted in stages, this means, in the normal case, that redemption is still possible until the end of a period of six months from the date when the mortgage account is certified by the Master. The decree is thus an order *nisi* which will be made absolute on a subsequent application, provided that in the meanwhile the right to redeem has not been exercised. A foreclosure order absolute will never be granted in the first instance, unless the persons interested in the equity of redemption agree to that course.[72] The order therefore usually takes this form: It is directed that upon the payment of the sum certified by the Master on a day six months after the date of this certificate and at the time and place specified therein, the mortgagee shall give the defendant a receipt in accordance with the provisions of section 115 of the Law of Property Act 1925,[72a] and shall deliver up the title deeds, but that in default of such payment the defendant shall be fore-

---

[68] *Exchange and Hop Warehouses Ltd.* v. *Association of Land Financiers* (1886) 34 Ch.D. 195.
[69] For the details of the account, see *post*, pp. 434 *et seq*.
[70] These are a charge upon the property, but are not a personal debt of the mortgagor: *Frazer* v. *Jones* (1846) 5 Hare 475.
[71] *Farrer* v. *Lacy, Hartland & Co.* (1885) 31 Ch.D. 42.
[72] *Patey* v. *Flint* (1879) 48 L.J.Ch. 696.
[72a] s.115 of the L.P.A. 1925 is applied with qualifications by the Building Societies Act 1986, s.13(7), Sched. 4, para. 2. See *ante*, pp. 130 *et seq*. and *post*, p. 475.

closed.[72b] If the mortgagee has applied for possession, there will be added a direction that the defendant shall deliver up possession to the plaintiff, and in the case of an equitable mortgagee there must be a special direction for the conveyance of the legal title to the mortgagee.[73]

But, as in redemption actions, there may be several parties before the court with distinct rights to redeem, and the decree must provide in detail for the exercise of those rights. Questions may arise as to priority and as to successive periods for redemption, because foreclosure means the destruction of the equity of redemption of every person who acquired an interest in the property subsequently to the plaintiff's mortgage.[74] The determination of these questions, however, proceeds in decrees for foreclosure on the same lines as in decrees for redemption, and the rules will not be repeated here.[75] It should be added that it is also possible for the court to give the mortgagees successive periods of redemption, the party first entitled to redeem being allowed six months, and each of the others successive periods of three months more.[76]

In the case of dwelling-houses the court in foreclosure actions now has a statutory discretion to adjourn the proceedings, or to suspend executions of its order, or to postpone the date for delivery of possession as it thinks fit whether or not possession is sought in the same proceedings.[77]

Sale in lieu of foreclosure

Judicial sale.   In a foreclosure action the court's jurisdiction to order a sale in lieu of foreclosure does not depend on a sale having been asked for in the statement of claim. Under section 91(2) of the Law of Property Act 1925, the court, on the request of the mortgagee or *of any interested person*[78] may direct a sale (a "judicial sale") on such terms as it thinks fit, including the deposit in court of a sum to meet the expenses of sale and to secure performance of the terms. The jurisdiction is entirely discretionary both as to making the order for sale and as to the terms of the sale. The court may order the sale notwithstanding the dissent or non-appearance of any person,[79] and without allowing time for redemption.[80]

If a sale is requested, the order is not given, as of course, but a special case has to be made out for the exercise of the court's discretion.[81] It is unusual for the court to order an immediate sale unless the mortgagor consents. The rule is not to direct a sale unless it will confer a benefit on one of

---

[72b] R.S.C. Ord. 88, r. 7.
[73] *Lees* v. *Fisher* (1882) 22 Ch.D. 283; the order must also be preceded by a declaration of the equitable mortgage: *Marshall* v. *Shrewsbury* (1875) L.R. 10 Ch. 250.
[74] See *Briscoe* v. *Kenrick* (1832) 1 L.J.Ch. 116.
[75] See *post*, pp. 313 *et seq.*
[76] *Smithett* v. *Hesketh* (1840) 44 Ch.D. 161; *Platt* v. *Mendel* (1884) 27 Ch.D. 246.
[77] Administration of Justice Act 1973, s.8(3), and see *ante*, p. 245.
[78] *e.g.* a subsequent mortgagee or the mortgagor, and see *Twentieth Century Banking Corporation* v. *Wilkinson* [1977] Ch. 99.
[79] Which includes the mortgagee, and see *Wade* v. *Wilson* (1882) 22 Ch.D. 235.
[80] Or determining the priorities of interested parties: s.91(4) of the Law of Property Act 1925.
[81] *Provident Clerks' Mutual Life Assurance Association* v. *Lewis* (1892) 62 L.J.Ch. 89.

the parties sufficient to justify the expenses of a sale.[82] Nor will a sale be ordered if it will prejudice the position of any person interested.[83-84]

The usual direction given is that the accounts be certified and a period allowed to the mortgagor for redemption.[85-86] Indeed, if the statement of claim is for foreclosure only, the court will not order a sale at all unless the mortgagor has been notifed of the application for a sale.[87] But an immediate sale may be directed if the property is small and the security deficient.[88] The actual application for a sale may be made at any stage of the proceedings[89] and upon an interlocutory application,[90] the court's jurisdiction to order the sale being only terminated by decree absolute.

Conduct of the sale.   The conduct and conditions of the sale are always within the court's discretion. The general practice is to give the conduct of the sale to the mortgagor since he is the person whose interest is to obtain the best price[91]; on the same principle, if the mortgagor declines the privilege, the conduct of the sale will be given to the incumbrancer lowest in priority in preference to the mortgagee.[92] It seems, moreover, that this course will sometimes be followed, even when the first mortgagee has objected and claimed the right to carry out the sale.[93] But if the security is deficient, a first mortgagee's claim to be given the conduct of the sale will be allowed[94]: again, the court may prefer the first mortgagee's claim, on the ground that expense may be saved by allowing the person in possession of the deeds to conduct the sale.[95] Thus, there is no rule that the mortgagor shall conduct the sale, although the general practice very much favours that course.[96] Furthermore, the court will readily permit the sale to take place altogether out of court, the proceeds of the sale being ordered to be paid into court: but in such cases the order must be prefaced by a declaration that all interested parties are before the court.[97]

The fact that a first mortgagee does not agree to the mortgagor having the conduct of the sale will affect the terms on which the order is made; the mortgagor (or the puisne incumbrancer) will usually have to deposit a sum to cover the expenses of an ineffectual attempt to sell, and the court will fix

---

[82] *Lloyd's Bank* v. *Colston* (1912) 106 L.T. 420.
[83-84] *Merchant Banking Co. of London* v. *London & Hanseatic Bank* (1886) 55 L.J.Ch. 479; *Silsby* v. *Holliman* [1955] Ch. 552.
[85-86] *Green* v. *Biggs* (1885) 52 L.T. 680; see also *Smith* v. *Robinson* (1853) 1 Sm. & G. 140.
[87] *South Western District Bank* v. *Turner* (1882) 31 W.R. 113.
[88] *Oldham* v. *Stringer* (1884) 33 W.R. 251; but *cf. Hopkinson* v. *Miers* (1889) 34 S.J. 128.
[89] *Union Bank of London* v. *Ingram* (1882) 20 Ch.D. 463.
[90] *Woolley* v. *Colman* (1882) 21 Ch.D. 169.
[91] *Davies* v. *Wright* (1886) 32 Ch.D. 220; *cf. Re Jordan, ex p. Harrison* (1884) 13 Q.B.D. 228.
[92] *Norman* v. *Beaumont* [1893] W.N. 45.
[93] *e.g. Brewer* v. *Square* [1892] 2 Ch. 111.
[94] *Re Jordan, ex p. Harrison* (1884) 13 Q.B.D. 228; but not if a sum is deposited in court as a guarantee against loss: *Norman* v. *Beaumont* [1893] W.N. 45.
[95] *Hewitt* v. *Nanson* (1858) 28 L.J.Ch. 49.
[96] *Christy* v. *Van Tromp* [1886] W.N. 111; the language of Chitty J. goes further than the cases warrant.
[97] R.S.C. Ord. 31, r. 2. See *Cumberland Union Banking Co.* v. *Maryport Hematite Iron & Steel Co.* [1892] 1 Ch. 92.

a reserved price sufficient to cover the first mortgagee's claim.[98] If the first mortgagee's objection arises from the fact that he is himself anxious to exercise his powers of realising the security, the court will fix a time within which the sale must take place, and, on default, the first mortgagee may proceed to realise the security.[99] If no objection has been made to the sale by the first mortgagee, the mortgagor will not be made to give security for the expenses of the sale,[1] but if the sale is to take place altogether out of court, special directions will be given as to a reserved price and other conditions. A reserved price will also be fixed if the first mortgagee is given leave to bid at auction for the property.[2] Whoever conducts the sale acts primarily for himself and is not liable for improper activities of other parties to the action.[3]

Application of the proceeds of sale.   The proceeds of a judicial sale are applied in the same way and in the same order as the proceeds arising from a sale out of court under a power of sale. The rules governing the distribution of the proceeds of sale will therefore be found set out elsewhere.[4]

Foreclosure absolute

After the order *nisi*, the accounts are taken and certified in chambers, and the Master's certificate fixes the time and place for redemption, but a mortgagor's failure to pay on this date in accordance with the certificate does not automatically complete the mortgagee's title. The equity of redemption is not finally destroyed until a further decree, the foreclosure absolute, has been obtained making the mortgagee the sole owner both in law and in equity and free from any subsequent mortgages but subject to any prior incumbrances.[5] In consequence a forclosure *nisi* is by itself no defence to an action for redemption.[6] Moreover, although the mortgagor's further default entitles the mortgagee as of course to have his order *nisi* made absolute, yet the court will require the fact of non-payment to be strictly proved by the mortgagee by affidavit.[7] An affidavit must be sworn by the mortgagee or by the person who acted on his behalf that attendance was made at the time and place fixed by the certificate, and that the mortgagor did not appear[8]; but there must in addition be a positive statement by the mortgagee himself that he has not paid. An affidavit to that effect by his attorney is insufficient, and even in the case of co-mortgagees an

---

[98] *Whitbread* v. *Roberts* (1859) 28 L.J.Ch. 431; *Brewer* v. *Square* [1892] 2 Ch. 111.
[99] *Ibid.*
[1] *Davies* v. *Wright* (1886) 32 Ch.D. 220; but the mortgagor is personally liable for the expenses.
[2] *Re Commercial Bank of London* (1864) 9 L.T. (N.S.) 782.
[3] *Union Bank of London* v. *Munster* (1887) 37 Ch.D. 51.
[4] See *ante*, p. 234.
[5] See the L.P.A. 1925, ss.88(2), 89(2), and *ante*, p. 248. Also see *Sheriff* v. *Sparks* (1737) Westtemp. Hard. 130.
[6] *Senhouse* v. *Earl* (1752) 2 Ves.Sen. 450.
[7] *Patey* v. *Flint* (1879) 48 L.J.Ch. 696.
[8] *Moore and Robinson's Nottinghamshire Banking Co.* v. *Horsfield* [1882] W.N. 43.

affidavit by one on behalf of the others will not be accepted except where a mortgagee is out of the jurisdiction.[9] But in any case a mortgagee, who has received rents or other profits after the decree *nisi* but before default was made, must inform the court of this and *cannot proceed* to a decree absolute: such a receipt reopens the account and a new date for redemption will be allowed.[10] If, however, the receipt of profits did not occur until *after* the mortgagor's default under the decree *nisi*, the account is not reopened and the mortgagee upon producing the proper affidavits may obtain an order absolute.[11] The actual application for an order absolute is made either upon motion in court or, more usually, by summons in chambers, and this course is permissible whether the proceedings for foreclosure were begun by writ or summons. Notice of the proceedings must be served on the owner of the equity of redemption, but, with one exception, the application may be made *ex parte*: the exception is the case of a deceased defendant, when the court will insist on the presence of a properly appointed representative of the deceased.[12]

A foreclosure order absolute takes the form of a recital of the mortgagor's default under the decree *nisi*, and an order absolutely debarring and foreclosing him from all equity of redemption in the mortgaged property. In addition, the court will order the delivery to the plaintiffs of any title deeds to the property which are still in the defendants' hands; the deeds, which were executed subsequently to the plaintiff's mortgage, and which therefore relate only to the equity of redemption, will not be included in such an order, although their possession may be of advantage to the plaintiff.[13] The effect of foreclosure absolute, it must be repeated, is merely to destroy the equity of redemption and transfer the beneficial ownership to the mortgagee; it is not a conveyance of the legal title. Consequently, in the case of an equitable mortgage, if the mortgagor is obstructive, the order absolute must provide for the transfer of the legal title to the plaintiff.[14] This is achieved by a declaration that the mortgagor is a trustee for the mortgagee, followed by a vesting order in favour of the mortgagee-beneficiary under section 44 of the Trustee Act 1925. For the same reason an order absolute is not enough to give the plaintiff possession of the mortgaged property. For some purposes a foreclosure action is an action for the recovery of land,[15] but it is not an action for the recovery of *the possession of land*, and is not enforceable by writ of possession under R.S.C. Ord. 45, r. 3.[16] If, however, application is made, the court will add an order for pos-

---

[9] *Barrow* v. *Smith* (1885) 52 L.T. 798; *Docksey* v. *Else* (1891) 64 L.T. 256; *Kinnaird* v. *Yorke* (1889) 60 L.T. 380.

[10] *Prees* v. *Coke* (1871) L.R. 6 Ch. 645; nor will the mortgagor be put under conditions as to payment of arrears of interest.

[11] *National Permanent Mutual Benefit Building Society* v. *Raper* [1892] 1 Ch. 54.

[12] *Aylward* v. *Lewis* [1891] 2 Ch. 81.

[13] *Greene* v. *Foster* (1882) 22 Ch.D. 566.

[14] *Lees* v. *Fisher* (1882) 22 Ch.D. 283, and see *ante*, p. 257.

[15] *Heath* v. *Pugh* (1881) 6 Q.B.D. 345, affirmed (1882) 7 A.C. 235.

[16] *Wood* v. *Wheater* (1882) 22 Ch.D. 281.

session to the order absolute, whether or not the order *nisi* directed delivery of possession, and whether or not such an order was asked for in the pleadings.[17] Indeed, an order for possession will even be made, as ancillary to the judgment, after decree absolute.[18]

Re-opening foreclosure

The effect of a foreclosure absolute is to constitute the mortgagee beneficial owner of the property, so that he may at once deal with it as owner. The proceedings between the parties, theoretically, are at an end and, apart from an ancillary order for possession, the court cannot add to its decree as, for example, by appointing a receiver.[19] Nevertheless, as Jessel M.R., pointed out,[20] the finality of a decree absolute is nearly as illusory as the mortgage contract itself, since the court reserves for itself a discretion to discharge the final decree if the mortgagor makes out a special case for indulgence.[21] Of course a decree absolute, like any other decree, is liable to be set aside for actual fraud, and, similarly, oppression by the mortgagee will be sufficient to reopen the foreclosure. Again, the mortgagee himself may cause the foreclosure to be opened by suing the mortgagor or guarantor[22] on his personal covenant, for this automatically revives the right to redeem.[23] But there is an absolute discretion in the court to reopen the foreclosure[23a] and fix a new date for redemption, without the mortgagee having been guilty of misconduct or having taken collateral proceedings against the mortgagor. In truth, the court's tenderness towards a mortgagor is so extreme that it is prepared in special circumstances to treat his property as still essentially security, even after decree absolute, and to give him a last chance of redeeming. When the court exercises its discretion, the procedure is not immediately to vacate the decree, but to fix a new date for redemption, notwithstanding the decree, and to discharge the decree if redemption then takes place.[24] But, since a mortgagor is not entitled, as, of course, to an enlargement of time for redemption before the decree absolute, *a fortiori* he must make out a special case for the opening of foreclosure absolute. The opening of a foreclosure is completely within the court's discretion, and no precise rules have been laid down. In *Campbell* v. *Holyland*,[25] however, Jessel M.R. made some valuable comments on

---

[17] *Salt* v. *Edgar* (1886) 54 L.T. 374; see also *Best* v. *Applegate* (1887) 37 Ch. 42; *Keith* v. *Day* (1888) 39 Ch.D. 452.

[18] *Keith* v. *Day* (1888) 39 Ch.D. 452; an order for possession should so describe the property that the sheriff may identify it from the terms of the order: *Thynne* v. *Sarl* [1891] 2 Ch. 79.

[19] *Heath* v. *Pugh* (1881) 6 Q.B.D. 345, affirmed (1882) 7 A.C. 235; *Wills* v. *Luff* (1888) 38 Ch.D. 197.

[20] *Campbell* v. *Holyland* (1877) 7 Ch.D. 166 at 171.

[21] Even possibly after sale of the property, but this would be most unusual especially if the purchaser had no notice of the circumstances.

[22] *Lloyds and Scottish Trust Ltd.* v. *Britten* (1982) 44 P. & C.R. 249, and see *post*, p. 263.

[23] *Perry* v. *Barker* (1806) 13 Ves. 198; *Lockhart* v. *Hardy* (1846) 9 Beav. 349.

[23a] See *Quarles* v. *Knight* (1820) 8 Price 630; *Eyre* v. *Hansom* (1840) 2 Beav. 478.

[24] *Ford* v. *Wastell* (1848) 6 Hare 229.

[25] (1877) 7 Ch.D. 166 at 172.

the exercise of the discretion which indicate clearly the grounds on which it is exercised. He there said:

> "On what terms is that judicial discretion to be exercised? It has been said by the highest authority that it is impossible to say *a priori* what are the terms. They must depend on the circumstances of each case. . . . There are certain things which are intelligible to everybody. In the first place the mortgagor must come, as it is said, promptly; that is within a reasonable time. He is not to let the mortgagee deal with the estate as his own—if it is a landed estate, the mortgagee being in possession of it and using it—and then without any special reason come and say, 'Now I will redeem.' He cannot do that; he must come within a reasonable time. What is a reasonable time? You must have regard to the nature of the property. As has been stated in more than one of the cases, where the estate is an estate in land in possession— where the mortgagee takes it in possession and deals with it and alters the property, and so on—the mortgagor must come much more quickly than where it is an estate in reversion, as to which the mortgagee can do nothing except sell it. So that you must have regard to the nature of the estate in ascertaining what is to be considered a reasonable time.
>
> Then again was the mortgagor entitled to redeem, but by some accident unable to redeem? Did he expect to get the money from a quarter from which he might reasonably hope to obtain it, and was he disappointed at the last moment? Was it a very large sum, and did he require a considerable time to raise it elsewhere? All those things must be considered in determining what is a reasonable time.
>
> Then an element for consideration has always been the nature of the property as regards value. For instance, if an estate were worth £50,000, and had been foreclosed for a mortgage debt of £5,000, the man who came to redeem that estate would have a longer time than where the estate was worth £5,100, and he was foreclosed for £5,000. But not only is there money value, but there may be other considerations. It may be an old family estate or a chattel, or picture, which possesses a special value for the mortgagor, but which possesses not the same value for other people; or it may be, as has happened in this instance, that the property, though a reversionary interest in the funds, is of special value to both the litigants; it may possess not merely a positive money value, but a peculiar value, having regard to the nature of title and other incidents, so that you cannot set an actual money value upon it. . . . All this must be taken into consideration."

This dictum suggests that three points will be likely to influence the court in favour of opening foreclosure: *(i)* promptness of application; *(ii)* the special value of the estate, whether monetary or otherwise; and *(iii)* the fact that the mortgagor had a reasonable expectation of redeeming, but was disappointed in his attempt to obtain the money. It may be added that there is little chance of obtaining the court's indulgence, unless it can be shown at the time of the application that the security is reasonably sufficient, and that there is a reasonable expectation of the money being obtained.[26] In any case it is now the practice to make it a condition of opening a foreclosure, that the mortgagor pay up immediately or within, at the most, one month, all arrears of interest and costs reported to be due. On failure to comply with this condition the foreclosure remains absolute.[27] Delay in applying for relief will prejudice the chance of reopening a foreclosure, unless it can be explained; if the mortgagee deals with the estate or expends money on it, laches in the mortgagor will be fatal.[28] But mere dealing with the estate by the mortgagee will not prevent the revival of the right to redeem, because a purchaser of a foreclosed estate must be taken to know that a foreclosure may be reopened, and if he purchases soon after the decree, the foreclosure may be reopened as against him. In *Campbell* v. *Holyland*[29] Jessel M.R. explained the position of a purchaser thus:

> "Then it is said that you must not interfere against purchasers . . . there are purchasers and purchasers. If the purchaser buys a freehold estase in possession after the lapse of a considerable time from the order of foreclosure absolute, with no notice of any extraneous circumstances which would induce the court to interfere, I for one should decline to interfere with such a title as that; but if the purchaser bought the estate within twenty-four hours after the foreclosure absolute, and with notice of the fact that it was of much greater value than the amount of the mortgage debt, is it to be supposed that a court of equity would listen to the contention of such a purchaser that he ought not to be interfered with? He must be taken to know the general law that an order for foreclosure may be opened under proper circumstances, and under a proper exercise of discretion by the court; and if the mortgagor in that case came the week after, is it to be supposed a court of equity would so stultify itself as to say that a title so acquired would stand in the way? I am of opinion it would not."

Action on the personal covenant to repay

A creditor's primary remedy to recover his money is to bring a personal action against his debtor[30] on the contract of loan, for a creditor by taking security only reinforces his personal remedy. As Maitland said,[31] a mort-

---

[26] *Patch* v. *Ward* (1867) L.R. 3 Ch. 203; and see *Lancashire and Yorkshire Reversionary Interest Co. Ltd.* v. *Crowe* (1970) 114 S.J. 435.
[27] See *Eyre* v. *Hansom* (1840) 2 Beav. 478; *Holford* v. *Yate* (1855) 1 K. & J. 677.
[28] See *Thornhill* v. *Manning* (1851) 1 Sim. (N.S.) 451.
[29] (1877) 7 Ch.D. 166 at 173.
[30] This includes a guarantor, see *Lloyds & Scottish Trust Ltd.* v. *Britten* (1982) 44 P. & C.R. 249.
[31] Maitland, *Equity* (2nd ed.), p. 182.

gagee is not the less a creditor because he is a secured creditor. All well-drawn mortgages[32] contain an express covenant by the mortgagor to pay both principal and interest. Even when there is no such covenant, a promise to pay is implied in law from the acceptance of the loan so that a simple contract debt is created. Every mortgage, therefore, contains within itself a personal liability to repay the amount advanced,[33] which the mortgagee may enforce by an action on the contract. This action, like the action for possession, must be prosecuted in the Chancery Division unless within the county court jurisdiction.[34]

The covenant to pay normally fixes a date on which payment is to be made, and then no right of action on the personal covenant accrues to the mortgagee until non-payment on the day named: for the affirmative covenant to pay implies a negative promise by the lender not to sue before that date.[35] If, on the other hand, the principal is made payable on demand, and there is no express or implied provision for notice to be given,[36] the right to sue on the personal covenant arises immediately on the execution of the mortgage,[37] and it is not even necessary to make a demand before beginning the action. But in the case of an instalment mortgage a written demand *is* necessary by reason of the alterations in the nature of the debtor's obligations from payment by instalments to the whole capital sum.[38] Any mode of service is sufficient which enables a mortgagor to realise that a demand has been made.[39] A well-drawn covenant stipulates expressly for payment of both principal and interest, so that the right to sue for interest is quite distinct from the right to sue for principal and the actions may be brought separately.[40]

If a mortgagee assigns the mortgage debt the assignee will be able to sue on the personal covenant. He can sue in his own name if the assignment meets the requirements of section 136 of the Law of Property Act 1925; otherwise he must join the original mortgagee.[41] On the mortgagee's death the right to sue on the covenant passes to his personal representatives and,

---

[32] The personal liability of the mortgagor to pay is sometimes registered by the mortgage deed itself.

[33] *Sutton* v. *Sutton* (1882) 22 Ch.D. 511 at 515, *per* Jessel M.R.

[34] See further *post*, Appendix III.

[35] *Bolton* v. *Buckenham* [1891] 1 Q.B. 278; *Twentieth Century Banking Corporation Ltd.* v. *Wilkinson* [1977] Ch. 99. But it is possible that a demand should be first made, see *Re Tewkesbury Gas Co., Tysoe* v. *Tewkesbury Gas Co.* [1912] 1 Ch. 1.

[36] *Esso Petroleum Co. Ltd.* v. *Alstonbridge Properties Ltd.* [1975] 1 W.L.R. 1474. If there is such a provision an actual demand in writing must be made before the right of action accrues, see *Lloyds Bank* v. *Margolis* [1954] 1 W.L.R. 644. See also Limitation of Actions, *post*, pp. 404 *et seq.* It is also necessary to make a demand in writing if the covenant is merely *collateral* to the security, *e.g.* if the right is being enforced against a surety, see *Re Brown's Estate, Brown* v. *Brown* [1893] 2 Ch. 300 at 304.

[37] *Evans* v. *Jones* (1839) 5 M. & W. 295.

[38] *Esso Petroleum Co. Ltd.* v. *Alstonbridge Properties Ltd.* [1975] 1 W.L.R. 1474. In practice a demand is usually made before action is commenced in any event.

[39] *Worthington & Co. Ltd.* v. *Abbott* [1910] 1 Ch. 588.

[40] *Dickenson* v. *Harrison* (1817) 4 Pri. 282.

[41] See *ante*, pp. 71 *et seq.* and *post*, p. 377.

after assent, to his legatees, provided that the latter give notice of the assent to the debtor.[42]

The right to sue on the personal covenant may be lost by the mortgagee's inability to reconvey the mortgaged property. Although a mortgagor's covenant for repayment is usually absolute in form, and is not expressed to be conditional on the reconveyance of the security, equity treats a mortgagor's liability to pay and a mortgagee's obligation to reconvey as reciprocal. A mortgagee will therefore be restrained from suing on the covenant if, without authority from the mortgagor, he has parted with the property mortgaged.[43] If the mortgagee is only temporarily disabled from making the reconveyance by allowing his solicitor to obtain a lien on the title deeds, he is restrained from suing on the covenant until the disability has been removed by the discharge of the lien.[44] If he forecloses he cannot afterwards sue on the personal covenant to make up the deficiency unless he still retains the mortgaged property in his hands.[45] In other words, a sale of the property after foreclosure extinguishes the mortgagor's liability for the contract debt.[46] It is for the same reason that if a mortgagee sues on the personal covenant after foreclosing, he reopens the foreclosure[47]: he cannot require the mortgagor or guarantor to repay his loan unless he is himself ready and willing to surrender the security.[48]

This rule still applies although the mortgagor has assigned his equity of redemption. A mortgagor cannot assign his personal liability, but if he is sued on the contract debt after assigning the equity of redemption he is still entitled to the reconveyance of his security.[49] Consequently, any bargain between an assignee of the equity of redemption and the mortgagee which prevents reconveyance will discharge the original mortgagor from his liability on the contract of loan.[50] On the other hand, a mortgagor surrenders his right to recover his security by authorising the mortgagee to part with it. Thus, a mortgagee does not lose his right to sue on the personal covenant if he sells the mortgaged property either with the express concurrence of the mortgagor or under an express or implied power of sale in the mortgage deed.[51] Nor does he lose his right if, when realising his security, he asks the

---

[42] Administration of Estates Act 1925, ss.1(1), 3(1)(ii), 36.

[43] *Walker* v. *Jones* (1866) L.R. 1 P.C. 50; *Palmer* v. *Hendrie (No. 2)* (1860) 28 Beav. 341; this principle applies equally to mortgages of personalty, though its application there may be more flexible: *Ellis & Co.'s Trustee* v. *Dixon-Johnson* [1925] A.C. 489.

[44] *Schoole* v. *Sall* (1803) 1 Sch. & Lef. 176.

[45] *Perry* v. *Barker* (1806) 13 Ves. 198; a puisne mortgagee does not, however, lose his right to sue on the personal covenant by consenting to a decree for foreclosure absolute in favour of a prior mortgagee: *Worthington* v. *Abbott* [1910] 1 Ch. 588.

[46] *Lockhart* v. *Hardy* (1846) 9 Beav. 349; *Gordon, Grant & Co.* v. *Boos* [1926] A.C. 781; see also *Lloyds and Scottish Trust Ltd.* v. *Britten* (1982) 44 P. & C.R. 249.

[47] *Perry* v. *Barker* (1806) 13 Ves. 198, and see *ante*, p. 261.

[48] See *Lloyds and Scottish Trust Ltd.* v. *Britten* (1982) 44 P. & C.R. 249.

[49] *Kinnaird* v. *Trollope* (1888) 39 Ch.D. 636, subject, of course, to the equity of redemption. For the form of conveyance, see *Pearce* v. *Morris* (1869) L.R. 5 Ch.App. 227.

[50] *Palmer* v. *Hendrie* (1859) 27 Beav. 349.

[51] *Rudge* v. *Richens* (1873) L.R. 8 C.P. 358.

court for a judicial sale instead of for foreclosure. Such a sale is a sale by the court and not by the mortgagee, so that although the mortgagee can no longer reconvey, he is entitled to recover any deficiency from the mortgagor by suing on the covenant.[52]

Appointment of a receiver by the court

Before the Judicature Act 1873, courts of equity always acted on the principle that they would never grant a receiver where the party applying for the receiver had a legal right to the possession, so that an equitable mortgagee could get a receiver, but a legal mortgagee could not.[53] But section 25(8) of that Act, which is now replaced by section 37 of the Supreme Court Act 1981,[53a] empowered the court to grant a receiver by interlocutory orders whenever it should appear just or convenient to do so. The Court of Appeal has decided that a receiver will now be granted at the instance of a legal mortgagee in the same way as at the instance of an equitable mortgagee, because, although a legal mortgagee has power to take possession, yet there are obvious conveniences in granting a receiver, so as to relieve a legal mortgagee from assuming the responsibilities of a mortgagee in possession.[54] It should be added, however, that the statutory power usually renders it unnecessary to apply to the court.

But, although the court may now appoint a receiver in all cases in which such a course appears just or convenient, the principles on which this jurisdiction is exercised are well defined. Except in very special cases[55] the court will not make an appointment, unless an action is pending.[56] If an action is pending, so that the parties are already at arm's length, it is preferable that the appointment should be made by the court in all cases, rather than that the mortgagee himself should appoint under a power.[57] It appears that a mortgagee is entitled to a receiver in any of the following cases:

(1) if the property would be in jeopardy if left in the mortgagor's possession until the hearing of the action[58];

---

[52] *Gordon Grant & Co.* v. *Boos* [1926] A.C. 781. This is a particularly strong case, as the mortgagee had obtained leave to bid and had actually bought the mortgage property, subsequently reselling it at an enhanced value.

[53] *Berney* v. *Sewell* (1820) 1 J. & W. 647; *Sollory* v. *Leaver* (1869) L.R. 9 Eq. 22 at 25.

[53a] Although the power to appoint a receiver and manager under subs. (1) is wide, the duty of maintaining houses owned by a local authority is expressly entrusted to the local authority under the Housing Act 1957, s.111 (now repealed and replaced, with amendment by Housing Act 1985, s.21), and the court will not usurp that duty by appointing a receiver and manager: *Parker* v. *Camden London Borough Council* [1986] Ch. 162.

[54] *Anglo-Italian Bank* v. *Davies* (1878) 9 Ch.D. 275; *Re Pope* (1886) 17 Q.B.D. 743 at 749, *per* Cotton L.J.

[55] *e.g.* where the mortgagee is a patient under the Mental Health Act 1983, see *ante*, p. 166.

[56] For this purpose an originating summons is an action.

[57] *Tillett* v. *Nixon* (1883) 25 Ch.D. 238.

[58] *Stevens* v. *Lord* (1838) 2 Jur. 92; *Re Victoria Steamboats, Ltd.* [1897] 1 Ch. 158; *Re London Pressed Hinge Co. Ltd.* [1905] 1 Ch. 576.

(2) if default has been made in payment of the principal[59];

(3) if any interest is in arrear[60]; nor does it make any difference that the mortgagee has covenanted not to call in his loan until some future date.[61]

When there are two or more mortgagees later mortgagees may obtain the appointment of a receiver, but without prejudice to the rights of prior mortgagees.[62] Nevertheless, if the order appointing the receiver does not contain an express reservation of the rights of prior incumbrancers, the latter cannot interfere with the receiver without an application to the court, for the receiver is an officer of the court.[63] When a prior legal mortgagee has already gone into possession the court will not appoint a receiver at the instance of a later incumbrancer, who is not offering to redeem the legal mortgagee.[64] But if a mortgagee in possession cannot assert on oath that there is something still due to him on his mortgage, the court will appoint a receiver at the instance of a later incumbrancer.[65]

Although the selection of a receiver appointed by the court is in its discretion, a nomination by the party applying for the appointment will usually be accepted. One person will not, however, be appointed, namely, the mortgagee's solicitor, for it is his duty to check the accounts of the receiver.[66] But when the mortgagee himself appoints a receiver under a power, he frequently appoints his own solicitor to act as receiver. The duties of a receiver appointed by the court cannot be exhaustively discussed here,[67] but it may be observed that in some important aspects they differ substantially from those of a receiver appointed by the mortgagee. Thus, a receiver appointed by the court is not strictly an agent, and is personally liable for what he does as receiver: consequently, the court almost invariably requires him to give security before entering into office.[68] Indeed, his appointment is normally incomplete until he has actually given security.[69] His duties are regulated by the terms of the order appointing him, but in general he is bound to assume possession of the mortgage property, to get in the rents and profits, and to pay these, after deducting outgoings and his own salary, into court or according to the court's direction. Not being the mortgagor's agent, it is his duty to take possession himself and to compel tenants to attorn tenant to himself. He must keep down outgoings, and has power to grant leases for a term not exceeding three

---

[59] *Curling* v. *Marquis of Townshend* (1816) 19 Ves. 628 at 633.
[60] *Strong* v. *Carlyle Press* [1893] 1 Ch. 268.
[61] *Burrowes* v. *Molloy* (1845) 2 J. & L. 521.
[62] *Berney* v. *Sewell* (1820) 1 J. & W. 647.
[63] *Aston* v. *Heron* (1834) 2 My. & K. 390.
[64] *Berney* v. *Sewell* (1820) 1 J. & W. 647.
[65] *Quarrell* v. *Beckford* (1807) 13 Ves. 377.
[66] *Re Lloyd* (1879) 12 Ch.D. 447.
[67] See *Halsbury's Laws of England* (4th ed., 1980), Vol. 39, Receivers; and Coote, *Mortgages* (9th ed., 1927), Vol. 2, p. 977.
[68] R.S.C. Ord. 30, r. 2.
[69] *Edwards* v. *Edwards* (1876) 2 Ch.D. 291.

years,[70] and to do necessary repairs[70a]; for any other repairs he should first obtain the leave of the court. If he requires any further powers not specially sanctioned by the terms of the order appointing him, he must make an application to the court. A receiver, for example, has no power to carry on a business, and, if such a power is desired, the court must be asked to appoint a receiver and manager.[71]

RIGHTS, REMEDIES AND DUTIES OF EQUITABLE MORTGAGEES AND CHARGEES

Equitable mortgagees[72]

Foreclosure

Since the equitable mortgagee has no legal estate, foreclosure is his primary remedy. It is available whether the charge relates to land or to personalty. But in the case of land as the mortgagee has no legal estate the foreclosure order absolute will direct the mortgagor to convey the land in question freed from any right to redeem.[73] In the case of a chose in action the court will direct the execution by the mortgagor of a power of attorney.[74] In the case of land, provided that there is evidence of an agreement, express or implied, on the part of the mortgagor to execute a legal mortgage the remedy is available to the mortgagee. Thus, it arises when the mortgage is made merely by deposit of title deeds[75] or is accompanied by a written memorandum.[76] In the case of a chose in action, it is available, for example, in the case of the deposit of the share certificates,[77] policies of insurance,[78] and of a share in a partnership.[79]

Sale

The statutory power of sale[80] applies only where the mortgage was made by deed.[81] Thus, it is usual for equitable mortgages to be made by deed and

---

[70] *Daniel's Chancery Practice* (8th ed.), p. 1443. But see *Stamford Banking Co.* v. *Keeble* [1913] 2 Ch. 96 at 97, where it was laid down that no lease can be granted without leave of the court. The court, however, can approve the granting of any lease which it concludes is necessary for the protection of or making fruitful the mortgated property. See also *Re Cripps* [1946] Ch. 265 and *The Supreme Court Practice 1988*, Vol. 1, para. 88/2–731.

[70a] Not amounting to more than £1,000 in any one accounting period, see *Practice Direction*, July 1, 1985, and *The Supreme Court Practice 1988*, Vol. 1, para. 88/2–7/30.

[71] See *Re Manchester & Milford Rly. Co.* (1880) 14 Ch.D. 645 at 653.

[72] At one time equitable mortgages were in common use as a means of avoiding or mitigating the payment of stamp duty. Now that stamp duty has been abolished, legal mortgages are almost invariably used, the exception being where deposits of deeds are made to secure temporary facilities.

[73] *James* v. *James* (1873) L.R. 16 Eq. 153. Foreclosure of an equity of redemption also occurs occasionally through the dismissal of an action for redemption, see *Cholmley* v. *Countess of Oxford* (1741) 2 Atk. 267.

[74] *James* v. *Ellis* (1871) 19 W.R. 319 (and see *post*, p. 269).

[75] *Backhouse* v. *Charlton* (1878) 8 Ch.D. 444.

[76] *York Union Banking Co.* v. *Artley* (1879) 11 Ch.D. 205.

[77] See *Harrold* v. *Plenty* [1901] 2 Ch. 314.

[78] See *Re Kerr's Policy* (1869) L.R. 8 Eq. 331 at 336.

[79] See *Redmayne* v. *Forster* (1866) L.R. 2 Eq. 467

[80] See *ante*, pp. 221 *et seq.*

[81] L.P.A. 1925, s.101(1).

mortgages by deposit are accompanied by a memorandum under seal. But, there still may be difficulties, for the reasons expressed elsewhere[82] arising from the decision in *Re Hodson & Howes Contract*,[83] in that the mortgagee can sell only the interest which he himself holds.[84]

Therefore, in order to avoid such difficulties, the practice has arisen of employing either or both of two conveyancing devices which enables the mortgagee, in effect, to convey the legal estate.

Power of attorney. A power of attorney is inserted into the mortgage deed granting a power of attorney to the mortgagee or his assigns[85] to convey the legal estate which remains vested until sale in the mortgagor. Under section 4(1) of the Powers of Attorney Act 1971[86] as the power is given for value to secure a proprietary interest of the donee of the power it may be made irrevocable in perpetuity. Thus, neither the mortgagee nor any purchaser from him will be affected by any act on the part of the mortgagor, or by his death.[87] Accordingly, by virtue of section 5(3) of the 1971 Act, such persons are protected as they are entitled to assume that the power is incapable of revocation.[88]

Declaration of trust. A clause is inserted in the mortgage deed whereby the mortgagor declares that he holds the legal estate on trust for the mortgagee and authorises the mortgagee to appoint himself or his nominee as trustee in place of the mortgagor.[89] By this method the mortgagee can vest the legal estate in himself or in a purchaser.[90]

It goes without saying that an equitable mortgagee is subject to the same duties and restrictions on sale of the mortgaged property as a legal mortgagee.[91]

In the case of other equitable mortgages not made by deed, there is no statutory power of sale out of court. But, by virtue of section 91(2) of the Law of Property Act 1925 the court itself has the power to order a judicial sale on the application of the mortgagee or of any interested person and may vest a legal term of years in the mortgagee so that he can sell as if he were a legal mortgagee.[92]

Possession

Right to take possession. The position with regard to the right of an equitable mortgagee to take possession of the mortgaged property is unclear. It

---

[82] See *ante*, p. 237.
[83] (1887) 35 Ch.D. 668.
[84] But this interpretation has been doubted in the case of *Re White Rose Cottage* [1965] Ch. 940 at 951, and see *ante*, p. 239.
[85] See Powers of Attorney Act 1971, s.11(2) and Sched. 2.
[86] As amended by the Supreme Court Act 1981, s.152(4) and Sched. 7.
[87] See Powers of Attorney Act 1971, s.11(2) and Sched. 2.
[88] See *Re White Rose Cottage* [1965] Ch. 940.
[89] See *London and County Banking Co.* v. *Goddard* [1897] 1 Ch. 642.
[90] Under the Trustee Act 1925, s.40.
[91] See *ante*, pp. 221 *et seq*.
[92] L.P.A. 1925, ss.90, 91(7), and see *ante*, pp. 257 *et seq*.; *Oldham* v. *Stringer* (1884) 33 W.R. 251.

is generally stated in the authorities (including the second edition of Waldock, *The Law of Mortgages*) that an equitable mortgagee has no right to take possession.[93] It is clear that the equitable mortgagee has no right to take possession at law, for he has no legal estate. It is also clear that an equitable mortgagee can take possession if there is an express provision in the agreement giving him that right.[94] Thus, many agreements contain a clause empowering the mortgagee to take possession in the event of a default by the mortgagor. Also, as mentioned above, another device is to insert into the equitable mortgage a clause granting a power of attorney to the mortgagee making available to him all the rights and remedies of a legal mortgagee including the right to take possession of the mortgaged property. Further, the mortgagor may, by express permission, give the equitable mortgagee the right to take possession.[95]

But what is unclear is whether or not an equitable mortgagee has the right to take possession. In Megarry & Wade, *The Law of Real Property*[96] it is urged that in equity an equitable mortgagee should be entitled to the same rights as if he had a legal mortgage and that there would seem to be no reason why he should not take possession under the doctrine of *Walsh* v. *Lonsdale*,[97] as the basis of an equitable mortgage is the creation of an immediate relationship of mortgagor and mortgagee, rather than a mere contract for a future mortgage.[98] But the suggestion does not have universal approval.[99] It is possible that an equitable mortgage is an interest in property which is independent of the doctrine of *Walsh* v. *Lonsdale*. Further, it must be remembered that if this doctrine applies to equitable mortgages, it may produce a number of substantial difficulties with regard to the question of priority.[1]

Thus, the equitable mortgagee's right to take possession is uncertain. The court may in any event award him possession.[2] There is also some authority which indicates that the equitable mortgagee may take possession in his own right.[3] But the basis of the legality of such a right is uncertain. Unfortunately, the subject is not merely academic for if there is such a right on a claim to the court for an order for possession, the statu-

---

[93] Coote, *Law of Mortgages* (9th ed., 1927), p. 823; Halsbury, *Laws of England* (4th ed., 1980), Vol. 32 p. 309; Waldock, *The Law of Mortgages* (2nd ed., 1950) pp. 55, 235; and see *Barclays Bank Ltd.* v. *Bird* [1954] Ch. 274 at 280. See also the discussion in (1954) 70 L.Q.R. 161, and (1955) 71 L.Q.R. 204, where the authorities are reviewed.

[94] *Ocean Accident and Guarantee Corp. Ltd.* v. *Ilford Gas Co.* [1905] 2 K.B. 493.

[95] *Re Postle, ex p. Bignold* (1835) 2 Mont. & A. 214.

[96] (5th ed., 1984), pp. 951–952.

[97] (1882) 21 Ch.D. 9.

[98] And as indicated an action for the recovery of land will not be defeated merely for want of the legal estate, see *General Finance Mortgage and Discount Co.* v. *Liberator Permanent Benefit Building Society* (1878) 10 Ch.D. 15 at 24). *Re O'Neill* [1967] N.I. 129.

[99] See, *e.g.* Cheshire and Burn, *Modern Law of Real Property* (14th ed., 1988), p. 686.

[1] See Fairest, *Mortgages* (2nd ed., 1980), p. 109.

[2] *Barclays Bank Ltd.* v. *Bird* [1954] Ch. 274; *Re O'Neill* [1967] N.I. 129.

[3] See Megarry and Wade, *The Law of Real Property* (5th ed., 1984), p. 952 n. 71.

tory discretion pursuant to the provisions of the Administration of Justice Acts 1970 and 1973 would apply.[4]

Collection of rents.   As there is no privity of estate nor tenure between an equitable mortgagee and the tenants of the mortgagor, the equitable mortgagee has no right to direct the tenants of the mortgagor to pay over their rents to himself, nor to collect such rents,[5] without an order of the court.[6] If the tenants do pay the rents to the equitable mortgagee, his receipt will not discharge them from liability. But, at the same time, the tenants cannot demand the return of the rent if payment has been made under no mistake of fact.[7] Moreover, if a prior legal mortgagee is already in possession, the equitable mortgagee can intercept the surplus rents and profits of the prior legal mortgagee by requiring them to be paid over to himself instead of to the mortgagor.[8]

Appointment of receiver

In a proper case an equitable mortgagee can apply to the court for the judicial appointment of a receiver[9] and an equitable mortgagee has also the statutory power to appoint a receiver if the mortgage is by deed.[10] As we have seen, the statutory power usually renders it unnecessary to apply to the court to appoint a receiver.

Equitable chargees

An equitable chargee has no right to take possession.[11] Further, an equitable chargee cannot foreclose.[12] His primary remedies are to apply to the court for an order for sale or for the appointment of a receiver.[13] But, as the statutory definition of a mortgage extends to a charge,[14] an equitable chargee by deed will have the same statutory powers as an equitable mortgagee with regard to sale and the appointment of a receiver *out of court*.

RIGHT TO FIXTURES[14a]

In accordance with general principles fixtures affixed to mortgaged land form part of the security in the land whether affixed before or after the date

---

[4] See *ante*, pp. 243 *et seq.*
[5] *Re Pearson, ex p. Scott* (1838) 3 Mont. and A. 592; *Finck* v. *Tranter* [1905] 1 K.B. 427; *Vacuum Oil Co. Ltd.* v. *Ellis* [1914] 1 K.B. 693.
[6] The appropriate order is for the appointment of a receiver by way of equitable execution, see *Vacuum Oil Co. Ltd.* v. *Ellis* [1914] 1 K.B. 693 at 703.
[7] *Finck* v. *Tranter* [1905] 1 K.B. 427.
[8] *Parker* v. *Calcraft, Dunn* v. *Same* (1821) 6 Madd. 11.
[9] Supreme Court Act 1981, s.37; and see *ante*, p. 266.
[10] L.P.A. 1925, s.101(1)(iii); and see *ante*, p. 217.
[11] *Garfitt* v. *Allen, Allen* v. *Longstaffe* (1887) 37 Ch.D. 48 at 50.
[12] *Tennant* v. *Trenchard* (1869) 4 Ch.App. 537; *Re Lloyd, Lloyd* v. *Lloyd* [1903] 1 Ch. 385 at 404.
[13] *Tennant* v. *Trenchard* (1869) 4 Ch.App. 537; *Re Owen* [1894] 3 Ch. 220. Sale is also the remedy for the holder of an equitable lien, see *Neate* v. *Duke of Marlborough* (1838) 3 My. & Cr. 407. See also *ante*, pp. 247 *et seq.* and 266 *et seq.*
[14] See the L.P.A. 1925, ss.101(1), 205(1)(xvi).
[14a] For further discussion, see *ante*, p. 32.

of the mortgage. They pass automatically to the mortgagee of the land as realty unless a contrary intention appears in the mortgage.[15] Accordingly, the special exceptions ("tenant's fixtures") which have developed in the law of Landlord and Tenant do not apply.[16]

---

[15] *Reynolds* v. *Ashby & Son* [1904] A.C. 466.
[16] See Megarry & Wade, *The Law of Real Property* (5th ed., 1984), pp. 735–738.

CHAPTER 15

THE EQUITY OF REDEMPTION AS AN INTEREST IN PROPERTY

MORTGAGOR AS EQUITABLE OWNER

IN *Kreglinger* v. *New Patagonia Meat Co.*[1] Lord Parker pointed out that the equitable right to redeem which arises on failure to exercise the contractual right must be carefully distinguished from the equitable interest, which, from the first, remains in the mortgagor and is sometimes referred to as an equity of redemption. The equitable *right* to redeem does not exist until the mortgagor is in default and the mortgagee's estate has become absolute at law.[2] The equitable *interest*, on the other hand, arises simultaneously with the execution of the mortgage, since in equity the mortgage conveyance does not have the effect of transferring to the mortgagee the whole beneficial interest in the security, but separates the legal from the equitable ownership. Equity from the outset treats the mortgagor as continuing to be the owner of the property which he has conveyed away, subject only to the mortgagee's charge.[3] By like reasoning a mortgagee's interest is, in equity, not a right to the mortgaged property, but to the mortgage debt, and his beneficial interest in the security is only as a means for enforcing his right to the debt.[4] He is a mere incumbrancer.

The equity of redemption is therefore not only an equitable right, but an interest in property.[5] When personal chattels are the subject-matter of the security, the mortgagor's equity is an interest in personalty similar to any other equitable interest in a fund of personalty. Similarly, when the subject-matter is land, the equity of redemption is an equitable interest in land, which before 1926 was termed in equitable estate.[6] For a mortgagor *held* the same interest in equity as he had at law before the mortgage and, therefore, if he had mortgaged a legal estate in land, he retained afterwards a corresponding equitable estate. Lord Hardwicke, in *Casborne* v. *Scarfe*,[7] drew attention to the conception of the equity of redemption as an estate in the following well-known passage:

"An equity of redemption has always been considered as an estate

---

[1] [1914] A.C. 25 at 48.
[2] *Brown* v. *Cole* (1845) 14 Sim. 427, and see *ante*, pp. 249 *et seq.*
[3] *Casborne* v. *Scarfe* (1738) 1 Atk. 603; *Finch* v. *Earl of Winchelsea* (1715) 1 P.Wms. 277; *cf. English Sewing Cotton·Co.* v. *I.R.C.* (1947) 63 T.L.R. 306 at 307.
[4] *Thornborough* v. *Baker* (1675) 1 Ch.Cas. 283.
[5] A mortgagor has a title in equity "equitable right inherent in the land," *per* Hale C.B. in *Pawlett* v. *Att.-Gen.* (1667) Hard. 465 at 469. In view of s.1 of the L.P.A. 1925, it may now be safer to term it an equitable interest, or perhaps a mere equity.
[6] *Casborne* v. *Scarfe* (1738) 1 Atk. 603.
[7] *Ibid.* at 605.

in the land, for it may be devised, granted, or entailed with remainders, and such entail and remainders may be barred by a fine and recovery, and therefore cannot be considered as a mere right only, but such an estate whereof there may be a seisin. "

In *Casborne* v. *Scarfe*,[8] Lord Hardwicke gave a husband an estate by the curtesy in his wife's equity of redemption,[8a] and his decision resulted in the equity of redemption being placed on the same footing as the equity of a *cestui que trust*. A mortgagor's equity of redemption is therefore not only his right to redeem, but also his title to the beneficial ownership of the mortgaged property during the continuance of the mortgage. Having this equitable title he may deal with the beneficial ownership just as if he had never made a mortgage; he may sell it, settle it, create charges upon it, demise it; he may do anything he pleases with it, subject only to the mortgagee's incumbrance. Moreover, he will continue to have an equitable title to the property until his title is terminated by lapse of time, release, sale under a power of sale, or by a judgment of the court.[9]

This view of the equity of redemption was again asserted in the case of *Re Sir Thomas Spencer Wells*.[10] A company mortgaged certain leaseholds by assigning to the mortgagees the residue of the terms, subject to a proviso for redemption. In 1910 a liquidator was appointed, who, believing the equities of redemption to be then valueless, neither surrendered them to the mortgagees, nor made any attempt to sell them. In 1916 the company was dissolved. By 1931 the leaseholds had appreciated in value so considerably that the equities of redemption were claimed by the Crown as *bona vacantia*. Farwell J., at first instance, held[11] that whereas there was, immediately prior to the dissolution of the company, a legal entity entitled to redeem, that legal entity had ceased to exist, with the result that the leaseholds were vested in the mortgagee free of any right in any one to redeem. Such a result could be reached only by treating the equity of redemption, not as a title, but as a personal equity, and the Court of Appeal had no hesitation in reversing the decision and allowing the claim of the Crown. Lawrence L.J.[12] put the matter thus:

"In equity the mortgagor is regarded as the owner of the mortgaged land subject only to the mortgagee's charge, and the mortgagor's equity of redemption is treated as an equitable estate in the land of the same nature as other equitable estates . . . . It would be just as unconscionable for a mortgagee to set up a claim to hold the land comprised in his mortgage free from the equity of redemption as it would be for a trustee to set up a claim to retain the trust property in his hands for his own use. Consequently, the reasoning which has induced

---

[8] (1738) 1 Atk. 603.
[8a] Curtesy was abolished by Administration of Estates Act 1925, s.45.
[9] *Cf. Weld* v. *Petre* [1929] 1 Ch. 33 at 42, *per* Russell J.
[10] [1933] Ch. 29.
[11] [1932] 1 Ch. 380.
[12] [1933] Ch.29 at 52, 53.

the Court to hold that a trustee cannot on failure of the trusts set up his legal title so as to defeat the Crown's claim to bona vacantia applies with equal force to a mortgagee of leaseholds where the mortgagor, being an individual, has died intestate without next of kin, or being a company, has been dissolved."

EQUITY OF REDEMPTION UNDER THE LAW OF PROPERTY ACT 1925

In the case of *Re Sir Thomas Spencer Wells*[13] the Court of Appeal did not refer to the effect of the Law of Property Act 1925 on the nature of a mortgagor's rights, although some reference to the transitional provisions[14] of that Act might not have been inappropriate. For a mortgagor's position has, in the case of mortgages of legal estates, been technically changed by sections 85 and 86 of the Law of Property Act 1925, which alter the formal methods of creating such mortgages. A mortgagor now possesses not merely his equitable title, but also a legal reversion. Under sections 85 and 86, mortgages of both freeholds and leaseholds are created by demise, so that a mortgagor necessarily retains for himself at least a nominal reversion. Freeholds can no longer be mortgaged by the conveyance of the fee simple. Now on mortgaging a fee simple, for example, the mortgagor possesses simultaneously a legal reversion expectant on a 3,000 year lease and an equitable interest in the 3,000 year term. It is contended in *Halsbury's Laws of England*,[15] that the equitable interest in the term is co-extensive with, and therefore merged in, the legal reversion. For this premise it is concluded that "instead of the equity of redemption constituting an equitable estate or interest, it subsists only as a right in equity to redeem the property, this right being attached to his legal freehold estate." No doubt this view of the equity of redemption avoids any conveyancing complications and corresponds with the broad policy of the 1925 legislation. It may, however, be questioned whether the statement in *Halsbury* provides a completely satisfactory explanation of the position of the equity of redemption, in mortgages by demise. Certainly the equity of redemption, viewed simply as the equitable title arising from the right to pay off the mortgagee and recover the mortgaged property after the passing of the contract date, is co-extensive with the legal reversion. But, if the equitable interest in the 3,000 year lease is also to disappear by being merged in the fee, how is the mortgagor's right to the beneficial ownership of the lease before redemption to be accounted for? Even if the mortgagee takes possession under the lease, the mortgagor is in equity beneficially entitled to the profits, a fact which cannot be explained by reference to the fee simple title, since this is *subject to the lease*. In other words, the equity of redemption in the lease appears to be essentially distinct from, and additional to, the nominal legal reversion. For this reason there does not seem to be a true merger of the

[13] [1933] Ch. 29.
[14] Sched. 1, Pt. 7.
[15] Vol. 32, para. 571.

equitable interest in the fee[16] and the statement in *Halsbury* is thought to go too far. The view is preferred that sections 85 and 86 of the Law of Property Act 1925 are concerned only with conveyancing and do not effect any essential change in the character of the equity of redemption. It is clear that the substance of the mortgagor's rights is still his equitable right of redemption and that his legal reversion is a nominal estate meeting the requirements of the modern system of conveyancing. At the same time, the legislature undoubtedly regarded the equity of redemption and the legal reversion as inseparable interests, and the view in *Halsbury* that the equity of redemption is now attached to the legal reversion is perhaps correct. Otherwise, the two-fold nature of the mortgagor's interest might cause conveyancing complications.

DISPOSITION AND DEVOLUTION OF THE EQUITY OF REDEMPTION

Disposition inter vivos and by will

Since a mortgagor through the protection of equity remains substantially the owner of the property which he has mortgaged, he has as much power to deal with it as if he had never executed the conveyance, though the dealings will generally be subject to the mortgagee's charge.[17] Thus, an equity of redemption may be sold, leased,[18] settled, mortgaged, assigned for the benefit of creditors or disposed of by will. Dispositions by will must, of course, be in accordance with the provisions of the Wills Act 1837, and conveyances of equities of redemption, being conveyances of equitable interests, must be in writing under section 53(1)(c) of the Law of Property Act 1925. When the subject-matter of a mortgage is land, the equity of redemption is an interest in land, and thus any contract to assign it must be evidenced by a memorandum in writing, signed by the party to be charged, or by his lawfully authorised agent.[19] Moreover, in the case of land, although section 53(1)(c) only requires the conveyance of an equity of redemption to be in writing, it will usually be by deed. For on a mortgage of freehold or leasehold property the mortgagor necessarily retains, at least, a nominal reversion, which he will convey to his assignee, together with the equity of redemption.

The assignee of incumbered property generally takes it subject to the mortgagee's charge. The Law of Property Act 1925, however, provides special machinery, whereby a person selling or exchanging land which is

---

[16] Turner, *Equity of Redemption* (1931) pp. 186, 187. See also *Young* v. *Clarey* [1948] Ch. 191 at 198, where Harman J., seems to have regarded the reversion as a distinct interest.

[17] Provision is made by s.50 of the L.P.A. 1925 for the discharge of an incumbrance on the sale or exchange of land, if there is paid into court a sum sufficient to meet the mortgagee's claim.

[18] *Tarn* v. *Turner* (1888) 39 Ch.D. 456, C.A. When a mortgagor has no power to create leases binding on the mortgagee, a lease granted by him is valid on the principle of estoppel, and confers on the lessee an interest in the equity of redemption sufficient to entitle him to redeem. See *post*, pp. 317, 338.

[19] L.P.A. 1925, s.40; see *Massey* v. *Johnson* (1847) 1 Exch. 241.

subject to a charge, may transfer it free of the charge. Under section 50 an application may be made to the court to allow a fund to be brought into court to meet the charge, interest in it, if any, plus all necessary costs, and then to have the property declared free from the incumbrance. If the application is granted, the court may make appropriate vesting orders or orders for conveyance and give directions concerning the investment of the fund in court. The advantage of this machinery is that it enables land to be sold free of an incumbrance in cases when, by the terms of the charge, the incumbrance cannot immediately be paid off, for example, where an annual sum is charged on land, or where a capital sum is due on some future date. It is true that the incumbrancer loses the security of the land, but the fund in court is not his only protection; for, if by the depreciation of its investments the fund proves insufficient, the deficiency must be made up by the vendor. The fund is thus not substituted for the charge, but is a security for it, and consequently, if there is a surplus after discharging the incumbrance, the surplus belongs to the vendor.[20]

Settlement of equities of redemption

Since a large proportion of family estates are to some extent mortgaged, the settlement of an equity of redemption is a common occurrence. Even before 1926 an equity of redemption on freehold land, being an equitable estate of inheritance, could be entailed,[21] and the entail could be barred under the Fines and Recoveries Act 1833; the mortgaging of freehold estates did not therefore interrupt the continuity of a strict settlement. Section 130(1) of the Law of Property Act 1925 now enables an equity of redemption to be entailed whether the subject-matter of the mortgage be real or personal property. When entails or other successive interests are created in an equity of redemption, the question arises as to how far the tenant for life is obliged to keep down the interest on the mortgage debt. The general principle is that a tenant for life is bound on all paramount incumbrances to keep down the interest accruing during his period of enjoyment to the extent of the profits received by him.[22] Thus, if a tenant for life allows the interest to get into arrear when the rents and profits are sufficient to meet it, the persons subsequently entitled may bring an action to have the arrears discharged, and may enforce their right against the life tenant's personal representatives after his death.[23] Moreover, if incumbered and unincumbered property is included in the same settlement the tenant for life is bound to employ the profits from all the properties in discharging the interest on the incumbered portion.[24] Tenants in tail in possession, however, are not within the rule; although they are tenants for life

[20] *Re Wilberforce's Trusts* [1915] 1 Ch. 94.
[21] *Casborne* v. *Scarfe* (1738) 1 Atk. 603.
[22] *Revel* v. *Watkinson* (1748) 1 Ves.Sen. 93.
[23] *Lord Kensington* v. *Bouverie* (1859) 7 H.L.C. 557; *Makings* v. *Makings* (1860) 1 De G.F. & J. 355.
[24] *Frewen* v. *Law Life Assurance Society* (1896) 2 Ch. 511; *Honeywood* v. *Honeywood* [1902] 1 Ch. 347.

for the purposes of the Settled Land Act 1925, they are not under an obligation to keep down the interest on incumbrances, because by the power of breaking the entail they always have the reversioner and the remaindermen at their mercy.[25]

But the duty of a life tenant to keep down interest on charges is now owed to the incumbrancer; it exists only between the life tenant and persons subsequently entitled.[26] Consequently, when the income from the settled property is insufficient to meet the claim for interest, and the life tenant makes up the deficiency out of his own pocket, he does not necessarily obtain a charge on the property for the amount of the deficiency. He is presumed to intend a benefit to the inheritance, unless he intimates to those next entitled his intention to reserve a charge on the property before he meets the claim for interest.[27]

Equity of redemption as assets for payment of debts

An equity of redemption is part of the mortgagor's assets available for the payment of his debts, and therefore on his bankruptcy vests in his trustee for that purpose, and on his death in his personal representatives. An equity of redemption may also be taken by a judgment creditor to satisfy his judgment, the process varying with the nature of the property.

When the equity of redemption arises from the mortgage of land the appropriate remedy is for the judgment creditor to register his judgment in the Register of Writs and Orders at the Land Charges Register pursuant to the Land Charges Act 1972.[28]

Alternatively, the judgment creditor can obtain the appointment of a receiver by way of equitable execution (which the High Court and any county court is empowered to do in appropriate circumstances in relation to land and interests therein.)[29] It also relates to personal property.[30] The

---

[25] *Amesbury* v. *Brown* (1750) 1 Ves.Sen. 477; *Chaplin* v. *Chaplin* (1734) 3 P.Wms. 245. An infant tenant in tail cannot, of course, break the entail during his minority, and the interest must be kept down during that period: *Sergeson* v. *Sealey* (1742) 2 Atk. 412; *Burgess* v. *Mawbey* (1823) 1 T. & R. 167.

[26] *Re Morley* (1869) L.R. 8 Eq. 594.

[27] *Lord Kensington* v. *Bouverie* (1859) 7 H.L.C. 557. *Cf. Re Warwick's Settlement Trusts* [1937] Ch. 561.

[28] s.6. (If the title to the land is registered it should be protected by a caution, (Land Registration Act 1925, s.59(1)). Power is given to the High Court and to any county court for the purpose of enforcing any judgment or order of those courts for the payment of money to any person, to impose by order a charge on any such land or interest in land of the debtor as may be specified in the order, and for securing the payment of monies due or to become due under the judgment order. Such an order may be made absolute or on conditions, see Charging Orders Act 1979, s.1(1), (repealing Administration of Justice Act 1956, s.35). Formerly a mere interest under a trust for sale was not a interest in "land" for this purpose, (see *Irani Finance Ltd.* v. *Singh* [1971] Ch. 59, C.A.). But since the Charging Orders Act 1979, the court is now empowered to make an order charging a debtor's beneficial interests under any trust including a trust for sale, (see *National Westminster Bank* v. *Stockman* [1981] 1 W.L.R. 67).

[29] Supreme Court Act 1981, s.37; County Courts Act 1984, s.107; and see R.S.C. Ord. 30, r. 1, Ord. 51, r. 2; C.C.R. Ord. 32, r. 1. See also pp. 217 *et seq.* for the power to appoint a receiver under the L.P.A. 1925.

[30] *e.g.* such as stocks and shares.

power may be exercised whether or not a charging order has been imposed under the Charging Orders Act 1979 and R.S.C. Ord. 50 and is in addition to and not in derogation of any power of the court to appoint a receiver in proceedings by enforcing a charge created by a charging order.[31] The appointment of a receiver by way of equitable execution does *not* of itself create a charge on the property and will be void if not registered under the Land Charges Act 1972.[32]

When the equity of redemption is in personal chattels which have been mortgaged by a bill of sale, the chattels cannot be taken by the sheriff under a writ of *fi. fa.*, since the property in them has already passed to the holder of the bill of sale.[33] The judgment creditor may, however, under R.S.C. Ord. 29, r. 24, apply to the court for a sale of the chattels and will be entitled to any sum which is realised in excess of the amount due to the holder of the bill of sale. If it is doubtful whether there will be any excess, the court will not order a sale unless the creditor indemnifies the mortgagee against loss, while if it is certain that there will be no excess, an order for sale will not be granted.[34]

Devolution of equity of redemption on intestacy

Since a mortgagor continues in equity to be the owner of the mortgaged property, the mortgage does not affect the devolution of the property after the mortgagor's death. Thus, before 1926, an equity of redemption in freehold belonged to the heir-at-law, while an equity of redemption in chattels real or in pure personalty belonged to the next of kin. Moreover, in the case of land, if any special custom of descent was applicable to the land as, for example, gavelkind, the custom governed the descent of an equity of redemption in the land.[35] Today, of course, succession to an equity of redemption, whether of chattels or realty, is governed by the provisions of the Administration of Estates Act 1925.[36] Consequently, on the death of a mortgagor intestate, the equity of redemption passes to his personal representatives with the rest of his property.

Incidence of the mortgage debt

A mortgagor's liability for the mortgage debt has two aspects—his personal liability on the express or implied promise to pay, and his incumbered property's liability to be taken by the mortgagee. Liabilities under a contract cannot be assigned, and consequently, if a mortgagor assigns his equity of redemption (even if the assignee undertakes personal liability[37])

---

[31] *The Supreme Court Practice 1988*, Vol. 1, para. 51/1–3/5.
[32] s.6. It will not, however, be void if an order has also been made under the Charging Orders Acts 1979 (see *The Supreme Court Practice 1988*, Vol. 1, para. 51/1–3/5).
[33] *Scarlett* v. *Hanson* (1883) 12 Q.B.D. 213.
[34] *Stern* v. *Tegner* (1898) 1 Q.B. 37.
[35] *Fawcett* v. *Lowther* (1751) 2 Ves.Sen. 300.
[36] ss.45–52 as amended by the Family Law Reform Act 1987, ss.1, 18 and 33(1).
[37] *West Bromwich Building Society* v. *Bullock* (1936) 80 S.J. 654.

the assignee does not become personally liable to pay the mortgage debt,[38] although the mortgagee may, of course, still take the property to satisfy his debt. Moreover, even though an assignment is made subject to the mortgage debt, the original mortgagor is still liable to be sued on the personal covenant,[39] and thus usually takes an indemnity from his assignee to meet that contingency.[40] Of course, the mortgagee may consent to the assignee and not the original mortgagor taking over the liability to pay, by the assignee entering into a fresh covenant with the mortgagee.

The case is more complicated when the equity of redemption is transferred, not *inter vivos*, but on the death of the mortgagor, for his personal representatives succeed to the liability in contract,[41] whereas the incumbered property may devolve upon or be devised to beneficiaries who have not that liability. Until the law was altered by Locke King's Acts,[42] a deceased's personal estate was primarily liable to satisfy a debt charged upon land, so that an heir-at-law or a devisee was entitled to call on the personalty to exonerate lands from the debts charged upon them.[43] The rule was displaced if the deceased had signified a contrary intention,[44] and, being based upon succession to the deceased's contractual liability, it only applied on the death of the original mortgagor. An assignee of an equity of redemption had not himself created the charge and was not therefore under any personal liability.[45]

Today, however, the rule is reversed. Unless the deceased mortgagor has signified a contrary intention, the primary liability to satisfy charges upon his property is, as between persons claiming beneficially under him, upon the incumbered property. The personal estate is still, of course, liable to satisfy a mortgagee's claim in contract against the deceased, but, if called on to do so, has a right to be compensated out of the mortgaged property. This change was first effected in 1854, but the Administration of Estates Act 1925[46] extends the new rule to incumbered *personalty* as well as realty. Thus, specific personalty which has been mortgaged or pledged will not, after 1925, be entitled to exoneration at the expense of the general assets of the deceased, unless the latter has shown an intention by will, deed or other document to that effect. Under the Administration of

---

[38] *Oxford (Earl)* v. *Lady Rodney* (1808) 14 Ves. 417; *Re Errington, ex p. Mason* [1894] 1 Q.B. 11.

[39] *Kinnaird* v. *Trollope* (1888) 39 Ch. 636; subsequent proceedings (1889) 42 Ch.D. 610.

[40] Even if he does not (see *Mills* v. *United Counties Bank Ltd.* [1912] 1 Ch. 231), when the whole mortgaged property is assigned subject to the mortgage, such an indemnity will be implied (*Bridgman* v. *Daw* (1891) 40 W.R. 253) unless it is not made for value (*Re Best* [1924] 1 Ch. 42). See also Romer L.J. in *Re Mainwaring's Settlement Trusts* [1937] 1 Ch. 96 at 103.

[41] *Bartholomew* v. *May* (1737) 1 Atk. 487.

[42] Real Estates Charges Acts, 1854, 1867 and 1877.

[43] *Cope* v. *Cope* (1710) 2 Salk. 449; *Galton* v. *Hancock* (1742) 2 Atk. 436.

[44] *Morrow* v. *Bush* (1785) 1 Cox. 185; *Forrest* v. *Prescott* (1870) L.R. 10 Eq. 545; *Hancox* v. *Abbey* (1805) 11 Ves. 179.

[45] *Scott* v. *Beecher* (1820) 5 Madd. 96; *Butler* v. *Butler* (1800) 5 Ves. 534; *Earl of Ilchester* v. *Earl of Carnarvon* (1839) 1 Beav. 209.

[46] ss.35, 55(1)(xvii); this largely restates the old law.

Estates Act 1925, as under Locke King's Acts, the deceased's contrary direction in favour of exoneration must be clear and unambiguous. Thus, a general direction for the payment of debts, or even of *all* debts, out of the deceased's personal or residuary estate will not be sufficient to exonerate property mortgaged or charged[47] nor will a direction to charge all debts upon the personal or residuary estate. In fact, an intention to exonerate must be signified by words referring clearly to mortgage debts, and not to debts generally.[48] Such an intention can be shown in any document such as a letter.[49] It may be partial in that it applies to mortgages and not to liens,[50] but it is not enough to make a specific demise of one property comprised in a mortgage and not the whole.[51]

These provisions do not in any way affect a mortgagee's right to satisfy himself, either out of the incumbered property or, by suing on the personal promise, out of the deceased mortgagor's general assets. The changed incidence of the debt does not alter the mortgagee's remedies.[52] They do not apply to a person who is given the right to purchase part of the estate by will. He is not a devisee or legatee, but a purchaser.[53]

Contribution

When several estates, held in different ownership, are subject to the same mortgage, any one owner, who discharges the common debt, has a right to contribution from the others pro rata according to the value of their securities. The primary equitable rule is that, where different properties are charged with the same debt, the burden shall be distributed proportionately among the properties.[54] Thus the mortgagee may pursue his remedies against any estate he pleases, but he cannot, by so doing, throw the whole liability on the owner of one estate.[55] The same rule applies when a mortgagor has mortgaged several estates to secure the same debt, and then on his death the estates pass into the hands of several owners. Under section 35 of the Administration of Estates Act 1925, all the incumbered properties are responsible for the debt, and if one owner discharges the whole liability, he has a right to contribution.[56] The fundamental requirement for this right to contribution is that all the properties shall be subject to a common liability *of the same degree*.[57] It is not enough that a creditor has a charge on more than one property; the properties must, as

---

[47] s.35(2).
[48] *Re Valpy* [1906] 1 Ch. 531.
[49] See *Re Campbell* [1898] 2 Ch. 206; *Re Wakefield* (1943) 87 S.J. 371, C.A.; *Re Birmingham* [1959] Ch. 523.
[50] *Re Beirnstein* [1925] Ch. 12.
[51] *Re Neeld* [1962] Ch. 643, overruling *Re Biss* [1956] Ch. 243.
[52] s.35(3).
[53] *Re Fison's Wills Trust* [1950] Ch. 394.
[54] *Per* Tomlin J. in *Re Best* [1924] 1 Ch. 42 at 44.
[55] *Aldrich* v. *Cooper* (1803) 8 Ves. 382; *Johnson* v. *Child* (1844) 4 Hare 87.
[56] See *Carter* v. *Barnardiston* (1718) 1 P.Wms. 505; *Middleton* v. *Middleton* (1852) 15 Beav. 450.
[57] *Re Dunlop* (1882) 21 Ch.D. 583.

between themselves, be equally liable. For example, a property specifically charged with a debt has no right to contribution from property over which the creditor has only a general lien. It is for this reason that the owner of incumbered property, who is also under a personal obligation to pay a common debt, cannot claim contribution from another whose property is subject to the same incumbrance, but who has no personal liability in respect of the debt.[58] Nor must it be forgotten that the doctrine of marshalling may have the result of throwing the primary liability for a common debt upon one only of the mortgaged estates, so that the owner of that estate, not having an equal liability, will lose his right to contribution.[59] Again, even in the case of joint mortgagees there may be no right of contribution, because of the special circumstances of the mortgage; for example, of two co-mortgagors one may be acting as surety for the other so that, as between themselves, the primarily liability is upon the principal debtor.[60] In all these cases, where the primary liability is upon one debtor or property, the others are not only bound to contribute, but if they in fact discharge the debt, they have a right to be compensated.[61] This is important if a mortgagor mortgages two estates to cover the same debt, and afterwards assigns one of the estates. Under the principles just stated, the primary liability is upon the assignor so that, if he does not intend to exonerate his assignee's estate, he must be careful to preserve his own right to contribution.[62] This right he will preserve if he assigns the estate *subject to the mortgage*, because by so doing he shows that the primary liability is not to be all on the property which he retains, and thus restores the fundamental rule of equity which requires the imposition of proportionate burdens on properties charged with the same debt.[63] On the other hand, the assignment of one estate subject to the mortgage does not, by itself, shift the *whole* burden of the whole mortgage to the property assigned. Only an express indemnity covering the whole mortgage debt will have that effect.[64]

MORTGAGOR'S BENEFICIAL ENJOYMENT OF THE SECURITY

The notion that the mortgagor is the real owner of the security is carried in equity as far as it can be, without actually infringing the rights vested in the mortgagee by virtue of his legal estate. The mortgagee, is not a trustee for the mortgagor, for he has an interest in the mortgaged property adverse to that of the mortgagor.[65] In equity, however, that interest is rigidly confined to a right to hold the property as a security. A mortgagor, until his equity of redemption is lost to him by foreclosure, sale under a power of sale,

---

[58] *Re Darby's Estate* [1907] 2 Ch. 465.
[59] *Bartholomew* v. *May* (1737) 1 Atk. 487; and *post*, pp. 428 *et seq.*
[60] *Marquess of Bute* v. *Cunynghame* (1826) 2 Russ. 275.
[61] *Re Best* [1924] 1 Ch. 42.
[62] *Ibid.*
[63] *Re Mainwaring's Settlement Trusts* [1937] 1 Ch. 96.
[64] *Ibid.*
[65] *Dobson* v. *Land* (1850) 8 Hare 216 and see *ante*, pp. 194 *et seq.*

lapse of time or release, is entitled to the full beneficial enjoyment of the land. He is regarded as the owner of the land subject to a mere incumbrance. It is true that a mortgage contract usually confers on the mortgagee a legal right to take possession of the property immediately and without regard to the state of the mortgage debt, but equity treats this right as part of his security, and not as a right to beneficial enjoyment. Thus, if a mortgagee does take possession of his security, he will be called on to account with strictness for his use of it, and for the profits which he has taken or ought to have taken from the property.[66] For example, if the mortgagee occupies land the mortgagor is entitled to be credited with a fair occupation rent.[67] In consequence, not only is a mortgagee prevented from making any profit out of the mortgage property, but he is, by the strictness of the account, discouraged from exercising his legal right to take possession, except as a measure to preserve his security.[68] Equity stops short of restraining the mortgagee from taking possession by granting an injunction, but, if possession is taken, the mortgagor is considered as being entitled to the profits, subject only to the mortgagee's right to devote them to the satisfaction of the mortgage debt.

On the other hand, if, as generally happens, the mortgagor remains in possession, he is entitled to take all the profits from the security without being in any way obliged either to account for them or to apply them in discharging the mortgage interest.[69] This is so even though the security is insufficient. Thus, in a case[70] where the property mortgaged was land let out on lease and the mortgagor went bankrupt, Lord Eldon refused to compel the assignee in bankruptcy to account for past rents received by him. He insisted that a mortgagor does not receive the rents for the mortgagee, and that there is no instance of a mortgagor being directly called on to account for rents. Again, a mortgagor of land may cut and sell timber, and in so doing may even waste the inheritance, provided that he does not thereby render the security insufficient.[71] A mortgagor in possession cannot therefore be considered a bailiff of the mortgagee. He is equitable owner of the property, and as such is not liable to pay an occupation rent to the mortgagee.[72] Correspondingly, he has the ordinary liabilities of an owner and is, for example, responsible for the maintenance of dykes and sea walls.[73]

---

[66] *Hughes* v. *Williams* (1806) 12 Ves. 493; *Shepherd* v. *Spansheath* (1988) E.G.C.S. 35; *Chaplin* v. *Young (No. 1)* (1864) 33 Beav. 330; *Parkinson* v. *Hanbury* (1867) L.P. 2 H.L. 1.

[67] *Marriott* v. *Anchor Reversionary Co.* (1861) 3 De G.F. & J. 177 at 193.

[68] It is the nature of the transaction that the mortgagor shall continue in possession. *Per* Lord Selborne, *Heath* v. *Pugh* (1881) 6 Q.B.D. 345 at 359.

[69] *Trent* v. *Hunt* (1853) 9 Exch. 14; *Heath* v. *Pugh* (1881) 6 Q.B.D. 345 at 359, *per* Lord Selborne; affirmed (1882) 7 A.C. 235, H.L.

[70] *Ex p. Wilson* (1813) 2 V. & B. 252; *cf. Colman* v. *Duke of St. Albans* (1796) 3 Ves. 25; *Hele* v. *Lord Bexley* (1855) 20 Beav. 127.

[71] *Usborne* v. *Usborne* (1740) 1 Dick. 75; *Hippesley* v. *Spencer* (1820) 5 Mad. 422; *Harper* v. *Aplin* (1886) 54 L.T. 383.

[72] *Yorkshire Banking Co.* v. *Mullan* (1887) 35 Ch.D. 125.

[73] *Reg.* v. *Baker* (1867) 2 Q.B. 621.

MORTGAGOR IN POSSESSION

General

Although in equity a mortgagor remains owner of the property, by the mortgage conveyance he parts with an estate or interest which carries with it the immediate right to possession.[74] It is true that he usually remains in occupation, and that equity discourages the mortgagee from going into occupation, but the fact remains that the mortgagee holds the legal title to possession, and that the court will never prevent him from insisting on his title.[75] It follows that as a mortgagee has the immediate right to possession, the mortgagor can only lawfully remain in occupation as the mortgagee's tenant, and that in the absence of any special agreement the tenancy will be precarious. For unless the mortgage contract makes express provision for the mortgagor's continued possession of the property, his tenancy depends solely on his *de facto* possession, and is terminable by the mortgagee at any moment. The exact nature of this precarious tenancy is a subject of controversy, three distinct theories being put forward: *(i)* that the mortgagor is a tenant at will[76]; *(ii)* that he is a tenant at sufferance[77]; and *(iii)* that as a tenant he is *sui generis*, and cannot be assigned to any of the well-known classes.[78] The first theory has frequently been criticised[79] and can scarcely be correct, because a mortgagee may bring ejectment against a mortgagor without any previous demand for possession,[80] and a mortgagor, when ejected, is not entitled to emblements.[81] It is not, of course, suggested that a mortgagor is never a tenant at will of the mortgagee, because he may be made such a tenant by actual agreement,[82] or by the mortgagee expressly or impliedly recognising him as a tenant. The receipt of interest by the mortgagee is, however, referable to the mortgage, and is by itself no recognition of a tenancy in the mortgagor.[83] The second theory has more to recommend it, because the position of a mortgagor in possession, who has not been recognised as a tenant, largely corresponds to that of a tenant at

---

[74] Thus, under the old law a heriot could not be taken from a mortgagor, because he was not seised: *Copestake* v. *Hoper* [1908] 2 Ch. 10.

[75] *Per* Plumer, M.R., *Marquis Cholmondely* v. *Lord Clinton* (1817) 2 Mer. 171 at 359; *Pope* v. *Biggs* (1829) 9 B. & C. 245.

[76] Lord Mansfield in *Keech* v. *Hall* (1778) 1 Doug. 21; *cf. Moss* v. *Gallimore* (1779) 1 Doug.K.B. 279; Fortescue, M.R., in *Leman* v. *Newnham* (1747) 1 Ves.Sen. 51.

[77] Lord Ellenborough, *Thunder d. Weaver* v. *Belcher* (1803) 3 East. 449 at 451; Vaughan-Williams J. in *Scobie* v. *Collins* [1895] 1 Q.B. 375. See Turner, *Equity of Redemption* (1931), p. 102.

[78] Parke B. in *Litchfield* v. *Ready* (1850) 20 L.J.(N.S.) Ex. 51 at 52; Turner, *Equity of Redemption* (1931), p. 110.

[79] *e.g.* by Buller J. in *Birch* v. *Wright* (1786) 1 Term. 378 at 381.

[80] *Doe d. Griffith* v. *Mayo* (1828) 7 L.J.(O.S.) K.B. 84; *Jolly* v. *Arbuthnot* (1859) 4 De G. & J. 224.

[81] *Per* Buller J. in *Birch* v. *Wright* (1786) 1 Term. 378 at 387; *Christophers* v. *Sparke* (1820) 2 Jac. & W. 223. Even Lord Mansfield, who is chiefly responsible for the description of the mortgagor as tenant at will, was constrained by these differences to admit that he is a tenant at will only *quodam modo*: *Moss* v. *Gallimore* (1779) 1 Doug.K.B. 279.

[82] *e.g.* by the mortgagor attorning tenant to the mortgagee. See *ante*, p. 207.

[83] *Doe d. Rogers* v. *Cadwallader* (1831) 2 B. & Ad. 473; *Scobie* v. *Collins* [1895] 1 Q.B. 375.

sufferance: he begins lawfully, holds over without title, may be ejected without previous demand for possession, and is not entitled to emblements. Moreover, there are clear statements by Lord Ellenborough[84] and Lord Tenterden[85] that the mortgagor is at most a tenant at sufferance. On the other hand, unlike a tenant at sufferance, a mortgagor in possession, who pays his interest, will not find time running in his favour under the Limitation Act 1980,[86] although he is not thereby recognising the mortgagee as his landlord. Furthermore, statute[87] has given to a mortgagor in possession wide powers of bringing actions in respect of the mortgaged property, and of granting leases without the concurrence of the mortgagee, so that his position is, in fact, rather different from that of a tenant at sufferance. In the past[88] analogies from tenancies at will or at sufferance may have influenced judges in deciding questions concerning the mortgage relationship, but today the rights, powers and interests of mortgagor and mortgagee are well settled.[89] Therefore, while recognising that the closest analogy to the possession of a mortgagor is the possession of a tenant at sufferance,[90] it is sufficient to describe mortgagors as being in possession as mortgagors.[91]

A mortgagor, when his contract makes no provision for his continued occupation, holds precariously from the mortgagee, being liable to be ejected not only without notice, but without even a previous demand for possession. In fact it is then at the option of the mortgagee to treat his mortgagor in possession, either as his tenant or as a trespasser.[92] It is by no means uncommon, however, for a mortgagor to stipulate in the mortgage the right to continue in possession of the security.[93] Such a stipulation will sometimes amount to a redemise of the property, sometimes only to a personal covenant by the mortgagee not to interfere with the mortgagor's enjoyment, and, if the language is not precise, it is not always easy to distinguish between a redemise and a mere covenant. The cases suggest the following propositions:

(1) If there is an *affirmative* covenant[94] for the mortgagor's enjoy-

---

[84] *Thunder* d. *Weaver* v. *Belcher* (1803) 3 East 449.

[85] *Doe* d. *Roby* v. *Maisey* (1828) 8 B. & C. 767; *cf.* Littledale J. in *Pope* v. *Biggs* (1829) 9 B. & C. 245.

[86] See *post*, p. 404.

[87] Now the L.P.A. 1925. ss.98 and 99. See *post*, p. 284.

[88] Turner, *Equity of Redemption* (1931), p. 104.

[89] Thus Buller J. in *Birch* v. *Wright* (1786) 1 Term. 378 at 383, said, perhaps somewhat prematurely: "A mortgagor and mortgagee are characters as well known and their rights, powers and interests are well settled, as any in the law."

[90] See I Smith, *Leading Cases* (13th ed.), p. 594; Turner, *Equity of Redemption* (1931), Chap. 5.

[91] *Litchfield* v. *Ready* (1850) L.J.Ex. 51; Turner, *Equity of Redemption* (1931), p. 110.

[92] *Partridge* v. *Bere* (1822) 5 B. & Ald. 604; *Hitchman* v. *Walton* (1838) 4 M. & W. 409; *Moss* v. *Gallimore* (1779) 1 Doug.K.B. 279; *Re Ind, Coope & Co. Ltd.* [1911] 2 Ch. 223.

[93] This is sometimes effected by an "attornment clause," by which the mortgagor attorns tenant to the mortgagee. If there is such an attornment clause it can have certain consequences in a mortgagor's claim for possession. See *ante*, pp. 23, 207 *et seq* and *post*, p. 467.

[94] *Wilkinson* v. *Hall* (1837) 3 Bing.N.C. 508; *Doe* d. *Parsley* v. *Day* (1842) 2 Q.B. 147.

ment of the property, and a determinate period[95] is indicated as the length of the term the mortgage contract operates as a redemise for a term.

(2) If the agreement contains an affirmative covenant that the mortgagor shall continue in possession, or have quiet enjoyment until he makes default on the date fixed for repayment, he is a tenant for the intervening period.[96]

(3) In either case, if the mortgagor remains in occupation after the term as expired, he becomes a tenant at sufferance.[97]

(4) If the mortgagor is expressed to hold at the will and pleasure of the mortgagee, a tenancy at will is created, and it may still be a tenancy at will, although a yearly rent is payable.[98] On the other hand, the tenancy may be a periodic tenancy, although the mortgagee reserves a right to determine it without notice.[99] In each case it is a question of the true intention of the parties.

(5) If there is a covenant, which is negative, for example, that the mortgagee shall not interrupt the mortgagor's possession, or which does not indicate any period for the lease, it will be a personal covenant, and no demise.[1] In such cases a mortgagor is tenant as mortgagor, and his position is very like that of a tenant at sufferance.

Right of a mortgagor in possession to bring actions in respect of the mortgaged property

Although the tenancy of a mortgagor is usually precarious, it is plain that, when he is in possession of the mortgaged property, he will have the protection which the law always affords to a possessory title.[2] Except against the person entitled, a disseisor or a tenant at sufferance has all the remedies, legal or equitable, which the true owner has to protect his property.[3] So, too, has a mortgagor who is in personal occupation. But when the mortgage property is let out on lease, the mortgagor is, of course, only a reversioner, though technically still in possession. As owner of the property in equity he has always had available to him equitable remedies to protect his interest.[4] Thus he may bring an action for an injunction against his

[95] *Doe* d. *Roylance* v. *Lightfoot* (1841) 8 M. & W. 553; *Doe* d. *Parsley* v. *Day* (1842) 2 Q.B. 147.
[96] *Wilkinson* v. *Hall* (1837) 3 Bing.N.S. 508. See Coote, *Law of Mortgages* (9th ed., 1927), p. 677 (n.).
[97] *Gibbs* v. *Cruickshank* (1873) L.R. 8 C.P. 454.
[98] *Doe* d. *Bastow* v. *Cox* (1847) 11 Q.B. 122.
[99] *Re Knight, ex p. Voisey* (1882) 21 Ch.D. 442; *Re Threlfall, ex p. Queen's Benefit Building Society* (1880) 16 Ch.D. 274.
[1] *Doe* d. *Parsley* v. *Day* (1842) 2 Q.B. 147.
[2] *Perry* v. *Clissold* [1907] A.C. 73.
[3] *Graham* v. *Peat* (1801) 1 East. 244; *Asher* v. *Whitlock* (1865) L.R. 1 Q.B. 1.
[4] *Per* Channel J. in *Turner* v. *Walsh* [1909] 2 K.B. 484 at 487.

lessee or against a third party to prevent an injury to the property,[5] or to enforce a restrictive covenant.[6] Legal remedies, however, at common law attach only to the legal estate, and in days when mortgages were usually created by assignment, passed with the legal estate to the mortgagee.[7] A mortgagor was, indeed, allowed to recover the rents from his lease, and even distrain for them on the basis that he had an implied authority from the mortgagee,[8] but that at common law was the limit of his rights. Having at law no estate he was unable, against third parties, to bring an action for damages for injury to the reversion,[9] and having parted with the reversion to the mortgagee he was unable against his lessee to bring ejectment or any action on the covenants in the lease.[10] His course was either to induce the mortgagee to sue or to ask the court to compel the mortgagee to lend his name to the action, but this he could do only on the terms of offering to redeem.[11]

The power of a mortgagor in possession of mortgaged land to sue in respect of the land was, however, considerably enlarged by section 25(5) of the Judicature Act 1873 and section 10 of the Conveyancing Act 1881, which are now replaced by, respectively, sections 98 and 141 of the Law of Property Act 1925. These sections apply to all mortgages, whether made before or after January 1, 1926, and their effect is as follows. So long as the mortgagee has not given an effective[12] notice of an intention to take possession or to enter into receipt of the rent and profits, a mortgagor may, in his own name, sue for possession or for the recovery of rents and profits, and may bring an action for damages against a trespasser or against any other wrongdoer.[13] Similarly, whilst still a mortgagor in possession, he may, in his own name, enforce all covenants and conditions which are contained in leases of the mortgaged land.[14] It is immaterial whether the mortgage[15] or lease[16] was made before or after the statutory amendment. Finally, these statutory powers do not in any way prejudice a mortgagor's right to bring actions, which may be vested in him independently of the Act, for example, by virtue of the possession of a legal estate.

---

[5] *Van Gelder, Apsimon & Co.* v. *Sowerby Bridge, & United District Flour Society* (1890) 44 Ch.D. 374.

[6] *Fairclough* v. *Marshall* (1878) 4 Ex.D. 37; *Rogers* v. *Hosegood* [1900] 2 Ch. 388.

[7] *Doe* d. *Marriot* v. *Edwards* (1834) 5 B. & Ad. 1065. But if the mortgage was made *before* the lease there was no difficulty.

[8] *Ibid. Cf.* also *Trent* v. *Hunt* (1853) 9 Ex. 14.

[9] *Per* Bramwell B., at Assizes, *Rumford* v. *Oxford, Worcester & Wolverhampton Rly Co.* (1856) 1 H. & N. 34.

[10] *Matthews* v. *Usher* [1900] 2 Q.B. 535. See also *Molyneux* v. *Richard* [1906] 1 Ch. 34.

[11] *Per* Farwell L.J. in *Turner* v. *Walsh* [1909] 2 K.B. 484 at 495.

[12] Possession proceedings which are defective by means of a technicality are not sufficient, see *Kitchen's Trustee* v. *Madders and Madders* [1949] Ch. 588 affd. [1950] Ch. 134.

[13] s.98(1).

[14] s.141(2).

[15] s.98(3).

[16] s.141(4).

CHAPTER 16

THE RIGHTS, DUTIES AND REMEDIES OF THE MORTGAGOR OR CHARGOR

THE RIGHT OF REDEMPTION

Legal right to redeem

The legal right to redeem is the right specifically reserved to the mortgagor in the mortgage contract to recover his property upon discharging the obligations to secure which the mortgage was created. At law the contract is construed strictly, so that a mortgagor exercising his legal right to redeem must comply punctiliously with the proviso for redemption. Thus a mortgage to secure a money loan ordinarily fixes a definite date for repayment, and at law repayment must be made precisely on that date. Before the stipulated date the mortgagor has no right to redeem either at law or in equity,[1] nor has the mortgagee, in the absence of a special agreement to that effect, any right to call in his money. Even the fact that the mortgagor is in default upon other covenants not touching the proviso for redemption will not accelerate the mortgagee's right to call in his money.[2] After the stipulated date the mortgagor ceases at law to have any right to redeem his property.

The date for redemption usually prescribed by the mortgage contract is six months after the date of its execution. The period before which the property may be redeemed at law may, however, be shorter and indeed the mortgage may be made redeemable and repayable on demand, in which case the demand fixes the date for redemption. Normally the period is a short one, because[3] it is an advantage to the mortgagee to place the mortgagor in default as soon as possible. But at law there is no restriction upon the parties making their own arrangements. Accordingly the date for repayment and redemption may be suspended for any period, however long, provided that the mortgage contract does not infringe the equitable rules for the protection of the equity of redemption discussed below. Broadly, the position under these rules is that there is no limit to the length of a mortgage contract if the date for redemption is fixed genuinely upon an investment basis and the contract is neither a device to render the right of redemption illusory nor otherwise a cloak for an unconscionable bargain.[4]

---

[1] *Brown* v. *Cole* (1845) 14 Sim. 427.
[2] *Williams* v. *Morgan* [1906] 1 Ch. 804.
[3] See *ante*, p. 10 and pp. 273 *et seq*.
[4] *Knightsbridge Estates Trust Ltd.* v. *Byrne* [1939] Ch. 441; see *post*, pp. 291 *et seq*. and 308 *et seq*.

Equitable right to redeem

The equitable right to redeem[5] is the right of a mortgagor to recover his security by discharging his obligations under the mortgage, although the time fixed by the contract for the performance of those obligations has passed, and even though under the express terms of his agreement the security may be stated to be the absolute property of the mortgagee. Similarly, in the case of a charge, it is the right to have the security freed from the charge, although default was made at the time fixed by the contract for the performance of the obligations in respect of which the charge was given. The right to redeem in equity is therefore a right given in contradiction to the declared terms of the contract between the parties.[6] Today, however, the nature of the equitable right to redeem is so well known that when a mortgage is made in the usual form to secure a money payment on a certain day, it may generally be taken to be a term of the real bargain between the parties that the property is to remain redeemable after default on the day named.[7] As Maitland said,[8] the common form of mortgage by conveyance "is one long *suppressio veri* and *suggestio falsi*."

The equitable right to redeem is thus the right to recover the mortgaged property *after* the expiry of the legal right to redeem through its non-exercise on the contract date.[9] After the passing of the contract date equity superimposes on the mortgage agreement a condition giving the mortgagor a continuing right to redeem, which he may exercise at any time before the right is destroyed by foreclosure, sale, release, or lapse of time. In general, this equitable right is dependent on the mortgagor giving the mortgagee reasonable notice of his intention to redeem, and on his fully performing his obligations under the mortgage. In special cases the mortgagor is absolved from giving notice,[10] and sometimes may even be allowed to recover his security on giving the mortgagee less than what he is entitled to under the provisions of the mortgage.[11] But in every case the terms of redemption in equity[12] are imposed on the parties *ab extra* by the settled custom of the court, which regulates every mortgage contract. Nor can the court's control be ousted by any agreement in the mortgage itself. Lord Eldon in *Seton* v. *Slade*[13] said:

"I take it to be so in the case of a mortgage; that you shall not by

---

[5] The equitable right to redeem should be distinguished from the "equity of redemption," which has a wider meaning. See *post*, pp. 273 *et seq*.

[6] *Per* Lord Bramwell in *Salt* v. *Marquess of Northampton* [1892] A.C. 1 at 18.

[7] *Per* Lord Parker in *Kreglinger* v. *New Patagonia Meat and Cold Storage Co. Ltd.* [1914] A.C. 25 at 50.

[8] *Equity* (2nd ed.), p. 182.

[9] The right can arise *before* the legal date for redemption if the mortgagee has demanded payment, *e.g.* by entering into possession of the security, see *Bovill* v. *Endle* [1896] 1 Ch. 648.

[10] See *post*, pp. 314 *et seq*.

[11] *e.g.* in the case of a mortgage executed under undue influence.

[12] These terms are set out in full, *post*, pp. 319 *et seq*.

[13] (1802) 7 Ves. 265 at 273.

special terms alter what this Court says are the special terms of that contract."

Accordingly, if property is transferred with the object of providing security, and with the intention that it should be restored to the mortgagor, it is not competent for the parties so to frame their bargain that the mortgagee has a right under its terms to obtain an absolute title to the property overriding the equity of redemption. Thus, a person who has taken property by way of security will not be allowed to deprive the mortgagor of his equity of redemption by formulating the bargain as a conditional sale, or by any similar device.[14] The jurisdiction of the court over mortgages cannot be ousted by any trick of conveyancing. Moreover, the question whether a transaction is a mortgage is one of substance, not of form, so that the court will freely admit parol evidence for the purpose of establishing that the true intention was merely to give a security, even if the parol evidence contradicts the plain terms of a deed.[15] The equity of redemption is thus an inseparable incident of a contract of mortgage. As counsel said in *Howard* v. *Harris*,[16] a mortgage can no more be made irredeemable than a distress for a rentcharge can be irrepleviable. The legislature has established one statutory exception to this principle; the Companies Act 1985 specifically authorises the creation of irredeemable mortgages in the form of irredeemable debentures or redeemable only on the happening of a contingency or the expiration of a period of time.[17]

Equity, therefore, interferes directly with freedom of contract between mortgagor and mortgagee. Today this interference is sometimes explained as being an illustration of the principle that equity looks to the intent rather than to the form. Historically, however, the Chancellor's intervention was the result partly of a desire to extend his jurisdiction,[18] and partly of the position held by mortgages in the life of the sixteenth and seventeenth centuries. Mortgages, during that period, were very generally securities taken by creditors from persons in circumstances of financial embarrassment, so that the mortgagors were not free agents in making their contracts.[19] At first the Chancellor justified his interference, either on the

---

[14] *Barnhart* v. *Greenshields and Ors* (1853) 9 Moo.P.C.C. 18.

[15] *England* v. *Codrington* (1758) 1 Eden 169; *Lincoln* v. *Wright* (1859) 4 De G. & J. 16. In the latter case, Turner L.J., puts this upon the general principle that in equity parol evidence will be admitted to prove a fraud. *Cf. Rochefoucauld* v. *Boustead* [1897] 1 Ch. 196. See also *Barton* v. *Bank of New South Wales* (1890) 15 App.Cas. 379; *Grangeside Properties Ltd.* v. *Collingwoods Securities Ltd.* [1964] 1 W.L.R. 139 (an assignment of a lease treated as a mortgage so as to enable the assignee–mortgagee to claim relief from forfeiture of the lease by the head-lessor).

[16] (1683) 1 Vern. 191 at 192.

[17] s.193, re-enacting s.89 of the Companies Act 1948. Strictly an irredeemable debenture is not a mortgage, see *Samuel* v. *Jarrah Timber and Wood Paving Corporation Ltd.* [1904] A.C. 323 at 330. See also *post*, pp. 294, 295.

[18] Turner, *Equity of Redemption* (1931), p. 42, thinks that this was the main reason for the development of the equity of redemption.

[19] "For necessitous men are not, truly speaking, free men, but, to answer a present exigency, will submit to any terms the crafty may impose on them." *per* Lord Northington in *Vernon* v. *Bethell* (1761) 2 Eden 110 at 113.

ground of protecting the mortgagor against an unscrupulous creditor, or on the ground that relief should be given to a debtor who had been prevented from discharging his obligation only by reason of some mistake, accident or special hardship. At the same time and for the same reasons he was giving similar relief against penal clauses in bonds. Early in the seventeenth century, however, the Chancellor[20] decided to give relief against penal conditions in all cases, although no special ground for relief could be shown, and the equity of redemption became part of the settled custom of the court.

Protection of the right to redeem

But the protection of embarrassed mortgagors could not be achieved by the mere creation of the equitable right of redemption. As soon as the practice in equity to allow redemption after the contract date became known, mortgagees sought to defeat the intervention of equity by special provisions in the mortgage deed. These provisions were designed either to render the legal right to redeem illusory, and thus prevent the equity of redemption from arising at all, or to defeat or clog the equity of redemption after it had arisen. For example, the mortgage contract might provide for an option for the mortgagee to purchase the mortgaged property, thus defeating both the legal and equitable right to redeem, or might allow redemption after the contract date only upon payment of an additional sum or upon performance of some additional obligation. Consequently, the Chancellor began to relieve mortgagors against such restrictions and fetters on the legal and equitable rights to redeem imposed by special covenants in the mortgage.

The protection of a mortgagor against all attempts to defeat or clog his right of redemption involved the creation of subsidiary rules of equity, invalidating the various contrivances which ingenious conveyancers devised. These rules are sometimes summed up in a maximum of equity "once a mortgage always a mortgage."[21] This means that once a contract is seen to be a mortgage no provision in the contract will be valid if it is inconsistent with the right of the mortgagor to recover his security on discharging his obligations. Provisions offending against the maxim may either touch the contractual terms of redemption, rendering the right to redeem illusory, or they may touch only the equitable right to redeem after the passing of the contract date, hampering the exercise of the right. Provisions of the latter kind are termed "clogs" on the equity of redemption. Greene M.R. in *Knightsbridge Estates* v. *Byrne*, emphasised that provisions touching the *contractual right* to redeem are not properly to be classed as clogs on the equity of redemption. But it is evident that such

---

[20] Turner, *Equity of Redemption* (1931), p. 32, suggests that the Chancellor who took this step was none other than Lord Bacon.
[21] *Per* Lord Eldon L.C. in *Seton* v. *Slade* (1802) 7 Ves. 265 at 273.

provisions are in substance clogs on the equity of redemption, since they tend to defeat it altogether.

Provisions infringing the equitable principle, "once a mortgage always a mortgage" are invalid, not merely against the mortgagor, but against any person subsequently interested in the equity of redemption. For, although the object of the rules against clogs on the equity of redemption is the protection of the mortgagor himself, yet the operation of the rules is to invalidate altogether any provisions which offend against them. The reason for this was clearly explained by Lord Tomlin in the case of *Mehrban Khan* v. *Makhna*[22]:

> " . . . the provisions in question, being a clog upon the equity of redemption, were void and could have no more binding force against the assign of the mortgagor than they had against the mortgagor himself. They are not provisions of general validity avoided against the mortgagor personally by reason of pressure or undue influence brought to bear on him. They are provisions which, when forming part of the actual mortgage contract, have under the general law no validity at all. If it were otherwise, an illogical result would follow. The mortgagor, if he redeemed, would escape from the burden, but, if he sold to another he would necessarily bear the burden, as the validity of the provisions as against the assign would be reflected in the price which he received."[23]

Formerly the court's jurisdiction to intervene in mortgage contracts was wider than it is today, owing to the existence of usury laws. The court, in mortgages securing money loans, asserted a general jurisdiction to invalidate the contractual terms of redemption, if inconsistent with the policy of those laws. The economic fact that in the seventeenth and eighteenth centuries a mortgagee had an ascendancy over a mortgagor was taken into account by courts of equity as well as by the legislature, and they jealously scrutinised the terms of redemption. The usury laws were, however, repealed in 1854 and the court no longer invalidates the terms of a mortgage merely on the ground that they are exorbitant or unreasonable. Today the parties to a mortgage are free to make what bargain they like, subject to the protection extended by the court to a mortgagor: (i) through the special equitable rules safeguarding the right to redeem; (ii) in cases of undue influence or duress at common law and under general equitable principles; (iii) in transactions falling within the provisions of the Consumer Credit Act 1974 as extortionate credit bargains or as regulated mortgages; and (iv) other instances where the court will intervene pursuant to its statutory or equitable jurisdiction.[23a]

---

[22] (1930) 57 Ind.App. 168.
[23] *Ibid.* at 172.
[23a] See *e.g.* Insolvency Act 1986, ss.244, 245.

Special equitable rules against clogs on the equity of redemption

The following are the special equitable rules protecting the right of redemption which permit the mortgagor to redeem as if there had been no such restrictions.

(1) *A mortgage must be redeemable*

A mortgage may not be framed with the design to render the security irredeemable.[24] It is the essence of a mortgage, in the conception of equity, that it shall be redeemable and the rule cannot be evaded by dressing up the mortgage as a conditional sale or by any other conveyancing device.[25] Equally it cannot be circumvented by a provision which, while not extinguishing the equity of redemption, has the result of making the right nugatory. Therefore, in *Fairclough* v. *Swan Brewery Co. Ltd.*,[26] where the security was a lease with 210 months still to run, and the mortgage was made redeemable only by 209 monthly payments, the mortgagor was permitted to disregard the instalment arrangement and to redeem at once on giving reasonable notice. For in substance the leasehold security was made irredeemable by the terms of the mortgage. This rule, as previously stated,[27] no longer applies to debentures, for section 193 of the Companies Act 1985 provides that debentures shall not be invalid by reason only that they are made irredeemable, or redeemable only on the happening of a contingency, however remote. Otherwise the only limitation upon the principle appears to be that where a short-lived asset, such as a lease or insurance policy, is mortgaged to secure a longer dated obligation, the fact that the property owing to its nature will not be restored to the mortgagor freed from the mortgage is not enough by itself to invalidate the mortgage contract.[28]

Accordingly, any condition in a mortgage is invalid if its effect is to vest the security absolutely in the mortgagee on any event whatsoever.[29] The mortgage must not only begin by being redeemable; it must continue so. Lord Northington said in *Vernon* v. *Bethell*[30]:

> "This Court as a Court of conscience is very jealous of persons taking securities for a loan and converting such securities into purchases, and therefore I take it to be an established rule that a mortgagee can never provide, at the time of making the loan, for any event or condition on which the equity of redemption shall be discharged and the conveyance absolute."

A condition which confines redemption to any particular person or

---

[24] *Newcomb* v. *Bonham* (1681) 1 Vern. 7; *Re Sir Thomas Spencer Wells* [1933] Ch. 29 at 52.
[25] *See ante*, pp. 291 *et seq.*
[26] [1912] A.C. 562.
[27] See *ante*, p. 290.
[28] *Knightsbridge Estates Trust Ltd.* v. *Byrne* [1939] Ch. 441, 462; 1940 A.C. 613.
[29] *Toomes* v. *Conset* (1745) 3 Atk. 261.
[30] (1761) 2 Eden 110 at 113.

period is therefore void. In *Howard* v. *Harris*[31] the agreement only allowed redemption by the mortgagor, or his heir male, yet it was held that *any* heir might redeem. Again, where life policies were mortgaged and redemption was confined to a period covering the life of the mortgagor himself, it was held that his executor might redeem.[32]

Similarly a mortgagee cannot, by a stipulation in the mortgage contract, obtain for himself an option on the property mortgaged. A contract cannot at once be a mortgage and a conditional sale even if the transaction is not oppressive.[33] So, too, if a mortgagor holds an option to purchase the fee or to renew a lease, and assigns it to a mortgagee by way of security, the mortgagee cannot exercise the option and then claim the purchased property or new lease as against the mortgagor. In *Nelson* v. *Hannam*[34] the mortgage comprised an assignment of a 99 years' building lease plus the option to purchase the freehold, and the mortgagee exercised the option after he had taken out a summons for foreclosure but before the decree had become absolute. The Court of Appeal held that the mortgagor was entitled—and, indeed, bound if called upon—to redeem not merely the lease but also the freehold reversion. Greene M.R. stated that, if an option is an essential part of a mortgage transaction, whether as the sole security or merely as one element in the security, the mortgagee cannot retain against the mortgagor what is directly the fruit of the mortgaged property. The mortgagee may improve his security by exercising the option and may add the expense incurred in so doing to the mortgage account, but he cannot thus defeat the mortgagor's right to recover the fruit of the option. The court, in so deciding, acted on the analogy of cases dealing with mortgages of renewable leases, in which it has consistently been held that a mortgagee who exercises the right to renew must hold the renewed lease subject to the same equity of redemption as existed in relation to the original lease.[35]

The maxim, "once a mortgage always a mortgage," does not, however, mean that a mortgagee can never purchase the mortgaged property while the relationship of mortgagor and mortgagee subsists. If the contract for the purchase of the mortgaged property is a transaction independent of the mortgage or genuinely collateral to the mortgage, the mortgagee is fully entitled either to buy it or to obtain an option for himself[36] provided that the agreement cannot be struck down as being in restraint of trade or is unfair or unconscionable.[37] Similar considerations probably apply to a

---

[31] (1583) 1 Vern. 32 and 190; *cf. Spurgeon* v. *Collier* (1758) 1 Eden 55.
[32] *Salt* v. *Marquess of Northampton* [1892] A.C. 1. See also *Newcomb* v. *Bonham* (1681) 1 Vern. 7.
[33] *Samuel* v. *Jarrah Timber and Wood Paving Corporation Ltd.* [1904] A.C. 323; *cf. Jennings* v. *Ward* (1705) 2 Vern. 520; *Price* v. *Perrie* (1702) Free.Ch. 258; *Re Edwards' Estate* (1861) 11 Ir.Ch.R. 367.
[34] [1943] Ch. 59.
[35] *Rakestraw* v. *Brewer* (1729) 2 P.W. 511; *Re Biss* [1903] 2 Ch. 40 at 62.
[36] *Reeve* v. *Lisle* [1902] A.C. 461, where the option was granted to the mortgagee some 10 days after the mortgage itself.
[37] See *post*, pp. 306–307, 308 *et seq.*

right of pre-emption.[38] For a mortgagee may take a release of the equity of
redemption from the mortgagor without in any way being subject to the
stringent rules which affect purchases by a trustee from his *cestui que
trust*.[39] It make no difference that the only consideration for the release is
the discharge of the mortgage debt itself.[40] It follows *a fortiori* that the
mortgagee of a lease containing no option to purchase the fee or renew the
lease should on principle be entitled to purchase or obtain an option on the
fee or obtain a renewal for his own account from a third party without
being liable to have the new title redeemed by the mortgagor of the lease
even if it wholly or partially destroys the equity of redemption.[41] An option
is also plainly valid if it was obtained *before* the execution of the
mortgage.[42] But in a case where the executors of a deceased mortgagee
sought to call in a loan and the mortgagor procured the transfer of the
mortgage to a new mortgagee, it was held (following the principles set out
in *Samuel* v. *Jarrah Timber and Wood Paving Corporation Ltd.*[43]) that the
options to purchase part of the mortgaged property imposed as a condition
of the transfer by the new mortgagees was void. In effect, it was a new loan
purportedly made subject to an option to purchase.[44]

(2) *Suspension of the right to redeem*

A stipulation postponing or suspending the right to redeem until some
date in the future longer than the customary six months may not be framed
with the design of rendering the right illusory under the rule just explained,
and in addition it may not be so framed as to be actually repugnant to the
expressed right to redeem. Otherwise such a stipulation is valid unless it
forms part of a mortgage contract which was extorted from the mortgagor
oppressively or unconscionably or through undue influence when the
contract will be set aside under the general equitable principles applying to
such cases which are set out in the next section.[45] But the cases are difficult
to reconcile. In effect it seems to be a question of degree.

Stipulations postponing or suspending the contractual right to redeem
for a period of years clearly have a tendency to defeat the equity of
redemption or render it illusory and until recently the court adopted a
reserved attitude towards any considerable postponement or suspension of

---

[38] *Orby* v. *Trigg* (1722) 9 Mod. 2.
[39] *Knight* v. *Marjoribanks* (1849) 2 Mac. & G. 10.
[40] *Melbourne Banking Co.* v. *Brougham* (1882) 7 A.C. 307.
[41] For a case where there was a lease by the plaintiffs to an oil company and a re-lease at a
higher rent by the oil company to the directors with an exclusive tie to sell the oil company's products after the grant of mortgage which was redeemed by the new arrangement.
See *Alec Lobb (Garages) Ltd.* v. *Total Oil (Great Britain) Ltd.* [1985] 1 W.L.R. 173
approving *Multiservice Bookbinding Ltd.* v. *Marden* [1979] Ch. 84). See also *Davies* v. *Directloans Ltd.* [1986] 1 W.L.R. 823.
[42] *London and Globe Finance Corporation* v. *Montgomery* (1902) 18 T.L.R. 661.
[43] [1904] A.C. 323.
[44] See *Lewis* v. *Frank Love Ltd.* [1961] 1 W.L.R. 261.
[45] See *post*, pp. 308 *et seq.*; *cf. Cowdry* v. *Day* (1859) 1 Giff. 316.

redemption.[46] Nevertheless, in individual cases the court did accept postponement of the right to redeem for five years[47]; eight years[48]; 10 years[49] and 14 years.[50] In all these cases, however, the obligation to continue the mortgage was *mutual, i.e.* the mortgagee could not call in his money during the period when the mortgagor was precluded from redeeming. Moreover, the dicta in the cases suggested the equitable principle to be that a suspension of the right to redeem must be shown to be reasonable between the parties in the circumstances of the particular mortgage and that the mutuality of the obligation is the best evidence of reasonableness.[51] In *Morgan* v. *Jeffreys*[52] Joyce J. held invalid a postponement of the right to redeem for 28 years unaccompanied by a corresponding forbearance on the part of the mortgagee during the same period. Again, in *Davis* v. *Symons*[53] Eve J. was prepared to uphold a postponement for 20 years, but only if the covenant for postponement was genuinely mutual and the longer the period of postponement the more closely the ostensible mutuality required, he thought, to be scrutinised. In the particular case two insurance policies were mortgaged, and redemption was postponed for a period of 20 years, during which the mortgagee was not to call in his money. But the mortgage provided that the policy moneys, on maturity, were to be paid over to the mortgagee and applied in the reduction of the mortgage debt, and both policies were due to mature before the end of the 20-year period, one four years, and the other eight days before that time. This provision was held by the learned judge to destroy the mutuality[54] and to render the postponement of redemption invalid.

Recognition of the fact that today mortgages are normally genuine investments and not oppressive exactions from the mortgagor had thus already caused a considerable relaxation in the court's attitude towards postponement or suspension of redemption, so that Eve J. could envisage a genuinely mutual postponement for 20 years as unobjectionable. In *Knightsbridge Estates Trust Ltd.* v. *Byrne*[55] it led the Court of Appeal entirely to reject the view that a postponement of the contractual right to redeem is only permissible if reasonable between the parties.[56] A large estates company mortgaged freehold properties to the trustees of a friendly society to secure a loan of £310,000. The mortgagors covenanted to repay

---

[46] See *e.g. Fairclough* v. *Swan Brewery Co. Ltd.* [1912] A.C. 562, (redemption allowed after only three years).
[47] *Biggs* v. *Hoddinott* [1898] 2 Ch. 307.
[48] *Re Hones Estate* (1873) 8 I.R.Eq. 65.
[49] *Re Fortescue's Estate* (1916) 1 I.R. 268.
[50] *Williams* v. *Morgan* [1906] 1 Ch. 804.
[51] *e.g.* Sir Edward Burtenshaw Sugden L.C. in *Lawless* v. *Mansfield* (1841) 1 Dr. & W. 557 at 598.
[52] [1910] 1 Ch. 620.
[53] [1934] Ch. 442 at 448.
[54] This provision rendered part of the security irredeemable but more owing to the nature of the security than to the contrivance of the mortgagee.
[55] [1939] Ch. 441; affirmed on other grounds [1940] A.C. 613.
[56] See *e.g.* the explanation of the judgments in *Fairclough* v. *Swan Brewery Co. Ltd.* ([1912] A.C. 565) in [1939] Ch. 441 at 460–462.

the principal and interest in 80 half-yearly instalments, combining principal and interest, redemption being thus suspended for 40 years. The mortgagees in turn covenanted that if the mortgagors made no default in respect of any of their covenants the money would only be called in by the 80 half-yearly instalments. There was thus mutuality in the covenant to continue the mortgage for 40 years, and the contract was made between two powerful corporations at arm's length. The only reason why the mortgagors desired a release from their covenant was that they had miscalculated the future trend of interest rates and that money was now obtainable at easier rates than the mortgage rate. A less meritorious claim to the protection of equity it would be difficult to imagine and the court upheld the postponement for 40 years on the grounds that (i) as the covenant did not render the right to redeem illusory,[57] nor form part of an oppressive or unconscionable bargain,[58] the court could not interfere; and (ii) the covenant was in any event reasonable between the parties. But, although the court thus upheld this long suspension even upon the test of reasonableness, the main ground for their decision was that only a covenant which renders redemption illusory, or alternatively forms part of an oppressive or unconscionable mortgage, is bad. Greene M.R. who delivered the judgment of the court, stated roundly that the proposition that a postponement of the contractual right of redemption is only permissible for a reasonable time is ill-founded. He denied that there is any general jurisdiction to reform mortgage transactions because the court considers them unreasonable—a view which is undoubtedly correct.[59]

Although the covenant postponing redemption in the instant case was, in fact, mutual, the Court of Appeal by rejecting the test of reasonableness appears also to have rejected mutuality as essential to the validity of a postponement of redemption. The absence of mutuality may in a particular case be confirmatory evidence of an oppressive or unconscionable bargain but the covenant will not be invalidated unless the mortgage in its totality is found to be oppressive or unconscionable.

Greene M.R. in the course of a discussion of the earlier authorities, also emphasised that a covenant suspending redemption may be invalid for actual repugnancy to the legal and equitable rights to redeem set up by the proviso for redemption. This will be so when, as in *Morgan* v. *Jeffreys*[60] and *Davis* v. *Symons*,[61] there is an express proviso for redemption after a few months, followed by a stipulation binding the mortgagor not to redeem for a longer period. Neither of the two judges who decided those cases made this feature of the mortgages a ground of their decision, but it was on this ground of repugnancy to the legal and equitable rights to redeem that

[57] *Ibid.* at 456, 457.
[58] *Ibid.* at 463.
[59] Subject now, of course, to the provisions of the Consumer Credit Act 1974 and the Insolvency Act 1986, and prossibly to the Treaty of Rome; see *ante*, pp. 140 *et seq*. and *post*, p. 307.
[60] [1910] 1 Ch. 620.
[61] [1934] Ch. 442.

the Court of Appeal alone thought that the decisions in the two older cases could be supported.

When *Knightsbridge Estates Trust Ltd.* v. *Byrne*[62] came before the House of Lords, it was unanimously decided that the mortgage constituted a debenture within the meaning of the Companies Act 1929, so that the long postponement of redemption was in any event covered by the statutory authority to create irredeemable debentures contained in section 74 of that Act. The House of Lords vouchsafed no opinion on the correctness of the views expressed by the Court of Appeal—an omission to be regretted, as the matter is of general importance to conveyancers. Although it is difficult to accept the Court of Appeal's explanation of the earlier authorities, as never having intended the word "reasonable" to denote anything more than "not unconscionable" or "not rendering the right to redeem illusory," it is considered that the principles stated by the Court of Appeal can be confidentially accepted as representing the true modern doctrine of equity concerning postponement of the right to redeem. These principles are fully in accord with the opinions expressed by the House of Lords in *Kreglinger* v. *New Patagonia Meat and Cold Storage Co. Ltd.*,[63] upon the rules concerning the validity of collateral advantages.

The House of Lords in *Knightsbridge Estates Trust Ltd.* v. *Byrne*,[64] and both the courts below, were unanimous in holding that the rule against perpetuities has no application to a covenant in a mortgage suspending the contractual right to redeem for more than 21 years. The result, therefore, is that the modern principles concerning suspension of redemption are as stated in the opening paragraph of the discussion of this subject. Provided that a covenant suspending redemption is framed genuinely on an investment basis, and not as a cloak for oppression, it will be valid unless (i) it renders the right to redeem illusory, or (ii) it is directly repugnant to the contractual and equitable rights to redeem.

But in many of the more recent cases there has been the added factor to be considered of a contract made in unlawful restraint of trade in which the mortgagor has been "tied" by a "solus agreement" to sell the mortgagee's products for the duration of the mortgage. In *Esso Petroleum Co. Ltd.* v. *Harper's Garage (Stourport) Ltd.*[65] it was held that a covenant by a mortgagor to sell only the mortgagee's brand of petrol for 21 years and not to redeem the mortgage which was repayable by instalments over a 21-year period, before the expiry of 21 years was void as it was in unreasonable restraint of trade. The mortgage was therefore redeemable.

It seems, however, that a postponement for a shorter period may be

---

[62] [1940] A.C. 613, and see now the Companies Act 1985, s.193 and see *ante*, p. 290.

[63] [1914] A.C. 25.

[64] [1940] A.C. 613.

[65] [1968] A.C. 269, following and extending the decision in *Petrofina (Great Britain) Ltd.* v. *Martin* [1966] Ch. 146; see also *Hill* v. *Regent Oil Co. Ltd.* [1962] E.G.D. 452 and *Regent Oil Co. Ltd.* v. *J. A. Gregory (Hatch End) Ltd.* [1966] Ch. 402 (an earlier case reported later), in which the doctrine of restraint of trade was not mentioned.

valid (as in *Texaco Ltd.* v. *Mulberry Filling Station*[66]). Further, if the tying provisions and the mortgage are separate and independent transactions, the restrictions being freely negotiated prior to the mortgage, the tie may well be valid provided that it is not unreasonable in duration.[67] It should also be added that in the *Esso* case[68] the House of Lords held valid a tie in respect of another garage owned by Harpers Ltd. But in this case the tie was for four-and-a-half years and no mortgage was involved.

Further, it has been stated that the doctrine only applies to an agreement where a person is required to give up an existing freedom to trade as opposed to a position where there was no such previous right.[69]

In conclusion it should be noticed that sometimes the very nature of the obligation secured by a mortgage may render the security irredeemable for a considerable period without the mortgage being invalidated. Thus a mortgage may be made to secure an annuity during the life of some person or as an indemnity against contingent charges or for some other object not capable of immediate pecuniary valuation. Redemption in these cases is necessarily suspended for an uncertain period.[70]

(3) *Clogs on the equity of redemption*

A covenant is invalid if it imposes a penalty on the mortgagor for his failure to redeem on the contract date. Equity grants relief against penalties[71] in all kinds of contracts, but in the case of mortgages there is the added consideration that such covenants are designed, or at any rate calculated, to render redemption more difficult and are, therefore, clogs on the equity of redemption. Consequently, any additional sum expressed to be due from the mortgagor by reason of his default on the contract date is not recoverable by the mortgagee.[72] This principle does not, however, avoid a stipulation which obliges the mortgagor, when he redeems, to pay in respect of principal a sum greater than that actually advanced. This is not a penalty, but a bonus or commission for making the advance. Since the repeal of the usury laws there is no objection to such a stipulation if the mortgage is not otherwise unconscionable.[73]

---

[66] [1972] 1 W.L.R. 814.

[67] *Re Petrol Filling Station, Vauxhall Bridge Road* (1968) 20 P. & C.R. 1.

[68] [1968] A.C. 269.

[69] See *Esso Petroleum Ltd.* v. *Harper's Garage (Stourport) Ltd.* [1968] A.C. 269 at 298, 306–309, 316–317. See also *Alec Lobb (Garages) Ltd.* v. *Total Oil (Great Britain) Ltd.* [1985] 1 W.L.R. 173, and *contra, Cleveland Petroleum Ltd.* v. *Dartstone Ltd.* [1969] 1 W.L.R. 116. There is the somewhat questionable practice imposed by some finance houses which provides that if the mortgagor redeems within two or three years he pays three or six months additional "penalty" interest in any event and not in lieu of notice. Whether or not such a clause is a clog is yet to be decided.

[70] *Fleming* v. *Self* (1854) 3 De G. M. & G. 997 at 1024; *cf.* Lindley L.J. in *Secretary of State in Council of India* v. *British Empire Mutual Life Assurance Co.* (1892) 67 L.T. 434 at 439.

[71] See Snell's *Principles of Equity* (28th ed., 1982), pp. 527–530.

[72] *Booth* v. *Salvation Army Building Association (Ltd).* (1897) 14 T.L.R. 3.

[73] *Potter* v. *Edwards* (1857) 26 L.J.Ch. 468; *cf. James* v. *Kerr* (1889) 40 Ch.D. 449 where in all the circumstances the mortgage itself was unconscionable; *Bucknell* v. *Vickery* (1891) 64 L.T. 701.

An analogous rule invalidates a provision whereby the rate of interest is increased if it is not paid punctually. Such a provision constitutes a penalty and is accordingly void.[74] This particular rule is not, however, of much importance, since it has been decided that there is no objection to a provision which stipulates for a higher rate of interest, *reducible on punctual payment* to the rate agreed by the parties.[75] Conveyancers naturally frame the covenant in the latter form. Nor does the rule invalidate a stipulation for compound interest. Formerly objection was taken to such stipulations on the ground of usury.[76] But after the abolition of the usury laws in 1854 and their subsequent replacement by the Moneylenders Acts 1900–1927 objection was no longer taken (unless the transactions fell within the provisions of the latter Acts which, *inter alia*, forbade the charging of compound interest in moneylending transactions).

Now, in addition to the courts' general equitable jurisdiction to interfere with a mortgage transaction where one of the terms is oppressive and unconscionable[77] since the repeal of the Moneylenders Acts the courts have a statutory jurisdiction to interfere in all non-commercial extortionate credit bargains under the provisions of Consumer Credit Act 1974.[78]

(4) *Collateral advantages*

A stipulation which, being a term of a mortgage, secures to the mortgagee an advantage outside his principal and interest is invalid if it (i) defeats or renders illusory the right to redeem under the first rule set out above; (ii) is repugnant to the right to redeem under the second rule; (iii) clogs the equity of redemption under the third rule; or (iv) forms part of a mortgage contract obtained oppressively or through undue influence under the rules set out below.[79]

Before the repeal of the usury laws, equitable principles concerning collateral advantages were somewhat obscured by the existence of absolute limitations on the rate of interest which might legally be charged for a loan: for a mortgagee who insisted on an advantage additional to his interest might well appear to be evading the usury laws. At any rate, it appears that before 1854 collateral advantages were not enforceable. Thus, in *Jennings* v. *Ward*,[80] Trevor M.R. said:

> "A man shall not have interest for his money and a collateral advantage besides for the loan of it, or clog the redemption with any by-agreement."

---

[74] *Holles* v. *Wyse* (1693) 2 Vern. 289.
[75] *Strode* v. *Parker* (1694) 2 Vern. 316; this provision is construed strictly against the mortgagor, so that his payments must be exactly punctual if he is to be entitled to pay the lower rate, *Maclaine* v. *Gatty* [1921] 1 A.C. 376.
[76] *Clarkson* v. *Henderson* (1880) 14 Ch.D. 348.
[77] See *post*, pp. 308 *et seq.*
[78] See *ante*, pp. 140 *et seq.*
[79] See *post*, pp. 308 *et seq.*
[80] (1705) 2 Vern. 520 at 521.

It is evident that this much quoted dictum propounds two distinct principles: (i) that a mortgagee may not obtain an advantage additional to his interest; (ii) a collateral covenant must not operate to impede redemption. If the first proposition is correct, the second is unnecessary; but there is ample authority that the first proposition is no longer law. In *Biggs* v. *Hoddinott*[81] the Court of Appeal went so far as to declare that in all previous cases in which a collateral advantage had been disallowed, it had been such as either to clog the equity of redemption or to render the mortgage oppressive. The court went on to decide that, since the repeal of the usury laws, collateral advantages are not in themselves objectionable, and that they will be valid provided that: (i) they do not make the bargain harsh and unconscionable and; (ii) they do not clog the equity of redemption. As to the first test, we shall see that a mortgage is not unconscionable merely because it appears unduly favourable to the mortgagee, and is therefore unreasonable as regards the mortgagor. Collateral advantages will not be considered unconscionable unless they were extorted from the mortgagor by active exploitation of his weakness, through oppression or undue influence under the rules set out in the next section. It is the application of the second test which is here mainly discussed, namely, when a collateral advantage "clogs" the equity of redemption.

A collateral stipulation is plainly a clog if its effect is to render the security irredeemable on any event whatever. In these cases, which have already been explained, the collateral stipulation may be repugnant not only to the equitable, but also to the legal right to redeem.[82] For example, the grant of an option to purchase is inconsistent with the contractual right to redeem, as well as with the equity of redemption, when the option is exercisable before the contract date for redemption. On the other hand, it is equally evident that a collateral advantage is no clog if it ceases to affect both the security and the mortgagor the moment the legal or the equitable right to redeem is exercised. Thus, in *Biggs* v. *Hoddinott*, a hotel was mortgaged to a brewery company, with mutual covenants by mortgagor and mortgagee to continue the mortgage for five years. In addition, the mortgagor covenanted that during the five years and afterwards, whilst any money was still due on the mortgage, he would purchase from the company all the beer sold or consumed at the hotel. The court held that (i) five years was in the circumstances a reasonable period for the suspension of the contractual right to redeem; and (ii) the equity of redemption was not in any way clogged by a covenant which was to be operative only until redemption took place. This decision has received the emphatic approval of the House of Lords.[83]

But what if the collateral stipulation is expressed to bind the mortgagor

---

[81] [1898] 2 Ch. 307.

[82] *Kreglinger* v. *New Patagonia Meat and Cold Storage Co. Ltd.* [1914] A.C. 25 at 50, *per* Lord Parker.

[83] *Noakes and Co. Ltd.* v. *Rice* [1902] A.C. 24; *Bradley* v. *Carritt* [1903] A.C. 253; *Kreglinger* v. *New Patagonia Meat and Cold Storage Co. Ltd.* [1914] A.C. 25.

absolutely during a specified period, while the mortgage allows for redemption before the end of that period? Is the mortgagor to be bound until the end of the named period, or do the doctrines of equity demand that he be automatically released from the stipulation if he redeems before that time?[84] At the outset it must be clear that the mortgage does give a right to redeem before the collateral advantage comes to an end. For a covenant may be so framed that the collateral advantage is as much charged on the security as the principal and interest itself, in which case the mortgagor, by the contract, is not entitled to a reconveyance of his security until the end of the period during which the collateral advantage is intended to operate. Thus, in *Santley* v. *Wilde*[85] the tenant of a theatre borrowed £2,000, at 6 per cent., on a mortgage of her lease, which still had 10 years to run: in addition she agreed to pay to the mortgagee during the rest of the lease one-third of the net profits to be derived from any underleases of the theatre. Moreoever, she gave an express covenant that even if she repaid the loan, the mortgage should continue in existence to secure the payment of the share of profits.

The Court of Appeal pointed out that a mortgage can be redeemed only when all the obligations have been discharged for which the mortgage was given; and that in this case redemption, by the contract of the parties, could not take place until the covenant to pay a share of the profits had been fully performed. The covenant was a business agreement between parties at arm's length and was upheld. Lindley M.R. in a classic passage,[86] explained the doctrine of clogs on the equity of redemption:

> "A mortgage is a conveyance of land or an assignment of chattels as a security for the payment of a debt or the discharge of some other obligation for which it is given. This is the idea of a mortgage: and the security is redeemable on the payment or discharge of such debt or obligation, any provision to the contrary notwithstanding. . . . Any provision inserted to prevent redemption on payment or performance of the debt or obligation for which the security was given is what is meant by a clog or fetter on the equity of redemption, and is therefore void. It follows from this that "once a mortgage always a mortgage"; but I do not understand that this principle involves the further proposition that the amount or nature of the further debt or obligation, the payment or performance of which is to be secured, is a clog or fetter within the rule. . . . Of course, the debt or obligation may be impeachable for fraud, oppression or overreaching. . . . But putting such cases out of the question, when you get a security for a debt or obligation, that security can be redeemed the moment the debt or obligation is paid or performed, but on no other terms."

---

[84] The stipulation is never void *ab initio*, unless it is actually unconscionable; it is void, if at all, only after redemption.
[85] [1899] 2 Ch. 474.
[86] *Ibid.* at 475.

The principles stated by Lindley M.R. in the above passage have frequently been approved, although the actual decision in *Santley* v. *Wilde* was strongly criticised by Lords Macnaghten and Davey in *Noakes* v. *Rice*.[87] It is open to the objection that it takes no account of the fact that the mortgagor was prevented from discharging his obligations until a time when his security ceased to exist. The collateral covenant made the security irredeemable and there is thus some difficulty in reconciling the decision with that of the House of Lords in *Fairclough* v. *Swan Brewery Co. Ltd.*[88] Although there is no objection in principle to a mortgagee retaining a security for the performance of a collateral stipulation even *after* payment of principal and interest, yet the covenant, it is submitted, must not be such as to defeat or render illusory the right to redeem, nor such as to be repugnant to it. In the light of later cases, the only way in which it seems possible to support the admittedly desirable decision in *Santley* v. *Wilde*[89] is by holding that the transaction was not in essence one of mortgage, but a partnership agreement to share in the profits of the theatre.[89a]

Normally the collateral advantage is not made a charge on the security. Although the additional stipulation is expressed to be binding until a named date, yet redemption is allowed *before* that date on payment of principal, interest and costs, without more. In consequence, the performance of the collateral stipulation is not one of the terms of redemption. Thus, in *Noakes* v. *Rice*[90]:

> "On mortgaging the lease of a public-house a mortgagor covenanted that during the whole remainder of the lease (which still had twenty-six years to run) no beer would be sold at the public-house, except beer bought from the mortgagees. The mortgage moneys, on the other hand, were made repayable on demand by either side, and there was an express proviso for reconveyance of the security on payment of principal, interest and costs."

The House of Lords decided unanimously that the collateral advantage was a clog upon redemption, because it was repugnant to the mortgagor's right to recover his security *intact and unimpaired by the mortgage*: the covenant turned a free public-house into a tied house. In this case the fetter on the mortgaged property was direct, but a covenant will, it seems, be just as much a clog if it indirectly impairs the enjoyment of the property, not by fettering the property itself, by but imposing personal obligations on the mortgagor which make it advisable (though not compulsory) for him to enjoy his property in a particular way. In *Bradley* v. *Carritt*[91] the defendant, who had a controlling interest in a tea company, mortgaged his shares to the plaintiff, who was a tea-broker, and, as part of the consideration,

[87] [1902] A.C. 24.
[88] [1912] A.C. 565.
[89] [1899] 2 Ch. 474.
[89a] See Waldock, *Law of Mortgages* (2nd. ed., 1950), p. 187.
[90] [1900] 2 Ch. at 445 and [1902] A.C. 24, H.L.
[91] [1903] A.C. 253.

covenanted to use his best endeavours always thereafter to secure that the company should continue to employ the mortgagee as their broker; if the company should cease to do so he was to pay to the mortgagee the amount of commission the latter would have earned, had his services been retained. The collateral stipulation was personal to the mortgagor, and its performance was not made a charge on the security.

The mortgagor redeemed his shares, and the House of Lords (Lords Lindley and Shand dissenting) decided that the collateral covenant was no longer binding, since it was a clog on the equity of redemption. The difference of opinion between the majority of the court (Lords Macnaghten, Davey and Robertson), and Lords Lindley and Shand, lay not so much in the principle to be applied, as in its application to the particular case.[92] Thus, Lord Macnaghten found in the covenent a contrivance calculated to impede redemption because, by making it advisable for the mortgagor to retain control of his shares after redemption, the covenant indirectly fettered his right to recover his security unimpaired by the mortgage. Lord Lindley, on the other hand, was unable to comprehend how the covenant, which was purely personal to the mortgagor and did not *bind* him to deal with the shares in any particular way, could possibly clog the equity of redemption, when it was open to the mortgagor to recover his security merely by paying up principal, interest and costs.

The difficulty in reconciling *Bradley* v. *Carritt* with the later decision of the House of Lords in *Kreglinger* v. *New Patagonia Meat Co.*[93] has led some writers to treat the earlier case as no longer of any importance. But, although some of the dicta of Lords Macnaghten and Davey in *Bradley* v. *Carritt*[94] are disapproved by the judges in *Kreglinger* v. *New Patagonia Meat Co.*, the decisions in the two cases are not irreconcilable. Consequently the earlier case must, it is submitted, still be treated as laying down that a collateral covenant, which is a term of the mortgage, and may endure *after* redemption, may constitute a clog on the equity, although it imposes a purely personal obligation on the mortgagor.

In *Bradley* v. *Carritt* Lords Macnaghten and Davey both expressed the opinion that collateral advantages are only another form of interest, and therefore must come to an end when the principal sum is repaid. Consequently it appeared to have been settled that in no circumstances could a collateral advantage survive redemption. In *Kreglinger*'s case, however, this reasoning was decisively rejected by a unanimous court, who pointed out that it was unnecessary for the decision in *Bradley* v. *Carritt*.

In *Kreglinger*'s case the House of Lords refused to admit that a covenant clogged the equity of redemption merely because it was contained in a mortgage deed, and by its nature might continue to impose obligations on the mortgagor after redemption. *Kreglinger*'s case appears to decide that,

[92] *Cf.* Lord Parker in *Kreglinger* v. *New Patagonia Meat Co.* [1914] A.C. 25 at 59.
[93] [1914] A.C. 25 at 59; applied in *Re Cuban Land and Development Co. (1911) Ltd.* [1921] 2 Ch. 147. See *post*, pp. 305 *et seq.*
[94] [1903] A.C. 253.

just as equity looks at the substance of a transaction, rather than at its form, to see if the transaction is really a mortgage, and even admits parol evidence to explain the deed, so will it look at the intention of the parties, rather than at the form of the documents, to see if a collateral covenant was intended to be truly a constituent element of the mortgage or an independent severable bargain[95] linked to a mortgage in a larger business transaction, but not constituting a term of the mortgage. In the latter case the collateral covenant does not touch the mortgage relationship and stands entirely outside the equitable principles protecting the right to redeem. This principle will more easily be understood if regard is had to the case of *De Beers Consolidated Mines Ltd.* v. *B.S.A. Co.*[96]:

De Beers, who had already lent the B.S.A. Co. £112,000, and were proposing to lend a further £100,000, contracted for the grant of a licence to work diamond mines in consideration of "the assistance rendered and to be rendered" by them to the company. The contract was not itself a mortgage, but contained a provision enabling the company, in lieu of repayment, to cover the loan by issuing debenture stock and assigning an appropriate amount of stock to De Beers. The grant of the loan was not, however, conditional on the issue of the debentures. The company issued debentures and assigned to De Beers sufficient stock to cover the loan. Subsequently they redeemed the debentures and claimed that the licence was no longer binding on them.

The House of Lords had no hesitation in rejecting this claim. The licence had been obtained by a contract independent of and preliminary to the mortgage transaction. This contract did not even compel the company to grant a mortgage, but, when they did so, they could only mortgage assets which were already bound by the licence. The protection of the equity of redemption does not require the court to free a man of pre-existing obligations when he mortgages his property to the obligee. Similarly, the court in *Kreglinger*'s case[97] held that there were two independent contracts, a contract for the grant of an option and a contract of mortgage, but the separation of the mortgage from the other contract was by no means so obvious as in *De Beers* v. *British South Africa Co.*[98]

The facts of *Kreglinger*'s case were these: the appellants, a firm of woolbrokers, consented to lend £10,000 to the respondents, a meat company, in consideration of obtaining an option on such sheep skins as the respondents might have for sale to the public. The £10,000 was lent at 6 per cent., and was secured by a floating charge on the assets of the meat company; if the latter paid the interest punctually, the appellants were not to call in their money for five years. The terms of the option[99] were that it was to extend over a period of five years, *but this period was not co-extensive*

---

[95] The test of "severability."
[96] [1912] A.C. 52.
[97] [1914] A.C. 25.
[98] [1912] A.C. 52.
[99] Perhaps a right of pre-emption.

with that during which the appellants were not to call in their loan. The price
to be paid for the skins was to be equal to the best price offered by any one
else, while the respondents were to pay a commission of one per cent. on
any skins sold to other buyers at the best market price. The respondents
repaid the loan after only two years, and claimed to be at once relieved of
their obligation to offer their sheep skins to the appellants.

The House of Lords decided unanimously that the option continued to
bind the mortgagors, notwithstanding the termination of the mortgage
relation. The construction placed upon the transaction by the court was
that it contained two distinct bargains—the sale of an option and the loan
of money on security—and that although these two bargains were contemporaneous, and in fact formulated in the same deed, yet they were
intended by the parties to be independent of each other. Thus, although
the sale of the option was a condition precedent to the grant of the *loan* it
was not intended to form a term *in the mortgage*, but rather to be a separate contract as much outside the terms of the mortgage as the grant of the
licence in *De Beers* v. *B.S.A. Co.*[1] In short, the collateral covenant was not
repugnant to the mortgagor's right to recover his security unfettered *by the
mortgage*, because, in the intention of the parties, the mortgage was the
grant of a security already subject[2] to the option.

The question whether a collateral stipulation is a condition independent
of the mortgage, not touching equitable principles concerning redemption
of mortgages, or an actual term of the mortgage is, of course, a question of
the intention of the parties in each case, so that no one case will be a
precise authority for another. *Bradley* v. *Carritt*[3] and *Kreglinger*'s case[4] can
be reconciled on this ground, although it must be admitted that the majority judges in *Bradley* v. *Carritt* held views widely divergent from those of
the unanimous court in *Kreglinger*'s case. The earlier case represents the
high-water mark of the old conception of a mortgage as an exaction from a
man who is not a free agent. *Kreglinger*'s case,[5] by excluding from equitable doctrines concerning mortgages those cases where collateral covenants do not in the true intention of the parties constitute a term of the
mortgage, has to this extent prevented genuine commercial bargains
between equal parties at arm's length from being upset by technical doctrines framed to defeat usury and oppression.

Maybe, at the end of the day, the distinction to be drawn between the
cases rests on the reluctance of the courts, on the one hand, to interfere in
commercial transactions freely negotiated at arm's length (albeit unfair to
one party), and the vigilance of the courts, on the other hand, to protect
individuals who have been persuaded to enter into a disadvantageous
trading transaction as a condition of the grant of the loans. But even this

---

[1] [1912] A.C. 52.
[2] Or at any rate, made subject to the option by an independent agreement.
[3] [1903] A.C. 253.
[4] [1914] A.C. 25.
[5] *Ibid.*

interpretation does not lay at rest the difficulties of reconciling the various cases. Perhaps the view expressed by Megarry and Wade in *The Law of Real Property*[6] that the "severability" test introduced in the *Kreglinger* case "provides a convenient but indefinable rule for dealing with such cases on their merits" sums up the difficulties in the attempts to reconcile the differences.

It should also be noted that it was not until *Esso Petroleum Co. Ltd.* v. *Harper's Garage (Stourport) Ltd.*[7] that the issue of restraint of trade had been raised in the "tie" cases with a mortgage element. Thus neither in *Biggs* v. *Hoddinott*[8] nor in *Noakes* v. *Rice*[9-10] was this issue canvassed, and they should now perhaps be regarded as of doubtful authority. As a result of the *Esso* case, such covenants in mortgages will be prima facie void unless they are shown to be reasonable[11] in the light of the circumstances irrespective of whether or not they are rendered void in accordance with equitable principles.[12]

Perhaps the moral to be drawn from these cases is that, if a mortgagee intends to impose the burden of a collateral advantage on the mortgagor for a specified period without also suspending redemption during that period, the deed or deeds must be so drawn that the court can reasonably infer an intention to keep the collateral advantage outside the terms of the mortgage.[13] For, although the substance of the agreement is the determining factor, the language of the deeds is, of course, the best evidence of the actual intention. Viscount Haldane L.C. indeed suggested in *Kreglinger's* case that[14]:

> "the validity of the bargain in such cases as *Bradley* v. *Carritt* and *Santley* v. *Wilde* might have been made free from serious question if the parties had chosen to seek what would have been substantially the same result in a different form."

To sum up, it is submitted that a covenant giving a mortgagee advantages beyond his principal and interest is valid if:

(1) the covenant is truly collateral to the mortgage in the sense that the covenant, as a matter of construction, is not one of the terms of the mortgage; or

---

[6] (5th ed., 1984), p. 971. See also para. 3.35 Law Commission's Working Paper No. 99, "Land Mortgages."

[7] [1968] A.C. 269; and see *ante*, pp. 298, 299.

[8] [1898] 2 Ch. 307.

[9-10] [1902] A.C. 24; nor indeed, in *Hills* v. *Regent Oil Co. Ltd.* [1962] E.G.D. 452 and *Regent Oil Co. Ltd.* v. *J. A. Gregory (Hatch End) Ltd.* [1966] Ch. 402.

[11] A more simple test than having regard to equitable principles.

[12] It is also possible that mortgage terms could be challenged on the grounds that they infringe the competition provisions of the Treaty of Rome, *e.g.* Article 85, which deals with restrictive agreements, and Article 86, which deals with abuse of a dominant position.

[13] Although the point is not noted in the judgments, it is submitted that in *Kreglinger's* case it would have been more difficult to construe the sale of the option as an independent bargain if the period during which the option was to be exercisable had been coincident with the period during which the mortgagees were not to call in their money.

[14] [1914] A.C. 25 at 43.

(2) the covenant, though a term of the mortgage, does not conflict with the three preceding equitable rules for the protection of the equity of redemption and does not form part of a mortgage extorted by oppression or undue influence; and

(3) the stipulation is not in restraint of trade; and

(4) it is not otherwise oppressive or unconscionable.[15]

REDEMPTION OF OPPRESSIVE AND UNCONSCIONABLE MORTGAGES

The terms of a mortgage must not be such as to render the conditions on which redemption may take place unconscionable. This is part of the well-established jurisdiction in equity to set aside oppressive bargains executed under the principle of "undue influence,"[16] meaning the victimisation of one party by another.[17] Hence it is a general principle[18] that a mortgagor, from whom a mortgage has been extorted by the unconscionable use of his position by the mortgagee may obtain relief and have the transaction set aside, or be permitted to redeem on payment only of such sums as were actually advanced with interest at a reasonable rate fixed by the court. But to establish undue influence it must be demonstrated not only from the evidence of the relationship of the parties but also from evidence that the transaction itself was wrongful " . . . in that it constituted an advantage taken of the person subjected to the influence which, failing proof to the contrary, was explicable only on the basis that undue influence

---

[15] See below.

[16] There is at common law the corresponding principle of duress.

[17] See *National Westminster Bank plc* v. *Morgan* [1985] A.C. 686 at 705.

[18] See *National Westminster Bank plc* v. *Morgan* [1985] A.C. 686. In this case possession proceedings were commenced against a house jointly owned by husband and wife by reason of the husband's inability to meet the mortgage repayments owing to business difficulties. To avoid this the husband entered into re-financing arrangements with the plaintiff bank, the re-financing being secured by a legal charge in favour of the bank which was aware of the urgency of the matter. The bank manager called at the home in order to obtain the wife's signature to the charge. During the course of this visit the wife made it clear to the manager that she had little faith in her husband's business ventures and that she did not want the legal charge to cover his business liabilities. Wrongly, but in good faith, the bank manager stated to the wife that the legal charge was limited to the amount advanced to re-finance the mortgage (this being the bank's intention), when in fact it was unlimited and was capable of extending to all the husband's liabilities to the bank. The wife did not receive independent legal advice before executing the charge. Subsequently the husband and wife fell into arrears with the mortgage payments and the bank obtained an order for possession of the home. Shortly afterwards the husband died with no indebtedness on his part to the bank for business advances. The wife appealed against the order for possession contending that the charge had been executed by her by reason of the undue influence of the bank and that therefore it should be set aside. Held, reversing the decision of the Court of Appeal, that the transaction could not be set aside on the grounds of undue influence unless it was shown that the transaction was to the manifest disadvantage of the persons influenced. The basis of the principle justifying the court in setting aside such a transaction is not public policy but the victimisation of one party by another. On the facts of the case the bank manager had not crossed the line between an ordinary banking transaction and a relationship in which he had a dominating influence. The transaction was not unfair to the wife and the bank, therefore, was under no duty to ensure that she had independent advice.

had been exercised to procure it."[19] Further, although the doctrine is not limited to transactions of gift, but also extends to commercial relationships, it should not be subsumed under the general principle of "equality of bargaining power."[20]

This principle has induced the court to interfere in the following classes of cases:

(1) Fiduciary

Where the mortgagee stands in a fiduciary relationship to the mortgagor, for example, if he is the mortgagor's parent,[21] guardian,[22] fiancé,[23] medical attendant,[24] spiritual adviser,[25] solicitor,[26] husband,[27] bank,[28] or if he has in any other way gained an ascendancy over the mortgagor sufficient to impeach the transaction, the transaction may be set aside.

The principle has been further established in cases[29] where a debtor (at the instigation of the creditor who entrusts him to do so) procures the execution of a guarantee or mortgage by his wife without the creditor ensuring that the wife seeks independent legal advice, the creditor acts at his peril. The relationship between the parties is such that undue influence may well result. Thus the creditor is tainted by any such influence exercised by the debtor and cannot enforce the security or guarantee against the wife.[30] This principle was also applied in a case where a son procured the

[19] Ibid. per Lord Scarman at 704.
[20] Ibid. at 708 disapproving Lloyds Bank v. Bundy [1975] Q.B. 326 at 339, (per Lord Denning). See also Allcard v. Skinner 36 Ch. D. 145; Bank of Montreal v. Stuart [1911] A.C. 120 at 137; Poosathurai v. Kannappa Chettiar [1919] 47 Ind.App. 1 at 3, 4; and see Alec Lobb (Garages) Ltd. v. Total Oil (Great Britain) Ltd. [1985] 1 W.L.R. 173.
[21] London & Westminster Loan and Discount Co. Ltd. v. Bilton (1911) 27 T.L.R. 184.
[22] Powell v. Powell [1900] 1 Ch. 243.
[23] Re Lloyds Bank Ltd. [1931] 1 Ch. 289.
[24] Mitchell v. Homfray (1881) 8 Q.B.D. 587, although the gift was not inpeached since on the facts the donor had chosen to confirm the gift after the confidential relationship had ceased.
[25] Huguenin v. Baseley (1807) 14 Ves. 273; Allcard v. Skinner (1887) 36 Ch.D. 145.
[26] McPherson v. Watt (1877) 3 App. Cas. 254; Wright v. Carter [1903] 1 Ch 27.
[27] Cresswell v. Potter [1978] 1 W.L.R. 255; Backhouse v. Backhouse [1978] 1 W.L.R. 243; Bank of Montreal v. Stuart [1911] A.C. 120.
[28] Lloyds Bank v. Bundy [1975] Q.B. 326 (but see National Westminster Bank plc v. Morgan [1985] A.C. 686).
[29] Chaplin & Co. Ltd. v. Brammall [1908] 1 K.B. 233; Turnbull & Co. Ltd. v. Duval [1902] A.C. 429.
[30] This principle was applied in Kings North Trust Ltd. v. Bell [1986] 1 W.L.R. 119: where the husband fraudulently misrepresented the purpose of the loan to his wife who signed the deed without obtaining independent legal advice. The finance company through its solicitors entrusted the husband with the responsibility for procuring the execution of the wife's signature. It was held that the wife's signature had been obtained by undue influence and the mortgagee's action for possession failed. The husband had acted as agent of the finance company binding them by his actions. There was no difference in principle between a husband who procured his wife to execute a document without giving her any explanation and a husband who deliberately gave his wife a false explanation. See also Cornish v. Midland Bank plc [1985] 3 All E.R. 513 (no agency); contra Coldunell Ltd. v. Gallon [1986] Q.B. 1184, and see Davies v. Directloans Ltd. [1986] 1 W.L.R. 823. See also Bristol & West Building Society v. Henning [1985] 1 W.L.R. 778; Paddington Building Society v. Mendelsohn (1985) 50 P. & C.R. 244; City of London Building Society v. Flegg [1987] 2 W.L.R. 1266 (all of which were concerned with the rights of third parties in occupation of the

execution of a mortgage on the home of his elderly parents without informing them of the circumstances. The finance company, acting through the son as their agent, did not ensure that the parents took independent legal advice.[31] In another case it was held that where the bank had assumed a duty to give proper advice to a customer it was liable for damages in negligence for an explanation made by the bank's employee given to the plaintiff prior to her execution of a mortgage to secure the borrowing of a third party, her then husband. The explanation had constituted a negligent misstatement on the part of the bank for which it was liable. But as no unfair advantage had been taken of the plaintiff the presumption of undue influence did not arise, and accordingly the mortgage itself could not be set aside.[32]

In such cases, if the transaction is impeached, the onus is on the mortgagee to prove that the mortgage was not in fact made under the pressure of his influence.[33] He may, for example, show that the mortgagor executed the bargain after receiving independent advice from a person

---

mortgagor's land as against the mortgagee). A comparison between the *Henning* and *Mendelsohn* cases and the *Bell* case produces the odd result that a mortgagee who seeks to protect his position by taking precautions (*e.g.* by insisting on a signed document agreeing to their interest taking priority as is the *Bell* case may be worse off than one who makes no enquiries at all. See [1986] Conv. 57 (M. P. Thompson); [1986] Conv. 131 (D. J. Hayton); [1986] 49 M.L.R. 245 (M.P. Thompson) and see below.

[31] *Avon Finance Co. Ltd.* v. *Bridger* [1985] 2 All E.R. 281; and see *Davies* v. *Directloans Ltd.* [1986] 1 W.L.R. 823. It is probable that this decision would have been decided differently in the light of *National Westminster Bank* v. *Morgan* [1985] A.C. 686.

[32] *Cornish* v. *Midland Bank plc* [1985] 3 All E.R. 513 following *National Westminster Bank* v. *Morgan* [1985] A.C. 686; and applying *Hedley Byrne and Co. Ltd.* v. *Heller & Partners Ltd.* [1964] A.C. 465. See also *Coldunell Ltd.* v. *Gallon* [1986] 2 W.L.R. 466—where the undue influence exerted by the son of elderly mortgagors was not imputed to the mortgagee. In this case although the mortgagee's solicitors dealt with the son throughout the transaction, the mortgage deed was sent direct by them to the mortgagors for execution together with covering letters advising the mortgagors to seek independent legal advice before signing the documents. These letters never reached the parents but they did receive the charge documents. The parents' signatures to these documents were procured by the son in the presence of his own solicitor who merely explained the consent form to the mother and witnessed the signatures but failed to advise the parents as to the nature and effect of the transaction. The son then forged his father's endorsement on the cheque made in favour of the father by the mortgagees for the net amount of the loan and kept the money. It was held, *inter alia*, the mortgagees were not liable for the son's unconscionable conduct as his conduct was an unauthorised intervention in the transaction. Thus, where a third party had not been appointed as agents for the mortgagee in the conduct of the transaction the lender's only duty was to indicate the desirability of the mortgagors taking independent legal advice before execution of the documents and to require the documents to be executed in the presence of a solicitor. The duty of the mortgagee did not extend to ensuring the mortgagors were separately advised. It followed that the mortgagees were not tainted by the son's undue influence as a result of the son's unauthorised intervention—considering *Turnbull & Co.* v. *Duval* [1902] A.C. 429; *Chaplin & Co. Ltd.* v. *Brammall* [1908] 1 K.B. 233; *Avon Finance Co. Ltd.* v. *Bridger* [1985] 2 All E.R. 281; and *Kings North Trust Ltd.* v. *Bell* [1986] 1 W.L.R. 119. It was further held that the rate of interest charged in this transaction was not unreasonable and since the plaintiffs had acted in the way that an ordinary commercial lender would be expected to act, they had discharged the burden of proving that the bargain was not "extortionate" within the meaning of s.138(1)(*b*) of the Consumer Credit Act 1974, (see *ante*, p. 140 and *post*, p. 312).

[33] See generally *National Westminster Bank* v. *Morgan* [1985] A.C. 686.

competent to advise. This, of course, is the familiar principle of equity, which applies equally to transactions other than those of mortgage. But it is, perhaps, necessary to say something more of mortgages taken by a trustee from his *cestui que trust*, and by a solicitor from his client. In neither case is there any rule against the mortgage being taken, but in each case the conduct of the mortgagee will be carefully scrutinised, because of the special relationship between the parties.[34] Moreover, a trustee will not be allowed to foreclose a mortgage on the trust property, because it is his duty, as trustee, to protect the estate.[35] Where a solicitor takes a mortgage from his client there must be no unusual provisions[36] in the mortgage which may prejudice the client and the solicitor must be ready to prove not only that he has taken no advantage of his client, but that he has given the latter all the protection which he would have had if he had employed an independent solicitor.[37] Further such security will be valid only if the sum secured was eventually advanced or already owed and the amount due if unascertained at the time of the mortgage is capable of being ascertained. A solicitor may take security for future cost charges and disbursement and the amount due if not fixed at the time of the mortgage can be ascertained on taxation.

(2) Other instances

The court has both an equitable and statutory jurisdiction to modify, set aside or avoid executed conveyances (including mortgages) in cases of fraud, fraudulent misrepresentation,[39] or if given for an illegal consideration, or if opposed to public policy. But since the conveyance is voidable and not void, it passes a good title to an innocent purchaser who has no notice of the circumstances unless and until it is avoided. Since the enactment of the Misrepresentation Act 1967 it is now possible to obtain damages in addition or alternative to recision of a contract.[40]

Further, Part XVI of the Insolvency Act 1986 contains provisions against debt avoidance.[41] Section 423 of the Act relates to transactions entered into at an undervalue.[42] The court must be satisfied that the transaction

---

[34] And partly because of the mortgagee's special knowledge of the property to be mortgaged. *McPherson* v. *Watt* (1877) 3 A.C. 254.

[35] *Tennant* v. *Trenchard* (1869) L.R. 4 Ch. 537.

[36] Although there may be special provisions where the mortgage is made solely as security for costs; see *Pooley's Trustee* v. *Whetham* (1886) 33 Ch. D. 111.

[37] *Savery* v. *King* (1856) 5 H.L.C. 627; *cf. Wright* v. *Carter* [1903] 1 Ch. 27; *Cockburn* v. *Edwards* (1881) 18 Ch.D. 449.

[38] Solicitors Act 1974, s.65(1), modifying the position at common law.

[39] See, *e.g. Kings North Trust Ltd.* v. *Bell* [1986] 1 W.L.R. 119.

[40] s.2(2). See generally, *Chitty on Contracts* (26th ed., 1989).

[41] See ss. 423–425 of the Act, which apply to England and Wales only. The predecessor to these sections was the L.P.A. 1925, s.172 which rendered conveyances made with intent to defraud creditors voidable. This section was repealed by Insolvency Act 1985, s.235(3), Sched. 10, Pt IV.

[42] A transaction at an undervalue arises where a person enters into a transaction with another if (a) he makes a gift to the other person or he otherwise enters into a transaction with the other on terms that he provide for him to receive no consideration; (b) he enters into a

was entered into for the purpose of putting assets beyond the reach of a person who is making, or may at sometime make, a claim, or of otherwise prejudicing the interest of such a person in relation to the claim which he is making or may make. In such circumstances the court[43] may make such order as it thinks fit for restoring the position to what it would have been if the transaction had not been entered into and for protecting the interest of persons who are victims of the transaction.[44] Section 424 of the Act specifies those persons who may make an application for an order under section 423.[45]

Section 425 of the Act (without prejudice to the generality of section 423) provides for the form of order which may be made under that section[45a] and further provides[45b] that an order under section 423 may affect the property of, or impose any obligation on, any person whether or not he is the person with whom the debtor entered into the transaction; but such an order (a) shall not prejudice any interest in property which was acquired from a person other than the debtor and was acquired in good faith, for value and without notice of the relevant circumstances, or prejudice any interest deriving from such an interest; and (b) shall not require a person who received a benefit from that transaction in good faith, for value and without notice of the relevant circumstances to pay any sum unless he were a party to the transaction.

Every voluntary disposition of land made with intent to defraud a subsequent purchaser is voidable at the instance of that purchaser.[46] But a subsequent conveyance of value is not in itself evidence of fraudulent intent.[47]

Also, in certain circumstances a mortgage may be set aside when the mortgagee has failed in its duty to proffer an adequate explanation of the nature and legal effect of the mortgage having chosen to give such advice especially where the advice went beyond that which was sought.[48]

---

transaction with the other in consideration of marriage; (c) he enters into a transaction with that other person for a consideration the value of which, in money or money's worth, is significantly less that the value, in money or money's worth of the consideration provided by himself.

[43] Meaning the High Court or (a) if the person entering into the transaction is an individual, any other court which would have jurisdiction in relation to a bankruptcy petition relating to him; (b) if that person is a body capable of being wound up under Part IV or V of the Act, any other court having jurisdiction to wind it up.

[44] *Ibid.* s.423(2) A victim of the transaction is a person who is, or is capable of being, prejudiced by it, and is referred to as "the debtor," see s.423(5) of the Act.

[45] *e.g.* the victim, see s.424(1).

[45a] *Ibid.* s.425(1)(*a*)–(*f*).

[45b] *Ibid.* s.425(2).

[46] L.P.A. 1925, s.173(1).

[47] *Ibid.* s.173(2).

[48] See *Lloyds Bank Ltd.* v. *Bundy* [1975] Q.B. 326; *National Westminster Bank plc* v. *Morgan* [1985] A.C. 686; *Cornish* v. *Midland Bank* [1985] F.L.R. 298; *Hedley Byrne & Co. Ltd.* v. *Heller & Partners Ltd.* [1964] A.C. 465. In *National Westminster Bank plc* v. *Morgan, ibid* at 708–709; the advice given went beyond explaining the legal effect of the document and into the wisdom of entering into the agreement.

(3) Mortgages of reversionary interests and expectancies

The courts have a general equitable jurisdiction to interfere and set aside mortgages of reversionary interests and expectancies (and the terms of redemption modified) if it is established that the mortgagor has been overreached.[49] This jurisdiction may also operate where the mortgagor is poor and ignorant or in weak health.[50] The onus of proof is on any person who acquires an expectancy to show that the bargain was not "catching" or extortionate.[51] Formerly undervalue was always a ground for setting aside such bargains, but section 174 of the Law of Property Act 1925 provides that no acquisition of a reversionary interest, made in good faith, is to be set aside merely on that ground. This section does not, however, in any way limit the general jurisdiction of the court to disallow and modify unconscionable agreements. Undervalue is still a material element in considering whether the contract is oppressive, and the section has done nothing to shift the onus of proof.[52] Here the fact that the "expectant" mortgagor has had independent advice will be important to rebut the presumption of overreaching, but the court will look into all the circumstances of the loan. The special jurisdiction of the court to reopen dealings with expectancies will not, however, now be so often called into play owing to the extensive powers conferred on the court to interfere in cases where the Consumer Credit Act 1974 applies.

(4) Control under the Consumer Credit Act

By reason of the 1974 Act the court now has a general and additional power to reopen extortionate[53] credit agreements[53a] if the debtor or mortgagor is an "individual," as defined.[54] It is therefore possible that the case of *Cityland and Property (Holdings) Ltd.* v. *Dabrah*[55] would not have been decided any differently in view of the court's power under section 139 of the 1974 Act.[56]

Finally it must also be remembered that in a relatively few cases, where

---

[49] In the sense of having been overpowered, see *Croft* v. *Graham* (1863) 2 De G. J. & S. 155.

[50] *Bromley* v. *Smith* (1859) 26 Beav. 644; *Croft* v. *Graham* (1863) 2 De G.J. & S. 155; *Fry* v. *Lane* (1889) 40 Ch.D. 312; *Cresswell* v. *Potter* [1978] 1 W.L.R. 255.

[51] Re-enacting the provisions of the Sales of Reversions Act, 1867.

[52] *Earl of Aylesford* v. *Morris* (1873) 8 Ch. App. 484.

[53] By virtue of s.138(1) a bargain is "extortionate" only if it requires payments which are "grossly exorbitant" or if it "otherwise grossly contravenes ordinary principles of fair dealing." For a recent case, see *Coldunell Ltd.* v. *Gallon* [1986] Q.B. 1184.

[53a] See *ante*, pp. 146 *et seq.*

[54] s.137(1) and s.189(1), the latter defining "individual". The powers are contained in s.139(2). See also the similar powers of the court under the Insolvency Act 1986, s.244 in the case of companies and s.343 in the case of bankrupts.

[55] [1968] Ch. 166, In this case there was no provision for interest, but the payment of an extra sum as a "premium" representing 57% interest on the capital sum. The stipulation struck down as "unreasonable and oppressive". This case is difficult to reconcile with *Knightsbridge Estates Ltd.* v. *Byrne* [1939] Ch. 441, see *ante*, pp. 296 *et seq.*

[56] Although it is unclear as to the extent to which the definition of "extortionate" differs from "unfair and unconscionably," see *e.g. Davies and Hedley Cheney* v. *Directloans Ltd.* [1986] 1 W.L.R. 823 at 831.

the mortgage is a "regulated agreement" within the meaning of section 189(1) of the Consumer Credit Act 1974, the mortgagor has an overriding right of redemption exercisable at any time.[57]

REDEMPTION IN COURT OR OUT OF COURT

Generally

Redemption takes place when a mortgagor, either under the terms of his covenant or under the principles of equity, discharges the obligations imposed by the mortgage and thus becomes entitled to have his property revested in him free of the charge. But until the debt has been paid and the money accepted the mortgage remains in being.[58] The mortgagor's right is to have his property returned to him contemporaneously with the due discharge of his obligations, so that it is the duty of the mortgagee at once to execute the instruments necessary to terminate the mortgage. In *Graham* v. *Seal*,[59] Swinfen Eady M.R. said:

> "The obligation of a mortgagee is, as against payment of what is due to him, to reconvey and deliver up the deeds of the mortgaged premises. It is like the obligation of a vendor to convey and hand over the title deeds and the conveyance as against payment of the purchase-money. It contemplates that the handing over of the conveyance and payment of the purchase-money shall be a simultaneous transaction, so that neither party is at risk for any time without either the money or the estate; so in the paying off of a mortgage a mortgagee is not entitled to insist upon payment of the mortgage money with a view to his reconveying at some future time."

Consequently, if a mortgagee has been fully satisfied and yet refuses to reconvey the security, he will have to pay the costs of any proceedings taken by the mortgagor to recover his property.[60] Even a valid tender of the mortgage debt is not, however, *equivalent* to payment. A tender may have the effect of stopping the running of interest and of throwing the risk of the costs of a redemption action on the mortgagee,[61] but the mortgagor's obligations are not finally discharged until his tender has been accepted, or if not accepted, the money is set aside.[62] Thus, in the case of a mortgage with a deposit of title deeds, if the mortgagee improperly refuses

---

[57] See *ante*, pp. 140 *et seq.*
[58] *Samuel Keller (Holdings) Ltd.* v. *Martins Bank Ltd.* [1971] 1 W.L.R. 43.
[59] (1918) 88 L.J.Ch. 31 at 35.
[60] *Walker* v. *Jones* (1866) L.R. 1 P.C. 50.
[61] See Lindley M.R. in *Greenwood* v. *Sutcliffe* [1892] 1 Ch. 1 at 10; *Graham* v. *Seal* (1918) 88 L.J.Ch. 31.
[62] *Barratt* v. *Gough-Thomas (No. 3)* [1951] W.N. 309; and see *post*, pp. 328 *et seq.*

a tender, an action for wrongful interference with goods under the Torts (Interference with Goods) Act 1977 will probably not lie for the deeds at the suit of the mortgagor.[63] If the mortgagor disputes the amount claimed by the mortgagee, his only remedy[64] is to bring an action for redemption.

A mortgagor exercises his right to redeem in one of two ways—either (i) out of court, by inducing the mortgagee to accept a tender of the money due under the mortgage; or (ii) by bringing the mortgagee into court in an action for redemption, and afterwards complying with the court's order for the payment of the mortgage debt. He has, of course, no right whatever to redeem, either at law or in equity, until the day named in the mortgage as the date for repayment.[65] Before that date he cannot maintain an action for redemption against the mortgagee, while if he tenders to the mortgagee a sum representing principal and full interest right up to the contract date, plus costs, the latter is not bound to reconvey the security nor, indeed, to accept the money. The case is, however, different if the mortgagee, by demanding payment, or by taking steps to enforce payment (for example, by taking possession) himself disturbs the relation between the parties set up by the contract. The mortgagor may then redeem at once and need only tender the amount of the principal, plus interest, *up to the date of the tender*, and costs.[66]

Notice of intention to redeem

A mortgagor who is redeeming on the contract date need not give notice of his intention to redeem.[67] He need only attend on the day named and tender to the mortgagee the full amount of the mortgage debt, plus costs, observing any conditions there may be as to time and place of payment. If the contract allows the mortgagor to redeem on demand, he need do no more than give the mortgagee a reasonable opportunity to look up the deeds and prepare the instrument for the discharge of the mortgage.[68] Moreover, redemption may be made on demand in all cases where the mortgage contains no proviso for redemption, or express covenant for payment. Equitable mortgages by deposit of title deeds do not, as a rule, fix any date, either for redemption or repayment, and either party may terminate the mortgage on demand.[69]

But if, as usually happens, the mortgagor allows the contract date for payment to pass without redeeming, so that at law he is in default, it is a

---

[63] *Bank of New South Wales* v. *O'Connor* (1889) 14 App. Cas. 273, where a claim for detinue was rejected. Similarly, a mortgagee cannot be held liable for negligence for loss of the deeds, see *Browning* v. *Handiland Group Ltd.* (1978) 35 P. & C.R. 345.
[64] He is, however, advised to make a tender in order to put the respoansibility for the extra costs on the mortgagee: *Greenwood* v. *Sutcliffe* [1892] 1 Ch. 1.
[65] *Brown* v. *Cole* (1845) 14 Sim. 427.
[66] *Bovill* v. *Endle* [1896] 1 Ch. 648.
[67] See *Crickmore* v. *Freeston* (1870) 40 L.J.Ch. 137.
[68] *Toms* v. *Wilson* (1863) 4 B. & S. 442.
[69] *Fitzgerald Trustees* v. *Mellersh* [1892] 1 Ch. 385.

settled rule of equity that he must give the mortgagee six months' notice of his intention to redeem.[70] The reason for this is that the mortgagor, having lost his estate at law, will only be allowed to redeem in equity on the terms that he does equity to the mortgagee by giving the latter a reasonable opportunity to find a new investment for his money.[71] A mortgagee may, of course, agree to accept repayment at shorter notice, but his right is to a clear six months' notice. Even though it may be possible to find suitable investments in less than six months, it is now settled practice that a mortgagee is entitled to that amount of notice, regardless of the nature of the property mortgaged.[72] Indeed, the only exceptions to the rule are when a mortgagee either demands his money, or takes proceedings (for example, foreclosure proceedings,[73] or steps to enforce payment[74] (for example, by taking possession). The mortgagor may then redeem at any moment by paying up the principal, plus interest up to the date of payment and costs,[75] and he is not deprived of this right even if he has previously given notice of an intention to redeem in six months' time.[76] It need scarcely be said that a mortgagor may always dispense with the giving of notice by offering to pay six months' interest in lieu of notice.[77]

Since a mortgagee is entitled to have six months' notice of the date of payment, it follows that if the mortgagor fails to tender the amount due on the date fixed by his notice, he is bound either to give a fresh notice, or its equivalent in additional interest.[78] Otherwise the mortgagee might be put to inconvenience and loss in finding a new investment. In this instance, however, there is no rigid rule that the further period of notice must be one of six months. At the most the mortgagee is entitled to a reasonable amount of further notice. Thus, in one case,[79] a mortgagee had agreed to take payment if he were given three months' notice. Notice was duly given, but owing to conveyancing difficulties payment could not be made on the due date. Maugham J. held that the mortgagee was entitled in the circumstances to the benefit of only three months' further notice, but he also pointed out that even this period of notice would not have been allowed if the mortgagor had not failed to communicate with the mortgagee for

---

[70] *Shrapnell* v. *Blake* (1737) West. T. Hard. 166. *Smith* v. *Smith* [1891] 3 Ch. 550; *cf.* Maugham J. in *Cromwell Property Investment Co.* v. *Western and Toovey* [1934] Ch. 322 at 331, 332.

[71] *Browne* v. *Lockhart* (1840) 10 Sim. 420 at 424, *per* Shadwell V.-C.

[72] *Cromwell Property Investment Co.* v. *Toovey* [1934] Ch. 322 at 331, 332, *Centrax Trustees Ltd.* v. *Ross* [1979] 2 All E.R. 952 at 955–956.

[73] *Hill* v. *Rowlands* [1897] 2 Ch. 361 at 363; or, *e.g.* giving the mortgagor notice to repay the debt so as to entitle the mortgagee to sell on default being made, *Edmondson* v. *Copland* [1911] 2 Ch. 301.

[74] *Per* Romer J. *Smith* v. *Smith* [1891] 3 Ch. 550 at 552.

[75] *Bovill* v. *Endle* [1896] 1 Ch. 648; *Letts* v. *Hutchins* (1871) L.R. 13 Eq. 176; the same rule applies in the case of a bill of sale: *Ex p. Wickens* [1898] 1 Q.B. 543.

[76] *Re Alcock* (1883) 23 Ch.D. 372 at 376. Although the court would have considered the point had the mortgagee altered his financial position as a result of the mortgagors notice.

[77] *Johnson* v. *Evans* (1889) 61 L.T. 18; and see *post*, p. 439.

[78] *Bartlett* v. *Franklin* (1867) 15 W.R. 1077; *Re Moss* (1885) 31 Ch.D. 90.

[79] *Cromwell Investment Co.* v. *Western and Toovey* [1934] Ch. 322.

several days after the expiry of the first notice. He declared that the right to further notice is by no means automatic, and that if the mortgagor gives a reasonable explanation of the reason why a short delay is necessary, and keeps the mortgagee advised as to when payment may be expected, redemption will be allowed on payment of principal, plus the interest due only up to the actual date of payment, plus, of course, costs. In any case, a mortgagee will not be entitled to six months' further notice where the security is a fund in court and he has been a party to an order directing payment of his debt out of that fund. By accepting the order he assents to be governed by all the contingencies to which the completion of the order may be subject.[80]

Once the contract date has passed, the mortgagor insisting on redemption must pay interest on the loan. This applies even if the mortgage makes no provision for the payment of interest, and it includes statute-barred interest.[81] If necessary, the court will fix the rate of such interest.[82] He must also pay the mortgagee's proper costs in any redemption action brought by the mortgagor, including any expenses incurred by the mortgagee in protecting his security.[83]

Persons entitled to redeem[84]

The right to redeem is not confined to the mortgagor or even to those claiming through him, but is exercisable by any person who either has an interest in the mortgaged property,[85] or is under a liability to pay the mortgage debt[86] irrespective of the size of their interest.[87] The mortgagor himself does not lose his right to redeem until he has made an absolute assignment of his equity of redemption,[88] and even then his right will revive if he is sued on the personal covenant.[89] If he assigns his equity of redemption by way of mortgage only, he does not, of course, lose his right to redeem the first mortgage; but he does alter his position to some extent, because, as we shall see,[90] the maxim redeem up, foreclose down, prevents him from redeeming a prior mortgagee *by action* without at the same time redeeming all intermediate incumbrancers.

Present owners of the ultimate equity of redemption have the same right

---

[80] *Re Moss* (1886) 31 Ch. D. 90.

[81]

[82] See *Cityland and Property (Holdings) Ltd.* v. *Dabrah* [1968] Ch. 166.

[83] See *Sinfield* v. *Sweet* [1967] 1 W.L.R. 1489. A mortgagor, however, is not personally liable for these expenses.

[84] A stranger has no right to redeem. But a person who is entitled to redeem the mortgage may, instead of redeeming, insist that the mortgage be transferred to a stranger who is discharging the mortgage debt; L.P.A. 1925, s.95. See *post*, pp. 379 *et seq*.

[85] *Pearce* v. *Morris* (1869) L.R. 5 Ch. App. 227.

[86] *Green* v. *Wynn* (1869) L.R. 4 Ch. App. 204.

[87] *Hunter* v. *Macklew* (1846) 5 Hare 238.

[88] *Moore* v. *Morton* (1886) W.N. 196.

[89] *Kinnaird* v. *Trollope* (1888) 39 Ch.D. 636.

[90] See *post*, p. 321.

to redeem as the original mortgagor whom they replace,[91] even if they are statute-barred,[92] and it makes no difference whether they are purchasers for value[93] or mere volunteers.[94] If the property is only subject to one incumbrance, their right to redeem is the only right to redeem, but if there are successive incumbrances, the primary right to redeem the first incumbrance is in the holder of the second, and so on, and it is only the ultimate equity of redemption which remains in the mortgagor or those who represent him.[95] Consequently, the latter can only redeem a first mortgage after the other incumbrancers have had the opportunity of exercising their prior rights. Persons who may redeem as holders of the ultimate equity of redemption are:

(1) Assignees.[96] It makes no differences that the assignee acquires only a partial or limited interest in the property.[97] For example, a lessee under a lease, which is not binding on the mortgagee, may redeem.[98]

(2) Persons taking the equity of redemption under an intestacy or under a will.[99] On the death of a mortgagor the right to redeem first belongs to his personal representatives, but will pass to the persons beneficially interested when an assent has been made in their favour.

(3) Trustees for sale and life tenants under the Settled Land Act 1925. On the mortgage of settled property, the primary right to redeem is in either the trustees for sale or, in the case of settled land, the estate owners. Consequently, when an equity of redemption is in settlement the beneficiaries, though they may redeem, must do so through their trustees or through the life tenant.[1] It is only when the trustees or estate owners are in collusion with the mortgagee, or otherwise refuse improperly to act, that the beneficiaries may take proceedings for redemption.[2] In any case, it must be remembered that a remainderman cannot redeem if the tenant for life objects.[3]

(4) Joint tenants and tenants in common. Each co-owner has a right

---

[91] *Fell* v. *Brown* (1787) 2 Bro.C.C. 276.

[92] *Cotterell* v. *Price* [1960] 1 W.L.R. 1097.

[93] A purchaser for value, if he redeems, has no right to a conveyance of the legal estate from the mortgagee, or to delivery of the title deeds, unless he has already accepted his assignor's title: *Pearce* v. *Morris* (1869) L.R. 5 Ch. App. 227.

[94] *Thorne* v. *Thorne* (1683) 1 Vern. 182; *Howard* v. *Harris* (1683) 1 Vern. 191; *Rand* v. *Cartwright* (1664) 1 Cas. in Ch. 59.

[95] *Teevan* v. *Smith* (1882) 20 Ch.D. 724 at 730.

[96] *Kinnaird* v. *Trollope* (1889) 58 L.J.Ch. 556.

[97] *Hunter* v. *Maclew* (1846) 5 Hare 238.

[98] *Tarn* v. *Turner* (1888) 39 Ch.D. 456.

[99] Administration of Estates Act 1925, ss.1 and 2.

[1] *Troughton* v. *Binkes* (1801) 6 Ves. 573; *Mills* v. *Jennings* (1880) 13 Ch.D. 639.

[2] *Troughton* v. *Binkes* (1801) 6 Ves. 573.

[3] *Prout* v. *Cock* (1896) 2 Ch. 808.

to redeem provided that he discharges the whole debt and does not claim to redeem merely his own share.[4] Since 1925, however, co-ownership of land involves statutory trusts, and presumably the rule that beneficiaries ought to redeem through their trustees applies. Consequently, in the case of land, a co-owner of the equity of redemption should proceed through the trustees.

(5) In the case of two properties mortgaged to secure one debt, the owner of each property has an individual right to discharge the whole debt; indeed, since the mortgagee cannot be made to accept payment in instalments, if only one owner redeems he must redeem the whole mortgage and not merely his own share.[5]

(6) A surety, or any person whose property is under any liability to satisfy the mortgage debt, will be allowed to redeem.[6] For example, the doctrine of consolidation may render the purchaser of an equity of redemption in Blackacre liable to discharge a mortgage on Whiteacre in addition to that on Blackacre. This entitles him to redeem Whiteacre.

(7) But a stranger, who has no title to the equity of redemption, cannot redeem; against him the mortgagee's title is absolute.[7]

(8) Creditors. General creditors of a mortgagor cannot redeem except in special circumstances, as when there is collusion between mortgagor and mortgagee.[8] Similarly, when the mortgaged property has been assigned to a trustee for the benefit of creditors, creditors who were parties to the deed must proceed through their trustee, but, if the latter acts improperly, they will be admitted to redeem.[9] Again, a judgment creditor, as such, has no right to redeem, but he will become entitled to do so if he has obtained a charging order[10] or he has obtained the appointment of a receiver by way of equitable execution provided that the order making the appointment is similarly registered.[11]

(9) Bankruptcy. Bankruptcy divests a mortgagor of his right to redeem, and it passes to the trustee[12]; creditors of a bankrupt can thus only redeem through the trustee.[13] The mortgagee has the option either to prove in the bankruptcy as a secured creditor, in which case he puts a value on the security and proves for the

[4] *Marquis of Cholmondeley* v. *Lord Clinton* (1820) 2 J. & W. 1 at 134; *Pearce* v. *Morris* (1869) L.R. 5 Ch. App. 227.
[5] *Hall* v. *Heward* (1886) 32 Ch.D. 430.
[6] *Green* v. *Wynn* (1869) L.R. 4 Ch. App. 204.
[7] *James* v. *Biou* (1813) 3 Swanst. 234.
[8] *White* v. *Parnther* (1829) 1 Knapp 179; but see *Beckett* v. *Buckley* (1874) L.R. 17 Eq. 435.
[9] *Troughton* v. *Binkes* (1801) 6 Ves. 573.
[10] See Charging Orders Act 1979, ss.1, 2(2)(*a*), 3(2)(3)(4); the Land Charges Act 1972, s.6; and the Land Registration Act 1925, s.59(1).
[11] As to equitable execution, see Supreme Court Act 1981, s.37 and R.S.C. Ord. 51.
[12] *Spragg* v. *Binkes* (1800) 5 Ves. 583; see *post*, pp. 387 *et seq.*
[13] *Troughton* v. *Binkes* (1801) 6 Ves. 573.

deficiency,[14] or else to stand outside the bankruptcy and rest on his security. If he elects to do the former, the trustee may redeem at the valuation[14a]; if he does the latter, the trustee can only redeem on the terms of an ordinary redemption.

(10) The Crown. If the equity of redemption is left vacant, whether by a failure of persons entitled to take on intestacy, or by the dissolution of a company, the right to redeem vests in the Crown by reason of its right to *bona vacantia*. For the equity of redemption, being an estate or interest, and not a mere personal equity, is not extinguished by a failure of persons representing the mortgagor.[15]

(11) Spouses. Where a spouse has statutory rights of occupation of the matrimonial home under the Matrimonial Homes Act 1983, that spouse will be entitled to redeem the mortgage as a person interested in the equity of redemption if able to do so.[16] Further the spouse is entitled to make such payments, *inter alia*, in respect of the mortgage due from the other spouse in respect of the matrimonial home.[17] Also the spouse is entitled to be made a party to any action brought by the mortgagee to enforce his security if such person is able to meet the mortgagor's liabilities under the mortgage and the court does not see any special reason against it. Further the court must be satisfied that the spouse may be expected to make such payments towards the mortgagor's liabilities which might affect the outcome of the proceedings.[18] The spouse is also entitled to be served with notice of the action if a class F land charge has been registered at the Land Charges Registry (in the case of unregistered land) or a registration of notice at the Land Registry (in respect of registered land).[19]

Redemption by action

In earlier chapters it was emphasised that once default is made under the contract relations between mortgagor and mortgagee are strictly regulated by the practice of the court. This does not, however, mean that redemption invariably, or even usually, takes place in court. On the contrary, the parties, as a rule, agree to the accounts out of court, and the mortgage is discharged by payment of the agreed sum. It is only when there is a dispute

---

[14] The mortgagee must prove in the bankruptcy in accordance with Insolvency Act 1986, s.332.

[14a] The trustee may redeem upon 28 days' notice at the mortgagee's value, subject to the mortgagee's right to revalue (Insolvency Rules 1986, rr.6115, 6.117). It is also subject to the trustees' right to sell the property if he considers that the mortgagee's value is excessive (r.6.118).

[15] *Re Sir Thomas Spencer Wells* [1933] 1 Ch. 29; Administration of Estates Act 1925, s.46 as restricted by the Inheritance (Provisions for Family and Dependants) Act 1975, s.24.

[16] If the court is satisfied that the spouse is likely to be able to pay off the mortgage, see *Hastings and Thanet Building Society* v. *Goddard* [1970] 1 W.L.R. 1544, and see *ante*, p. 172.

[17] Matrimonial Homes Act 1983, s.1(5).

[18] *Ibid.* s.8(2) if a dwelling-house.

[19] *Ibid.* s.8(3) if a dwelling-house. A caution may no longer be lodged, s.8(9).

that an action is necessary. Nevertheless, it is convenient to deal first with redemption by action, since the practice in redemption suits largely controls the rights of the parties in settlements out of court.

Parties

All persons interested in the equity of redemption are entitled to redeem and this means that persons with very diverse interests in the mortgaged property may have such a right. The importance of this rule in actions for redemption is considerable, since the general principle is that all persons with a right to redeem must be represented in the action.[20] The reason is that the mortgagee has a right to account once and for all, which entails the presence of all persons who are entitled to an account.[21] It follows that all persons known to have any interest in the equity of redemption must be joined as parties, either personally or through their representatives. It is no excuse that the interest of an omitted person is very small.[22] The result is that if a co-mortgagor or other person with only a partial interest seeks to redeem, the remaining mortgagors or interested parties ought to be joined.[23] The only exception to the rule that interested parties ought to be joined, is when a life tenant, trustees, executors, administrators, or the trustee under a deed of assignment, represent the persons for whom they act.[24] Even then it is in the discretion of the court to allow beneficiaries to be made parties, if their rights cannot adequately be protected by the decree. It is not often necessary to allow this in redemption actions, but in foreclosure actions the court will always bring in beneficiaries if there is a danger of the trustees having insufficient funds for redemption.[25] Again, all persons interested in the mortgage debt are necessary parties.[26] If there are co-mortgagees all must be joined. If the right to the mortgage money has been assigned, or otherwise passed into different hands, the new owners are the proper persons to be redeemed. If there has been a sub-mortgage the original mortgagor, in bringing his action, must join the sub-mortgagee; the mortgagee may, however, redeem the sub-mortgage without adding the mortgagor. But, although all persons known to be interested ought to be joined, yet the joinder of the parties is in the discretion of the court, who will sometimes allow the action to proceed without the representation of a party who cannot be found, provided that the mortgagee runs no risk.[27] In such a case the decree will expressly preserve the rights of the absent party.[28]

[20] *Fell* v. *Brown* (1787) 2 Bro.C.C. 276; *Johnson* v. *Holdsworth* (1850) 1 Sim.(N.S.) 106.
[21] *Palk* v. *Clinton* (1805) 12 Ves. 48.
[22] *Hunter* v. *Maclew* (1846) 5 Hare 238.
[23] *Marquis of Cholmondeley* v. *Lord Clinton* (1820) 2 J. & W. 1 at 134.
[24] See R.S.C. Ord. 15, r. 12.
[25] *Goldsmit* v. *Stonehewer* (1852) 9 Hare App. xxxviii.
[26] *Wetherell* v. *Collins* (1818) 3 Mad. 255.
[27] *Faulkner* v. *Daniel* (1843) 3 Hare 199.
[28] *Francis* v. *Harrison* (1889) 43 Ch.D. 183.

"Redeem up, foreclose down"

The rule that a mortgagee is entitled to account once and for all is of the utmost importance where there are successive incumbrances, since it prevents a puisne incumbrancer from redeeming an earlier mortgagee by action, without at the same time foreclosing on subsequent mortgagees and on the mortgagor.[29] The subsequent incumbrancers and the mortgagor have successive[30] rights to redeem, and the accounts taken in the puisne incumbrancer's action for redemption will inevitably fix the price at which any later redemption can be effected. Therefore it is essential that in the puisne incumbrancer's action all persons with later rights to redeem should be before the court in order that they may be bound by the accounts. On the other hand, it would be onerous to the mortgagor and to the later incumbrancers to allow them to be dragged before the court merely that they might watch the accounts being taken.[31] Indeed, they cannot be joined for this limited purpose, and it is the rule that a puisne incumbrancer who redeems an earlier mortgage by action must at the same time foreclose on all later incumbrancers, and on the mortgagor. For the same reason, any one who redeems an earlier mortgage, which is not the immediately preceding incumbrance, must also redeem any intermediate mortgages. If, for example, a third mortgagee redeems the first, it is obvious that the first mortgagee's account will affect the rights of the second, so that the latter must be joined as a party and redeemed.[32] This principle applies also in foreclosure actions with this result—a mortgagee who forecloses must join all persons with interests in the security subsequent to his,[33] since his account will fix the price of redemption for them all. Foreclosure on the mortgagor means foreclosure also on intermediate mortgagees. The general result is that actions to discharge incumbrances are multiple actions, and this is commonly expressed by the maxim, *redeem up, foreclose down*. Two consequences of this principle should be noticed in relation to the right to redeem: (i) a puisne mortgagee cannot redeem an earlier mortgage in court without at the same time exposing himself to redemption by the mortgagor and later incumbrancers; (ii) there cannot be a redemption action in the absence of the mortgagor, so that a puisne mortgagee, who, by stipulating not to call in his money for a stated period, has precluded himself from bringing the mortgagor before the court, cannot during that period bring a redemption action against any prior mortgagee.[34]

---

[29] *Fell* v. *Brown* (1787) 2 Bro.C.C. 276.

[30] The first right to redeem a first mortgage is in the second mortgagee, the next right in the third mortgagee and so on: *Teevan* v. *Smith* (1882) 20 Ch.D. 724.

[31] *Ramsbottom* v. *Wallis* (1835) 5 L.J. (N.S.) Ch. 92; *Slade* v. *Rigg* (1843) 3 Hare 35; *Rose* v. *Page* (1829) 2 Sim. 471; *Briscoe* v. *Kenrick* (1832) 1 L.J.Ch. 116.

[32] *Teevan* v. *Smith* (1882) 20 Ch.D. 724.

[33] See *ante*, pp. 252 *et seq*.

[34] *Ramsbottom* v. *Wallis* (1835) 5 L.J.(N.S.) Ch. 92; there is, however, no objection to the prior mortgagee being paid off out of court; indeed, the prior mortgagee ought to accept payment in such circumstances: *Smith* v. *Green* (1844) 1 Coll. 555.

Procedure[35]

The proceedings may be by writ or by originating summons,[36] and any person who has the right to redeem any mortgage, whether legal or equitable, can, as of course seek redemption, reconveyance and delivery of possession.[37]

In a redemption action the plaintiff's claim is for an account and for redemption. If the parties wish to redeem, the statement of claim or the affidavit in support of the originating summons must expressly or by implication contain an offer to redeem, and, if the plaintiff makes out a case for redemption without such an offer, he will be compelled to amend his plea,[38] or at any rate to give an undertaking to redeem.[39] It is only in exceptional circumstances that a mortgagor can bring the mortgagee into court without offering to redeem him[40]: namely;

(1) if he claims a sale instead of redemption;
(2) when the proceedings are merely for the purpose of determining questions of the construction of the mortgage deed[41]; and
(3) when the mortgagee is a party to a trust deed affecting the equity of redemption, for the trust may be enforced without an offer to redeem.[42]
(4) possibly where the mortgagee is not exercising his power of sale bona fide.

Nor need the mortgagor offer to redeem if he denies the existence of the mortgage, or is asking that it be avoided. But in such a case, if the mortgage is upheld, he cannot redeem in the same action unless he has pleaded in the alternative for redemption.[43]

Sale in lieu of redemption

A mortgagor in his plea may claim a sale in lieu of redemption, and this requires further explanation, since neither the mortgage contract nor the rules of equity give him this right. Section 91(1) of the Law of Property Act 1925 provides as follows:

> "Any person entitled to redeem mortgaged property may have a judgment or order for sale, instead of for redemption in an action brought by him, either for redemption alone, or for sale alone or for sale or redemption in the alternative."

---

[35] For jurisdiction see *post*, Appendix III; and see *ante*, pp. 253 *et seq* for procedure in foreclosure actions.
[36] See R.S.C. Ord. 88. The choice is governed by Ord. 5, see *ante*, p. 254.
[37] In general, a mortgagor has to pay the costs of a redemption action, but there are occasions when the mortgagee by his conduct renders himself liable to pay the costs.
[38] *Palk* v. *Lord Clinton* (1805) 12 Ves. 48.
[39] *Balfe* v. *Lord* (1842) 2 Dr. & W. 480.
[40] *Tasker* v. *Small* (1837) 3 My. & Cr. 63.
[41] *Re Nobbs* [1896] 2 Ch. 830.
[42] *Jefferys* v. *Dickson* (1866) L.R. 1 Ch. 183.
[43] *Martinez* v. *Cooper* (1826) 2 Russ. 198; *Bagot* v. *Easton* (1877) 7 Ch.D. 1.

The language of this subsection would appear to confer an absolute right on a plaintiff to apply for a sale in lieu of redemption, rather than to give a discretionary power to the court to order a sale.[44] It is submitted that the subsection must be so interpreted, although under the Conveyancing Act 1881, Kekewich J. undoubtedly treated the whole question of sale as a matter of discretion.[45] Section 91 does, on the other hand, provide that, when a person interested in the equity of redemption is a plaintiff asking for a sale, the court may, on the application of any defendant, direct the plaintiff to give security for costs, and may give the conduct of the sale to any defendant, with appropriate directions as to costs. Moreover, although, as we have suggested, the court may have no discretion to refuse an order for sale in lieu of redemption, the terms of the order for sale are very much within its discretion: for section 91 further provides:

> "In any action, whether for foreclosure, or for redemption, or for sale, or for the raising and payment in any manner of mortgage money, the court on the request of the mortgagee, or of any person interested, either in the mortgage money or in the right of redemption, and notwithstanding that—
> (a) any other person dissents; or
> (b) the mortgagee or any person so interested does not appear in the action;
> and without allowing any time for redemption or for payment of any mortgage money, may direct a sale of the mortgaged property on such terms as it thinks fit, including the deposit in Court of a reasonable sum fixed by the Court to meet the expenses of sale and to secure performance of the terms."

The practice in sales by the court has already been considered,[46-47] but here it may be said that in redemption actions the order for sale may be made at any time before the final decree for redemption, and may, indeed, be made on an interlocutory application before the trial.[48]

Order

In the ordinary case the court's order is that an account be taken of what is due to the mortgagee in respect of his mortgage, including the costs of the redemption action, and that upon the mortgagor paying to the mortgagee the amount certified by the Master to be due within six (calendar[49]) months after the date of his certificate and at a time and place to be appointed in the certificate, the mortgagee shall surrender his mortgage term or give a receipt in accordance with section 115 of the Law of Property Act 1925, and deliver up the title deeds. The order further directs

---

[44] *Clarke* v. *Pannell* (1884) 29 S.J. 147.
[45] *Brewer* v. *Square* [1892] 2 Ch. 111.
[46-47] See *ante*, pp. 247 *et seq*.
[48] *Woolley* v. *Colman* (1882) 21 Ch.D. 169.
[49] R.S.C. Ord. 3, r. 1.

that, if the mortgagor makes default in such payment, his action is to stand dismissed with costs.[50] The order may be varied by an order for sale in lieu of redemption, and it may be necessary to add an order for possession if the mortgagee has exercised his right to take possession. Again, the circumstances may make it necessary to give special directions for the account; for example, if the order for redemption is made after the mortgagee has refused a proper tender, the account must be stopped on the date of the tender, and there must be alternative orders to meet the possibilities that the tender may or may not have been sufficient. Similarly, if the mortgagee is in possession the account must be taken on the footing of wilful default, and further variations in the order will be necessary if the mortgagee in possession has been charged with waste, improper management or improper sale of the security. Moreover, the account of a mortgagee in possession may sometimes be ordered with annual rests. The accounts taken between mortgagor and mortgagee have already been considered in detail in connection with the mortgagee's interest.[51]

Successive redemptions

Special directions will be necessary when there are several parties to the action with successive rights to redeem; the order must not only notice their priorities,[52] but must also provide distinctly for the possibility of any party redeeming or failing to redeem. To take a simple case, if a second mortgagee is claiming to redeem the first and to foreclose on the mortgagor, the order is: on payment by the plaintiff of the amount due to the first mortgagee within six months of the certificate, the first mortgagee to surrender his mortgage term or give the statutory receipt—in default the action to be dismissed with costs; if the plaintiff shall pay off the first mortgagee, interest to be computed on what he shall pay, and an account to be taken of what is due on the plaintiff's own mortgage and for his costs of action; and, on payment by the mortgagor within three months of the certificate of the amount reported due to the plaintiff, the plaintiff to surrender his mortgage term or give a statutory receipt to the mortgagor—in default, the mortgagor to be foreclosed. The introduction of other parties further complicates the order which, as we said, will provide for every contingency.

Two further points must be noticed in the form of the order given above: (i) when a mesne incumbrancer brings the action for redemption and fails to redeem, not only is his action dismissed, but he is made to pay the costs both of the first mortgagee and also of the mortgagor[53]; (ii) in special circumstances the mortgagor may be given a longer period to redeem.[54] The

---

[50] See Seton, *Judgments and Orders* (7th ed.), Vol. 3, p. 1853.
[51] See *ante*, pp. 212–216.
[52] *Jones* v. *Griffith* (1845) 2 Coll. 207; *Duberly* v. *Day* (1851) 14 Beav. 9.
[53] *Hallett* v. *Furze* (1885) 31 Ch.D. 312.
[54] See *Lewis* v. *Aberdare and Plymouth Co.* (1884) 53 L.J.Ch. 741.

limitation of a successive period for redemption in case an intermediate incumbrancer redeems is obviously necessary, since a new account has to be taken, but in the redemption of a first mortgage, when the plaintiff is the mortgagor or a third or later incumbrancer, the question will arise whether distinct periods are to be allotted to each party for the redemption of the *first mortgage*. Formerly, the practice was to give a period of six months to the person entitled to the first equity of redemption, and further periods of three months to each later incumbrancer with an additional three months for the mortgagor. This rule applied only to incumbrancers, so that a life tenant and remainderman under a settlement of the equity of redemption had only one period between them.[55] Nor did it even apply to incumbrancers when their mortgages were created on the same day,[56] or when it was plain that the security would be insufficient to give anything to the later incumbrancers.[57] It is not, however, going too far to say that the practice of the court today is the reverse.[58] A mortgagee may be seriously inconvenienced by the delay caused by allowing successive periods for redemption, and now, as a general rule, one period only of six months will be allotted to the puisne incumbrancers and the mortgagor together: if there is any ground for successive periods, the incumbrancers must appear and make out a special case for such an order.[59] The mortgagor himself cannot apply for the special order, because he cannot enlarge his own time for redemption by merely dealing with the equity of redemption.[60] It follows that a special order will never be made if the puisne incumbrancers are not before the court. To make an order in such a case would be equivalent to giving judgment between co-defendants without their having asked for it.[61] Nor will a special order be made when the priorities are in dispute. The determination of the priorities will cause delay and is a question in which the first mortgagee has no interest.[62] But where, as is now usual, there is only one period of six months for all the defendants, there is, of course, liberty to apply to the court in case any one of the defendants shall redeem. The court will then determine the rights of the defendants *inter se*. If a special order for successive periods is made, the procedure is as follows: The first right to redeem is in the second mortgagee, and if he defaults he is foreclosed; a further three months' interest is then added to the mortgage account, and the person next entitled has an opportunity to redeem, and so on: if a puisne incumbrancer does redeem, the action continues between him and later incumbrancers and the mortgagor; his own debt is added to

[55] *Beevor* v. *Luck* (1867) L.R. 4 Eq. 537.
[56] *Long* v. *Storie* (1849) 3 De G. & Sm. 308.
[57] *Cripps* v. *Wood* (1882) 51 L.J.Ch. 584.
[58] *Bartlett* v. *Rees* (1871) L.R. 12 Eq. 395; *Smith* v. *Olding* (1884) 25 Ch.D. 462; *Platt* v. *Mendel* (1884) 27 Ch.D. 246.
[59] *Platt* v. *Mendel* (1884) 27 Ch.D. 246; *Doble* v. *Manley* (1885) 28 Ch.D. 664.
[60] *Ibid* at 248.
[61] *Doble* v. *Manley* (1885) 28 Ch.D. 664.
[62] *Bartlett* v. *Rees* (1871) L.R. 12 Eq. 395; *General Credit and Discount Co.* v. *Glegg* (1883) 22 Ch.D. 549.

the first mortgage debt, with an allowance of three months' interest, and the person next entitled must redeem or be foreclosed, and so on.

Effect of the decree

The rules for payment by the mortgagor and for the execution of the necessary instruments by the mortgagee are the same whether redemption takes place under the order of the court or by agreement, and will be found dealt with fully in connection with redemption out of court. But it must be emphasised that *in redemption actions* payment has to be made strictly in accordance with the terms of the Master's certificate. In foreclosure actions the court will readily grant an extension of time for redemption, but not so when the proceedings are initiated by the mortgagor. He comes of his own volition to the court professing to have his money ready, and if he has not, he cannot claim the indulgence which he receives when the mortgagee is pressing him for payment. Consequently, a failure to pay on the date specified results in the final dismissal of the action.[63] This is so even when after his default the mortgagor has made a tender of the full amount reported due with subsequent interest.[64] It is only in the rare case of a bona fide mistake, as when the court's order is misunderstood, that any enlargement may be obtained.[65]

The dismissal of an action for redemption is obtained as of course upon production of the certificate of the amount due, and of an affidavit of attendance for payment resulting in no payment. In the case of a legal mortgage the dismissal of the action for any cause, except want of prosecution,[66] operates as a decree for foreclosure absolute against the plaintiff. As James L.J. said[67]:

> "The mortgagor, by filing the bill, admits the title of the mortgagee, and admits the mortgage debt, and the dismissal of the bill operates as a decree for foreclosure, because he cannot afterwards file another bill for the same purpose; he is not allowed thus to harass the mortgagee."

The plaintiff's equity of redemption is extinguished, and in the case of a legal mortgage this completes the mortgagee's title. In the case of an equitable mortgage the effect is somewhat different. The plaintiff is not allowed to take subsequent proceedings for the same purpose, but a mere dismissal of his action cannot complete the mortgagee's title. The mortgagee must either rely on the acquisition of a title by lapse of time under the Limitation Act 1980,[68] which is only possible if he is in possession, or else must take fresh proceedings in order to obtain a conveyance and possession. It is just possible that after 1925, even in the case of a legal mort-

---

[63] *Novosielski* v. *Wakefield* (1811) 17 Ves. 417.
[64] *Faulkner* v. *Bolton* (1835) 7 Sim. 319.
[65] *Collinson* v. *Jeffery* [1896] 1 Ch. 644.
[66] *Hansard* v. *Hardy* (1812) 18 Ves. 455.
[67] *Marshall* v. *Shrewsbury* (1875) L.R. 10 Ch. 250 at 254.
[68] See *post*, p. 400.

gage, the mortgagee does not acquire the mortgagor's whole title. Sections 89 and 90 of the Law of Property Act 1925 carefully provide that a fore-closure decree is to pass the mortgagor's legal reversion to the mortgagee, but there is no similar provision for the dismissal of an action for redemption.

The dismissal of the action operates against the plaintiff only, and therefore, in the case of successive incumbrancers if the mortgagor is the plaintiff, the dismissal of his action places the final equity of redemption in the last incumbrancer, who becomes quasi-mortgagor.[69] If a puisne incumbrancer is the plaintiff and fails to redeem, he is not only foreclosed, but must pay the costs of all parties, including the mortgagor, whom he must, of course, have made a defendant.[70] Finally, it must be remembered that proceedings for redemption are a pending action, and therefore the dismissal will not bind an assignee for value between the date of the writ and the dismissal, unless the action has been registered as a pending action.

Redemption out of court

This is effected by an accord and satisfaction out of court, which usually resolves itself into a tender of the mortgage moneys and an acceptance of the tender. For the most part the conditions under which redemption may be claimed out of court are the same as those under which it is allowed in an action. Thus, the right to make a tender only arises at the same time as the right to redeem by action, and the mortgagee, after default, is entitled to six months' notice, or to six months' interest in lieu of notice, unless the mortgage contract otherwise provides. Similarly, tender must be made by some one entitled to redeem, for, as we have seen, a mortgagee's estate is absolute against a stranger.[71] A mortgagee may, if he pleases, transfer his mortgage to a stranger, but he cannot be compelled to accept payment from any one who is not entitled to bring an action for redemption.

But the maxim, *redeem up, foreclose down*, does not apply to redemption out of court. That maxim is founded on the court's anxiety to make a complete decree which will bind all parties interested in the estate, and redemption out of court is not governed by the same considerations. On the contrary, it is well established that a prior mortgagee ought to accept a proper tender of his money if it is made by any person interested in the equity of redemption, and that he rejects such a tender at the peril of paying the costs of a redemption action.[72] Consequently, a puisne mortgagee or any person claiming through the mortgagor may redeem the first mortgage by payment out of court, without at the same time discharging intermediate incumbrances. Of course, a satisfied mortgagee is strictly a trustee for the persons entitled to the equity of redemption, so that he must be careful to preserve the rights of such other persons of whose interests he

---

[69] *Cottingham* v. *Shrewsbury* (1843) 3 Hare 627.
[70] *Hallett* v. *Furze* (1885) 31 Ch.D. 312.
[71] *James* v. *Biou* (1818) 3 Swanst. 234 at 237.
[72] *Smith* v. *Green* (1844) 1 Coll. 555.

has notice. This does not, however, prevent him from being under an obligation to transfer his mortgage to the person who has redeemed him, subject to an express reservation of the rights of the other interested parties of whom he knows.[73] If several persons are claiming to redeem the first mortgagee at the same time, the right to redeem first out of court clearly belongs to the puisne incumbrancer, whose charge has priority.[74] Accounts which have been agreed out of court are not conclusive against third parties, but they are binding on all persons interested until they are impeached. They may be impeached for error or fraud, and then in a proper case the court will set aside the settled account.

Tender

A tender, to be effective, must be made to the mortgagee himself, and not to his solicitor, or other agent,[75] unless the agent has been expressly authorised to receive payment of the money and to reconvey the estate.[76] But under section 69 of the Law of Property Act 1925, the validity of a tender cannot be questioned if it was made to the mortgagee's solicitor,[76a] who at the time produced a deed executed by the mortgagee and having attached to it a receipt for the mortgage moneys. Again, a tender on the contract date must conform strictly to any conditions as to time and place of payment which may have been fixed by the mortgage deed if it is to stop interest running.[77] But, if a particular hour has been appointed for payment, the mortgagor may appear to make his tender at any time during the currency of the hour named, because in law a named hour is not an individual moment of time, but the whole hour.[78] For the same reason, if the mortgagee does not appear or is late, the mortgagor himself must continue to attend during the whole hour or his tender will be bad.[79] Today, when the fact that a mortgage is redeemable after default is well known, it is unusual to find a special hour or place for payment fixed by the mortgage deed. If, as usually happens, payment is not made until after the contract date, or, in any case, if no place is named for payment, the mortgagor must seek out the mortgagee and tender the money either to him personally or to his authorised agent. Tender on the mortgaged land is not sufficient, because mortgage moneys are a sum in gross and do not issue out of the land like a rent.[80] Consequently, a mortgagor will, as a rule, suggest a time and place for payment when he notifies the mortgagee of his intention to redeem. Then, if the suggested place is reasonably near the mortgagee's

[73] *Pearce* v. *Morris* (1869) L.R. 5 Ch. App. 227.
[74] *Teevan* v. *Smith* (1882) 20 Ch.D. 724.
[75] *Withington* v. *Tate* (1869) L.R. 4 Ch. App. 288.
[76] *Bourton* v. *Williams* (1870) L.R. 5 Ch. App. 655; and see *Bonham* v. *Maycock* (1928) 138 L.T. 736.
[76a] And licensed conveyancer, see Administration of Justice Act 1985, s.34(1).
[77] *Gyles* v. *Hall* (1726) 2 P.Wms. 378.
[78] *Knox* v. *Simmons* (1793) 4 Bro.C.C. 433.
[79] *Bernard* v. *Norton* (1864) 10 L.T. 183.
[80] Co.Lit. Vol. II, 210 b.

residence, or is for other reasons convenient to the mortgagee, and if the latter has made no objection, an effective tender may be made at that place.[81] A tender must, of course, be a "legal tender" and in the proper currency, and, except by special agreement, the mortgagor is not entitled to deduct any sum by way of set-off from the amount of principal, interest and costs.[82] Again, a tender must not be clogged with a condition[83]; for example, the tender of a sum on condition that it is accepted in full satisfaction of all claims is a bad tender, even though the sum tendered turn out to be all that is due.[84] But a tender may always be made under protest, the mortgagor reserving a right afterwards to dispute the mortgagee's claim.[85] Nor is a tender conditional if the mortgagor does no more than demand what he is by law entitled to. Thus a demand that a reconveyance be executed at the time of the tender does not invalidate the tender because, on payment, a mortgagor's right is to the immediate discharge of the mortgage.[86] In any case a tender, otherwise invalid, will be good, if the mortgagee makes no objection except to dispute the amount of the mortgage debt.[87]

Payment to joint creditors

Creditors who advance money on a joint mortgage are, in equity, entitled in common[88] even if the legal estate was conveyed to them as joint tenants. Consequently, although at law payment to one joint creditor discharges the debt to all,[89] in equity a receipt from one creditor does not release the debtor from the claims of the others.[90] The receipt must, therefore, be taken from all the creditors. Formerly, a conveyancing difficulty arose when one of the creditors died. Since his interest was an interest in severalty, it passed to his personal representatives,[91] who must also therefore join in the receipt.[92-93] This would obviously be inconvenient in the case of mortgages by trustees, and so it was customary to insert in the mortgage a statement that the moneys were advanced on a *joint account* (a "joint account clause") in order that on the death of one trustee the receipt

---

[81] Coote, *Mortgages* (9th ed., 1927), Vol. 1, p. 739; it has, indeed, been said that a tender for redemption need not always be such as would afford a defence to an action at law on the covenant: *Manning* v. *Burges* (1663) 1 Cas.in Ch. 29; *Webb* v. *Crosse* [1912] 1 Ch. 323.

[82] *Searles* v. *Sadgrave* (1855) 5 E. & B. 639. In general, the money must actually be produced; but see *Dickinson* v. *Shee* (1801) 4 Esp. 67.

[83] *Jennings and Turner* v. *Major* (1837) 8 C. & P. 61.

[84] *Strong* v. *Harvey* (1825) 3 Bing. 304 (an insurance case).

[85] *Manning* v. *Lunn and Thrupp* (1845) 2 C. & K. 13; *Greenwood* v. *Sutcliffe* [1892] 1 Ch. 1.

[86] *Rourke* v. *Robinson* [1911] 1 Ch. 480.

[87] *Jones* v. *Arthur* (1840) 8 Dowl.P.C. 442.

[88] *Vickers* v. *Cowell* (1839) 1 Beav. 529.

[89] *Rigden* v. *Vallier* (1751) 2 Ves.Sen. 252 at 258.

[90] *Husband* v. *Davis* (1851) 10 C.B. 645.

[91] *Matson* v. *Dennis* (1864) 4 De G.J. & S. 345; *Powell* v. *Brodhurst* [1901] 2 Ch. 160. The case would, of course, be different if one creditor was specially authorised by the others to receive payment for them all.

[92-93] *Petty* v. *Styward* (1632) 1 Rep. Ch. 31; no survivorship; *Vickers* v. *Cowell* (1839) 1 Beav. 529.

of the survivors would be sufficient to release the mortgagor. Although the joint account clause is still frequently included in a joint mortgage it is no longer necessary. Section 111 of the Law of Property Act 1925 provides that in all joint mortgages, not merely those of trustees, the moneys shall be deemed to have been advanced on a joint account unless the deed expresses a contrary intention. Consequently, in such cases, unless the mortgage contract otherwise provides, payment may safely be made to the survivors (or survivor) of joint mortgagees. This enables the surviving mortgagees to overreach the beneficial interests in the mortgaged property. But it does not affect the right of the mortgagees *inter se* nor does it alter the presumptions as to a tenancy in common.

Effect of a proper tender when refused

A mortgagee is bound to know the state of the mortgage debt so that if a proper tender is made he rejects it at his peril.[94] By the contract and by the practice of the court a mortgagee is entitled to all the costs of the mortgage, including those of redemption, but he cannot be allowed to swell the costs and thereby render redemption more difficult. He will have to reimburse the mortgagor for such additional costs (usually the costs of a redemption action)[95] as the latter may be put to by the refusal of his tender. Clearly, therefore, even if it is known that a proper tender will be rejected, it is of the first importance that the tender should be made and the risk of further expense placed upon the mortgagee. As Lindley L.J. said[96]:

> "What is the object of a tender? It is not necessarily to put an end to all controversy. It may have that effect and very often has, but its main object is to throw the risk of further controversy on the other party."

But, apart from the question of costs, a tender may have the effect of terminating the mortgagee's right to interest. It is true that a tender by itself will not altogether stop the running of interest, because tender is not equivalent to payment, and a mortgagor who continues to have the use of the mortgagee's money will have to pay interest for its use.[97] But if, after tender, the mortgagor continues to keep the money set aside[98] and available for payment of the mortgage debt, the running of interest is absolutely stopped as from the date of tender.[99] Presumably he need not keep the money completely idle, and if, for example, he places it to deposit, he will only have to account to the mortgagee for the interest earned by the money while on deposit.[1] But even if he does not keep the money available, his tender afterwards enables him to enforce redemption without giving any further notice to the mortgagee, and consequently by payment of the

[94] Provided they were created after December 31, 1881.
[95] *Harmer* v. *Priestly* (1853) 16 Beav. 569.
[96] *Greenwood* v. *Sutcliffe* [1892] 1 Ch. 1 at 10.
[97] *Edmondson* v. *Copland* [1911] 2 Ch. 301.
[98] *Ibid.* at p. 310.
[99] *Rourke* v. *Robinson* [1911] 1 Ch. 480.
[1] *Edmondson* v. *Copland* [1911] 2 Ch. 301, *per* Joyce J. at 310.

principal plus interest *only up to the date of payment*.[2] If the mortgagee unequivocally refuses a proposed tender, then this is equivalent to a waiver by the mortgagee and a formal tender is not necessary.[3]

Effect of a proper tender when accepted

Usually a proper tender is accepted and the mortgage thereby discharged. The mortgagee is then bound to execute such instruments as are necessary to release the security from the debt. Accordingly, he must be given a reasonable time in which to prepare and execute the deeds, especially when he is not the original mortgagee, but a derivative holder of the mortgage. The cost of preparing these deeds falls on the mortgagor, as being part of the general costs of the mortgage, and this is true even when the costs have been increased by complications in the title caused by the mortgagee's activites. For example, in a case where one trustee-mortgagee absconded, the cost of obtaining a vesting order from the court vesting the estate in the remaining trustees was included in the general costs of the mortgage, and added to the mortgage debt.[4]

---

[2] *Edmondson* v. *Copland* [1911] 2 Ch. 301 at 307.

[3] *Chalikani Venkatarayanim* v. *Zaminder of Tun* (1922) L.R. Ind. App. 41.

[4] In the case of several incumbrances, the person *immediately* entitled to the equity of redemption, is, of course, the second incumbrancer. For discharge of mortgages, see *post*, pp. 390 *et seq*.

CHAPTER 17

OTHER MATTERS INCIDENTAL TO THE SECURITY

INSURANCE[1]

By virtue of section 101 of the Law of Property Act 1925[2] the mortgagee has the statutory power to insure and keep insured the mortgaged property at the expense of the mortgagor in order to preserve his security in respect of loss or damage by fire.[3] The premiums paid for any such insurance shall be a charge on the mortgaged property carrying interest at the same rate as the mortgage debt. But the premiums cannot be recovered from the mortgagor as a debt in the absence of any express covenant. The power is exercisable as soon as the mortgage is made.[4]

The disadvantages of the statutory power arise not only by virtue of this express restriction as to loss or damage by fire, but also from the terms of section 108(1)[5] of the Law of Property Act 1925 in that the power is limited to an insurance not exceeding the amount specified in the mortgage deed, or if no amount is so specified, two-thirds of the sum necessary to restore the mortgaged property in the event of total destruction. Further, by section 108(2) the statutory power cannot be exercised by the mortgagee:

"(i) where there is a declaration in the mortgage deed that no insurance is required;
 (ii) when an insurance is kept by or on behalf of the mortgagor in accordance with the mortgage deed;
(iii) where the mortgage deed contains no stipulation respecting insurance, and an insurance is kept up by or on behalf of the mortgagor with the consent of the mortgagee to the amount to which the mortgagee is by the Act authorised to insure."

The mortgagee may require that the insurance moneys received be applied by the mortgagor in making good the loss or damage in respect of which it has been paid.[6-7]

Thus, owing to the inadequacy of the statutory power it is usual for the mortgage deed to contain an express covenant on the part of the mortgagor

---

[1] For a criticism of the limitations of the present legal position, see the Law Commission, Working Paper No. 99, *Land Mortgages*, paras. 3.27, 3.28.
[2] ss.101(1)(ii), 108, replacing (with slight variations) the Conveyancing Act 1881, ss.18(1)(ii), 23.
[3] The power may be varied or extended by the mortgage deed, and the section only applies if and so far as a contrary intention is not expressed in the deed—L.P.A. 1925, s.101(3), (4).
[4] L.P.A. 1925, s.101(1)(ii).
[5] *Ibid.* s.108(3).
[6-7] *Ibid.* s.101(1)(ii).

to insure the security for a specified amount, or for the full value of the property. The covenant also usually contains an agreement by the mortgagor to produce receipts for the premiums on demand, and to repay to the mortgagee any sums paid by him in respect of those premiums.

The effect of such an express covenant on the part of the mortgagor enables the mortgagee, in the case of default by the mortgagor, to recover those sums paid by the mortgagee in respect of premiums as a debt and as a breach of the covenant by the mortgagor instead of having to add such premiums to the mortgage debt which occurs in the case of the statutory power. Breach of such a covenant is a default which at once sets up the mortgagee's statutory power of sale. Further, and without prejudice to any obligation to the contrary imposed by law or by special contract, a mortgagee may require that all money received under an insurance effected as mentioned above be applied in or towards the discharge of the mortgage money.[8] But, it should be mentioned that if the mortgagor has effected a further insurance which is independent of the security, the mortgagee will not be entitled to its benefit.[9] Thus, if the insurance policy contains a clause limiting the insurers' liability in the event of the security in question being the subject of any other insurance, the result may be that the amount payable to the mortgagee is diminished and the mortgagee will have no right to the benefit of the further insurance moneys.[10]

POWER TO GRANT LEASES

Generally

The power of a mortgagor to grant and enforce leases well illustrates the compromise between the equitable ownership of the mortgagor and the legal rights inherent in the title of the mortgagee.[11] Having parted with his legal right to possession by demise or legal charge and merely retaining the reversion subject to a long term of years[12] (together with the equity of redemption), the mortgagor might be expected to have no power to grant

---

[8] L.P.A. 1925, s.108(4). In the case of loss or damage by fire and reinstatement of the mortgaged property from the insurance proceeds the position is somewhat complicated, see the Fire Prevention (Metropolis) Act 1774, s.83, the operation of which is not confined to the metropolis. It is generally assumed that the mortgagee's rights under s.108(4) or the mortgagee's contractual rights are subsumed to the rights of "any person interested" under s.83 of the 1774 Act to require the insurance company to utilise the insurance proceeds towards reinstatement of the building (see, e.g. Fisher & Lightwood, *Law of Mortgage* (10th ed., 1988), p. 52; but see MacGillivray and Parkington, *Insurance Law* (8th ed., 1988), para. 1650). Even if this is a correct interpretation of the law in relation to fire insurance, a third party with no interest in the mortgage but who is a "person interested" under s.83 of the 1774 Act, can insist on reinstatement.
[9] See *Halifax Building Society* v. *Keighley* [1931] 2 K.B. 248.
[10] *Ibid.*
[11] For the position with regard to leases granted *before* the mortgage, see *ante*, Chap. 14.
[12] See *ante*, pp. 284 *et seq.*

leases to take effect during the continuance of the mortgage.[13] But, unless
he has actually been dispossessed by the mortgagee, he can create legal
tenancies which are binding on himself and his lessee upon the principle of
estoppel.[14] For a tenant is estopped from denying his landlord's title, and a
landlord from denying the validity of his lease. Consequently, the mortgagor may sue or distrain for rent.[15] Such a lease will not, however, be
binding on the mortgagee, if the latter asserts his paramount title to possession.[16] But a problem can arise when a purchaser of the legal estate purports to grant a lease[17] of the land he has contracted to purchase. On
completion of the purchase the estoppel created by the grant of the lease is
"fed" and a legal tenancy arises in the place of the tenancy by estoppel
which binds the mortgagee in priority to the mortgage and in effect is a
mortgage of the reversion only.[18]

Thus a mortgagor cannot—apart from express or statutory power (or, in
the limited circumstances explained above) grant leases which bind the
mortgagee because he has conveyed away the title to possession.
Further,[19] although the mortgagor may remain in possession of the mortgaged property and receive the rents and profits and sue in his own name[20]
until demand by the mortgagee, it is the mortgagee who is always entitled
to take possession or after an effective demand[21] to require the rent includ-

---

[13] See *ante*, pp. 284 *et seq*.

[14] *Doe* d. *Marriot* v. *Edwards* (1834) 6 C. & P. 208; *Webb* v. *Austin* (1844) 7 Man. & G. 701;
Cuthbertson v. *Irving* (1860) 4 H. & N. 742 at 754 (*affd.* (1860) 6 H. & N. 135); *Trent* v.
Hunt (1853) 9 Exch. 14.

[15] *Trent* v. *Hunt* (1853) 9 Ex. 14; and see *ante*, p. 287.

[16] *Rogers* v. *Humphreys* (1835) 4 Ad. & El. 299; *Trent* v. *Hunt* (1853) 9 Ex. 14; unless, of
course, the lease was authorised by the mortgagee; *Corbett* v. *Plowden* (1884) 25 Ch.D.
678; or his concurrence in the tenancy could be implied from some act or conduct on his
part, *e.g.* by the acceptance of the mortgagees' tenant, see *Stroud Building Society* v. *Dela-
mont* [1960] 1 W.L.R. 431, approved in *Chatsworth Properties Ltd.* v. *Effiom* [1971] 1
W.L.R. 144. But such a tenancy binding the mortgagee will not arise merely because the
mortgagee does not object, (*Re O'Rourke's Estate* (1889) 23 L.R.Ir. 497); or the mortgagee
fails to evict the tenant, (*Parker* v. *Braithwaite* [1952] W.N. 504), even though the mortgagor was in default at the time, (*Taylor* v. *Ellis* [1960] Ch. 368); see also *Barclays Bank* v.
Kiley [1961] 1 W.L.R. 1050.

[17] On the assumption that the grant of the lease is under seal or capable of being a valid parol
lease (see the L.P.A. 1925, s.52 (as amended by the Insolvency Act 1986, s.439(2), Sched.
14 and s.437 Sched. 11. part II) and s.54(2)).

[18] Notwithstanding the normal practice for the conveyance and the mortgage deed to form
substantially the same transaction, see *Church of England Building Society* v. *Piskor* [1954]
Ch. 553 following *Woolwich Equitable Building Society* v. *Marshall* [1952] Ch. 1 and
Universal Permanent Building Society v. *Cooke* [1952] Ch.95, and overruling *Coventry Permanent Economic Building Society* v. *Jones* [1951] W.N. 218. See also *Lloyds Bank* v. *Rossett* [1988] 3 W.L.R. 1301. This position will not arise if there is evidence of fraud on the
part of the mortgagor and the tenant in which case the lease will be voidable, see Insolvency Act 1986, ss.423–425; and see *Lloyds Bank* v. *Marcan* [1973] 1 W.L.R. 339. *Quaere*
the position where there is simultaneous registration of the lease and mortgage. See also
Grace Rymer Investments Ltd. v. *Waite* [1958] Ch. 831, and contrast *City Permanent Building Society* v. *Miller* [1952] Ch. 840.

[19] See *ante*, pp. 286 *et seq*.

[20] L.P.A. 1925, s.98, and see *ante*, p. 287.

[21] See *Kitchen's Trustee* v. *Madders and Madders* [1950] Ch. 134.

ing any arrears[22] to be paid to himself.[23] This right to possession on the part of the mortgagee cannot be fettered by the mortgagor[24] and against the mortgagee the tenant has no defence.[25]

The corollary to this ought to be that the mortgagee, having the legal title to possession, should be able to create legal tenancies to the full extent of the estate mortgaged to him, though, of course, the exercise of the power would mean that he took possession of the security. Equity, however, in pursuance of the principle that the mortgagee's estate belongs to him only as a security, refuses to recognise that leases granted by him are binding on the mortgagor after redemption.[26] Consequently, unless special powers of leasing are granted in the mortgage there may be difficulty in the management of the property, for during the continuance of the mortgage it is impossible for either mortgagor or mortgagee to grant an indefeasible term without the concurrence of the other. The result was that mortgage contracts frequently contained express powers to grant leases binding on both parties and this practice eventually received statutory recognition.[27]

Statutory power

The Law of Property Act 1925[28] makes elaborate provision for the creation of indefeasible tenancies by a mortgagor in possession, and by a mortgagee who has gone into occupation. Where the mortgage contract does not limit the statutory powers of leasing,[28a] and was itself executed after December 31, 1881,[29] the mortgagor in possession,[30] or the mortgagee if he is in possession[31] or has appointed a receiver who is still acting[32-33] (in which case the mortgagee's powers of leasing may be delegated in writing to the receiver), is vested by section 99 with the power to grant leases[34] so that they will bind all persons.

---

[22] *Moss* v. *Gallimore* (1779) 1 Doug. K.B 279.

[23] *Pope* v. *Biggs* (1829) 9 B. & C. 245.

[24] See *Thunder* d. *Weaver* v. *Belcher* (1803) 3 East. 449.

[25] *Rogers* v. *Humphreys* (1835) 4 Ad. & El. 299; *Dudley and District Benefit Building Society* v. *Emerson* [1949] Ch. 707; *Rust* v. *Goodale* [1957] Ch. 33; and see *post*, pp. 337–338.

[26] *Franklinski* v. *Ball* (1864) 33 Beav. 560; and see *Chapman* v. *Smith* [1907] 2 Ch. 97 at 102. s.99 of the L.P.A. 1925 empowers a mortgagee to make certain leases which will bind the mortgagor even after redemption: a lease made *ultra vires* these powers would still, however, be void against the mortgagor after redemption.

[27] Conveyancing Act 1881, s.18; and now the L.P.A. 1925, s.99.

[28] s.99.

[28a] See s.99(13) as amended by Agricultural Holdings Act 1986, s.100 Sched. 14, para. 12 and Landlord and Tenant Act 1954, s.36(4). See *post*, p. 337 nn. 51 & 52.

[29] The Conveyancing Act of that year first introduced the statutory powers; in cases where a mortgage was executed before 1822, the parties may now by agreement introduce the statutory powers in the mortgage.

[30] L.P.A. 1925, s.99(1).

[31] *Ibid.* s.99(2).

[32-33] *Ibid.* s.99(19).

[34] The provisions of this section extend to agreements for a lease as well as to leases, and specific performance of such agreements will therefore be decreed. See *post*, p. 336.

Duration

A lease may be granted for the following terms:

(1) Agricultural or occupation leases for any term not exceeding 50 years.[35]

(2) Building leases for any term not exceeding 999 years.[36]

No power is, however, given to create mining leases.

Conditions

All leases within the terms of the statute must comply with the following conditions:

(1) The lease must be limited to take effect in possession not later than 12 months after its date.[37]

(2) The lease must reserve the best rent that can reasonably be obtained, and with certain qualifications no fine may be taken[38] though in a building lease the rent may be nominal for the first five years.[39]

(3) The lease must contain a covenant by the lessee for the payment of rent, and a condition of re-entry on the rent not being paid within a time not exceeding 30 days.[40]

(4) In the case of a building lease there must be a covenant by the lessee that within five years improvements will be effected on the land in connection with buildings, repairs to buildings, or building purposes.[41]

(5) A counterpart of the lease must be executed by the lessee and delivered to the lessor.[42]

(6) Where it is the mortgagor who grants the lease, he must within one month deliver to the mortgagee, first in priority, a counterpart of the lease duly executed by the lessee.[43]

The provisions of the section extend to agreements for a lease.[44] But some doubt has been raised as to whether the covenant by the lessee for the payment of rent and the condition of re-entry in the event of rent not

---

[35] 21 years if the mortgage was executed before January 1, 1926. See L.P.A. 1925, s.99(3)(i).
[36] 99 years if the mortgage was executed before January 1, 1926. See L.P.A. 1925, s.99(3)(ii).
[37] L.P.A. 1925, s.99(5).
[38] *Ibid.* s.99(6).
[39] *Ibid.* s.99(10).
[40] *Ibid.* s.99(7).
[41] *Ibid.* s.99(9).
[42] *Ibid.* s.99(8).
[43] *Ibid.* s.99(11). The lessee is not, however, concerned to see that this provision has been complied with. But non-compliance does not invalidate the lease although it renders the power of sale exercisable; see *Public Trustee* v. *Lawrence* [1912] 1 Ch. 789; and see *Rhodes* v. *Dalby* [1971] 1 W.L.R. 1325.
[44] L.P.A. 1925, s.99(17), " . . . as far as circumstances admit . . . [the definitions of lease] . . . to an agreement, whether in writing or not, for leasing or letting."

being paid can apply in the case of an oral letting. In any event such a condition, if imposed, will be strictly construed.[45]

A lease by the mortgagor of agricultural land does not cease to be such if it includes chattels and sporting rights not included in the mortgage.[46] But it will not bind the mortgagee if it commprises both the mortgaged land and other land at a single inclusive rent.[47]

Contrary agreement

The above powers are subject to exclusion[48] or extension[49] by the mortgage agreement, (which in fact frequently does modify the mortgagor's statutory power[50]) or otherwise in writing by the parties. But the statutory power cannot be excluded in any mortgage of agricultural land after March 1, 1948,[51] and in the case of business premises the exclusion of the statutory power does not prevent the court from ordering the grant of a new tenancy.[52]

Leases not made under the statutory power

Section 99 of the Law of Property Act 1925, does not, however, take away the mortgagor's ordinary power, outside the statute, to create leases binding on himself by estoppel, although not binding on the mortgagee, should the latter assert his paramount title to possession.[53] Thus, if the mortgage deed altogether excludes the statutory power to grant leases binding on the mortgagee, the mortgagor may still create leases effective between himself and his lessee.[54] The same is true if, as frequently happens, the mortgage deed merely restricts the statutory power by making its exercise subject to the previous consent of the mortgagee. Indeed, in a case where the mortgagors had covenanted not to exercise the statutory power without the previous consent of the mortgagees and had then created a yearly tenancy without their consent, Farwell J. held that the mortgagors must be assumed to have been exercising their general

---

[45] See *Pawson* v. *Revell* [1958] 2 Q.B. 360; *Rhodes* v. *Dalby* [1971] 1 W.L.R. 1325; Wolstenholme & Cherry, *Conveyancing Statutes* (13th ed.), pp. 198, 200. But even if the letting does not comply with the statutory requirements, provided that it is made in good faith and the tenant has taken possession it may be effective in equity at the tenant's option as a contract for a lease subject to such variations as may be necessary to comply with the above conditions; see L.P.A. 1925, s.152, replacing the Leases Acts 1849, 1850.

[46] *Brown* v. *Peto* [1900] 2 Q.B. 653.

[47] *King* v. *Bird* [1909] 1 K.B. 837.

[48] L.P.A. 1925, s.99(13).

[49] *Ibid.* s.99(14).

[50] As, for instance, by requiring the mortgagee's consent before the powers can be exercised; *Iron Trades Employers Insurance Association Ltd.* v. *Union of Land & House Investors Ltd.* [1937] 1 Ch. 313.

[51] Agricultural Holdings Act 1986, s.100, Sched. 14, para. 12. See also *Pawson* v. *Revell* [1958] 2 Q.B. 360; *Rhodes* v. *Dalby* [1971] 1 W.L.R. 1325.

[52] Landlord and Tenant Act 1954, s.36(4).

[53] See *ante*, p. 334.

[54] *Dudley and District Benefit Building Society* v. *Emerson* [1949] Ch. 707. *Rust* v. *Goodale* [1957] Ch. 33.

power to create leases by estoppel and had therefore not committed a breach of the covenant.[55]

Consequently, at the very least, a demise by a mortgagor in possession will create a lease which is effective between the parties.[56] Thus the mortgagor can distrain for rent and enforce the covenants and his interest will pass to his personal representatives or to assignees, so as to enable them to sue upon the covenants.[57] The lessee, on his side, may not only enforce the lease but obtains an interest in the equity of redemption which is sufficient to entitle him to redeem.[58] He cannot insist that the mortgagee shall accept him as tenant but he may, if he thinks fit, take over the mortgage by redeeming. If he does not redeem and is dispossessed by the mortgagee, his only relief against the mortgagor is an action for damages because the court will not compel a mortgagor to redeem for the purpose of giving efficacy to his lease.[59] The mortgagee's right to eject the mortgagor's lessee by estoppel is absolute, for he is asserting a title to possession paramount to that of the mortgagor himself. There is no contractual nexus of any kind between the lessee and the mortgagee so that the latter is not a landlord for the purpose of the Rent Act 1977[60] and the lessee cannot claim the protection of the Act.

Thus, it is now usual for the mortgage deed to contain a clause not only excluding the statutory power of leasing, but also a clause which makes the grant of any lease or tenancy, or otherwise parting with possession of the mortgaged property a breach of the mortgagor's obligations under the lease.

The importation of such a clause will cause the power of sale to arise in the event of any breach on the part of the mortgagor.

If the mortgage permits the mortgagor to exercise the statutory power of leasing with the consent of the mortgagee, the onus is on the lessee to prove that the mortgagee gave his consent.[61] If the deed provides that the proposed lessee shall not be concerned to inquire as to such consent, the mortgagee is estopped from denying the lease was made with his consent.[62]

The result is that a mortgagor's power to grant leases will either be expressly stated by the agreement, or will depend on section 99 of the Law of Property Act 1925. Leases granted in conformity with the express or statutory power will be binding on the mortgagee and, equally, on his

---

[55] *Iron Trades Employers Insurance Association Ltd.* v. *Union of Land & House Investors Ltd.* [1937] 1 Ch. 313.

[56] This appears to be so whether or not the lease discloses on its face the existence of the mortgage: *Morton* v. *Woods* (1869) L.R. 4 Q.B. 293.

[57] *Cuthbertson* v. *Irving* (1860) 6 H. & N. 135.

[58] *Tarn* v. *Turner* (1888) 39 Ch.D. 456, C.A.

[59] *Howe* v. *Hunt* (1862) 31 Beav. 420.

[60] *Dudley and District Benefit Building Society* v. *Emerson* [1949] Ch. 707; *Rust* v. *Goodale* [1957] Ch. 33. *Quaere* whether a statutory tenant can claim the protection of the Act, see dicta in *Jessamine Investment Co. Ltd.* v. *Schwartz* [1978] Q.B. 264 at 273; and see P. W. Smith, (1977) Conv. 197.

[61] *Taylor* v. *Ellis* [1960] Ch. 368.

[62] *Lever Finance Ltd.* v. *Needlemans Property Trustee* [1956] Ch. 375.

assuming possession, the benefit of the covenants will pass to the mortgagee in virtue of section 141 of the Law of Property Act 1925.[63]

POWER TO ACCEPT SURRENDER OF LEASES

Complementary to the power to grant leases is the power given by section
100 of the Law of Property Act 1925, to the mortgagor or mortgagee to
accept surrenders of leases. This power was first introduced by the Conveyancing Act 1911,[64] and now extends to all mortgages executed after
December 31, 1911. Its purpose is to allow a mortgagee or mortgagor to
accept a surrender in order to enable another lease to be granted.

The surrender may be accepted:

(1) by the mortgagee, if he is in possession[65] or has appointed a
receiver who is still acting[66] (in which case the mortgagee may
delegate his powers of accepting surrenders to the receiver in
writing[67]);

(2) by the mortgagor, if he is in possession.[68]

For the surrender to be valid the following conditions must apply:

(a) a fresh authorised lease of the property concerned must be
granted to take effect within one month of the surrender; and

(b) the new lease must be for a term not less than the unexpired term
of the surrendered lease; and

(c) the rent must be at least equivalent to the rent reserved in the surrendered lease.[69]

These provisions also apply to agreements for a lease and are subject to the
parties expressing a contrary intention either in the mortgage deed or
otherwise in writing.[70] But the power may be extended by an agreement in
writing between the parties whether in the mortgage or not.[71] A surrender
which does not comply with these conditions is void.[72]

---

[63] *Municipal Permanent Investment Building Society* v. *Smith* (1888) 22 Q.B.D. 70.
[64] s.3. Prior to the 1911 Act a mortgagor who had granted a lease under his statutory powers
could not accept its surrender unless the mortgagee consented.
[65] L.P.A. 1925, s.100(2).
[66] *Ibid.* s.100(13).
[67] *Ibid.*
[68] *Ibid.* s.100(1).
[69] *Ibid.* s.100(5).
[70] *Ibid.* s.100(7).
[71] *Ibid.* s.100(10).
[72] *Barclays Bank* v. *Stasek* [1957] Ch. 28; *Rhyl U.D.C.* v. *Rhyl Amusements Ltd.* [1959] 1
W.L.R. 465.

CHAPTER 18

PRIORITY OF MORTGAGES

PRINCIPLES OF PRIORITY BEFORE 1926

General rules

As a mortgagor is able to obtain successive advances on the same property and circumstances may arise in which the property is insufficient to satisfy all the securities, there is a need for rules which regulate priorities among the various mortgagees. Unlike the unsecured creditors of a bankrupt, mortgagees do not share rateably if there is not sufficient to satisfy them all. The simplest way of regulating priorities is by order of creation. While this would be fair in many cases, it would not be fair when, by the misconduct of the mortgagor or an earlier mortgagee, the existence of that earlier mortgage was concealed from a later mortgagee.

For mortgages (including sub-mortgages) of realty, the basic rule of priority, ranking by order of creation (*qui prior est tempore, potior est jure*) was modified in two ways. The first is normally expressed by the phrase "where the equities are equal, the law prevails." In *Bailey* v. *Barnes*[1] Lindley L.J. said that equality meant "the non-existence of any circumstance which affects the conduct of one of the rival claimants, and makes it less meritorious than that of the other." The result of this is that, where a legal and an equitable mortgagee have, in that sense, equal claims to be preferred, the legal mortgagee will rank first even though his mortgage was created later.

The second modification was that any priority, whether depending on earlier creation or superiority of the legal estate, could be lost if the conduct of the mortgagor or the prior mortgagee was inequitable. Priorities of mortgages of realty, therefore, were regulated by general equitable principles, subject to the two following exceptions. The first depended on registration. Between 1703 and 1735, registers of transactions in land were set up for Yorkshire and Middlesex. The principle of the registration system was that an earlier transaction by A would be void against a later purchaser, B, unless A's deed was registered before B's. The efficacy of this system was severely reduced by the insistence of courts of equity on applying the doctrine of notice, so that B took subject to A's incumbrance if he knew of its existence, irrespective of registration. The system no longer exists, since both counties are now wholly subject to compulsory registration of title.

Although the Land Charges Act 1888, a consolidating Act, provided for

[1] [1894] 1 Ch. 25 at 36, C.A.

the registration of, *inter alia*, deeds of arrangement and certain statutory charges affecting land, it made no provision for registration of mortgages of land.

The second exception was by means of tacking, a device whereby a later mortgagee can gain priority over an earlier mortgagee by amalgamating his debt with that owned to a still earlier mortgagee. The opportunities for this device to be used were cut down by the 1925 legislation and its operation is now regulated entirely by statute.[2]

The rules regulating priorities of mortgages of personalty developed rather differently. Legal mortgages of personal chattels have been dealt with in Chapter 6; they are only regulated by the Bills of Sale Acts 1878 and 1882. Mortgages of choses in action are governed by the general law of assignment, though sub-mortgages, which are mortgages of mortgage debts and, therefore, choses in action, are treated as interests in land and are subject to the same rules of priority as mortgages.[2a]

Mortgages of equitable interests in personalty were subject to the rule in *Dearle* v. *Hall*.[3] In its original form the rule provided that priority depended on the order in which notice of the mortgages or other transactions was received by the owner of the legal estate or interest in the subject-matter, except where the subsequent mortgagee had, at the time he lent the money, actual or constructive notice of the earlier transaction. Although the rule now applies to equitable interests in land arising out of a trust for sale,[4] it did not do so before 1926.

Priorities between legal and equitable mortgages of land

Two successive legal mortgages

Legal mortgages of land before 1926 were almost invariably created by a conveyance of the fee simple with a proviso for reconveyance on redemption, therefore the opportunity for any priority question to arise rarely occurred.

Successive legal mortgages could arise from the grant of successive terms of years, in which case priority would normally be determined by the order of creation, on the basis that the first lease would be a lease in possession, to which the second, as a lease in reversion, would be postponed.[5]

The earlier mortgagee could, as in *Jones* v. *Rhind*,[6] lose priority by parting with the title deeds. In that case, S mortgaged a leasehold property first to J, then to R, handing over the lease to R when he made the second mortgage. R had no notice of the first mortgage and he was held to have

---

[2] L.P.A. 1925, s.94.
[2a] *Taylor* v. *London & County Banking Co.*; *London and County Banking Co.* v. *Nixon* [1901] 2 Ch. 231.
[3] (1828) 3 Russ. 1. See *post*, pp. 350–353.
[4] L.P.A. 1925, s.137. See *post*, p. 354.
[5] *Ex p. Knott* (1806) 11 Ves. 609.
[6] (1869) 17 W.R. 1091; applying *Perry-Herrick* v. *Attwood* (1857) 2 De G. & J. 21. See also *Abbey National Building Society* v. *Cann*, *The Times*, March 15, 1989.

priority over J. In *Mason* v. *Rhodes*,[7] W created three mortgages, an equitable mortgage to G, followed by legal mortgages to B and then to R. R, who had no notice of B, arranged to pay off G, and received the title deeds. It was held on appeal that R had priority over M (B's trustee in liquidation) to the extent of G's security.

One source of successive legal mortgages was the portions term[8] contained in a strict settlement. The trustees of the portions term were empowered to raise money for the younger children by mortgaging a long term, usually 1,000 years. In *Hurst* v. *Hurst*[9] it was held that a tenant for life, who had power, by the settlement, to create portions terms, could not do so to the prejudice of the mortgagees with whom he had covenanted not to exercise that power, even though the portions term was not made subject to the mortgage term.

Legal mortgage followed by equitable mortgage

In this case the legal mortgagee has a claim to priority based both on earlier creation and the superiority of the legal estate.[10] This double protection can be lost. Usually the cases on such loss of protection are considered under the three headings of fraud, estoppel (or misrepresentation) and gross negligence in relation to the title deeds.

The so-called *estoppel* cases fall into two classes. First, there are those where the prior mortgagee puts into the hands of a mortgagor a document containing within it a statement that money has been received by the mortgagee. As against an innocent person who lends money on the property on the faith of that receipt, he cannot deny that the money has been received.[11]

The second class involves a representation, express or implied, that the person in possession of the title-deeds is the mortgagee's agent to raise money or otherwise deal with the property. Thus, where a mortgagee expressly authorises the mortgagor to raise money on the security of the property, and gives him control of the title deeds, he represents to innocent third parties who advance money that the mortgagor has that authority to deal with the property which possession of the title deeds implies, and he cannot, against such a third party, rely on any secret limitation of the mortgagor's apparent authority.[12]

Thus, where the prior legal mortgagee returned the deeds to the mortgagor to enable him to raise a further loan, he was postponed to a later equitable mortgagee who lent without notice of the earlier mortgage, even

---

[7] (1885) 53 L.T. 322.
[8] See Megarry and Wade, *The Law of Real Property*, (5th ed., 1984), pp. 413–414.
[9] (1852) 16 Beav. 372.
[10] *Peter* v. *Russell* (1716) 1 Eq.Cas.Abr. 321.
[11] *Bickerton* v. *Walker* (1885) 31 Ch.D. 151; *cf. Rice* v. *Rice* (1854) 2 Drew. 73.
[12] *Rimmer* v. *Webster* [1902] 2 Ch. 163; *Fry* v. *Smellie* [1912] 3 K.B. 282; *Abigail* v. *Lapin* [1934] A.C. 491; *Brocklesby* v. *Temperance Permanent Building Society* [1895] A.C. 173; *Lloyds Bank* v. *Cooke* [1907] 1 K.B. 794; *Edmunds* v. *Bushell* (1865) L.R. 1 Q.B. 97.

though the mortgagor exceeded the limit that he was authorised to borrow.[13] This similarly arose where the mortgagor had undertaken to inform the later mortgagee of the existing mortgage, but failed to do so.[14]

Priority will not be lost where the title deeds are left with another for safe-keeping, or without reference to any transaction regarding the property.[15] The pre-1926 rule as to questions of priority depending on possession of deeds is preserved.[16]

The fraud and gross negligence cases are considered together. In *Peter* v. *Russell*[17] it was held that a prior mortgagee who deliberately assists or connives in a scheme of the mortgagor designed to defeat later incumbrancers is postponed to them. The same applies if the fraud is that of the party's solicitor, provided that the solicitor-client relationship existed at the time of the fraud. In *Evans* v. *Bicknell*,[18] Lord Eldon held that a prior mortgagee would be postponed if his conduct in relation to the deeds displayed gross negligence that amounted to a fraudulent intention. In *Colyer* v. *Finch*,[19] however, it was held that, in order to deprive a first mortgagee of his legal priority, the party claiming by title subsequent must satisfy the court that the first mortgagee has been guilty of either fraud or gross negligence, but for which he would have had the deeds in his possession.

Clarke v. *Palmer*[20] seems to have been decided in accordance with that principle. X, the first mortgagee, negligently failed to obtain the title deeds, after which the mortgagor further mortgaged part of the property to Y, then all of it to Z. Z knew of Y but neither of them knew of X, who was, on account of his negligence, postponed to both of them.

In his analysis of the authorities in *Northern Counties of England Fire Insurance Co.* v. *Whipp*,[21] Fry L.J. held *Clarke* v. *Palmer* to have been rightly decided. He considered six types of case. In the first three, the prior legal mortgagee retains priority:

> (1) Where he has a reasonable excuse for not obtaining the deeds. This has been extended, in *Grierson* v. *National Provincial Bank of England Ltd.*[22] where F, a leaseholder, deposited his lease with another bank as security for a loan, and then granted a legal mortgage to G which was made expressly subject to the prior equitable mortgage. He then redeemed the equitable mortgage and deposited the lease with the defendant bank, who knew nothing

---

[13] *Perry-Herrick* v. *Attwood* (1857) 2 De G. & J. 21; *Abbey National Building Society* v. *Cann*, *The Times*, March 15, 1989.

[14] *Briggs* v. *Jones* (1870) L.R. 10 Eq. 92.

[15] *Shropshire Union Railways and Canal Co.* v. *R.* (1875) L.R. 7 H.L. 496; *Re Vernon, Ewens & Co.* (1886) 33 Ch.D. 402. *Cf. Waldron* v. *Sloper* (1852) 1 Drew. 193.

[16] *Beddoes* v. *Shaw* [1937] Ch. 81; L.P.A. 1925, s.13.

[17] (1716) 1 Eq.Cas.Abr. 321.

[18] (1801) 6 Ves. 174 at 189.

[19] (1856) 5 H.L.C. 905.

[20] (1882) 21 Ch.D. 124.

[21] (1884) 26 Ch.D. 482, C.A.

[22] [1913] 2 Ch. 18.

of G, as security for a loan. It was held that G retained priority over the defendant bank,

(2) Where he reasonably believes that he has been given all the deeds, though he has not, in fact, been given all of them. *Walker* v. *Linom*,[23] which is discussed later, is against this proposition.

(3) Where he has lent them to the mortgagor who has given a reasonable excuse for requiring them as in *Peter* v. *Russell*[23a] and *Martinez* v. *Cooper*.[23b]

In the remaining three, priority would be lost.

(4) Where the legal mortgagee has made no inquiry for the deeds, he will be postponed to a prior equitable estate or to a subsequent equitable owner who used diligence in inquiring for the deeds. In the first case, of which he cites *Worthington* v. *Morgan*[24] as an example, his reasoning was that the conduct of the mortgagee in making no inquiry was evidence of fraudulent intent to escape notice of a prior equity. In the second case, exemplified by *Clarke* v. *Palmer*,[25] he considered that a subsequent mortgagee who was misled by the mortgagor taking advantage of fraudulent conduct on the part of the legal mortgagee could, against him, take advantage of the fraudulent intent;

(5) and (6) These are the cases, already dealt with under estoppel, such as *Perry-Herrick* v. *Attwood*,[26] and *Briggs* v. *Jones*,[27] where the legal mortgagee has conferred apparent authority on the mortgagor to deal with the property without restriction, although there were conditions as between mortgagee and mortgagor of which a third party would be unaware.

In arriving at his decision in *Northern Counties of England Fire Insurance Co.* v. *Whipp*,[28] Fry L.J. relied on *Evans* v. *Bicknell*[29] and cases which followed it, and seems to have ignored the plain words of *Colyer* v. *Finch*.[30] He has used a later passage,[31] which refers to "gross negligence, so gross as to be tantamount to fraud" in order to reconcile those two cases and make fraud a requirement for postponement.

In *Walker* v. *Linom*,[32] Parker J. reviewing the authorities and particu-

---

[23] [1907] 2 Ch. 104; see *Cottey* v. *National Provincial Bank of England* (1904) 48 S.J. 589.
[23a] 1 Eq. Cas. Abr. 321.
[23b] (1826) 2 Russ. 198.
[24] (1849) 16 Sim. 547.
[25] (1882) 21 Ch.D. 124.
[26] (1857) 2 De G. & J. 21. See also *Abbey National Building Society* v. *Cann, The Times,* March 15, 1989.
[27] (1870) L.R. 10 Eq. 92.
[28] (1884) 26 Ch.D. 482, C.A.
[29] (1801) 6 Ves. 174.
[30] (1856) 5 H.L.C. 905, in the headnote and at 928.
[31] *Ibid.* at 929.
[32] [1907] 2 Ch. 104.

larly the judgment of Fry L.J. referred to above, concluded that the principle should be stated as follows:

> "Any conduct on the part of the holder of the legal estate in relation to the deeds which would make it inequitable for him to rely on his legal estate against a prior equitable estate of which he had no notice ought also to be sufficient to postpone him to a subsequent equitable estate the creation of which has only been rendered possible by the possession of deeds which but for such conduct would have passed into the possession of the owner of the legal estate."[33]

In that case, W conveyed land to solicitor trustees to hold on the trusts of his marriage settlements. The title-deeds, except for the conveyance to W, were handed over to the trustees, who failed to discover the omission. They were found to have been negligent but not dishonest in that failure which had enabled W, using the conveyance, to mortgage the property to X, who then sold it to Y; and were postponed to Y.

Although that decision is inconsistent with Fry L.J.'s judgment in *Northern Counties* v. *Whipp*,[34] it is suggested that Parker J.'s formulation of the principle is correct, the more so since Hall V.-C. did not find any fraudulent conduct in *Clarke* v. *Palmer*,[35] but postponed the prior mortgagee on the grounds of his negligence.

The attempt to reconcile the decisions in the *Northern Counties* case and *Walker* v. *Linom*[36] on the basis that the first refers to negligence in failing to retain, and the second to negligence in failing to obtain the title deeds, cannot be supported. As Waldock[37] has pointed out, it is not satisfactory to argue that by carelessly failing to keep the title-deeds, the legal mortgagee could prejudice only himself and his carelessness would thus not tend to convict him of fraud. The owner of the legal estate is the one person who could not be prejudiced by misuse of the title-deeds. Normally the person prejudiced is one who enters into a transaction with the person who wrongly has them. The prejudice arises whether the deeds fall into the wrong hands by failure to retain or failure to obtain.

It may be, as Waldock suggests, that Fry L.J. was influenced by the doctrine of constructive fraud.[38] Commenting on the decision in *Ratcliffe* v. *Barnard*,[39] Jeune P. said in *Oliver* v. *Hinton*[40]:

> "I think that what he [James L.J.] meant was . . . negligence so gross as would justify the Court of Chancery in concluding that there had been fraud in an artificial sense of the word—such gross negligence,

[33] *Ibid.* at 114.
[34] (1884) 26 Ch.D. 482.
[35] (1882) 21 Ch.D. 124.
[36] [1907] 2 Ch. 104.
[37] *Waldock on Mortgages* (2nd ed., 1950), p. 397.
[38] *Ibid.*; and see *Le Lievre* v. *Gould* [1893] 1 Q.B. 491.
[39] (1871) 6 Ch.App. 652, C.A.
[40] [1899] 2 Ch. 264 at 275.

for instance, as omitting to make any inquiry as to the title to the property."

It is clear, also, from the judgments in *Derry* v. *Peek*[41] that fraud and gross negligence are to be regarded as two different causes of action and from the above cases, that each of them constitutes a ground for postponing a prior legal mortgagee.

Equitable mortgage followed by legal mortgage

Where the prior interest was equitable, it was liable to be defeated by a bona fide purchaser for value of the legal estate without notice of that prior equitable interest.[41a] A mortgagee is a purchaser for this purpose, and a person who, although not the purchaser of a legal estate, has a better title to the legal estate than the equitable mortgagee, can also displace his priority.

The onus is on the legal mortgagee to show that he is a bona fide[42] purchaser[43] without notice. It is not sufficient for him to show lack of actual notice; if he fails to make such inquiries as would normally be made by a reasonably prudent man of business, he is fixed with constructive knowledge of what he would have discovered by making them. Not only the failure to enquire for the title deeds, but the inability of the mortgagor to produce them or to provide a reasonable excuse for their non-production, would amount to constructive notice of some prior interest.

In addition, where he employed an agent to carry out the transaction, the knowledge of prior interests which his agent obtained or should have obtained was imputed to him so as to prevent him being a purchaser without notice.[44] Originally this rule was applied very strictly, it being possible to impute to the purchaser the knowledge acquired by his agent in an entirely separate transaction on behalf of some other principal.[45] By section 3(2) of the Conveyancing Act 1882, however, the doctrine of imputed notice was restricted to cases in which the agent's knowledge was obtained in the same transaction as that which led to the question of notice being raised.[46] This provision is re-enacted by the Law of Property Act 1925, section 199(1)(ii)(*b*).

The words "ought reasonably to enquire" did not fix the purchaser with any legal duty to inquire but rather meant that he "ought, as a matter of prudence, [to make the inquiries] having regard to what is usually done by men of business under similar circumstances."[47] It was generally considered that the following inquiries ought reasonably to have been made:

[41] (1889) 14 App. Cas. 337.
[41a] *Re Hardy, ex p. Hardy* (1832) 2 Deac. & Ch. 393.
[42] *Att.-Gen.* v. *Biphosphated Guano Co.* (1879) 11 Ch.D. 327.
[43] A mortgagee is a purchaser; *Pilcher* v. *Rawlins* (1872) L.R. 7 Ch. 259.
[44] *Sheldon* v. *Cox* (1764) 2 Eden. 224; *Berwick & Co.* v. *Price* [1905] 1 Ch. 632; *Kennedy* v. *Green* (1834) 3 My. & K. 699.
[45] *Hargreaves* v. *Rothwell* (1836) 1 Keen 154.
[46] *Re Cousins* (1886) 31 Ch.D. 671.
[47] *Per* Lindley L.J. in *Bailey* v. *Barnes* [1894] 1 Ch. 25 at 35.

(1) Inspection of the land. Failure to inspect land occupied by a third party would fix the purchaser with knowledge of the third party's rights.[48]

(2) Investigation of the title for the statutory period applicable to an open contract. Failure so to investigate would fix the purchaser with knowledge of all that he would have discovered by doing so, even if he had stipulated for a shorter contractual root of title[49];

(3) Examination of deeds executed within the statutory period if they actually affected the title. Failure to do so would fix a purchaser with notice of their contents.[50] If, however, the character of the deed was such that it was uncertain whether it would affect the title, he was permitted to rely on an assurance that it did not[51];

(4) Inquiry into the terms of any trust, affecting the land, of whose existence he knew. Knowledge of the trust fixed him with knowledge of the interests of the beneficiaries.[52]

Whether the purchaser had actual notice was a fact to be established by evidence, but the decided cases are at variance as to whether information must be given by a person interested in the property in order to fix the purchaser with notice.[53]

In spite of the principle that a subsequent purchaser of a legal estate would be fixed with notice of a prior incumbrance if the mortgagor was unable to produce the title deeds, the courts found it necessary to develop a separate doctrine of "gross negligence" in relation to their non-production.

In *Hewitt* v. *Loosemore*[54] and in *Hunt* v. *Elmes*[55] it was said that to deprive a man of the protection of the legal estate he must have been guilty of either fraud or gross and wilful negligence. In *Oliver* v. *Hinton*[56] Lindley M.R. followed these authorities, holding that a purchaser for value of a legal estate, without notice of a prior equitable incumbrance, would not be permitted to assert the superiority of the legal estate if he had, himself, been guilty of such gross negligence as to render it unjust to deprive the equitable incumbrancer of his priority. An attempt to describe the requisite degree of negligence was made in *Hudston* v. *Viney*[57] where Eve J. said:

---

[48] *Hunt* v. *Luck* [1902] 1 Ch. 428; *Lloyds Bank* v. *Rossett* [1988] 3 W.L.R. 1301.

[49] *Re Nisbet and Potts' Contract* [1906] 1 Ch. 386.

[50] *Bisco* v. *Earl of Banbury* (1676) 1 Ch.Cas. 287.

[51] *English and Scottish Mercantile Investment Trust* v. *Brunton* [1892] 2 Q.B. 700.

[52] *Perham* v. *Kempster* [1907] 1 Ch. 373.

[53] *Barnhart* v. *Greenshields* (1853) 9 Moo.P.C. 18 at 36; explained in *Reeves* v. *Pope* [1914] 2 K.B. 284; *cf. Lloyd* v. *Banks* (1868) L.R. 3 Ch. 488, where the court was dealing with notice under the rule in *Dearle* v. *Hall*. The effect of notice, to trustees, of dealings with equitable interests is regulated by the L.P.A. 1925, s.137(3).

[54] (1851) 9 Hare. 449.

[55] (1860) 2 De G., F. & J. 578.

[56] [1899] 2 Ch. 264.

[57] [1921] 1 Ch. 98 at 104.

"It must at least be carelessness of so aggravated a nature as to amount to the neglect of precautions which the ordinary reasonable man would have observed, and to indicate an attitude of mental indifference to obvious risks."

It is not clear why such conduct would not be held to fix the purchaser of the legal estate with constructive notice of the prior incumbrance,[58] and in view of the repeated failure of courts to give anything but the most general description of "gross negligence," one must sympathise (*pace* Lord Chelmsford) with the views of Rolfe B. in *Wilson* v. *Brett*[59]:

"I said that I could see no difference between negligence and gross negligence—that it was the same thing with the addition of a vituperative epithet."

In *Oliver* v. *Hinton*,[60] X deposited the deeds of some property with O, then two years later purported to convey it to H. H's agent asked to see the deeds but X replied that he could not, as they related also to other property. At first it was held that O retained priority because H had constructive notice of the prior incumbrance. The Court of Appeal affirmed the decision, but on the ground that H's agent had acted with such gross carelessness that it would be unjust to deprive O of priority.

However unnecessary the doctrine of postponement by gross negligence may be, it is undoubtedly part of the law and the decided cases are authority for the following propositions as to when a prior equitable mortgagee[61] will be postponed:

(1) The weight of the authorities favours the view that the degree of negligence needed to bring about a postponement is the same whether the prior mortgagee is a legal or an equitable mortgagee, though a contrary view had been expressed.[62]

(2) A prior equitable mortgagee will be postponed if:
   (a) his title depends on the deeds and he fails to acquire any of them,[63] and
   (b) he has a right to obtain them and not only fails to do so but fails to give a reasonable explanation for such failure.[64]

(3) A prior equitable mortgagee will not be postponed if:
   (a) he inquired for the deeds and was given a reasonable excuse for their non-production[65];

---

[58] *Le Neve* v. *Le Neve* (1748) 3 Atk. 646.
[59] (1843) 11 M. & W. 113 at 116.
[60] [1899] 2 Ch. 264.
[61] *Taylor* v. *Russell* [1891] 1 Ch. 8 at 14–20; [1892] A.C. 244 at 262.
[62] *National Provincial Bank* v. *Jackson* (1886) 33 Ch.D. 1, C.A.
[63] See *Rice* v. *Rice* (1854) 2 Drew. 73 at 81 *per* Kindersley V.-C.; *Farrand* v. *Yorkshire Banking Co.* (1889) 40 Ch.D. 182.
[64] *Worthington* v. *Morgan* (1849) 16 Sim. 547; *Colyer* v. *Finch* (1856) 5 H.L.C. at 905; *Clarke* v. *Palmer* (1882) 21 Ch.D. 124.
[65] *Hewitt* v. *Loosemore* (1851) 9 Hare. 449; *Agra Bank* v. *Barry* (1874) L.R. 7 H.L. 135; *Barnett* v. *Weston* (1806) 12 Ves. 130; *Manners* v. *Mew* (1885) 29 Ch.D. 725.

(b) he received some of the deeds but reasonably believed he was receiving all of them.[66] The same applies if it was represented to him that the packet of deeds, handed to him contained all the necessary deeds and he honestly believed that to be true. He would not lose priority by failure to examine them[67];

(c) he lent the deeds to the mortgagor on a reasonable representation of his requiring them, and was diligent in inquiring for them[68];

(d) he allowed the deeds to be in the custody of someone in a fiduciary relationship to him, who fraudulently or negligently parted with them.[69] But he would be postponed by estoppel[70] if the fiduciary had authority to deal with them.

If he was a second mortgagee and at the time of making the advance the deeds were in the hands of a prior mortgagee, he would not be deprived of his priority by failure to give notice of his interest to the earlier incumbrances, even though that resulted in the deeds being returned to the mortgagor on discharge of the earlier mortgage. The same applied if the deeds had not come into existence at the time of the mortgage, as where the leasehold was mortgaged before the head lessor executed the lease.

Where a mortgagee left deeds in the hands of his trustee with authority to deal with them, he was not protected against subsequent equitable incumbrances by setting limits on that authority.[71] But beneficiaries who so act are protected if the trustee exceeds his apparent authority.[72]

Two successive equitable mortgages[73]

As with successive legal mortgages, priority normally depended on the order of creation, but with the additional condition that, for that rule to apply, the equities had to be equal. Inequitable behaviour on the part of the prior mortgagee could cause him to be postponed. Generally this consisted of misconduct in relation to the title-deeds, which has already been discussed.

[66] *Ratcliffe* v. *Barnard* (1871) L.R. 6 Ch. 652.
[67] *Dixon* v. *Muckleston* (1872) App. 8 Ch. 155; *Colyer* v. *Finch* (1856) 5 H.L.C. 905.
[68] *Peter* v. *Russell* (1716) 1 Eq.Cas.Abr. 321; *Martinez* v. *Cooper* (1826) 2 Russ 198; *Layard* v. *Maud* (1867) L.R. 4 Eq. 397.
[69] *Shropshire Union Railways and Canal Co.* v. *R.* (1875) L.R. 7 H.L. 496; *Re Vernon Ewens & Co.* (1886) 33 Ch.D. 402; *Re Richards* (1890) 45 Ch.D. 589; *Hill* v. *Peters* [1918] 2 Ch. 273. In *Carritt* v. *Real and Personal Advance Co.* (1889) 42 Ch.D. 263 it was held that where trustees advanced trust moneys on mortgage, the beneficiaries were not postponed to a subsequent equitable incumbrancer simply because they allowed the deeds to be taken by the trustees, who had subsequently misused them.
[70] *Rimmer* v. *Webster* [1902] 2 Ch. 163; see also *Heid* v. *Reliance Finance Corp. Pty.* (1984) 49 A.L.R. 229, High Ct. of Australia.
[71] *Perry-Herrick* v. *Atwood* (1857) 2 De.G. & J. 21. And see *Abbey National Building Society* v. *Cann*, *The Times*, March 15, 1989.
[72] *Capell* v. *Winter* [1907] 2 Ch. 376.
[73] *Rice* v. *Rice* (1853) 2 Drew. 73; *cf. Rimmer* v. *Webster* [1902] 2 Ch. 163. See also *Heid* v. *Reliance Finance Corp. Pty.* (1984) 49 A.L.R. 229, High Ct. of Australia.

Priority of mortgages of equitable interests in personalty

As between equitable interests, there is a rule that where the equities are equal, the first in time prevails. *Dearle* v. *Hall*[74] was a case in which a person having a beneficial interest in a fund assigned parts of that interest to D and to S respectively for valuable consideration, and then, advertising the fund as unencumbered, sold his entire beneficial interest to H. H made enquiries of the trustees and, learning of no prior incumbrance, completed the purchase and gave the trustees notice to pay the dividends of the fund to him. It was held that H gained priority over the prior interests of D and S.

In so holding, Plumer M.R. cited the case of *Ryall* v. *Rolle*.[75] There it was said that, if a person had a right to possession and failed to exercise it, leaving the property in possession of another and thereby enabling him to gain a false and delusive credit, he must take the consequences. This may include loss of priority to a subsequent purchaser who does exercise his right in the appropriate way, that is, by giving notice to the owner of the legal estate or interest in the property. In affirming that decision,[76] Sir Thomas Plumer M.R. held that D and S, by neglecting to give the trustees notice of the assignments to them, could not assert the priority arising from the earlier creation of their interests, against H.

Before *Dearle* v. *Hall*, there had never been a case in which a prior mortgagee of an equitable interest in personalty had been postponed to a subsequent mortgagee except where there was fraud on the part of the prior mortgagee.[77] Although the rule in *Dearle* v. *Hall* was approved by the House of Lords in *Foster* v. *Cockerell*,[78] the reasons for its adoption were not clearly and consistently expressed and those reasons were criticised in *Ward* v. *Duncombe*.[79] The rule, itself, however, continued to be accepted, and was developed in a series of cases dealing with the nature of notice, the manner in which it was given or received, and the effect of the subsequent incumbrancer's knowledge of a prior mortgage. As the rule applied to equitable interests in all forms of personalty, it regulated the priorities of successive mortgages of equitable interests in land, such interests being treated as interests in personalty by virtue of the doctrine of conversion.[80] It does not apply "until a trust has been created" and this has been held to exclude its application to interests of purchasers under a contract of sale or a lease.[81]

---

[74] (1823) 3 Russ. 1; affirmed on appeal, *ibid.* at 55. The appeal in the similar case of *Loveridge* v. *Cooper* (1823) 3 Russ. 30,was heard together with that in *Dearle* v. *Hall*.

[75] (1750) 1 Ves.Sen. 348.

[76] *Dearle* v. *Hall* (1823) 3 Russ. 29.

[77] *Cooper* v. *Fynemore* (1814) 3 Russ. 60, a decision by Plumer V.-C.

[78] (1835) 3 Cl. and F. 456.

[79] *Ward* v. *Duncombe sub nom. Re Wyatt* [1892] 1 Ch. 188, C.A., at 209; [1893] A.C. 369 at 392, *per* Lord Macnaghten; *B.S. Lyle Ltd.* v. *Rosher* [1959] 1 W.L.R. 8, H.L.

[80] *Lee* v. *Howlett* (1856) 2 K. & J. 531.

[81] *Property Discount Corporation Ltd.* v. *Lyon Group Ltd.* [1981] 1 W.L.R. 300.

In *Dearle* v. *Hall*, it was not necessary to consider what would have been the situation if H had known, at any time, of the existing interests of D and S, because he had no such knowledge, either actual or constructive. It was later decided[82] that the subsequent incumbrancer who gave notice first would gain priority provided that, at the time he advanced the money, he had no such knowledge. He was not adversely affected if he later acquired such knowledge and then gave notice, that being the very event which would cause him to give notice.[83]

Although the rule is expressed in terms of gaining priority by giving notice, it is in fact the receipt of the notice by the trustee, or other legal owner, not the giving of notice by the subsequent incumbrancer, that affords priority.[84] Thus in *Lloyd* v. *Banks*,[85] priority was given to the earlier incumbrancer over a later incumbrancer who gave notice when the trustee's knowledge of the earlier incumbrancer had been derived from a newspaper report. Knowledge on which a reasonable man, or an ordinary man of business, would act in the execution of the trust, would be sufficient. Oral notice would be sufficient, provided that it was clear and distinct[86]; but this did not include knowledge imparted in the course of a casual conversation.[87] It does not appear that the decision in *Lloyd* v. *Banks* would apply so as to give a later incumbrancer priority over an earlier incumbrancer who had not given notice[88]; as Megarry[89] puts it, "stronger measures are needed to upset the natural order of the mortgages than are needed to maintain it."

It was laid down in *Addison* v. *Cox*[90] that notice, to be effective, must be given to the legal owner of the fund. Notice given to an executor or administrator who renounces probate is therefore ineffective,[91] as is notice given to a trustee before his appointment. In *Ipswich Permanent Money Club Ltd.* v. *Arthy*,[92] this was done and held to be effective on the principle of *Lloyd* v. *Banks*, but it is thought that the effect would be only to preserve existing priorities, not to prefer a later incumbrancer to one earlier who had not given notice.

Where the legal owner is a bank, notice is given when, in the ordinary

---

[82] *Spencer* v. *Clarke* (1878) 9 Ch.D. 137; *Mutual Life Assurance Society* v. *Langley* (1886) 32 Ch.D. 460; *Re Holmes* (1885) 29 Ch.D. 786. These cases show that the later incumbrancer who gives notice first obtains priority provided he does not know of the earlier incumbrance when he advances the money; his state of knowledge when he gives notice to the trustees is immaterial.

[83] *Wortley* v. *Birkhead* (1754) 2 Ves.Sen. 571.

[84] *Calisher* v. *Forbes* (1871) 7 Ch.App. 109; *Johnstone* v. *Cox* (1881) 19 Ch.D. 17, C.A.

[85] (1868) 3 Ch. App. 488. See *ante*, p. 347.

[86] *Browne* v. *Savage* (1859) 4 Drew 635; *cf. Re Worcester* (1868) 3 Ch.App. 555 where a statement of a directors' meeting was held sufficient notice.

[87] *Re Tichener* (1865) 35 Beav. 317.

[88] *Arden* v. *Arden* (1885) 29 Ch.D. 702.

[89] Megarry & Wade, *The Law of Real Property* (5th ed., 1984), p. 994.

[90] (1872) 8 Ch.App. 76.

[91] *Re Dallas* [1904] 2 Ch. 385.

[92] [1920] 2 Ch. 257.

course of business, it would be read. In *Calisher* v. *Forbes*,[92a] A left notice with the bank after closing hours on one day, while B gave notice immediately the bank opened the next day. It was held that the two notices were to be treated as having been received simultaneously, with the result that the charges ranked in order of creation.[93] Had the charges been created simultaneously, A and B would have shared the fund rateably.[94] Notice given to the solicitors of the trustees was held to be effective in *Foster* v. *Cockerell*[95] but later decisions held that this will be the case only where the solicitors are agents to receive notice on the trustees' behalf.[96]

Where the fund is in court, notice given to the trustees before the fund was paid into court is effective, and it is the duty of the trustees to inform the court of such notice.[97] A notice given to the trustees after payment into court is not effective, and only a stop order will gain priority.

Where there is more than one trustee, it is advisable to give notice to all, since that notice will continue to be effective even if they all retire or die without communicating the notice to their successors.[98] If notice is given to only one trustee, it will be effective against all incumbrances created during his trusteeship, even after his death or retirement.[99] But it will not be effective against an incumbrance created after his trusteeship has come to an end, unless he has communicated that notice to at least one of the remaining trustees.[1] The creator of the earlier incumbrance will have to give a fresh notice in order to protect himself.

If the mortgagor is a trustee, his knowledge does not constitute notice so as to affect priorities. Clearly it would be in his interest to conceal his knowledge from subsequent incumbrancers.[2] Where the mortgagee is a trustee, his knowledge does constitute notice, as it is in his interest to disclose the existence of an existing incumbrance.[3]

The rule in *Dearle* v. *Hall* does not apply to a judgment creditor[4] or

---

[92a] (1871) 7 Ch.App. 109.

[93] *Boss* v. *Hopkinson* (1870) 18 W.R. 725. If notices bearing different dates are received on the same day, the notice dated earlier ranks first.

[94] *Re Metropolitan Rail Co.*, *Re Tower Hill Extension Act*, *Re Rawlins' Estate*, *ex p. Kent* (1871) 19 W.R. 596.

[95] (1835) 3 Cl. & Fin. 456. See *ante*, p. 350.

[96] *Saffron Walden Second Benefit Building Society* v. *Rayner* (1880) 14 Ch.D. 406; *Arden* v. *Arden* (1885) 29 Ch.D. 702 at 709.

[97] *Livesey* v. *Harding* (1856) 23 Beav. 141; *Brearcliffe* v. *Dorrington* (1850) 4 De G. & Sm. 122.

[98] *Re Wasdale, Brittin* v. *Partridge* [1899] 1 Ch. 163. For the complications which occur when there are two trustees and successive incumbrancers give notice to one only, see Fisher and Lightwood, *The Law of Mortgage* (10th ed., 1988) n. (a) at p. 501.

[99] *Ward* v. *Duncombe*, [1893] A.C. 369 at 394, *per* Lord Macnaghten.

[1] *Timson* v. *Ramsbottom* (1837) 2 Keen 35; criticised in *Ward* v. *Duncombe* [1893] A.C. 369 and followed in *Re Phillips Trusts* [1903] 1 Ch. 183. Although criticised in *Ward* v. *Duncombe* it was accepted by Lord Herschell in the same case, at 381, as it has been in *Meux* v. *Bell* (1841) 1 Hare 73; *Re Hall* (1880) 7 L.R.Ir. 180; *Re Wyatt, White* v. *Ellis*, [1892] 1 Ch. 188, C.A.

[2] *Browne* v. *Savage* (1859) 4 Drew 635 at 641; *Lloyds Bank* v. *Pearson* [1901] 1 Ch. 865.

[3] *Newman* v. *Newman* (1885) 28 Ch.D. 674.

[4] *Scott* v. *Lord Hastings* (1858) 4 K. & J. 633.

assignee in bankruptcy[5] of an incumbrancer to enable him to gain, by giving notice, a priority which he has lost by failure to do so, since they stand in his shoes and take subject to prior equities.[6] Nor can a volunteer gain priority over earlier incumbrances by giving notice,[7] though he can protect his priority against later incumbrances by doing so.

It is not altogether clear whether the right to tack applies to mortgages of equitable interests in personalty. In *West* v. *Williams*[8] it was held that it did, where the mortgage was expressed to be made to cover further advances. In *Re Weniger's Policy*[9] it was decided that notice of further advances must be given to the trustees if the mortgage did not cover them. It has been suggested[10] that a further advance should not be made without inquiring of the trustees whether notice of a subsequent incumbrance has been received.

At any given time a trustee is entitled to pay out the capital or income of a trust fund to those persons of whose interests he is aware. So, while notice is not essential to the validity of a mortgage (as between the mortgagor and mortgagee),[11] a mortgagee who gives notice to a trustee protects his own interests by so doing. A trustee will be presumed to have knowledge of such interests as would have been revealed to him by inspection of the documents handed over to him.[12]

He is not liable to a prior assignee of whose interest he is unaware,[13] if he pays out the fund or any part thereof to a subsequent incumbrancer of whom he is aware. He is bound only to pay out to all those of whose existence he knows.[14] If he is a successor trustee, he is not bound to make inquiry of his predecessor as to what notices he received. In *Low* v. *Bouverie*,[15] it was decided that a trustee was under no duty to answer enquiries, from a beneficiary or a prospective mortgagee, as to the extent to which the property was incumbered. If he did make such answers, he was bound only to answer to the best of his knowledge and belief and did not have to make enquiries to ascertain whether his existing knowledge was adequate.

The effect of this is somewhat to reduce the value of the rule in *Dearle* v. *Hall*, since a purchaser who received an honest but incorrect reply from a trustee as to the non-existence of prior incumbrances would have no remedy if these existed, unless the trustee was estopped from denying such non-existence. The purchaser's situation has, in this respect, been somewhat improved by the Law of Property Act 1925, section 137(8).

[5] *Re Anderson* [1911] 1 K.B. 896.
[6] *Re Atkinson* (1852) 2 De G. M. & G. 140.
[7] *Justice* v. *Wynne* (1860) 12 I.Ch.Rep. 289.
[8] [1899] 1 Ch. 132.
[9] [1910] 2 Ch. 291.
[10] Fisher and Lightwood, *The Law of Mortgages* (10th ed., 1988), p. 487 and note (u).
[11] *Burn* v. *Carvalho* (1839) 4 My. & Cr. 690; *Gorringe* v. *Irwell India-Rubber and Gutta-Percha Works* (1886) 34 Ch.D. 128, C.A.
[12] *Hallows* v. *Lloyd* (1888) 39 Ch.D. 686.
[13] *Phipps* v. *Lovegrove* (1873) L.R. 16 Eq. 80.
[14] *Hodgson* v. *Hodgson* (1837) 2 Keen 704.
[15] [1891] 3 Ch. 82.

PRIORITY ACCORDING TO THE 1925 LEGISLATION

General rules

We have already seen that, before 1926, priorities of mortgages of interests in land depended on the date of creation and the superiority of the legal estate, while the rule in *Dearle* v. *Hall* governed priorities between equitable interests in pure personalty which included interests arising under a trust for sale of land.

The 1925 legislation reduced the number of legal estates and put the titles of limited owners "behind the curtain" as equitable interests. The registration system set up by the Land Charges Act 1925 was intended to provide a register of interests which would bind the legal estate in the hands of a subsequent purchaser. Consequently, equitable interests which are overreached and become charges on the proceeds of sale of the land have no place in such a register. It therefore follows that the rules for determining priority must depend on whether the interest mortgaged is legal (in which case it is capable of binding the land in the hands of a subsequent purchaser) or equitable, and not on whether the mortgage itself is legal or equitable.

The effect of the 1925 legislation is that priority of a mortgage of a legal estate in land depends either on possession of the title deeds or on registration, while priority of a mortgage of any equitable interest, whether in realty or personalty, is governed by the rule in *Dearle* v. *Hall* as altered by the Law of Property Act 1925, section 137(1).

Mortgages of legal estates in unregistered land

The Law of Property Act 1925 provides, by section 85(1), that a legal mortgage of a fee simple can be created only by a demise for a term of years absolute or by a charge by deed expressed to be by way of legal mortgage. Both these methods of creation admit the possibility of successive legal mortgages of a legal estate, in which case a system of priorities based on the superiority of the legal estate is inappropriate.

In the rare pre-1925 cases where successive legal mortgages were created by the grant of successive terms of years, priority would normally have been determined by the order of creation. This exposed a later mortgagee or purchaser who had made all reasonable inquiries to the risks that the mortgagor might fraudulently conceal a prior incumbrance. *Grierson* v. *National Provincial Bank of England Ltd.*[16] affords a good example of the difficulties caused by fraudulent concealment. The mortgagor created an equitable mortgage by deposit followed by a legal mortgage by conveyance of the fee simple. The legal mortgagee discovered the existence of the prior equitable mortgagee but did not inform the equitable mortgagee of his own interest. When the equitable mortgage was paid off the deeds were returned to the mortgagor, who negotiated another equitable mortgage by

---

[16] [1913] 2 Ch. 18. See *ante*, p. 343.

deposit with the bank. Although there was no way in which the bank could have discovered the existence of the concealed legal mortgage, it was held that priority went in order of creation.

Where a mortgage of a legal estate in unregistered land is protected by deposit of title deeds, it is not capable of being registered as a land charge. Priorities between such mortgages are regulated by the pre-1926 rules. It appears that a "protected" mortgage is one which was originally protected, rather than one which has been continuously protected.[17]

Mortgages which are not protected by a deposit of title deeds and were created after 1925, are registrable as land charges. They are of two types, 'puisne mortgages' and general equitable charges. The Land Charges Act 1972 section 2(4) defines these as follows: a puisne mortgage is a legal mortgage not protected by a deposit of documents relating to the legal estate affected. A general equitable charge is any equitable charge on land which:

(1) is not included in any other class of land charge; and
(2) is not secured by a deposit of documents relating to the legal estate affected; and
(3) does not arise, or affect any interest arising, under a trust for sale or settlement.

The Land Charges Act 1972, section 4(5) deals with the effect of failure to register such charges, and reads as follows:

> "A land charge of class B and a land charge of class C (other than an estate contract) created or arising on or after 1st January 1926 shall be void as against a purchaser of the land charged with it, or of any interest in such land, unless the land charge is registered in the appropriate register before the completion of the purchase."

The other provisions relevant to priorities between unprotected mortgages are section 13 of the Law of Property Act 1925, which reads:

> "This Act shall not prejudicially affect the right or interest of any person arising out of or consequent on the possession by him of any documents relating to a legal estate in land, nor affect any question arising out of or consequent upon any omission to obtain or any other absence of possession by any person of any documents relating to a legal estate in land"

and section 97 of the Law of Property Act 1925, as amended by section 18(1) and Sched. 3, para. 1 of the Land Charges Act 1972:

> "Every mortgage affecting a legal estate in land made after the commencement of this Act, whether legal or equitable (not being a mortgage protected by the deposit of documents relating to the legal estate affected) shall rank according to the date of registration as a land charge pursuant to the Land Charges Act 1972."

[17] Megarry and Wade, *The Law of Real Property* (5th ed., 1984), p. 997.

Priorities between unprotected mortgages are regulated by the above provisions, and three possibilities exist:

(1) If the first mortgage is registered before the second is made, then the first has priority over the second even if the first is equitable and the second is legal. By section 198(1) of the Law of Property Act 1925, registration under the Land Charges Acts of any instrument or matter required or authorised to be registered under the Act is deemed to constitute actual notice of the interest registered to all persons and for all purposes connected with the land affected, as from the date of registration or other prescribed date, and so long as the registration continues to be in force. This prevents the subsequent legal mortgagee from claiming to be a purchaser without notice of the prior equitable interest.

(2) If the first mortgage is made but remains unregistered, it will be void, by section 4(5) of the Land Charges Act 1972, against a later mortgagee. This is so regardless of the legal or equitable character of the two mortgages.

(3) In both the above cases, the same conclusions are reached regarding priorities whether section 4(5) of the Land Charges Act 1972 or section 97 of the Law of Property Act 1925 is applied.

Consider, however, the following sequence of events:

(a) L mortgages Blackacre to A.
(b) L mortgages Blackacre to B.
(c) A registers.
(d) B registers.

The effect of section 4(5) of the Land Charges Act 1972 would be to make A's mortgage void against B; thus the order of priority is B, A. On the other hand, section 97 of the Law of Property Act 1925 provides for priority to run according to order of registration, in which case the order is A, B. Earlier commentators disagree as to which of these two solutions is to be adopted and there is no judicial decision on the point.[18]

The arguments advanced in favour of the first view are as follows:

(a) If A's mortgage is void against B, it has no existence with respect to B, and thus it is difficult to see how its subsequent registration can adversely affect B.

(b) The Law of Property Act 1925, section 97, refers not simply to registration, but to registration as "a land charge pursuant to the Land Charges Act." It is thus possible to interpret section 97 of the Law of Property Act 1925 as incorporating by reference, the

---

[18] The problem was considered by Megarry ((1940) 7 C.L.J. 243) who, while stating that the subject is not one for dogmatism, comes down in favour of the first solution which is also adopted by Waldock (*Mortgages* (2nd ed., 1950), pp. 410 *et seq.*) and, more tentatively, by Fisher and Lightwood (*The Law of Mortgage* (10th ed., 1988), p. 509).

rule in section 4(5) of the Land Charges Act 1972 in which case there is no conflict.

(c) In relation to each of the five registers set up by the Land Charges Act 1972, it is provided that in respect of each type of incumbrance, failure to register it makes it void against a subsequent purchaser. It is thought improbable that the Law of Property Act 1925, section 97, was intended to destroy the symmetry of the scheme so set up by establishing a different rule for land charges.

(d) In the same way that, of two irreconcilable provisions in one Act, the later prevails, the provisions of the Land Charges Act 1925, the later statute, should prevail over those of the Law of Property Act 1925 where they conflict irreconcilably.

However, the arguments against this can be summarised as follows:

(e) The simple reading of the Law of Property Act 1925, section 97, is that the first mortgage to be registered has priority.[19]

(f) The general opinion appears to be that, probably, priority will depend on the date of registration as mentioned in the Law of Property Act 1925, section 97, because that section deals expressly with priority of mortgages. Whereas the Land Charges Act 1972, section 4(5) deals with the avoidance of charges as against purchasers, and mortgagees are only brought in by reference to the Land Charges Act 1972, section 17(1).[20]

Perhaps the solution lies in adopting (b) above, according to which argument the two statutes do not conflict, thus avoiding the unlikely conclusion that Parliament simultaneously enacted contradictory statutes, one expressly referring to the other.[21]

Insoluble problems involving three or more registrable mortgages have been discussed[22]; such problems have been solved in practice by resorting to the doctrine of subrogation. However, this solution is totally arbitrary since there is no reason for breaking into the circle in which the priorities run at one place rather than another; whatever is done, one creditor will lose a priority which he arguably has over another. It appears that the judicially favoured approach would be to take the mortgages in order of creation and begin by subrogating the latest mortgages to the earliest.[23]

No such difficulties arise where one mortgage is protected and the other is not. If only the first mortgage is protected, its priority runs from the date of its creation and it will have priority over the second, subject to the rules, discussed earlier, regarding loss of priority due to fraud or gross negligence. If only the second mortgage is protected, one of two situations can

---

[19] Hargreaves, (1950) 13 M.L.R. 534. Megarry and Wade (*The Law of Real Property* (5th ed., 1984)) regard the argument for this reading as unconvincing.

[20] *Emmet on Title* (19th ed., 1985), para. 25.103.

[21] See Megarry and Wade, *The Law of Real Property* (5th ed., 1984), p. 1001.

[22] *Ibid.*; (1968) Conv.(N.S.) pp. 325 *et seq.* (W. A. Lee).

[23] Megarry and Wade, *The Law of Real Property* (5th ed., 1984), p. 1002; (1961) 71 Yale L.J. 53 (G. Gilmore).

arise. Where the first mortgage is registered before the second is created, its priority ranks from the date of the registration by section 97 of the Law of Property Act 1925. Where it is not, it is void against the second mortgage for want of registration. The second mortgage takes priority from the date of its creation and therefore ranks first even if the first mortgage is subsequently registered.

Mortgages of a legal estate in registered land

The most important provision dealing with priorities among such mortgages is section 29 of the Land Registration Act 1925, which reads:

> "Subject to any entry to the contrary on the register, registered charges on the same land shall as between themselves rank according to the order in which they are entered on the register, and not according to the order in which they are created."

There is, or is deemed to be, a contrary entry on the register when:

(1) a charge contains provisions altering the normal rules as to priority;

(2) after the registration of two or more charges, a deed altering their priorities is noted on the register;

(3) a charge secures further advances. This fact will be noted in the register so as to give warning of the possible priority of any further advance;

(4) a chargee claims that a charge has priority by virtue of a statute. The fact of such claim is entered on the register. If the charge itself contains a statement about statutory priority, the registration of the charge constitutes a contrary entry.

Since, by sections 20 and 23 of the Land Registration Act 1925, the transferee of registered land or a legal estate therein takes subject only to overriding interests and to incumbrances appearing on the register, a subsequent registered charge has priority over an earlier charge not registered or protected on the register. In *De Lusignan* v. *Johnson*[24] it was held that a person who acquired a registered charge took free from an unprotected estate contract although he had express knowledge of its existence.

The creation and protection of unregistered mortgages of registered land is dealt with by section 106 of the Land Registration Act 1925, which, as substituted by section 26(1) of the Administration of Justice Act 1977, reads as follows:

> "(1) The proprietor of any registered land may, subject to any entry to the contrary on the register, mortgage by deed or otherwise, the land or any part thereof in any manner which would have been permissible if the land had not been registered, and with the like effect. Provided that the registered land comprised in the mortgage is described

---

[24] (1973) 230 E.G. 499.

(whether by reference to the register or in any other manner) in such a way as is sufficient to enable the registrar to identify the same without reference to any other documents.

(2) Unless and until the mortgage becomes a registered charge[25];

  (a) it shall take effect only in equity, and

  (b) it shall be capable of being overridden as a minor interest unless it is protected as provided by sub-section (3);

(3) A mortgage which is not a registered charge may be protected on the register by;

  (a) a notice under section 49 of this Act,

  (b) any such other notice as may be prescribed,

  (c) a caution under section 54 of this Act;

(4) A mortgage which is not a registered charge shall devolve and may be transferred, discharged, surrendered or otherwise dealt with by the same instruments and in the same manner as if the land has not been registered."

The amendment abolished the mortgage caution which was, formerly, the only way of protecting an unregistered mortgage by deed, and the Administration of Justice Act 1977, section 26(2) provided for the conversion of any mortgage already protected by a mortgage caution into a registered charge.

The effect of sections 101(2) and 106(4) of the Land Registration Act 1925 is that, until protected by notice or caution, mortgages created off the register take effect only in equity and, as minor interests, will be overridden by a disposition for valuable consideration.

There is no provision expressly regulating priorities among successive mortgages created off the register. It has been argued[26] that the Land Registration Act 1925, section 52, has the effect of giving priority among such mortgages in order of their creation, but this has been doubted.[27]

A lien on registered land can be created by deposit of the land certificate. The Land Registration Act 1925, section 66 reads:

"The proprietor of any registered land or charge may, subject to the overriding interests, if any, to any entry to the contrary on the register, and to any estates, interests, charges or rights registered or protected on the register at the date of the deposit, create a lien on the registered land or charge by deposit of the land certificate or charge certificate; and such lien shall, subject as aforesaid, be equivalent to a lien created in the case of unregistered land by the deposit of documents of title or of the mortgage deed by an owner entitled to his own benefit to the registered estate, or a mortgagee beneficially entitled to the mortgage, as the case may be."

[25] By the Land Registration Act 1925, s.3(xiii) the term "registered charge" includes a mortgage or incumbrance registered under that Act.
[26] (1977) 43 L.Q.R. 541 (R. J. Smith).
[27] Hayton, *Registered Land* (3rd ed., 1981), p. 141.

There is no statutory provision regulating priorities of mortgages so created, but rule 239 of the Land Registration Rules 1925, provides that the depositee may obtain protection against dealings with the land or charge by giving notice in writing to the registrar. Such a notice operates as a caution under section 54 of the Land Registration Act 1925. He is, of course, also protected against a subsequent registered disposition since the intending disponor cannot produce the certificate to the registrar.

Mortgages of equitable interests

Priorities among mortgages of equitable interests in land, arising under a trust, are regulated by the rule in *Dearle* v. *Hall* as amended by sections 137 and 138 of the Law of Property Act 1925.[27a] According to that rule, priority depends on the order in which notice of the mortgages is received by the trustees. By section 137(10), the rule does not apply until a trust has been created. It is considered that this provision excludes the interest of a purchaser under a contract of sale or lease.[28] Section 137(3) provides that the notice must be in writing, whereas under the original rule, oral notice was sufficient.[29]

Section 137(2) specifies the persons to whom notice must be given, namely, the trustees of the settlement if the interest is in settled land; the trustees of the trust for sale if the interest arises under such trust; and, in any other cases, the estate owner (*i.e.* the owner of the legal estate) of the land affected. Under the old law it was advisable to give notice to all the trustees,[30] and the 1925 legislation does not alter this position.

Section 137(4) sets out the procedure to be adopted where the valid notice cannot be served either because there are no trustees or because its service would involve unreasonable cost or delay. The purchaser may require the endorsement of a memorandum on the instrument creating the trust or (where the trust is created by statute or operation of law) on the document under which the equitable interest is acquired or which evidences its devolution. Such an indorsement has the same effect as notice to the trustees.

By section 138 of the Law of Property Act 1925, a trust corporation may be nominated to receive the notice and where this is the case, notice to the trustees is ineffective. Notice does not affect priorities until delivered to the corporation.

[27a] The Land Registration Act 1925, s.102(2) formerly made provisions for priorities between certain dealings of equitable interests in registered land to be determined in accordance with the lodging of priority cautions and inhibitions in the Minor Interests Index. This subs. has now been repealed by the Land Registration Act 1986, s.5(1). Consequently, s.137(1) now determines questions of priority both in respect of registered and unregistered land. For the way in which existing entries are to be treated, see 1986 Act, s.5(2)–(4).

[28] Megarry and Wade, *The Law of Real Property* (5th ed., 1984), p. 1003.

[29] *Browne* v. *Savage* (1859) 4 Drew 635; *Re Worcester* (1868) 3 Ch.App. 555.

[30] *Lloyds Bank* v. *Pearson* [1901] 1 Ch. 865; *Timson* v. *Ramsbottom* (1837) 2 Keen 35; *Re Wasdale, Brittin* v. *Partridge* [1899] 1 Ch. 163; *Ward* v. *Duncombe* [1892] 1 Ch. 188, C.A.

The Law of Property Act 1925, section 137(8), (9) brings about a change in the law relating to the duty to produce notices. In the case of *Low* v. *Bouverie*[31] it was held that trustees were not bound to answer inquiries by a prospective mortgagee or a beneficiary regarding the extent to which a beneficiary's share was incumbered. By section 137(8) any person interested in the equitable interest may require the trustee to produce all such notices; and section 137(9) places a corresponding liability on the estate owner.

PRIORITY BETWEEN MORTGAGEE AND BENEFICIAL OWNER

In the case of *Williams and Glyn's Bank* v. *Boland*[32] the husband was registered as sole proprietor of the matrimonial home in which he and his wife lived and towards the purchase of which she had substantially contributed. She had not protected the equitable interest thus acquired by entering a notice, caution or restriction on the register. The husband, without her consent, mortgaged the house to the bank to secure his business indebtedness and the bank made no inquiries of her. The question which arose was whether that equitable interest constituted an overriding interest by which the mortgagee Bank was bound.

Section 70(1)(g) of the Land Registration Act 1925 provides that the class of overriding interests shall include:

> "The rights of every person in actual occupation of the land or in receipt of the rents and profits thereof, save where enquiry is made of such person and the rights are not disclosed . . . "

Lord Wilberforce found no difficulty in concluding that a spouse, living in a house, has an actual occupation capable of conferring protection, as an overriding interest, upon his or her rights.[33] In so concluding, he rejected arguments that the occupation, to come within the section, must be inconsistent with the rights of the vendor.[34] He then went on to consider whether such equitable interests were "minor interests" as defined by section 3(xv) of the Land Registration Act 1925. Although holding that the interests of co-owners under the statutory trusts[35] are minor interests, he

---

[31] [1891] 3 Ch. 82 at 99.

[32] [1981] A.C. 487, varying the decision of the Court of Appeal at [1979] Ch. 312, which allowed the appeal of Mr. and Mrs. Boland against the decision of Templeman J. at (1978) P. & C.R. 448. This appeal was heard together with *Williams and Glyn's Bank* v. *Brown* in which at first instance H. H. Judge Clapham applied Templeman J.'s decision, making an order for possession in favour of the Bank.

[33] *Ibid.*, at p. 506.

[34] Disapproving *Caunce* v. *Caunce* [1969] 1 W.L.R. 286 and *Bird* v. *Syme-Thompson* [1979] 1 W.L.R. 440 at 444, and approving *Hodgson* v. *Marks* [1971] Ch. 892, C.A., at 934 *per* Russell L.J.

[35] Defined in s.35 of L.P.A. 1925.

considered that any such interests, if protected by actual occupation, acquired the status of an overriding interest, being, as section 70 of the Land Registration Act 1925 requires, interests subsisting in reference to land.[36]

This decision, as Lord Wilberforce recognised, had important consequences for conveyancers, which he formulated in these words:

> "What is involved is a departure from an easy-going practice of dispensing with enquiries as to occupation beyond that of the vendor and accepting the risks of doing so. To substitute for this a practice of more careful enquiry as to the facts of occupation, and, if necessary, as to the rights of occupiers can not, in my view of the matter, be considered as unacceptable except at the price of overlooking the widespread development of shared interest in ownership."

The Law Commission considered that the law in this field had been left in a most unsatisfactory state.[38] The report made three recommendations, one for overcoming the conveyancing problems faced by purchasers and mortgagees,[39] and the others for protecting and establishing the interests of married co-owners in the matrimonial home.[40]

A problem which soon become apparent was that no guidance had been given as to the extent and nature of the inquiries which would be necessary in order to ascertain the existence of persons in occupation and their equitable rights. That problem was considered in *Northern Bank Ltd.* v. *Henry*.[41] By section 3(1) of the Conveyancing Act 1882,[42] a purchaser (including, by virtue of section 1(4), a mortgagee) is not prejudicially affected by any matter unless, *inter alia*, it would have come to his knowledge if such inspections and inquiries as ought reasonably to have been made had been made by him. Henchy J. stated[43]:

> "The test of what inquiries ought reasonably to have been made . . . is an objective test which depends . . . on what a purchaser of the par-

---

[36] *Elias* v. *Mitchell* [1972] Ch. 652, *cf. Cedar Holdings Ltd.* v. *Green* [1981] Ch. 129; for cases in which it was held that equitable interests other than those of tenants in common could be overriding interests if protected by actual occupation, see *Bridges* v. *Mees* [1957] Ch. 475; *Hodgson* v. *Marks* [1971] Ch. 892, C.A.

[37] [1981] A.C. 487 at 508, 509.

[38] Law Commission Report No. 115, Cmnd. 8636 (1982), at paras. 2.52–2.54, *The Implications of Williams and Glyn's Bank* v. *Boland*.

[39] That co-ownership interests in land should be registrable at H.M. Land Registry and should be protected against purchasers and mortgagees if, and only if, they were so registered.

[40] That: (i) the interest of every married co-owner in the matrimonial home should carry with it a right to prevent any dealing being made without that co-owner's consent or a court order; and (ii) as a general rule married couples should, in the absence of agreement to the contrary, have an equal ownership of the matrimonial home.

[41] [1981] I.R. 1.

[42] Repealed in England, but similar provisions are contained in s.199(1)(ii)(*a*) of the L.P.A. 1925.

[43] [1981] I.R. 1 at p. 9.

ticular property ought reasonably to have done in order to acquire title to it,"

adding that "a reasonable purchaser would be expected to make such inquiries and inspections as would normally disclose whether the purchase will trench, fraudulently or unconscionably, on the rights of . . . third parties in the property." It was held, accordingly, that the wife's claim to be entitled to an equitable estate in the house would have come to the knowledge of the plaintiffs' agent if inquiries and inspections were made in accordance with the standard described in section 3(1) of the Conveyancing Act 1882, and hence the plaintiffs were deemed to have had constructive notice of the wife's claim. In *Ulster Bank Ltd.* v. *Shanks and others*,[44] it was stated that the doctrine of constructive notice was not to be extended further than was necessary. In that case the legal title to the house was in the sole name of the husband, but it was common ground that, prior to the husband executing a second mortgage on behalf of the plaintiff bank, the wife had acquired a one-third equitable interest in the house. Since the wife knew of the proposed mortgage which had been discussed by the bank in her presence, and had said nothing, the bank had done all that was reasonable and could not accordingly be saddled with constructive notice of the wife's interest under section 3 of the Conveyancing Act 1882. The court further took the view that if a person in the wife's position were deliberately to stay silent about her own equitable interest with a view to asserting it later if the mortgagee sought to realise his security, such conduct would leave that person open to the charge of not coming to court with clean hands. It was also pointed out that the relevant law differs from that in *Williams and Glyn's Bank* v. *Boland* in that the determining factor was not whether inquiry was made and rights were not disclosed, but whether that specific inquiry was one which ought reasonably to have been made.

There has been criticism of the fact that section 70(1)(g) does not limit the scope of the inquiries to be made by reference to any concept of "reasonable inquiry."[45] The section does not specify who must make the inquiry; it has been accepted that in most cases this could properly be done by the solicitor acting for the purchaser.[46] Nor does it specify when inquiry or disclosure ought to be made. It is clear, however, that the inquiry must be made of the person whose rights would otherwise amount to an overriding interest.[47] The difficulties facing a purchaser in making adequate

[44] [1982] N.I. 143. For a similar English approach to concealment of the existence of a beneficial interest, see *Midland Bank Ltd.* v. *Farmpride Hatcheries Ltd.* (1981) 260 E.G. 493, C.A.

[45] Law Commission Report no. 158, H.C. 269 (1987), para. 2.59. At para. 2.75 the Report recommends that all categories of overriding interest be made explicitly subject to the jurisdiction of the courts to postpone them in favour of subsequent purchasers and lenders on the general grounds of fraud or estoppel.

[46] *Winkworth* v. *Edward Baron Development Co. Ltd.* [1986] 1 W.L.R. 1512.

[47] *Hodgson* v. *Marks* [1971] Ch. 892; *Kling* v. *Keston Properties* (1985) 49 P. & C.R. 212 at 220.

inquiries have been extensively discussed.[48] In unregistered land conveyancing it had been decided in *Caunce* v. *Caunce*[49] that notice of the
presence of the wife in the matrimonial home was not, of itself, notice of
any interest that she might have. The decision came under judicial attack[50]
and was not followed in *Kingsnorth Trust Ltd.* v. *Tizard.*[51] In that case it
was held that the mortgagee had not made such inquiries as ought reasonably to have been made by him and was therefore fixed with constructive
notice of the wife's interest.[52] Two facts which (it was held) fixed
Kingsnorth with constructive notice of the wife's interest were T's informing the surveyor that he was married but separated from his wife, who lived
nearby, although he had described himself as single on the application
form, and evidence of occupation by teenage children. In addition, however, the judge took the view that, in the circumstances, the pre-arranged
inspection was not within the category of "such . . . inspections . . . as
ought reasonably to have been made."[53]

A legislative attempt to minimise the difficulties created by the *Boland*
decision was the Land Registration and Law of Property Bill, which would
have placed a spouse in a different position from that of all other equitable
co-owners. In unregistered land, only possesssion by the spouse would
affect a purchaser with notice of the beneficial interest, and in registered
land only the interest of a spouse in occupation would be capable of being
an overriding interest. The hostility to this proposal resulted in its withdrawal. Two recent decisions, *Bristol and West Building Society* v. *Henning*[54] and *Paddington Building Society* v. *Mendlesohn,*[55] have gone some
way towards restricting the effects of *Boland*, though in *Henning* that
decision was not considered. In both cases the person seeking to assert the
prior beneficial interest knew that the registered proprietor was acquiring
the property with the assistance of a mortgage, and an intention was
imputed to her that her interest should be postponed to that of the mortgagee. If those decisions are to be followed, *Boland* will hardly ever affect
building societies, since there can be few cases in which the equitable co-
owner will be unaware that the purchase is being financed by way of mortgage.[56] In the *Mendlesohn* case the decision at first instance raised another
problem.[57] The first instance decision did not rest on imputed intention but
on the date at which the rights under section 70(1)(g) bite against the regis-

---

[48] (1979) 95 L.Q.R. 501 (R.J. Smith); [1980] Conv. 85, 311 and 318; [1980] Conv. 361 (J.
Martin); *Kling* v. *Keston Properties, supra,* at 222; (1986) 136 New L.J. 771 (P. Luxton);
Kingsnorth Finance Co. v. *Tizard* [1986] 1 W.L.R. 783; K. Gray, *Elements of Land Law,*
(1st ed., 1987), pp. 189–92 and 852–862; *Emmet on Title,* (19th ed., 1985), para. 5–200.
[49] [1969] 1 W.L.R. 286.
[50] *Williams and Glyn's Bank* v. *Boland* [1981] A.C. 487 at 505–506.
[51] [1986] 1 W.L.R. 783.
[52] L.P.A. 1925, s.199(1)(ii)(a) and s.205(1)(xxi) ("purchaser" includes "mortgagee").
[53] [1986] 1 W.L.R. 783 at 795.
[54] [1985] 1 W.L.R. 778, C.A.
[55] (1985) 50 P. & C.R. 244, C.A.
[56] See [1986] Conv. 57 (M. Thompson).
[57] See [1986] Conv. 309 (P. Sparkes).

tered proprietor. The two main possibilities are the date of registration[58] and the date of transfer.[59] In that case, S arranged to purchase a property with the aid of a mortgage advance from the society together with a contribution from M. Completion took place on July 20, 1979, the transfer being made, the mortgage executed and S and his girl-friend moving in. On August 20, 1979 M moved in also. The mortgage was registered on October 1, 1979. The county court judge held that an occupier can claim an overriding interest only if in occupation at the time of execution of the charge, and thus M had no such interest. Although both parties wished the Court of Appeal to decide whether that was correct, the Court declined to do so. It was held that, once it was established (as the Court found) that an intention was to be imputed to M that her rights should be postponed to those of the mortgagee, the fact that they constituted overriding interests did not afford her any priority. In the recent case of *Lloyds Bank Ltd.* v. *Rossett*,[60] the Court of Appeal held that where a wife claims that she has a beneficial interest in a house registered in her husband's name and that her interest has priority over the rights of a mortgagee under a legal charge executed without her knowledge, then in order to claim protection afforded to overriding interests by section 70(1)(g) of the Land Registration Act 1925, the wife must have been in actual occupation of the house when the charge was executed as distinct from being in occupation when the charge was registered. Nicholls L.J., giving the leading judgment, stated "once the transfer or mortgage has been executed the die has been cast," thereby confirming the opinion of the court at first instance in the *Mendlesohn* case. In *Chhokar* v. *Chhokar and Parmar*,[61] it was held that the purchaser, who had bought the house at an undervalued price, and thereafter attempted to prevent the wife (who had contributed to the purchase price) acquiring an overriding interest by occupation, nevertheless took subject to that interest because she was in actual occupation at the time when registration of the purchaser's title was sought. Whilst it is clear that in the case of a first registration of title it is the date of registration which is decisive,[62] there appears to be no firm rule in the case of a transfer of an existing registered title.

It was not necessary to consider in *Boland* whether the interests of the

---

[58] This is the date on which an application for registration of the transfer is delivered to the Land Registry: Land Registration Rules 1925, r.42 and r.83(2). For delivery of applications see rr.24, 84 and 85.

[59] Assumed to be the date of completion.

[60] [1988] 3 W.L.R. 1301. This case is also authority for the proposition that a person could be in actual occupation by having agents there on his behalf. See Also *Abbey National Building Society* v. *Cann, The Times*, March 15, 1989.

[61] [1984] F.L.R. 313, C.A.; (1984) 14 Fam.Law 269, C.A.

[62] *Re Boyle's Claim* [1961] 1 W.L.R. 339. For discussion of what is actually decided by this case, see Farrand, *Contract and Conveyance*, (4th ed., 1983), p. 199; Emmet on Title (19th ed., 1985), para. 5–197; Ruoff and Roper, *Registered Conveyancing* (5th ed., 1986), p. 894; Megarry and Wade, *Law of Real Property* (5th ed., 1984) p. 228. So far as the proposition in the text is concerned, the case has been followed in *Schwab and Co.* v. *McCarthy* (1975) 31 P. & C.R. 196 at 204 and in *Kling* v. *Keston Properties* (1985) 49 P. & C.R. 212 at 218.

beneficial owners were overreached, as the mortgage money was paid to a sole registered proprietor. In that case, Lord Wilberforce said[63]:

> "Undivided shares in land can only take effect in equity behind a trust for sale upon which the legal owner is to hold the land. Dispositions of the land, including mortgages, may be made under this trust and, provided there are at least two trustees or a trust corporation, 'overreach' the trusts. This means the 'purchaser' takes free from them whether or not he has notice of them, and the trusts are enforceable against the proceeds of sale."

The question did arise in *City of London Building Society* v. *Flegg*.[64] In that case the registered proprietors of Bleak House were a Mr. and Mrs. Maxwell-Brown, the daughter and son-in-law of Mr. and Mrs. Flegg, who had contributed over half of the purchase price, having sold their own home in order to do so and with the intention that all four should live together. The Maxwell-Browns raised their contribution by means of a mortgage and later, without the knowledge or consent of the Fleggs, executed three more charges, the third being for the purpose of discharging all the earlier charges. The Fleggs had been in occupation throughout and no inquiries had ever been made of them as to whether they claimed any interest in the property. The Maxwell-Browns defaulted on the mortgage repayments and the mortgagee sought possession. At first instance this relief was granted, it being held that the Fleggs' overriding interest arising from their actual occupation coupled with their equitable interest under the resulting trust was overreached by the payment of the mortgage money to two trustees for sale. The Court of Appeal upheld the Fleggs' appeal, considering the case to be indistinguishable from *Boland* although the mortgage money had in the instant case been paid to two trustees for sale and also holding that section 14 of the Law of Property Act 1925 prevented the overreaching provisions of Section 2 of that Act from operating, the Fleggs being in occupation of the property.[65] That decision attracted some academic criticism[66] and was reversed in the House of Lords, where it was unanimously held that the Fleggs' interests under the trust for sale were overreached. Lord Templeman[67] considered that this was brought about by sections 27 and 28 of the Law of Property Act 1925, while Lord Oliver's more extensive analysis referred also to sections 2 and 26 of the same Act.[68] Although the decision of the House of Lords has been welcomed,[69] the basis of it has been questioned.[70] It is now thought that the safe prac-

---

[63] [1981] A.C. 487 at 503.
[64] [1986] Ch. 605, C.A.; reversed [1988] A.C. 54, restoring the decision of the judge at first instance.
[65] [1986] Ch. 605, C.A., at 618–620.
[66] (1986) New L.J. 210 (D.J. Hayton).
[67] [1988] A.C. 54 at 71–72.
[68] *Ibid.* at 80–81, 83, 90–91.
[69] See, *e.g.* Emmet on Title, (19th ed., 1985) para. 5–202.
[70] [1987] Conv. 451 (W.J. Swadling); [1988] Conv. 141 (P. Sparkes); [1980] Conv. 313 (draft Editorial Practice Note) entitled "Occupational Hazards."

tice is, as has previously been suggested,[71] to decline to deal with a sole registered proprietor and to insist on the appointment of a second trustee to receive capital money. The Law Commission's response to *Flegg*[72] favours the view that the law should adopt the Court of Appeal's position that any equitable co-owner of land who is in actual occupation of it should have the right to consent to dispositions affecting it, such that his or her interest should not be overreached without consent.

After the decision in *Boland*, institutional lenders in many cases sought to protect themselves against the rights of occupiers by requiring them to sign forms of acknowledgement, consent or waiver. This device was, for a number of reasons, less effective than the lenders would have wished. In the first place, it was inadequate to give protection against the rights of an equitable co-owner who was in constructive occupation.[73] Next, some persons may not be capable of giving a valid consent to the release of their rights.[74] Most importantly, however, an occupier who gives such a consent may seek to claim that the consent was vitiated by duress or undue influence. The doctrine of inequality of bargaining power, formulated in *Lloyds Banks Ltd.* v. *Bundy*[75] was invoked in several such cases.

In that case, Lord Denning M.R., having enumerated the categories where he considered the doctrine to apply, said[76]:

> "Gathering all together, I would suggest that through all these instances there runs a single thread. They rest on 'inequality of bargaining power.' By virtue of it, the English law gives relief to one who, without independent advice, enters into a contract which is very unfair . . . when his bargaining power is grievously impaired by reason of his own needs or desires, or by his own ignorance or infirmity, coupled with undue influence brought to bear on him by or for the benefit of the other."

This formulation initially met with some enthusiasm among commentators[77] but has more recently come under both judicial[78] and academic[79] attack. Lord Scarman considered that the true *ratio* of *Lloyds Bank* v. *Bundy* was to be found in the judgment of Sachs L.J.,[80] based on the well-

---

[71] See [1980] Conv. 316 (J. Martin); *ibid.*, 427 (C. Sydenham); [1981] Conv. 19 (S.M. Clayton); *ibid.*, 219 (J. Martin).

[72] *Trusts of Land: Overreaching* (1988) Working Paper No. 106.

[73] See *Strand Securities* v. *Caswell* [1965] Ch. 958, C.A., for discussion of what constitutes occupation for the purposes of s.70(1)(*g*) of Land Registration Act 1925.

[74] The Law Commission recognised this, referring in its Report no. 115, Cmnd. 8636 (1982) at para. 42(1)(*b*) to patients and minors.

[75] [1975] 1 Q.B. 326.

[76] *Ibid.* at 339.

[77] [1975] C.L.J. 21 (L. Sealey); (1975) 38 M.L.R. (Carr).

[78] *National Westminster Bank* v. *Morgan* [1985] A.C. 686, *per* Lord Scarman at 707–708.

[79] [1985] Conv. 387 (C.N. Barton and P.M. Rank); and see also (1985) L.S.Gaz. 1320 (P.H. Kenny) sub.title "A Mortgage Affected by Undue Influence" preceding the report of *Kings North Trust* v. *Bell* at p. 1329, and (1985) 48 M.L.R. 579 (D. Tiplady).

[80] [1975] Q.B. 326 at 347; cited by Lord Scarman in [1985] A.C. 686 at 708.

established principles laid down in *Allcard* v. *Skinner*.[81] Having reviewed the law relating to undue influence[82] and summarised the legislative developments restricting freedom of contract, he questioned the need for the principle laid down by Lord Denning.

It is clear that the relationship of banker and customer does not, of itself, give rise to a presumption of undue influence. There has to be evidence that the transaction was wrongful in that it had constituted an advantage taken of the person subjected to the influence which, failing proof to the contrary, was explicable only on the basis that undue influence had been exercised to procure it. In *National Westminster Bank* v. *Morgan*[83] M and his wife bought a house with the aid of a building society mortgage. M fell into arrears with the repayments and also encountered business difficulties. He requested the Bank to re-finance the loan; it agreed to advance a short-term bridging loan subject to a legal charge on the house in joint names. After M had signed the charge, the bank manager called at the house in order to obtain the wife's signature. The wife was concerned about the effect of the charge, but she signed it. She made it clear to the bank manager that she had little faith in her husband's business ventures and she did not want the charge to cover his business liabilities. Incorrectly, although in good faith, the bank manager told the wife that (as was the bank's intention) the legal charge was limited to the amount advanced to re-finance the mortgage. In fact it was unlimited and capable of extending to all M's liabilities to the Bank. At first instance it was found that the couple had been desperately anxious not to lose their home, that the transaction had not been manifestly disadvantageous to the wife, who knew that it was the only way in which the home could be saved and that there had been no pressure exerted on her to get her to sign the charge. It was also found that there was, in the circumstances, no duty on the bank manager to ensure that the wife received independent legal advice. The couple fell into arrears with the repayments to the Bank, which brought possession proceedings to recover the house. The wife's contention that the charge had been executed as a result of undue influence was rejected at first instance and, although her appeal to the Court of Appeal succeeded, the House of Lords reversed that decision.

National Westminster Bank v. *Morgan* was followed in *Cornish* v. *Midland Bank*.[84] In that case it was held that, where a bank chose to advise a customer as to the nature and effect of a mortgage in its favour prior to the

---

[81] (1887) 36 Ch.D. 145, C.A.; particularly *per* Lindley L.J. at 182–3, 185.
[82] *Huguenin* v. *Baseley* (1807) 14 Ves. 273; *Rhodes* v. *Bate* (1866) L.R. 1 Ch.App. 252; *Bank of Montreal* v. *Stuart* [1911] A.C. 120, P.C.; *Poosathurai* v. *Kanappa Chettiar* (1919) L.R. 47 Ind. App. 1 (a case involving consideration of s.16(3) of Indian Contract Act 1872). The doctrine of inequality of bargaining power has been considered in the field of restraint of trade: see *Alec Lobb Garages* v. *Total Oil (Great Britain) Ltd.* [1985] 1 W.L.R. 173, C.A., where an argument based on the doctrine failed. The law relating to undue influence was extensively reviewed by the Court of Appeal in *Goldsworthy* v. *Brickell* [1987] Ch. 378, a case involving a tenancy agreement.
[83] *National Westminster Bank* v. *Morgan* [1983] A.C. 85, C.A.: revsd. [1985] A.C. 686.
[84] [1985] 3 All E.R. 513, C.A.

execution of the mortgage by the customer, it was under a duty not to mis-state negligently the effect of the mortgage. As in *National Westminster Bank* v. *Morgan*, the mortgage was worded so as to secure not merely the amount of the advance, but unlimited further advances. It was held that if this was the case, it was something which the bank was under a duty to explain. The bank was held liable to the plaintiff in damages for breach of duty but the mortgage was not set aside.

There is also a series of cases in which the mortgagor has claimed to have a transaction set aside on the ground of undue influence or misrepresentation by a relative or friend. In the cases of *Avon Finance Company Ltd.* v. *Bridger*[85] and *Kings North Trust* v. *Bell*[86] the principles relied on were those stated in *Turnbull and Co.* v. *Duval*[87] and *Chaplin and Co.* v. *Brammall.*[88] Those authorities show that if a creditor, or a potential creditor of a husband, wishes to obtain a charge on the property of the wife, and if the creditor entrusts the husband with the task of ensuring that the wife executes the relevant document, the creditor cannot enforce the security against the wife if it is established that the execution of the document was procured by undue influence and the wife had no independent advice. In *Avon Finance Co. Ltd.* v. *Bridger* those principles were held to apply outside the marital relationship, provided that the creditor was, or should have been aware, that the relationship between the debtor and the person from whom the security was sought was such that the debtor could be expected to have influence over that person.

Those authorities were distinguished in *Coldunell* v. *Gallon*[89] where the undue influence exerted by the son of elderly mortgagors was not imputed to the mortgagee. Although the mortgagee's solicitors dealt with the son throughout, they sent the mortgage deed direct to the mortgagors for execution, together with covering letters advising them to seek independent legal advice before signing the documents. The mortgagors received the mortgage deed but not the letters. Their son procured their signatures in the presence of his own solicitor, who did not advise them as to the

---

[85] [1983] 2 All E.R. 281.
[86] [1986] 1 W.L.R. 119, C.A.
[87] [1902] A.C. 429.
[88] [1908] 1 K.B. 233.
[89] [1986] Q.B. 1184 (and see *Davies* v. *Directloans Ltd.* [1986] 1 W.L.R. 823). The authorities were reviewed in *Shephard* v. *Midland Bank plc* [1987] 2 F.L.R. 175, C.A. In that case H opened an account with the respondent bank. The account became overdrawn and it was proposed that a new account be opened in the names of H and W, both of whom signed a mandate which provided that any loan or overdraft would be the joint and several responsibility of each of them. H negotiated a loan, causing the new account to become overdrawn. W appealed against the order giving judgment for the bank on the ground that it was unenforceable against her, her signature to be mandate having been obtained by undue influence exerted by H. Held, the transaction was potentially disadvantageous to W and therefore the defence was not unarguable: but there was no evidence that H had made any fraudulent misrepresentation or concealment, or had exerted pressure on W to sign. Further, even if he had exercised a dominating influence over her, there was no evidence that the bank knew that he had or would use such influence, or that it used H in order to exert pressure on W.

nature and effect of the transaction, though he did explain the consent form to the mother. The son then forged his father's endorsement on the cheque made out to the father by the mortgagees and kept the money. It was held, *inter alia*, that the mortgagees were not liable for the son's unconscionable conduct as his intervention in the transaction was unauthorised.

These cases were referred to and explained in the recent case of *Bank of Baroda v. Shah*,[90] where it was held that where undue influence has been brought to bear by a debtor on a surety to give a legal charge over a property to secure the debtor's liability to the creditor, the creditor is not infected with the conduct of the debtor, and accordingly the charge will not be set aside if the creditor wishes to enforce it by obtaining possession of that property.

TACKING

Tacking has been described[91] as a special way of obtaining priority for a secured loan by amalgamating it with another secured loan of higher priority. Before 1926 there were two forms of tacking, of which one has been abolished by the 1925 legislation, and the law as to the other has been amended.

The form which has been abolished is the *tabula in naufragio* ("plank in the shipwreck"). The opportunity to tack in this manner occurred when a borrower B created a legal mortgage in favour of L followed by successive equitable mortgages in favour of M and N. If N then took a transfer of L's mortgage ("the plank") he would, provided he had no notice of M's mortgage when he advanced his money[92] obtain priority over M if B defaulted ("the shipwreck"). Tacking in this manner depended on the superiority of the legal estate[93]; provided the equities between M and N were equal,[94] N's possession of[95] or best right to call for the legal estate[96] upset the natural priorities which were governed by order of creation. Prior legal estates or rights to call for legal estates which were sufficient to bring the doctrine into operation included a term of years,[97] a judgment giving legal rights against the land,[98] an express declaration of trust by the owner of the legal

---

[90] [1988] 3 All E.R. 24.
[91] Megarry and Wade, *The Law of Real Property* (5th ed., 1984), p. 1005.
[92] *Brace* v. *Duchess of Marlborough* (1728) 2 P.Wms. 491.
[93] *Bailey* v. *Barnes* [1894] 1 Ch. 25 at 36, *per* Lindley L.J.; "a curious example of the deference paid by equity to the legal estate."
[94] *Lacey* v. *Ingle* (1847) 2 Ph. 413; *Rooper* v. *Harrison* (1855) 2 K. & J. 86, in which it was held that, if the mortgagee subsequently parts with the legal estate, he lost the right to tack.
[95] *Wortley* v. *Birkhead* (1754) 2 Ves.Sen. 571.
[96] *Wilkes* v. *Bodington* (1707) 2 Vern. 599; *ex p. Knott* (1806) 11 Ves. 609.
[97] *Willoughby* v. *Willoughby* (1756) 1 Term. Rep. 763; *Maundrell* v. *Maundrell* (1804) 10 Ves. 246; *Cooke* v. *Wilton* (1860) 29 Beav. 100.
[98] *Morret* v. *Paske* (1740) 2 Atk. 52.

estate in favour of the mortgagee who sought to tack,[99] or a transfer of the legal estate to a trustee for such a mortgagee.[1] The right to tack was lost as soon as the mortgagee parted with the legal estate[2] and did not arise unless the legal estate[2] and the mortgage were held in the same right.[3]

Notice acquired after the advance was made by N but before he got in the legal estate did not prevent him tacking.[4] Notice to L, the holder of the legal estate, was immaterial, so M could not prevent N taking by giving notice to L of his mortgage.[5] This opened the possibility of L and N conspiring to cheat M.[6]

If a legal estate was held on trust for M, and N has notice of the trust, he was bound by it and could not get that estate in so as to tack.[7]

The more important form of tacking was the tacking of further advances. The borrower might wish to raise further sums on the property at a later date (as where he was developing a building estate) or the lender might contemplate a variation in the state of the borrower's account and be prepared to make further advances. Where B mortgaged the property first to L, then to M, then took a further advance from L, it was possible, in certain circumstances, for L's further advance to be tacked on to the original advance, displacing M's priority.

Where L had no notice of the mortgage in favour of M, tacking was allowed provided one of two conditions was satisfied:

    (1) Where L was either a legal mortgagee[8] or an equitable mortgagee with the best right to call for the legal estate.[9] As with the *tabula in naufragio*, priority resulted from the superiority of the legal estate.

    (2) Where the mortgage to L expressly provided for the security to be extended to cover further advances, whether or not such further advances were obligatory. This form of tacking was independent of the legal estate. Originally it had been held that, where M had notice that L's mortgage was expressed to cover further advances, he took subject to L's right to tack further advances.[10] This, how-

---

[99] *Wilmot* v. *Pike* (1845) 5 Hare 14.

[1] *Earl of Pomfret* v. *Lord Windsor* (1752) 2 Ves.Sen. 472; *Stanhope* v. *Earl Verney* (1761) 2 Eden 81; *Pease* v. *Jackson* (1868) 3 Ch.App. 576; *Crosbie-Hill* v. *Sayer* [1908] 1 Ch. 866.

[2] *Rooper* v. *Harrison* (1855) 2 K. & J. 86.

[3] *Harnett* v. *Weston* (1806) 12 Ves. 130.

[4] *Taylor* v. *Russell* [1892] A.C. 244.

[5] *Peacock* v. *Burt* (1834) 4 L.J.Ch. 33.

[6] *West London Commercial Bank* v. *Reliance Permanent Building Society* (1885) 29 Ch.D. 954.

[7] *Sharples* v. *Adams* (1863) 32 Beav. 213; *Mumford* v. *Stohwasser* (1874) L.R. 18 Eq. 556; *Taylor* v. *London and County Banking Co.* [1901] 2 Ch. 231; *Saunders* v. *Dehew* (1692) 2 Vern. 271.

[8] *Wyllie* v. *Pollen* (1863) 3 De G.J. & S. 596.

[9] *Wilkes* v. *Bodington* (1707) 2 Vern. 599; *Wilmot* v. *Pike* (1845) 5 Hare. 14; *Taylor* v. *London and County Banking Co.* [1901] 2 Ch. 231; see also *McCarthy & Stone Ltd.* v. *Hodge & Co.* [1971] 1 W.L.R. 1547.

[10] *Gordon* v. *Graham* (1716) 2 Eq.Cas.Abr. 598.

ever, was overruled by a divided House of Lords[11] and the rule
that notice of a subsequent incumbrance prevented the first mortgagee from tacking further advances was applied even where the
first mortgage contained a covenant to make further advances.[12]
In that case, however, the creation of M's mortgage released L
from the obligation to make any further advances, since further
advances to him could no longer have the same priority as the
original mortgage.

Tacking could also take place if M agreed that further advances to L should
have priority over his mortgage. This was a matter of contract between the
parties and it was immaterial whether L was a legal or equitable mortgagee.

An unsuccessful attempt to abolish tacking was made by section 7 of the
Vendor and Purchaser Act 1874; that provision was retrospectively
repealed by section 129 of the Land Transfer Act 1875. The 1925 legislation abolished the *tabula in naufragio* rule and amended the law relating
to tacking of further advances.[13]

The law as to tacking is now set out in section 94 of the Law of Property
Act 1925, which reads:

"(1) After the commencement of this Act, a prior mortgagee shall
have a right to make further advances to rank in priority to subsequent
mortgages (whether legal or equitable)—

(*a*) if an arrangement has been made to that effect with the subsequent mortgagees; or

(*b*) if he had *no notice of such subsequent mortgages* at the time when
the further advance was made by him; or

(*c*) whether or not he had such notice as aforesaid, where the mortgage imposes an obligation on him to make such further
advances.

This subsection applies whether or not the prior mortgage was made
expressly for securing further advances.

(2) In relation to the making of further advances after the commencement of this Act a mortgagee shall not be deemed to have
notice of a mortgage merely by reason that it was registered as a land
charge[13a] was not so registered at the time when the original mortgage
was created or when the last search (if any) by or on behalf of the
mortgagee was made, whichever last happened.

---

[11] *Hopkinson* v. *Rolt* (1861) 9 H.L.C. 514; see also *London & County Banking Co. Ltd.* v.
Ratcliffe (1881) 6 App.Cas. 722; *Bradford Banking Co.* v. *Briggs & Co. Ltd.* (1886) 12
App.Cas. 29; *Union Bank of Scotland* v. *National Bank of Scotland* (1886) 12 App.Cas. 53;
Matzner v. *Clyde Securities Ltd.* [1975] 2 N.S.W.L.R. 293; *Central Mortgage Registry of
Australia Ltd.* v. *Donemore Pty. Ltd.* [1984] 2 N.S.W.L.R. 128.
[12] *West* v. *Williams* [1899] 1 Ch. 132, C.A.
[13] L.P.A. 1925, s.94(3).
[13a] Repealed by L.P.A. 1969, s.16(2), Sched. 2, Pt. 1.

This subsection only applies where the prior mortgage was made expressly for securing a current account or other further advances.

(3) Save in regard to the making of further advances as aforesaid, the right to tack is hereby abolished:

Provided that nothing in this Act shall affect any priority acquired before the commencement of this Act by tacking, or in respect of further advances made without notice of a subsequent incumbrance or by arrangement with the subsequent incumbrancer.

(4) This section applies to mortgages of land before or after the commencement of this Act, but not to charges registered under the Land Registration Act 1925, or any enactment replaced by that Act."

Section 94(1) extends the doctrine of tacking in two ways. It makes the nature of the prior mortgage immaterial and it applies to any prior mortgagee; thus if B successively mortgages the property to L, M, N and M again, M has the right to tack subject to any provisions as to notice. Section 94(1)(a) preserves the pre-1926 position as to tacking with the consent of subsequent mortgagees. Section 94(1)(b) again preserves the pre-1926 position as laid down in *Hopkinson* v. *Rolt*,[14] but, by the Law of Property Act 1925, section 198, registration of the subsequent mortgage as a land charge constitutes deemed actual notice. Section 94(1)(c) reverses the principle of *West* v. *Williams*[15] in that, where there is an obligation to make further advances, notice to the prior mortgagee does not affect his right to tack. Therefore, a mortgagee must make a search whenever he makes a further advance, unless the mortgage is made expressly to secure further advances or a current account. He is not affected by an unregistered mortgage unless he has actual notice of it.

Section 94(1) permits tacking of further advances to rank in priority to subsequent mortgages; thus the mortgagee who wishes to tack is bound by other intervening interests which are registered. It is suggested that the failure to give priority over such interests is a flaw in drafting.[16] Emmet[17] refers to the situation where an estate contract has been registered between dates of the original and a further advance. The mortgagee would be deemed to make the further advance with notice of the estate contract, and it would therefore seem that he could be compelled to release his security in favour of the purchaser on receiving only the amount of the original advance, if it was the case that the purchase price was insufficient to repay both the original and the further advance. The risk involved in not searching before making a further advance is discussed by Rowley,[18] as is the meaning of the words "for securing a current account or other further advances."[19]

[14] (1861) 9 H.L.C. 514.
[15] [1899] 1 Ch. 132.
[16] Maitland, *Equity* (8th ed., 1949), p. 214.
[17] *Emmet on Title* (19th ed., 1985), para. 25/106.
[18] (1958) 22 Conv.(N.S.) 44 at 56.
[19] *Ibid.* at 49.

Section 94(2)[20] provides an exception to the rule laid down by the Law of Property Act 1925, section 198(1) that registration constitutes deemed actual notice. If the prior mortgage is made expressly for securing a current account or further advances, registration of a subsequent charge is not equivalent to actual notice of that charge to the prior mortgagee and he can tack against that charge provided that he had no actual notice of it at the time of the further advance. He takes, of course, subject to any charges which were registered at the time of the original advance. The reason for this exception to section 198 is to make it unnecessary for a bank to have to search the register before cashing each cheque drawn by a borrower who has a secured overdraft, although the exception applies whenever the mortgagee contemplates further advances on the same security.

Consequently, a subsequent mortgagee who wishes to protect himself from loss of priority by tacking should give notice to all prior mortgagees, in case their mortgages are in a form which allows them to tack further advances against registered incumbrances. Giving notice to the immediately prior mortgagee also fixes him with the duty to hand over the deeds when that mortgage is discharged.

Banks are affected by the rule in *Clayton's Case*,[21] whose effect is that where there is an unbroken account between the parties, or "one blended fund" as in the case of a current account at a bank, then in the absence of any express appropriation, each payment is impliedly appropriated to the earliest debt that is not statute-barred. Thus, where a prior mortgage is made to secure a current account with a bank and notice of a subsequent mortgage is received, subsequent payments reduce the overdraft existing at the time of the notice and these improve the position of the later mortgagee.[22] The bank can avoid this result by closing the account and if it wishes opening a new account into which the mortgagor's subsequent payments are made.[23] The parties can agree to exclude the rule, which can also be displaced if an intention to exclude it appears from the circumstances.[24]

Section 94(4) of the Law of Property Act 1925 excludes charges on registered land under the Land Registration Act 1925. Further advances on the security of such charges are dealt with by section 30 of that Act:

> (1) Where a registered charge is made for securing further advances, the registrar shall, before making any entry on the register which would prejudicially affect the priority of any further advance hereunder, give the proprietor of the charge, at his registered address, notice by registered post of the intended entry, and the proprietor of the charge shall not, in respect of any further advance, be affected by

---

[20] As amended by the Law of Property (Amendment) Act 1926. The amendment safeguards a mortgage registered before the principal mortgage was created.

[21] (1816) 1 Mer. 572.

[22] *Deeley* v. *Lloyds Bank* [1912] A.C. 756, H.L.

[23] *Re Sherry* (1884) 25 Ch.D. 692.

[24] *Re James R. Rutherford & Sons* [1964] 1 W.L.R. 1211.

such entry, unless the advance is made after the date when the notice ought to have been received by registered post.

(2) If, by reason of any failure on the part of the registrar or the post office in reference to the notice, the proprietor of the charge suffers loss in relation to a further advance, he shall be entitled to be indemnified under this Act in like manner as if a mistake had occurred in the register; but if the loss arises by reason of an omission to register or amend the address for service, no indemnity shall be payable under this Act.

(3) Where the proprietor of a charge is under an obligation noted on the register, to make a further advance, a subsequent registered charge shall take effect subject to any further advance made pursuant to the obligation.

Where the proprietor of a registered charge to secure further advances (but without obligation to do so) receives notice of any subsequent registered charge he can refuse to make any further advance. If he does make an advance, it has priority over a subsequent charge which is not registered, but it has no priority over a subsequent charge which is registered before the further advance is made, unless the proprietor of the subsequent charge agrees to postpone his charge.

CHAPTER 19

TRANSFER AND DEVOLUTION OF RIGHTS UNDER THE SECURITY

INTER VIVOS TRANSFER OF THE MORTGAGE

General

A mortgagee, like any other owner, has a right to alienate his interest either absolutely or by way of sub-mortgage.[1] His interest comprises two distinct titles; his title to the mortgage debt and his title to the mortgaged property. Conceivably, therefore, he may assign the debt without the title and *vice versa*. Accordingly, before 1926, it was the practice expressly to provide both for the assignment of the debt and the conveyance of the security; and presumably this is still necessary when the transfer is not effected by deed. In the case of a deed executed after December 31, 1925, section 114(1) of the Law of Property Act 1925 provides that—subject to the expression of a contrary intention—the deed shall operate to transfer:

(a) the right to demand, sue for, recover, and give receipts for, the mortgage money or the unpaid part thereof, and the interest then due, if any, and thenceforth to become due thereon; and

(b) the benefit of all securities for the same, and the benefit of and the right to sue on all covenants with the mortgagee, and the right to exercise all powers of the mortgagee[2]; and

(c) all the estate and interest in the mortgaged property then vested in the mortgagee subject to redemption or cesser, but as to such estate and interest subject to the right of redemption then subsisting.[3]

In short, if the transfer is by deed, then without these details being set

---

[1] *Re Tahiti Cotton Co., ex p. Sargent* (1874) L.R. 17 Eq. 273 at 279, *per* Jessel M.R.; but it is not yet settled whether a building society mortgage (as opposed to the mortgage debt) is transferable without either an express contract to that effect or the actual concurrence of the mortgagor and in any event the transferee may not be able to exercise the power of sale. See *Re Rumney & Smith* [1897] 2 Ch. 351; *Sun Building Society* v. *Western Suburban & Harrow Road Permanent Building Society* [1920] 2 Ch. 144; reversed on other grounds [1921] 2 Ch. 438. It would seem to be difficult to separate the rights arising from membership of the building society from the rights arising under the mortgage. Since the Building Societies Act 1986 a transfer of a building society mortgage may be made under an amalgamation of transfer of engagements between societies. In such circumstances a mortgagor will be bound by the rules of the amalgamated or transferee society, (see ss.93(4), 94(8)). It is also now possible to transfer business from a building society to a commercial company, (see s.97). See also *ante*, p. 130.

[2] Express assignment of the benefit of covenants is therefore no longer necessary. Statutory powers are in any case exercisable by any person from time to time deriving title under the mortgagee: L.P.A. 1925, s.204(1)(xvi).

[3] L.P.A. 1925, s.114(1), (4), (5).

out, the transferee[4] steps into the shoes of the mortgagee.[4a] If, as is unlikely, a case should arise where the debt and the security have not been assigned together, the consequences are these: where the debt alone is transferred, the assignor remains the mortgagee and is the person to exercise the powers and remedies attached to that position. He must therefore be the party joined in redemption of foreclosure proceedings, but he is a trustee of the powers and remedies for his assignee, and must hand over to the assignee any moneys he obtains by exercising them.[5] When the security alone is transferred, the assignee becomes entitled to hold the security until he is redeemed by payment of the debt charged thereon. Moreover, as mortgagee, he may foreclose and thus holds the beneficial interest in the debt to the extent that it can be satisfied out of the security[6] but the transferee cannot sue on the covenant.

Form of transfer

Section 114(1) applies equally to mortgages of realty and personalty with the exception of mortgage bills of sale. Its provisions are comprehensive and render a transfer by deed a completely effective instrument. Therefore, in practice a transfer is nearly always carried out either by deed or by the newer method of transfer, *i.e.* a receipt endorsed upon the mortgage deed, to which method section 115 of the Law of Property Act 1925 gives the same effect as a transfer by deed.[7] It is, however, necessary to consider the minimum requirements of form for an effective transfer of mortgages of land. Moreover, it will be assumed that the assignor intends to transfer the debt and the security together. If the debt only is transferred, the assignment must be in writing and notice given to the mortgagor for the purpose of enabling the assignee to sue in his own name.[8]

A legal mortgage of land or a charge by way of legal mortgage requires, strictly speaking, a deed for its transfer in every case, because otherwise the legal title will not pass: a short precedent of such a deed is set out in the Schedule 3 to the Law of Property Act 1925.[9] If the security is a statutory charge by way of legal mortgage under section 117 of the Law of Property Act 1925, the transfer may be by one of the statutory deeds of transfer provided by section 118. This last section sets out for statutory transfers much the same benefits as section 114(1) contains for ordinary transfers, with an additional clause dealing with the case of a mortgagor concurring in the transfer. Again, transfers of legal charges on registered land must not only

---

[4] "transferee" includes his personal representatives and assignees (s.114(2)).
[4a] *Quaere* whether this is the position where further advances are then made by the transferee to the mortgagor after transfer in the absence of a supplement deed between the parties.
[5] *Morley* v. *Morley* (1858) 25 Beav. 253.
[6] *Jones* v. *Gibbons* (1804) 9 Ves. 407; *cf. Phillips* v. *Gutteridge* (1859) 4 De G. & J. 531.
[7] subs. (6); all that is necessary is that the receipt should on its face appear to have been given to a person not entitled to the immediate equity of redemption. See *post*, pp. 390 *et seq.* Such a transfer made before 1926 would not have passed the legal estate, (*Re Beachey, Heaton* v. *Beachey* [1904] 1 Ch. 67).
[8] L.P.A. 1925, s.136.
[9] But its use is not compulsory and its form may be modified or varied (*i.e.* s.114(3)).

be by deed, but must be in the prescribed form,[10] and the name of the transferee must be entered on the register as the new proprietor of the charge.[11] The transfer of an equitable mortgage need not, of course, be by deed, although in practice it usually is so effected. But transfers of equitable mortgages are caught by section 53 of the Law of Property Act 1925, and therefore, strictly, such transfers ought always to be made by an instrument in writing. Section 53 applies equally to an equitable security by deposit of title deeds, because the deposit creates an equitable mortgage which can only be assigned by a disposition in writing under section 53.[12]

Subrogation

Such are the rules to which, strictly, transfers should conform, yet it is idle to pretend that a transfer will be impossible without keeping to these rules, for equitable doctrines concerning the merger and non-merger of charges frequently allow a transfer to be effected by mere payment of the mortgage debt. Thus if a stranger discharges the mortgage debt, he will—unless he has manifested a contrary intention—be presumed to intend to keep the mortgage alive for his own benefit.[13] Moreover, the presumption in favour of the mortgage being kept alive is a strong one, because in one case it was held to apply although the person discharging the debt had actually contracted with the mortgagor to be given a new mortgage.[14] The result is that under this doctrine a transfer may be obtained by merely paying over the mortgage moneys, the effectiveness of the transfer being assured by the fact that in equity the person discharging the debt is *subrogated* to the rights of the mortgagee.[15] If the mortgagee holds the deeds, the person paying him will obtain delivery of the deeds. On the other hand, this apparently simple method is not usually employed because the transferee cannot thus obtain the legal estate and because there are strong reasons for making the mortgagor concur in a proper deed of transfer. Therefore, in the normal case, transfers are effected by deed, or by an endorsed receipt under section 115 of the Law of Property Act 1925.[16]

Transfers initiated by the mortgagor

Another form of transfer requires special mention, namely transfers which are not initiated by the mortgagee, but are instigated by the person redeeming. It is a common occurrence for a mortgagor, who is pressed for payment, or who can obtain his money more cheaply elsewhere, to discharge the mortgage with the money of a stranger, who will require the

[10] In either of the three forms (Nos. 2, 3 and 4) given in Schedule 4 to the L.P.A. 1925, with variations adapted to the particular case—see L.P.A. 1925, s.118.

[11] See *ante*, pp. 35 *et seq.*

[12] *Re Richardson, Shillito* v. *Hobson* (1885) 30 Ch.D. 396.

[13] *Chetwynd* v. *Allen* [1899] 1 Ch. 353.

[14] *Butler* v. *Rice* [1910] 2 Ch. 277 at 282, 283.

[15] See *Cracknall* v. *Janson* (1879) 11 Ch.D. 1; *Patten* v. *Bond* (1889) 60 L.T. 583; *Ghana Commercial Bank* v. *Chandiram* [1960] A.C. 732 at 744, 745.

[16] See *post*, pp. 390 *et seq.*

mortgage to be transferred to him.[17] The primary rule is that a stranger has no right to redeem, and cannot obtain a transfer except by contract with the mortgagee.[18] Section 95 of the Law of Property Act 1925 however, creates an exception to this rule when a stranger discharges the debt through the mortgagor. Subsection (1) provides[19] that, where a mortgagor is entitled to redeem, and the mortgage debt is discharged, he may require the mortgagee, instead of reconveying or surrendering, to assign the mortgage debt and convey the mortgaged property to any third person as the mortgagor shall direct, and the mortgagee is bound to assign and convey accordingly. This right is exercisable, not only by the original mortgagor, but by any person from time to time deriving title under him and by any person with any right to redeem. Mesne incumbrancers[20] are therefore entitled to call for a transfer, and subsection (2) expressly states that, where there are several incumbrancers, each incumbrancer and the mortgagor may call for a transfer, notwithstanding the existence of intervening incumbrances, but that in case of conflict the right is exercisable according to their priorities.

There are, however, two important limitations on the exercise of the right given by section 95, the first of which is that a mortgagee in possession cannot be compelled to make a transfer, unless he is brought into court for that purpose.[21] The reason for this is that a mortgagee who goes into possession will not be allowed to give up possession without the leave of the court if he makes a transfer and goes out of possession, he remains absolutely liable to account, as mortgagee in possession, for all rents and profits which have, or ought to have, been received after the transfer.[22] Even if the mortgagor were to concur in releasing him from liability, this would not be sufficient when there were any mesne incumbrancers, for the latter would not be bound by the release. It is only under the direction of the court that a mortgagee in possession can safely transfer.[23] The second limitation is that a person does not qualify to exercise the right by merely tendering the mortgage moneys; he must become entitled to a surrender or a reconveyance.[24] Therefore, if the mortgagee has notice that the mortgagor

---

[17] A stranger assisting a mortgagor to pay off the first mortgagee cannot safely take a new mortgage from the mortgagor because of the danger that the mortgagor has created mesne incumbrances; in the case of land he would be safeguarded by searching the register, but even so, if he discovers an incumbrance he must have a transfer instead of a new mortgage to preserve his priority: cf. *Teevan* v. *Smith* (1882) 20 Ch. 724 at 728.

[18] *James* v. *Biou* (1819) 3 Swanst. 234.

[19] Notwithstanding any stipulation to the contrary in the mortgage.

[20] This follows from the definition of mortgagor in L.P.A. 1925, s.205(1)(xvi). Accordingly, the right is exercisable by an equitable mortgagee or chargee or the holder of an equitable lien: see *Everitt* v. *Automatic Weighing Machine Co.* [1892] 3 Ch. 506.

[21] L.P.A. 1925, s.95(3).

[22] *Re Prytherch, Prytherch* v. *Williams* (1889) 42 Ch.D. 590; and see *Hinde* v. *Blake* (1841) 11 L.J.Ch. 26.

[23] *Hall* v. *Heward* (1886) 32 Ch.D. 430.

[24] But subs. (2) expressly allows a mortgagor to call for a transfer, notwithstanding mesne incumbrances, overruling *Teevan* v. *Smith* (1882) 20 Ch.D. 724, to this extent; for the reasons given in the text, subs. (2) is, however, of limited application.

is not entitled to a reconveyance to himself absolutely, he cannot be compelled to transfer the mortgage to the mortgagor's nominee absolutely.[25]
This limitation is important in connection with mesne incumbrancers, for a
prior mortgagee must give effect to the rights of any intervening mortgagees of whose mortgages he has notice,[26] and, therefore, a mortgagee
cannot under section 95 be compelled to transfer to a third party, when he
has notice of a mesne incumbrancer, whose consent has not been
obtained.[27]

Effect of transfer

When a mortgage is transferred without the concurrence of the mortgagor, the transferee takes subject to any equity, which at the date of the
transfer, the mortgagor might have asserted in taking the mortgage
account; for the debt, being a chose in action, can only be assigned, subject
to existing equities. It is true that in the transfer of a legal mortgage, the
transferee obtains a legal title, but it is apparent, upon the face of the title,
that it is a security only for a debt and that the real transaction is an assignment of a debt.[28] As was said by Loughborough L.C. in *Matthews* v.
Wallwyn[29] it is not consonant to the general course of equity to consider
the estate as more than a security for a debt. The result is that, as a rule, a
transferee's only right is to the sum actually owing by the mortgagor to the
mortgagee at the date of the transfer and after allowing the mortgagor the
benefit of any set-off or other equity which he had against the mortgagee.[30]
For example, in *Turner* v. *Smith*,[31] a mortgagor put into the hands of her
solicitor a sum sufficient to pay off the mortgage; the solicitor subsequently
himself took a transfer of the mortgage, having concealed from his client
that he had never paid it off; he then transferred it again to the defendant
for value, but the mortgagor was held entitled to redeem without further
payment, because the transferee could be in no better position than the
solicitor at the date of the assignment.

The moral of this story is that a man takes a transfer of a mortgage at his
peril if he does not obtain an acknowledgment from the mortgagor of the
sum actually due. Indeed, the transfer of a mortgage is an unsafe investment, unless the mortgagor concurs or joins in the transfer as a party to the

---

[25] *Alderson* v. *Elgey* (1884) 26 Ch.D. 567.
[26] *Corbett* v. *National Provident Institution* (1900) 17 T.L.R. 5.
[27] (1915) 84 L.J.Ch. 814.
[28] *Matthews* v. *Wallwyn* (1798) 4 Ves. 118; *Chambers* v. *Goldwin* (1804) 9 Ves. 254.
[29] *Ibid.* at 126. It seems, however, that a legal estate may be a protection to a transferee if the
original mortgage was voidable on equitable grounds; he will, if he is a bona fide purchaser,
be able to hold the estate as a security for money due under the mortgage at the date of the
transfer: *Judd* v. *Green* (1875) 45 L.J.Ch. 108; *Nant-y-glo and Blaina Ironworks Co. Ltd.* v.
Tamplin (1876) 35 L.T. 125. These decisions, both by Bacon V.C. are criticised in *Halsbury's Laws of England* (4th ed.), Vol. 32, para. 654.
[30] *Bickerton* v. *Walker* (1885) 31 Ch.D. 151 at 158. He cannot, in general add the costs of the
transfer to the mortgage debt. The mortgagee must pay such costs himself (see *Re Radcliffe*
(1856) 22 Beav. 201).
[31] [1901] 1 Ch. 213.

transaction[32] whereby he enters into a new covenant for the payment of the debt and interest. The risk is well illustrated by the case of *Parker* v. *Jackson*.[33] Real property was mortgaged for £700, and the mortgage then transferred to the mortgagor's solicitor. Before he took the transfer the solicitor had sold other property of his client, so that he held in his hands £2,000 of his client's money. He did not appropriate the money to the discharge of the mortgage, nor pay it over to the client, but, without informing his client, transferred the mortgage again and went bankrupt. Farwell J. held that the fact that the money had not been appropriated to the mortgage debt was immaterial, and that the transferee could be redeemed without payment. But, although a transferee is as a rule entitled to no more than the sum actually due at the date of the transfer—plus subsequent interest—the mortgagor may sometimes estop himself from relying on his equity. For example, where a mortgage is executed containing an acknowledgment of the receipt of the sum expressed to be advanced, the mortgagor cannot afterwards claim that only a lesser sum was actually advanced, as against a transferee who acted on the faith of the receipt, and was not aware of any special circumstances to put him upon inquiry.[34] This does not mean that where there is such a receipt, the concurrence of the mortgagor is superfluous, because there will always remain the risk that the mortgage was paid off, either in part or in full, between the date of the mortgage and that of the transfer.

There is a further danger. A debtor, who has no notice of an assignment of the debt, is entitled to pay it to the assignor.[35] Consequently, a transferee takes, subject not only to the equities existing in favour of the mortgagor at the date of the transfer, but also to any equities which arise after that date and before notice of the transfer.[36] Payments made by the mortgagor to the mortgagee after, but without notice of, the transfer are binding as against the transferee.[37] If the whole debt is thus discharged the mortgagor may redeem from the transferee without further payment.[38] Indeed, any agreement made for value to discharge the debt will be effective against the transferee in the absence of collusion.[39] The result is that, if a transferee makes the initial mistake of not obtaining the concurrence of the mortgagor, it is vital that notice of the transfer should at once be given.

Since a transferee takes the mortgage subject to the state of the accounts at the date of transfer, he is, unless a contrary intention is expressed,

---

[32] See *Matthews* v. *Wallwyn* (1798) 4 Ves. 118 at 126(a). In the case of a transfer of statutory mortgage the covenant will be implied if the transferee is joined in the transfer (L.P.A. 1925, s.118(3)).

[33] (1936) 155 L.T. 104.

[34] *Bickerton* v. *Walker* (1885) 31 Ch.D. 151; L.P.A. 1925, s.68. *Cf.* also *Dixon* v. *Winch* [1900] 1 Ch. 736, where the mortgagor's equity was lost on the ground of imputed notice.

[35] *Stocks* v. *Dobson* (1853) 4 De G.M. & G. 11.

[36] *Williams* v. *Sorrell* (1799) 4 Ves. 389.

[37] *Dixon* v. *Winch* [1900] 1 Ch. 736 at 742, *per* Cozens-Hardy J.

[38] *Norrish* v. *Marshall* (1821) 5 Madd 475; *Re Lord Southampton's Estate* (1880) 16 Ch.D. 178.

[39] In *Norrish* v. *Marshall* (*ante*) the mortgagor paid in goods, not money.

entitled to arrears of interest.[40] But, in accordance with the general rule that arrears may not be capitalised, except by agreement, a transferee has no right to treat the arrears as part of the principal merely because he has had to pay the aggregate sum to obtain his investment.[41] This right may be obtained if the mortgagor is made to join in the transfer and to assent to the capitalisation of the arrears, because it will be assumed that his assent was given in return for forbearance by the creditor.[42] If the transfer is properly drawn it will contain such an agreement for capitalisation in express terms, but it seems that the court will also infer the agreement from the mere fact of the mortgagor's concurrence.[43]

It should also be noticed that the sum paid to the mortgagee on a transfer does not determine the amount to which his transfer entitles him against the mortgagor. The market value of a mortgage is not necessarily the amount due on the security, because the soundness of the security and the general credit of the debtor materially affect its attractiveness as an investment.[44] Therefore, a transferee, who purchases his mortgage at a price less than the amount of the mortgage debt, may stand on his rights as assignee of the mortgagee and claim the full amount of the debt from the mortgagor.[45] This is true, whether the transferee is a stranger,[46] a mesne incumbrancer,[47] or a person otherwise beneficially interested in the estate.[48] But the mortgagor himself and his personal representatives, who succeed to his liability on the contract for payment, cannot, of course, buy up the first mortgage at an under value and hold it against mesne incumbrancers, for they have no right to keep the mortgage alive at all, and it is wholly extinguished on the transfer being taken.[49] Again, in special circumstances a transferee may not be permitted to hold the mortgage as security for more than its purchase price on the ground that he is in a fiduciary relation with the mortgagor. Thus, a trustee,[50] solicitor,[51] agent[52] or any other person, whose position gives him special opportunities of buying up the mortgage, and of knowing its real value, will hold the mortgage subject to redemption only at the price for which he bought it.[53]

---

[40] *Cottrell* v. *Finney* (1874) 9 Ch. App. 541.
[41] *Ashenhurst* v. *James* (1845) 3 Atk. 270; *Matthews* v. *Wallwyn* (1798) 4 Ves. 118.
[42] *Cf. Porter* v. *Hobbard* (1677) Freem. Ch. 30. But a mesne incumbrancer will not be bound by such an agreement, if the prior mortgagee had notice of his incumbrance: *Digby* v. *Craggs* (1762) Amb. 612.
[43] *Agnew* v. *King* [1902] 1 I.R. 471.
[44] See *Anon.* (1707) 1 Salk 155.
[45] *Davis* v. *Barrett* (1851) 14 Beav. 542.
[46] *Phillips* v. *Vaughan* (1685) 1 Vern. 336.
[47] *Darcy* v. *Hall* (1682) 1 Vern. 49.
[48] *e.g.* a reversioner (*Davis* v. *Barrett* (1851) 14 Beav. 542); but a life tenant under the Settled Land Act 1925, would be in a fiduciary position.
[49] *Otter* v. *Lord Vaux* (1856) 6 De G.M. & G. 638; *Morrett* v. *Paske* (1740) 2 Atk. 52; see *post,* p. 391.
[50] *Darcy* v. *Hall* (1682) 1 Vern. 49.
[51] *Macleod* v. *Jones* (1883) 24 Ch.D. 289.
[52] *Carter* v. *Palmer* (1841) 8 Cl. & F. 657.
[53] *Hobday* v. *Peters (No. 1)* (1860) 28 Beav. 349. Similarly a surety: *Reed* v. *Norris* (1837) 2 My. & Cr. 361.

Transfer part of mortgage debt

If the mortgagee wishes to transfer part of the mortgage debt and not the whole, it is necessary either to execute a transfer of the whole debt and mortgaged property to a trustee for both the transfer and transferee, or for the mortgagee to execute a declaration of trust. The reason for this is that the mortgagee's powers of redemption, foreclosure or sale are indivisible and the executors of a trust deed or declaration of trust are the only methods available.

Transfer of registered charge

In the case of the transfer of a registered charge the proprietor of such a charge may transfer it by means of Form 54. Completion of the transfer then occurs when the registrar enters the transferee in the register as the proprietor.[54] Provided that he had no notice of any irregularity or invalidity in the original charge, a registered transferee for valuable consideration and his successors in title should not be affected thereby.[55] Once registration has been effected the term granted rests in the proprietor for the time being of the charge without any consequence or assignment.[56] But until the registration formalities have been completed the transferee of the charge does not become the proprietor. The effect of this is that until registration is completed the transferee cannot exercise his statutory powers, for example, the power to appoint a receiver.[57]

Transfers of local authority mortgages

Since the enactment[58] of the Local Government Act 1986, section 7, a local authority wishing to transfer any interests in land which they hold as mortgagee must obtain the prior written consent of the mortgagor.

The Act makes specific provision for the local authority to ensure that the mortgagor has the opportunity to make an informed decision whether or not to give consent. Thus the consent must specify the name of the transferee, it may be withdrawn by notice in writing at any time before the date of the transfer, and it ceases to have effect if the transfer does not take place within six months after the consent is given.[59] Further, the Local Authorities (Disposal of Mortgages) Regulations 1986[60] impose requirements in the case of transfers taking place on or after September 1, 1986. In particular, the mortgagor's consent must be in the form set out in the Schedule to the Regulations, and the local authority must supply the mortgagor with information specified by the Regulations. A transfer made with-

---

[54] Land Registration Act 1925, s.33(1), (2).
[55] *Ibid.* s.33(3).
[56] *Ibid.* s.33(4), (5).
[57] *Lever Finance Ltd.* v. *Trustee of the Property of Needleman* [1956] Ch. 375.
[58] Applying to all transfers made *after* April 1, 1986 (unless pursuant to a contract made before that date).
[59] Local Government Act 1986, s.7(1) and (2).
[60] S.I. 1986 No. 1028.

out consent is void.[61] It is to be presumed that failure to comply with the requirements set out in section 7 and in the regulations has the same effect. There is also special provision in the case of transfers which appear on their face to be valid. Thus it is provided[62] that a transfer made following an initially valid consent is valid even if the consent has expired or been withdrawn by the date of the transfer, provided that the transfer contains a certificate by the transferor that consent has not been withdrawn or ceased to have effect. In such a case, however, the mortgagor is entitled to have the transfer set aside and the mortgage re-vested in the transferor by serving notice to that effect on the local authority within six months of the transfer.

Sub-mortgages

A sub-mortgage is in essence a transfer of a mortgage subject to a proviso for redemption. In other words, it is a mortgage of a mortgage and it arises when a mortgagee wishes to borrow money upon the security of a profitable mortgage and it avoids the calling in of the whole of the loan. Therefore, the rules set out above apply *mutatis mutandis* to sub-mortgages.

But, after 1925 if the original mortgage was of the legal estate and created by demise, the sub-mortgage cannot be effected by assignment of the estate. It can only be created by *the transfer* of the mortgage debt, together with a separate sub-demise of the estate, or with a separate legal charge or equitable mortgage of the estate.[63] This means that the simple form of transfer provided by section 114 is not appropriate,[64] but otherwise the effect of the transaction is the same as if a transfer were made subject to a proviso for redemption.[65] In all other cases the sub-mortgage can be effected by a transfer of the benefit of the head mortgage by a deed under section 114.[66] Whatever its form, a sub-mortgage should contain an express covenant for payment of the monies due under the sub-mortgage and a proviso for redemption of the sub-mortgage. Further, the original mortgagor should join in the transaction or be given immediate notice of it in order to avoid the problems which can arise under cases such as *Norrish* v. *Marshall* and *Parker* v. *Jackson*.[67]

Therefore, a sub-mortgage makes the sub-mortgagee a transferee of the original mortgage subject to an equity of redemption in the mortgagee. As

---

[61] Local Government Act 1986, s.7(3).

[62] *Ibid.* s.7(4), (5).

[63] L.P.A. 1925, s.86(1), (3).

[64] It can, however, be used, since s.86(2) provides that an attempt to mortgage a term of years by assignment shall take effect as a sub-demise.

[65] See Key & Elphinstone, *Precedents in Conveyancing*, (15th ed., 1953–54), Vol. 2, pl. 230.

[66] Some doubt has been expressed, however, as to the appropriateness of this method, see (1948) 12 Conv.(N.S.) 171 (H. Woodhouse).

[67] *Norrish* v. *Marshall* (1821) 5 Madd. 475; *Parker* v. *Jackson* (1936) 155 L.T. 104. A sub-mortgagee being in the position of a transferee, takes subject to the state of the accounts between the mortgagor and the mortgagee at the date of the sub-mortgage. If the mortgagor's concurrence is not obtained notice must be given to him to avoid the consequences of any equities arising after the date of the transfer.

such, he may exercise all the powers of the original mortgagee and may sell, foreclose, dispose of the fee simple or lease under sections 88(5) or 89(5) of the Law of Property Act 1925, or otherwise realise the mortgaged property.[68]

For example: A mortgages Blackacre for £1,000 to B. Owing to arrears of interest the mortgage debt stands at £1,500 when B sub-mortgages to C for an advance of £500. A, the mortgagor, is made to concur and C thus holds a mortgage for £1,500 as security for his advance of £500.

C, if he subsequently wishes to realise his security, has two choices. He may either realise on his sub-mortgage alone, or on the original mortgage which necessarily involves terminating the sub-mortgage as well. If he sells his sub-mortgage to X for £600, and his own account against B remains at £500, he must pay over the surplus to B whilst X becomes transferee of the mortgage. If, on the other hand, he sells Blackacre itself for £2,000, he pays himself his £500, then discharges A's debt to B, deducting £500 from B's claim, and finally hands over any surplus to A. On the same principle, he may foreclose on the mortgagee without disturbing the original mortgagor or making him a party, but if he forecloses on the mortgagor, the mortgagee must be joined as a party and given an opportunity to redeem.

In the case of registered land a proprietor of a registered charge may charge the mortgage debt with the payment of money in the same way as a proprietor of registered land may charge the land. Such charges are referred to as sub-charges.[69] This must be completed by registration[70] and thereupon the sub-chargee will be entered as proprietor of the sub-charge and be issued with a sub-charge certificate.[71] Subject to any entry to the contrary, the proprietor of the sub-charge has the same powers of disposition in relation to the land as if he had been registered as proprietor of the principal charge.[72]

INTER VIVOS TRANSFER OF EQUITY OF REDEMPTION

In the absence of any express provisions or statutory enactment to the contrary,[73] a mortgagor can at any time transfer the mortgaged property without the mortgagee's consent. But he remains personally liable on the covenant to pay despite such transfer.[74]

---

[68] A sub-mortgage, which transfers the original power of sale to the sub-mortgagee, appears at the same time to deprive the original mortgagee of the power, see *Cruse* v. *Nowell* (1856) 25 L.J.Ch. 709.

[69] Land Registration Act 1925, s.36; Land Registration Rules 1925, r. 163(1).

[70] Land Registration Rules 1925, r. 164(1).

[71] *Ibid.* r. 166.

[72] *Ibid.* r. 163(2).

[73] Under the Small Dwellings Acquisition Acts 1899 to 1923 the mortgagor was restricted from transferring the mortgaged property. These Acts have now been repealed by the Housing (Consequential Provisions) Act 1985. But the Housing Act 1985, s.456 and Sched. 18, contain provisions applicable to existing mortgages made under the previous legislation. Most building society mortgages contain restrictions on transfer.

[74] See *ante*, pp. 279 *et seq.*

A mortgagor is only able to convey his property unincumbered if:

(1) the mortgagee consents to the transfer; or
(2) the mortgagor redeems the mortgage; or
(3) a declaration is obtained from the court by the mortgagor that the property is free from incumbrances upon sufficient money being paid into court.[75]

DEVOLUTION ON DEATH

In *Thornborough* v. *Baker*,[76] Lord Nottingham settled conclusively that, whatever the nature of the property mortgaged, a mortgagee's interest in his mortgage is personalty. The result was that until 1882 freehold estates in mortgage caused difficulty upon the mortgagee's intestacy, for the estate passed to the heir-at-law while the debt belonged to the personal representatives,[77] and since the estate was in equity only a security, the heir-at-law held it on trust for the personal representatives.[78] The Conveyancing Act 1881[79] (superseded by the Land Transfer Act 1897[79a]), however, provided that a mortgaged estate should pass to the personal representatives as if it were a chattel real, notwithstanding any testamentary disposition to the contrary. The point is merely of historical interest, though it may arise in an occasional search on title. The Law of Property Act 1925 removes all difficulties by its initial provision that mortgages of freehold cannot be created by the conveyance of the title, but must be effected through terms of years, the result being that both the security and the debt are in their own nature personalty. Furthermore, the Administration of Estates Act 1925,[80] has instituted a single system of devolution upon intestacy for both realty and personalty. On the death of a mortgagee the mortgage and the debt devolve on his personal representatives who, until the mortgage is discharged, or until they have assented in favour of the persons next entitled, may exercise all the powers of the mortgagee.[81] But the basic principle in *Thornborough* v. *Baker*[82] is still of importance; the benefit of the mortgage passes under a general bequest of personalty, not a general devise of realty,[83] whilst a specific devisee takes the mortgage as personalty. This rule is on the assumption that the equity of redemption is still subsisting. If the equity of redemption is destroyed by foreclosure, or by the mortgagee

---

[75] L.P.A. 1925, s.50(1), (2); see *ante*, pp. 276, 277.
[76] (1675) 3 Swann. 628.
[77] *Ibid.*
[78] *Re Loveridge, Drayton* v. *Loveridge* [1902] 2 Ch. 859.
[79] s.30.
[79a] s.1(1).
[80] ss.1(1), 3(1).
[81] In the case of the death of one of several mortgagees, see *ante*, pp. 329, 330, and the operation of the joint account clause in the case where two or more persons lend money.
[82] (1675) 3 Swann. 628.
[83] Even a specific devise of Blackacre will not give the devisee the beneficial interest in a mortgage held by the testator if he also held a reversionary interest in the property: the devisee will get the reversionary interest only: *Bowen* v. *Barlow* (1872) L.R. 8 Ch. 171.

having been in possession for the statutory period without acknowledging the debt, a conversion takes place and his interest acquires the nature of the property mortgaged, so that in the case of freehold it becomes realty.[83a]

Assent by personal representatives

Although a mortgage term is "an estate or interests in real estate" for the purposes of section 36(1) of the Administration of Estates Act 1925, a mortgage debt is not. Thus there is some doubt as to whether an assent by personal representatives is sufficient to pass both the legal estate and the debt. But as such a debt passes if there is a clear intention that it should,[84] it seems that no difficulty would arise in most cases.

DEVOLUTION ON INSOLVENCY[84a]

Insolvency of mortgagee

In the case of an individual insolvency of an individual mortgagee,[85] any mortgage, like the rest of the bankrupt's estate vests (with certain exceptions) in his trustee.[86] Thus his trustee may exercise all the mortgagee's powers and remedies, including the right to sue for foreclosure.[87]

In the case of registered land the trustee is entitled to be registered as the proprietor in the place of the bankrupt,[88] but he may deal with the charge before registration.[89]

Where a company mortgagee has been dissolved all property and rights whatsoever, vested in or held in trust for the company immediately before its dissolution is deemed to be *bona vacentia* and devolves to the Crown.[89a]

Insolvency of mortgagor

In the case of the insolvency of the mortgagor, again the insolvent's estate vests (with certain exceptions) in his trustee. The effect of this is that the bankrupt cannot mortgage or further mortgage his property. His insolvency also divests him of his right to redeem any mortgaged property, such right passing to his trustee under statutory powers.[89b]

But the mortgagor's insolvency does not prevent him from mortgaging whatever excepted property remains vested in him[90] or from mortgaging

---

[83a] See *Garrett* v. *Evers* (1730) Mos. 364; *Thompson* v. *Grant* (1819) 4 Madd. 438; *Re Loveridge, Pearce* v. *Marsh* [1904] 1 Ch. 518.

[84] *Re Culverhouse* [1896] 2 Ch. 251.

[84a] See also *ante*, p. 192.

[85] For a more detailed analysis of the positions of both the mortgagee and mortgagor on insolvency, see further *Williams & Muir Hunter on Bankruptcy* (19th ed., 1979).

[86] Insolvency Act 1986, s.306.

[87] *Waddell* v. *Toleman* (1878) 9 Ch.D. 212.

[88] Land Registration Act 1925, s.42.

[89] *Ibid.* s.37; Land Registration Rules 1925, r. 170.

[89a] Companies Act 1985, s.654.

[89b] Insolvency Act 1986, s.306.

[90] *Bird* v. *Philpott* [1900] 1 Ch. 822.

any property acquired after the commencement of his bankruptcy if his trustee has not intervened to exercise his rights to such property.[91] The insolvency of the mortgagor does not affect a right of the mortgagee as a secured creditor of the bankrupt to enforce his security.[92] Thus, a secured creditor can choose not to come in under the bankruptcy but to use the ordinary remedies available to him for enforcing his security.[93] He cannot, however, prove twice for the same debt.[94] Nor can he retain his security and at the same time prove for the value of the debt. He can only prove for the deficiency after allowing for the security.[95] Further, where any express or statutory power of sale or power to appoint a receiver is made exercisable by reason of the bankruptcy of the mortgagee, such power is not to be exercised only on the account of the adjudication without the leave of the court.[96-97]

Remedies of mortgagee

The mortgagee may exercise his rights under the mortgage on the insolvency of the mortgagor. Thus, the mortgagee may commence proceedings for foreclosure or other appropriate remedy. Such an action will be against the mortgagor's trustee.[98] But is must be noted that in the place of a company at anytime after the presentation of a winding-up petition and before a winding-up order has been made, the company or any creditor or contributory may where any action or proceeding against the company is pending in the High Court or Court of Appeal apply to the court in which the action or proceeding is pending for a stay of proceedings. Where any other action or proceeding is pending against the company such person may apply to the court having jurisdiction to wind-up the company to restrain further proceedings on such terms as the court thinks fit.[99] When a winding-up order has been made or a provisional liquidator appointed, no action or proceeding shall be proceeded with or commenced against the company or its property except by leave of a court and subject to such terms as the court may impose.[99a]

In the case of an individual at any time when proceedings on a bank-

---

[91] Insolvency Act 1986, ss.283(2), 307(4); *Cohen* v. *Mitchell* (1890) 25 Q.B.D. 262.
[92] *Ibid.* s.285(4). By virtue of the s.383(1), (2), a "secured creditor" is a creditor who holds a security for the debt (whether a mortgage, charge, lien or other security) over any property of the person by whom the debt is owed.
[93] *White* v. *Simmons* (1871) 6 Ch.App. 555.
[94] *Deering* v. *Bank of Ireland* (1887) 12 App.Cas. 20.
[95] See the Insolvency Rules 1986, rr. 4.88(1), 6.109(1). See also *Re Rushton (a bankrupt), ex p. National Westminster Bank Ltd.* v. *Official Receiver* [1972] Ch. 197.
[96-97] See the L.P.A. 1925, s.110(1), as altered by the Insolvency Act 1985, s.235(3), Sched. 10, pt. III.
[98] *Re Wherly, ex p. Hirst* (1879) 11 Ch.D. 278; and see *Re Hutton (a bankrupt)* [1969] 2 Ch. 201. Where the statutory, or an express, power to sell or appoint a receiver is made exercisable by reason of the mortgagor being adjudged bankrupt, such power is not to be exercised only on account of the adjudication without leave of the court, L.P.A. 1925, s.110(1) as amended by the Insolvency Act 1985, s.235, Sched. 10, Pt. III.
[99] Insolvency Act 1986, s.126(1).
[99a] *Ibid.* s.130(2).

ruptcy petition are pending or an individual has been adjudged bankrupt, the court[1] may stay any action, execution or other legal process against the property or person of the debtor or, as the case may be, of the bankrupt.[2] Any court in which proceedings are pending against any individual may, on proof that a bankruptcy petition has been presented in respect of that individual or that he is an undischarged bankrupt, either stay the proceedings or allow them to continue on such terms as it thinks fit.[3]

After the making of a bankruptcy order no person who is a creditor of the bankrupt in respect of a debt provable in the bankruptcy shall (a) have any remedy against the property or person of the bankrupt in respect of that debt; or, (b) before the discharge of the bankrupt commence any action or other legal proceedings against the bankrupt except with the leave of the court and on such terms as the court may impose,[4] but this provision shall not affect the right of a secured creditor of the bankrupt to enforce his security.[5]

In the case where an interim receiver has been appointed under the Act[6] during the period between the appointment and the making of a bankruptcy order on the petition, or the dismissal of the petition, no creditor of the debtor, other than a secured creditor, shall commence any action or other legal proceedings against the debtor except with the leave of the court and on such terms as the court may impose.[7]

Acquired property

In the case where a bankrupt mortgages an equitable chose in action and his trustee has not perfected his title by notice[8] the mortgage will be effective against the trustee. A similar position arises where the trustee has stood by and allowed the mortgagee to advance the loan upon the belief that the bankrupt could dispose of his property.[9] Also a mortgage by a bankrupt will be effective against his trustee in favour of the mortgagee where the receiving order or bankruptcy petition has not been registered pursuant to the Land Charges Act 1972[10] provided that the mortgagee is acting in good faith.

---

[1] The High Court and those county courts upon which jurisdiction in insolvency matters has been conferred: see Insolvency Act 1986, ss.373, 374. Those county courts upon which jurisdiction in insolvency matters has been conferred have all the powers and jurisdiction of the High Court: Insolvency Act 1986, s.373.

[2] Insolvency Act 1986, s.285(1).

[3] *Ibid.* s.285(2).

[4] *Ibid.* s.285(3). This is subject to certain exceptions.

[5] *Ibid.* s.285(4) and see s.285(5).

[6] *Ibid.* s.286.

[7] *Ibid.* s.286(6).

[8] *Stuart* v. *Cockerell* (1869) L.R. 8 Eq. 607; *Palmer* v. *Locke* (1881) 18 Ch.D. 381. But if the trustee first gives notice his title will prevail see *Re Beall, ex p. Official Receiver* [1899] 1 Q.B. 688.

[9] *Troughton* v. *Gitley* (1766) Amb. 630; *Re Bourne, ex p. Bourne* (1826) 2 Gl. & J. 137 at 141; *Tucker* v. *Hernaman* (1853) 4 De G.M. & G. 395.

[10] ss.6, 7, 8.

Mortgages by trustee in bankruptcy

With the consent of the creditors' committee or order of the court, the trustee in bankruptcy may mortgage any part of the property of the bankrupt which has passed to him under the bankruptcy for the purpose of raising money for the payment of the debts of the bankrupt.[11]

---

[11] Insolvency Act 1986, s.314(1)(*a*), Sched. 5, para. 4.

CHAPTER 20

EXTINGUISHMENT OF THE SECURITY

DISCHARGE OF THE MORTGAGE OR CHARGE

The precise character of the instrument necessary to release the security depends on the nature of the mortgage, though the Law of Property Act 1925 has made it largely a matter of an appropriate receipt. Prior to 1926, when mortgages of freehold were usually made by conveyance of the legal estate, redemption involved a deed of reconveyance executed by the mortgagee, or the mortgagor's chain of title would be incomplete.[1] Again, in mortgages of leasehold made, as a rule, by sub-demise, redemption necessitated an express surrender of the sub-lease, because the Satisfied Terms Act 1845, did not apply to terms created out of leaseholds.[2] Equitable mortgages, on the other hand, did not require any instrument of reconveyance, because the receipt of the mortgage moneys automatically terminated the equity[3]: nevertheless it was in fact quite common to have a reconveyance even in these cases. In one class of mortgage, however, namely, building society mortgages, special legislation[4] enabled the discharge of such mortgages to be effected by a receipt indorsed on or annexed to the mortgage deed. In these cases the receipt operated as an automatic reconveyance of the property mortgaged.

Indorsed receipt

The Law of Property Act 1925 has simplified the machinery of redemption by extending this principle to all mortgages of land, except those of registered land. Thus, under section 115 a receipt for the mortgage moneys indorsed on, written at the foot of, or annexed to the mortgage instrument, and executed by the mortgagee[5] operates:

(1) in the case of a mortgage by demise or sub-demise, as an automatic surrender of the term, so that the term is merged in the reversion, which is immediately expectant on the term;

(2) in other cases, as an automatic reconveyance of the mortgaged interest to the person who, immediately before the execution of the receipt, was entitled to the equity of redemption.

---

[1] *Webb* v. *Crosse* [1912] 1 Ch. 323.
[2] *Re Moore & Hulm's Contract* [1912] 2 Ch. 105.
[3] *Firth & Sons* v. *I.R. Commissioners* [1904] 2 K.B. 205.
[4] Building Societies Act 1986, s.
[5] The receipt need not be under seal; all that the statute requires is that it should be executed under the hand of the mortgagee: *Simpson* v. *Geoghehan* [1934] W.N. 232. The production by a solicitor of his client's indorsed receipt is a sufficient authority to the debt to make his payment to the solicitor; see the L.P.A. 1925, s.69.

The result is that an indorsed receipt at once exonerates the property from the mortgage, but does not alter the position of any one with an interest in the property paramount to the discharged mortgage. Thus it operates to discharge the mortgagor in respect of all claims against the mortgaged property.

In one case where the mortgagee had made an arithmetical error in calculating the redemption figure it was held that the mortgage had been validly discharged.[6]

Payment by persons not entitled to the immediate equity

A mortgage is not always redeemed by the person immediately entitled to the equity of redemption[7] but sometimes by a person—for example, a third or later mortgagee—who is entitled to have the charge kept alive against the second incumbrancer. In such cases, if the receipt were allowed to effect a surrender of the term or reconveyance of the security, the charge would be extinguished: accordingly, it is provided that if the receipt clearly indicates[8] that the money was not paid by the person entitled to the immediate equity of redemption, the indorsement is to operate as a *transfer* of the mortgage by deed to the person actually named as the payer.[9] Of course, if the latter does not wish to keep the charge alive, his intention not to take a transfer can be stated in the receipt by means of a declaration to this effect, in which case the indorsement will have its usual effect. Section 115, in fact, takes care to preserve the law as to merger of charges intact, and by subsection (3) prevents a mortgagor from making use of these provisions to redeem and keep alive a first mortgage against a later incumbrance which he himself has created. This was forbidden in *Otter* v. *Lord Vaux*[10] and subsection (3), perhaps *ex abundanti cautela*, warns that this case is still good law.

Use of the simple receipt

Although the extended use of the indorsed (or statutory) receipt has simplified the conveyancing side of redemption, it is important to remember that in the case of mortgages of legal estates, sections 5 and 116 of the Law of Property Act 1925 afford an alternative[11] means of discharging the mort-

---

[6] *Erewash Borough Council* v. *Taylor* (1979) C.L. 1831 C.C.
[7] In the case of several incumbrances, the person *immediately* entitled to the equity of redemption is, of course, the second incumbrancer.
[8] There need not be an express statement to that effect, provided that the fact sufficiently appears: *Simpson* v. *Geoghehan* [1934] W.N. 232.
[9] s.115(2). See also *Cumberland Court (Brighton) Ltd.* v. *Taylor* [1964] Ch. 29 where it was held that although the receipt had operated as a transfer of the charge to the *vendor* (as the receipt was dated *after* the conveyance), there was no defect in title as there was an estoppel from the recitals in the conveyance which was "fed" on transfer and passed the interest in the property to the purchaser.
[10] (1856) 6 De G.M. & G. 638. For the rules regarding merger of charges see *post*, pp. 393 *et seq.*
[11] And prior to the Finance Act 1971, s.64, (which abolished stamp duty on mortgages), a cheaper means of discharging the mortgage.

gage[12] if it has been created by demise. Section 5 affirms the provisions of the Satisfied Terms Act 1845 and extends them to sub-terms created out of leaseholds. Section 116 expressly brings mortgage terms and sub-terms within the same principle, so that (provided that there is written evidence) mortgages by demise or sub-demise may now be discharged by a mere payment of the mortgage debt, the term thereby being automatically merged in the reversion. Here again merger does not take place if the person making payment has a right to have the charge kept alive, and he may in these circumstances obtain a transfer of the mortgage instead. But it must be said that conveyancers in practice do not rely on such an "ordinary" receipt and prefer the statutory form, as the ordinary form is only prima facie evidence of payment.

But, in any case, the Law of Property Act 1925 reserves for a person who redeems an absolute right to demand a reconveyance in place of the indorsed receipt.[13] This right will not, however, be frequently exercised, because a reconveyance only increases the cost of redemption. There are, however, occasions when a reconveyance is still not merely convenient, but an actual necessity. For example, if a mortgagor is redeeming only as to part of the debt, so that only a portion of the mortgaged property is being exonerated, an indorsed receipt cannot be employed. Section 115 in terms confines the use of a receipt to occasions when *all* the moneys charged upon the property under the mortgage are being repaid. In cases, therefore, of partial redemption a reconveyance is essential.

After redemption the title deeds should be returned to the mortgagor. If there is another person, such as a subsequent mortgagee, with a better title, the Law of Property Act 1925, section 96(2) (as amended) provides that the mortgagee whose mortgage is surrendered or otherwise extinguished is not liable on account of delivering the deeds to the person not having the best right thereto, unless he has notice of the better right. It is further expressly provided that notice does not include statutory notice implied by reason of registration under the Land Charges Act 1972.

Mortgages of registered land

Mortgages of registered land are outside section 115, and are dealt with by section 35 of the Land Registration Act 1925. Under this Act mortgages are discharged by a notification in the register that the charge has been cancelled, and the registrar will enter this notification, either at the request of the mortgagee or upon sufficient proof that the mortgage has been paid off.[14] The effect of such a notification is to extinguish any term of years created by the mortgage. The Land Certificate will then be redelivered to the mortgagor. Alternatively, under rule 160 of the Land Registration

---

[12] Either a mortgage by demise or a charge by way of legal mortgage, see *Edwards* v. *Marshall-Lee* (1975) 235 E.G. 901.

[13] s.115(4).

[14] A discharge should be in Form 53, see Land Registration Rules 1925, r. 151 and Sched. The charge certificate and discharge must be lodged at the Land Registry with Form A4.

Rules 1925, the person paying off the charge may himself be registered as the proprietor of the charge, a step which is necessary when the charge is to be kept alive.

Discharge of equitable mortgages

The statutory method of discharge is inappropriate in the case of equitable mortgages. But, although not strictly necessary as a simple receipt will suffice, there is usually a reconveyance of the property to the mortgagor.

Discharge of legal choses in action

In the case of the discharge of a legal chose in action a statutory receipt or reassignment is necessary.

MERGER OF A MORTGAGE OR CHARGE

Equitable doctrine of merger—a question of intention

The purchase of an equity of redemption by the mortgagee or the redemption of a mortgage by a person entitled to redeem seems, at first sight, certain to put an end to the mortgage and such, in fact, was the result at common law.[15] In equity, however, the merger, both of charges and of estates, was purely a question of intention,[16] and did not occur automatically on the union in one hand of a charge with an estate, or of a lesser estate in a greater. Indeed, so free from technicalities were the equitable rules, that the intention to extinguish a charge might produce a merger, although the estate was outstanding in a trustee, so that there would be no merger at common law.[17] Equitable principles now prevail,[18] and, in any case, section 185 of the Law of Property Act 1925[19] expressly provides that "there is no merger by operation of law only of any estate the beneficial interest in which would not be deemed to be merged or extinguished in equity," while section 116 recognises that the discharge of the mortgage debt does not necessarily extinguish the mortgage.

The main object of keeping alive a charge, which has been paid off, is that it may afford a protection against subsequent incumbrances. The doctrine of equity is based on the principle that a later incumbrancer has no claim to benefit gratuitously from a transaction to which he himself contributes nothing.[20] For when merger takes place the result is that a second incumbrancer is raised to the position of first incumbrancer without any

---

[15] Either by analogy to the merger of estates or on the principle that a man cannot be his own debtor.

[16] *Forbes* v. *Moffatt* (1811) 8 Ves. 384.

[17] *Astley* v. *Milles* (1827) 1 Sim. 298, 344; *Forbes* v. *Moffatt* (1811) 18 Ves.Jr. 384 at 390.

[18] Supreme Court Act 1981, s.49(1), re-enacting the Judicature Act 1873, s.25(11) and the Supreme Court (Consolidation) Act 1925, s.44.

[19] Re-enacting s.25(4) of the Judicature Act 1873.

[20] *Cf.* Fletcher-Moulton L.J., in *Manks* v. *Whiteley* (1912) 1 Ch. 735 at 764.

effort of his own. Equity, therefore, does not, except in one case, consider a charge to be extinguished by the mere fact of its being paid off, but makes merger a question of intention. The one exception is that where a mortgagor himself pays off an incumbrance he can in no circumstances set it up as a protection against a later mortgage which he has himself created.[21] Not even an express declaration of intention in the deed of discharge will avail him to keep the incumbrance alive. The reason is that a second mortgage, as between the parties, is a grant of the mortgagor's entire interest in the property, saving only the rights of the prior incumbrancer, and the mortgagor cannot derogate from his grant by holding the first mortgage against the second mortgagee.[22] This is the position even in the case where a third party provides the mortgagor with the necessary money to redeem the mortgage.[23-24]

A purchaser of the equity of redemption is not, however, under this disability, for the same considerations do not apply. He may pay off a charge and take a transfer of the mortgage. He can then keep it alive to protect himself against a subsequent incumbrance which he has not himself created, because he has no personal contract with the subsequent incumbrancer.[25] Consequently, in the case of a purchaser of the equity of redemption, the general rule applies, and merger depends on intention.

The intention to extinguish a charge is a question of fact to be established by the evidence. There are, however, certain presumptions as to intention which are made by the court, and decide the onus of proof.[26] The principle on which all these presumptions are based is that a person intends a charge to be kept alive or merged, according as to whether it is of advantage or of no advantage to him that the charge be kept alive.[27] The result is that:

(a) If a life tenant or any other limited owner (not a tenant in tail)[28] acquires or pays off a charge, there is a presumption against merger, because merger would operate as a gift of the charge to those in remainder.[29]

(b) If a person entitled in possession to either a fee simple or a fee tail acquires a charge on the estate, whether by devolution or by paying off the chargee, the presumption is in favour of merger, unless the estate is defeasible by the operation of a condition. In

---

[21] *Otter* v. *Lord Vaux* (1856) 6 De G.M. & G. 638.

[22] A mortgagor " . . . cannot derogate from his own bargain by setting up the mortgage so purchased against a second mortgagee." *Per* Lord Haldane L.C. in *Whiteley* v. *Delaney* [1914] A.C. 132 at 145. See also *Frazer* v. *Jones* (1846) 5 Hare 475.

[23-24] *Parkash* v. *Irani Finance Ltd.* [1970] Ch. 101. *Adams* v. *Angell* (1877) 5 Ch.D. 634; *Thorne* v. *Cann* (1895) A.C. 11; *Whiteley* v. *Delaney* [1914] A.C. 132.

[25] *Burrell* v. *Earl Egremont* (1844) 7 Beav. 205.

[26] *Per* Parker J. in *Manks* v. *Whiteley* (1911) 2 Ch. 448 at 458.

[27] A tenant in tail is for this purpose an absolute owner, because he has it in his power to become owner of the whole fee.

[28] *Burrell* v. *Lord Egremont* (1844) 7 Beav. 205; *Lord Gifford* v. *Lord Fitzhardinge* (1899) 2 Ch. 32.

[29] *Donisthorpe* v. *Porter* (1762) 2 Eden 162.

general, there is no advantage in a man having a charge on his
own estate, and the removal of the charge simplifies the title.

(c) If a person entitled in remainder to a fee simple or a fee tail
acquires a charge, no merger takes place until the estate comes
into possession. When this occurs, the question of merger
depends on the intention which the owner of the estate is presumed to have had *at the time when he acquired the charge*. Therefore, the presumption is against merger (if he acquired the charge
by paying it off himself) because he cannot have intended to
benefit the inheritance at a time when it was uncertain that he
would ever succeed to it.[30] On the other hand, if he acquired the
charge by devolution, he is presumed to have intended it to merge
in the inheritance, and merger takes place when the inheritance
comes into possession.[31]

The above presumptions as to the intention of a person who pays off a
charge are derived from the nature of his interest in the incumbered property. All are founded on the principle that he intends what is for his own
benefit, and does not intend to confer gratuitous benefits on strangers. It is
evident that at the time when a charge is acquired, there may exist other
circumstances which make it clearly beneficial for the person acquiring the
charge to keep it alive. If this is so, the court presumes that he does not
intend to extinguish his charge, and this presumption will displace the
ordinary presumption in favour of merger, when an absolute owner pays
off a charge on his estate. For example, the circumstance that a charge
acquired by the owner of an estate has priority over other incumbrances,
raises a presumption that he intends to keep it alive as a protection against
the other charges.[32] This does not, as we have seen, apply to incumbrances
created by the owner of the estate himself, because he can never keep alive
a charge against his own incumbrancers.[33] But a purchaser of an equity of
redemption may keep alive a charge, which he acquires, to protect himself
against mesne incumbrances, if such was his intention at the time when he
acquired the charge.[34] Similarly, a prior mortgagee, who takes a release of
the equity of redemption, may keep his own charge alive against later
mortgagees. In these cases, as in others, merger is a matter of intention.[35]

It would, therefore, be expected that, when the purchaser of an equity of
redemption pays off a charge, the existence of mesne incumbrances would
automatically raise a presumption against merger, under the general rule
that the intention is to be gathered from what is advantageous to the owner
of the charge. But the decision of Sir William Grant in *Toulmin* v. *Steere*[36]

[30] *Horton* v. *Smith* (1857) 4 K. & J. 624.
[31] *Ibid*.
[32] *Forbes* v. *Moffatt* (1811) 8 Ves. 384.
[33] *Otter* v. *Lord Vaux* (1856) 6 De G.M. & G. 638.
[34] *Whiteley* v. *Delaney* [1914] A.C. 132.
[35] *Adams* v. *Angell* (1877) 5 Ch.D. 634.
[36] (1817) 3 Mer. 210.

suggests that if the purchaser of an equity of redemption has actual or constructive notice of mesne incumbrances when he pays off a charge on the estate, the court will not presume an intention to keep alive the prior charge, so that the presumption is in favour of merger.[37] If this is correct, the intention to keep the charge on foot must be affirmatively proved, either by an express declaration to that effect in the deed of discharge, or otherwise by circumstances surrounding the transaction.[38]

The authority of *Toulmin* v. *Steere*, however, is very doubtful. It has been severely criticised by eminent judges,[38a] and runs counter to the general principle on which presumptions in favour of and against merger are based. There is no good reason for denying to a purchaser of an equity of redemption the benefit of a presumed intention to keep his charge alive in circumstances when it is clearly to his advantage to do so. Knowledge of the mesne incumbrances is irrelevant, because he can never be under any obligation to confer a gratuitous benefit on third parties. Indeed, notice of the puisne incumbrances only assists the presumption against merger, because it is sheer madness for the owner of an estate, who acquires a prior charge, to extinguish it when he knows of mesne incumbrances. *Toulmin* v. *Steere* was considered by the House of Lords in *Thorne* v. *Cann*,[38b] in *Liquidation Estates Purchase Co.* v. *Willoughby*,[38c] and in *Whiteley* v. *Delaney*.[39] It is probably not going too far to say that the case has not been expressly overruled only because of the great reputation of the judge who decided it and the accident that, for the decision of the cases before the House of Lords, it was unnecessary to do so.[39a] In *Thorne* v. *Cann* the court, in deciding that the purchaser of an equity of redemption intended to keep alive the charge which he had acquired, found indications of his intention, not only in the form of the instruments, but in the circumstances surrounding the transaction. It is difficult to believe that the existence of mesne incumbrances is not a circumstance from which such an indication of intention can be derived.[39b] After this decision, and the language of Lord Haldane in *Whiteley* v. *Delaney*, it is probably safe to say that *Toulmin* v. *Steere* will no longer be followed, and that the existence of mesne incumbrances raises a presumption against merger in all cases.

The foregoing presumptions do no more than establish the onus of

---

[37] Sir William Grant's decision actually went further than this and denied that even actual intention could in such a case keep the charge alive. This part of his decision has been clearly overruled by *Adams* v. *Angell* (1877) 5 Ch.D. 634, and *Thorne* v. *Cann* (1895) A.C. 11.

[38] *Thorne* v. *Cann* (1895) A.C. 11.

[38a] *e.g.* James L.J. in *Stevens* v. *Mid-Hants Rly. Co.* (1873) L.R. 8 Ch. 1064 at 1069; Lords Herschell and Macnaghten in *Thorne* v. *Cann* (1895) A.C. 11 at 16, 18; Fletcher-Moulton L.J. in *Manks* v. *Whiteley* (1912) 1 Ch. 735 at 759.

[38b] [1895] A.C. 11.

[38c] [1898] A.C. 321.

[39] [1914] A.C. 132, in particular at 144, 145.

[39a] In *Liquidation Estates Purchase Co.* v. *Willoughby* and *Whiteley* v. *Delaney* the cases were decided on other grounds; in *Thorne* v. *Cann* an actual intention was established.

[39b] Lindley L.J. in *Liquidation Estates Purchase Co.* v. *Willoughby*, thought that the dicta in *Thorne* v. *Cann* have overruled *Toulmin* v. *Steere* (1896) 1 Ch. 726 at 734.

proof, and do not prevail when there is sufficient evidence that the actual intention was otherwise. Such evidence is usually to be found in the instrument under which the property and the benefit of the charge become united in the same hand. Thus, if it is intended to keep a charge on foot, the proper course is to insert in the instrument an express declaration to that effect, for this will usually be conclusive of the intention.[40] But the form of the instrument itself may indicate the intention, either to keep alive or merge the charge; for example, if the instrument is in terms a transfer of the charge, it suggests that the charge is to be kept alive, but if the instrument is merely a reconveyance of the security, the merger of the charge appears to be the intention. In neither case, however, is the form of the transaction decisive, unless the surrounding circumstances point to the same conclusion.[41] Similarly, the fact that the charge is assigned to a trustee to be held for the owner of the estate, is not by itself sufficient evidence of an intention to keep the charge alive. In one case, however, the circumstances point conclusively to an intention to extinguish the charge, namely, when a mortgagee takes a conveyance of the equity of redemption in consideration not only of releasing his own debt, but of paying off all other incumbrances.[42]

In determining the question of merger or no merger, evidence of intention is therefore usually derived either from the language or the circumstances of the instrument by which the charge is acquired. It appears, however, that the court will allow parol evidence of intention to be given, for in *Astley* v. *Milles*[43] the solicitor, who had prepared the instruments by which a charge was acquired, was permitted to depose that the actual intention of the parties had been to keep the charge on foot. When the evidence establishes an intention to extinguish, this is decisive, since a charge, once merged, is destroyed for ever. If, on the other hand, a charge has been kept alive either by express declaration or by reason of the circumstances of its acquisition, this will not be conclusive if a subsequent alteration in the intention is proved; for example, when property is afterwards mortgaged or settled without the deeds noticing the charge, an intention to cancel the charge will be inferred.[44]

DESTRUCTION OR LOSS OF MORTGAGED PROPERTY

If the mortgaged property is lost or destroyed the benefit of the security may also be lost. This can arise for instance, in a case where a mortgaged leasehold is forfeited.[45] The mortgagor's personal liability on the covenant remains.[46]

[40] *Re Gibbon* [1909] 1 Ch. 367.
[41] *Hood* v. *Phillips* (1841) 3 Beav. 513.
[42] *Brown* v. *Stead* (1832) 5 Sim. 535.
[43] (1827) 1 Sim. 298 at 345.
[44] *Tyler* v. *Lake* (1831) 4 Sim. 351; *Hood* v. *Philipps* (1841) 3 Beav. 513.
[45] But see the L.P.A. 1925, s.146(4).
[46] See *ante*, p. 263.

DISCHARGE OR MODIFICATION BY STATUTE

Under the Housing Act 1985

The Housing Act 1985, Part XVII contains special provisions with regard to the discharge or modification of liabilities under a mortgage or instalment purchase agreement.[47] This part of the legislation was designed to provide for the removal by demolition or closure of unfit houses incapable of being rendered fit at reasonable expense, and also to provide for slum clearance. Provision is made for the payment of compensation in such circumstances.

Under the Leasehold Reform Act 1967

The purpose of this Act is to enable tenants of dwelling-houses held on long leases who fulfil the requisite residential qualification to acquire the freehold or an extended lease provided that the premises are within the appropriate rateable value limits and the tenancy is a long tenancy at a low rent. Where the tenant gives notice of his desire to have the freehold or an extended lease the landlord is bound subject to the Act to convey to him the fee simple absolute or a new tenancy for a term expiring 50 years after the existing tenancy. In such circumstances mortgages of both the landlord's and the tenant's interest in the premises may be affected.

The Act therefore provides for the discharge of mortgages on the landlord's estate. A conveyance executed to give effect to the tenant's right to acquire the freehold shall as regards any charge on the landlord's estate (however created or arising) to secure the payment of money or the performance of any other obligation by the landlord or any other person, not being a charge subject to which the conveyance is required to be made or which would be overreached apart from this section, be effective by virtue of this section to discharge the house and premises from the charge, and from the operation of any order made by the court for the enforcement of the charge, and to extinguish any term of years created for the purposes of the charge, and shall do so without the persons entitled to or interested in the charge or in any such order or term of years becoming parties to or executing the conveyance.[48]

Where in accordance with section 12(1) the conveyance to a tenant will be effective to discharge the house and premises from a charge to secure the payment of money then except as otherwise provided by section 12 it shall be the duty of the tenant to apply the price payable for the house and premises, in the first instance, in or towards the redemption of any such charge (and, if there are more than one, then according to their priorities).[49] If any amount payable in accordance with section 12(2) to the per-

---

[47] See further Hague, *Leasehold Enfranchisement* (2nd ed., 1987) for a detailed analysis of this area of law.

[48] Leasehold Reform Act 1967, s.12(1).

[49] *Ibid.* s.12(2).

son entitled to the benefit of a charge is not so paid nor paid into court, in accordance with section 13 of the Act, then for the amount in question the house and premises shall remain subject to the charge and to that extent section 12(1) of the Act shall not apply.[50] Where the house and premises are discharged by section 12 of the Act from a charge (without the obligations secured by the charge being satisfied by the receipt of the whole or part of the price), the discharge of the house and premises shall not prejudice any right or remedy for the enforcement of those obligations against other property comprised in the same or any other security, nor prejudice any personal liability as principal or otherwise of the landlord or any other person.[51]

The tenant acquiring the freehold may pay into court on account of the price for the house and premises the amount, if known, of the payment to be made in respect of the charge or, if that amount is not known, the whole of the price or such less amount as the tenant thinks right in order to provide for that payment.[52] This can occur if:

(a) for any reason difficulty arises in ascertaining how much is payable in respect of the charge; or

(b) for any reason mentioned in section 13(2) difficulty arises in making a payment in respect of the charge.

Such difficulty is envisaged in the following cases:

(a) because a person who is or may be entitled to receive payment cannot be found or ascertained; or

(b) because any such person refuses or fails to make out a title, or to accept payment and give a proper discharge, or to take any steps reasonably required of him to enable the sum to be ascertained and paid; or

(c) because a tender of the sum payable cannot, by reason of complications in the title to it or the want of two or more trustees or for other reasons, be effected, or not without incurring or involving unreasonable costs or delay.[53]

The tenant must pay the purchase price into court if before execution of the conveyance written notice is given to him:

(a) that the landlord or a person entitled to the benefit of a charge on the house and premises so requires for the purpose of protecting the rights of persons so entitled, or for reasons related to any application made or to be made under section 36 of the Act, or to the bankruptcy or winding up of the landlord; or

(b) that steps have been taken to enforce any charge on the landlord's

---

[50] *Ibid.* s.12(2).
[51] *Ibid.* s.12(6).
[52] *Ibid.* s.13.
[53] *Ibid.* s.13(2).

interest in the house and premises by the bringing of proceedings in any court, or by the appointment of a receiver, or otherwise.[54]

Where payment is made into court by reason only of a notice under section 13(3) and the notice is given with reference to proceedings in a court specified in the notice other than the county court, payment shall be made into the court so specified.[55]

In certain cases the court is able to grant relief in respect of mortgages on the landlord's estate in order to avoid or mitigate any financial hardship that might otherwise be caused by the rights conferred on tenants by the Act.[56]

Under the Landlord and Tenant Act 1987

The Act provides for the compulsory acquisition of the landlord's interest and entitles qualifying tenants of blocks of flats to apply to the court for an acquisition order.[57] This contains provision for the discharge of mortgages on the landlord's interest, if such order is made.[58]

Under the Rent Act 1977

Variation of the terms of regulated mortgages.[59]

Under the Consumer Credit Act 1974

Refusal of enforcement orders and other aspects.[60]

Under the Lands Clauses Consolidation Act 1845

Redemption on compulsory purchase.[61]

EXTINCTION OF MORTGAGE BY LAPSE OF TIME

Loss of the mortgagor's right to redeem by lapse of time

Land

Where the security is land,[62] the Limitation Act 1980, section 16, provides that when a mortgagee "has been in possession of any of the mortgaged land for a period of 12 years, no action to redeem the land of which

---

[54] Leasehold Reform Act 1967, s.13(3).
[55] *Ibid*. The court for the purposes of s.13(1) and (unless the landlord's notice specifies another court) s.13(3), is the county court, see s.20(1).
[56] *Ibid*. s.36.
[57] Landlord and Tenant Act 1987, Pt. 111.
[58] *Ibid*. s.32, Sched. 1. See further *Woodfall's Law of Landlord and Tenant* (28th ed., 1978).
[59] See *ante*, p. 247.
[60] See *ante*, pp. 140 *et seq.* and p. 246.
[61] For a treatment of this subject see [please specify].
[62] "Land" is defined in s.38(1) of the Limitation Act 1980.

he has been so in possession shall be brought after the end of that period by the mortgagor or any person claiming through him." This section means that time begins to run against the mortgagor at once from the mortgagee's entry into possession, whether or not the right of redemption has yet arisen.[63] It begins to run in respect of any part of which the mortgagee is in possession, although the mortgagor remains in possession of the rest of the land.[64] Formerly, the fact that the mortgagor was under a disability made no difference, for actions for redemption were not actions to recover land within section 16 of the Real Property Limitation Act 1833, which made allowance for disability.[65] Section 22 of the 1939 Act, however, extended the allowance for disability to all cases where the Act imposed a limitation and therefore to actions for redemption of mortgages of land.[66] This is now incorporated into section 28 of the 1980 Act.

Acknowledgment and part payment

By section 29(4) the running of time under the Limitation Act 1980, is stopped if the mortgagee:

" . . . either:
(a) receives any sum in respect of the principal or interest of the mortgage debt; or
(b) acknowledges the title of the mortgagor, or his equity of redemption."

The 12-year period then runs from the date of the last payment or acknowledgment. A receipt, to have this effect, must be of money paid "in respect of the principal or interest," so that the receipt of rents or proceeds of sale by a mortgagee in possession without accounting for them to the mortgagor will not stop the period from running. An acknowledgment must be in writing, signed either by the mortgagee or his agent, and must be made to the owner of the equity of redemption or his agent.[67] The actual form of the instrument is immaterial so long as it contains an unequivocal recognition of the fact that the estate is mortgaged.[68]

Where there are two or more mortgagors, an acknowledgment to one is deemed to be made to all and so stops time from running against any of them.[69] But an acknowledgment by one of two or more mortgagees does not bind the other mortgagees. Section 31 of the 1980 Act provides:

"(3) Where two or more mortgagees are by virtue of the mortgage in

---

[63] *Re Metropolis and Counties Permanent Investment Building Society* [1911] 1 Ch. 698. But the mortgagee must have entered in the character of mortgagee: *Hyde* v. *Dallaway* (1843) 2 Hare 528.

[64] *Kinsman* v. *Rouse* (1881) 17 Ch.D. 104.

[65] *Ibid.*

[66] Preston & Newsom, *Limitation of Actions* (1953), p. 219.

[67] s.30. *Cf. Wright* v. *Pepin* [1954] 1 W.L.R. 635, where the authority was inferred. There had been an acknowledgment by the mortgagor's solicitor which was held sufficient.

[68] *Cf. Stansfield* v. *Hobson* (1853) 3 De G.M. & G. 620.

[69] s.31(5).

possession of the mortgaged land, an acknowledgement of the mortgagor's title or of his equity of redemption by one of the mortgagees shall only bind him and his successors and shall not bind any other mortgagee or his successors.

(4) Where in a case within subsection (3) above the mortgagee by whom the acknowledgement is given is entitled to a part of the mortgaged land and not to any ascertained part of the mortgage debt the mortgagor shall be entitled to redeem that part of the land on payment, with interest, of the part of the mortgage debt which bears the same proportion to the whole of the debt as the value of the part of the land bears to the whole of the mortgaged land.''

The effect of this somewhat difficult language appears to be that:

(a) An acknowledgment by one mortgagee can in no case bind the other mortgagees.

(b) Where the mortgage moneys are not held by the mortgagees on a joint account, an acknowledgment by one binds him and the mortgagor may redeem him as to his share thus acquiring an equitable right to his interest in the mortgage. But the other mortgagees hold their shares in the mortgage free of the equity of redemption.

(c) Where the mortgage moneys are held on a joint account (*i.e.* no ascertained share) but the mortgagees have entered separately into possession of distinct parts of the mortgaged land, an acknowledgment by one binds him and exposes him to redemption of the part of which he is in possession. As he is not entitled to any ascertained part of the mortgaged debt, the price of redemption is worked out by attributing to him a share of the mortgage debt corresponding to the proportion of the mortgaged land which his part bears to the whole.

(d) Where the mortgage moneys are held on a joint account and the mortgagees are jointly in possession, an acknowledgment by one is wholly ineffective to stop the running of the period in favour of all.[70]

Once the right of redemption has been barred by the mortgagee's continuance in possession for the statutory period no subsequent acknowledgment can revive it; for section 17 of the 1980 Act expressly extinguishes the title to the equity of redemption.[71]

Personalty

Although the 1939 Act placed forclosure actions for mortgaged personalty on the same footing as for realty, barring them after 12 years, it did not

---

[70] *Cf. Richardson* v. *Younge* (1871) L.R. 6 Ch. 478; Preston & Newsom, *Limitation of Actions* (1953), p. 238.

[71] *Cf. Young* v. *Clarey* [1948] Ch. 191; and under the former law; *Re Alison* (1879) 11 Ch.D. 284.

subject actions to redeem mortgaged personalty to the limitations governing actions to redeem realty. The Law Revision Committee justified this
differential treatment of realty and personalty in regard to redemption on
the ground that, whereas a mortgagee of land does not ordinarily take possession except by way of enforcing his security, the mortgagee of personalty may have possession of the property from the outset. The Committee
thought that, for this reason, serious practical difficulties might arise if the
statutory limitations were applied to the redemption of mortgaged personalty. It had in mind particularly the case of bonds or shares deposited with
a bank by way of equitable mortgage and left with the bank more or less
indefinitely to cover an overdraft.[72] Consequently, the 1939 Act, like previous Statutes of Limitation, left actions to redeem personalty without any
statutory limit. Moreover, it was well established under the former statutes
that equity will not, by analogy, extend to personalty statutory limitations
whose operation is expressly restricted to land.[73] This position remains
unchanged under the 1980 Act.

Since no Statute of Limitation operates, whether directly or by analogy,
to bar actions to redeem personalty, lapse of time will defeat such actions
only on the general principle *æquitas vigilantibus non dormientibus succur-
rit.* The rules on which the court acts in refusing its assistance to stale
demands cannot be stated with precision, because in cases where no Statute of Limitation applies judges have refrained from fixing a definite period
within which equitable remedies must be brought. In *Weld* v. *Petre*,[74]
counsel invited the court to say that no action to redeem personalty would
be entertained after 20 years, but the court refused to lay down any rigid
rule. A defence based on lapse of time depends in equity primarily on the
balance of justice or injustice in affording or refusing relief.[75] Under such a
test each case will clearly be governed by its own special circumstances.
Thus, in *Erlanger* v. *New Sombrero Phosphate Co.*,[76] Lord Blackburn said:

> "I think, from the nature of the inquiry, it must always be a question
> of more or less, depending on the degree of diligence which might
> reasonably be required, and the degree of change which has occurred,
> whether the balance of justice or injustice is in favour of granting the
> remedy or withholding it."

The doctrine of laches, which is the name given to this principle, thus really
provides two distinct grounds on which a remedy may be refused:

   (*i*) conduct by the plaintiff which suggests that he has waived his
        right;

[72] Fifth Interim Report (1936), Cmd. 5334, p. 15.
[73] *London & Midland Bank* v. *Mitchell* [1899] 2 Ch. 161; *Weld* v. *Petre* [1929] 1 Ch. 33. But in
the case of a mixed fund of personalty and realty it was held in one case that the right to
redeem personalty was barred as the equity was indivisible, see *Charter* v. *Watson* [1899] 1
Ch. 175.
[74] [1929] 1 Ch. 33.
[75] *Lindsay Petroleum Co.* v. *Hurd* (1874) L.R. 5 P.C. 221.
[76] (1878) 3 App.Cas. 1218 at 1279.

(*ii*) a change in the circumstances of the defendant which renders it practically unjust to enforce the remedy.

The leading case on the application of the doctrine to the right to redeem personalty is *Weld* v. *Petre*,[77] in which it was held that:

   (a) Mere inaction by the mortgagor, laches in the narrow sense, is not sufficient evidence of an intention to waive his rights, and will not bar the right to redeem under the doctrine of laches. Thus, Russell J. at first instance,[78] expressly said: "Equity should not, in my opinion, deprive mortgagors of their right to redeem if, when they assert it, the debt has been or can be repaid, the security is available and no one's position has been altered in the meanwhile. If these circumstances co-exist, the mortgagor should be allowed to redeem unless his right has been destroyed by statute, foreclosure, sale or release."

   (b) Where the mortgagee (*i*) has not altered his position by expending money on the property in the reasonable belief that the property was now his own; (*ii*) has not, by reason of the delay, lost any evidence which will make it difficult for him to render his accounts; and (*iii*) has not otherwise altered his position to his prejudice, the mortgagor will be admitted to redeem.

   (c) The fact that on the death of the mortgagee the mortgaged property has been included in the mortgagee's assets and estate duty paid in respect of it is not a sufficient ground for refusing relief to the mortgagor.

Barring a Mortgagee's Remedies under the Limitation Act 1980

The rules limiting the exercise of a mortgagee's remedies before the Limitation Act 1939 came into force contained some glaring anomalies primarily owing to the absence of any general statutory limitation on the enforcement of mortgages of personalty. The Real Property Limitation Acts 1833 and 1874, prescribed a 12 years' period of limitation for enforcing mortgages of land and of the proceeds of sale of land, but there was no statutory provision for pure personalty.[79] The result was that if, as in *Re Jauncey*,[80] a mixed fund of realty and personalty had been mortgaged in a single mortgage, the remedy against the land was barred after 12 years, but that against the personalty remained alive indefinitely, being subject only to the equitable doctrine of laches.[81] When the property mortgaged was a reversionary interest the anomaly was made worse by the fact that section 2 of the 1874 Act, which in a mortgage of land postponed the running of the

---

[77] [1929] 1 Ch. 33.
[78] *Ibid*. at 42.
[79] *London & Midland Bank* v. *Mitchell* [1899] 2 Ch. 161; *Re Stucley* [1906] 1 Ch. 67.
[80] [1926] Ch. 471; *Re Edwards' Will Trusts* [1937] 1 Ch. 553.
[81] But see *post*, p. 403.

statutory period until the interest fell into possession, did not apply to the proceeds of sale of land.[82] Consequently, three quite separate rules operated in the case of reversionary interests. If the interest was in land, the period did not begin to run until the interest fell in; if it was in the proceeds of sale of land, the period began to run immediately from the date of the mortgagor's default under the mortgage contract; if, however, it was in a fund of pure personalty, there was no statutory limitation at all. The Limitation Act 1939, removed these and other anomalies by assimilating the rules relating to personalty to those formerly governing realty, though it still differentiated between land and personalty with regard to foreclosure.[83] The Limitation Act 1939 is now consolidated in amended form in the Limitation Act 1980 (replacing the 1939 Act, the 1975 Act, parts of the Limitation Act 1963 and parts of the Limitation Amendment Act 1980).[84]

The limitations imposed by the Limitation Act 1980 ("the 1980 Act") on the enforcement of a mortgagee's remedies require to be considered under five main heads:

(1) Personal actions on the contract for payment;
(2) Actions to recover principal sums of money secured by mortgage or charge;
(3) Actions for foreclosure or possession;
(4) Actions to enforce mortgages of future interests; and
(5) Actions for the recovery of arrears of interest.

In addition the rules laid down for these actions are affected by the general provisions of the Act relating to disability, acknowledgment, part payment, fraud, concealment and mistake.

(1) Personal actions on the contract for payment

When the mortgage is not under seal, an action on the express or implied promise to pay the debt is one "founded on simple contract" within section 5 of the 1980 Act and, as such, is barred "after the expiration of six years from the date when the cause of action accrued," *i.e.* after the date for repayment.[84a] It was, however, well settled under the old law that the barring of the personal action on the contract after six years did not preclude the subsequent enforcement of the remedies against the security. The reason was that the statute only barred the action and did not extinguish the debt.[85] The position in regard to the debt is still the same under the 1980 Act, so that the remedies against the security are not touched by section 5 but fall under section 20, being barred only after 12 years.[86]

---

[82] *Re Witham* [1922] 2 Ch. 413.
[83] *Cotterell* v. *Price* [1960] 1 W.L.R. 1097.
[84] The Limitation Amendment Act came into force on August 1, 1980 and the Limitation Act itself came into force on May 1, 1981.
[84a] This will depend on whether the covenant gives the date for repayment and whether a demand is necessary.
[85] *London & Midland Bank* v. *Mitchell* [1899] 2 Ch. 161.
[86] See *post*, p. 406.

When the mortgage is under seal, the action on the covenant for payment is one "upon a specialty" within section 8 of the 1980 Act, and the period of limitation is thus 12 years.[87–88]

(2) Actions to recover principal sums of money secured by mortgage or charge

Section 20(1) of the 1980 Act provides:

"(1) No action shall be brought to recover—
(a) any principal sum of money secured by a mortgage or other charge on property (whether real or personal); or
(b) proceeds of the sale of land;
after the expiration of 12 years from the date on which the right to receive the money accrued."

Thus, quite apart from the limits imposed on contractual actions to recover the principal, the Act specifically bars any action to recover the principal by enforcing the security after the elapse of 12 years. The extension of this statutory limitation on enforcing securities to mortgages of personalty, as explained above, was an innovation. The limitation of 12 years now applies to all forms of property.

Foreclosure actions are in fact subject to a 12 years' period of limitation, but they are not within section 20(1). The former Limitation Acts did not deal with actions to foreclose mortgages of land as actions to recover money charged on land but as actions to recover land.[89] The 1980 Act, both in regard to land and personalty, also separates foreclosure actions from other remedies. Section 20(1) therefore covers remedies other than foreclosure. On the other hand, the personal action on the covenant for payment was held in *Sutton* v. *Sutton*[90] to be an action for the recovery of money charged on land and therefore subject to the 12 years' limitation in section 8 of the 1874 Act as well as to the 12 years' limitation applicable to specialty debts. It is thus arguable that personal actions for simple or specialty debts secured by mortgage are within section 20(1) of the 1980 Act as well as section 5. The point is somewhat academic in regard to mortgages of present interests as, quite apart from section 20(1), the personal actions are barred after six and 12 years respectively from the date when the right to receive the money accrued. But, if this part of the decision in *Sutton* v. *Sutton* is still good law, personal actions for the mortgage debt have the benefit of the provision in section 20(3) whereby in mortgages of future interests the right to receive the money is not deemed to accrue until the interest falls into possession. The debt would thus be kept alive until six or 12 years *after* the mortgaged property fell into possession—a point of poss-

---

[87–88] It is not sufficient for the obligation to be merely acknowledged or evidenced by the security, it must be created or secured by it—*Re Compania de Electricidad de la Provincia de Buenos Aires Ltd.* [1980] Ch. 146.

[89] See *post*, pp. 407 *et seq*.

[90] (1883) 22 Ch.D. 511.

ible importance in the event of the mortgagor's bankruptcy, should the security prove insufficient.

(3) Actions for foreclosure or possession

Foreclosure actions, as already mentioned, are dealt with by the 1980 Act as actions to recover the property rather than to recover the debt by realising the security. Formerly, the Real Property Limitation Acts did not specify foreclosure actions as actions to recover land but it was settled in a series of decisions that in the case of land foreclosure actions, for purposes of the limitation of actions, are actions to recover land.[91] These decisions were not perhaps entirely logical because foreclosure is not, either in law or in equity, an action to recover the mortgagor's interest. It is an action to complete the mortgagee's title to an interest already vested in him by removing the stop on the title imposed by equity.[92] Moreover, a foreclosure action always invites redemption and is in substance an action to recover the amount of the debt by realising the security. The courts, however, looked primarily to the fact that in equity the mortgagor remains beneficial owner and that a foreclosure order absolute for the first time vests the beneficial ownership in the mortgagee.[93] On this basis, they decided to treat foreclosure actions as actions to recover land. They had a strong inducement to do so in that some of the provisions postponing the running of the statutory period applied, owing to the erratic policy of the Acts, to actions for the recovery of land, but not to actions for the recovery of money charged on land.[94] Although the 1980 Act maintains the distinction between foreclosure and other remedies, happily the distinction has lost most of its importance owing to the rules relating to actions for the recovery of money charged on property having been assimilated to those governing actions to recover land.

In the case of land,[95] section 20(4), re-enacting the former law, declares that foreclosure actions are not within section 20 at all but are governed by the provisions of the Act relating to actions to recover land in particular by section 15. The period prescribed by section 15(1) in ordinary cases is 12 years from the date on which the right of action accrued under the mortgage.[96] In the case of personalty where formerly there was no statutory limit on foreclosure actions, the Act does not carry logic to the extent of applying the provisions relating to recovery of chattels. Instead, section 20(2) simply enacts that foreclosure actions in respect of mortgaged per-

---

[91] e.g. Heath v. Pugh (1881) 6 Q.B.D. 345; Pugh v. Heath (1881) 7 A.C. 235; Harlock v. Ashberry (1882) 19 Ch.D. 539.

[92] See ante, pp. 247 et seq.

[93] See Heath v. Pugh (1881) 6 Q.B.D. 345 at 360.

[94] A good example is the case of future interests discussed, post, p. 410.

[95] "Land" includes corporeal hereditaments, tithes and rentcharges and any legal or equitable estate or interest therein, including an interest in the proceeds of the sale of land held upon trust for sale, but except as provided above in this definition does not include an incorporeal hereditament, as defined by s.38(1).

[96] Sched. 1, para. 10, prescribes 30 years in the case of the Crown and spiritual or eleemosynary corporations sole.

sonalty shall be barred after 12 years from the date on which the right to foreclose accrued. The general rule is thus the same both for land and personalty: foreclosure actions are barred 12 years after the right to foreclose accrued.

The right to foreclose accrues when the mortgagor is in default on the proviso for redemption and the mortgagee's estate has become absolute at law.[97] Although any default which touches the terms of the proviso for redemption gives rise to the right of foreclosure, the right usually accrues on a default in the covenant to pay the mortgage moneys on the date specified. Where, however, the moneys are repayable on demand, the right accrues immediately on the execution of the mortgage unless the demand has been made a condition precedent to the enforcement of the mortgage.[98] Such are the basic rules concerning the first accrual of the right of foreclosure and the date when the statutory period begins to run. But the Act contains several provisions which, for the purposes of the limitation of actions, suspend the accrual of the right of action of a mortgagee. The most important of these provisions, covering future interests, disabilities, acknowledgments and part payment, apply generally to all remedies, and are dealt with separately below. One provision, however, affects foreclosure alone. If a mortgagee, whether of land[99] or of personalty,[1] has been in possession of the mortgaged property after the right of foreclosure has accrued, the right is deemed not to have accrued until he has been dispossessed or has discontinued his possession.

A mortgagee's right to take possession of the security is also a right to recover the land and is barred 12 years after the right accrued. In this instance the period does normally begin to run immediately from the execution of a legal mortgage because the conveyance carries the right to possession. If, however, the mortgage provides for quiet enjoyment by the mortgagor until default, it operates as a redemise to him from the mortgagee and the period only begins to run from the date of the default.[2] As an equitable mortgagee has no right to possession except by special agreement, the date when the right accrues can only be ascertained from the agreement if such an agreement exists.[3] The running of the statute against the right to enter into possession is, as with other remedies, interrupted by acknowledgment or part payment or by disability.

A mortgagee, who exercises his rights and obtains a foreclosure order absolute, acquires, it was decided in *Heath* v. *Pugh*,[4] an entirely new title so that time only runs against his new right to eject the mortgagor as from the date of the order being made absolute.

---

[97] See *ante*, p. 247.
[98] See *Re Brown's Estate* [1893] 2 Ch. 300; *Lloyds Bank* v. *Margolis* [1954] 1 W.L.R. 644.
[99] Limitation Act 1980, Sched. 1, para. 1.
[1] *Ibid.* s.20(2).
[2] *Wilkinson* v. *Hall* (1837) 3 Bing N.C. 508; *ante*, pp. 285 *et seq*.
[3] *Ocean Accident & Guarantee Corp.* v. *Ilford Gas Co.* [1905] 2 K.B. 493.
[4] (1881) 6 Q.B.D. 345.

(4) Actions to enforce mortgages of future interests

The distinction between actions for foreclosure of land and actions to recover money charged on land was formerly of particular importance in regard to the mortgage of future interests. Section 2 of the 1874 Act provided that the operation of the statute against actions to recover land should, in the case of a future interest, be postponed until the interest fell into possession. In *Hugill* v. *Wilkinson*,[5] North J. decided that foreclosure actions, being actions to recover land, also had the benefit of section 2, with the result that foreclosure of a mortgage of a remainder was not barred until 12 years after the remainder became vested in possession. There was, however, no similar provision to effect a postponement in the case of actions to recover money charged on land. Consequently, in the absence of acknowledgment, part payment or disability a mortgagee's other remedies were barred 12 years after the mortgagor's default in redeeming, although the security might not yet have fallen into possession.[6] This meant that in charges, properly so called, where foreclosure was not an available remedy, the creditor might lose his charge on a future interest altogether 12 years after his charge first became payable.[7] Moreover, owing to the particular language of section 2, its operation was confined to land in the strict sense and it did not, like other sections, extend to the proceeds of sale of land. The result, as previously mentioned, was that the unlucky mortgagee of a future interest in proceeds of sale found that his security was land for the purpose of attracting the 12 years' limit imposed on foreclosure actions for the recovery of land, but not "land" for the purpose of working a postponement under section 2.[8] On the other hand, the mortgagee of a future interest in pure personalty had nothing to worry about because to him no statute of limitations applied at all.[9]

The decision in *Hugill* v. *Wilkinson*[10] was a literal application of section 2 of the 1874 Act in the light of the decisions that foreclosure is an action to recover land. The principle of the case was not, however, really the same as that of section 2. Foreclosure operates between mortgagee and mortgagor; the right to foreclose arises immediately on the mortgagor's default whether the property be present or future and there is no legal obstacle to the prosecution of the action. Foreclosure, as stated, is really an action to terminate the equity of redemption. Even if it be regarded as an action to recover the mortgagor's interest, it is not, where the security is a future interest, a future right of action for the recovery of the land but an immediate right of action to recover the mortgagor's present right to future possession. The fact that foreclosure of a future interest does not vest in the

---

[5] (1888) 38 Ch.D. 480.
[6] *Re Owen* [1894] 3 Ch. 220.
[7] *Re Witham* [1922] 2 Ch. 413.
[8] *Re Hazeldine's Trusts* [1908] 1 Ch. 34; *Re Fox* [1913] 2 Ch. 75.
[9] See *Re Witham* [1922] 2 Ch. 413 where part of the property was personalty.
[10] (1888) 38 Ch.D. 480. For a discussion of this case see Preston & Newsom, *Limitation of Actions* (1953), pp. 110–114.

mortgagee an immediate right to the rents and profits is immaterial. Foreclosure does effectively vest in him an immediate title to the property mortgaged. This point was taken by Cozens-Hardy M.R. in *Wakefield and Barnsley Union Bank Ltd.* v. *Yates*[11]: "the object of foreclosure is to destroy the mortgagor's right to redeem and it is only as an incident that the right to receive the rents and profits arises." The Court of Appeal in that case refused to regard the fact that the mortgaged property was a reversion after a 21 years' lease as any reason for postponing the running of the statute. Yet, for purposes of the limitation of actions, leasehold reversions are treated as future interests in the same category as the remainder in *Hugill* v. *Wilkinson*. Consequently, the decision of the Court of Appeal in *Yates' Case* is scarcely consistent with that of North J. in *Hugill* v. *Wilkinson*, although the latter case was referred to in *Yates' Case* without disapproval.

On the other hand, the principle of *Hugill* v. *Wilkinson*, if open to question on technical grounds, has practical advantages. There is much to be said for a rule which does not constrain a mortgagee to realise his security before the asset to which the mortgagor looked as the means for repaying his debt has materialised. At any rate the Law Revision Committee so far approved the principle of *Hugill* v. *Wilkinson*[12] that section 18(3) of the 1939 Act incorporated it in statutory form now repeated in section 20(3) of the 1980 Act. This provides as follows:

> "The right to receive any principal sum of money secured by a mortgage or other charge and the right to foreclose on the property subject to the mortgage or charge shall not be treated as accruing so long as the property comprises any future interest or any life insurance policy which has not matured or been determined."

The effect of this provision is that time does not run against remedies to enforce mortgages comprising any future interest until the future interest falls into possession; and a life insurance policy that has not yet matured or been determined is treated as a future interest for this purpose. Section 20(3) applies to all remedies for the recovery of money charged on real or personal property and to foreclosure of mortgages of personalty. It does not, however, apply to foreclosure of mortgages of "land" which falls under section 15 and Schedule 1, which govern actions for the recovery of land.

Section 15 substantially re-enacts the provisions of the former Acts relating to the postponement of the statutory period of limitation in the case of future interests in land. But the primary rule is now contained in Schedule 1, paragraph 4 to the 1980 Act which provides:

> "The right of action to recover any land shall, in a case where—

---

[11] [1916] 1 Ch. 452 at 458.
[12] Fifth Interim Report (1936), Cmnd. 5334, p. 14.

(*a*) the estate or interest claimed was an estate or interest in reversion or remainder or any other future estate or interest; and

(*b*) no person has taken possession of the land by virtue of the estate or interest claimed;

be treated as having accrued on the date on which the estate or interest fell into possession by the determination of the preceding estate or interest."

Section 15(2) qualifies this rule in cases where the holder of a preceding estate, other than a term of years, has been dispossessed during its continuance by allowing to the person entitled to the future interest either 12 years from the dispossession or six years from the date when his own interest vested in possession, whichever is longer. Certain other points of detail are covered in the Act to which detailed reference should be made. The result is that section 15 makes provision for the postponement of the operation of the statute in actions for the recovery of land comparable to the general provision for postponement in section 20(3) in regard to actions for the recovery of money charged on real and personal property. Ironically enough, it is doubtful whether the benefit of postponement under section 6 extends to actions to foreclose mortgages of future interests in land owing to the questionable authority of the decision in *Hugill* v. *Wilkinson*.[13] If the decision in *Wakefield and Barnsley Union Bank Ltd.* v. *Yates*[14] is correct, foreclosure actions are not within section 15 and Schedule 1; and there is nothing in the 1980 Act to bring them within that section. Yet the intention plainly was that in the case of land foreclosure actions should have the benefit of postponement no less than the actions now covered by section 20(3). For the Law Revision Committee assumed that *Hugill* v. *Wilkinson* was good law and recommended its extension in the manner effected by the predecessor to section 20(3).[15]

The position in regard to foreclosure of future interests in land is, therefore, scarcely satisfactory. The courts may be inclined, in interpreting the 1980 Act, to overlook the difficulty of reconciling *Hugill* v. *Wilkinson* with *Yates' Case* and simply give foreclosure actions the benefit of postponement under section 15 on the basis of the decisions holding foreclosure actions to be actions for the recovery of land. Otherwise, an arbitrary distinction will be created between foreclosure of mortgages of land and other actions to enforce mortgages of realty and personalty, a distinction which would be the precise opposite of that which the Law Revision Committee intended to remove.[16]

If *Hugill* v. *Wilkinson* is followed in applying the 1980 Act, the status of *Yates' Case* necessarily comes into question particularly in regard to the

[13] (1888) 38 Ch.D. 480; see *ante*, p. 409.
[14] [1916] 1 Ch. 452.
[15] *Hugill* v. *Wilkinson* had been mentioned without disapproval in more than one case, *e.g.* *Re Witham* [1922] 2 Ch. 413.
[16] See Preston & Newsom, *Limitation of Actions* (1953), p. 113.

position of second mortgagees. Under the similar provisions of the earlier Acts it had been decided that:

- (a) The existence of a prior mortgage, under which possession has not been taken, does not make a second mortgage a mortgage of a future interest so that it does not postpone the operation of the statute against a second mortgagee's right to foreclose.[17]
- (b) The same is true, if the prior mortgagee goes into possession after the creation of the second mortgage.[18]
- (c) Similarly the existence of a 21 years' lease under which possession has been taken before the execution of a mortgage does not postpone the running of the statute against the right to foreclose.[19]

All these decisions are obviously good sense. It would be absurd to postpone the running of the statute against a second mortgagee merely because of the existence of a prior mortgage term, even when the prior mortgagee has taken possession. A second mortgagee obtains the mortgagor's right to redeem the first mortgagee and there is nothing to stop him either from foreclosing the mortgagor or redeeming the first mortgagee whenever he chooses. What case is there for postponement? *Yates' Case* has a particular importance owing to mortgages now being made by demise and it is believed to be fundamentally sound. It certainly has to be accepted if any sense is to be made of the position of a second mortgagee. Yet, if foreclosure is regarded as an action for the recovery of land, *Yates' Case* is not easy to square with the general principles of the Limitation Acts under which a reversion upon a term of years is treated as a future interest. The courts are likely to uphold both *Yates' Case* and *Hugill* v. *Wilkinson*, but by what process of reasoning remains to be seen.

In any event, the 1980 Act seems to have created minor anomalies. Thus section 20(3) postpones the operation of the statute so long as the property mortgaged "comprises any future interest." These words can only mean that, where present and future interests are mortgaged together, section 20(3) protects the mortgagee's remedies in respect of *all* the property against the operation of the statute until the future interest falls into possessin. No such provision is to be found in regard to foreclosure of mortgages of land, although a single mortgage comprising both a present interest in land and a future interest in realty or personalty is by no means impossible.

Again, section 15(3) excludes from the category of future interests estates or interests which fall into possession after an entail capable of being barred. There is no similar provision under section 20, although entails of personalty are now permissible.

---

[17] *Kibble* v. *Fairthorne* [1895] 1 Ch. 219.
[18] *Samuel Johnson & Sons Ltd.* v. *Brock* [1907] 2 Ch. 533.
[19] *Wakefield & Barnsley Union Bank Ltd.* v. *Yates* [1916] 1 Ch. 452.

(5) Actions for the recovery of arrears of interest

So long as the right to the principal remains alive, the right to interest also continues, since interest is accessory to principal. But section 20(5) of the 1980 Act requires actions for the recovery of arrears of interest payable in respect of sums secured by mortgage or charge to be brought within six years of the date when the interest became due. In other words, the maximum amount of interest recoverable in such an action is six years' arrears. The same limit is imposed on actions to recover arrears by way of damages, in cases where there is no covenant for payment of interest and the court gives interest by way of damages.[20] There are, however, two qualifications on the general limit of six years by section 20(6) and (7) of the Act:

(a) Where a prior incumbrancer has been in possession of the property mortgaged, a subsequent incumbrancer, if he brings his action within one year of the discontinuance of the prior mortgagee's possession, may recover all interest which fell due during the period of that possession. The reason, of course, is that the prior incumbrancer's possession disables the second mortgagee from keeping down the interest of his own mortgage out of the rents and profits.[21]

(b) Where the mortgaged property comprises any future interest or life insurance policy and it is a term of the mortgage that arrears of interest shall be treated as part of the principal debt secured by the mortgage, then the interest is deemed not to be due until the right to receive the principal is deemed to accrue. This means that when the statute does not run against the mortgagee of future property until the property falls into possession, all arrears of interest accruing during the time when the property was still future are deemed to accrue only on the date when the property vested in possession. Consequently all such arrears are recoverable within six years of that date.

This is not, however, a general exception in favour of a mortgagee of future property. It is only when the mortgage provides for capitalisation of arrears of interest that the second exception operates. In other cases the six years' limit runs against the right to interest from the date when the interest was actually due whether or not the running of the statute against the right to the principal is postponed under section 20(3).

The six years' limit under section 20(5) applies to an action to recover arrears of interest, which includes an action to recover the principal with the interest thereon. On the basis of the decisions taken under the similar provision in section 42 of the Real Property Limitation Act 1833, the six years' limit would also apply to all proceedings by the mortgagee to enforce the mortgage. For it was settled that no more than six years' arrears of

---

[20] *Cf. Mellersh* v. *Brown* (1890) 45 Ch.D. 225.

[21] Unless the prior mortgagee pays over surplus rents and profits to the second mortgagee which rarely happens.

interest might go into the mortgagee's account in proceedings for fore-closure, judicial sale or the appointment of a receiver.[22] The 1980 Act, however, by wholly excluding foreclosure of mortgages of land from the provisions of section 20(4) appears inadvertently to have enacted that more than six years' arrears of interest may be claimed in foreclosure of land. Thus, while only six years' arrears will be allowed in computing the mortgagor's personal debt, the full amount of the arrears will, in the case of land, be allowed in actions against the security.[23]

In any event, it is well settled that the six years' limit does not apply in actions *by the mortgagor* for redemption,[24] and this is so even when the mortgagee has instituted proceedings for foreclosure and the mortgagor counterclaims for redemption.[25] A mortgagor who has lost his estate at law will only be allowed to redeem it in equity on the terms of discharging all his obligations under the mortgage. The mortgagor's neglect to pay the interest is just as culpable as the mortgagee's failure to enforce his rights. The rule is the same where the mortgagee has sold the security under a power of sale and the mortgagor seeks to recover the surplus proceeds of sale, for this is in essence an action for redemption. The mortgagee may thus retain out of the proceeds the full amount of the arrears.[26] The pos-ition is, however, not entirely clear when the property has been sold not in pursuance of the mortgagee's power of sale but under a paramount power outside the mortgage, and the proceeds of sale have been paid into court. In *Re Stead's Mortgaged Estates*[27] the property had been sold under the Land Clauses Acts and the mortgagee petitioned to have the amount of his debt with full arrears of interest paid out to him. Malins V.-C. only allowed him six years' arrears. But in *Re Lloyd*[28] the Court of Appeal allowed the mortgagee his full arrears when the property had been sold in an adminis-tration suit and the proceedings for payment out of court were initiated by the mortgagor. The court expressed no view as to the correctness of *Re Stead's Mortgaged Estates* and treated the mortgagor's claim as in sub-stance one for redemption. The only observable difference between the two cases was in the party who took the first step in the proceedings for payment out. But this difference can scarcely be material because in fore-closure the mortgagor's counterclaim for redemption, although made under the pressure of the mortgagee's proceedings, is outside the six years' limitation on arrears of interest. Indeed, if this is the difference between the cases, money may lie in court because neither party wishes to take the first step in the proceedings. It is therefore hoped that *Re Lloyd* will be regarded as having impliedly overruled *Re Stead's Mortgaged Estates*.

---

[22] *Sinclair* v. *Jackson* (1853) 17 Beav. 405; *Re Lloyd* [1903] 1 Ch. 385.
[23] See Preston & Newsom, *Limitation of Actions* (1953), p. 165.
[24] *Elvy* v. *Norwood* (1852) 5 De G. & Sm. 240; *Edmunds* v. *Waugh* (1866) L.R. 1 Eq. 418.
[25] *Dingle* v. *Coppen* [1899] 1 Ch. 726; *Holmes* v. *Cowcher* [1970] 1 W.L.R. 834.
[26] *Edmunds* v. *Waugh* (1866) L.R. 1 Eq. 418; *Holmes* v. *Cowcher, supra.*
[27] (1876) 2 Ch.D. 713.
[28] [1903] 1 Ch. 385.

Disability

It is not possible here to deal in detail with the rules governing the extension of the period of limitation by reason of the disability of the person entitled to sue.[29] The main rule laid down in section 28 is that, if on the date when the right of action accrued the person to whom it accrued was under a disability, the action may be brought within six years of the cessation of the disability. The disability must therefore subsist on the date when the right of action accrues which, in the case of a mortgagee's remedies is normally the date when the mortgagor defaults on the covenant for redemption.[30] It is not enough if the disability arises after the date fixed for redemption.[31]

Section 28(4) contains a provision with a special bearing on remedies to enforce a mortgage of land. Notwithstanding any disability, no action to recover land (including, of course, foreclosure) or to recover money charged on land may be brought more than 30 years after the right of action accrued. In other words, there is an absolute limit of 30 years even in cases of disability.

Acknowledgments and part payments

The Act provides in sections 29 to 31 for the fresh accrual of actions—and thus for the extension of the statutory period—when an acknowledgment or part payment is made. It lays down slightly different rules for the remedies their effect against the security and those in respect of the personal debt, so that the two forms of remedy have to be considered separately.

1. Remedies against the security. Section 29(1) to (3), which applies equally to realty and personalty, enacts that when there has accrued to a mortgagee any right of action to recover the mortgaged property, including a foreclosure action, and:

(1) the person in possession of the land acknowledges the title of the mortgagee[32]; or
(2) the person in possession or the person liable for the mortgage debt makes any payment in respect of the debt whether principal or interest;

---

[29] See Preston & Newsom, *Limitation of Actions* (1953), Chap. VII.
[30] See *ante*, p. 247.
[31] *Purnell* v. *Roche* [1927] 2 Ch. 142. In this case the remedies of a lunatic mortgagee were held not to have been saved by the disability, although interest had been paid after the disability supervened. Now, however, under s.29(3) of the 1980 Act, in a foreclosure or other action by the mortgagee, payment of principal or interest by the person in possession of the property causes the accrual of the right of action to be deemed to be postponed until the date of such payment, and facts similar to those in *Purnell* v. *Roche* would today give a different result.
[32] Or as agent on his behalf, see, *e.g.* *Wright* v. *Pepin* [1954] 1 W.L.R. 635.

the right shall be deemed to have accrued on the date of the acknowledgment or payment.

An *acknowledgment* is thus effective only when made by the person in possession, or an agent on his behalf, while a *payment* is effective not only when made by the person in possession but also when made by the person liable for the mortgage debt. Both acknowledgments and payments, when effective, bind "all other persons in possession during the ensuing period of limitation."[33] In other words, the mortgagee's remedies against the property are protected against everybody for a further period of 12 years from the date of the acknowledgment or payment. Section 31 which establishes these rules refers only to mortgages and mortgagees and there is no definition clause in the Act, which extends the meaning of "mortgage" to cover charge. It is therefore arguable that acknowledgments and part payments under section 31 do not extend a chargee's remedies against the security. The argument gains point from the fact that section 20, which does cover charges, refers specifically to "a mortgage or other charge." The omission of charges[34-35] from the operation of section 31 can hardly have been intended and the courts may resort to the definition of mortgage in section 205(1)(xvi) of the Law of Property Act 1925, in order to avoid this result.[36]

Mortgagor dispossessed by third party. If after the execution of the mortgage a third party obtains possession and occupies the property under such conditions that time begins to run in his favour against the mortgagor, the mortgagee's rights will be unaffected so long as the mortgagor continues to make payments in respect of the debt (whether of principal or interest). In such a case the protection afforded by section 29(3) of the 1980 Act is absolute.[37] If, on the other hand, the mortgagor was already dispossessed at the date of the mortgage and time was already running against him, the execution of the mortgage does not confer on the mortgagee a new right of entry, so that subsequent payments by the mortgagor cannot prevent time from running in favour of his disseisor.[38]

2. Remedies in respect of the personal debt. Subject to section 29(6), section 29(5) enacts that where any right of action has accrued to recover any debt or other liquidated pecuniary claim or any claim to the personal estate of a deceased person or to any share or interest in any such estate and the person liable or accountable for the claim acknowledges the claim or makes any payment in respect of it, the right shall be treated as having accrued on and out before the date of the acknowledgment or payment. This is subject to the provision that a payment of a part of the rent or interest due at any-

---

[33] s.31(1) and (2).
[34-35] A charge by way of legal mortgage is presumably in the same position as a legal mortgage by virtue of ss.88 and 89 of the L.P.A. 1925.
[36] "Mortgage" in the L.P.A. 1925, "includes any charge or lien on any property "for securing money or money's worth."
[37] See *Doe d. Palmer* v. *Eyre* (1851) 17 Q.B.D. 366; *Ludbrook* v. *Ludbrook* [1901] 2 K.B. 96.
[38] *Thornton* v. *France* [1897] 2 Q.B. 143.

time shall not extend the period for claiming the remainder then due, but any payment of interest shall be treated as a payment in respect of the principal debt.[39]

The effect of an acknowledgment is different from that of a payment. A *payment* binds all persons liable in respect of the debt, including, of course, the successors of the person paying.[39a] But an *acknowledgment* only binds the acknowledgor and his successors, *i.e.* his personal representatives and any person on whom the liability for the debt devolves on his death or bankruptcy or by disposition of property or by the terms of a settlement or otherwise.[40]

The effect of acknowledgment or payment made after the relevant period of limitation has run.   Formerly there existed a rule of law that where the effect of the expiration of the prescribed period of limitation was merely to bar the remedy and not the right, an acknowledgment or payment could cause a right of action to accrue once again even though it was made after the expiry of the prescribed period of limitation unless the statute had extinguished the right itself. It is now provided by section 29(7) that a current period of limitation may be repeatedly extended under the section by further acknowledgments or payments, but a right of action once barred shall not be revived by any subsequent acknowledgment or payment.[41]

Section 17 extinguishes the title of a mortgagees of land who fails to exercise his remedies within the prescribed period and so a subsequent acknowledgment or payment does not revive his rights against the security.[42]

There is no corresponding provision which extinguishes the title of a mortgagee of personalty, so that a subsequent acknowledgment or payment appears to revive the mortgage as well as the personal debt.[43] This difference between realty and personalty in regard to the effect of acknowledgments and payments on a mortgagee's rights is to be explained more by reference to the history of the drafting of the relevant provisions than on rational grounds.

In any event, acknowledgments and payments made after the statutory

---

[39] Limitation Act 1980, s.29(6).

[39a] *Ibid.* s.31(7).

[40] *Ibid.* s.31(6)(9). s.31(6) and (7) re-enact s.25(5) and (6) of the 1939 Act but omit provisos which formally existed to both sub-sections. Those limited the effect of an acknowledgement or payment made *after* the expiration of the period of limitation prescribed the commencement of an action to recover a debt or other liquidated pecuniary claim and were repealed by the Limitation Amendment Act 1980, ss.6(3), 13(2), and Sched. 2.

[41] This is subject to the Limitation Act 1980, s.29(6). This change came as a result of the recommendation made by the Law Reform Committee in its 21st Report (Final Report on Limitations of Actions) (Cmmd. 6923), para. 2.71.

[42] *Kibble* v. *Fairthorne* [1895] 1 Ch. 219. After the mortgagee's remedies have been barred against the land, the mortgagor is entitled to the return of the deeds; *Lewis* v. *Plunket* [1937] Ch. 306.

[43] It is true that s.3(2) extinguishes the title to chattels after an action for conversion has been barred, but this does not cover the case of mere inactivity by mortgagor and mortgagee.

period has once run may operate to revive the personal action for the mortgage debt. Section 5 bars the remedy for simple contract and section 8 in the case of specialty debts but neither extinguishes the debt. The right to the debt is therefore revived and under section 31[44] it is revived not only against the person making the acknowledgment or payment but against his successors and all persons liable in respect of the debt, respectively, with one exception. The exception is that the revival of the debt by a limited owner under a settlement antedating the acknowledgment or payment does not bind other persons taking under that settlement.[45]

Conditions of an effective acknowledgment or payment.   Payment need only be proved as a fact. An acknowledgment to have the effects described above, must, however, be in writing signed by the person making it.[46]

The acknowledgment or payment has further to be made by the person specified in section 29, that is:

(1) in the case of an acknowledgment of the mortgage, by the person in possession;

(2) in the case of a payment keeping the mortgage alive, by the person in possession or by the person liable for the mortgage debt;

(3) in the case of an acknowledgment or payment keeping the personal debt alive, by the person liable or accountable for the debt.

The acknowledgment or payment may also be made by the agent of the person required to make it.[47]

The "person in possession" for the purposes of section 29 is the person in possession of the interest mortgaged. It does not include a tenant from the mortgagor and a payment of rent by a tenant direct to the mortgagee does not bind the mortgagor unless made at the latter's express direction. A tenant is not the implied agent of the mortgagor for making acknowledgments or payments to the mortgagee.[48] On the other hand, a receiver, whether appointed by the court or by the mortgagee under a power, is in law the agent of the mortgagor and entitled to make payments on the mortgagor's behalf. Consequently, a receiver's acts do bind the mortgagor.[49]

The "person liable or accountable" for the debt means a person liable or accountable in connection with the discharge of the mortgage debt. A

---

[44] Subs. (6) and (7).

[45] *Cf. Gregson* v. *Hindley* (1846) 10 Jur. 383.

[46] Limitation Act 1980, s.30(1).

[47] *Ibid.* s.30(2). *cf. Wright* v. *Pepin* [1954] 1 W.L.R. 635 (acknowledgment by mortgagor's solicitor held to be sufficient).

[48] *Harlock* v. *Ashberry* (1882) 19 Ch.D. 539. A payment of rent made by a tenant of mortgaged property to a mortgagee in consequence of a notice by the mortgagee requiring the rent to be paid to him is not a receipt of any sum in respect of the mortgage debt and accordingly not a payment to prevent the barring by the Limitation Act of a foreclosure action.

[49] *Chinnery* v. *Evans* (1864) 11 H.L.C. 115 at 134.

surety[50] or a co-mortgagor[51] is clearly such a person, and their payments
bind the mortgagor. But it is otherwise with a third party who is liable to
make payments to the mortgagee in connection with the mortgaged property but not in relation to the discharge of the mortgage debt. The case of
rent paid by a tenant to the mortgagee has already been mentioned.[52] Payments of rent at the request of the mortgagee convert him into a mortgagee
in possession but do not constitute payments by the mortgagor. If an insurance policy is assigned by way of mortgage and notice is given to the
insurers, the latter become liable to pay the moneys to the mortgagee. But
a payment under the policy is not a payment in respect of the debt and does
not keep the mortgagee's remedies alive against other securities comprised
in the mortgage.[53] Similarly, if a beneficiary mortgages his interest in a
trust fund, a payment by the trustees direct to the mortgagee in pursuance
of their duty to give effect to all interests of which they have notice does
not bind the mortgagor.[54] On the other hand, the "person liable or accountable" is not limited to persons contractually liable to the mortgagee. It is
enough if the person paying is "concerned to answer the debt."[55] In *Bradshaw* v. *Widdrington*[56] a father borrowed money on mortgage for the benefit of his son who executed a bond for the money in favour of his father.
Payments by the son in respect of mortgage interest were held sufficient to
keep the mortgage alive since, as between him and the mortgagor, he was
bound to discharge the mortgage debt. There need not even be a contractual obligation for the discharge of the debt between the mortgagor and the
person making payment. All that is necessary is that the person paying
should, by reason of the relations between himself and the mortgagor, be
entitled in law to discharge the debt.[57] Thus when the property mortgaged
is settled, a payment by any one beneficiary is sufficient to save the mortgagee's remedies against the property.[58] The rule appears to be that whenever a number of persons stand in peril of suit by a creditor so that all
benefit by the discharge of the liability, a payment by one keeps the creditor's remedies alive.[59]

Logically, the same rule should apply in assignments of the equity of
redemption so that a payment either by the mortgagor[60] or by the
assignee[61] would keep the mortgagee's remedies alive. It has in fact been

[50] *Lewin* v. *Wilson* (1886) 11 A.C. 639.
[51] *Re Earl Kingston's Estate* [1869] 3 I.R. 485.
[52] See *ante*, p. 53.
[53] *Re Lord Clifden* [1900] 1 Ch. 774.
[54] *Re Edwards' Will Trusts* [1937] Ch. 553.
[55] *Lewin* v. *Wilson* (1886) 11 A.C. 639 at 644.
[56] [1902] 2 Ch. 430.
[57] *Bradshaw* v. *Widdrington* [1902] 2 Ch. 430 at 439, *per* Buckley, J.
[58] *Barclay* v. *Owen* (1889) 60 L.T. 220. A life tenant, who is also the mortgagee of the settled
    property, is presumed to be keeping down the interest on his own incumbrance so that the
    statute does not run against his mortgage: *Wynne* v. *Styan* (1847) 2 Ph. 303.
[59] *Re Lacey* [1907] 1 Ch. 330 at 346, *per* Farwell L.J.; also *Roddam* v. *Morley* (1857) 1 De G.
    & J. 1.
[60] *Bradshaw* v. *Widdrington* [1902] 2 Ch. 430.
[61] *Dibb* v. *Walker* [1893] 2 Ch. 429.

so decided in the case of an equity of redemption assigned *free from incum-brances* when the original mortgagor is, as between himself and his assignee, bound to discharge the mortgage debt.[62] If, however, the assignment is made *subject to incumbrances*, the position is not free from doubt. In *Newbould* v. *Smith*[63] the Court of Appeal held that payments by the original mortgagor would not bind the assignee. This decision is inconsistent with the language of Westbury L.C. and Lord Cranworth in *Chinnery* v. *Evans*[64] and it seems to have been doubted by the House of Lords in *Newbould* v. *Smith* itself, the court finding other reasons for dismissing the appeal. The decision, although the Court of Appeal was a strong one, is submitted to be entirely unacceptable. A mortgagee who receives regular payments of interest from his mortgagor should not be concerned to inquire into the latter's dealings with the equity of redemption. Any other rule would be very alarming to mortgagees.[65]

Finally, an acknowledgment or payment must be made to the person whose remedies are to be kept alive, *i.e.* to the person entitled to the mortgage or to his agent. Who is the right person to receive an acknowledgment or payment naturally depends on the dealings with the mortgage debt and on the notices of those dealings given to the mortgagor. If the mortgagee has died, his personal representatives are the persons concerned to receive acknowledgments or payments.[66] Similarly, if the mortgage debt has been settled, the trustees are the right persons to be paid. But a payment direct to the proper beneficiary is regarded as paid to him as agent for the trustees,[67] and may be sufficient to prevent time from running.

Institution of proceedings by the mortgagee

If an action is begun by the mortgagee within the statutory period, that will prevent his rights from being barred, even though the hearing does not take place before time has run out.[68] But it must be remembered that the institution of proceedings does not have the same effect as an acknowledgment and saves the remedies only for that action, so that upon their discontinuance the benefit of the saving will not be available in a subsequent action.[69] On the other hand, if a judgment for foreclosure absolute is obtained, the effect is to vest a new title in the mortgagee, so that although the mortgagor may remain continuously in possession, the statutory period begins to run afresh from the decree.[70]

---

[62] *Bradshaw* v. *Widdrington, supra*.
[63] (1886) 33 Ch.D. 127, affirmed (1889) 14 A.C. 423 but on other grounds, the House of Lords reserving their opinion on this point.
[64] (1864) 11 H.L.C. 115.
[65] *Ibid.* at 139, *per* Lord Cranworth.
[66] *Barclay* v. *Owen* (1889) 60 L.T. 220.
[67] *Re Somerset* [1894] 1 Ch. 231.
[68] *Wrixon* v. *Vize* (1842) 3 Dr. & W. 104 at 123.
[69] *Pratt* v. *Hawkins* (1846) 15 M. & W. 399.
[70] *Heath* v. *Pugh* (1881) 6 Q.B.D. 345 affirmed (1882) 7 App. Cas. 235. Unless, of course, the action is struck out.

Fraud, concealment and mistake

Section 32 of the 1980 Act provides that:

(1) where the action is based on the fraud of the defendant, his agent or any person through whom he claims and his agent;

(2) any fact relevant to the plaintiff's right of action has been deliberately concealed by fraud; or

(3) the action is for relief from the consequences of a mistake;

the period shall not begin to run until the plaintiff either discovered or could with reasonable diligence have discovered the fraud, concealment or mistake.

The section at the same time saves the rights of bona fide purchasers.[71]

---

[71] Limitation Act 1980, s.32(3) and see Preston & Newsom, *Limitation of Actions* (1953), Chap. IX.

CHAPTER 21

RIGHTS OF CONSOLIDATION AND MARSHALLING

The effect of these equitable doctrines is that, in certain circumstances, a mortgagee is enabled to enlarge his security beyond the property which he took to secure his debt.

CONSOLIDATION

Right to consolidate

If a borrower (B) has mortgaged two or more properties to a lender (L), L may have the right to refuse to allow B to redeem one mortgage unless he redeems all of them. Whereas equity normally extends the right to redeem, the application of the maxim "he who seeks equity must do equity"[1] results, where the doctrine of consolidation comes into play, in a restriction of that right. Normally, L will wish to exercise the right when one of the mortgaged properties depreciates in value so that by itself it is insufficient to satisfy the security; but he may do so even if each property is by itself a sufficient security for the debt.

The basis of the long-established right to consolidate is the practice of courts of equity in redemption actions. After the mortgagor is in default, he needs the assistance of equity in order to redeem, and equity demands, in such a case, that he shall not be able to redeem an estate which is sufficient security for the debt while leaving the mortgagee with another estate which is not.[2] This would suggest that the mortgagee can exercise the right only when one of the properties mortgaged depreciates; but it is settled law that the right exists in any circumstances where the mortgagor has to assert his equitable title. Thus it applies in a forfeiture action, since in such an action the mortgagor has to redeem then or not at all.[3] It applies also when the mortgagee has sold one property under his power of sale and the mortgagor is claiming to be paid the surplus remaining after the discharge of that mortgage; the effect of the doctrine is then to give the mortgagee the right to retain that surplus so as to satisfy a debt secured on another property.[4] Unlike the right to tack, the right to consolidate is independent of the possession of the legal estate.

---

[1] *Willie* v. *Lugg* (1761) 2 Eden 78; *White* v. *Hillacre* (1839) 3 Y. & C. Ex. 597; *Chesworth* v. *Hunt*, (1880) 5 C.P.D. 266; *Cummins* v. *Fletcher* (1880) 14 Ch.D. 699.
[2] *Jennings* v. *Jordan* (1881) 6 App.Cas. 698, H.L.; *Griffith* v. *Pound* (1890) 45 Ch.D. 553.
[3] *Cummins* v. *Fletcher* (1880) 14 Ch.D. 699; *Watts* v. *Symes* (1851) 1 De G.M. & G. 240.
[4] *Selby* v. *Pomfret* (1861) 3 De G.F. & J. 595; *Cracknall* v. *Janson* (1879) 11 Ch.D. 1, C.A.

Conditions for consolidation

The doctrine may cause difficulty to a purchaser of mortgaged property, since the mortgage may be liable to be consolidated against him although he has no means of knowing that to be the case. Consequently, the operation of the doctrine was abolished by statute for all mortgages made after December 31, 1881, except where a contrary intention is expressed in the mortgage. Section 93 of the Law of Property Act 1925, reproducing section 17 of the Conveyancing Act 1881, is as follows:

> "(1) A mortgagor seeking to redeem any one mortgage is entitled to do so without paying any money due under any separate mortgage made by him, or by any person through whom he claims, solely on property other than that comprised in the mortgage which he seeks to redeem.
>
> This subsection applies only if and so far as a contrary intention is not expressed in the mortgage deeds or one of them.
>
> (2) This section does not apply where all the mortgages were made before 1st January, 1882.
>
> (3) Save as aforesaid nothing in this Act, in reference to mortgages, affects any right of consolidation or renders inoperative a stipulation in relation to any mortgage made before or after the commencement of this Act reserving a right to consolidate."

The intention to exclude the statutory rule may be effectively manifested either by a clause in the mortgage deed that section 93(1) is not to apply to the security , or by a clause providing for the preservation of the right to consolidate.[5]

If either all the mortgages were made before January 1, 1882 or the parties have excluded section 93(1), the mortgagee's right to consolidate can be exercised subject to the following conditions:

(1) The legal dates of redemption of all the mortgages sought to be consolidated have passed.[6]
(2) All mortgages must have been made by the same mortgagor.
(3) The security must be in existence at the time that the mortgagee claims to consolidate.
(4) At one and the same time, all the mortgages must have been vested in some person, and all the equities of redemption in some other person.

These conditions are now considered in turn.

(1) The right to consolidate is an equitable right and does not override

---

[5] *Hughes* v. *Britannia Permanent Benefit Building Society* [1906] 2 Ch. 606. In *Re Salmon, ex p. the Trustee* [1903] 1 K.B. 147 it was held that a clause excluding the statute (at that time s.17 of the Conveyancing Act 1881) and contained in the first of several mortgages would preserve the right to consolidate; compare *Griffith* v. *Pound* (1890) 45 Ch.D. 553; a clause in a later mortgage is ineffective as to earlier mortgages.

[6] *Cummins* v. *Fletcher* (1880) 14 Ch.D. 699.

the legal right to redeem on the contractual date: the mortgagor does not require the assistance of equity to redeem on that date.

(2) The right can come into existence only if the mortgages were originally made by the same mortgagor,[7] with one possible exception; that is, where one mortgage is made by B and the other by persons claiming by devolution from him on his death.[8] Thus the right does not exist where one mortgage is made by B and the other jointly by A and B[9]; nor when B as beneficiary makes one and A, as B's trustee, makes the other[10]; nor when B as principal debtor makes one and A as surety makes the other[11]; nor when B makes one as security for a private debt and A and B as partners make the other as security for a partnership debt.

Various other differences between the mortgages are irrelevant to the existence of the right to consolidate. First, it does not matter that the mortgages were originally made to different mortgagees.[12] Next, the right is not affected by either the nature of the mortgage or the nature of the property mortgaged, except that no right to consolidation can arise in respect of personal chattels as defined by the Bills of Sale Acts 1878.[13] Thus two legal mortgages, or two equitable mortgages,[14] or a legal and an equitable mortgage can be consolidated,[15] as can a mortgage of realty and a mortgage of personalty other than personal chattels.[16]

(3) Where a mortgagee holds two mortgages, and one has ceased to exist because its subject matter has determined, as may be the case when it is a mortgage of a lease[17] or a life interest,[18] the mortgagee may not apply any surplus on the other to make good the deficiency on the one whose subject-matter has determined. As soon as it has determined, the debt is no longer secured and is a simple contract debt.

This does not apply when a security has ceased to exist because the mortgagee has realised it; the right to consolidate is not affected by realisation.[19]

This rule may be illustrated by the following examples: consider these events and assume that all other conditions for consolidation are satisfied:

---

[7] *Sharp* v. *Rickards* [1909] 1 Ch. 109.

[8] *White* v. *Hillacre* (1839) 3 Y. & C. Ex. 597.

[9] *Jones* v. *Smith* (1794) 2 Ves. Jun. 372; *Thorneycroft* v. *Crockett* (1848) 2 H.L.C. 239; *Cummins* v. *Fletcher* (1880) 14 Ch.D. 699.

[10] *Re Raggett, ex p. Williams* (1880) 16 Ch.D. 117.

[11] *Aldworth* v. *Robinson* (1840) 2 Beav. 287.

[12] Provided that they are united in the same mortgagee when the right to consolidation is claimed: *Pledge* v. *White* [1896] A.C. 187.

[13] *Chesworth* v. *Hunt* (1880) 5 C.P.D. 266.

[14] *Tweedale* v. *Tweedale* (1857) 23 Beav. 341.

[15] *Cracknall* v. *Janson* (1879) 11 Ch.D. 1, C.A.; *Watts* v. *Symes* (1851) 1 De G. M. & G. 240.

[16] *Cracknall* v. *Janson, supra. Tassell* v. *Smith* (1858) 2 De G. & J. 713 was overruled by *Jennings* v. *Jordan* (1881) 6 App.Cas. 698 which held that consolidation cannot occur so as to prejudice the purchaser of an equity of redemption by virtue of a mortgage created after the sale.

[17] *Re Raggett, ex p. Williams* (1880) 16 Ch.D. 117.

[18] *Re Gregson, Christison* v. *Bolam* (1887) 36 Ch.D. 223.

[19] *Selby* v. *Pomfret* (1861) 3 De G.F. & J. 595; *Cracknall* v. *Janson* (1879) 11 Ch.D. 14, C.A.

    (a) B mortgages a leasehold interest in Blackacre to L for £10,000.

    (b) B mortgages a freehold interest in Whiteacre to L for £40,000.

    (c) L realises his security in Whiteacre for £50,000.

    (d) The leasehold interest in Blackacre determines.

    (e) L gives B notice to pay off the debt on Blackacre, with a view to becoming entitled to exercise his power of sale.

If the events (a), (b), (e) happen, and in that order, L can consolidate against B and can refuse a tender by B of the money secured against Blackacre.[20]

If the events (a), (b), (d), (c) happen, and in that order, L can consolidate and apply the surplus on realisation of his security in Whiteacre to the payment of the debt secured on Blackacre, since both securities were in existence when L claimed to consolidate.[21]

If the events (a), (b), (c), (d) happen, and in that order, the security on Blackacre no longer exists at the time L realises his security in Whiteacre. The debt formerly secured on Blackacre has now become a simple contract debt and in respect of it, L is in the same position as any other of B's unsecured creditors. If there are such creditors L cannot, against them, claim to apply the surplus from Whiteacre to the payment of the Blackacre debt.[22]

Both mortgages must be vested solely in L at the time when he wishes to exercise his right to consolidate, so, if in either of the first two rules above, the mortgage in one property was vested in L and M jointly at the time L wished to exercise the right, he would not be permitted to do so.[23]

For the purposes of the first three rules, only the right to consolidate against the original mortgagor needs to be discussed. The fourth rule, however, involves consideration of the right to consolidate against an assignee of a mortgagor, as well as the right to consolidate against the original mortgagor.

Consolidation against the original mortgagor

Consider the following transactions:

    (a) B mortgages Blackacre to L;

    (b) B mortgages Blackacre to M;

    (c) B mortgages Whiteacre to M;

    (d) L buys M's mortgage;

    (e) K buys both mortgages;

    (f) B assigns the equity of redemption in one of the properties to N.

Provided the conditions previously discussed are all satisfied, M will have the right to consolidate against B if the events (b), (c) occur before (f),

---

[20] *Griffith* v. *Pound* (1890) 45 Ch.D. 553.

[21] *Selby* v. *Pomfret, supra; Cracknell* v. *Janson, supra.*

[22] *Re Gregson, Christison* v. *Bolam* (1887) 36 Ch.D. 223; *Talbot* v. *Frere* (1878) 9 Ch.D. 568.

[23] *Riley* v. *Hall* (1898) 79 L.T. 244.

while L will have the same right if the events (a), (c), (d), occur before (f). The equities of redemption are in B's hand throughout and whoever acquires both mortgages can consolidate against him. This applies equally if, instead of L buying M's mortgage, K buys both mortgages.

If, however, the equities are severed before both mortgages come into one hand, as in the sequences (b), (f), (c), or (a), (c), (f), (d) (or e); there can be no right to consolidate against B, because B never owns both equities of redemption at the same time that L or K owns both mortgages.[24] Subsequent transactions may, as explained below, create a right to consolidate against N.

It is for the mortgagee of the two properties to decide whether he wishes to take advantage of his right to consolidate, and the mortgagor cannot compel him to do so against his will. In *Pelly* v. *Wathen*,[25] after the events (a), (c), B created a second mortgage of both properties in favour of P. It was held that P was entitled, if he wished, to redeem only one of the first mortgages, even though he had the right to consolidate against B if he redeemed both.

The right to consolidate is not lost because the mortgagee does not choose to exercise it; if, following the events (a), (c), (e), K gives notice to B that he requires payment of the mortgage on Blackacre, he can refuse a tender by B if it is insufficient to discharge both mortgages.[26]

Consolidation against the mortgagor's assignee

The principle is that an assignee of the equity of redemption succeeds to whatever rights the mortgagor had at the time of the assignment.[27] The simple example is where a person purchases the freehold or leasehold interest of the mortgagor subject to one or more mortgages, but a person acquiring the equity of redemption under a will or intestacy[28] or under the bankruptcy law[29] will be in the same position.

Consider the following transactions:

   (a) B mortgages Blackacre to L;
   (b) B mortgages Whiteacre to L;
   (c) B mortgages Whiteacre to L and M;
   (d) B mortgages Whiteacre to M;
   (e) L buys M's mortgage;
   (f) B assigns both equities of redemption to N;
   (g) B assigns the equity of redemption in Blackacre to N.

In the events (a), (b), L can consolidate against B, and he will have the

---

[24] *Harter* v. *Coleman* (1882) 19 Ch.D. 630; *Minter* v. *Carr* [1894] 3 Ch. 498.
[25] (1849) 7 Hare 351; on appeal (1851) 1 De G.M. & G. 16; *cf. Re Thompson's Estates* [1912] 1 I.R. 194.
[26] *Griffith* v. *Pound* (1890) 45 Ch.D. 553.
[27] *Harter* v. *Coleman* (1882) 19 Ch.D. 630.
[28] *Harris* v. *Tubb* (1889) 42 Ch.D. 79.
[29] *Selby* v. *Pomfret* (1861) 3 De G.F. & J. 595; *Re Salmon, ex p. the Trustee* [1903] 1 K.B. 147.

same right in the events (a), (c), (d), or (a), (d), (e), since B has both equities of redemption and at the same time L has both mortgages. As soon as (f) occurs, L can consolidate against N, who takes subject to equities existing against B at the time of the assignment.[30] The same is true if (g) occurs, because N takes the assignment subject to the existing right to consolidate. If N wishes to redeem Blackacre, L can force him to redeem Whiteacre at the same time, though N will, if he redeems, be entitled to have Whiteacre transferred to him.[31]

In the events (a), (d), (f), (e), it would appear that there is no right to consolidate since, after the occurrence of (a) and (d) the two mortgages were in different hands; there would have been no right to consolidate against B and therefore no right to consolidate against N. On general principles N should not be prejudiced by the subsequent transaction between L and M. It is, however, an old-established rule[32] that, in such circumstances the assignee of both equities must be deemed to have taken the assignment with the knowledge that the two mortgages might come into one hand, with the result that the mortgagee would have the right to consolidate against him.[33] This leads to the possibility that a mortgagee whose security was inadequate could improve his position at the expense of the mortgagor's general creditors if the mortgagor became bankrupt. If, in the sequence of events (a), (d), (f), (f) takes place because N is B's trustee in bankruptcy, either L or M, if he thought his security to be inadequate, would be able to enlarge it by buying up the other's mortgage and consolidating against N, and would be unaffected by notice of B's bankruptcy.[34] It would be otherwise if the sequence were (a), (f), (d); there could be no consolidation of two mortgages, one created before and one after the start of the bankruptcy.

It might be thought that the same result would occur as a result of the sequence (a), (d), (g), (e); that is, that B assigns only one equity of redemption. If N is exposed to the risk of consolidation against himself when he buys both equities, the fact that he has bought only one should not make any difference. The decision in *Beevor* v. *Luck*[35] to that effect is, however, no longer considered to be good law, the practical reason being the risk that would be associated with the purchase of any equity of redemption. In this example, N when he took the equity of redemption in Blackacre would have no means of finding out from L that Whiteacre had been mortgaged to M by B and that, in consequence M, by buying L's mortgage, would be able to consolidate against him. As was said in *Pledge*

---

[30] *Willie* v. *Lugg* (1761) 2 Eden 78.

[31] *Cracknall* v. *Janson* (1871) 11 Ch.D. 1, C.A.; *Mutual Life Assurance Society* v. *Langley* (1886) 32 Ch.D. 460, C.A.

[32] *Bovey* v. *Skipwith* (1671) 1 Cas. in Ch. 201; *Tweedale* v. *Tweedale* (1857) 23 Beav. 341; *Vint* v. *Padget* (1858) 2 De G. & J. 611.

[33] As was decided, albeit with reluctance, in *Pledge* v. *White* [1896] A.C. 187.

[34] *Selby* v. *Pomfret* (1861) 3 De G.F. & J. 595.

[35] (1867) L.R. 4 Eq. 537.

v. *White*,[35a] a person in the position of N can see, if he buys two properties mortgaged by the same mortgagor, that there is a risk of the mortgages coming into the same hand. But if he buys one property, he can be aware of this risk only if B tells him that he has mortgaged other property.

Where the sequence of events is (a), (g), (d), (e) there can clearly be no consideration, since the equities of redemption in the two properties have been severed before there is even a potential right to consolidate.[36]

The general principle that the assignor of an equity of redemption should not be able to prejudice his assignee's position by subsequent transactions with third parties was qualified in *Jennings* v. *Jordan*[37] where it was suggested that the assignee might be affected by an express contractual term reserving to the assignor the right to consolidate future mortgages. That case was decided before the Conveyancing Act 1881 came into operation, and mortgage deeds did not then, as they commonly do now, contain clauses excluding the statutory prohibition on, or preserving the right of, consolidation.

The question therefore arises whether an assignee of an equity of redemption is liable, by reason of such a contractual term, to have consolidated against him mortgages created by the assignor which were not in existence at the time of the assignment. In *Andrews* v. *City Permanent Building Society*[38] it was held that, while a second mortgagee would not by virtue of the equitable doctrine be liable to have mortgages consolidated against him which were not in existence when he took the second mortgage, he was so liable if the first mortgage contained an express stipulation for a right to consolidate later mortgages. The liability arises whether or not the second mortgagee has notice of the stipulation because the mortgage contract prevents him from redeeming free of that right.

The same point arose in *Hughes* v. *Britannia Permanent Benefit Building Society*[39] where the much-criticised Kekewich J. arrived at what is generally considered to be the right decision. He held that the second mortgagee is affected by the contractual stipulation, but treated it as if it reserved the right to tack further advances, and applied the rule in *Hopkinson* v. *Rolt*[40] that is, that a mortgagee with notice of an intervening mortgage could not tack further advances. The rule has been criticised on the ground that a paramount right to tack created by a first mortgage should not be capable of being defeated by the action of a second mortgagee in giving notice of his charge, but, whatever substance there is in that criticism, it is settled law that a second mortgagee can prevent consolidation of later mortgages against him by giving actual notice to the first mortgagee. Registration of

[35a] [1896] A.C. 187.
[36] *Jennings* v. *Jordan* (1881) 6 App.Cas. 698, H.L.
[37] (1881) 6 App.Cas. 698 at 702.
[38] (1881) 44 L.T. 641.
[39] [1906] 2 Ch. 606.
[40] (1861) 9 H.L.C. 514; see Megarry and Wade, *The Law of Real Property* (5th ed., 1984), p. 1010.

the second mortgage is not notice for this purpose where a mortgage is expressly made for securing further advances.[41]

Registration of the right to consolidate

Where the land affected by the right to consolidate is registered land, the Land Registration Act 1925 and the Land Registration Rules 1925, rule 154 come into play.

The Land Registration Act 1925, section 25(3)(ii) states that any provision contained in a charge which purports to affect any registered land or charge other than that in respect of which the charge is to be expressly registered shall be void.

Rule 154 of the Land Registration Rules 1925, is as follows:

> "(1) Where a charge, whether affecting the whole or part of the land comprised in a title, reserves the right to consolidate, it shall not on that account be registered against any other land than that expressly described in it
>
> (2) But where the right reserved is to consolidate with a specified charge, or an application in writing is made to register the right in respect of a specified charge, the Registrar shall require the production of the [land] certificate of all the titles affected and, on the production thereof, shall enter in the register a notice that the specified charges are consolidated."

Since the Land Registration Act 1925, section 65, requires that, on registration of a charge or mortgage, the land certificate is to be deposited at the registry until the charge or mortgage is cancelled, it must be the charge certificate, not the land certificate, to which rule 154(2) should refer.

The right to consolidate does not depend on the entry of any notice under rule 154.

It has been suggested[42] that the right to consolidate mortgages of unregistered land is registrable as a class C (iii) land charge, but there is no direct authority in support of the suggestion and it is not easy to see how such a right can amount to a charge.

MARSHALLING

Principle underlying the doctrine

If B has two creditors, L and M, and L has recourse to only one security in order to satisfy his debt, while M has recourse to more than one, M will not be permitted to satisfy his debt in a way that prejudices L.[43] Although

---

[41] L.P.A. 1925, s.94(2).(as amended by the L.P.A. 1969, s.16(2), Sched. 2, Pt. I; and the Law of Property (Amendment) Act 1926, s.7).

[42] (1948) 92 S.J. 726.

[43] *Lanoy* v. *Duke of Athol* (1742) 2 Atk. 444; *Aldrich* v. *Cooper* (1803) 8 Ves. 382; *Trimmer* v. *Bayne (No. 2)* (1803) 9 Ves. 209, approved, *Webb* v. *Smith* (1885) 30 Ch.D. 192; *Averall* v. *Wade* (1835) L. & G. temp. Sugden 252.

the application of this doctrine will, like the application of the doctrine of consolidation, enlarge the creditor's security beyond what he contracted for, it is not a right which the creditor needs actively to assert, since in any case where it should apply, the court will automatically apply it without it being claimed as relief in the pleadings.[44]

An illustration of the doctrine is given by the following facts:

(a) B mortgages Blackacre to M;
(b) B mortgages Whiteacre to M;
(c) B mortgages Whiteacre to L.

The effect of the doctrine is that L may claim, against B, that B shall satisfy M's debt out of Blackacre so far as possible, leaving Whiteacre for the satisfaction of his own debt.[45] The doctrine applies to a fund of money as well as to realty and also applies whether the security is by way of mortgage, charge or lien.[46]

Suppose, in the above events, B had mortgaged the two properties to M to secure a loan of £25,000, and later mortgaged Whiteacre to L to secure a loan of £15,000, and suppose each of the two properties to be worth £20,000. If the doctrine of marshalling did not exist, then the primary rule[47] as to the satisfaction of M's debt would operate, and it would be satisfied as to £12,500 out of each property, leaving only £7,500 of the equity in Whiteacre for L. Thus, although the two properties would between them be sufficient to satisfy the total debts owing to L and M, L's would be only half satisfied.

If the securities are marshalled, M's debt is satisfied as to £20,000 out of Blackacre and as to the remaining £5,000 out of Whiteacre, leaving £15,000 equity in Whiteacre to satisfy L.

Conditions for marshalling

There are four such conditions which are now stated and discussed in turn:

(1) The right exists only where the prior mortgagee holds two securities (of whatever nature) which belong to the same owner.
(2) The right exists against the common mortgagor and against all persons, other than purchasers, claiming through him.
(3) The right is not enforced to the prejudice of third parties claiming as purchasers.
(4) A puisne incumbrancer's right to marshall does not affect the prior mortgagee's right to realise his securities in whatever manner or order he decides.

[44] *Gibbs* v. *Ougier* (1806) 12 Ves. 413.
[45] *Lanoy* v. *Duke of Athol, supra*; *South* v. *Bloxam* (1865) 2 H. & M. 457.
[46] *Re Westzinthus* (1833) 5 B. & Ad. 817; *Re Fry* [1912] 2 Ch. 86.
[47] *i.e.* that the debt is satisfied out of the two properties rateably to their values.

Rule 1

The two securities must originally have belonged to the same owner[48]; thus, where the two securities were a ship and its cargo and belonged to different owners, marshalling was not permitted.[49] It is not necessary for the securities to have been created at the same time, or to have been given in respect of each of the same debt. But if two securities are given, one in respect of each of two debts, marshalling is not permitted unless the debts are those of the same person.[50] As with consolidation, the right does not exist where one security is given by one person and the other security by the same person jointly with someone else.

If, in the example given above, M had satisfied his debt out of Whiteacre, L's right to marshall would be enforced by being subrogated to M's rights against Blackacre.[51]

Rule 2

The right may be exercised against the common mortgagor[52] or against persons claiming the property or part of it under him, unless those persons take by charge or assignment.[53] They are not subject to the right, even if they are volunteers.[54]

Because the right is exercisable against the common mortgagor's trustee in bankruptcy,[55] a puisne incumbrancer may be able to enlarge his security at the expense of the general creditors. The common mortgagor's judgment creditors[56] and real and personal representatives[57] are exposed to the operation of the doctrine.

The right is not lost by reason of the two funds or securities later becoming vested in different persons.[58]

Rule 3

The court will not interfere with a mortgagee in the exercise of his remedies, so if, in the example above, M chooses to satisfy his debt first out of Whiteacre, L's debt will be thrown on Blackacre, of which he becomes second mortgagee, and if L pays off the unsatisfied part of M's debt, he

---

[48] *Douglas* v. *Cooksey* (1868) 2 I.R.Eq. 311.
[49] *The Chioggia* [1898] P. 1, distinguishing *The Edward Oliver* (1867) L.R. 1. A. & E. 379; *contra Webb* v. *Smith* (1885) 30 Ch.D. 192, which is considered incorrect on this point.
[50] *ex p. Kendall* (1811) 17 Ves. 514.
[51] *Mason* v. *Bogg* (1837) 2 My. & Cr. 443; *Wallis* v. *Woodyear* (1855) 2 Jur.N.S. 179; *Dolphin* v. *Aylward* (1870) L.R. 4 H.L. 486.
[52] *Haynes* v. *Forshaw* (1853) 11 Hare. 93.
[53] *Barnes* v. *Racster* (1842) 1 Y. & C.Ch.Cas. 401; *Flint* v. *Howard* [1893] 2 Ch. 54, C.A.
[54] *Dolphin* v. *Aylward* (1870) L.R. 4 H.L. 486; *Hales* v. *Cox* (1863) 32 Beav. 118.
[55] *Re Cornwall, Baldwin* v. *Belcher* (1842) 3 Dr. & War. 173; *Re Tristram, ex p. Hartley* (1835) 1 Deac. 288; *Re Holland, ex p. Alston* (1868) 4 Ch.App. 168; *Heyman* v. *Dubois* (1871) L.R. 13 Eq. 158.
[56] *Gray* v. *Stone and Funnell* (1893) 69 L.T. 282.
[57] *Lanoy* v. *Duke of Athol* (1742) 2 Atk. 444; *Flint* v. *Howard* [1893] 2 Ch. 54, C.A.
[58] *Lanoy* v. *Duke of Athol, supra.*

becomes first mortgagee.[59] If M realises both securities, he holds the aggre-gate proceeds on trust to pay himself first, then L.[60]

Rule 4

The right to consolidate may, as *Pledge* v. *White*[61] shows, operate to the disadvantage of third parties claiming as purchasers, but the right to mar-shall does not.[62] This can be illustrated by considering what would happen if there was a fourth event added to the series above (see page 429), that is:

(d) B mortgages Blackacre to N.

This does not affect L's right to marshall against B; but if M satisfies him-self primarily out of Whiteacre, which is the only property to which L can resort, L can no longer throw his debt on Blackacre.[63] It is irrelevant that N had notice of the previous transactions,[64] or that he was a volunteer.[65]

There are only two cases in which L's right can affect N. In *Re Mower's Trusts*[66] it was held that N was bound by L's pre-existing right to marshall because his mortgage was expressly made subject to the payment of the two earlier mortgages. In *Stronge* v. *Hawkes*[67] there was an erroneous recital to the effect that the prior mortgagee had been paid off, so L thought that he was the prior mortgagee. N, taking with notice of the error and of L's consequent incorrect belief, was held to be subject to L's right to marshall.

The mere fact that N's second mortgage overrides L's right of marshall-ing does not altogether destroy the effect of the doctrine, as the following example shows:

(a) B mortgages Blackacre and Whiteacre to M for £20,000;
(b) B mortgages Whiteacre to L for £10,000;
(c) B mortgages Blackacre to N for £10,000.

Suppose that, on realisation, each property was found to be worth £20,000. If L were allowed to marshall, the effect would be that M would satisfy his entire debt out of Blackacre, L would satisfy his out of Whiteacre, leaving £10,000 equity in Whiteacre to which N would have no recourse.

The rule does not permit this, and the court preserves the right of all the incumbrancers, so far as possible, by apportioning M's charge, as between L and N, rateably between the two properties. There is no marshalling, strictly speaking; the rateable division simply prevents the loss from lying

[59] *Manks* v. *Whitely* [1911] 2 Ch. 448, affd. [1914] A.C. 132; and see *Noyes* v. *Pollock* (1886) 32 Ch.D. 53.
[60] *South* v. *Bloxham* (1865) 2 Hem. & M. 457.
[61] [1896] A.C. 187, H.L.
[62] *Baglioni* v. *Cavalli* (1900) 83 L.T. 500.
[63] *Barnes* v. *Racster* (1842) 17 Y. & C.Ch.Cas. 401.
[64] *Baglioni* v. *Cavalli* (1900) 93 L.T. 500; *Flint* v. *Howard* [1893] 2 Ch. 54, C.A.; *Smyth* v. *Toms* [1918] 1 I.R. 338.
[65] *Dolphin* v. *Aylward* (1870) L.R. 4 H.L. 486.
[66] (1869) L.R. 8 Eq. 110.
[67] (1859) 4 De G. & J. 632.

where it falls as a result of the way in which M elects to satisfy his debt. If M, in the above example, were to satisfy his debt entirely out of Whiteacre, N's debt would be satisfied out of Blackacre and L would get nothing; with the converse result if he satisfied it entirely out of Blackacre.[68]

Suppose, in the example above, M chose to satisfy his debt primarily out of Whiteacre, and that Whiteacre was worth £10,000 and Blackacre £30,000. The court would treat the matter as if M had satisfied his debt rateably out of the two properties, that is, £5,000 out of Whiteacre (notionally leaving £5,000 equity) and £15,000 out of Blackacre (notionally leaving £15,000 equity). To the extent of the £5,000 which he would have had out of Whiteacre had M in fact satisfied his debt rateably, L will be subrogated to N's rights in Blackacre.[69]

As M satisfied his debt so as to leave no equity in Whiteacre and £20,000 in Blackacre, that £20,000 will go first towards the rights to which L is subrogated (£5,000) then towards the satisfaction of N's debt (£10,000) leaving a surplus of £5,000 which L is entitled to claim as against B.

EXONERATION

A right of exoneration, if enforced, has the effect of varying the incidence of a liability as between two or more properties. Primarily that incidence is determined by the doctrine of contribution, which is based on the principle that, where two properties or funds are equally liable to pay a debt, one shall not escape because the creditor has chosen to satisfy himself entirely out of the other.

If two or more properties, whether or not all owned by the same person, are mortgaged for or subject equally to one debt, they will, under the doctrine of contribution, be rateably liable for it, the value of each property being reduced by the amount of any other incumbrance affecting it. Thus if Blackacre and Whiteacre are each worth £20,000, and if Blackacre is mortgaged to secure a debt of £10,000, after which Blackacre and Whiteacre are mortgaged together to secure a debt of £15,000, the value of Blackacre for the purpose of determining its rateable share of the later debt is £10,000. Since Whiteacre is otherwise unincumbered in value for that purpose is £20,000. Thus Blackacre will bear one third and Whiteacre two thirds of the later debt.

Circumstances exist, however, in which the doctrine of contribution does not apply and the person entitled to one property or fund has a right to be exonerated at the expense of the other.

Consider the following series of transactions:

(a) B mortgages Blackacre and Whiteacre to L;
(b) B assigns Blackacre to M;
(c) B assigns Whiteacre to N.

---

[68] *Barnes* v. *Racster* (1842) 1 Y. & C.Ch.Cas. 401; *Flint* v. *Howard* [1893] 2 Ch. 54, C.A.; *Bugden* v. *Bignold* (1843) 2 Y. & C.Ch.Cas. 377.
[69] *Cracknall* v. *Janson* (1879) 11 Ch.D. 1.

Suppose only events (a) and (b) occur. B as mortgagor is personally liable and therefore the property remaining in his hands, that is, Whiteacre, is the primary fund for payment.[70] If B has paid the debt there is no equity to compel any contribution to be made out of Blackacre, unless the assignment to M was expressly made subject to the prior mortgage.[71]

If, however, L has enforced payment out of Blackacre, M is entitled to be exonerated out of Whiteacre, whether the assignment to him was voluntary or for value.[72]

If events (a), (b), (c), occur, the doctrine of contribution cannot be displaced by the above argument, neither M nor N being personally liable. The earlier assignee, M, will have a right to exoneration if:

(i) the assignment to him contains a covenant against incumbrances, or for further assurance; or

(ii) when he took the assignment it was represented to him, even orally, by B, that Blackacre was free from incumbrances,[73]

and, in either case, that the later assignee, N was not a purchaser of the legal estate in Whiteacre for value and without notice.

It would appear that M has no right of exoneration on the second of these two grounds if he himself is a volunteer.

The right of exoneration may also exist as a result of the following series of transactions:

(a) B mortgages Blackacre and Whiteacre to L;

(b) Both properties vest in A subject to B's mortgage which is paramount to A's title;

(c) A assigns Blackacre to M.

Since A did not create the mortgage, the doctrine of contribution is not displaced by the existence of any personal liability; so if A pays off the mortgage, he is entitled to contribution from M, unless he made the assignment to M on the basis that Blackacre was free from incumbrances. In that case, M has a right to exoneration, which will enable him to marshall against Whiteacre unless and until it comes into the hands of a purchaser for value of the legal estate without notice.[74]

---

[70] *Re Darby's Estate, Rendall* v. *Darby* [1907] 2 Ch. 465.

[71] *Re Mainwaring's Settlement Trusts, Mainwaring's Trustee in Bankruptcy* v. *Verden* [1937] Ch. 96.

[72] *Re Best, Parker* v. *Best* [1924] 1 Ch. 42; *Ker* v. *Ker* (1869) 4 Ir.R.Eq. 15.

[73] *McCarthy* v. *M'Cartie* [1904] 1 I.R. 100; see *Finch* v. *Shaw, Colyer* v. *Finch* (1854) 19 Beav. 500.

[74] *Ocean Accident & Guarantee Corporation Ltd. and Hewitt* v. *Collum* [1913] 1 I.R. 337.

CHAPTER 22

THE MORTGAGEE'S DEBT AND THE MORTGAGE ACCOUNT

LIABILITY TO ACCOUNT

The mortgagee's substantial interest in the mortgaged property is his security for recovering his debt. The extent of that debt depends primarily on the terms of the mortgage contract, but it also depends on the rules of equity. Some of those rules have already been mentioned in connection with the equity of redemption and the rights of the mortgagee; others depend on the practice of the court in actions for redemption and foreclosure.[1] Many of these rules are relevant in that they fix the terms of the mortgage account; for example, consolidation vitally affects the price of redemption. Nevertheless, to prevent repetition, only incidental reference can be made to such rules here in the course of explaining the contents of the account.

Assessment of the mortgage debt takes place either upon the discharge of the mortgage or the realisation of the security. Even a foreclosure action, in which the mortgagee asks for the cancellation of the right to redeem, necessitates an account, because the court will not decree foreclosure without first giving the mortgagor an opportunity to redeem.[2] But it must not be supposed that accounts are invariably or even usually taken in court: the respective rights of mortgagor and mortgagee are well defined, so that the account is generally agreed by the parties out of court. It is only in case of dispute that the account need be brought into court, and then the court directs the account to be taken in chambers. Moreover, a mortgagor cannot bring his mortgagee into court for the purpose of having the accounts taken, unless either he is offering to redeem, or he is seeking to recover surplus proceeds of sale.[3] The court directs an account only in actions for redemption, foreclosure, judicial sale, or for the recovery of moneys resulting from the exercise of a power of sale.

The liability to account is not, as is sometimes thought, a liability only of the mortgagee, but also of the mortgagor. A mortgagor will not be admitted to redeem in equity, except on the terms of allowing, to the mortgagee, all sums properly expended in the maintenance or defence of the mortgaged property, in addition to what is allowed him by his contract. Indeed, the account is primarily taken against the mortgagor, and it is only a mortgagee in possession who has special liabilities in the account.

---

[1] See *ante*, pp. 247 *et seq.* and pp. 275 *et seq.*
[2] Later incumbrancers, for the purpose of the account, are in the same position as the mortgagor, so that they may assert against the first mortgagee any equity which the mortgagor himself might assert: *Mainland* v. *Upjohn* (1889) 41 Ch.D. 126.
[3] *Cf. Troughton* v. *Binkes* (1801) 6 Ves. 573; *Tasker* v. *Small* (1837) 3 My. & Cr. 63.

THE ACCOUNT

In *Re Wallis*,[4] Fry L.J. stated that a mortgagee's claim may comprise the following five items:

(1) the principal debt;
(2) the interest thereon;
(3) his costs in proceedings for redemption or foreclosure of the security;
(4) all proper costs, charges and expenses incurred by the mortgagee in relation to the mortgage debt or the mortgage security;
(5) the cost of litigation properly undertaken by the mortgagee in reference to the mortgage debt or security.

Of these items the first three, subject to any misconduct proved against the mortgagee, are automatically included in the account; the last two items will also be allowed if a case is made out for them. R.S.C. Order 43, rule 6 provides that in taking any account directed by any judgment or order, all "just allowances" shall be made without any direction to that effect. It is now settled that the words "all just allowances" cover all payments to which a mortgagee is entitled under the terms of his security, *i.e.* all payments properly incurred in the enforcement of the rights given to him by the terms of his mortgage.[5] Accordingly, the costs of proceedings taken to obtain possession, or of proceedings by an equitable mortgagee to compel the execution of a legal mortgage, and the costs of all necessary repairs and outgoings will be allowed to the mortgagee without the court having made any special direction in the decree. It is only when "permanent improvements" have been made by a mortgagee in possession, or extraordinary litigation has been pursued by the mortgagee in defence of the mortgage security, that the facts justifying an extraordinary allowance must be specially pleaded and a special direction given as to the account.[6]

Apart from the possibility of extraordinary allowances, the account may be complicated by the mortgagee having gone into possession and the mortgagee's items on the credit side are then offset by his receipt of rents and profits.

The following are a mortgagee's allowances:

(1) Principal debt

Under this heading a mortgagee is entitled not merely to the sums actually advanced, but also to any bonus, premium, or commission for which he has legitimately stipulated by way of a fee for advancing the

---

[4] (1890) 25 Q.B.D. 176 at 181.
[5] *Blackford* v. *Davis* (1869) 4 Ch.App. 304; *Wilkes* v. *Saunion* (1877) 7 Ch.D. 188.
[6] *Bolingbroke* v. *Hinde* (1884) 25 Ch.D. 795.

money.[7] The bonus or other fee in the nature of a bonus is provided for in the mortgage either by the mortgagee deducting the amount of the bonus from the sum expressed to be advanced,[8] or else by a condition that the mortgagor shall only be able to redeem on payment of a sum larger than that actually advanced.[9] The former is the usual method, but the latter is employed when the security is a reversionary interest whose immediate value is small. Whichever course is adopted, the mortgagee is entitled to recover the full amount for which he contracted. Again, where a mortgage is payable by instalments, and the instalments represent partly capital and partly interest—as in building society mortgages—commission or fines may payable on default upon a single instalment are not within the rule against penalties, and may be included in the account for principal.[10] Finally, if a bonus or other such sum is not claimed as part of the principal, it may be claimed specially as a "just allowance."[11]

A mortgagee not infrequently makes further advances upon the security of property already mortgaged to him, and such advances, if proved, go into the account for principal due on the original mortgage—at any rate, as against the mortgagor. Whether a puisne incumbrancer is subject to the further advances depends on the law of tacking contained in section 94 of the Law of Property Act 1925.[12]

But the further advance must be shown to have been in fact made upon the faith of the security,[13] and (in the case of mortgages granted prior to 1971) the total amount claimed for principal must not exceed the sum for which the original mortgage was stamped.[14] Where further advances are contemplated, it is usual for the first mortgage to be taken on the understanding that it will cover future advances either up to a specified amount or to the amount indicated by the stamp.[14] If a sum is so specified, it is a question of construction whether the sum named stands for principal only or for the total amount of the mortgage debt.[15] Again, the mortgage may be taken to secure not isolated advances but the general balance of an account; the burden of proving that the security is such a running security is upon the mortgagee,[16] but if he establishes it, he may prove the amount due by extrinsic evidence. If the requisite evidence is not forthcoming, the mortgagor can only be charged to the extent of his own admissions.[17] Special questions arise if the account is taken between a first mortgagee,

---

[7] *Potter* v. *Edwards* (1857) 26 L.J.Ch. 468; *cf. Bradley* v. *Carritt* [1903] A.C. 253, *per* Lord Davey.

[8] See *Mainland* v. *Upjohn* (1889) 41 Ch.D. 126.

[9] *Webster* v. *Cook* (1867) L.R. 2 Ch. 542.

[10] *General Credit and Discount Co.* v. *Glegg* (1883) 22 Ch.D. 549.

[11] *Bucknell* v. *Vickery* (1891) 64 L.T. 701.

[12] See, *ante*, pp. 370 *et seq.*

[13] *ex p. Knott* (1806) 11 Ves. 609.

[14] In relation to mortgages prior to the abolition of stamp duty on mortgages by the Finance Act 1971, s.64.

[15] See *Blackford* v. *Davis* (1869) 4 Ch.App. 304.

[16] *Re Boys* (1870) L.R. 10 Eq. 467.

[17] *Melland* v. *Gray* (1843) 2 Y. & C.C.C. 199.

who holds the mortgagor's current account, and a puisne incumbrancer. If the latter acted wisely and gave notice to the first mortgagee, the first mortgage becomes as against him security only for the amount due at the date of the notice. Further advances by the first mortgagee will thereafter only rank as a third mortgage. But unless the first mortgagee took the precaution of closing the first account upon receipt of the notice, he may find that, as against the puisne incumbrancer, his priority for principal has been seriously reduced by the operation of the rule in *Clayton's Case*.[17a] Subsequent payments into the account by the mortgagor must be set against the first advances to him. Thus all fresh payments in, as against the puisne incumbrancer, reduce the amount secured by the first mortgage, while any further withdrawals add to the debt which now can only rank after the second mortgage.[18] Banks who, of course, hold many securities for current accounts, direct their officials to close the account at once on receipt of notice of a subsequent incumbrance, thus obviating this risk.

(2) Interest

The rules as to allowance of interest may be shortly stated as follows:

(a) Except in cases of undue influence, or extortionate credit bargains under the Consumer Credit Act 1974 there is no rule to prevent a mortgagee from obtaining the agreed rate of interest, however high.[19]

(b) Similarly, there is no objection to compound interest as such,[20] but it will only be allowed if it was contracted for in the mortgage.[21] Such a contract may be either express or implied from the usage of a trade or business.[22] Compound interest will also be chargeable when, though not a term of the mortgage, it has been agreed to subsequently for a fresh consideration, for example, in consideration of the mortgagee's forbearance.[23]

(c) If there is no mention of interest in the mortgage, an agreement to pay interest will be implied, and the rate formerly allowed was 5 per cent.[24] (4 per cent. for equitable mortgages[25]). The court

---

[17a] (1816) 1 Mer. 572.

[18] *Deelay* v. *Lloyds Bank* [1912] A.C. 756, see *ante*, p. 374.

[19] See *ante*, pp. 000–000. Bargains will not be interfered with merely because they are unreasonable (*Knightsbridge Estates* v. *Byrne* [1939] Ch. 441 at 457) unless the provisions relating to interest could be seen as an unreasonable collateral advantage (see *Cityland and Property Holdings Ltd.* v. *Dabrah* [1968] Ch. 166).

[20] *Clarkson* v. *Henderson* (1880) 14 Ch.D. 348.

[21] *Daniell* v. *Sinclair* (1881) 6 A.C. 181.

[22] *Fergusson* v. *Fyffe* (1841) 8 Cl. & F. 121. See also *National Bank of Greece S.A.* v. *Pinios (No. 1)* [1989] 1 All E.R. 253.

[23] *Blackburn* v. *Warwick* (1836) 2 Y. & C. Ex. 92.

[24] *Mendl* v. *Smith* (1943) 169 L.T. 153; and see *Wallersteiner* v. *Moir (No. 2)* [1975] Q.B. 373; *Bartlett* v. *Barclays Bank Trust Co. Ltd. (No. 2)* [1980] Ch. 515; *International Military Services Ltd.* v. *Capital and Countries plc* [1982] 1 W.L.R. 575.

[25] *Re Kerr's Policy* (1869) L.R. 8 Eq. 331; *Re Drax* [1903] 1 Ch. 781.

will undoubtedly order a more commercial rate today.[26] The only
exception to this rule is when the mortgage agreement expressly
indicates that no interest is to be paid.[27] Whether the fact that the
proviso for reconveyance is upon payment only of principal is
such an indication now appears doubtful.[28]

(d) If the mortgage provides for payment of a stated rate down to the
date named for repayment of the loan,[29] but nothing is said of
interest to be paid afterwards, no agreement will be implied to
continue payment of interest at the mortgage rate after default.
Interest will, however, be recoverable for the period after default
not strictly as mortgage interest, but by way of damages for deten-
tion of the debt,[30] pursuant to statute. The former practice was to
allow the mortgage rate, if not in excess of 5 per cent., but to limit
it to 5 per cent. in other cases. The rate awarded today will presumably be current High Court rate.[31] This rule applies to foreclosure and redemption, as well as to an action on the personal
covenant: Fry J. in *Wallington* v. *Cook*[32] pointed out that foreclosure and redemption proceedings interest could not properly
be awarded as damages, but decided that it could be awarded by
way of consideration for allowing the loan to remain unpaid. Thus
equity once again follows the law.[33]

(e) A well-drawn mortgage deed provides for payment of interest at
the mortgage rate after default, so long as the security continues,
but even so the mortgage rate will not be allowed after a judgment has been obtained upon the personal covenant. The mortgagee's personal right merges in his judgment, and judgments
carry interest only at the statutory rate. This rule only affects
actions on the personal covenant,[34] and does not reduce the mortgagee's claim for interest in redemption or foreclosure accounts.
The fact that he obtains a personal judgment does not alter his
right to retain his security, and he cannot be redeemed, except on
the terms of payment of all that he contracted for in the mortgage.[35]

(f) A stipulation for a higher rate of interest in case the agreed rate is
not punctually paid is a penalty and void,[36] but a subsequent
agreement for a higher rate, made in consideration of the mort-

[26] *Cityland and Property Holdings Ltd.* v. *Dabrah* [1968] Ch. 166.
[27] *Thompson* v. *Drew* (1855) 20 Beav. 49.
[28] *Mendl* v. *Smith* (1943) 169 L.T. 153.
[29] *Cook* v. *Fowler* (1874) L.R. 7 H.L. 27.
[30] See Supreme Court Act 1981, s.35A; County Courts Act 1984, s.69.
[31] *Re Roberts* (1880) 14 Ch.D. 49.
[32] (1878) 47 L.J.Ch. 508 at 510.
[33] *Re Sneyd* (1883) 25 Ch.D. 338.
[34] Even to that extent it may be avoided by stipulation for the agreed rate to be paid "as well
before as after any judgment."
[35] *Economic Life Assurance Society* v. *Usborne* [1902] A.C. 147.
[36] *Wallingford* v. *Mutual Society* (1880) 5 A.C. 685.

gagee's further forbearance, is enforceable.[37] In any case, the higher rate is always obtainable by the simple device of drawing the covenant in the form that the higher rate is the agreed rate, but is reducible upon punctual payment.[38]

(g) In redemption actions the mortgagor must give six months' notice of his intention to redeem, or else give six months' interest in lieu of notice[39]; the only exceptions are: (*i*) if the mortgagee refuses a proper tender,[40] or otherwise improperly obstructs redemption[41]; (*ii*) if the mortgagee takes steps to obtain payment[42]; (*iii*) where the mortgage is payable on demand.[43]

(h) Whether the mortgage is of land or of personalty, no more than six years' arrears of interest are recoverable on the covenant for payment. The rule does not, however, apply in actions for redemption nor in foreclosure.[44]

(i) When a mortgagor is in arrears with his interest, the mortgagee as a condition of his further forbearance, may require that the arrears be capitalised and added to the principal, so that they too may bear interest.[45] Such an arrangement is enforceable, provided that the mortgagor's positive assent to it is proved. Mere absence of protest is not enough, and there must at least be evidence from which the court can infer that he agreed to the proposal.[46] In any case, capitalisation of arrears will not bind a mesne incumbrancer, of whose charge the first mortgagee had notice before the capitalisation occurred. To allow the first mortgagee the advantage of capitalisation in those circumstances would be to allow him to tack a further charge with notice.[47] Capitalisation often takes place when a mortgage is transferred to a third party, but it does not then bind the mortgagor without his concurrence.[48]

In certain circumstances there is compulsory deduction of income tax.[49]

---

[37] See *Law* v. *Glenn* (1867) L.R. 2 Ch. 634.
[38] *Union Bank of London* v. *Ingram* (1880) 16 Ch.D. 53.
[39] *Johnson* v. *Evans* (1889) 61 L.T. 18.
[40] *Rourke* v. *Robinson* [1911] 1 Ch. 480, only if the money is kept available. See *ante*, pp. 328 *et seq.*
[41] *e.g.* by losing the deeds.
[42] *Bovill* v. *Endle* [1896] 1 Ch. 648.
[43] *Fitzgerald's Trustee* v. *Mellersh* [1892] 1 Ch. 385.
[44] See *ante*, p. 414.
[45] As to the difference between capitalisation of arrears and compound interest, see *Re Morris Mayhew* v. *Halton* [1922] 1 Ch. 126.
[46] *Tompson* v. *Leith* (1858) 4 Jur.N.S. 1091.
[47] *Digby* v. *Craggs* (1762) Amb. 612.
[48] *Agnew* v. *King* [1902] 1 I.R. 471; *ante*, p. 382.
[49] For the question of deduction of income tax and tax relief for mortgage interest under the Income and Corporation Taxes Act 1970 (as amended) and the Finance Acts 1972, 1974, 1982 and 1984, reference should be made to a standard mark on taxation such as *Simon's Taxes* (revsd. 3rd ed.).

(3) Costs of proceedings for redemption or foreclosure[50]

A mortgagee's right to his costs in these proceedings is an equity arising from his contract, and is not therefore within the usual discretion of the court as to costs.[51] The right is not, however, contractual in the sense that the mortgagor is under a personal contract to pay the costs. Liability to pay the costs is rather part of the price which he must pay for being permitted to redeem, so that the costs are a charge upon the property, but not, without special agreement, a personal debt of the mortgagor.[52] Similarly, the right to costs being an equitable right, the mortgagee may forfeit his right by misconduct.[53]

Misconduct by the mortgagee when proved puts the costs in the discretion of the court,[54] whose order may be either that he be merely deprived of his costs or else be made to pay the costs of the mortgagor as well.[55] In the latter case the costs are not paid to the mortgagor direct, but are credited to him in the mortgage account.[56] The following are the main grounds upon which the court will depart from the normal rule as to costs:

(a) *Failure to accept a proper tender*

This may occur either because the tender is refused or the mortgagee has lost the deeds,[57] or because he is not ready with his receipt or conveyance.[58] On a proper tender a mortgagor is entitled to have his mortgage discharged, and the mortgagee must pay the costs of subsequent litigation necessary to enforce that discharge.[59]

(b) *Mortgage already paid off*

If, after receiving the full amount of his debt, a mortgagee either takes proceedings for foreclosure or defends an action for redemption, he will be made to pay the costs of the proceedings.[60] On the same principle a mortgagee, who is paid off after he has instituted proceedings, must pay any costs consequent on his failure to discontinue the action.[61]

---

[50] The costs are party and party costs.
[51] Therefore, contrary to the usual rule, an appeal will lie as to costs (*Cotterell* v. *Stratton* (1872) L.R. 8 Ch. 295); the costs are within the discretion of the court only when a charge of misconduct has been *made and proved*: *Charles* v. *Jones* (1886) 33 Ch.D. 80.
[52] *Frazer* v. *Jones* (1846) 5 Hare 475.
[53] *Cottrell* v. *Stantton* (1872) L.R. 8 Ch. 295 at 302.
[54] *Charles* v. *Jones* (1886) 33 Ch.D. 80. Therefore no appeal lies from the order as to costs when misconduct is established. *Ibid.*
[55] *Detillin* v. *Gale* (1802) 7 Ves. 583; *Kinnaird* v. *Trollope* (1889) 42 Ch.D. 610.
[56] *Wheaton* v. *Graham* (1857) 24 Beav. 483.
[57] *Stokoe* v. *Robson* (1815) 19 Ves. 385.
[58] *Rourke* v. *Robinson* [1911] 1 Ch. 480.
[59] *Graham* v. *Seal* (1918) 88 L.J.Ch. 31.
[60] *Barlow* v. *Gains* (1856) 23 Beav. 244; *National Bank of Australasia* v. *United Hand in Hand Co.* (1879) 4 A.C. 391; unless the mortgagor makes allegations against the mortgagee which he fails to substantiate when no order will be made.
[61] *Gregg* v. *Slater* (1856) 22 Beav. 314.

(c) *Untenable claim*

A mortgagee, who raises an untenable defence to an action for redemption, may also be deprived of his costs or even made to pay the mortgagor's costs. Nor is it a question of *male fides*.[62] If he sets up an unfounded claim to tack[63] or consolidate, or if he claims the conveyance to be absolute[64] and not by way of mortgage,[65] or otherwise denies or improperly obstructs the right to redeem,[66] he will be made responsible for the costs thus occasioned. But he will not, it seems, be deprived of costs which would have been incurred in any event.[67] Moreover, he will not be penalised if his claim, though mistaken, was fairly open to argument.[68]

(d) *Vexatious or oppressive conduct*

If the mortgage transaction is shown to have been tainted with fraud,[69] or if the mortgagee's subsequent conduct has been unreasonable or oppressive, he may be made to pay costs. For example, if he refuses to account or obstructs the taking of an account[70]; if he fails to allow the mortgagor a reasonable opportunity of tendering the mortgage moneys[71]; if he harasses the mortgagor by bringing simultaneous actions for foreclosure and for judgment on the personal covenant in separate proceedings[72]; in any of these cases he will have to pay the costs occasioned by his misconduct. On the other hand, not every mistake made by the mortgagee is oppression; for example, mere over-statement of his claim is not a sufficient ground for refusing him his costs.[73]

(e) *Improper joinder of parties*

A mortgagee is liable for all costs resulting from the wrongful joinder of parties, whether as defendants or plaintiffs.[74] This rule is of special importance for parties whose interest in a security is worthless owing to prior claims. A person who is made a party but disclaims before delivering any defence will be entitled to his costs after the date of disclaimer if the mort-

---

[62] *Credland* v. *Potter* (1874) 10 Ch.App. 8.
[63] *Ibid.*; *Kinnaird* v. *Trollope* (1889) 42 Ch.D. 610.
[64] *Squire* v. *Pardoe* (1891) 66 L.T. 243.
[65] *England* v. *Codrington* (1758) 1 Ed. 169.
[66] See *Whitfield* v. *Parfitt* (1851) 4 De G. & Sm. 240; *Ashworth* v. *Lord* (1887) 36 Ch.D. 545; *Hall* v. *Heward* (1886) 32 Ch.D. 430; *Heath* v. *Chinn* [1908] W.N. 120.
[67] *Harvey* v. *Tebbutt* (1820) 1 J. & W. 197.
[68] *Bird* v. *Wenn* (1886) 33 Ch.D. 215.
[69] *Baker* v. *Wind* (1748) 1 Ves.Sen. 160; *Morony* v. *O'Dea* (1809) 1 Ball & B. 109.
[70] *Detillin* v. *Gale* (1802) 7 Ves. 583.
[71] *Cliff* v. *Wadsworth* (1843) 2 Y. & C.C.C. 598.
[72] *Williams* v. *Hunt* [1905] 1 K.B. 512. Similarly, if he ought to have sued in the county court only county court costs will be allowed: *Crozier* v. *Dowsett* (1885) 31 Ch.D. 67.
[73] *Cotterell* v. *Stratton* (1872) L.R. 8 Ch. 295; *Re Watts* (1882) 22 Ch.D. 5.
[74] *Pearce* v. *Watkins* (1852) 5 De G. & Sm. 315.

gagee insists on taking him to the hearing.[75] It is not, however, the mortgagee's duty to invite a defendant to disclaim.[76]

The general rule, it may be repeated, is that a mortgagee is entitled to his costs of action, and that only misconduct can deprive him of that right. Judges have said time and again that the court is reluctant to depart from the normal rule.[77] But the court is by no means so favourable to a mortgagee who has sold the security and retains in his hands surplus proceeds of sale. He is a trustee for the persons next entitled, and if his conduct makes it necessary to bring an action to recover the money, he will be liable for the costs of the action.[78] In *Williams* v. *Jones*,[79] Eve J. said expressly that the general rule allowing a mortgagee his costs of action does not apply to an action for an account against a mortgagee who has exercised his power of sale.

(4) Costs, charges and expenses incurred in relation to the mortgage debt or security

Disbursements under this heading are for the most part within the terms of the mortgage contract as applied in equity, and will, therefore, be included in the account as "just allowances." They are not a personal debt of the mortgagor, for they are only one of the equitable terms of redemption, and are not covered by the covenant for payment unless expressly brought within it by the contract. There are four main grounds on which disbursements are admitted as just allowances:

(a) *Perfecting the security*

An equitable mortgagee is entitled to specific performance and will be allowed the costs of completing his security by the execution of a legal mortgage. These costs cover the preparation of the mortgage and the correspondence relating thereto; they do not include the investigation of title, because an equitable mortgagee only contracts to transfer such title as he himself possesses.[80] On the same principle a mortgagee has been allowed the costs of obtaining a stop order against a fund in court.[81] On the other hand, the costs of negotiating the loan and of preparing the original mortgage cannot be brought into the mortgage account without express contract. Farwell J. in *Wales* v. *Carr*,[82] said that such costs are a simple contract debt and a personal liability of the mortgagor, but are not part of the price fixed for redemption in equity. These costs may, however, be

---

[75] *Greene* v. *Foster* (1882) 22 Ch.D. 566.
[76] *Maxwell* v. *Wightwick* (1886) L.R. 3 Eq. 210.
[77] *e.g. Cotterell* v. *Stratton* (1872) L.R. 8 Ch. 295 at 302, *per* Selborne, L.C.
[78] See *Tanner* v. *Heard* (1857) 23 Beav. 555; *Charles* v. *Jones* (1887) 35 Ch.D. 544.
[79] (1911) 55 S.J. 500.
[80] *National Provincial Bank* v. *Games* (1886) 31 Ch.D. 582. See *Pryce* v. *Bury* (1853) 2 Drew. 41.
[81] *Waddilove* v. *Taylor* (1848) 6 Hare 307.
[82] [1902] 1 Ch. 860.

brought into the account by express contract,[83] indeed, it is the usual practice to deduct the amount of the initial expenses from the sum advanced.

(b) *Maintenance of property*

A mortgage is entitled to preserve his security, and to add to his debt expenses incurred in so doing. A mortgagee of leaseholds may bring into the account payments for rent, ground-rents[84] or renewal fines.[85] A mortgagee of an insurance policy may pay the premiums to prevent default.[86] Where the payments are not merely to protect, but to salve the security, a puisne incumbrancer who makes the payments is entitled to a charge for such payments in priority even to the first mortgagee.[87] A mortgagee's right to add fire insurance premiums to the mortgage debt will in general be provided for by section 101 of the Law of Property Act 1925, which gives that right to all mortgages, whose security is by deed, unless the mortgagor is keeping up a sufficient policy.[88] If the terms of the contract do not allow for the mortgagee insuring, it appears that any insurance policy he takes out is effected for his own benefit, and that he cannot charge the premiums in the account.[89]

(c) *Management*

A mortgagee in possession is entitled to bring into the account the reasonable expenses of managing the property. He will thus be credited with the amount of any wages paid to such servants or agents as would reasonably be employed by an owner of the property[90]; and in most cases he will be allowed the salary or commission of a bailiff or other general agent employed to look after the whole property.[91]

Similarly, a mortgagee will be reimbursed expenditure incurred in running a business,[92] or working existing mines.[93] It appears also that, although as a rule he will only be allowed to balance his losses against his receipts, yet if a business is mortgaged as a going concern, losses may be

---

[83] *Blackford* v. *Davis* (1869) 4 Ch. App. 304.

[84] *Brandon* v. *Brandon* (1862) 10 W.R. 287; *Shepherd* v. *Spansheath* (1988) E.G.C.S. 35.

[85] *Lacon* v. *Mertins* (1743) 3 Atk. 4; *Hamilton* v. *Denny* (1809) 1 Ball & B. 199.

[86] *Bellamy* v. *Brickenden* (1861) 2 J. & H. 137; *Gill* v. *Downing* (1874) L.R. 17 Eq. 316; *Re Leslie* (1883) 23 Ch.D. 552.

[87] *Angel* v. *Bryan* (1845) 2 Jo. & Lat. 763; but it must really have been a case of salvage: *Landowners, etc. Drainage and Inclosures Co.* v. *Ashford* (1880) 16 Ch.D. 411.

[88] L.P.A. 1925, s.108(2).

[89] *Dobson* v. *Land* (1850) 8 Hare 216; but a mortgagee in possession may include such payments as part of his management expenses under just allowances: *Scholefield* v. *Lockwood* (1863) 11 W.R. 555.

[90] *Brandon* v. *Brandon* (1862) 10 W.R. 287; *Shepherd* v. *Spansheath* (1988) E.G.C.S. 35.

[91] *Bank of London* v. *Ingram* (1880) 16 Ch.D. 53; *Leith* v. *Irvine* (1883) 1 My. & Cr. 277.

[92] *Bompas* v. *King* (1886) 33 Ch.D. 279.

[93] *County of Gloucester Bank* v. *Rudry, Merthyr Steam and House Colliery Co.* [1895] 1 Ch. 629; but not for working new mines: *Hughes* v. *Williams* (1806) 12 Ves. 493 and *Shepherd* v. *Spansheath* (1988) E.G.C.S. 35.

made a charge upon the corpus of the mortgaged property.[94] But he is not, apart from express contract, allowed to make any charge for his own time and trouble.[95] He may not charge commission for collecting rents,[96] or for any other business done in connection with the mortgaged property.[97] Formerly, an express contract that such commission should be allowed made no difference, because the agreement for commission was held to come within the rule against collateral advantages.[98] But after the decision in *Biggs* v. *Hoddinott*[99] it is clear that collateral advantages are not bad as such, and so an agreement for commission is valid, provided the bargain is not otherwise unconscionable.[1] In any case, by virtue of section 3 of the Mortgagees' Legal Costs Act 1895, (now replaced by Solicitors Act 1974, section 58) solicitor mortgagees may charge the usual professional fees for all business done in relation to the security, whether or not the mortgage contains an express stipulation to that effect.

A mortgagee may also include in his account sums expended on repairs, improvements and other outgoings. He has, for example, been allowed the amount of compensation payable to a tenant at the end of his tenancy.[2] Repairs and improvements require careful examination. Concerning "necessary repairs" there is no doubt; a mortgagee in possession is under a duty to execute them, and will be entitled to his expenditure under the heading of just allowances.[3] But what may be called substantial repairs or permanent improvements are only allowed if the value of the property has been increased.[4] In any event a special case must be made out for their allowance at the hearing, or no inquiry will be directed. Jessel M.R. in *Shepard* v. *Jones*,[5] stated the established practice to be that the mortgagee must plead that he has made a lasting improvement, and then, if he adduces evidence of laying out money, and that the works were prima facie lasting improvements, he will be entitled to an inquiry. The older cases[6] suggest that even an admitted improvement, if substantial, will not be allowed to a mortgagee unless it was consented to by a mortgagor. The reason for this was that a mortgagee by increasing the price of redemption might prevent redemption altogether. But the Court of Appeal in *Shepard* v. *Jones*[7] greatly modified this doctrine, and stated the following rules:

---

[94] *Bompas* v. *King* (1886) 33 Ch.D. 279.
[95] *Bonithon* v. *Hockmore* (1685) 1 Vern. 316; *Nicholson* v. *Tutin* (1857) 3 K. & J. 159; *Cf. Re Wallis* (1890) 25 Q.B.D. 176.
[96] *Langstaffe* v. *Fenwick* (1805) 10 Ves. 405.
[97] *Leith* v. *Irvine* (1883) 1 My. & Cr. 277.
[98] See *Chambers* v. *Goldwin* (1804) 9 Ves. 254.
[99] [1898] 2 Ch. 307.
[1] See *Bucknell* v. *Vickery* (1891) 64 L.T. 701 at 702, though the case is not absolutely in point.
[2] *Oxenham* v. *Ellis* (1854) 18 Beav. 593.
[3] *Tipton Green Colliery Co.* v. *Tipton Moat Colliery Co.* (1877) 7 Ch.D. 192.
[4] But not, apparently, if he alters the nature of the property: *Moore* v. *Painter* (1842) 6 Jur. 903.
[5] (1882) 21 Ch.D. 469 at 476.
[6] *e.g. Sandon* v. *Hooper* (1843) 6 Beav. 246.
[7] (1882) 21 Ch.D. 469.

(1) If the improvement is reasonable and produces a benefit, the mortgagor's consent is unnecessary.

(2) If the improvement is unreasonable and produces no benefit it will be allowed, if the mortgagor either expressly agreed to it or did what in law amounted to acquiescing to it.

(3) If the improvement is unreasonable and was not agreed to, it will not be allowed in any circumstances. The mortgagee cannot force the improvement on the mortgagor by merely serving a notice upon him, whatever the terms of the notice.

Finally, it must be observed that repairs and improvements are not "salvage" advances and do not entitle a mesne incumbrancer, who executes them, to priority for his expenditure over earlier mortgagees.[8]

(d) *Exercising his power of sale*

A mortgagee is entitled to claim in the account the expenses not merely of an actual sale, but also of an abortive attempt to sell.[9] But in accordance with the general principle that he may not charge for his own time and trouble, he may not, if he is an auctioneer,[10] or a broker,[11] be credited with a commission on the sale, unless he has expressly contracted for such commission.[12]

(5) Costs of litigation in connection with the mortgage

In *Dryden* v. *Frost*,[13] Cottenham L.C. expressed the rule thus:

"This Court, in settling the account between a mortgagor and mortgagee, will give to the latter all that his contract, or the legal or equitable consequences of it entitle him to receive, and all the costs properly incurred in ascertaining or defending such rights."

The decision in this case was that litigation is not properly undertaken when an equitable mortgagee institutes an action available only to a legal mortgagee, and in another case a mortgagee was refused his costs when, in exercising his power of sale, he brought an action against the purchaser for specific performance and lost because of errors in the description of the property sold.[14] In other words, the litigation must have been reasonable. Costs of litigation, with one exception, will not be allowed unless they have been specially pleaded and claimed at the hearing.[15] The one exception is

[8] *Landowners West of England & South West Drainage and Inclosure Co.* v. *Ashford* (1880) 16 Ch.D. 411.
[9] *Corsellis* v. *Patman* (1867) L.R. 4 Eq. 156; *Farrer* v. *Lacy, Hartland & Co.* (1885) 31 Ch.D. 42.
[10] *Matthison* v. *Clarke* (1854) 3 Drew. 3.
[11] *Arnold* v. *Garner* (1847) 2 Ph. 231.
[12] *Biggs* v. *Hoddinott* [1898] 2 Ch. 307. But after redemption he cannot insist on being made auctioneer of the property when it is to be sold; the clause allowing him commission must terminate at redemption: *Browne* v. *Ryan* [1901] 2 I.R. 635.
[13] (1838) 3 My. & Cr. 670 at 675.
[14] *Peers* v. *Ceeley* (1852) 15 Beav. 209.
[15] *Millar* v. *Major* (1818) Coop.temp.Cott. 550.

costs of proceedings to obtain possession which are included under "just allowances."[16] Costs may be allowed to the mortgagee whether he is plaintiff or defendant in the litigation. If his title is impeached by the mortgagor, he is entitled to be fully reimbursed, so that if he was successful and received costs in the action, he may still recover the difference between the taxed costs and his actual costs.[17] Similarly, if the mortgagor's title to the mortgaged property is questioned, the mortgagee may defend it and charge his full costs in the account.[18] But if his own title is attacked by third parties, he must pay his own expenses, for the mortgagor cannot be made to bear the loss caused by the litigious activities of third parties.[19] As plaintiff, his proceedings may either be against third parties or, more usually, the mortgagor. He is entitled to the costs of an ejectment against third parties,[20] and of proceedings against a surety for the recovery of the debt, even although the proceedings prove fruitless.[21] Similarly, the costs of an ejectment against the mortgagor and of a judgment on the personal covenant previously obtained may be included in the account.

TAKING THE ACCOUNT

The general rule for taking a mortgage account is to take it as a continuous debtor and creditor account. A mortgagor, apart from express contract, is never compelled to pay interest on interest in arrear[22] so that, when the mortgagee is not in possession, there is no occasion for stopping the account. At the end of the account the amount of unpaid interest is added to the principal, and the resulting sum, plus any special allowances, is the price of redemption. Where the mortgagee is not in possession, the only possible exceptions to the rule are when the parties have themselves struck a balance at some date during the currency of the mortgage,[23] or when part of the mortgaged property has previously been sold. In the latter case the proceeds are applied first in discharging the expenses of sale and any interest already accrued due at the date of the sale, and then the residue, if it was not handed over to the mortgagor, must be taken to have satisfied the principal debt *pro tanto*. Thus, in the final account interest will only be allowed, as from the date of the sale, on the diminished amount of the principal.[24]

---

[16] *Wilkes* v. *Saunion* (1877) 7 Ch.D. 188.
[17] *Ramsden* v. *Langley* (1706) 2 Vern. 536. *Cf.* also *Re Leighton's Conveyance* [1937] Ch. 149.
[18] *Godfrey* v. *Watson* (1747) 3 Atk. 517; *cf. Sclater* v. *Cottam* (1857) 29 L.T.O.S. 309.
[19] *Parker* v. *Watkins* (1859) John. 133.
[20] *Owen* v. *Crouch* (1857) 5 W.R. 545.
[21] *National Provincial Bank* v. *Games* (1886) 31 Ch.D. 582.
[22] *Parker* v. *Butcher* (1867) L.R. 3 Eq. 762.
[23] *Cf. Wilson* v. *Cluer* (1840) 3 Beav. 136.
[24] *Thompson* v. *Hudson* (1870) L.R. 10 Eq. 497; here the mortgagee was in possession, but the reasoning of Romilly M.R. applies generally.

Mortgagee in possession

The general rule in most cases applies equally to the account of a mortgagee in possession, since it is only in special circumstances that the court will direct the account to be taken against the mortgagee with rests.[25] On the other hand, a mortgagee's entry into possession always complicates the account, because he must be debited with the amount of rents and profits which he actually received or which, but for his wilful default, he ought to have received. In practice, it means that the account is split into three distinct amounts:

(1) The account of principal, interest and costs.
(2) The account of the mortgagee's expenditure in managing, repairing, or improving the property, plus interest on the expenditure.
(3) The account of rents, profits and other sums received by the mortgagee.

The price of redemption is, of course, calculated by adding together the first two accounts and then deducting the third from the aggregate so obtained.[26]

Again, the continuity of the account may be interrupted either by the parties having struck a balance during the currency of the mortgage or by a sale of part of the security. In the latter case the net proceeds are appropriated first to the discharge of the interest in account number (1), and then to the reduction of the principal debt with a consequent reduction in the amount of interest due in account number (1). But the rest in that account is not accompanied by a simultaneous rest in the other accounts. The mere fact of the sale cannot entitle the mortgagor at the date of the sale to have the amount of the rents and profits received before the sale immediately set off against the mortgage debt. In other words, without a general direction for rests throughout the account, the mortgagor has no right to have the items of account number (1) in any way affected by the state of account number (3) until the final accounts are taken.[27]

Since the account of a mortgagee in possession is in the normal case a continuous debtor and creditor account, the mortgagee will derive an indirect profit from his possession if the amount of his receipts exceeds that of the interest due. He may retain the balance and have the use of the money without debiting himself with interest upon it. If, on the other hand, the receipts are less than the interest, the mortgagor does not pay interest on the unpaid arrears of interest, and so he has the advantage.[28] The object and effect of directing the account to be taken with periodic rests is to prevent the mortgagee from deriving any advantage from an excess of receipts over interest due. Such a direction is unusual and, as we have seen, only to

---

[25] See *ante*, pp. 212–217.
[26] Interest is usually allowed.
[27] *Wrigley* v. *Gill* [1905] 1 Ch. 241; *Ainsworth* v. *Wilding* [1905] 1 Ch. 435.
[28] *Union Bank of London* v. *Ingram* (1880) 16 Ch.D. 53 at 56, *per* Jessel M.R.

penalise the mortgagee.[29] The procedure then is to strike a balance at the end of each year or half-year, as the case may be, and to appropriate at once the surplus receipts—after discharging the interest—to the reduction of the principal debt with a consequent reduction in the future interest due on the debt. Furthermore, if by this method of accounting it is found that the whole mortgage debt had been satisfied before the end of the account, the result is that the periodic rests make the mortgagee liable to account for the subsequent receipts with compound interest in favour of the mortgagor.[30]

---

[29] *Wrigley* v. *Gill* [1905] 1 Ch. 241; *cf. Cowens* v. *Francis* [1948] n. 2 L.R. 567.
[30] Seton, *Judgments and Orders* (7th ed.), Vol. 3, p. 1885.

PRECEDENTS

A: Legal Charges and Mortgages

1. Skeleton of Legal Charge or Mortgage

THIS [MORTGAGE]
    [LEGAL CHARGE] is made   (date)

between
    PARTIES[1]

WHEREAS

    RECITALS

TESTATUM 1
    NOW THIS DEED (receipt of advance *or*
                      acknowledgment of existing debt)

    WITNESSETH AS FOLLOWS
    Borrower's covenant to pay principal and interest
    Reduction of interest on punctual payment

TESTATUM 2
    Demise, sub-demise or charge of mortgaged property
    Proviso for redemption or discharge
    Date on which mortgage money falls due
    Borrower's covenants

    Other operative clauses including lender's powers

    Attestation clause

THE SCHEDULE(S)

2. Recitals

(a) Borrower's Title

(1) Borrowers' freehold title
    The Borrower is seised for his own benefit of the property described in the Schedule hereto ("the mortgaged property") for a legal estate in fee simple in possession (subject as hereinafter mentioned but otherwise)[2] free from incumbrances

---

[1] The Borrower and Lender (not the Mortgagor and Mortgagee, to avoid errors in copying) may be defined with reference to their respective successors in title: (a) "the Borrower" shall where the context admits include persons deriving title under the Borrower or entitled to redeem this security; (b) "The Lender" shall where the context admits include persons deriving title under the Lender.

[2] Include these words if there are restrictive covenants or easements and list them in the Schedule.

(2) Borrower's leasehold title

The Borrower is possessed of the property described in the Schedule hereto ("the mortgaged property") for a legal estate for the residue of the term of years granted by the lease short particulars of which are set out in the said Schedule subject to the rent reserved and the covenants and conditions herein contained but otherwise free from incumbrances[3]

In recitals (3) to (7) below, omit the words "for his own benefit" but otherwise use (1) and continue after "incumbrances" as follows:

Where the Borrowers are personal representatives,[4] add:

(3) Personal representatives

as the personal representatives[5] of (name of deceased) late of (address as in probate or letters of administration) [whose Will was proved by] [letters of administration to whose estate were granted to] the Borrowers on (date) [in] [out of] the [Principal] [name of district] Probate Registry

Where the Borrowers are trustees for sale, add one of the following:

(4) Trustees for sale solely in that capacity

as trustees upon an immediate binding trust for sale hereof

(5) Trustees for sale beneficially entitled to the whole property

as trustees upon trust to sell the same and hold the proceeds of sale on trust for themselves beneficially as [joint tenants] [tenants in common in equal shares] [part of their partnership property]

(6) Trustees for sale with an express power to mortgage

    (a) as trustees for sale thereof declared by (instrument, date, parties)
    (b) (. . . recite the express power)

If the Borrower is a tenant for life, add the following[6]:

(7) Tenant for life

    (i) The said property is settled land the legal estate herein having been duly vested in the Borrower upon the trusts of the settlement by a Principal Vesting Deed (date) made between (parties) pursuant to the Settled Land Act 1925 and the Borrower accordingly has and can exercise the powers of a tenant for life under the said Act over the said property
    (ii) The Trustees are the trustees of the said settlement for the purpose of the said Act as stated in the said Vesting Deed

---

[3] This form is suitable for an unincumbered lease where the whole of the property is mortgaged.

[4] If the property is being charged to raise money for administration, include in the recital of the loan agreement the phrase "which is required by the Borrowers as personal representatives as aforesaid for the purposes of administration."

[5] A person who covenants as trustee, mortgagee or personal representative impliedly covenants that he has not created any incumbrances: L.P.A. 1925, s.76(1)(*F*) and Sched. 2, Pt. VI.

[6] See p. 452 for a form of loan agreement.

(b) Loan Agreement and Acknowledgment of Debt

(1) Loan agreement

The Lender has agreed with the Borrower to lend him (the sum advanced) upon having the repayment thereof with interest thereon secured as appears herein

(2) Acknowledgment of existing debt

The Borrower is indebted to the Lender in the sum of (amount of debt) and it has been agreed that in consideration of the Lender forbearing to enforce the immediate repayment thereof, repayment of the said debt with interest thereon shall be secured as appears herein

(3) Loan agreement where building is to be financed: obligation to make further advances

    (i) The mortgaged property includes a dwelling-house now under construction and the Borrower has requested the Lender to lend him (total sum to be advanced) for the purpose of enabling him to complete the said dwelling-house which the Lender has agreed to do upon having the repayment thereof and of any other further advances which the Lender may agree to make to the Borrower with interest thereon secured as appears herein

    (ii) Upon the treaty for the said loan it was agreed that the sum of (amount of initial advance) part of the sum of (total sum to be advanced) should be paid by the Lender to the Borrower on the execution of this deed and that the residue of the said (total sum to be advanced) should be paid as appears herein

(4) Loan agreement where security extends to further advances but without obligation to make them

The Lender has agreed to lend to the Borrower the sum of (amount of initial advance) upon having the repayment thereof and of every other sum which may be advanced by the Lender to the Borrower with interest thereon secured as appears herein

(5) Further security for loan already secured by legal charge on other land

    (i) By a legal charge ("the Mortgage") (date) between the parties to this deed certain property known as (address and brief description) was charged to the Lender to secure repayment of the sum of (amount advanced under the Mortgage) and interest at the rate of ( ) per cent. per annum thereon

    (ii) (Recite title of Borrower to subject-matter of further security)

    (iii) Upon the treaty for the advance of (amount advanced under the Mortgage) it was agreed that the repayment of the moneys made payable by it should be further secured by a mortgage of [(description of property which is the subject-matter of the further security)] [the property described in the Schedule hereto]

(6) Loan agreement where the borrower wishes to raise money for the purposes of the Settled Land Act 1925

The Borrower requires to raise the sum of £— for purposes authorised by section 71 of the said Act and the Lender has agreed to lend the same to the Borrower upon having the repayment thereof with interest at the rate hereinafter mentioned secured in a manner hereinafter appearing

(c) Subsisting Prior Mortgages

(1) Borrower's title—freehold property

The Borrower is seised of the property described in the First Schedule hereto ("the Mortgaged Property") for a legal estate in fee simple in possession subject (as mentioned in the said Schedule) and to the [Legal Charge(s)] [Mortgage(s)] ("the Prior Mortgage(s)") particulars of which are contained in the Second Schedule hereto

(2) Borrower's title—leasehold property

The Borrower is possessed of the property described in the First Schedule hereto ("the Mortgaged Property") for a legal estate for the residue of the term of years granted by the Lease mentioned in the said Schedule subject to the rent reserved and the covenants and conditions thereby contained and (subject also as further mentioned in the said Schedule and) to the [Legal Charge(s)] [Mortgage(s)] ("the Prior Mortgage(s)") particulars of which are contained in the Second Schedule hereto but otherwise free from incumbrances

(3) State of Mortgage debt

The principal sum of £( ) remains owing on the security of the prior mortgage
[but all interest thereon has been paid up to the date hereof]
[together with the sum of £( ) for interest thereon]
Or:
There are now owing on the security of the prior mortgages the sums specified in the particulars contained in the Second Schedule hereto
[but all interest thereon has been paid up to the date thereof]
[together with the sums specified in the said particulars for interest thereon]

(d) Persons Joining In or Consenting

(1) Surety's agreement to act as such

The Surety has agreed to join in this deed as surety for the Borrower in manner hereinafter appearing

(2) Lessor's consent to charge of leasehold property

The consent of the Lessor (as required by the said lease) has been duly obtained

(3) Agreement of prior incumbrancer to postpone[7]

The (holder of the prior charge) has agreed to join in this deed for the purpose of postponing (the prior charge) to the security hereby created in manner hereinafter appearing

3. Testatum 1

NOW in pursuance of the said agreement and in consideration of

[the sum of (amount advanced) now paid to the Borrower by the Lender, the receipt of which the Borrower hereby acknowledges]
or
[the forbearance of the Lender to enforce immediately the payment of the said debt of (amount of debt)]

(a) Covenants to Pay

(1) Covenant to pay principal and interest
THIS DEED WITNESSETH AS FOLLOWS:
The Borrower HEREBY COVENANTS with the Lender to pay to the Lender on (repayment date) the sum of (amount advanced) with interest thereon from the date hereof at the rate of (rate) per cent. per annum AND FURTHER if the said sum of (amount advanced) shall not be so paid to the Lender interest at the rate aforesaid by equal (interval) payments on (payment dates) in each year on the principal moneys for the time being remaining due on this security or on any order or judgment which may be recovered hereunder

Covenants for payment by instalments or lender's agreements to accept instalment payments (covenants (2) to (5))*

(2) Covenant to pay by instalments where loan is interest-free
The Borrower HEREBY COVENANTS with the lender to pay to the Lender the said sum of £ (amount advanced) by equal (interval) instalments of £(amount of instalment) to be made on (payment dates) the first payment to be made on (first payment date) until the whole of the said sum of £(amount advanced) has been duly paid and satisfied (and no right to interest on the said sum shall be implied hereby)

(3) Flat rate system
If the Borrower shall pay to the Lender the said principal sum of £(amount advanced) with interest hereon at the rate [aforesaid][8] from the date hereof by the instalments at the times and in the manner set out

---

[7] This is a suitable form where the spouse with the right of occupation under the Matrimonial Homes Act 1983 agrees to postpone his or her charge to another security.

[8] If there is a provision for reduction of interest on punctual payment, replace "aforesaid" by the following: (higher rate) reducible to (lower rate) as provided in clause ( ) hereof.

herein, namely, by (number of instalments) equal (interval) instalments of £(aggregate amount of principal and interest) each the first instalment to be paid on the (date)[9] and a subsequent instalment on every (payment dates) or within ( )[10] days after each such day and if

[there has been no breach of any provision contained in this deed or implied by law and on the part of the Borrower to be observed or performed (other than the covenant for payment of the mortgage money and interest contained in clause (number of clause))[11] of this deed][12]

[the power of sale applicable hereto (which notwithstanding this present provision shall be deemed to arise on (date)[13] shall not have become exercisable][14]

then the Lender shall apply each such instalment in payment of the interest for the time being due on this security and subject thereto in reduction of the said principal moneys and shall accept payment of the said principal sum and the interest thereon by the instalments at the times and in the manner aforesaid.[15]

(4) Repayment by fixed instalments[16]

If the Borrower shall pay to the Lender on (first payment date) and thereafter every (interval) the sum of £( ) on account of the principal sum

---

[9] This should be the date for repayment which is normally six months from the date of the mortgage deed.

[10] Usually 14 days.

[11] The number of the clause containing the borrower's covenant to repay principal and interest.

[12] This alternative should be used if the mortgage deed contains a clause excluding the operation of s.103 of L.P.A. 1925. The author of *Hallett's Conveyancing Precedents* (1965) considers that it would be fairer to omit such a clause where the mortgage is of a dwelling-house and the borrower is in personal occupation (see p. 629, n. 3) but it is frequently found nowadays in building society mortgages.

[13] Usually 14 days.

[14] Should be used if s.103 of L.P.A. 1925 has not been excluded.

[15] No notice is required if the borrower wishes to exercise his right to pay off the mortgage on the contractual date for repayment: *Crickmore* v. *Freeston* (1871) 40 L.J.Ch. 137. It appears to be a settled rule of practice that once the borrower has failed to pay principal and interest on the legal redemption date, he must either give the lender six months' notice of his intention to pay off the mortgage, or pay six months' interest in lieu: *Fitzgerald's Trustee* v. *Mellersh* [1892] 1 Ch. 385 at 388; *Smith* v. *Smith* [1891] 3 Ch. 550 at 552. In the latter case it was said that there were recognised exceptions to the rule: see *Bovill* v. *Endle* [1896] 1 Ch. 648 where it was held that the rule does not apply where the lender takes proceedings to recover the mortgage money from the borrower or his estate, and that going into possession is equivalent to taking proceedings. The mere fact that the mortgage is an instalment mortgage and contains a term precluding the lender from making immediate demand for payment or otherwise immediately enforcing his security does not displace the lender's right "to go into possession before the ink is dry on the mortgage" (*per* Harman J., *Four-Maids Ltd.* v. *Dudley Marshall (Properties) Ltd.* [1957] Ch. 317): see *Esso Petroleum Co. Ltd.* v. *Alstonbridge Properties* [1975] 1 W.L.R. 1474 at 1483–1484 and *Western Bank* v. *Schindler* [1977] Ch. 1 at 10, C.A.

[16] In the flat-rate system, the repayment is by fixed regular instalments in which the proportion of capital to interest increases throughout the mortgage period: but in the fixed-instalment system, the amount of the principal repaid is the same in every instalment and the interest decreases throughout the term.

due hereunder and also shall pay to the Lender on (dates as before) interest at the rate aforesaid on the principal moneys for the time being unpaid

[   ][17]

then the Lender shall accept payment of the said principal sum hereby secured and the interest thereon by the instalments at the times and in the manner aforesaid

(5) Repayment by equal instalments[18]

If the Borrower shall pay to the Lender on (first payment date) and thereafter for the next subsequent (number of instalments) (intervals) instalments of combined principal and interest of £(amount of instalment) each apportioned as to £(   ) to principal and as to the balance to interest

[   ][19]

then the Lender[20] . . .

*Note to (2)–(5) above

The Borrower can covenant directly to pay by instalments and a provision can be inserted whereby the whole debt shall become immediately payable in the event of default in payment of any instalment. Such a clause is not a penalty.[21] In order to exercise his power of sale the Lender has to prove that the instalments are in arrears. If there is a direct covenant to repay by instalments and no redemption date is specified in the mortgage deed, the borrower may not be able to redeem until the date of the final payment. In *De Borman* v. *Makkofaides*[22] it was held that, on the true construction of the special stipulations (*infra*), the principal outstanding did not not become due so long as the instalments were paid before the expiration of the stipulated notice period:

"3. The statutory power of sale shall be exercisable in any of the following events:
  (a) If default is made in payment of the principal moneys for the time being owing on this security or any instalment thereof for one month after notice requiring payment thereof shall have been served on the borrower.
  (b) If the borrower fails to observe any of his obligations hereunder after reasonable notice (not being less than one month) has been served on the borrower by the lender requiring him to perform the same.
  (c) If the borrower commits any act of bankruptcy or if execution is levied against him or if distress is levied on the chattels of the borrower on the said property.

[17] Use nn. 12 or 14 above, depending on whether the operation of s.103 of L.P.A. 1925 has been excluded.
[18] This form is suitable where the total sum to be repaid consists of the advance plus a lump sum representing interest at the agreed rate, not reducing over the period of the mortgage.
[19] See n. 17, (fixed-instalment system).
[20] Continue as for fixed-instalment system ((4) above).
[21] *Sterne* v. *Beck* (1863) 1 De G.J. & Sm. 595; *Wallingford* v. *Mutual Society* (1880) 5 App. Cas. 685, H.L., *per* Lord Hatherley at 702; *Protector Endowment and Annuity Loan Co.* v. *Grice* (1880) 5 Q.B.D. 592, C.A., *revsing* (1880) 5 Q.B.D. 121; *Cityland and Property (Holdings) Ltd.* v. *Dabrah* [1968] Ch. 166 (provision that not only the whole debt but the whole of an added premium became due on default, held unreasonable on the facts).
[22] (1971) 220 E.G. 805

4. If the borrower shall pay to the lender the quarterly instalments herein-before referred to in repayment of the said sum of £18,000 the lender shall not (except as aforesaid) enforce the security hereby constituted."

The more usual form of a covenant for repayment by instalments is a covenant to repay at a fixed date with a proviso that if the specified instalments are paid on the payment dates or within a specified time-limit, the lender will not require payment in any other manner.

(b) Proviso for Reduction of Interest Rate on Punctual Payment[23]

If the Borrower shall on [any] [every][24] day on which interest is hereby made payable or within (number of days) thereafter pay to the Lender interest on the principal moneys for the time being owing on this security at the rate of (reduced rate) per annum and if the power of sale applicable hereto[25] has not become exercisable[26] then the Lender will accept interest at such reduced rate for the (period)[27] for which such interest shall be so paid to him.

4. Testatum 2

(a) Form of Charge or Demise

(1) Charge of freeholds

The Borrower as (capacity)[28] HEREBY CHARGES BY WAY OF

---

[23] This clause is sometimes found in non-building society mortgages. It must provide for reduction on punctual payment, not for an increase on non-punctual payment; a clause of the latter type is bad as being a penalty, see Nicholls v. Maynard (1747) 3 Atk. 519, following Holles v. Wyse (1693) 2 Vern. 289 (increase for non-punctual payment relievable in equity), cf. Marquis of Hallifax v. Higgens (1689) 2 Vern. 134; Strode v. Parker (1694) 2 Vern. 316. For the position where interest is omitted from the mortgage deed, see ante, pp. 437 et seq.

[24] If the word "every" is used, the right to reduction is terminated on the occasion of the first non-punctual payment: if "any," then it is lost for that period.

[25] See s.101 of L.P.A. 1925.

[26] See s.103 of L.P.A. 1925. The operation of this section is often excluded.

[27] Usually a quarter or half-year.

[28] The covenants implied in a conveyance by a person conveying and being expressed to convey as a beneficial owner are the same as those implied in a mortgage by such a person. In a mortgage, however, they extend to persons from whom the mortgagor derives title, whether or not for value: see s.76(1)(C), (D) of, and Pts. III, IV of Sched. 2 to L.P.A. 1925. Hallett, Conveyancing Precedents (1965), at pp. 156–157 and 611, n. 16(ii) considers that the "beneficial owner" covenants are implied if the form of words in the text is used, whether or not the borrower actually is the beneficial owner. In Eastwood v. Ashton [1915] A.C. 900 at 921, it was held that a purchaser could sue a vendor on the implied covenants for title as beneficial owner although the vendor's title had at the time of the case been extinguished by adverse possession. In Pilkington v. Wood [1953] 1 Ch. 770 at 777, Harman J. said, obiter, that it was a sine qua non that the covenantor must be, in fact, as well as being expressed to be, the beneficial owner. The learned editor of Emmet on Title (19th ed.), para. 14.003, considers that the words "conveys and is expressed to convey" ought to be construed as "expressly purports to convey," and that the views expressed in Pilkington v. Wood (and see also Fay v. Miller, Wilkins & Co. [1941] Ch. 360, C.A.: Re Robertson's Application [1969] 1 W.L.R. 109 at 112) are in conflict with the idea behind s.76 and with

LEGAL MORTGAGE[29] All That the mortgaged property (subject as stated in the Schedule hereto)[30] with the payment to the Lender of the principal moneys interest and other money[31] hereby covenanted to be paid by the Borrower (or otherwise secured)[32]

(2) Charge of leaseholds

The Borrower as (capacity)[33] HEREBY CHARGES BY WAY OF LEGAL MORTGAGE[34] All That the mortgaged property (and all other (if any) the premises comprised in and demised by the Lease mentioned in the Schedule hereto)[35]

(3) Mortgage of freeholds by demise

The Borrower as (capacity)[36] HEREBY DEMISES unto the Lender All That the mortgaged property to hold the same unto the Lender for the term[37] of [   ][38] years from the date hereof without impeachment of waste[39] (subject as is mentioned in the said Schedule)[40] and subject also to the proviso for cesser on redemption contained herein[41] namely:

(4) Mortgage of leaseholds by sub-demise

The Borrower as (capacity) HEREBY DEMISES unto the Lender All That the property described in the Schedule hereto and comprised in and

direct authority not cited in those cases. Nevertheless, the latest direct authority cited in support of the view expressed in Emmet is *Parker* v. *Judkin* [1931] 1 Ch. 475 and it may well be advisable to provide expressly that the "beneficial owner" covenants be implied. Hallett, *op. cit.* at p. 611 proposes the following: "Covenants by the Borrower with the Lender on the terms set forth in [Part III] [Parts III and IV] of the Second Schedule to the Law of Property Act 1925 shall be implied in this Legal Charge."

[29] See s.87 of L.P.A. 1925 for the power, protections and remedies of a chargee by way of legal mortgage. The section refers to "a charge by deed expressed to be by way of legal mortgage." The italicised words are unnecessary in a charge of registered land: *Cityland and Property (Holdings) Ltd.* v. *Dabrah* [1968] Ch. 166 at 171, but Goff J. (as he then was) did not express any opinion as to the need for them in a charge of unregistered land.

[30] Include these words if the mortgaged property is subject to easements or restrictive covenants.

[31] See L.P.A. 1925, Sched. 5, Form 1. The words "other money" apply to costs which the borrower has specifically covenanted to pay.

[32] The words "or otherwise secured" refer to moneys which may become due under the mortgage but which there is no specific covenant to pay.

[33] See n. 28 above.

[34] See n. 29 above.

[35] Omit these words if the mortgaged property is part only of the property originally demised.

[36] See nn. 28 and 29 above.

[37] The term granted is a legal term of years: s.1(1)(*b*), L.P.A. 1925. S.149 of that Act makes it clear that entry is not required before it can take effect: *cf.* the position before 1926, see *Lewis* v. *Baker* [1905] 1 Ch. 46: *Re Moore and Hulm's Contract* [1912] 2 Ch. 105.

[38] The most usual length of term granted is 3,000 years from the date of the mortgage: but see the first specimen abstract to Sched. 6 to L.P.A. 1925. There is no general rule as to the minimum length of the term; but see s.10(2) of the Trustee Act 1925 for a case where a minimum of 500 years is required.

[39] In accordance with the provisions of Pt. VII, Sched. I to L.P.A. 1925. "Waste" means voluntary waste, that is, doing that which ought not to be done. For a discussion of waste, see Megarry and Wade, *Law of Real Property* (5th ed., 1984), pp. 95–98.

[40] Include these words if the mortgaged property is subject to restrictive covenants or easements.

[41] The date mentioned in the proviso for cesser should be the same as the date for repayment in the covenant to repay.

demised by the Lease mentioned herein TO HOLD unto the Lender henceforth for all the residue of the term of years created by the Lease except the last 10 days thereof subject to the said rents covenants and conditions and subject also to the proviso for cesser on redemption contained herein namely:

(5) Second mortgage of freeholds by demise

As in (3) up to the word "years," then continue:

... and [one][42] day from the date hereof without impeachment of waste (subject as is mentioned in the said Schedule and) subject to the prior mortgage and to the principal moneys and interest thereby secured and also subject to the proviso for cesser on redemption contained herein namely:

(b) Provisos for cesser or discharge

(1) Discharge of legal charge

If the Borrower shall on (date)[43] pay to the Lender the sum of £(amount of advance) with interest thereon from the date hereof at the said rate[44] the Lender will at the request and cost of the Borrower duly discharge this security[45]

(2) Proviso for cesser on redemption

PROVIDED that if the Borrower shall on (date)[46] pay to the Lender the sum of £(amount of advance) with interest hereon from the date hereof at the said rate[47] the said term hereby granted shall absolutely cease and determine[48]

(c) Date on which Mortgage falls Due

The mortgage money shall become due and the statutory power of sale and of appointing a receiver shall arise on (repayment date)[49]

---

[42] Where there is a series of mortgages, each term is normally made one day longer than the mortgage term immediately prior to it, but this is not necessary: L.P.A. 1925, s.149(5).

[43] The date specified should be the same date as that in the covenant for repayment.

[44] Insert before "rate" the word "reduced" if the deed contains a covenant for reduction of interest on punctual payment.

[45] This provision is not always included in a legal charge. The purpose of it is to make ascertainable the date when the right to foreclosure arises, but in its absence it is normally accepted that the right arises on the date specified in the covenant for repayment.

[46] See n. 43 above.

[47] See n. 44 above.

[48] See n. 45 above. The provision is normally included in a mortgage by demise or sub-demise, for the reason given in n. 45. The term ceases automatically on repayment, having become a satisfied term (L.P.A. 1925, s.116) and merging in the reversion expectant on the term out of which it was created (*ibid.* s.5).

[49] Normally six months after the date of the mortgage deed. If there is no express provision, the power of sale *arises* when the mortgage money has become due (L.P.A. 1925, s.101). In the absence of any term specifying that date, it is the date for repayment of the mortgage money or, if repayable by instalments, the date of the first instalment: see *Payne* v. *Cardiff*

Borrower's Covenants and other Operative Clauses

(a) Covenants to Insure and Maintain the Security

(1) To (repair and)[50] insure[51]

To keep the
[mortgaged property][52]
[buildings for the time being comprised in or subject to this security][53]
insured against loss or damage by fire (and such other risks as the Lender from time to time in writing directs)

[in the name of the Lender] [in the joint names of the Lender and the Borrower][54] to the full value thereof with some insurance office or underwriters approved by the Lender and duly and punctually to pay all premiums and other payments required for effecting and keeping up such insurance as and when the same shall become due and when required by the Lender to produce to him the policy or policies of such insurance and the receipt for each such payment

(2) To (repair and) insure, where the property charged is leasehold property and there are adequate repairing and insuring covenants in the lease

To keep the mortgaged property in repair and insured in accordance with the covenants in that behalf contained in the said Lease and to pay duly and punctually all premiums necessary for keeping up such insurance and to produce to the Lender on demand (the policy or policies of such insurance[55] and) the receipt for every such payment

---

R.D.C. [1932] 1 K.B. 241. In the case of a mortgage for securing further advances, it is usual for the mortgage money to be deemed to have become due at the date for repayment of the initial advance.

[50] The obligation to keep in repair may be expressed by inserting the following words: "in good and substantial repair (allowing the Mortgagee to enter and view the state of repair of the same at all reasonable times without becoming liable as mortgagee in possession)" and it is prudent for the mortgagee to insert the non-accountability clause since, once a mortgagee has gone into possession he remains accountable, in the absence of some such provision, after he has gone out of possession: *Re Prytherch* (1889) 42 Ch.D. 590, at 599–560.

[51] Statutory powers relating to insurance are conferred on a mortgagee by deed, but they can be varied or extended, or displaced by contrary intention expressed in the mortgage deed: see L.P.A. 1925, ss.101(1)(ii) and 108. A person interested is also given the right to have insurance moneys expended in reinstatement: Fire Prevention (Metropolis) Act 1774, s.83. In spite of its title, it is a general, not a local, Act, and it applies as between mortgagor and mortgagee: *Sinnott* v. *Bowden* [1912] 2 Ch. 414; *Portavon Cinema Co. Ltd.* v. *Price and Century Insurance Co. Ltd.* [1939] 4 All E.R. 601 at 607.

[52] If defined or described in a Schedule.

[53] See n. 50 above.

[54] Neither phrase need be used.

[55] If the policies are in the borrower's possession.

(3) Application of insurance moneys[56]

All moneys received on any insurance whatsoever in respect of loss or damage by fire or otherwise to the mortgaged property or any part thereof shall if the Lender so requires be applied in making good the loss or damage or in or towards the discharge of the money for the time being owing thereon

(4) To repair buildings—short form

To keep the buildings for the time being comprised in this security in good condition and repair . . .

(5) To enter, inspect and execute repairs

Add to (4) after "repair" where lender is to be entitled to enter, inspect and execute repairs:

. . . and if the borrower shall fail to do so the lender may at any time thereafter enter upon the premises or any part thereof and execute such repairs as (in the opinion of the lender) may be necessary or proper without thereby becoming liable as mortgagee in possession and the borrower will on demand[57] repay to the lender all the expenses thereby incurred by the lender and will pay interest at the rate of (rate) per cent. per annum from the date of demand until repayment on any moneys not repaid on demand as aforesaid and all such expenses and interest shall be charged on the property hereby mortgaged [charged][58]

(6) To appoint a surveyor to survey the property

Add to (4) after "repair" where lender is to be entitled to appoint a surveyor to survey the property, numbering (4) as sub-clause (i):

(ii) For the purpose of ascertaining whether the said buildings are for the time being in good condition and repair the lender may from time to time cause the same to be surveyed by a competent sur-

---

[56] It is important to include this covenant because otherwise the borrower would not be liable to apply moneys received under a policy, not effected under the mortgage, in making good or in discharge of the mortgage debt. In *Halifax Building Society* v. *Keighley* [1931] 2 K.B. 248 it was held that, where a borrower effects an insurance elsewhere independently, and a claim arises which is met by the two companies in their due proportions, the mortgagee has no claim to the proportion paid by the independent company.

It is not considered that the alternative way of dealing with this problem (*i.e.* a covenant not to insure in any other office) is a satisfactory protection for the mortgagee, as any breach of the covenant would normally come to light only when the claim had been made.

[57] This obligation may, alternatively, form part of a covenant for payment and charge of costs, charges and expenses: see *Encyclopedia of Forms and Precedents* (4th ed.) Vol. 14, forms 2.30, 2.36 at pp. 129, 134, respectively.

[58] The power given by this covenant should be cautiously exercised by the lender, as he will be liable, to the extent the repairs executed are not necessary or proper, as mortgagee in possession. He will be allowed the cost of necessary and proper repairs: see *Sandon* v. *Hooper* (1843) 6 Beav. 246: affd. (1844) 14 L.J.Ch. 120. Alternatively, where income-producing property is in disrepair, he could appoint a receiver and give him written directions as to the necessary or proper repairs, the cost of which the receiver must pay out of money received by him. For the power to appoint a receiver, see L.P.A. 1925, s.101(1)(iii), and for the manner in which the receiver is to apply money received by him towards repairs, see s.109(8)(iii) of that Act.

veyor appointed by the lender and such surveyor may without rendering the lender liable as a mortgagee in possession at all reasonable times enter upon the said premises or any part thereof for the purpose of making a survey of the said buildings and the certificate of such surveyor shall be conclusive as to the state of repair and condition of the said buildings;

(iii) If the borrower shall fail to do any repairs to the said buildings certified by any such surveyor as aforesaid to be necessary and proper the lender may at any time thereafter enter upon the premises and execute the same without thereby becoming liable as mortgagee in possession;

(iv) On demand to repay to the lender (the reasonable remuneration of any surveyor appointed by the lender for making any such survey of the said buildings and) all expenses incurred by the lender in the execution of such repairs as aforesaid and will pay interest at the rate of . . . per cent. per annum from the date of demand until repayment on any moneys not repaid on demand as aforesaid all which moneys and interest shall be charged on the property hereby mortgaged.

(b) To Observe and Perform Conditions, etc.

(1) To observe and perform conditions (short form)[59]

To observe and perform all covenants provisions and regulations affecting the mortgaged property

(2) The same (longer form)[60]

To observe and perform all restrictive and other covenants all building regulations and all restrictions conditions and stipulations (if any) for the time being affecting the mortgaged property or the mode of user or enjoyment of the same or any part thereof

(3) To pay outgoings, etc.

To pay all outgoings and to keep the mortgaged property free from any charges taking priority over the money hereby secured[61]

---

[59] Some such clause as this is desirable so as to make the mortgagee's power of sale exercisable on breach of an obligation.

[60] See n. 59 above.

[61] Where a local authority has a charge in respect of the expense of executing works required to render a house fit for human habitation, or on premises of frontagers for expenses incurred in making up private streets, it has the same powers and remedies as if it were a mortgagee by deed having powers of sale and lease and of appointing a receiver. See the Housing Act 1985, ss.200, 229 (works executed pursuant to repair and improvement notices respectively); Highways Act 1980, s.212(3) where the powers arise by virtue of s.7 of the Local Land Charges Act 1975, pursuant to registration of the charge under s.5 thereof.

(4) Not to commit waste, etc.

Not to commit any waste upon or injure or in any manner or by any means lessen the value of the mortgaged property or any part thereof

(c) In Respect of Building and Planning

(1) To erect dwelling-house, where the purpose of the charge is to finance building

To proceed with and continue the erection of the said dwelling-house in a proper manner and with due diligence and to the satisfaction of the surveyor for the time being of the Lender within such time as shall be reasonably required by the Lender and to expend in the erection of the said dwelling-house

[the sum of £(amount to be spent)]

[the sum named in the said contract dated (date)].

(2) The same, including lender's power to re-enter and complete if the borrower fails to do so

To construct and complete the said dwelling-house at his own cost and before the (date) in a proper and workmanlike manner fit for immediate habitation with proper drains sewers and conveniences and in accordance with the plans and specifications therefor and the byelaws and regulations applicable thereto (and to the satisfaction of [the surveyor for the time being of the Lender] [the surveyor or other proper officer of (the local authority)]) and to expend (continue as in (1) above)

If the Borrower shall fail to construct and complete the said dwelling-house as aforesaid in accordance with the covenant by him hereinbefore contained the Lender may at any time enter upon the mortgaged property and complete the same and may for that purpose use any plant or materials belonging to the Borrower and all expenses incurred by the Lender under this power shall be deemed to have been properly incurred under this security.[62]

(3) Authorised use of premises: lender's powers on default

Not without the consent of the Lender and of the competent authority to use or suffer or permit the use of the mortgaged property[63] for any other purpose than its present use and if such consent is given by the competent authority to deliver a copy of the said consent to the Lender

---

[62] If there is a charging clause (see (8) below) the costs and expenses may be made subject to it.

[63] "Suffer" is said to have a wider meaning than "permit" in that its meaning includes allowing something to be done which the covenantor is fully able to prevent: see *Barton* v. *Reed* [1932] 1 Ch. 362 at 375. To sell land, knowing that the purchaser intends to use it for some purpose other than the specified purpose is not to "permit" that use: see *Tophams* v. *Earl of Sefton* [1967] 1 A.C. 50.

And if the Borrower persists in such other use after a refusal of consent on the part of the Lender any and every power or remedy conferred on the Lender by the Law of Property Act 1925 (as varied and extended by this deed) shall become exercisable by the Lender

(4) To produce notices[64]

To produce to the Lender immediately on receipt any order direction requisition permission notice or other matter affecting or likely to affect the mortgaged property and served on the Borrower by any third party and [allow the Lender to make a copy thereof];

[allow the Lender to retain the same but the Borrower shall be entitled to retain a copy thereof]

(5) To comply with statutory conditions

If at any time permission be obtained for any development of the mortgaged property within the provisions of the Town and Country Planning Act 1971 or any statutory amendment or replacement thereof or order made thereunder, to comply with all conditions subject to which permission is granted

(6) To comply with enforcement notices: lender's power to comply on default

To comply in all respects and at his own expense with the requirements of any valid enforcement notice or order made or served by a competent authority under or by virtue of the Town and Country Planning Act 1971 or any statutory amendment or replacement thereof or any order made thereunder requiring the discontinuance of or imposing conditions on the use of the mortgaged property or any part thereof or requiring the removal or alteration of any works or buildings thereon within the time specified therein (or within (period) from the date thereof whichever is the shorter)

In the event of the Borrower failing to comply as covenanted hereinbefore with any such requirement as is mentioned herein the Lender may in so far as the same may be necessary to comply with such requirement enter upon the mortgaged property and execute any works and do anything thereon necessary to ensure such compliance upon giving the Borrower (number) days' notice in writing of the intention to do so and all costs and expenses incurred by the Lender under this power shall be deemed to have been properly incurred under this security

(7) Power of attorney

The Borrower hereby irrevocably appoints the Lender and the persons deriving title under him to be his attorney to apply for and procure on his behalf any licences permissions or other things from any competent auth-

---

[64] The very wide powers given to Ministers and authorities to serve notices requiring things to be done or requisitioning property make it advisable that all parties interested in the property should be fully aware of such notices.

ority necessary for the execution of the repairs and other works hereby authorised to be executed by the Lender on default of the Borrower

(8) Covenant to repay money properly paid under the security, costs charges and expenses

The Borrower will on demand repay to the Lender all money properly paid and all costs charges and expenses properly incurred hereunder by the Lender (as to such costs charges and expenses on a full indemnity basis)[65] together with interest thereon from the time of paying or incurring the same until repayment at the rate aforesaid and until so repaid such costs charges and expenses shall be charged upon the property for the time being subject to this security and shall be added to the principal money hereby secured and interest thereon as aforesaid shall be charged upon the same property and shall be payable by equal [half yearly] payments on the respective dates hereinbefore appointed for payment of interest on the said principal money

(d) Modifications of Statutory Powers

(1) Retention of power to consolidate[66]

The restriction on the right of consolidating mortgage securities contained in section 93 of the Law of Property Act 1925 shall not apply to this [Legal Charge] [Mortgage]

(2) Borrower's covenant not to grant leases or accept surrenders without lender's consent[67]

During the continuance of this security the borrower shall not without the consent[68] in writing of the lender grant or agree to grant any lease or

---

[65] Unless this clause is included the costs charges and expenses do not constitute a debt for which the borrower can be sued: they are added to the security. In the absence of any contractual provision the costs in a mortgage action are recoverable by the mortgagee on the standard basis. The view of the majority of commentators is that it is possible to contract that the costs should be recovered on an indemnity basis: see Hallett, *Conveyancing Precedents*, (1965), p. 613, n. 29(i) summarising the views up to 1965, and *Fisher and Lightwood's Law of Mortgage* (10th ed., 1988) p. 660 and cases there cited. Prideaux, *Precedents in Conveyancing* (25th ed.) Vol. 2, p. 443 suggests that such a provision might be considered harsh and unconscionable and thus be held invalid.

[66] This clause need be inserted only where there is to be a series of charges of different properties in favour of the lender. It is advisable to register the right, if reserved, as a general equitable charge.

[67] It is advisable to frame the provision in this form rather than merely to exclude the exercise of the statutory powers by the borrower for, if that is done and the borrower grants a lease without the mortgagee's consent, it is a lease outside the statute and is not a breach of the terms of the mortgage: see *Iron Trades Employers Insurance Association Ltd.* v. *Union Land and House Investors Ltd.* [1937] Ch. 313.

[68] It is for the lessee to prove that the mortgagee gave his consent and if he fails to do so, the lease does not bind the mortgagee: *Taylor* v. *Ellis* [1960] Ch. 368. The provision sometimes found in the clause, that no intending lessee shall be concerned to inquire as to such consent, is best omitted, since, if it is included, the mortgagee is estopped from denying that consent was given: *Lever Finance Ltd.* v. *Needleman Property Trustee* [1956] Ch. 375.

tenancy of the mortgaged property or any part thereof or accept or agree to accept a surrender of any lease or tenancy

(3) Extension of lender's leasing power

The statutory power of leasing conferred on the Lender shall be extended so as to authorise the Lender to grant leases and make agreements for leases for any term and at any rent with or without payment of a fine or premium (provided that any such fine or premium paid to the Lender shall be applied by the Lender as if it were money paid to the Lender on the exercise of the power of sale conferred or implied by this deed)

(4) Exclusion of section 103 of the Law of Property Act 1925 and extension of the powers of sale and of appointing a receiver

Section 103 of the Law of Property Act 1925 shall not apply to this security and the statutory powers of sale and appointing a receiver shall arise on (repayment date) and shall become exercisable by the Lender without notice to the Borrower immediately on the happening of any one or more of the following events:

   (i) if the Lender demands payment of any money secured by this deed and repayable on demand and it is not repaid immediately;

  (ii) if any payment of any money secured by this deed payable in any other manner or interest payable under it is not paid on the due date whether demanded or not;

 (iii) if the Borrower makes default in fulfilling or observing any of his obligations under this deed or any deed made by way of further assurance or supplemental to it;

 (iv) if the powers of sale or appointing a receiver become exercisable under any other security given before or after this deed by the Borrower to the Lender or to any third party or if any money payable to the Borrower under any such other security is not paid within 14 days of the due date;

  (v) if any distress or execution is levied or issued against any property of the Borrower or any steps are taken by any person to enforce any rights against the mortgaged property;

 (vi) if the Borrower dies or is adjudicated bankrupt[69] or enters into any agreement or composition with his creditors or becomes of unsound mind or otherwise incapable of managing his affairs.

(5) Power to sell by instalment sale

The statutory power of sale is hereby modified so that any sale by the Lender may be in such form as to the manner thereof as to the method of payment of the purchase price and otherwise as the Lender may think fit.

---

[69] A petitioner in bankruptcy must establish that the debtor cannot pay, or has no reasonable prospect of being able to pay: Insolvency Act 1986, s.267(2).

(6) Covenant against registration[70]

No person or persons shall be registered under the Land Registration Acts 1925 to 1986 or any Act amending or reamending the same as proprietor or proprietors of the mortgaged property or any part thereof without the consent in writing of the Lender (and the costs incurred by the Lender of entering any caution against registration of the mortgaged property shall be deemed to be costs properly incurred by the Lender under this security)[71]

(e) Surety Covenants

(1) Where as between the borrower and the surety the borrower is primarily liable[72]

As between the Borrower and the Surety the Borrower and the mortgaged property shall be primarily liable for the payment of the moneys hereby secured but this provision shall not prejudice the Lender in the exercise of any of his rights and remedies for enforcing this security

(2) Where as between the surety and the lender the surety is a principal debtor

As in (1) up to "hereby secured" then continue as follows:

But as between the Surety and the Lender the Surety shall be treated as principal debtor for the moneys hereby secured And[73] the Surety shall not be released from liability hereunder by time given to the Borrower or any other variation of the provisions of this deed or by anything by reason of which but for this provision the Surety would have been released

---

[70] This clause is very rarely required. Its purpose is to prevent the borrower from registering his title in H.M. Land Registry without the knowledge of the mortgagee and obtaining a land certificate. It is unnecessary (i) if the land is already registered; (ii) when, as in the case of a first mortgage, the documents of title are handed over to the mortgagee; and (iii) if the land is to be registered on completion of the conveyance and a contemporaneous mortgage, since in that case the mortgagee will insist on a completed application form for first registration being handed over to him, which he will then lodge at H.M. Land Registry together with the title deeds. He will receive a charge certificate on completion of registration.

[71] When the clause is used, the words in brackets should be omitted if the mortgage deed contains a covenant to repay money properly paid, costs charges and expenses (see (8) p. 464 above).

[72] If this clause is used, the surety may in certain circumstances be released from his obligation. Thus if time is given to the borrower by way of a binding agreement for good consideration, the surety is released: *Rouse* v. *Bradford Banking Co.* [1894] A.C. 586 at 594. Although in general he is discharged by the creditor dealing with the principal debtor in a manner inconsistent with the contract the performance of which the surety had guaranteed, it has been held that he will not be discharged if there is a variation which is to his benefit or is insubstantial.

[73] This provision is effective to prevent waiver of the lender's rights against the surety by reason of a variation of the terms of the contract between the lender and the borrower.

Other Operative Clauses and Provisos

(1) Warranty that borrower is in personal occupation

The Borrower HEREBY WARRANTS to the Lender that the Borrower is in personal occupation of the whole of the mortgaged property and that neither it nor any part of it is now let or agreed to be let[74]

(2) Freedom from accountability as mortgagee when out of possession

If the Lender shall enter into possession of the mortgaged property or part thereof he may from time to time at pleasure go out of such possession and shall not be liable to account as mortgagee in possession while in fact out of such possession PROVIDED that notice of such fact shall within seven days after its happening be served on the Borrower[75]

(3) Attornment clause[76]

The Borrower hereby attorns tenant to the Lender of the mortgaged property during the continuance of this security at the yearly rent of a peppercorn if demanded but nothing in this clause shall prevent the Lender from at any time entering on and taking possession of the mortgaged property and so determining the tenancy hereby created [after giving the Borrower or leaving upon the said property at least seven days' notice in writing to quit][77]

(4) Lender's covenant to make further advances

The Lender HEREBY COVENANTS with the Borrower that he will

---

[74] This clause reinforces the borrower's covenant not to lease or agree to lease without the mortgagee's consent. If the warranty is given fraudulently and the tenant is a party, the mortgagee is not bound by the tenancy granted: *Church of England Building Society* v. *Piskor* [1954] Ch. 553 at 614, and damages are available for breach of such warranty, whether or not the breach is fraudulent. See also *Lloyds Bank* v. *Rossett* [1988] 3 W.L.R. 1301.

[75] The purpose of this clause is to prevent the lender being permanently liable to account on the footing of wilful default on the ground that, having gone into possession, he can never be held to go out: *Re Prytherch* (1889) 41 Ch.D. 590 at 599.

[76] The original purpose of an attornment clause was to enable a lender to distrain for money due from the borrower and to obtain summary judgment. It is now invalid so far as it purports to confer a right of distress, unless it is registered as a bill of sale (Bills of Sale Act 1878, s.6). In *Alliance Building Society* v. *Pinwill* [1958] Ch. 788 it was held that an attornment clause did not create the relationship of landlord and tenant so as to bring s.16 of the Rent Act 1957 (now s.5 of the Protection from Eviction Act 1977) into operation, and a similar decision was reached in *Steyning and Littlehampton Building Society* v. *Wilson* [1951] Ch. 1018 where an attornment clause relating to agricultural land was held not to create a tenancy within the Agricultural Holdings Act 1948. It is said, on the basis of the decision in *Regent Oil Co. Ltd.* v. *J.A. Gregory (Hatch End) Ltd.* [1966] Ch. 402 that an attornment clause enables restrictive covenants in the deed on the part of the borrower to be enforced against his successors in title. See *ante*, pp. 23, 24, 207.

[77] There is no need to serve a notice terminating the tenancy but if it is provided that a notice should be served, proceedings cannot be begun until it has been served and the time limit has expired: *Woolwich Equitable Building Society* v. *Preston* [1938] Ch. 129; *Hinckley and Country Building Society* v. *Henny* [1953] 1 W.L.R. 352.

from time to time advance to the Borrower[78] within [10] days after being so requested such further sums as the Borrower shall by notice in writing to the Lender request to be advanced not exceeding in the whole the sum of £( ) (total amount of further advances) (making the sum of £( ) (the initial advance) now advanced the said sum of £( ) (total amount to be advanced))[78]

PROVIDED ALWAYS that:

(i) the obligation of the Lender to make further advances shall only apply if and so long as the Borrower shall pay all interest payable hereunder within (14) days from the time hereby appointed for payment thereof and shall perform all his obligations under the covenants on his behalf herein contained or implied by statute (other than in regard to the payment of principal and interest);

(ii) no request shall be made as aforesaid for the payment of a larger sum than £( ) or a smaller sum than £( ) and the sum so requested shall be a multiple of £(100);

(iii) the aggregate amount of such advances shall not at any time exceed (three-quarters) of the sum for the time being certified in writing by a surveyor to be approved by the Lender and whose charges shall be paid by the Borrower as having been expended in material and labour for the construction of the said dwelling-house or works incidental thereto[79]

(5) Proviso that debt shall not be called in for term certain[80]

If the Borrower shall comply with all his obligations hereunder the Lender shall not before the ( ) day of ( )[81] call in the said principal money hereby secured or any part thereof or take any other steps to enforce this security.[82] PROVIDED nevertheless that the statutory power of sale shall as aforesaid be exercisable at any time after the said (date)

---

[78] It may be desired to make the covenant a personal covenant between the original lender and borrower, in which case the following proviso may be added:

(iv) the benefit of this covenant shall be personal to (name of borrower) and the burden of this covenant shall be personal to (name of lender) and such benefit and burden shall not pass to their respective personal representatives or any other persons respectively deriving title under them.

See Hallett, *Conveyancing Precedents* (1965), pp. 624–626 for other variations.

[79] The proviso will be used, *inter alia*, where there is a charge to secure present and future advances to finance building.

[80] At the earliest, the estimated date of completion of the building.

[81] This proviso does not affect the borrower's right to redeem on the contractual date. *Cromwell Property Investment Co.* v. *Western and Toovey* [1934] Ch. 322. s.10(2) of the Trustee Act 1925 authorises trustees lending on mortgage to contract that the principal shall not be called in for a period not exceeding seven years.

[82] Where there is an obligation to make further advances.

(6) Proviso restricting redemption for term certain[83]

The Borrower shall not be entitled to redeem this security during the period of ( ) years[84] from the date thereof unless the Lender shall have gone into possession or appointed a receiver of the mortgaged property or taken any other steps to enforce this security

(7) Proviso restricting dealings with equity

Not without the written consent of the Lender to convey assign transfer mortgage or otherwise howsoever dispose of the mortgaged property

(8) Lender's power (if lending on second mortgage) to settle and pass accounts

The Lender may settle and pass the accounts of any person in whom the First Mortgage may for the time being be vested and all accounts so settled and passed shall be conclusive in favour of the Lender and shall bind the Borrower

(9) Stipulation negativing borrower's personal liability[85]

The Borrower shall not be liable personally for any of the principal money interest or other money secured by this deed

---

[83] Even if there is a term restricting the lender from calling in the debt, the term must not be unduly long. Each case depends on its facts: see *Teevan* v. *Smith* (1882) 20 Ch.D. 724 at 729 (five or seven years considered reasonable; *Fairclough* v. *Swan Brewery Co.* [1912] A.C. 562, P.C.; *Knightsbridge Estates Trust* v. *Byrne* [1939] Ch. 441 C.A., where a 40-year postponement was held not to be unreasonable, but at [1940] A.C. 613 the House of Lords decided the case independently of the Court of Appeal's reasoning, on the ground that the mortgage, being a debenture, could be made irredeemable. 10 years was held not unconscionable or unreasonable in *Multiservice Bookbinding L.A.* v. *Marden* [1979] Ch. 84. (See also *Davies* v. *Directloans Ltd*. [1986] 1 W.L.R. 823).

[84] The same date as in the proviso not to call in, if the charge is as in n. 29.

[85] It is appropriate to include this clause if the borrowers are personal representatives or trustees with no beneficial interest in the mortgaged property.

B: Equitable Mortgages and Notices of Deposit or Intended Deposit

1. Memorandum under Seal[86] to Accompany Deposit of Title Deeds[87]

MEMORANDUM dated (date) by (name, address, description) ("the Borrower") whereby:

(i) The documents of title[88] specified in the Schedule hereto have this day been deposited by the Borrower with (name, address, description) ("the Lender") to the intent that the [freehold] [leasehold] [freehold and leasehold] property to which they relate ('the Property') be equitably charged and THE BORROWER as beneficial owner CHARGES it with payment to the Lender of the sum of £(the amount of advance) now advanced by the Lender to the Borrower (the receipt of which the Borrower hereby acknowledges) together with interest[89] at the rate of (rate) per cent. per annum payable by equal (interval) payments on (payment dates) (and with all further sums which the Lender while retaining the said documents shall from time to time advance to the Borrower with interest from the date of each such advance payable at the rate and in the manner mentioned hereinabove)

---

[86] Where the memorandum is under seal, the powers conferred by s.101 of L.P.A. 1925 apply.

[87] Such a mortgage does not require to be registered. The definition of a general equitable charge (Land Charges Act 1972, s.2(4)) specifically excludes equitable mortgages accompanied by a deposit of title deeds. However, every equitable mortgage either expressly or impliedly contains an agreement to create a legal mortgage, and it has been argued that a protected equitable mortgage is registrable as an estate contract: see Hallett, *Conveyancing Precedents* (1965), p. 691, nn. 1(v) and 4(i) and footnotes thereto.

[88] The documents deposited should be those affecting the legal estate. The lender then has an equitable interest protected by a deposit of documents relating to the legal estate affected (L.P.A. 1925, s.2(3)(i); Settled Land Act 1925, s.21(2)(i)), so the interest cannot be overreached by an ad hoc trust for sale or settlement. On the other hand, an equitable mortgage not protected by a deposit of documents, but registered as a general equitable charge (Class C(iii) land charge, Land Charges Act 1972, s.2(4)) can, by virtue of s.72(3) of the Settled Land Act 1925, be overreached by a disposition under that Act, and possibly by a disposition by trustees for sale (L.P.A. 1925, s.28(1)). If title to the land is registered, it will be necessary for the equitable mortgagee to protect his interest. A proprietor of registered land or of a registered charge may create a lien on the land or charge by deposit of the land or charge certificate: Land Registration Act 1925, s.66. A deposit of the certificate alone may be protected by a notice of deposit: Land Registration Rules 1925, s.239. Form 85A is used, and the notice of deposit operates as a caution. Where the depositor is a transferee, notice of intended deposit should be given, using Form 85C. This also operates as a caution: Land Registration Rules 1925, r. 242. The equitable mortgagee can also protect his interest by notice under s.49 of the Land Registration Act 1925, if he can produce the land certificate to the Registrar: or by caution under s.54. See *Re White Rose Cottage* [1965] Ch. 940, C.A. As to the priority over subsequent equitable charges on interests protected by caution, see also *Barclays Bank* v. *Taylor* [1973] Ch. 63, revsd. [1974] Ch. 137, C.A. and the commentary at (1977) L.Q.R. 541 at 542, 558 (R. J. Smith).

[89] An equitable mortgage by deposit of title deeds carries interest whether or not there is an express provision: *Re Drax, Savile* v. *Drax* [1903] 1 Ch 781 C.A. The court has in a number of previous cases adopted the rate of 5 per cent., though more recently higher rates have been allowed: see, *e.g. Cityland and Property (Holdings) Ltd.* v. *Dabrah* [1968] Ch. 166 (7 per cent.); *Wallersteiner* v. *Moir (No. 2)* [1975] Q.B. 373, C.A. (1 per cent. above minimum lending rate). See *ante*, pp. 437 *et seq.*

(ii) THE BORROWER UNDERTAKES[90] to execute at his own cost whenever called upon to do so a legal charge or mortgage of the Property in favour of the Lender to secure all moneys for the time being due or to become due to the Lender on this security with interest as above in such form and containing such powers and provisions as the Lender may reasonably require including provisions relating to sections 93[91] and 99(1)[92] of the Law of Property Act 1925

(iii) THE BORROWER HEREBY DECLARES[93] that he will henceforth hold the Property as trustee for executing such charge or mortgage as aforesaid in favour of the Lender and the statutory power of appointing a new trustee in his place shall be exercisable by the Lender and the persons deriving title under him who shall have full power to make such appointment and to remove the Borrower from his trusteeship at his or their sole and unfettered will and pleasure notwithstanding that none of the events referred to in the said statutory power as conditions precedent to its exercise shall have occurred and further that on any such exercise of the said statutory power the party or parties exercising the same may appoint himself or one or more of themselves to be the new trustee or trustees

(iv) THE BORROWER HEREBY IRREVOCABLY APPOINTS the Lender and the persons deriving title under him to be the attorney or attorneys of the Borrower and the persons deriving title under him and in his or their names and on his or their behalf to vest the legal estate in the Property on any purchaser or other person in exercise of the statutory powers conferred on mortgagees free and discharged from all rights of redemption

IN WITNESS, etc.

THE SCHEDULE
(List of documents deposited)

---

[90] This undertaking is not strictly necessary, since the decided cases show that it is implied from the mere fact of deposit. See *Parker* v. *Housefield* (1834) 2 Myl. & K. 419 at 421; *Pryce* v. *Bury* (1853) 2 Drew. 41; *Carter* v. *Wake* (1877) 4 Ch.D. 605 at 606. If it is given, there should be registration as an estate contract (Class C(iv), Land Charges Act 1972, s.2(4)).

[91] Excluding this section and thus preserving the mortgagee's right to consolidate. The mere undertaking to execute a legal mortgage, without such provision, does not entitle the mortgagee to have s.93 excluded: *Farmer* v. *Pitt* [1902] 1 Ch. 954.

[92] s.99(13) gives the parties power to exclude the mortgagor's leasing powers by expression of a contrary intention in the mortgage deed or otherwise in writing.

[93] There are conflicting views as to whether the declaration of trust and the power of attorney are both necessary and, if not, which, see *Re Hodsen and Howes' Contract* (1887) 35 Ch.D. 668; *Re White Rose Cottage* [1965] Ch. 940, C.A.: *Encyclopedia of Forms and Precedents* (Vol. 14), p. 616 n. 18; *Kelly's Draftsman* (15th ed., 1986), p. 479, n. 13: Fisher and Lightwood, *Law of Mortgage*, (10th ed., 1988), pp. 69, 70, 718, 719.

2. Memorandum Under Hand[94] to Accompany Deposit of Title Deeds

MEMORANDUM dated (date) by (name, address, description) ("the Borrower")

(i) [95]THE BORROWER HEREBY DECLARES that he has deposited the documents specified in the Schedule hereto with (name, address, description) ("the Lender") to secure the repayment to the Lender on demand the sum of £(amount advanced) now lent by the Lender to the Borrower (the receipt of which the Borrower hereby acknowledges) (and of every further sum which the Lender may hereafter advance to the Borrower) together with interest thereon at the rate of (rate) per cent. per annum from the date hereof (and as to every further sum advanced from the date of such advance) until payment

(ii) (If desired, give the undertaking as in clause (ii) of precedent (1) above)

Dated (date)

THE SCHEDULE
(List of documents deposited)

Signature
Signature of attesting witness

3. Equitable Charge of Land[96]

I, (name, address, description) ("the Borrower") (as beneficial owner) HEREBY CHARGE the [freehold] [leasehold] [freehold and leasehold] property described in the Schedule hereto with the payment to (name, address, description) ("the Lender") on the (date) of the sum of £(amount advanced) now paid by the Lender to the Borrower (the receipt whereof the Borrower hereby acknowledges) together with interest thereon at (rate) per cent. per annum from the date hereof and also if the said sum of £(amount advanced) shall not be paid on the date aforesaid with the payment on the (payment dates) in every year of interest at the rate aforesaid on the principal money for the time being secured

---

[94] If the mortgage is under hand only, the powers under s.101 of L.P.A. 1925 do not apply and the mortgagee, if he desires to exercise the power of sale, has to seek the aid of the court: see s.91(2) of that Act.

[95] If there is merely an agreement to create a mortgage, and there has not been a deposit, precede these words by the phrase "In consideration of (name, address, description) ('the Lender') forbearing from pressing for immediate repayment of the sum of £(amount) now owing to him by the Borrower." and then continue as in precedent (2) above but omitting the definition of the Lender and instead referring to him as such.

[96] If the charge is under hand only the chargee has the remedies of sale and appointment of a receiver on application to the court, but is not entitled to possession or foreclosure. A chargee by deed has the statutory powers of sale and appointment of a receiver.

Dated (date)

THE SCHEDULE
(particulars of property charged)

Signature of borrower

4. Notice of Deposit of a Land (or Charge) Certificate (Form 85A)

H.M. LAND REGISTRY
Land Registration Acts 1925 to 1986

County and district (or London borough)
Title number
Property

Registered proprietor of land (or charge no.) [Full names of proprietor]
    (i) [I] [We] having accepted the [land certificate] [charge certificate
no. (   )] of the title above-mentioned by way of lien as security for money,
hereby apply for the following notice to be entered in the register
    Notice of deposit of [land certificate] [certificate of charge no.   ] with
(name, address of depositee)
    (ii) The Application is made by (name of solicitor, address)
Solicitor's reference (   ) Telephone No. (   )
(date)
Signature of applicant or solicitor

5. Notice of Deposit of a Land Certificate on a Dealing (Form 85C)

H.M. LAND REGISTRY
Land Registration Acts 1925 to 1986

County and district (or London Borough)
Title number
Property

    (i) I [name of borrower] of [address] having this day applied for registra-
tion as proprietor of the above-mentioned property under an instrument of
transfer dated the [date] and intending to deposit the certificate by way of
lien as security for money, hereby apply for the following notice to be
entered in the charges register:
    Notice of intended deposit of Land Certificate with [name and address of
lender]
    (ii) I hereby request that, on completion of the registration, the land cer-
tificate be delivered to [name of depositee, usually the lender's solicitor] of
[address]
[date]
[Signature of borrower]

C: Receipts: Surrenders and Releases

1. Skeleton Form of Receipt[97] on Discharge[98] of Mortgage

[I] [We] the [within named][99] [above named][99] Mortgagee(s) [(names) the Mortgagee(s) named in the Mortgage annexed][99] (identity of recipient as in forms (1) to (9) on pages 475–476).

HEREBY ACKNOWLEDGE that [I] [We] have this (date) received the sum of £(amount) representing the (balance remaining owing in respect of the)[1] principal money secured by the [within written] [above written] [annexed][2] [Legal Charge] [Mortgage] and by a further charge dated (date)[3] together with all interest and costs the payment having been made by (identity of payer as in forms on pp. 476–477 below) [the within named Borrower] [(name, address, description) the person entitled to the immediate equity of redemption][4]

AS WITNESS whereof [I] [We] have set [my] [our] hand(s) and seal(s)

Signed by the above named (name(s))   Signature(s) of recipient(s)
in the presence of

Signature, etc., of attesting witness

---

[97] The statutory form of receipt is form 2 of Sched. 3 to L.P.A. 1925. S.115(5)(*F*) provides that a receipt may be given in that form, with such variations and additions if any as are deemed expedient. L.P.A. 1925, S.120 and Form 5, Sched. 4. s.120 provides that a statutory mortgage may be surrendered or discharged by a receipt in that form with such variations or additions, if any, as circumstances may require.

[98] s.115 sets out the requirements of a statutory receipt extinguishing a single mortgage of unregistered land. S.115(10) excludes the operation of the section in respect of a charge or incumbrance registered under the Land Registration Act 1925.

[99] Alternatives arise from the provision in s.115(1) that the receipt may be written at the foot of, indorsed on or annexed to a mortgage for all the money hereby secured. The same subsection also provides that it must state the name of the person who pays the money and that it must be executed by the person who is legally entitled to give a receipt for the mortgage money. In *Simpson* v. *Geoghegan* [1934] W.N. 232 it was held that no seal is necessary: a document under hand is sufficient. But if payment is to be made to the mortgagor's solicitor (or licensed conveyancer, see Administration of Justice Act 1985, s.34(1)), he should produce a receipt under seal: see s.69 of L.P.A. 1925.

[1] Omit these words if no part of the principal has been repaid.

[2] See n. 99 above.

[3] This is a convenient way of referring to the further charge if there is only one such charge. If there are more, it may be more convenient to refer to them in a Schedule.

[4] s.115(2) provides that, if by the receipt the money appears to have been paid by a person who is not entitled to the immediate equity of redemption, the receipt shall operate as if the benefit of the mortgage had by deed been transferred to him, unless: (a) it is otherwise expressly provided; or (b) the mortgage is paid off out of capital money, or other money in the hands of a personal representative or trustee properly applicable for the discharge of the mortgage, and it is not expressly provided that the receipt is to operate as a transfer. A statutory receipt under the Building Societies Act 1986 (Sched. 4, para. 2) cannot operate as a transfer, as there is no requirement under that Act for the receipt to state the name of the payer; see *ante*, pp. 130 *et seq*. S.115(3) provides that the receipt does not operate as a transfer where there is no right to keep the mortgage alive. That provision preserves the rule in *Otter* v. *Vaux* (1856) 6 De G.M. & G. 638 that a mortgagor cannot keep a mortgage alive in his own favour so as to prejudice a subsequent incumbrancer.

2. Recitals

(a) Identity of Recipient

(1) Original mortgagee, an individual
   I, the within named mortgagee (name)

(2) Sole recipient, not the original mortgagee
   I, (name, address, description)

(3) Personal representatives of mortgagee[5]
   We (name, address, description of PR 1); and (name, address, description of PR 2) personal representatives of (name) late of (address, description) [whose will dated (date) was proved by us on (date) in the [Principal] [name of District] Probate Registry]

Or

[letters of administration to whose estate were granted to us on (date) out of the [Principal] [name of District] Probate Registry].

(4) Original corporate mortgagee
   I, the within named mortgagee (name of company)

(5) A company other than the original mortgagee
   I, (name of company) whose registered office is situated at (address of registered office)

(6) Duly-appointed liquidator
   If the recipient is in liquidation, add to (4) or (5) above:

   acting by (name, address, description) its duly appointed liquidator.[6]

(7) Survivor of joint beneficial mortgagees
   I, the within named (name) the surviving mortgagee

(8) Original trustees for sale
   We, the within named mortgagees

(9) Trustees for sale other than the original trustees
   We (name, address, description of T1) and (name, address, description of T2) (Trustees)

---

[5] After stating the name of the person making payment, the receipt should continue: AND DECLARE that we have not previously hereto given or made any conveyance or assent in respect of any legal estate in the property comprised in the said [Legal Charge] [Mortgage] or in any part thereof AND ACKNOWLEDGE the right of the said (name of payer) to the production of the said [probate of the said Will] [letters of administration] (the possession of which is retained by us) and to delivery of copies thereof

[6] A suitable testimonium and attestation clause where the receipt is given by a corporate mortgagee in liquidation is: IN WITNESS whereof (name of company) acting by its liquidator (name) has caused its common seal to be affixed hereunto this (date) THE COMMON SEAL of (name of company) was affixed to this receipt by the direction of (name of liquidator) and in his presence Signed by the above named (name of liquidator) in the presence of (name of attesting witness)

(b) Identity of Payer

Insert after the words "payment having been made by":

(1) The original borrower, an individual
   the within named borrower (name)

(2) Personal representatives of the original borrower

As in (3) replacing "us" by "them" and omitting the initial "We" and continue:

   out of a fund properly applicable to the discharge of the said [Legal Charge] [Mortgage][7-8]

(3) Original borrower, a body corporate
   the within named borrower (name of company)

(4) Liquidator of original corporate borrower
   the within named borrower (company name) acting by its duly appointed liquidator (name, address, description)

(5) Survivor of joint beneficial mortgagors
   the within named (name) the surviving borrower

(6) Trustees for sale
   the within named (name of T1) and (name of T2) the present trustees of the within mentioned [assent] [conveyance] [will] out of a fund properly applicable to the discharge of the said [Legal Charge] [Mortgage][7-8]

(7) Trustees of settlement, named in the mortgage
   the within named (name of T1) and (name of T2) the present trustees of the settlement referred to in the [within mentioned] [above written] [annexed] Vesting [Deed] [Assent] dated (date) and made between (names of parties) out of capital money properly applicable to the discharge of the said [Legal Charge] [Mortgage]

(8) Trustees of settlement, not named in the mortgage

Replace the words preceding "the present trustees" by:

   (name, address, description of T1) and (name, address, description of T2)

[7-8] See s.115(2) of L.P.A. 1925 and the note to Form 2, Sched. 3. It is considered that, where the statutory receipt is intended to extinguish the mortgage and the mortgagee is paid off out of capital or other money in the hands of a personal representative or trustee, properly applicable to the discharge of the mortgage, the receipt should state that the money is paid "out of a fund applicable to the discharge of the mortgage." The payer should, having accepted a receipt in that form, be estopped from denying the statement: but in any event the situation may be made plain by adding the words "and this receipt shall not operate as a transfer."

3. Release and Surrender

(b) Part of Mortgaged Property[9]

THIS SURRENDER AND RELEASE[10] made (date) BETWEEN (name, address, description) (the "Lender")[11] of the one part and (name, address, description) (the "Borrower") of the other part

SUPPLEMENTAL to a [Legal Charge] [Mortgage] dated (date) and made between the Lender of the one part and the Borrower of the other part

WHEREAS

(1) (recite state of mortgage debt)
(2) The Lender has agreed with the Borrower for the consideration hereinafter appearing to execute the surrender and release of such part of the mortgaged property as is described in the First Schedule hereto

Now in pursuance of the said agreement and in consideration of the sum of £(amount) paid by the Borrower to the Lender (the receipt whereof the Lender hereby acknowledges) in reduction of the said mortgage debt[12] THIS DEED WITNESSETH as follows:

The Lender as Mortgagee HEREBY SURRENDERS AND RELEASES unto the Borrower ALL THAT the property described in the First Schedule hereto TO HOLD the same unto the Borrower discharged from all principal money and interest secured by and from all claims and liability under the said [Legal Charge] [Mortgage] (and to the intent that the term of years created by the said mortgage shall as respects the property hereby surrendered and released merge in the reversion immediately expectant hereon and be extinguished)[13] PROVIDED ALWAYS that nothing

---

[9] A statutory receipt is not available where only part of the mortgage money is being repaid: L.P.A. 1925, s.115(1). A mortgage may be discharged by statutory receipt (before the conveyance) where the whole of the mortgaged property is being released so that the mortgagor can sell free from the mortgage: alternatively the mortgagee can join in the conveyance to surrender and release the property sold. See Hallett, *Conveyancing Precedents* (1965), precedents 48–51 at pp. 269–273.

[10] Although such a deed is often called a reconveyance (by contrast with a statutory receipt) there is nothing to reconvey where the mortgage was by way of legal charge, while if it was by demise or subdemise the term ceases on satisfaction. L.P.A. 1925, s.116 provides as follows: "Without prejudice to the right of a tenant for life or other person having only a limited interest in the equity of redemption to require a mortgage to be kept alive by transfer or otherwise, a mortgage term shall, when the money secured by the mortgage has been discharged, become a satisfied term and cease."

[11] Or "the Lender" if he is the original mortgagee and so referred to in the mortgage.

[12] It is a general rule that if payments are made and not specifically appropriated to either the principal or the interest of the mortgage, they are applied first in reduction or extinction of the interest: but the rule yields to a contrary intention expressed in the deed. See *Chase* v. *Box* (1702) Freem. Ch. 261: *Parr's Banking Co.* v. *Yates* [1898] 2 Q.B. 460 at 466, C.A.; *Wrigley* v. *Gill* [1906] 1 Ch. 165, C.A.

[13] Include the words in brackets where the mortgage is by demise.

herein contained shall prejudice or affect the security of the Mortgagee under the said [Legal Charge] [Mortgage] in respect of property not surrendered or released for the payment to the Lender of so much of the said principal moneys as remains owing thereunder and the interest thereon

The Lender HEREBY ACKNOWLEDGES[14] the right of the Borrower to the production of the documents mentioned in the Second Schedule hereto (the possession of which is retained by the Lender) and to delivery of copies hereof

IN WITNESS whereof the parties[15] have hereunto set their respective hands and seals (date)

SIGNED SEALED and DELIVERED
by the above named (name)
in the presence of

(Signature of attesting witness,
address, description)

THE FIRST SCHEDULE

(Description of the property released)

THE SECOND SCHEDULE

(Documents retained by lender)

(b) *Whole of Mortgaged Property*[16]

THIS SURRENDER AND RELEASE made (date)
BETWEEN
(parties as in previous precedent)

WITNESSETH that in consideration of the sum of £(amount) representing the (balance owing in respect of the)[17] principal money secured by the within written [Legal Charge] [Mortgage] together with all interest and costs (the receipt whereof the Lender hereby acknowledges) the Lender as Mortgagee[18] HEREBY SURRENDERS AND RELEASES unto the Borrower ALL THAT the property mortgaged by the said [Legal Charge] [Mortgage] TO HOLD

(*continue as in previous precedent, including the words in round brackets*

---

[14] This acknowledgment is for the benefit of a purchaser of the released property. The borrower cannot give it, since he does not have them. The right to such acknowledgment is recognised: *Yates* v. *Plumbe* (1854) 2 Sm. & G. 174.
[15] Both parties should execute the deed.
[16] In a form suitable for indorsement on the original legal charge or mortgage.
[17] Omit these words if no part of the principal has been repaid.
[18] The words "as Mortgagee" imply a covenant that he has not encumbered the property: L.P.A. 1925, s.76(1)(*F*) and Pt. VI of Sched. 2.

if the mortgage is by demise, but omitting the proviso and acknowledgment for production)

IN WITNESS, etc.

(c) Property Charged as Collateral security

THIS DEED OF RELEASE made (date)
BETWEEN (name, address, description) "the Lender")
          (name, address, description) ("the Borrower")[19]
          (name, address, description) ("the Mortgagor")

WHEREAS

   (1) By a mortgage ("the Principal Mortgage") dated (date) and made between the Borrower and the Lender certain property was charged by way of legal mortgage with the payment to the Lender of the principal money interest and other moneys mentioned in the Principal Mortgage

   (2) By a mortgage ("the Collateral Mortgage") dated (date) and made between the Mortgagor and the Lender the property described in the Schedule hereto ("the Property") was charged by way of legal mortgage with the payments to the Lender of the moneys secured by the Principal Mortgage (and the Mortgagor covenanted with the Lender as security for the Borrower to pay the moneys secured by and to observe and perform the covenants and other conditions contained in the Principal Mortgage)[20]

   (3) The Lender being satisfied that the property comprised in the Principal Mortgage is a sufficient security for the moneys remaining due thereunder has agreed to release the Property from the Collateral Mortgage (and the Mortgagor from his covenants contained herein)[20] (upon the payment of £(amount))[21]

(The Lender HEREBY ACKNOWLEDGES the receipt of £(amount) paid to him on (date) by [the Borrower] [the Mortgagor])[21]

The Lender as Mortgagee releases the Property to the Mortgagor freed and discharged from the Collateral Mortgage and all principal money interest and other moneys secured by it and from all claims and liability under it (and releases the Mortgagor from all moneys now or in the future payable under the Principal Mortgage and from all the covenants on the part of the Mortgagor contained therein (or in the Collateral Mortgage))[22]

IN WITNESS, etc.

---

[19] He needs to be a party only if he made the payment to the Lender.
[20] These words are included only if the Mortgagor has covenanted with the lender as surety for the borrower.
[21] Include if appropriate.
[22] See n. 20 above.

(d) Rights of Occupation under the Matrimonial Homes Act 1983[23]

THIS DEED[24] OF RELEASE is made (date)
BETWEEN (the spouse entitled to the charge—name, address, description)
("the Wife" or "the Husband") of the one part
and (the other spouse—name, address, description)
("the Husband" or "the Wife") of the other part

WHEREAS

(1) By a conveyance[25] dated ( ) and made between (names, addresses, descriptions of parties) the property described in the Schedule hereto ("the Property") was conveyed[25] to (name of purchaser) in fee simple (subject as mentioned in the Schedule but otherwise free from incumbrances)[26]

(2) The Wife[27] is entitled to a charge ("the Wife's charge") on the property by virtue of the Matrimonial Homes Act 1983 and such charge is registered under the Land Charges Act 1972[28] as a land charge class F under registration number (000)

(3) The Wife has agreed with the Husband to release the property from the Wife's rights of occupation in respect of the property and the Wife's charge

(4) In the negotiations leading up to the said agreement the Wife (as she hereby admits) has been advised by (name and address of solicitors) as to the effect of this release

NOW in pursuance of the said agreement the Wife as mortgagee HEREBY RELEASES the property from the Wife's rights of occupation and from the Wife's charge to the intent that the Husband shall hold the property freed and discharged from the Wife's rights of occupation and the Wife's charge (and UNDERTAKES with the Husband to apply to H.M.

---

[23] Repealing the Matrimonial Homes Act 1967. The rights of occupation are set out in s.1(1), (10) of the Matrimonial Homes Act 1983. The priority date of the charge is the latest of the three dates specified in s.2(1) of the 1983 Act. See also n. 30 below and *ante*, pp. 170–172 and p. 319.

[24] s.6(1) of the 1983 Act provides that a release may be in writing, and may apply to part only of the dwelling-house.

[25] Or "transfer," "transferred" as the case may be.

[26] Include if appropriate.

[27] In the remainder of this precedent the wife is treated as being entitled to the charge.

[28] s.2(8)(*g*) of the 1983 Act provides that, where the title to the legal estate by virtue of which a spouse is entitled to occupy a dwelling-house is registered under the Land Registration Act 1925, registration of a land charge affecting the dwelling-house by virtue of the 1983 Act shall be effected by registering a notice under the 1925 Act. s.2(8)(*b*) provides that a spouse's rights of occupation shall not be an overriding interest within the meaning of the Act affecting that dwelling-house notwithstanding that the spouse is in actual occupation of the dwelling-house; and s.2(9) provides that a spouse's rights of occupation (whether or not constituting a charge) shall not entitle that spouse to lodge a caution under s.54 of the Land Registration Act 1925. The recital must be adapted if the title is registered.

Land Registry for the cancellation of the registration of the Wife's charge)[29]

IN WITNESS, etc.

THE SCHEDULE
(Description of property)

4. Legal Charge with Spouse Joining in to Postpone Charge to which he or she is Entitled under the Matrimonial Homes Act 1983[30]

THIS LEGAL CHARGE is made (date)
BETWEEN (name, address, description) ("the Borrower")[31] of the first part
    and (name, address, description) ("the Lender")[31] of the second part
    and (name, address, description) (["the Wife"] ["the Husband"]) of the third part

WHEREAS

(1) as in recital (1) on page 480.
(2) as in recital (2) on page 480.
(3) The Lender has agreed to lend to the Borrower the sum of £(the amount) upon having the repayment thereof with interest thereon at the rate hereinafter mentioned secured in the manner herein appearing such security to have priority to the Wife's Charge[32]
(4) The Wife has agreed to join herein for the purpose of postponing the Wife's Charge to the security hereby created in manner hereinafter appearing

NOW in pursuance of the said agreement and in consideration of the sum of £(amount) paid by the Lender to the Borrower the receipt of which the Borrower hereby acknowledges)
THIS DEED WITNESSETH as follows:

(1) The Borrower HEREBY COVENANTS with the Lender to pay to the Lender on (date) the sum of £(amount advanced) with interest thereon from the date hereof at the rate of (rate) per cent. per annum and also if the said sum of £(amount advanced) shall not be so paid to the Lender (as well after as before any

---

[29] Land Charges Act 1972, s.16(1); Land Charges Rules 1974 (S.I. 1974 No. 1286); Land Registration (Matrimonial Homes) Rules 1983 (S.I. 1983 No. 40).
[30] s.6(3) of the Matrimonial Homes Act 1983 provides that a spouse entitled by virtue of s.2 of that Act to a charge on an estate or interest of the other spouse may agree in writing that any other charge on or interest in that estate rank in priority to the charge to which that spouse is so entitled.
[31] Insert if necessary the reference to persons deriving title under these parties.
[32] See n. 27 above.

judgment) interest at the rate aforesaid by equal (interval) instalments on the (payment dates) in each year on the principal moneys or such part hereof as shall from time to time remain owing

(2) For the purpose of postponing the Wife's Charge to the security hereby created but not further or otherwise the Wife as mortgagee HEREBY RELEASES and the Borrower as beneficial owner HEREBY CHARGES BY WAY OF LEGAL MORTGAGE All That the property (subject as mentioned in the said Schedule) with the payment to the Lender of the principal moneys interest or other moneys hereby covenanted to be paid by the Borrower or otherwise hereby secured PROVIDED THAT if the Borrower shall on (date) pay to the Lender the said sum of £(amount advanced) thereon from the date hereof at the said rate the Lender will at the request and cost of the Borrower duly discharge this security. Nothing herein contained shall as between the Borrower and the Wife affect or prejudice any of the rights or remedies of the Wife under the Wife's Charge which shall remain in force subject to this Legal Charge and the postponement of the Wife's Charge shall be deemed to relate only to the moneys expressed to be secured by this deed and shall not in respect of any further moneys advanced by the Lender be deemed to confer on the Lender any like right of priority over the Wife's Charge

IN WITNESS, etc.

THE SCHEDULE
(description of property)

D: TRANSFERS

1. Skeleton Form of Transfer[33]

THIS TRANSFER OF MORTGAGE made (date)
BETWEEN[34]
(parties: either Mortgagee (1), Transferee (2)
                 or Mortgagee (1), Borrower (2), Transferee (3))
SUPPLEMENTAL TO[35] a [Legal Charge] [Mortgage] dated (date)
between (name of borrower) of the one part and the Mortgagee of the
other part[36] affecting (short particulars of the mortgaged property) (or as
in forms on page 483–484).
WHEREAS
(recitals)[37]
(see page 484–485).
TESTATUM
(*in statutory form or in alternative form where there are recitals*).
IN WITNESS, etc.

    (To be executed and attested
    by the mortgagee, the borrower if a party
    and the transferee if desired)

---

[33] The skeleton is based on the statutory form (Form No. 1, Sched. 3 to L.P.A. 1925). In that
form there is no provision for the borrower to be made a party. s.95(1) of L.P.A. 1925 provides that, where the mortgagor is entitled to redeem, he may require the mortgagee,
instead of reconveying or surrendering, and on the terms on which he would be bound to
reconvey or surrender, to assign the mortgage debt, and convey the mortgaged property to
any third person as the mortgagor directs, and the mortgagee is bound to assign and convey
accordingly notwithstanding any stipulation to the contrary.

    Although this is the usual case where the borrower is a party to a transfer, it is always
advisable, if he is willing, that he should be made a party. This enables him to admit the
state of the mortgage debt and interest and he is fixed with notice of the transfer. If he is
not a party, the transferee should inquire from him as to the true state of the mortgage
account between him and the mortgagee. The transferee takes subject to the true state of
the account (see *Matthews* v. *Wallwyn* (1798) 4 Ves. 118; *Chambers* v. *Godwin* (1804) 9
Ves. 254; *Dixon* v. *Winch* [1900] 1 Ch. 736; *Turner* v. *Smith* [1901] 1 Ch. 213; *De Lisle* v.
Union Bank of Scotland [1914] 1 Ch. 22; *Parker* v. *Jackson* [1936] 2 All E.R. 281) though,
in the absence of notice to the contrary he is entitled to rely on the receipt clause in the
mortgage deed as showing that the original amount was in fact advanced: see *Bickerton* v.
Walker (1885) 31 Ch.D. 151; *Powell* v. *Browne* (1907) 97 L.T. 854; and s.68(1) of L.P.A.
1925. A mortgagee is a "purchaser": s.205(1)(xxi).

[34] It is not always necessary to define the parties as including persons deriving title under
them. Where there is a transfer of the whole mortgage debt and the borrower is not a party
there is no need so to define the mortgagee or the transferee. If the borrower joins in, both
the borrower and the transferee should be so defined, to show that the admission by the
borrower of the state of the mortgage debt is intended to bind persons taking under him
and to benefit the transferee and persons taking under the transferee.

[35] Alternative forms on pp. 483–484.

[36] If there is a further charge or further charges insert here the following: "and to a further
charge dated (date) and made between (parties)" or "and to the further charges referred to
in the Schedule hereto."

[37] See Form (1) pp. 484 *et seq.*

2. Further Charge(s)

(1) One further charge transferred

SUPPLEMENTAL TO a legal Charge dated (date) and to a further charge dated (date) both made between (name of borrower) of the one part and (name of mortgagee) of the other part and affecting (short particulars of the mortgaged property)

(2) Several further charges transferred

SUPPLEMENTAL to the Legal Charge and to the several Further Charges specified herein

3. Recitals

(1) State of mortgage debt[38]

There is now owing upon the security of the said Legal Charge (as the Borrower hereby admits) the principal sum of £(amount) [but all interest has been paid up to the date hereof] [together with the sum of £(amount of interest) for interest thereon]

(2) State of mortgage debt

If Form (1) or (2) on pages 483–484 are used, as above except:

 (i) replacing the words "upon the security of the said Legal Charge" by the words "to the Mortgagee"
 (ii) inserting the word "aggregate" before "principal"

(3) Agreement to transfer mortgage

The Transferee has agreed (at the request of the Borrower)[39] to pay to the Mortgagee the sum of £(amount) upon having such transfer of the benefit of the [Legal Charge] [Mortgage] (and Further Charge(s)) as is hereinafter contained

(4) Agreement by transferee to make further advance

The Transferee has at the request of the Borrower agreed to pay to the Mortgagee the said sum of £(amount of principal owing) and to advance to the Borrower the further sum of £(amount of intended further advance) upon having such transfer of the benefit of the said [Legal Charge] [Mortgage] as is hereinafter contained and upon having the repayment of the aggregate sum of £(aggregate of principal owing and intended further advance) with interest at the rate hereinafter mentioned secured in manner hereinafter appearing

---

[38] The recital of the state of the mortgage debt will bind the mortgagor (and his successors on title if "mortgagor" is appropriately defined.

[39] Omit these words if the transfer is not made at the borrower's request.

(a) Transferor's Title

(1) Transferee from original mortgagee
The benefit of the said [Legal Charge] [Mortgage] (and Further Charges) [is now] [remains] vested in the Mortgagee[40]

(2) Personal representatives of original mortgagee
[The Mortgagees proved the Will of the said (name of original mortgagee) in] [Letters of administration to the estate of the said (name of original mortgagee) were granted to the Mortgagees out of] the [Principal] [name of district] Probate Registry on (date)

(3) Personal representatives of transferee from original mortgagee
The benefit of the said [Legal Charge] [Mortgage] is vested in the Mortgagees as personal representatives of the late (name of transferee) and *(continue as in (2) inserting the name of the transferee as appropriate)*

(b) Personal Representative Transfers[41] Mortgage to Beneficiary

(1) Death of deceased where original mortgagee, and title of personal representatives
The (name of original mortgagee) died on (date) and . . . *(Continue as in (2) or (3) above)*

(2) Death of deceased and his entitlement to the benefit of the mortgage

    (a) the (name of deceased) was at the date of his death hereinafter recited entitled to the benefit of the said [Legal Charge] [Mortgage]
    (b) the (name of deceased) died on (date) and . . .

(Continue as in (2) or (3) above)

(3) Payment of debts by personal representatives
The personal representatives have duly paid and discharged all debts funeral and testamentary expenses and taxes payable out of the estate of the said (name)

(4) Beneficiary's entitlement
In the administration of the said estate the Beneficiary is entitled to have the [Legal Charge] [Mortgage] transferred to him and the personal representatives have agreed to make this transfer accordingly

---

[40] It is not necessary to recite the immediate title of the transferor: *cf. Encyclopedia of Forms and Precedents* (4th ed.), Form 12.40.
[41] The personal representatives can, of course, assent rather than transfer.

(5) Recital where transfer is made on the appointment of new trustees

The Transferees have become jointly entitled in equity[42] to the benefit of the said [Legal Charge] [Mortgage]

4. Testatum Forms

(1) Testatum as in statutory form

WITNESSETH that in consideration of the sums of £(amount of principal) and £(amount of current interest) now paid by the Transferee to the Mortgagee being the respective amounts of the mortgage money and interest owing in respect of the said [Legal Charge] [Mortgage] (the receipt of which sums the Mortgagee hereby acknowledges)[43] the Mortgagee as Mortgagee HEREBY CONVEYS AND TRANSFERS to the Transferee the benefit of the said [Legal Charge] [Mortgage]

(2) Alternative form of testatum where agreements have been recited

Now in pursuance of the said agreement and in consideration of the sum of £(amount) now paid by the Transferee to the Mortgagee (the receipt whereof the Mortgagee hereby acknowledges) THIS DEED WITNESSETH (that the Mortgagee as Mortgagee HEREBY CONVEYS AND TRANSFERS to the Transferee the benefit of the said [Legal Charge] [Mortgage])

In (3) and (4) below, replace the words in parentheses by "as follows" and add the following clauses as necessary:

(3) Transfer made at borrower's request[44]

   (a) The Mortgagee as Mortgagee by the direction of the Borrower directing as Beneficial Owner HEREBY CONVEYS AND TRANSFERS to the Transferee the benefit of the said [Legal Charge] [Mortgage]

   (b) The same covenants shall be implied in this Deed by virtue of the

---

[42] It is still usual to recite the fact that the transferees are jointly entitled in equity. Such a recital is a convenient method of indicating that the trustees are entitled to a transfer, without referring to any trusts: the recital itself is not notice of a trust (see *Re Harman and Uxbridge Railway* (1883) 24 Ch.D. 720 and *Carritt* v. *Real and Personal Advance Co.* (1889) 42 Ch.D. 263). Apart from this, the trusts are kept off the title by s.113(1) of L.P.A. 1925 and, by virtue of that section, a purchaser who discovers the existence of a trust in the course of the examination of title no longer has to satisfy himself that the trustees have been properly appointed: *cf. Re Blaiberg and Abrahams' Contract* [1899] 2 Ch. 340.

[43] If the borrower is a party, the concluding words of the phrase in brackets should read "the Mortgagee and the Borrower hereby acknowledge."

[44] The purpose of clause (b) is that, if the borrower directs simply as beneficial owner, the covenants implied on his part are merely those contained in a conveyance for value other than a mortgage: See s.76(1)(A) of L.P.A. 1925 and Pt. I, Sched. 2, for these, and s.76(1)(C) and Pt. III, Sched. 2 for the unqualified covenants implied on the part of a mortgagor under a fresh mortgage and on which the transferee should insist. A transfer of a mortgage is a conveyance, not a mortgage.

Borrower directing as Beneficial Owner in manner aforesaid as would be implied therein if the Deed were a conveyance by way of mortgage

(4) Transfer made by personal representatives

    (a) In exercise of powers vested in them in this behalf enabling[45] the Mortgagees as personal representatives[46] of the said (name of original mortgagee or transferee, as the case may be) deceased HEREBY CONVEY AND TRANSFER to the Transferee the benefit of the said [Legal Charge] [Mortgage]

    (b) The Mortgagees HEREBY DECLARE that they have not previously hereto given or made any conveyance or assent in respect of any legal estate in the mortgaged property or any part thereof[47]

    (c) the Mortgagees HEREBY ACKNOWLEDGE the right of the Transferee to the production of [the probate of the said Will][48] [the said letters of administration] (the possession of which is retained by the Mortgagees) and to delivery of copies thereof

Form of testatum, transfer on appointment of new trustees

Now in consideration of the premises THIS DEED WITNESSETH that the Mortgagees as Mortgagees HEREBY CONVEY AND TRANSFER to the Transferees the benefit of the said [Legal Charge] [Mortgage]

Form of testatum, transferee making further advance

Now in pursuance of the said agreement and in consideration of the sum of £(amount of principal owing) now paid by the Transferee to the Mortgagee (the receipt of which sum the Mortgagee hereby acknowledges) and of the sum of £(amount of further advance) now paid by the Transferee to the Borrower (the payment and receipt respectively of which sums of £(principal) and £(further advances) making together the aggregate sum of £(total of principal and further advance) the Borrower hereby acknowledges THIS DEED WITNESSETH AS FOLLOWS

---

[45] Where the transfer is made on sale, the inclusion of these words enables reliance to be placed on s.17 of the Trustee Act 1925, which reads: "No purchaser or mortgagee, paying or advancing money on a sale or mortgage purporting to be made under any trust or power vested in trustees, shall be concerned to see that such money is wanted, or that no more than is wanted is raised, or otherwise as to the application thereof."

    By s.68(17) of that Act, "trustee" where the context admits includes a personal representative.

[46] Implying a covenant that they have not created an incumbrance.

[47] This clause is desirable since it protects a purchaser against any beneficiary who has taken an earlier assent without obtaining an indorsement on the grant of probate or letters of administration. s.36 of the Administration of Estates Act 1925 applies since the transfer is a conveyance. A transferee for value will obtain a good title against anyone except a previous purchaser, provided that no notice of a previous assent or conveyance affecting the estate has been placed on or annexed to the probate or letters of administration. A personal representative making a false statement in regard to such matters is liable as if he had made a false statutory declaration.

[48] Or "the documents mentioned in the Schedule hereto" if there are other documents retained by the personal representatives.

(a) (Clause (a) of Form (3), page 486)
(b) (Clause (b) of Form (3), page 486)

Borrower's covenant to repay

(c) The Borrower HEREBY COVENANTS with the Transferee to pay to the Transferee (date) the said aggregate sum of £(total, as above) being the outstanding principal sum of £(principal) together with the further advance of £(further advance) AND FURTHER if the said aggregate sum shall not be so paid to pay to the Transferee interest at the rate of (rate) per cent. per annum by equal [interval] instalments on the (payment dates) in every year on the principal moneys for the time being remaining due on this security (or under the said Legal Charge)[49] or on any order or judgment which may be made or recovered hereafter

Charge

(d) The Borrower as Beneficial owner HEREBY CHARGES BY WAY OF LEGAL MORTGAGE the premises contained in the said Legal Charge (subject as therein provided)[50] with the payment to the Transferee of the principal money and interest hereinbefore covenanted so to be paid [and all other moneys secured by this Deed]

Covenants in Legal Charge to apply to the deed

(e) The covenants powers and provisions contained in the said Legal Charge shall operate and take effect in like manner for protecting and enforcing this security as if such covenants powers and provisions were herein repeated.[51]

---

[49] To make it clear that the original legal charge is still subsisting. Since, by s.114(1)(b) of L.P.A. 1925, the transferee has the benefit of the borrower's covenants with the mortgagee, there is strictly no need for a covenant to pay the aggregate (rather than the further) sum: but in this way the borrower is made liable to the transferee as if he had taken a fresh mortgage.

[50] These words may be included where the land is affected by easements or restrictive covenants, as they limit liability on the covenants for title.

[51] This clause should be inserted if the legal charge contains provisions other than the covenant for payment and the charge itself.

FORMS

Statutory Forms

1. Law of Property Act 1925, Schedule 3

(a) Form No. 1: Transfer of Mortgage (s.114)

This Transfer of Mortgage made the   day of   19   between *M.* of [&c.] of the one part and *T.* of [&c.] of the other part, supplemental to a Mortgage dated [&c.], and made between [&c.], and to a Further Charge dated [&c.], and made between [&c.] affecting &c. (*here state short particulars of the mortgaged property*).
WITNESSETH that in consideration in the sums of £   and £   (for interest) now paid by *T.* to *M.*, being the respective amounts of the mortgage money and interest owing in respect of the said mortgage and further charge (the receipt of which sums *M.* hereby acknowledges) *M.*, as mortgagee, hereby conveys and transfers to *T.* the benefit of the said mortgage and further charge.
  In witness, &c.

(b) Form No. 2: Receipt on Discharge of a Mortgage (s.115)

I, *A.B.* of [&c.] hereby acknowledge that I have this   day of   19 , received the sum of £   representing the [aggregate] [balance remaining owing in respect of the] principal money secured by the within [above] written [annexed] mortgage [and by a further charge dated, &c., *or otherwise as required*] together with all interest and costs, the payment having been made by *C.D.* of [&c.] and *E.F.* of [&c.]
  As witness, &c.
  Note.—If the persons are not entitled to the equity of redemption state that they are paying the money out of a fund applicable to the discharge of the mortgage.

2. Law of Property Act 1925, Schedule 4

(a) Form No. 1: Statutory Charge by Way of Legal Mortgage (s.117)

This Legal Charge made by way of Statutory Mortgage the   day of   19 , between *A.* of [&c.] of the one part and *M.* of [&c.] of the other part Witnesseth that in consideration of the sum of £   now paid to *A.* by *M.* of which sum *A.* hereby acknowledges the receipt *A.* As Mortgagor and As Beneficial Owner hereby charges by way of legal mortgage

All That [&c.] with the payment to *M.* on the day of 19 , of the principal sum of £ as the mortgage money with interest thereon at the rate of per centum per annum.

In witness, &c.

Note.—Variations in this and the subsequent forms in this Schedule to be made, if required, for leasehold land or for giving effect to special arrangements. *M.* will be in the same position as if the Charge had been effected by a demise of freeholds or a subdemise of leaseholds.

(b) Form No. 2: Statutory Transfer, Mortgagor not Joining (s.118)

This Transfer of Mortgage made by way of statutory transfer the day of 19 , between *M.* of [&c.] of the one part and *T.* of [&c.] of the other part supplemental to a legal charge made by way of statutory mortgage dated [&c.] and made [&c.] Witnesseth that in consideration of the sum of £ now paid to *M.* by *T.* (being the aggregate amount of £ mortgage money and £ interest due in respect of the said legal charge of which sum *M.* hereby acknowledges the receipt) *M.* as Mortgagee hereby conveys and transfers to *T.* the benefit of the said legal charge.

In witness, &c.

Note.—This and the next two forms also apply to a transfer of a statutory mortgage made before the commencement of this Act, which will then be referred to as a mortgage instead of a legal charge.

(c) Form No. 3: Statutory Transfer, a Covenantor Joining (s.118)

This Transfer of Mortgage made by way of statutory transfer the day of 19 , between *A.* of [&c.] of the first part *B.* of [&c.] of the second part and *C.* of [&c.] of the third part Supplemental to a Legal Charge made by way of statutory mortgage dated [&c.] and made [&c.] Witnesseth that in consideration of the sum of £ now paid by *A.* to *C.* (being the mortgage money due in respect of the said Legal Charge no interest being now due or payable thereon of which sum *A.* hereby acknowledges the receipt) *A.* as Mortgagee with the concurrence of *B.* who joins herein as covenantor hereby conveys and transfers to *C.* the benefit of the said Legal Charge.

In witness, &c.

(d) Form No. 4: Statutory Transfer and Mortgage Combined (ss.117, 118)

This Transfer and Legal Charge is made by way of statutory transfer and mortgage the day of 19 , between *A.* of [&c.] of the first part *B.* of [&c.] of the second part and *C.* of [&c.] of the third part Supplemental to a Legal Charge made by way of statutory mortgage dated [&c.] and made [&c.] Whereas a principal sum of £ only remains due in respect of the said Legal Charge as the mortgage money and no interest is now due thereon And Whereas *B.* is seised in fee simple of the land comprised in the said Legal Charge subject to that Charge.

Now this Deed Witnesseth as follows:

1. In consideration of the sum of £   now paid to *A.* by *C.* (the receipt and payment of which sum *A.* & *B.* hereby respectively acknowledge) *A.* as mortgagee hereby conveys and transfers to *C.* the benefit of the said Legal Charge.

2. For the consideration aforesaid B† as beneficial owner hereby charges by way of legal mortgage All the premises comprised in the said Legal Charge with the payment to *C.* on the   day of   19   of‡ the sum of £   as the mortgage money with interest thereon at the rate of   per centum per annum In Witness &c. [or in the case of a further advance after "acknowledge" at *insert* "and of the further sum of £   now paid by *C.* to *B.* of which sum *B.* hereby acknowledges the receipt" *also at* † *before* "as beneficial owner" *insert* "as mortgagor and" *as well as where B. is not the original mortgagor. And after* "of" *at* ‡ *insert* "the sums of £   and £   making together"].

Note.—Variations to be made, as required, in case of the deed being by indorsement, or in respect of any other thing.

(e) Form No. 5: Receipt on Discharge of Statutory Legal Charge or Mortgage (s.120)

I *A.B.* of [&c.] hereby acknowledge that I have this   day of   19 received the sum of £   representing the [aggregate] [balance remaining owing in respect of the] mortgage money secured by the [annexed] within [above] written statutory legal charge [*or* statutory mortgage] [and by the further statutory charge dated [&c.] *or otherwise as required*] together with all interest and costs the payment having been made by *C.D.* of [&c.] and E.F. of [&c.]

As witness &c.

Note.—If the persons paying are not entitled to the equity of redemption state that they are paying the money out of a fund applicable to the discharge of the statutory legal charge or mortgage.

REGISTERED LAND FORMS

1. Charge of Whole of Land in Title (Form 45)

H.M. LAND REGISTRY
Land Registration Acts 1925 to 1986
[County and district] [London Borough]
Title no.
Short description of property
(date) In consideration of £(amount) the receipt whereof is hereby acknowledged I (name, address of borrower) (capacity) hereby charge the land comprised in the title(s) above mentioned with the payment to (name, address of lender) on the (date) of the principal sum of £(amount) with interest at (rate) per cent. per annum payable on (payment dates)
(To be executed by the borrower and attested)

2. Stipulations to be Inserted in a Registered Charge
(Forms 45A, B, C with Variations)

(a) Stipulations Negativing the Covenants Implied in Charges by Section 28 of the Land Registration Act 1925

1. No covenant is hereby implied to pay the principal or interest secured by the charge.
2. No covenant is hereby implied as to payment of rent or performance or observance of the covenants or conditions of the registered lease, or as to indemnity in respect thereof.

(b) Stipulations Excluding the Provisions of Section 34 of the Land Registration Act 1925

1. The lender shall have no power to enter upon the land.
2. The lender shall have no power to enforce foreclosure or sale of the land.
3. The lender shall have no power of sale.
4. The lender may exercise the power of sale without notice.

(c) Stipulations Altering the Priority of Charges under Section 19 of the Land Registration Act 1925

1. This charge shall rank *pari passu* with a charge of even date in favour of [*chargee*] of [*address, etc.*] to secure £ . . .

2. This charge shall be the first [*or* second] [*or* third] in order of priority of three charges of even date, one of which is to (*chargee*) of (*address, etc.*) to secure £ . . . , another is to (*chargee*) of (*address, etc.*) to secure £ . . . , and the other is this charge:

3. This charge shall have priority to a charge dated . . . and registered on the . . . day of . . . in favour of (*chargee*) of (*address, etc.*) for £ . . .

4. All monies up to but not exceeding a total of £ . . . advanced on the security of charge dated . . . and registered on the . . . day of . . . in favour of (*chargee*) of (*address, etc.*) shall have priority over this charge.

(d) Miscellaneous Stipulations

1. The rate of interest to be secured by the charge shall be reduced to . . . per cent. in every half-year [quarter] [other interval] in which it shall be paid within [seven] days after it becomes due.

2. None of the principal secured by the charge shall be called in till the . . . day of . . . unless the interest [*or* some instalment of interest] shall fail to be paid for . . . days after it becomes due [unless the said [*registered proprietor*] shall fail to observe some one of his obligations hereunder other than those relating to the payment of principal].

3. None of the principal money secured by this charge shall be paid off before the . . . day of . . . unless the proprietor of the charge shall be willing to accept it.

4. If the interest secured by the charge shall be paid within . . . days after it becomes due the principal shall be payable by instalments of £ . . . each, to be paid on the . . . day of . . . and the . . . day of . . . in every year, the first of such instalments to be paid on the . . . day of . . . save that on failure of payment of any instalment within . . . days after it becomes due the whole of the principal remaining owing on the said security shall become payable at once. PROVIDED nevertheless that the whole or any part (not less than £ . . . at any one time) of the above mentioned principal may be paid off on giving one month's notice in writing of the intention to do so and on paying up all arrears of interest that may be due at the time of such payment of principal.

5. The said (*chargee*) reserves the right to consolidate this charge with a charge dated . . . and registered on the . . . day of . . . as entry No. . . . in the charges register of Title No. . . . and of which he is registered as proprietor.

3. Transfer of Registered Charge (Form 54) (Clause 2 if Borrower's Consent Required. Heading as in Form 45 above, page 492)

(date)

 (1) In consideration of £(amount) the receipt of which is hereby acknowledged I (name, address of registered proprietor of charge) (capacity) hereby transfer to (name, address of transferee) the charge dated (date) and registered on (date) of which I am the registered proprietor

 (2) I (name, address of registered proprietor of land) hereby consent to this transfer

To be executed by the chargee (and the proprietor of the land) and attested

4. Discharge of Registered Charge (Form 53) (Heading as in Form 45 above, page 492)

(date) I (name, address of registered proprietor) hereby admit that the charge dated (date) and registered on (date) of which I am the proprietor has been discharged

5. Discharge of Registered Charge by a Corporation (Form 53 (Co))

(date) (Name of corporation, registered chargee) of (address) hereby admits . . . [continue as in Form 53 above, replacing "I am" by "it is"]

The Common Seal of [name of corporation]

was hereto affixed (by order of the Board of Directors)

in the presence of (proper officers)

JURISDICTION AND PROCEDURE IN MORTGAGE ACTIONS

Jurisdiction of High Court

Generally, the High Court has jurisdiction in *any* action (whether begun by Writ or Originating Summons) by a mortgagee or mortgagor, or by any person having the right to foreclose or redeem any mortgage, being an action in which there is a claim for any of the following reliefs,[1] namely:

(a) payment of monies secured by the mortgage[2];

(b) sale of the mortgaged property;

(c) foreclosure[3];

(d) delivery of possession (whether before or after foreclosure or without foreclosure) to the mortgagee by the mortgagor or by any other person who is or who is alleged to be in possession of the property;

(e) redemption[4];

(f) reconveyance of the property or its release from the security;

(g) delivery of possession by the mortgagee[5].

In this context "mortgage" includes a legal and an equitable mortgage and a legal and an equitable charge, and references to a mortgagor, mortgagee and mortgaged property shall be construed accordingly, and any such action is known as a "mortgage action."[6]

Further, and without prejudice to section 61 of the Supreme Court Act 1981 (which provides for the assignment to the Chancery Division of causes or matters for the purposes of, among others, the redemption or forclosure of mortgages and the sale and distribution of the proceeds of property subject to any lien or charge) any action in which there is a claim for:

(a) payment of monies secured by a mortgage of any real or lease hold property; or

(b) delivery of possession (where before or after foreclosure) to the mortgagee of any such property by the mortgagor or by any other person who is or is alleged to be in possession of the property,

shall be assigned to the Chancery Division[7].

---

[1] R.S.C. Ord. 88, r.1.
[2] See *ante*, pp. 263 *et seq.*
[3] See *ante*, pp. 247 *et seq.*
[4] See *ante*, pp. 313 *et seq.*
[5] See *ante*, pp. 240 *et seq.*
[6] R.S.C. Ord. 88, r.1(2), (3).
[7] *Ibid.* Ord. 88, r.2.

JURISDICTION OF COUNTY COURT

In all claims for possession of a *dwelling-house* the county court has, with certain exceptions, exclusive jurisdiction[8]. The exceptions are where:

    (a) the property is situated in the Greater London area; or

    (b) the net annual value for rating of the land is above the County Court limit[9]; or

    (c) the property does not consist of or include a dwelling-house[10].

Further, the county court has such exclusive jurisdiction notwithstanding that a claim in excess of the county court limit is also made in the action for payment by the mortgagor of the amount owing in respect of the mortgage or for payment of that amount by any person who guaranteed the debt secured by the mortgage[11]. It should be mentioned that a claim for possession under a mortgage is an action for the recovery of land within the meaning of section 21(1) of the County Courts Act 1984 and is not an action for foreclosure under section 23 of that Act[12]. The county court also has jurisdiction under section 21 to determine a mortgagee's claim for payment of a sum owed in respect of the mortgage in excess of the county court jurisdiction in contract actions and even though a prior mortgagee has been granted an order for possession[13].

---

[8] See County Courts Act 1984, s.21, and see *ante*, pp. 253 *et seq*.
[9] For the county court limit, see County Courts Act 1984, ss.21, 147(1). The current limit is £1,000, *ibid*. s.147(1). For the net annual value for rating, see *ibid*. s.147(2), (3), and *P.B. Frost* v. *Green* [1978] 1 W.L.R. 949 (where one of the two properties mortgaged was not liable to be rated). See also *ante*, pp. 253 *et seq*.
[10] See *ante*, pp. 253 *et seq*.
[11] See *R.V. Judge Dutton Briant, ex p. Abbey National Building Society* [1957] 2 Q.B. 497, and see *ante*, pp. 253 *et seq*.
[12] See *West Penwith* v. *Gunnell* [1968] 1 W.L.R. 1153, and see *ante*, pp. 253 *et seq*.
[13] *Universal Showcards and Display Manufacturing Ltd.* v. *Brunt* (1984) 128 S.J. 581.

PROCEDURE IN THE HIGH COURT

Commencement of Proceedings

Mortgage actions may be commenced by originating summons or by writ, the choice being governed by R.S.C. Ord. 5. In the Chancery Division mortgage actions are normally commenced by originating summons which is the appropriate procedure where questions of fact are not substantially in dispute and the matter is relatively straightforward[14]. If a writ is used when there is no need, the extra costs incurred by so doing will be disallowed[15]. Somtimes, however, there may be special reasons for commencing proceedings by way of writ. This can arise, for instance, when the facts are complicated[16]. When the facts are in dispute[17] and when questions of priority may have to be determined[18].

A writ by which a mortgage action is begun may not be issued out of a district registry, which is not a Chancery district registry, unless the mortgaged property is situated in the district of the Registry. Without prejudice to R.S.C. Ord. 7, r.5, insofar as it authorises an originating summons to be issued out of a Chancery district registry, an originating summons by which a mortgage action is begun may be issued out of any other district registry if, but only if, the property to which the action relates is situated in the district of that other registry[19]. The writ or originating summons by which a mortgage action is begun shall be endorsed with or contain a statement showing (a) where the mortgaged property is situated, and (b) if the plaintiff claims possession of the mortgaged property and it is situated outside Greater London, whether the property consists of or includes a dwelling-house and, if so, whether the net annual value for rating of the property exceeds £1,000[20]. Certain further procedural requirements are contained in R.S.C. Ord. 88 and reference should be made to *The Supreme Court Practice*[21].

---

[14] See Ord. 5, r.4; and see *Re Giles, Real and Personal Advance Co.* v. *Mitchell* (1890) 43. Ch. D. 391 at 398, 400.

[15] *O'Kelly* v. *Culverhouse* (1887) W.N. 36; *Barr* v. *Harding* (1887) 36 W.R. 216.

[16] *Re Giles, Real and Personal Advance Co.* v. *Mitchell* (1890) 43 Ch. D. 391 at 400.

[17] *Beamish* v. *Whitney* [1908] 1 I.R. 38.

[18] *Re Giles, Real and Personal Advance Co.* v. *Mitchell* (1890) 43 Ch. D. 391.

[19] R.S.C. Ord. 88, r.3(1), (2).

[20] R.S.C. Ord. 88, r.3(3).

[21] In a claim for possession where there has been failure by the defendant to acknowledge service, see Ord. 88, r.4. Where the action in the Chancery Division for possession or payment has been commenced by way of originating summons the affidavit in support should comply with the provisions of Ord. 88, r.5. There are special rules with regard to any mortgage action commenced in the Chancery Division to enforce a charging order by sale of the property charged, see Ord. 88, r.5A. In an action commenced by Writ judgment on failure to give notice of intention to defend or in default of defence shall not be entered except with the leave of the court and any application for the grant of leave must be made in accordance with Ord. 88, r.6.

PROCEDURE IN THE COUNTY COURT

Commencement of Proceedings

Generally any action in the county court by a mortgagee for possession of a dwelling-house (being an action to which section 36 of the Adminstration of Justice Act 1970 applies) shall be dealt with in chambers unless the court otherwise directs[22]. Further, evidence in support of or in opposition to the claim for possession is usually giveny by affidavit[23].

By virtue of C.C.R. Ord. 4, r.3 proceedings for the recovery of land or for the foreclosure or redemption of any mortgage, or, subject to Ord. 31, r.4, for enforcing any charge or lien on land, or for the recovery of monies secured by a mortgage or charge on land, may be commenced only in the court for the district in which the land or any part thereof is situated.

Further, by virtue of C.C.R. Ord. 6, r.5 where a plaintiff claims as mortgagee payment of monies secured by a mortgage of real or leasehold property or possession of such property, he shall set out in his particulars of claim the various matters specified in this sub-rule[24].

Where a plaintiff claims as mortgagee possession of land which consists of or includes a dwelling-house, he shall state in his particulars of claim whether there is any person on whom notice of the action is required to be served in accordance with section 8(3) of the matrimonial Homes Act 1983 and, if so, he shall state the name and address of that person and shall file a copy of the particulars of claim for service on that person[25].

---

[22] C.C.R. 1981 Ord. 49, r.1.

[23] There is no specific provision that evidence should be given by affidavit, but C.C.R. Ord. 20, r.5 provides that evidence is to be given by affidavit in proceedings in chambers.

[24] See *post*, p. 000.

[25] R.S.C. Ord. 6, r.5(1A). This statement may be based upon a search of the appropriate register. But such a search may be unnecessary where it is obvious that no charge or notice under the Act would be revealed.

Court Forms

1. Originating Summons by First Legal Mortgagee of Land

IN THE HIGH COURT OF JUSTICE   CH (year) (B) No.
CHANCERY DIVISION[26]

    BETWEEN   A.B.   Plaintiff
                              and
                              C.D.   Defendant

To C.D. of (address) (description)[27] under the mortgage hereinafter mentioned

LET the Defendant within (14 days) after service of this summons on him, counting the day of service, return the accompanying acknowledgment of service to the Court Office

By this summons, which is issued on the application of the Plaintiff A.B. of (address) who claims to be the mortgagee[28] under the mortgage hereinafter mentioned, the Plaintiff seeks the following relief,[29] namely

   (1) Payment of £(amount) being principal and £(amount) interest outstanding at the date hereof at the rate of (rate) per cent. per annum and further interest at (rate) per cent. until payment due to the Plaintiff under the covenant in (description of mortgage)[30] and such costs as would be payable if this claim were the only relief granted

   (2) An account of what is due to the Plaintiff under and by virtue of the mortgage for principal, interest and costs

   (3) An order that the said mortgage may be enforced by foreclosure or sale

   (4) [the appointment of a receiver]
        [An Order that C.D. shall do all acts necessary to enable the Plaintiff to receive the rents and profits of the mortgaged property]

   (5) Possession of the mortgaged property

   (6) Further or other relief

[26] As to issuing proceedings out of a district registry, see R.S.C. Ord. 88, r. 3(1).

[27] *i.e.* as mortgagor, second mortgagee, assignee, beneficiary, trustee in bankruptcy, person entitled to redeem. If the mortgage or charge uses the words "borrower," "lender," use those words.

[28] If the mortgage or charge uses the words "borrower," "lender," use those words.

[29] For other forms of relief, see Atkin, *Court Forms* (1986), Vol. 28, Form 6.

[30] As charge, demise, etc.

(7) Costs

The [freehold] land and premises are situate at (address)[31] ([No part of the said premises consists of a dwelling-house] [Part of the premises consists of a dwelling-house. The rateable value of the premises is £(amount)])

If the Defendant does not acknowledge service such judgment may be given or order made against or in relation to him as the Court may think just and expedient

Dated:

NOTE: This summons may not be served later than 12 calendar months beginning with the above date unless renewed by order of the court

This summons was taken out by (name, address of solicitors) Solicitors for the Plaintiff A.B. who resides at (address)

IMPORTANT
Directions for Acknowledgment of Service are given with the accompanying form

2. Affidavit Supporting Originating Summons[32]

Plaintiff
(Initials of deponent)
(Number of affidavit)
(Date sworn)

(Heading as in previous form)

1, [A.B.] (address, description) make oath and say as follows

(a) I am [the Plaintiff] (description of office held) of the Plaintiff] (and am duly authorised to make this affidavit on its behalf

(2) By a (describe mortgage, as in previous form) A true copy[33] of that mortgage ("the Mortgage") is now produced and shown to me marked "A.B1"

(3) The Mortgage contains the following provisions which are material to these proceedings[34]:

---

[31] See R.S.C. Ord. 88, r. 3(3). By s.37 of the Administration of Justice Act 1970 the county court has exclusive jurisdiction in possession cases unless (a) the property is in Greater London; or (b) its annual value is over £1,000; or (c) it does not consist of or include a dwelling-house.

[32] In a form whereby the Plaintiff is the deponent. See Atkin, *Court Forms* (1986), Vol. 28, Form 6 where the affidavit is drafted as if sworn by an officer of a body corporate.

[33] Required by R.S.C. Ord. 88, r. 5(2).

[34] *i.e.* covenants for repayment, clauses requiring any steps to be taken before instituting proceedings, provisions as to service of notices, variations of statutory provisions, attornment clause.

(4) (Statement of any transfer, devolution or assignment, or express notice given to the defendant)[35]

(5) The Defendant (and his family) [is] [are] the only person(s) in possession of the mortgaged property and the Defendant is in default in payment of principal and interest and [a] [no] class F land charge has been registered][36] [a] [no] notice or caution pursuant to the Matrimonial Homes Act 1983 has been entered [proceedings have been served on (name, address, description) who is the person on whose behalf the said [land charge] [notice] [caution] has been registered]

(*Alternative paragraph 5 if the Plaintiff is a mortgagee in possession*)

(5) The Plaintiff took possession on and has received the rents and profits of the mortgaged property from (date) and is ready to account as mortgagee in possession from that date

(6) (Statement of any breach of covenant and of any sums expended by the plaintiff in preserving the security)

(7)–(11) (Include the following paragraphs if necessary)
Appointment of receiver
Determination of tenancy created by an attornment clause[37]
Statement of notices
Requirement for appointment of receiver
Statement of outgoings, rents and profits

(12) The state of the account between the parties is as follows[38]

Amount of advance	£
Amount of periodic payments required to be made	£
Amount of [interest or instalments] in arrear at the date of the originating summons	£
Amount of [interest of instalments] in arrear at the date hereof	£
Total amount due at the date hereof	£

(13) (Statement that neither the amount referred to in the previous paragraph nor any part thereof has been received by or on behalf of the Plaintiff)

(14) (Statement as to source of knowledge of the facts and matters deposed to)

Sworn, etc.

---

[35] For descriptions, see Atkin, *Court Forms* (1986), Vol. 28, Form 5.

[36] See R.S.C. Ord. 88, r. 5(4)(*b*)(i) (requirement to state whether such a land charge, etc., has been registered) and (ii) (requirement to state that notice has been served).

[37] If the mortgagor has attorned tenant it must be shown that the tenancy has been properly determined. See precedent section 1, note 69 and R.S.C. Ord. 88, r. 5(5).

[38] R.S.C. Ord. 88, r. 5(3), (6), (7).

3. Particulars of Claim by Mortgagee for Possession of Dwelling-house[39]

IN THE (   ) COUNTY COURT   Case no.

BETWEEN   A.B.   Plaintiff
                                 and
                                 C.D.   Defendant

PARTICULARS OF CLAIM

1. By a mortgage dated . . . . . . 19 . . . and made between (1) the Plaintiff and (2) the Defendant, the land and dwelling-house (which is a dwelling-house within the meaning of Part IV of the Administration of Justice Act 1970, known as . . . . . . was mortgaged by the Defendant to the Plaintiff to secure the repayment by the Defendant to the Plaintiff of the principal sum of £ . . . advanced by the Plaintiff to the Defendant, and interest thereon at the annual rate of £ . . . per cent., and the Defendant covenanted to repay to the Plaintiff the principal sum together with interest thereon on . . . . . . 19 . . . and further covenanted that so long as the principal sum should remain unpaid he would pay to the Plaintiff interest as aforesaid by equal half-yearly instalments on . . . . . . and . . . . . . in every year.

2. The Defendant failed to pay the instalments of interest due on . . . . . . 19 . . . namely £ . . . , and the same is in arrears.

3. The amount remaining due under the mortgage is:

Principal	£
Arrears of interest	£
Interest from .... 19....	£
	———
	£
	———

4. The Plaintiff has not before the commencement of this action taken any proceedings against the Defendant in respect of the principal money or interest.

5. No land charge of Class F has been registered in relation to the land and dwelling-house or any part thereof.

6. The rateable value of the land and the dwelling-house does not exceed £1,000.

---

[39] See C.C.R. Ord. 6, r. 5 as to what particulars must be included.

AND the Plaintiff claims the sum of £ . . . or in default possession of the land and dwelling-house.

Dated, etc.,   (Signature)
                                            Plaintiff's Solicitors, of (address)
                                                where they will accept service
                                                of proceedings on behalf of the
                                                                     Plaintiff

To the Registrar of the [   ] County Court
and to the Defendant

STATUTORY ENACTMENTS AND RULES

1. County Courts Act 1984, sections 21, 23, 147(1)

21. Actions for recovery of land and actions where title is in question

(1) A county court shall have jurisdiction to hear and determine any action for the recovery of land where the net annual value for rating of the land does not exceed the county court limit.

(2) A county court shall have jurisdiction to hear and determine any action in which the title to any hereditament comes in question, being an action which would otherwise be within the jurisdiction of the court,—

> (a) in the case of an easement or licence, if the net annual value for rating of the hereditament in respect of which the easement or licence is claimed, or on, through, over or under which the easement or licence is claimed, does not exceed the county court limit; or
>
> (b) in any other case, if the net annual value for rating of the hereditament in question does not exceed the county court limit.

(3) Where a mortgage of land consists of or includes a dwelling-house and no part of the land is situated in Greater London then, subject to subsection (4), if a county court has jurisdiction by virtue of this section to hear and determine an action in which the mortgagee under that mortgage claims possession of the mortgaged property, no court other than a county court shall have jurisdiction to hear and determine that action.

(4) Subsection (3) shall not apply to an action for foreclosure or sale in which a claim for possession of the mortgaged property is also made.

(5) If an action in which the mortgagee under a mortgage of land claims possession of the mortgaged property would, by virtue of this section, be within the jurisdiction of a county court had that claim been the only claim made in the action, a county court shall have jurisdiction to hear and determine the action notwithstanding that a claim is also made in the action for payment by the mortgagor of the amount owing in respect of the mortgage or for payment of that amount by any person who guaranteed the debt secured by the mortgage and that by reason of the amount claimed the last mentioned claim is not within the jurisdiction of a county court.

(6) Nothing in subsection (5) shall be taken as empowering a county court to hear and determine an action for foreclosure or sale which is not within the jurisdiction of a county court.

(7) In this section—

> "dwelling-house" includes any building or part of a building which is used as a dwelling;
>
> "mortgage" includes a charge and "mortgagor" and "mortgagee" shall be construed accordingly;
>
> "mortgagor" and "mortgagee" includes any person deriving title under the original mortgagor or mortgagee.

(8) The fact that part of the premises comprised in a dwelling-house is used as a shop or office or for business, trade or professional purposes shall not prevent the dwelling-house from being a dwelling-house for the purposes of this section.

(9) This section does not apply to a mortgage securing an agreement which is a regulated agreement within the meaning of the Consumer Credit Act 1974.

23. Equiety jurisdiction

A County Court shall have all the jurisdiction of the High Court to hear and determine—

(a) . . .
(b) . . .
(c) proceedings for foreclosure or redemption of any mortgage or for enforcing any charge or lien, where the amount owing in respect of the mortgage, charge or lien does not exceed the County Court limit;
(d) . . .
(e) . . .
(f) . . .
(g) . . .

147. Interpretation

(1) In this Act, unless the context otherwise requires . . . "the County Court limit" means—

(a) in relation to any enactment contained in this Act for which a limit is for the time being specified by an Order under section 145, that limit,
(b) (subject to paragraph (a)), in section 21(1), (2)(*a*) and (*b*) . . . , £1,000 . . .
(c) . . .

2. Administration of Justice Act 1970, ss.36, 39

36. Additional powers of court in action by mortgagee for possession of dwelling-house

(1) Where the mortgagee under a mortgage of land which consists of or includes a dwelling-house bring an action in which he claims possession of the mortgaged property, not being an action for foreclosure in which a claim for possession of the mortgaged property is also made, the court may exercise any of the powers conferred on it by subsection (2) below if it appears to the court that in the event of its exercising the power the mortgagor is likely to be able within a reasonable period to pay any sums due under the mortgage or to remedy a default consisting of a breach of any other obligation rising under or by virtue of the mortgage.

(2) The court—

(a) may adjourn the proceedings, or

(b) on giving judgment, or making an order, for delivery of possession of the mortgaged property, or at any time before the execution of such judgment or order, may—

    (i) stay or suspend execution of the judgment or order, or

    (ii) postpone the date for delivery of possession, for such period or periods as the court thinks reasonable.

(3) Any such adjournment, stay, suspension[40] or postponement as is referred to in subsection (2) above may be made subject to such conditions with regard to payment by the mortgagor of any sum secured by the mortgage or the remedying of any default as the court thinks fit.

(4) The court may from time to time vary or revoke any condition imposed by virtue of this section.

(5) This section shall have effect in relation to such an action as is referred to in subsection (1) above begun before the date on which this section comes into force unless in that action judgment has been given, or an order made, for delivery of possession of the mortgaged property and that judgment or order was executed before that date.

(6) In the application of this section to Northern Ireland, "the court" means a judge of the High Court of Northern Ireland, and in subsection (1) the words from "not being" to "made" shall be omitted.

39. Interpretation of Part IV

(1) In this Part of the Act

"dwelling-house" includes any building or part thereof which is used as a dwelling.

"mortgage" includes a charge and "mortgagor" and "mortgagee" shall be construed accordingly.

"mortgagor" and "mortgagee" includes any person deriving title under the original mortgagor or mortgagee.

(2) The fact that part of the premises comprised in a dwelling-house is used as a shop or office or for business, trade or professional purposes shall not prevent the dwelling-house from being a dwelling-house for the purposes of this Part of this Act.

3. Administration of Justice Act 1973, s.8

8. Extension of powers of court in action by mortgagee of dwelling-house

(1) Where by a mortgage of land which consists of or includes a dwelling-house, or by any agreement between the mortgagee under such a mortgage and the mortgagor, the mortgagor is entitled or is to be permitted to pay

---

[40] The Court has no jurisdiction to order a stay or suspension of an order without defining or rendering ascertainable the period for which the order should be stayed or suspended: *Royal Trust Co. of Canada* v. *Markham* [1975] 1 W.L.R. 1416.

the principal sum secured by instalments or otherwise to defer payment of it in whole or in part, but provision is also made for earlier payment of the event of any default by the mortgagor or of a demand by the mortgagee or otherwise, then for purposes of section 36 of the Administration of Justice Act 1970 (under which a court has power to delay giving a mortgagee possession of the mortgaged property so as to allow the mortgagor a reasonable time to pay any sums due under the mortgage) a court may treat as due under the mortgage on account of the principal sum secured and of interest on it only such amounts as the mortgagor would have expected to be required to pay if there had been no such provision for earlier payment.[41]

(2) A court shall not exercise by virtue of subsection (1) above the powers conferred by section 36 of the Administration of Justice Act 1970 unless it appears to the court not only that the mortgagor is likely to be able within a reasonable period to pay any amounts regarded (in accordance with subsection (1) above) as due on account of the principal sum secured, together with the interest on those amounts, but also that he is likely to be able by the end of that period to pay any further amounts that he would have expected to be required to pay by then on account of that sum and of interest on it if there had been no such provision as is referred to in subsection (1) above for earlier payment.

(3) When subsection (1) above would apply to an action in which a mortgagee only claimed possession of the mortgaged property, and the mortgagee brings an action for foreclosure (with or without also claiming possession of the property), then section 36 of the Administration of Justice Act 1970 together with subsections (1) and (2) above shall apply as they would apply if it were an action in which the mortgagee only claimed possession of the mortgaged property, except that—

(a) section 36(2)(*b*) shall apply only in relation to any claim for possession; and
(b) section 36(5) shall not apply.

(4) For purposes of this section the expressions "dwelling-house," "mortgage," "mortgagee" and "mortgagor" shall be construed in the same way as for the purposes of Part IV of the Administration of Justice Act 1970.

(5) This section shall have effect in relation to an action begun before the date on which this section comes into force if before that date judgment has not been given, nor an order made, in that action for delivery of possession of the mortgaged property and, where it is a question of subsection (3) above, an order nisi for foreclosure has not been made in that action.

---

[41] s.8(1) can apply only if: (i) the mortgage itself or some agreement made under it has the effect that the mortgagor was to be permitted to defer payment of the principal sum in whole or in part after it had become due; and (ii) the mortgage itself must make provision for earlier payment in the event of any default by the mortgagor or of a demand by the mortgagee or otherwise.

(6) In the application of this section to Northern Ireland, subsection (3) shall be omitted.

4. R.S.C. Ord. 88, rr. 1–7

Application and Interpretation (O. 88, r. 1)

1.—(1) This Order applies to any action (whether begun by writ or originating summons) by a mortgagee or mortgagor or by any person having the right to foreclose or redeem any mortgage, being an action in which there is a claim for any of the following reliefs, namely—

(*a*) payment of moneys secured by the mortgage,

(*b*) sale of the mortgaged property,

(*c*) foreclosure,

(*d*) delivery of possession (whether before or after foreclosure or without foreclosure) to the mortgagee by the mortgagor or by any other person who is or is alleged to be in possession of the property,

(*e*) redemption,

(*f*) reconveyance of the property or its release from the security,

(*g*) delivery of possession by the mortgagee.

(2) In this Order "mortgage" includes a legal and an equitable mortgage and a legal and an equitable charge, and references to a mortgagor, mortgagee and mortgaged property shall be construed accordingly.

(3) An action to which this Order applies is referred to in this Order as a mortgage action.

(4) These rules apply to mortgage actions subject to the following provisions by this Order.

Assignment of certain actions to Chancery Division (O. 88, r. 2)

2. Without prejudice to section 61(1) of the Act (which provides for the assignment to the Chancery Division of causes or matters for the purposes, among others, of the redemption or foreclosure of mortgages and the sale and distribution of the proceeds of property subject to any lien or charge) any action in which there is a claim for—

(a) payment of moneys secured by a mortgage of any real or leasehold property, or

(b) delivery of possession (whether before or after foreclosure) to the mortgagee of any such property by the mortgagor or by any other person who is or is alleged to be in possession of the property,

Shall be assigned to the Chancery Division.

Commencement of action in registry (O. 88, r. 3)

3.—(1) A writ by which a mortgage action is begun may not be issued out of a district registry, which is not a Chancery district registry, unless the mortgaged property is situated in the district of the registry.

(2) Without prejudice to Ord. 7, r. 5, in so far as it authorises an orig-

inating summons to be issued out of a Chancery district registry, an originating summons by which a mortgage action is begun may be issued out of any other district registry if, but only if, the property to which the action relates is situated in the district of that other registry.

(3) The writ or originating summons by which a mortgage action is begun shall be indorsed with or contain a statement showing—

(a) where the mortgaged property is situated, and

(b) if the plaintiff claims possession of the mortgaged property and it is situated outside Greater London, whether the property consists of or includes a dwelling house and, if so, whether the net annual value for rating of the property exceeds £1,000.

Claim for possession: failure by a defendant to acknowledge service (O.88, r.4)

4.—(1) Where in a mortgage action in the Chancery Division begun by originating summons, being an action in which the plaintiff is the mortgagee and calims delivery of possession or payment of moneys secured by the mortgage or both, any defendant fails to acknowledge service of the originating summons, the following provisions of this rule shall apply, and references in those provisions to the defendant shall be construed as references to any such defendant.

This rule shall not be taken as affecting Ord. 28, r. 3, or r. 5(2) in so far as it requries any document to be served on, or notice given to, a defendant who has acknowledged service of the originating summons in the action.

(2) Not less than 4 clear days before the day fixed for the first hearing of the originating summons the plaintiff must serve on the defendant a copy of the notice of appointment for the hearing and a copy of the affidavit in support of the summons.

(3) Where the plaintiff claims delivery of possession there must be indorsed on the outside fold of the copy of the affidavit served on the defendant a notice informing the defendant that the plaintiff intends at the hearing to apply for an order to the defendant to deliver up to the plaintiff possession of the mortgaged property and for such other relief (if any) claimed by the originating summons as the plaintiff intends to apply for at the hearing.

(4) Where the hearing is adjourned, then, subject to any directions given by the Court, the plaintiff must serve notice of the appointment for the adjourend hearing, trogether with a copy of any further affidavit intended to be used at that hearing, on the defendant not less than 2 clear days before the day fixed for the hearing.

A copy of any affidavit served under this paragraph must be indorsed in accordance with paragraph (3).

(5) Service under paragraph (2) or (4) and the manner in which it was effected, may be proved by a certificate signed by the plaintiff, if he sues in person, and otherwise by his solicitor.

The certificate may be indorsed on the affidavit in support of the summons or, as the case may be, on any further affidavit intended to be used at an adjourned hearing.

(6) A copy of any exhibit to an affidavit need not accompany the copy of the affidavit served under paragraph (2) or (4).

(7) Where the plaintiff gives notice to the defendant under Ord. 3, r. 6, of his intention to proceed, service of the notice, and the manner in which it was effected, may be proved by a certificate signed as mentioned in paragraph (5).

Action in Chancery Division for possession or payment (O. 88, r. 5)

5.—(1) The affidavit in support of the originating summons by which an action (other than an action to which rule 5A applies) to which this rule applies is begun must comply with the following provisions of this rule.

This rule applies to a mortgage action in the Chancery Division begun by originating summons in which the plaintiff is the mortgagee and claims delivery of possession or payment of moneys secured by the mortgage or both.

(2) The affidavit must exhibit a true copy of the mortgage and the original mortgage or, in the case of a registered charge, the charge certificate must be produced at the hearing of the summons.

(3) Where the plaintiff claims delivery of possession the affidavit must show the circumstances under which the right to possession arises and, except where the Court in any case or class otherwise directs, the state of account between the mortgagor and mortgagee with particulars of—

(*a*) the amount of the advance,

(*b*) the amount of the periodic payments required to be made,

(*c*) the amount of any interest or instalments in arrear at the date of issue of the originating summons and at the date of the affidavit, and

(*d*) the amount remaining due under the mortgage.

(4) Where the plaintiff claims delivery of possession the affidavit must—

(*a*) give particulars of every person who to the best of the plaintiff's knowledge is in possession of the mortgaged property; and

(*b*) state, in the case of a dwelling house, whether—

(i) a land charge of Class F has been registered, or a notice of caution pursuant to s.2(7) of the Matrimonial Homes Act 1967 (or notice registered under section 2(8) of the Matrimonial Homes Act 1983) has been entered, and, if so, on whose behalf; and

(ii) he has served notice of the proceedings on the person on whose behalf the land charge is registered or the notice or caution entered.

(5) If the mortgage creates a tenancy other than a tenancy at will between the mortgagor and mortgagee, the affidavit must show how and

when the tenancy was determined and if by service of notice when the notice was duly served.

(6) Where the plaintiff claims payment of moneys secured by the mortgage, the affidavit must prove that the money is due and payable and give the particulars mentioned in paragraph (3).

(7) Where the plaintiff's claim includes a claim for interest to judgment, the affidavit must state the amount of a day's interest.

Action by writ: judgment in default (O. 88, r. 6)

6.—(1) Notwithstanding anything in Order 13 or Order 19, in a mortgage action begun by writ judgment on failure to give notice of intention to defend or in default of defence shall not be entered except with the leave of the Court.

(2) An application for the grant of leave under this rule must be made by summons and the summons must, notwithstanding anything in Order 65, rule 9, be served on the defendant.

(3) Where a summons for leave under this rule is issued in an action in the Chancery Division, rule 4(2) to (7) shall apply in relation to the action subject to the modification that for references therein to the originating summons, and for the reference in paragraph (2) to the notice of appointment, there shall be substituted references to the summons.

(4) Where a summons for leave under this rule is issued in an action to which rule 5 would apply had the action been begun by originating summons, the affidavit in support of the summons must contain the information required by that rule.

Foreclosure in redemption action (O. 88, r. 7)

7. Where foreclosure has taken place by reason of the failure of the plaintiff in a mortgage action for redemption to redeem, the defendant in whose favour the foreclosure has taken place may apply by motion or summons for an order for delivery to him of possession of the mortgaged property, and the Court may make such order thereon as it thinks fit.

5. C.C.R. Ord. 6, r. 5

Mortgage action (O. 6, r. 5)

5.—(1) Where a plaintiff claims as mortgagee payment of moneys secured by a mortgage of real or leasehold property or possession of such property, he shall in his particulars of claim—

(a) state the date of the mortgage;
(b) show the state of account between the plaintiff and the defendant with particulars of—
   (i) the amount of the advance,
   (ii) the amount of the periodic payments required to be made,
   (iii) the amount of any interest or instalments in arrear at the commencement of the proceedings, and
   (iv) the amount remaining due under the mortgage;

(c) state what proceedings, if any, the plaintiff has previously taken against the defendant in respect of the moneys secured by the mortgage or the mortgaged property and, where payment of such moneys only is claimed, whether the plaintiff has obtained possession of the property; and

(d) state, where possession of the property is claimed, whether or not the property consists of or includes a dwelling-house within the meaning of Part IV of the Administration of Justice Act 1970.

(1A) Where a plaintiff claims as mortgagee possession of land which consists of or includes a dwelling-house, he shall state, in his particulars of claim, whether there is any person on whom notice of the action is required to be served in accordance with section 8(3) of the Matrimonial Homes Act 1983 and, if so, he shall state the name and address of that person and shall file a copy of the particulars of claim for service on that person.

(2) In this rule "mortgage" includes a legal or equitable mortgage and a legal or equitable charge, and references to the mortgaged property and mortgagee shall be construed accordingly.

INDEX

Absolute owner. *See* **Owner.**
Accounts,
  costs,
    foreclosure, proceedings for, 446–448
    litigation, of, 451–452
    mortgage debt, in relation to, 448–451
    redemption, proceedings for, 436–448
    security, in relation to, 448–451
  foreclosure, 258–259
  interest, 443–445
  items comprised in, 441
  liability to account, 440
  mortgagee in possession, liability of,
    214–218, 440
  principal debt, 441–443
  taking, 452–454
Acknowledgment,
  chose in action, mortgage of, 72
Action,
  costs of, 451–452
  foreclosure. *See* **Foreclosure.**
  future interests, enforcement of mortgage
    of, 414–417
  interest, recovery of arrears of, 418–419
  mortgaged property, in respect of, 289–290
  mortgagee, institution by, 425
  personal covenant to repay, on, 266–269
  possession, for. *See* **Possession.**
  redemption by,
    decree, effect of, 330–331
    generally, 317–318, 323–324
    order, 327–328
    parties, 324
    procedure, 326
    redeem up, foreclose down, 325
    sale in lieu, 326–327
    successive redemptions, 328–330
Administration of Justice Acts 1970 and 1973,
  possession, proceedings for, 246–249
Advances,
  building society. *See* **Building society.**
  corporate body, to, 120
  further, right to tack, 43–44
  instalments, paid by, 122
  land, secured on, 116–119
  local authority, powers of, 155–157
  overseas property, secured on, 128
Agreement,
  consumer credit. *See* **Consumer credit**
    agreement.
  equitable assignment by, 73

Agreement—*cont.*
  non–commercial, 145
  partially regulated, 141
  regulated. *See* **Regulated agreement.**
  types of, 141
  unregulated, 141
Agricultural charge,
  Bills of Sale Acts, exemption from, 53
  creation of, 136–138
  nature of, 136–138
  priority of, 140
  registration of, 138–140
Agricultural land,
  crops growing on, 136
  meaning, 134
  oral tenancy, 135
  ordinary mortgage, 134–136
Agricultural Mortgage Corporation,
  statutory powers, 192
Aircraft,
  mortgage of, exemption from Bills of Sale
    Acts, 53
Assets,
  class 3, 128
  equity of redemption as, for payment of
    debts, 281–282
  other agricultural, meaning, 137–138
Assignee,
  redemption by, 321
Assignment,
  choses in action, of. *See* **Choses in action.**
  consideration,
    defective statutory assignment, 85–86
    future property, 82–83
    generally, 82
    need for, 82
    rights of action, 83–84
    voluntary equitable assignment, 84–85
  life assurance policy, of, 88–92
  partnership, share in, 92–93
  statutory. *See* **Law of Property Act 1925.**
  stocks and shares, of, 93–97
  trust property, of, 87–88
  voluntary equitable, 84–85
Attorney, power of,
  equitable mortgagee, granted to, 272
Attornment clause,
  deed of mortgage by demise, 23–24

Bank,
  meaning, 137